WITHDRA

FOREIGN AND COMMONWEALTH OFFICE

DOCUMENTS ON BRITISH POLICY OVERSEAS

EDITED BY

TONY INSALL

AND

PATRICK SALMON

SERIES I

Volume IX

LONDON AND NEW YORK

WHITEHALL HISTORIES: FOREIGN AND COMMONWEALTH OFFICE PUBLICATIONS
Series Editors: Keith Hamilton and Patrick Salmon
ISSN: 1471–2083

FCO historians are responsible for editing *Documents on British Policy Overseas (DBPO)* and for overseeing the publication of FCO Internal Histories.

DBPO comprises three series of diplomatic documents, focusing on major themes in foreign policy since 1945, and drawn principally from the records of the Foreign and Commonwealth Office. The latest volumes, published in Series III, are composed almost wholly of documents from within the thirty-year 'closed period', which would otherwise be unavailable to the public.

Since the early 1960s, several Internal Histories have been prepared by former or serving officers, the majority of which concentrated upon international developments and negotiations in which the UK has been directly involved. These were initially intended for use within the FCO, but some of the more substantial among them, studies that offer fresh insights into British diplomacy, are now being declassified for publication.

Published DBPO volumes:

SERIES I: 1945–1950

Volume I: The Conference at Postdam, July–August 1945
    0 11 591682 2
Volume II: Conferences and Conversations, 1945: London, Washington and Moscow
    0 11 591683 0
Volume III: Britain and America: Negotiation of the US Loan, 3 August–7 December 1945
    0 11 591684 9
Volume IV: Britain and America: Atomic Energy, Bases and Food, 12 December 1945–31 July 1946
    0 11 591685 7
Volume V: Germany and Western Europe, 11 August–31 December 1945
    0 11 591686 5
Volume VI: Eastern Europe, August 1945–April 1946
    0 11 591687 3
Volume VII: The UN, Iran and the Cold War, 1946–1947
    0 11 591689 X
Volume VIII: Britain and China, 1945–1950
Volume IX: The Nordic Countries: From War to Cold War, 1944–1951
    978 0 415 59476 9

SERIES II: 1950–1960

Volume I: The Schuman Plan, the Council of Europe and Western European Integration, May 1950–December 1952
　　0 11 591692 X
Volume II: The London Conference: Anglo-American Relations and Cold War Strategy, January–June 1950
　　0 11 591693 8
Volume III: German Rearmament, September–December 1950
　　0 11 591694 6
Volume IV: Korea, June 1950–April 1951
　　0 11 591695 4

SERIES III: 1960–

Volume I: Britain and the Soviet Union, 1968–1972
　　0 11 591696 2
Volume II: The Conference on Security and Co-operation in Europe, 1972–1975
　　0 11 591697 0
Volume III: Détente in Europe, 1972–1976
　　0 7146 5116 8
Volume IV: The Year of Europe: America, Europe and the Energy Crisis, 1972–1974
　　0 415 39150 4
Volume V: The Southern Flank in Crisis, 1973–76
　　0 7146 5114 1
Volume VI: Berlin in the Cold War, 1948–1990
　　978–0–415–45532–9
Volume VII: German Unification, 1989–1990
　　978–0–415–55002–4

DOCUMENTS ON BRITISH POLICY OVERSEAS

Series I, Volume IX

The Nordic Countries:
From War to Cold War, 1944–1951

First published 2011
by Routledge
2 Park Square, Milton Park, Abingdon, Oxon, OX14 4RN

Simultaneously published in the USA and Canada
by Routledge
711 Third Avenue, New York, NY 10017

Routledge is an imprint of the Taylor & Francis Group, an informa business

© 2011 Crown Copyright

The right of the editor to be identified as the authors of the editorial material, has been asserted in accordance with sections 77 and 78 of the Copyright, Designs and Patents Act 1988.

Printed and bound in Great Britain by
CPI Antony Rowe, Chippenham, Wiltshire

All rights reserved. No part of this book may be reprinted or reproduced or utilised in any any form or by any electronic, mechanical, or other means, now known or hereafter invented, including photocopying and recording, or in any information storage or retrieval system, without permission in writing from the publishers.

Published on behalf of the Whitehall History Publishing Consortium. Applications to reproduce Crown copyright protected material in this publication should be submitted in writing to: HMSO, Copyright Unit, St Clements House, 2–16 Colegate, Norwich NR3 1BQ. Fax: 01603 723000. E-mail: copyright@hmso.gov.uk

British Library Cataloguing in Publication Data
A catalogue record for this book is available from the British Library

Library of Congress Cataloging-in-Publication Data
A catalog record has been requested for this book

ISBN13: 978–0–415–59476–9 (hbk)
ISBN13: 978–0–203–82865–6 (ebk)

CONTENTS

		PAGES
Preface		ix
Abbreviations for Printed Sources		xxvii
Abbreviated Designations		xxviii
List of Persons		xxix
Document Summaries		xxxvi
Map		lviii
Chapter I	1944-1945	1
Chapter II	1946-1947	80
Chapter III	1948	201
Chapter IV	1949-1951	287
Index		371

PREFACE

Writing in 1951, a contemporary expert noted that 'the importance of the Scandinavian countries in world affairs has lately increased to an extent which is almost startling'.[1] He continued: 'In a world divided, as at present, by an "iron curtain" following roughly a line from the Arctic Ocean down the Baltic to the Adriatic, it is obvious that the Scandinavian peninsula no longer occupies a remote grand-stand in which its inhabitants can be passive or neutral spectators of any future conflict, but constitutes more than 1,200 miles of the front line dividing the forces of East and West.' The present volume documents the transition from war to cold war in the United Kingdom's relations with the five Nordic countries: Denmark, Iceland, Finland, Norway and Sweden.[2]

Between the wars the Nordic countries had been among Britain's most valuable trading partners, but their remoteness from the likely theatres of any future war (on land, at least) and the absence of serious conflicts among themselves or with their immediate neighbours had led the Foreign Office and the British military authorities to pay them only intermittent and limited attention. This was the normal peacetime state of affairs. In war, naturally, it was different. Indeed for a short time in the winter of 1939-40 Scandinavia became the main focus of strategic interest, as the British and French Governments contemplated military intervention in support of the Finns in their conflict with the Soviet Union and sought to deprive Germany of its supplies of Swedish iron ore while Germany, for its part, prepared the surprise assault that rapidly brought Denmark and Norway within its grip. What differed after 1945 (unlike, for example, 1815 or 1918), was that the Nordic region did not immediately revert to strategic insignificance. The heightened importance of the Nordic region after 1945 derived in part from the shared experience of war, including, for example, the exceptionally close relations established between the British Government and the Norwegian Government in exile. It was also due to common economic difficulties and a strong ideological affinity between the British Labour Government of 1945-51 and its social democratic counterparts in the Nordic countries. But it was due most of all to the development of air power and the atomic bomb, the break-up of the wartime alliance and the growing perception of the Soviet Union as the chief threat to the security of the United Kingdom.

In 1945 it seemed quite possible that the international engagement of the Nordic countries—while not, perhaps, reverting to the largely passive neutrality of the inter-war years—would be confined to membership of the new United Nations organisation. By 1949 only Sweden remained neutral. In April 1948 Finland had signed a Treaty of Friendship, Co-operation and Mutual Assistance with the Soviet Union; exactly one year later Denmark, Iceland and Norway had become founding

---

[1] G.M. Gathorne-Hardy, preface to *The Scandinavian States and Finland: A Political and Economic Survey* (London and New York: Royal Institute of International Affairs, 1951), p. vii.

[2] Terminology presents problems when dealing with the Nordic region, and we may not have been entirely consistent in resolving them. 'The Nordic countries', denoting the four Scandinavian countries—Denmark, Iceland, Norway and Sweden—together with Finland was not a term commonly used at the time; its appearance in this volume is therefore mainly confined to the title and to editorial material. 'Scandinavia' is often used in the documents to denote only the three continental Scandinavian countries (i.e. excluding Iceland), but sometimes to describe the Nordic region more generally, while 'the Scandinavian peninsula' refers to Norway and Sweden alone.

signatories of the North Atlantic Treaty. From the point of view of Scandinavian or Nordic solidarity, and especially because it appeared to consign Finland to the Soviet sphere of influence, this outcome was a disappointment. But as an alternative to a power vacuum that would have left Western Europe's northern flank open to continued Soviet penetration, and as a vital element in the emerging North Atlantic security system, it was an undoubted success. Within a few years, moreover, the Nordic region had settled into a state of equilibrium in which neutral Sweden acted as pivot between its westward-leaning and eastward-leaning neighbours, and which enabled the region to preserve a measure of detachment from the main zones of cold war confrontation to the south.

Great Britain was still, in these immediate post-war years, the Nordic countries' most important international interlocutor, and played a key role in bringing about this outcome. But Britain and the Nordic countries naturally entered the post-war period with differing as well as shared experiences. Norway and Denmark which, like Iceland, had attempted to maintain a policy of neutrality at the beginning of the war, had been invaded by Germany in April 1940 and had been occupied for more than five years. Finland had fought against the Soviet Union twice, and after the conclusion of an armistice in September 1944 had then fought against Germany. Sweden had remained neutral throughout the war, while Iceland had accepted British and then subsequently American troops which had established a series of bases in the country from 1940 onwards. All (apart from Sweden) faced the challenges of post-war reconstruction and all aimed to achieve economic growth as well as a large measure of social justice in their respective societies. They also needed to come to terms with the presence of a powerful Soviet Union which at the end of the war occupied a part of both Norway and Denmark and which, after the signature of the armistice with Finland, was to exercise a considerable influence on that country throughout this period.

The United Kingdom was exhausted by nearly six years of war and facing serious economic problems which verged on bankruptcy. Although it took time before the extent of Britain's financial difficulties became clear to the new Labour Government, it gradually became apparent that economic constraints were going to affect foreign policy as much as domestic policy as, in the aftermath of the war, Britain sought to maintain its world-wide economic and military commitments. The Foreign Office started to collect information about the situation as early as March 1945, sending out a circular about the effect of Britain's external financial position on foreign policy, to which the mission in Helsinki provided a reasonably optimistic response (No. 16). It continued to report regularly on Finnish progress in fulfilling its reparations requirements, reflecting concerns about the extent to which the Soviet Union might wish to integrate the Finnish economy with its own at the expense of Finnish trade with the UK (e.g. No. 74). Throughout this period the Foreign Office continued to seek information about bilateral trade in the Nordic countries and its impact on Britain's external financial position (e.g. Nos. 90 and 91).

The task of reconstruction was made more difficult when on 17 August 1945 President Truman approved a memorandum ending lend-lease to Britain. This sudden and unexpected decision had significant effects, and required the negotiation with the United States of an agreement, signed in December 1945, concluding a settlement of the loan agreement by Britain on payment of US$620 million and a dollar loan of US$3,750 million to be repaid over 50 years at 2 per cent interest.[3] A significant part of these negotiations took place at a time when Britain was also discussing with the United States a revised agreement on overseas bases, including bases in the Nordic and Arctic regions. The situation began to improve markedly in 1948 following the introduction of the Marshall Plan, which enabled all these countries, apart from Finland, to overcome their short-term dollar shortages and to begin to plan for long-term economic growth. Apart from differences over fisheries issues, there were few economic problems between Britain and Norway, and the Foreign Secretary, Ernest Bevin, supported a positive response to a proposal from the Vice-President of the Norwegian *Storting* that a Norwegian delegation should visit the UK to discuss closer economic collaboration (No. 145). Although nothing came directly from this, it was followed a year later by another Norwegian proposal at the OEEC for a Scandinavian regional grouping with which they wished Britain to be associated. This produced a positive response, leading to the establishment of the organisation which became known as UNISCAN (No. 199).

Norway

As early as the beginning of 1944, the Norwegian Government in exile had expressed concerns about the possibility of the Soviet army beginning to liberate Norway before the other allied armies were able to do so. In January 1944 the Norwegian Foreign Minister, Trygve Lie, approached Christopher Warner, head of the Northern Department at the Foreign Office, drawing attention to the possibility that this might happen once hostilities ended between the Soviet Union and Finland and Soviet forces would be free to undertake the task. He and Ambassador Erik Colban made a further approach to Sir Orme Sargent (then a Deputy Under-Secretary) on the same subject in February. Lie hoped that the allied planners would not confine themselves to considering the liberation of southern Norway, but would also consider taking steps to occupy northern Norway once it had been evacuated by the Germans, so as to avoid a situation where 'the Russians would break in and occupy the country indefinitely'. Sargent referred his representations to the Chiefs of Staff (No. 1). Lie's concerns were shown to have been justified when, on 18 October 1944, a few weeks after Britain and the Soviet Union had signed an armistice with Finland, the Soviet army crossed the border into Norway. Although Soviet troops did not pursue the German army very deeply into Norwegian territory, they were still occupying the eastern part of Finnmark when Lie visited Moscow to meet Vyacheslav Molotov, the Soviet Commissar for Foreign Affairs. At a meeting on 11 November Molotov demanded the cession of the Norwegian territory of Bear Island, an end to the demilitarised status of Svalbard (known to the British at that time as Spitzbergen) and the establishment of a Norwegian-Soviet condominium over the archipelago. Rolf Andvord, the Norwegian Ambassador in Moscow, ignored Lie's instructions not to discuss this with his British counterpart and confided Molotov's demands to the British Ambassador, Sir Archibald Clark Kerr. He added that Lie wished to have a private and unofficial conversation with Anthony Eden (Foreign Secretary in the wartime coalition Government) so as to seek his advice, as soon as he returned to London (No. 3).[4] Although their army withdrew from Finnmark later in 1945, Soviet

---

[3] Documents on the negotiations for the US loan agreement are printed in DBPO, Series I, Vol. III.
[4] Although Eden did not report Molotov's demands to Churchill until January 1945, his diary showed that Lie did consult him privately on 24 November (Avon papers, University of Birmingham, AP 20/1/24).

The Nordic Countries, 1944-1951

pressure on Norway over Svalbard was to continue for two years more. The subject was initially very tightly held: Sir Laurence Collier, the British Ambassador, was not briefed on it by the Foreign Office until after he had reported a discussion on the subject with Lie in July 1945 (No. 15). Molotov raised the subject once more with Lie (who was by then the United Nations Secretary-General) in July 1946, and again with the new Foreign Minister Halvard Lange in Paris the following November. Collier was impressed by the firmness with which Lange responded to this approach (No. 80). Lange subsequently referred the matter to the *Storting*, which decided in secret session not to have any discussions of a military nature with a foreign power (No. 87). This effectively marked the end of Soviet attempts to put pressure on Norway to accommodate their demands over Svalbard.

In early 1946 the Foreign Office expressed concerns about a growing Norwegian inclination towards pacifism, given as a reason by Lie for the unwillingness of his Government to send Jens Christian Hauge, Minister of Defence, to Britain to discuss equipment purchases. Collier was asked whether he thought that pressure from the Soviet Union might also be responsible for this decision (No. 47). He suggested later that this consideration might have influenced the Norwegian decision in March 1946 to request that Winston Churchill should cancel his planned visit to Norway, shortly after he had made his celebrated speech at Fulton, Missouri.[5] Not long afterwards, Lange gave a speech in which he outlined and developed the concept of bridge-building, exacerbating fears that Norway might revert to a position of isolation (No. 66). By December 1947, however, Collier began to detect signs that Norway might be starting to move away from this policy (No. 105), and Churchill's visit was rearranged for May of the following year (No. 138).

While there were problems in bilateral relations, they never escalated to the level experienced by Britain in relations with Norway's Nordic neighbours. In November 1945 Collier reported Lie's comment that there was 'a certain *malaise*' in Anglo-Norwegian relations, linked to issues such as the recent Payments Agreement, the removal of German fishing boats from Norwegian ports, the extension of the Mutual Aid Agreement and the disposal of the German whaling fleet (No. 40). Other difficulties developed over the participation of Norwegian troops in the occupation of Germany and the dispute over fisheries. The Chiefs of Staff had hoped that Norway would provide a division for Germany but the Norwegians found it difficult to meet the costs involved. The matter was resolved after a visit by Hauge and Erik Brofoss (Nos. 57, 59 and 64). The fisheries dispute, resolved in favour of Norway after reference to the International Court at The Hague, was probably the most serious bilateral problem during this period (Nos. 154 and 164), but it did not affect the broader relationship at a time when Britain and Norway were closely involved in the sensitive negotiations which led to the signing of the Atlantic Treaty in April 1949.

In his valedictory despatch, written in November 1950, Collier commented that while close relations had developed between Britain and Norway during the war,

> it hardly seemed possible to me, when I came back here in 1945 just after the liberation of Norway, that Anglo-Norwegian relations, then at the crest of a wave, should not subsequently suffer some diminution of cordiality, if only through a natural reaction from the emotional high tension of the war years: there was a strong tradition of neutrality in Norway and several grounds for

---

[5] Collier despatch of 21 March 1946, FO 371/56284, N/4710/219/30.

friction with her former allies, and if the Soviet Government had played their cards with skill they might have taken advantage of these factors and of the considerable Russophile feeling in Norway at the end of the war to drive a serious wedge between the two countries (No. 212).

Collier's long association with Norway—he had started in Northern Department in 1925—no doubt gave him an advantage over most of his ambassadorial colleagues. He was well placed to be able to develop very close relations with many leading Norwegian personalities. Though he initially shared the reservations of the Foreign Office about the appointment of Lange to replace Lie as Foreign Minister (Nos. 49, 50 and 51), he subsequently got to know him extremely well, later describing him as a European figure, head and shoulders above the foreign ministers of the other Scandinavian states (No. 195). Collier launched some productive initiatives, for example encouraging the development of closer links between the British and Norwegian labour movements as a means of strengthening bilateral relations (No. 55). This process was facilitated by the closeness of the contacts between the Labour Party and the Foreign Office.

Denmark

The occupation by Soviet troops of a part of Norwegian territory (from which they withdrew in September 1945) was never as big an issue in Soviet-Norwegian relations as the Soviet occupation of the Baltic island of Bornholm in May 1945 was in Danish-Soviet (as well as Danish-British) relations. It is likely that the decision to occupy Bornholm was the consequence of the unexpected decision by SHAEF to inform the Soviets of their intention to occupy Bornholm themselves, rather than to act straight away, as the Foreign Office had intended. The Soviet Union reacted quickly to SHAEF's message and sent 3,500 troops to subdue the garrison of some 20,000 German troops and take its surrender (No. 9). Anxious to achieve the withdrawal of Soviet troops as soon as possible, the Danish Government explored in July 1945 the possibility of linking the ultimate withdrawal of British troops from Denmark with the withdrawal of Soviet troops from Bornholm (No. 13). The Danes continued to put pressure on the British to speed up the rate of the withdrawal of their forces (many of whom were engaged in training Danish troops), making clear that they had no other levers which they could use with the Soviet Union (Nos. 27 and 30). There is no evidence that the Danish Government took the British into their confidence over the progress of their negotiations to secure Soviet withdrawal: the first indication received by the Foreign Office that this might happen was obtained from the British Embassy in Moscow.[6] Soviet troops finally left Bornholm in early April 1946.

Another complex wartime legacy, which occupied both British and Danish Governments for over three years, was the question of treatment of the Danish minority in South Schleswig. The issue first came to prominence when Alec Randall, the Minister in Copenhagen, challenged the reluctance of the Commander in Chief, Germany, to allow the Danish Foreign Minister John Christmas Møller to visit both the Danish minority there and the grave of his son, who had been killed in fighting near Flensburg shortly before the end of the war (No. 14). Sargent, by then Permanent Under-Secretary at the Foreign Office, directed that a paper summarising the situation should be prepared for Bevin to submit to the Cabinet Overseas Reconstruction Committee (No. 26). The paper concluded that there were

---

[6] Moscow telegram No. 970, 10 March 1946, FO 371/56107, N3249/62/15.

insufficient grounds for a revision of the frontier, that there would be practical difficulties in the way of an exchange of populations and that during the period of military government, the United Kingdom could not admit the right of the Danish Government to make approaches on behalf of German citizens of Danish origin. The administration of British policy on this subject was not always even-handed: Eden had earlier been given cause to question whether a member of the Control Commission in Germany was not anti-Danish.[7] The Danish Government continued throughout this period to seek to intervene on behalf of members of the Danish minority (e.g. No. 75). The basis of an agreement was finally achieved during a series of meetings in London in October 1948 (No. 153), although the issue was not finally resolved until rather later.

The Danish Government was not only concerned to find ways of protecting the interests of citizens of Danish origin in Germany: it was also keen to find ways of removing from Denmark the 200,000 German refugees who had found their way there by the end of the war. This was difficult to achieve, for there was little available space available in which to resettle them in the already crowded and impoverished zones of post-war Germany and all the occupation powers were understandably reluctant to take on additional burdens. A significant number of the refugees consisted of the elderly or very young, rather than able-bodied workers. The Danish Government found it extremely difficult to persuade the allies to be more accommodating to their requests for assistance. In order to draw attention to their difficulties, they suggested to Randall that they would not be able to provide the contingent of troops which they had committed to the occupation of Germany (No. 71). This commitment had originally been made explicit by Foreign Minister Christmas Møller during a meeting with Bevin in August 1946, when he had said that by April 1946, 10,000 Danish troops would be ready to participate in the occupation of the British zone of Germany (No. 23). While this number may have been unrealistically large, Northern Department reacted very strongly to the possibility that no Danish troops would be made available, particularly since by then it was thought that the Norwegians would be able to send 4,000. This led to some wrangling, and to brinkmanship over the question of costs which was resolved by an approach from Christopher Mayhew, the Parliamentary Under Secretary, to his opposite number at the War Office, Lord Pakenham (No. 78). However even this did not fully resolve matters, and in January 1947 Eduard Reventlow, the Danish Minister in London, sought to obtain a British undertaking to resolve the refugee problem in the course of the next few months, and to spread over a longer period the cost of sterling payments for military equipment for Danish occupation forces, before the question was put to the Danish *Rigsdag*.[8] Danish troops finally began to arrive in Germany in June 1947.[9] The final German refugees left Denmark in February 1949, and British assistance in facilitating this process was acknowledged by Reventlow in a courteous letter to Sir Ivone Kirkpatrick (No. 187).[10]

Other issues also caused friction during the post-war period. In a despatch of early January 1946, Randall drew attention to what he perceived as the influence of

---

[7] See footnote to No. 45.
[8] Record of a meeting between Warner and Reventlow, 24 January 1947, FO 371/65854, N895/121/15.
[9] Rose despatch to Bevin of 7 June 1947, FO 371/65854, N6980/121/15.
[10] Reventlow's memoirs offer a personal perspective on UK-Danish relations in this period: Eduard Reventlow, *I dansk tjeneste* (Copenhagen: Thaning & Appels Forlag, 1956), pp. 177-226.

Preface

the 'small nation complex' in Danish relations with Britain, and advised that any hint of patronage in relations should be avoided. He pointed out that there had been suggestions that Britain was indifferent to long-term Danish interests in South Schleswig, that Britain had allowed the Danish accumulation of sterling to grow to excessive proportions and that the food prices to which the previous Danish Government had agreed were being kept down, while the prices of British exports to Denmark increased out of all proportion (No. 46). A few months later, in July 1946, he also complained that there had not been a single British ministerial visit to Denmark since the liberation—though it is worth noting that in view of post-war travel restrictions and the press of business of the new Government, there had not been many ministerial visits elsewhere in the Nordic countries by that time either.[11] These factors remained significant issues, and were frequently raised both by Danish ministers with Randall, and by Randall with the Foreign Office.

Given the significance of the United Kingdom as a trading partner, it is not surprising that trade was a further source of tension during this period, as Britain's economic circumstances worsened. In his response to a Foreign Office circular of February 1947, requesting comments on Britain's external financial position, Randall demonstrated the extent to which the two economies were interdependent: before the war Britain had been Denmark's best customer, and Denmark had been Britain's third best customer in Europe. After the war, Britain had again become Denmark's best customer, while Denmark was Britain's best customer outside the British Empire. Moreover, Britain enjoyed a favourable trade balance approaching £40 million and Denmark had few opportunities to earn hard currency elsewhere (No. 90). As Denmark's economic situation worsened later that year (No. 94), so Danish perceptions of British inflexibility during the food price negotiations led to some heated exchanges, exacerbated by press comments (No. 96), but the Foreign Office did not recommend a very conciliatory approach to the subsequent negotiations (No. 106) and the Prime Minister, Clement Attlee, concurred. The most difficult period in UK-Danish relations followed the announcement in October 1949 of a sharp increase in coal export prices, following soon after a statement by the leader of a British trade delegation to Denmark which implied that no such increase was foreseen. This led to a sharp complaint from Randall, who drew attention to previous Danish objections to the differentiation in coal prices for domestic consumption and for export (No. 197). Bevin became involved, and complained to Attlee (No. 200). In view of the extent of Danish economic dependence on Britain, it was also inevitable that the British devaluation in 1950 would exacerbate Danish economic difficulties. Bevin intervened with Attlee on several occasions in the following year, when it appeared that the National Coal Board was intending to break the contract to supply coal to Denmark (and also to Sweden). Although reductions were made in the quantity supplied, they were smaller than originally planned (No. 209).

Finland

Eden described the armistice agreement which was shortly to be concluded with Finland in a memorandum of 24 September 1944 (No. 2), noting that the British had been able to deflect the Soviets from their original intention of signing an immediate peace treaty. He also described the extent of the territorial concessions which Finland had been obliged to make, including the cession of the port of

---

[11] Letter to Warner, 4 July 1946, FO 371/56109, N8829/63/15.

The Nordic Countries, 1944-1951

Petsamo, Finland's outlet to the Arctic Ocean. The armistice agreement established an Allied Control Commission, which was dominated by the Soviet Union but on which Britain was also represented (though with limited influence). Its purpose was to see that the Finnish Government fulfilled the terms of the armistice (No. 2). The relations of Frank Shepherd, Britain's political representative, with Andrei Zhdanov, the senior Soviet representative on the Commission, were not straightforward and the conduct of business during their infrequent meetings could be tortuous (No. 5). During this uncertain period, there were often difficulties in distinguishing truth from rumours which could not easily be substantiated. Shepherd reported a conversation with assistant Foreign Minister Reinhold Svento, when he asked about press reports of a treaty of Mutual Assistance between Finland and Russia. Svento denied that this was on the agenda, though rumours continued to circulate during the following few weeks and the Foreign Office judged it necessary to prepare a brief on the subject for the British delegation at the Potsdam Conference (No. 11).

When the Soviet Union announced the resumption of diplomatic relations with Finland (No. 20), the Foreign Office advised that it was not possible for Britain to resume diplomatic relations with a state with which Britain was technically still at war. However, there was no objection to the establishment of quasi-diplomatic relations with Finland on the model of the relations which then existed with Italy (No. 21). Although the United Kingdom's influence was limited, it tried during this period not to do anything which might make Finland's precarious position any worse. Shepherd also sought to find other ways of accommodating Finland's position, for example by supporting a paper put forward by Colonel Magill, a member of the Control Commission, which advocated the adoption of a co-ordinated policy towards Scandinavia as a whole, including Finland. Northern Department agreed with Shepherd's observation that whereas Finland should from a military point of view be considered as being within the Russian orbit, it was in all other ways a part of Scandinavia, and that as such it had 'strong political, commercial and cultural affinities with Britain, which we should try by all means to foster. But we shall have difficulties in doing so while the communists remain in their present strong position' (No. 41). Warner agreed generally with this paper, though he pointed out that it would perhaps be better to let the Finns look to the United Nations to support their independence, rather than to Britain alone (No. 53).

Shepherd considered that the resignation of Field-Marshal Mannerheim from the Presidency in 1946 had a significant psychological effect on Finland, for he had been the personification of Finnish independence and 'a rigid and unfailing symbol which has been conspicuous in Finnish affairs ever since the achievement of her independence'. He noted that it was only after his departure that Foreign Minister Carl Enckell began to speak candidly about the Finnish fear of Russia during their discussions about the negotiation of the Peace Treaty (No. 62). This was a few months after Stalin had announced the extension by two years of the time-limit for the conclusion of reparations deliveries (No. 35). At this stage, Robin Hankey considered that the Soviet Government was pursuing a moderate line both economically and politically, though Northern Department continued to be worried about indications that the Soviet Union and the extreme left in Finland might want to increase Finnish-Soviet trade at the expense of trade with the West (No. 68).

Preface

Concerns continued to be expressed about the extent to which the Soviet Union might be planning a campaign to exert a greater domination over Finland. However, Shepherd felt that

> Finland has no intention of subsiding gently behind any sort of Russian curtain. Although there is a genuine realisation that a policy of friendship with Soviet Russia is essential for the present, there is little doubt that the Finns would once again be seriously tempted if the rift between East and West developed, and if there were a reasonable chance of effective Western support. The Russians, in fact, have very little reason to conclude that they can count on any sort of loyalty from the Finns (No. 95).

He also considered that as long as it remained satisfied that Norway and Denmark would not provide bases for operations against its territory, the Soviet Union would not seek the same level of security as it had striven for in South-Eastern Europe (No. 95). In the longer term, this judgement was proved correct. However, towards the end of 1947 a large Finnish delegation visited Moscow and the Foreign Office eventually learned that the subject of a military understanding had been raised (Nos. 102 and 104). In February 1948 Enckell informed Shepherd that Stalin had written to President Paasikivi, proposing a pact of mutual assistance between Finland and the Soviet Union (No. 115). This was at a time of considerable tension in East-West relations, for it came just a couple of days after the conclusion of the coup in Czechoslovakia which established a Communist government there: the Chiefs of Staff went so far as to consider sending a task force to the Baltic so as to bolster morale elsewhere in Scandinavia. Since the Foreign Office advised against such a step, they did not make a formal recommendation to do so, deciding instead to inform the Secretary of State that such a force could be provided at three days notice (No. 116).

Shortly afterwards, Collier reported that the Norwegian Government had received information from three different sources indicating that it might soon be faced with a Soviet demand for a mutual assistance pact. It was this development, (further considered below in the section on Scandinavian defence) which led Bevin to make an approach to the United States to discuss the establishment of an Atlantic security system. The Finnish-Soviet Treaty of Friendship, Co-operation and Mutual Assistance was signed in Moscow on 6 April (No. 131). Bevin informed the Cabinet that the firm attitude adopted by the Finnish Government had resulted in a treaty which appeared to preserve Finland from Soviet interference in her internal affairs, treating her more as a neutral buffer state than as a Soviet satellite: it did not require the provision of any further Soviet bases in Finland (No. 132). Considerations about Finland did not play a major part in British deliberations as the policy on Atlantic security was developed. However, Shepherd drew attention to a speech by Karl-August Fagerholm, the Prime Minister, in which he highlighted Finland's position and stated that if Sweden decided to associate herself more directly with the Western Powers, there was a risk that the Soviets might occupy Finland as a counter-measure. Hankey, by then head of Northern Department, commented that Russian pressure on Finland was really aimed at Sweden, and that it was not serious, because Russia had recently concluded a good trade agreement with Finland (No. 160). Moreover, the Finnish Legation in London kept in close contact with the Foreign Office throughout the early part of 1949, to ensure that the Finnish position was given due weight (No. 186).

The Nordic Countries, 1944-1951

Sweden

There were still reservations in British attitudes towards Sweden in early 1945. Swedish opposition to allied intervention in the Finnish-Soviet Winter War of 1939-40, and its appeasement of Germany during the early part of the Second World War had created resentments which were slow to disperse, although there was at the same time some understanding of the difficult position in which Sweden had been placed. Some of the early documents in this volume provide background and comments on the Swedish position, for example an account by Sir Victor Mallet (Minister in Stockholm) of Foreign Minister Christian Günther's explanation of Swedish policy towards Germany and Russia in 1940-41 (No. 4), Mallet's valedictory despatch (No. 12) and his report of a speech in which Günther set out clearly his view of neutrality as the keystone of Swedish foreign policy (No. 10). Commenting on this speech, Anthony Haigh of the Northern Department observed with some foresight that if Britain had organised a Western Security *bloc* before the end of hostilities with Germany, there would have been every chance of getting the Norwegians and (on liberation) the Danes to join. Haigh thought that there was still a chance of achieving such a grouping at that time, but he expected that in due course the Swedish view of neutrality would commend itself more to the Norwegian and the Danes.[12]

Shortly afterwards, a meeting was held in the Foreign Office with senior American diplomats to discuss how to ensure that the exploitation of large deposits of uranium (estimated at about 80,000 tons) which were known to be in Sweden and which might be used for the development of atomic weapons, was properly controlled. Guidance was sent to Stockholm which set out the background, and which described the means by which an approach was to be made to the Swedish Government by Johnson, the American Minister in Stockholm (No. 17). The United States wished to buy up large quantities of uranium, while the British preference was to make sure of full Swedish control over the extraction and use of the uranium. The negotiations were protracted, and complicated by the dislike of the new Foreign Minister, Östen Undén, for the request to maintain the confidentiality of the discussions from his Cabinet colleagues. Sweden eventually undertook to introduce legislation forbidding the exploitation of uranium-bearing material without government permission, and also forbidding export.

British reservations about Swedish attitudes took some time to be dispelled. In early 1946 the Joint Intelligence Committee decided that Sweden should remain in Category C as far as the exchange of information was concerned, meaning that no classified military information would be passed to Sweden, while Norway and Denmark, in Category B, would receive information up to the level of Confidential (though it determined that an exception should be made for Sweden in respect of potential aircraft sales). At the same time the Legation in Stockholm was requested to weaken the position of, and to attempt to secure the removal of, officers in the Swedish armed forces who were considered to be anti-British (No. 48). Cecil Jerram, the new Minister, challenged this instruction, pointing out the practical difficulties involved and questioning the extent to which there might still be German sympathisers in the Swedish military. He suggested an approach to Undén, an idea Northern Department initially supported though subsequently dropped (No. 54): the Chiefs of Staff then decided to upgrade Sweden to Category B 'for purely Service reasons'. In a letter to Hankey of 16 May, Jerram sought

---

[12] Minute of 23 June 1945, FO 371/48042, N7135/1106/42.

guidance on the policy of 'coolness' on which he had been briefed before he left London. He noted that the Government had been anxious to send a Minister out to a not very important agricultural exhibition, to be followed by the Lord Chancellor shortly afterwards, though this had been cancelled for quite different reasons. Hankey replied that there had not been any real change in policy, but that there had been nuances as the general situation had changed, especially as far as changes in relations with the Soviet Union were concerned, which altered the position of countries on the periphery such as Sweden (No. 63).

In 1947 there were further exchanges about a conversation between R.A. Butler, then Parliamentary Under-Secretary of State at the Foreign Office, and Björn Prytz, the Swedish Minister, in June 1940. This had been recorded by Prytz in a telegram which described a greeting to him from Halifax, then Foreign Secretary, which included his comment that 'common sense not bravado would determine the British Government's policy': in other words, that the Government might be prepared to consider a compromise peace with Nazi Germany. When the White Books about relations between Sweden and Norway were published in Stockholm in February 1947, the Swedish Government noted in the preface that the British Government had not agreed to the inclusion of his telegram of 17 June 1940. This comment was picked up by the press, and the Foreign Office began to think that it might have been better if agreement to publish had not been withheld. Hankey suggested this to Jerram, drawing attention to the linkage between this telegram and the decision to allow the transit of German troops through Sweden to Norway. In fact, the decision had been taken on the day before arrival of Prytz's telegram (No. 101). Jerram concluded that it would be better to leave things as they were.

In his Western Union speech of 22 January 1948, Bevin condemned the political ambitions of the Soviet Union, whose policy was 'to use every means within their power to get Communist control in Eastern Europe, and, as it now appears, in the West as well'. He called for greater unity among the countries of Western Europe, proposing a defence union of France and the Benelux countries. He subsequently made clear to Lange (No. 127) that he had avoided mentioning the Scandinavian countries as he did not wish to frighten Swedish and Danish public opinion away from any move towards a defence pact. Jerram reported that Undén was most unwilling to express any opinion about Bevin's speech (No. 112). Undén's further development of a policy of Swedish neutrality was crystallised in a speech to the *Riksdag* shortly afterwards which disappointed Hankey, who had thought that the Scandinavian countries had gradually been moving towards some closer association with the West. Now, it seemed, these hopes had been premature and it was the Swedish attitude which had mainly been responsible for the lack of progress (No. 114). Commenting on the outcome of Bevin's separate meetings with the Scandinavian foreign ministers in Paris on 15 and 16 March, Jerram advised that the policy should now be to encourage Norway and Denmark to align themselves with Western Union in some form, and to hope that their affiliation might at the right moment encourage and attract Sweden.[13]

Senior Swedish military officers soon began to express concerns that Swedish neutrality might have an effect on their prospects of continuing to obtain military supplies from the United Kingdom (No. 121). Bevin chose to disregard advice from the Chiefs of Staff to use this as a means of putting pressure on Sweden to adopt a more accommodating attitude towards the West, and did so again

---

[13] Despatch of 30 March 1948, FO 371/71451, N4021/637/63.

following a submission from Charles Bateman which drew attention to the fact that 'certain Swedish newspapers are taking a truculent anti-British line in an effort to support M. Undén's policy for the formation of a neutral Scandinavian *bloc*' (No. 144). Shortly afterwards the Foreign Office also decided not to submit to American pressure over a British contract to supply Vampire aircraft to Sweden, at a time when the United States was also seeking to apply pressure to Sweden (No. 147). Northern Department raised this again with Bevin in December (when it appeared that the Swedish position had hardened and when it also became known to the Foreign Office that Britain was supplying night fighters to Sweden), requesting that the Chiefs of Staff should be asked to review the matter. Bevin moderated his position slightly, maintaining that the treatment Britain accorded to Sweden should be governed by availability and priority. He still believed that 'if handled wisely, Sweden is not hopeless' (No. 159). After the signature of the Atlantic Treaty, Sweden continued to exert diplomatic pressure to ensure that existing contracts for the supply of advanced radar equipment and Vampire airframes were maintained. On one occasion the Swedish Ambassador, Gunnar Hägglöf, approached Attlee to request him to revoke a decision to abrogate a contract for the supply of more than 200 Vampire airframes to Sweden: the Prime Minister agreed to do so (No. 210).

Iceland

As the end of the war approached, the main problem facing the British Government was how to fulfil undertakings given to the Icelandic Government to withdraw from the bases which it had established in Iceland after the conclusion of hostilities, while retaining scope for their renewed use in an uncertain post-war period, and how to develop a common policy with the United States for the achievement of these objectives. Eden sought to do this as early as March 1945 (No. 8). This proved not to be straightforward, for the Americans preferred to retain their bases in Iceland (and Greenland) and there was a difference of views about how this might be achieved: the British wished to avoid giving the Soviets a pretext to try to obtain similar bases elsewhere, for example in Bornholm (Nos. 28 and 32). Bevin's attempts to persuade the Americans to adopt a different tactic, by asking the Icelandic Government for a temporary lease, were not successful (Nos. 33, 34 and 37). Shortly afterwards James Byrnes, the US Secretary of State, sought British assistance both in an American approach to the Icelandic Government and in obtaining a range of bases and base facilities across the world (No. 37). As the British withdrawal continued in early 1946, there were discussions about how to retain traffic rights for British airlines, even if they were not operating a service to Iceland, so as to prevent the Soviets from obtaining those concessions. This meeting also reviewed the American decision not to approach the Icelandic Government over bases until after the general elections there (No. 58). A particular concern had been to reach a position where the United Kingdom could reserve the right, if engaged in a war in which the United States was neutral, to claim to participate in whatever bases the United States might obtain. Once the Americans had obtained temporary transit rights, it was decided that it was no longer necessary for Britain to seek such rights for itself (No. 92).[14]

The Legation in Reykjavik continued to report on the relationship between the United States and Iceland and also about the extent to which the Communist Party

---

[14] Further details of UK-US discussions on bases in Iceland in 1945-46 are contained in DBPO, Series I, Vol. III, Nos. 48, 90, 102-3, 127, 135; and Series I, Vol. IV, Nos. 15, 23, 69.

might be able to continue to play a part in government. A letter early in 1948 from Charles Baxter, the Minister, to Bateman covered both subjects (No. 109). The Communist Party continued to be active: a despatch of April 1949, describing the debate in the *Althing* which ratified the Icelandic decision to participate in the Atlantic Pact, painted a vivid picture of the extent to which the Communists had disrupted the proceedings (No. 192).

Relations with the Soviet Union and Scandinavian defence

In the immediate post-war period, despite concerns about the Soviet presence in northern Norway and Bornholm, and Soviet demands over Svalbard, the United Kingdom took no particular steps to develop a comprehensive strategy to enhance security in the Nordic area. Britain's primary interests lay elsewhere in Western Europe. Moreover, as Sweden began to make clearer its continued policy of neutrality, and Norway evolved its concept of 'bridge-building', there was initially little reason to attempt to consider any significant alternative. Gradually, this view changed, especially after clarifications in early 1946 by both the British and American Embassies in Moscow of the nature of Soviet policy, which they described as a settled policy of expansion that should be met by a firm policy of containment.[15] By the end of the year, it was becoming apparent that measures needed to be taken to create some sort of barrier in the region. A significant step was taken by the Chiefs of Staff in June 1947 when, in response to a request from Hankey, they produced a paper on the strategic considerations involved in the question of a common arrangement by Norway, Denmark and Sweden for the defence of Scandinavia. They concluded that by virtue of their geographical position, these countries would assume great strategic importance in a war between Russia and the West and that both sides would gain considerable advantage by occupying them first. Their paper recommended that 'we should put in hand an examination of the potentialities of both a Scandinavian and a Western European *bloc*, to enable us to judge whether we can give more practical encouragement to a Scandinavian *bloc*' (No. 93).

However, apart from the discreet encouragement of staff talks, there was little scope for active measures before the beginning of 1948, although in December 1947 Collier did report some signs that Norway was beginning to move away from its policy of bridge-building (No. 105). Shortly afterwards several key developments led to a sharp increase in the level of tension in the region. First came confirmation of the news of the negotiations which were to lead to the Finnish-Soviet Mutual Assistance Treaty. This was followed by the Communist coup in Czechoslovakia, to which the Norwegian Prime Minister, Einar Gerhardsen reacted in a speech at Kråkerøy on 29 February, where he declared an ideological war against Communists in Norway. Finally, as noted earlier, there was information given by Lange to Collier and his American colleague that the Norwegian Government had heard from three different sources that it might soon be faced with a Soviet demand for a mutual assistance pact (No. 120). Norway was now the only country facing the western frontier of the Soviet Union which did not have a similar treaty. It was this information which led Bevin to telegraph Lord Inverchapel, the Ambassador in Washington, suggesting that the Norwegian concerns about Russian intentions might be justified, and instructing him to

---

[15] The important telegrams and despatches sent by Frank Roberts from Moscow in March 1946 are printed in DBPO, Series I, Vol. VI, Nos. 77, 79–80, 82–87.

approach General George C. Marshall, the Secretary of State, to discuss the establishment of an Atlantic security system (No. 122).[16]

The US Government responded positively to Bevin's proposal, and he took the opportunity of meetings shortly afterwards in Paris with Lange, Undén and the Danish Foreign Minister Gustav Rasmussen, and to brief them on his ideas (although he did not go into as much detail with Undén) (Nos. 127, 128 and 129). The Brussels Treaty, between Britain, France and the Benelux countries, was signed on 17 March 1948. Preliminary talks on an Atlantic security arrangement began in Washington in late March. Substantive negotiations between the United States, Canada, Britain, France and the Benelux countries began on 6 July. In May, Sweden reacted by proposing the creation of a neutral non-aligned Scandinavian alliance, which was a significant move away from its previous position of isolated neutrality. British policy thereafter concentrated on trying to find a way of resolving the differences between the three Scandinavian countries. Hankey wrote a paper in September on 'The Relation of Sweden to Scandinavian Co-operation and Atlantic and Western Union' (which became known as the first Hankey plan) in which he set out proposals for a series of interlocking pacts, which he hoped might provide a means by which Norway and Denmark might be encouraged into an Atlantic pact, with Sweden being drawn in afterwards by a closer attachment to Norway and Denmark (No. 148). On 9 September, a meeting of Scandinavian foreign ministers announced that an inter-Scandinavian study of common security problems would be begun, thus raising the prospect of a neutral Scandinavian defence pact as an alternative to an Atlantic arrangement. It was largely for this reason that both Lange and Rasmussen requested the postponement of any invitation to participate in a conference to discuss Atlantic security (No. 149).

However, although the Chiefs of Staff supported Hankey's plan, it was rejected by the Norwegians: Lange made clear that it would create internal political difficulties for the Norwegian cabinet if Sweden and Norway were treated differently. This was considered at a meeting with the Ambassadors in Oslo, Copenhagen and Stockholm in late October, which discussed the tactics which Britain and the Western powers should pursue in order to achieve Scandinavian inclusion in an alliance (No. 152). It was agreed that it would be preferable not to press the Scandinavian powers further until they had made progress with their own discussions, and the Americans were informed to this effect. The Foreign Office

---

[16] No evidence has yet been found to demonstrate that these concerns were well founded. M. Korobochkin, 'Soviet Policy towards Finland and Norway 1947-49', *Scandinavian Journal of History* 20 (1995), p. 202, concludes, on the basis of research in Russian Foreign Ministry archives, that this was a false alarm and that the available Soviet sources give no indication that the idea of proposing such a treaty was ever contemplated. Some clues to the sources of Norwegian alarm are given in documents printed in S. Holtsmark (ed.), *Norge og Sovietunionen 1917-55. En utenrikspolitisk dokumentasjon* (Oslo: J.W. Cappelens Forlag, 1995). One is a telegram of 7 March from the Norwegian Ambassador in Moscow H.C. Berg, reporting a conversation with a Russian contact who had told him about a non-aggression pact which had been proposed by the then Norwegian Prime Minister in 1930 (p. 415). The contact had remarked that the negotiations had come to nothing because the Norwegian Government fell and the Russian Ambassador was posted elsewhere. The source of Berg's information is thought by the editor to have been Aleksandra Kollontay, the Soviet Ambassador to Sweden, who had been posted there from Oslo in 1930. Another is a telegram of 7 March from the Norwegian Minister in Warsaw A. Danielsen, which reported information from a diplomatic colleague who had quoted a well-informed source, close to the Polish Government, as saying that after Finland it would be the turn of Norway (p. 416). Although Danielsen, did not name his colleague, it is believed by the editor to have been C.A.H. Westring, the Swedish Minister in Warsaw.

Preface

hoped this would also achieve a better co-ordination of policy between Britain and the United States, for there were times when it had been felt in London that the United States was pressing Sweden too hard, with results that were counter-productive (No. 155).

Towards the end of the year, it became clear that the Swedish attitude towards some kind of accommodation with the West was cooling not least, in Hankey's view, because the memory of the Czech *coup* was fading, and because the Swedish predisposition towards neutrality was again coming to the fore (No. 158). Some American officials wished to take a tougher line towards Sweden, particularly over the issue of arms sales but, when approached again by Northern Department, Bevin declined to change his view significantly, arguing that the treatment which Britain accorded to Sweden should be governed by availability and priority (No. 159). When the United States made clear to the Swedes that they could only expect to receive a very low priority for the supply of arms if they did not join the Atlantic Pact, this did not result in any change in the Swedish attitude (No. 162).

Hankey agreed with Harold Farquhar, the new Ambassador, that it would be a mistake to put any further pressure on the Swedish Government (No. 163). He was still of the view that Scandinavian defence made no sense without some kind of Swedish co-operation. After the meeting of Scandinavian prime ministers at Karlstad, he put forward a further compromise solution based on a system of interlocking pacts. This envisaged that the three Scandinavian countries would sign a mutual assistance pact, and that Norway and Denmark would not join the Atlantic Pact, but that they would make certain specific security arrangements with Britain and the United States instead. He hoped that this might facilitate the supply of arms to all three countries (No. 166). It did not prove possible to make much progress with these ideas: when Hauge heard of them, he expressed his reservations to Collier and the idea was dropped (Nos. 172 and 173).

A number of factors combined to add varying degrees of uncertainty during what was a very fast-moving situation. During the meeting at Karlstad, the Swedes had made an offer to supply from Bofors all Norwegian requirements for war material: it was thought that the Swedish Government had made this offer on the assumption that Bofors would be supplied with the means to increase its production (No. 165). When, shortly afterwards, the Joint Intelligence Bureau undertook research which disproved Swedish claims that Bofors could satisfy the defence requirements of all three Scandinavian countries, Hankey recommended to Bateman, the Assistant Under-Secretary, that Lange and Rasmussen should be discreetly informed (No. 171). Some further, temporary, confusion was created by a telegram from Stockholm, containing a report quoting a Swedish military officer to the effect that if Norway were to join the Atlantic Pact, then Finland would place some of its airfields at the disposal of the Russians. This turned out to have no substance, but it was drawn to Bevin's attention and caused considerable concern in the Foreign Office (No. 176). A further and potentially more serious intervention came from a Soviet note, presented to the Foreign Ministry and simultaneously published in Moscow, which sought clarification of the Norwegian position on the negotiations. This attempt to put pressure on Norway was robustly and publicly rebuffed (Nos. 174 and 175) as was a second note which was delivered shortly afterwards. Finally, in the light of further questions from the negotiators in Washington about how the strategic interests of the West would best be served, Bateman drew attention to the latest views of the Chiefs of Staff, who favoured a Scandinavian defence pact based on neutrality. This was wholly unacceptable to the Foreign Office, and in a series of minutes on 9 February Gladwyn Jebb, Bateman and Sargent worked out how they were going to deal with it. Sargent concluded:

> what is absolutely certain is that if Norway does not join the Atlantic pact it will be recognised throughout the world as a Soviet victory—to be followed I should think by a further diplomatic offensive in order to forbid the formation of even a neutral Scandinavian pact (No. 182).

Lange visited Washington to put a series of questions to Dean Acheson, the new Secretary of State, which he subsequently discussed with Bevin on his way back to Norway (No. 183). The final major step was the debate at the Norwegian Labour Party conference where Lange sought and obtained an overwhelming endorsement for his handling of the negotiations hitherto, and a free hand in future negotiations (No. 185). Despatches from Randall and Grace Thornton (in Reykjavik) provided comments on the debates in the *Rigsdag* and the *Althing* which ratified Danish and Icelandic participation in the Atlantic Pact (Nos. 191 and 192). The North Atlantic Treaty was signed on 4 April 1949.

Information Research Department

Concerned by the extent and effectiveness of Soviet rhetoric in the early postwar period, the Foreign Office sought from the beginning of 1946 to find ways of countering Soviet propaganda. In response to a request from the PUS, Sir Orme Sargent, Christopher Warner drafted in March 1946 a paper entitled 'The Soviet campaign against this country and our response to it'.[17] Copies were sent to selected posts overseas, including all five Nordic missions. Responses from Stockholm and Oslo illustrated the concerns that heads of posts already felt about the extent of the Soviet campaign against the United Kingdom and British interests, even in countries where they did not consider that the local Communist Party was likely to be able to take part in government (Nos. 67 and 69). Shepherd expressed similar views, but acknowledged that the situation in Finland was quite different and would limit the ability of the Finns to take action (No. 70). Bevin, concerned also by domestic political constraints, subsequently decided that the proposed campaign was too negative and so it was not implemented on a wide scale.

However, as the Soviet campaign continued, a number of factors contributed to a change in attitude towards the Soviet Union. The first was the establishment by the Soviet Union and eight other European Communist parties of the Communist Information Bureau (Cominform) in September 1947. Soon afterwards, in December, the London Council of Foreign Ministers broke up, principally over its failure to reach agreement over the German problem. The third factor was the effects of the continuing Soviet attacks at the UN, which the British delegation was not well-equipped to refute. On his return from the UN, Mayhew drafted a paper entitled 'Third Force Propaganda' which provided the stimulus for the decision in January 1948 to establish Information Research Department (IRD). Overseas posts reacted to the opportunities which this presented with varying degrees of enthusiasm and imagination: some Nordic posts put forward a range of suggestions (Nos. 124 and 137), and there is an early example of the use of IRD material in Norway (No. 139). Warner's reply to Collier (No. 140) describes the response of the Foreign

---

[17] DBPO, Series I, Vol. VI, No. 88.

Preface

Office to his ideas at a time when the new department was still feeling its way. In 1949 the Icelandic delegation at the United Nations approached the British mission with a request on behalf of the Icelandic Foreign Minister, Bjarni Benediktsson, for a supply of IRD material for use in the forthcoming election campaign, where the Communists would form the main opposition party (No. 196).

The Labour Party provided assistance to IRD in a range of ways, particularly by suggesting suitable foreign contacts for the receipt of IRD material. This was but one example of the very close relationship which the party enjoyed with the Foreign Office throughout this period, which was to the mutual advantage of both. In November 1946 Bevin issued instructions that arrangements should be made to give confidential briefings on foreign policy issues to Denis Healey, the International Secretary of the Labour Party (No. 73)—an unprecedented arrangement which reflected the value Bevin placed on these links. Healey quite frequently carried out commissions on behalf of the Foreign Office, writing for example to Väinö Leskinen of the Finnish Social Democratic Party to express concern about internal political stability and to invite him to visit London (No. 95). He also passed through the Foreign Office briefings or messages of support to Haakon Lie, Secretary of the Norwegian Labour Party, at critical moments, for example before a meeting of the party's Executive Committee in preparation for the meeting of Scandinavian socialist parties which was to discuss Western Union.[18]

In addition to documents describing political and economic issues, we have chosen to include a number of documents which help to illuminate the atmosphere of the period and the diverse range of the activities in which both Ministers and officials were involved. These include a speech by Bevin to a visiting Danish parliamentary delegation (No. 142); an account of an elk hunt in the freezing winter in Finland (No. 38); a description of the procedures involved in arranging to send two reindeer—the gift of a Norwegian general—to London Zoo (No. 77); a detailed account by the Labour Attaché of the difficulties of everyday life in the spartan conditions of post-war Helsinki (No. 61) and British involvement in Danish plans to sell Eva Braun's diamond watch to raise money for charity (No. 85). We have also included Jerram's description of the change in status of the British Legation in Stockholm together with a footnote recording the circumstances when one of his predecessors refused to yield precedence to the Danish Ambassador in 1654, which we believe is by some margin the oldest diplomatic exchange to have been included in any of these volumes (No. 98).

It will be noted that there are relatively few documents covering the period after the North Atlantic Treaty was signed in Washington on 4 April 1949. This reflects the fact that, once the main issue of Atlantic security had been satisfactorily resolved, there were relatively few significant problems in British relations with the Nordic countries which required much attention from the Foreign Office.

We have not changed the spellings of names and places as they appear in the documents. Variations may therefore be noticed, for they were not always spelt consistently at that time. Thus Spitzbergen (now known as Svalbard) will sometimes be rendered as Spitsbergen, and Vuori (the Finnish minister in London) as Wuori. Other examples of these differences are Flensburg and Flensborg, Helsinki and Helsingfors, Schleswig and Slesvig, and Skagerrak and Skagerak.

---

[18] FO Tel. No. 64 to Oslo of 29 January 1948, FO 371/71485, N1336/34/30.

The Nordic Countries, 1944-1951

A small number of documents which appear in previous volumes of DBPO are also printed in this volume because of their significance and relevance to the subject. They are indicated by an appropriate footnote reference.

Acknowledgements

In accordance with the Parliamentary announcement cited in the Introduction to the Series, the Editors have had the customary freedom in the selection and arrangement of documents including full access to all classes of FO documentation. There have, however, in the case of the present volume been a number of exceptional instances when for security reasons it has been necessary to excise certain passages from selected documents. These omissions are indicated with square brackets and appropriate footnote references.

The main source of documentation in this volume has been the records of the Foreign Office held at The National Archives (TNA). We should like to thank the staff at TNA for their advice and assistance in providing information and in making facilities available during their reconstruction project. We are also grateful to the staff of the Foreign and Commonwealth Office archive at Hanslope Park, particularly Rachel Cox, for their help in identifying and declassifying a number of documents still in their charge, and to Sally Falk and Chris Grindall of the Knowledge and Information Unit of the Cabinet Office for facilitating access to documents in the CAB and PREM series.

We should like to thank the present and former Heads of the FCO's Information Management Group (IMG), Christine Ferguson and Jane Darby, and their staff for their help and support. We should also like to express thanks to Mariot Leslie, formerly HM Ambassador to Norway, for her assistance during some of the early research for this project, and to Kjersti Brathagen of the University of Oslo for her helpful advice. We are grateful to all those current and former members of FCO Historians who have helped on this volume, in particular Alastair Noble, Isabelle Tombs and Gill Bennett, former Chief Historian of the FCO. In addition, valuable technical assistance has been provided by Grant Hibberd, Giles Rose, Elaine Alahendra and Rosalind Pulvermacher.

The publication of this volume would not have been possible without the generous support of a grant from the FCO's Cash for Change Fund. We are grateful to James Bevan, Director General Change and Delivery at the FCO, and to colleagues in the Change Unit for their assistance in administering this grant. We should also like to acknowledge the generosity of the Department of War Studies, King's College London, in the provision of research facilities.

TONY INSALL					PATRICK SALMON

August 2010

ABBREVIATIONS FOR PRINTED SOURCES

DBPO — *Documents on British Policy Overseas* (London: HMSO, 1984f.)

FRUS — *Foreign Relations of the United States* (Washington, DC: State Department, 1861f.)

IRD History Note — *IRD: Origins and Establishment of the Foreign Office Information Research Department 1946-48* (London: Foreign and Commonwealth Office Historians, History Note No. 9, 1995)

Parl. Debs., 5th ser., H. of C. — *Parliamentary Debates (Hansard), Fifth Series, House of Commons, Official Report* (London, 1909f.)

ABBREVIATED DESIGNATIONS

AA	Air Attaché	NATO	North Atlantic Treaty Organisation
ACC	Allied Control Commission		
APS	Assistant Private Secretary	NCO	Non-Commissioned Officer
AUS	Assistant Under-Secretary of State	NKVD	*Navodrony Kommissariat Vnutrevnikah Def* (People's Ministry of Internal Affairs, USSR)
BBC	British Broadcasting Corporation		
		OEEC	Organisation for European Economic Co-operation
BOAC	British Overseas Airways Corporation		
		PM	Prime Minister
BTH	British Thomson Houston Co.	PPS	Parliamentary Private Secretary
CEEC	Committee (*or* Council, *or* Conference) for European Economic Co-operation		
		PS	Private Secretary
C-in-C	Commander-in-Chief	PUS	Permanent Under-Secretary of State *or* Parliamentary Under-Secretary
COGA	Control Office for Germany and Austria		
		RAF	Royal Air Force
COI	Central Office of Information	RN	Royal Navy
COS	Chiefs of Staff	SHAEF	Supreme Headquarters Allied Expeditionary Force
DNI	Director of National Intelligence		
		SIS	Secret Intelligence Service
DUS	Deputy Under-Secretary of State	SKF	*Svenska Kullagerfabrikken* (Swedish company manufacturing ball bearings)
ERP	European Recovery Programme		
		SOE	Special Operations Executive
FO	Foreign Office	SoS	Secretary of State
HMG	His Majesty's Government	SOS	Maritime distress call
IRD	Information Research Department	SSR	Soviet Socialist Republic
		TUC	Trades Union Congress
JIB	Joint Intelligence Bureau	UKDel	United Kingdom Delegation
JIC	Joint Intelligence Committee	UN(O)	United Nations Organisation
JPS	Joint Planning Staff	UNGA	UN General Assembly
JWPS	Joint War Planning Staff	UNISCAN	United Kingdom-Scandinavia
LO	*Landsorganisasjonen i Norge* (Norwegian Trade Union Organisation)	US(A)	United States (of America)
		USSR	Union of Soviet Socialist Republics
MA	Military Attaché *or* Master of Arts		
		WO	War Office
MFA	Minister or Ministry of Foreign Affairs		
NA	Naval Attaché		

LIST OF PERSONS

Acheson, Dean G., US Secretary of State, 1949-53
Alexander, Albert V., Minister of Defence, 1946-50
Allen, W. Dennis, Northern Department, FO, 1944-46 (Assistant, 1946)
Andersen, Alsing, Danish Minister of Finance, 1942, and Interior Minister, November 1947
Anderson, Sir John, Chancellor of the Exchequer, 1943-45
Andvord, Rolf, Norwegian Ambassador in Moscow, 1944-46; Secretary-General, Norwegian Foreign Ministry, 1946-48
Attlee, Clement, Prime Minister, 1945-51
Barclay, Christopher F. R., Northern Department, FO, 1946-48
Barclay, Roderick E., PS to the Secretary of State for Foreign Affairs, 1949-51
Bateman, Charles, H., AUS, 1948-50
Baxter, Charles W., British Minister, Reykjavik, 1947-51
Bay, Charles U., US Ambassador, Oslo, 1946-53
Beckett, Sir W. Eric, Legal Adviser, Foreign Office, 1945-53
Beck-Friis, Hans, Secretary-General, Swedish Foreign Ministry, 1947-49
Beeley, Harold, Counsellor, British Embassy, Copenhagen, 1949-51
Benediktsson, Bjarni, Icelandic Foreign Minister, 1947-53
Berg, General Ole, Chief of Defence, Norway, 1946-53
Berthoud, Eric A., AUS, FO, 1948-52
Bevin, Ernest, Secretary of State for Foreign Affairs, 1945-51
Bidault, Georges, French Foreign Minister, 1944-46 and 1947-48; Chairman of the Provisional Government, 1946; President of the Council of Ministers, 1949-50
Boheman, Erik, Swedish Ambassador, Paris, 1944-47; London, 1947-48; Washington, 1948-58
Bottomley, Arthur G., Secretary for Overseas Trade, Board of Trade, 1947-51
Bovenschen, Sir Frederick, Joint PUS, War Office, 1942-45
Brofoss, Erik, Norwegian Minister of Finance, 1945-47; Minister of Trade and Shipping, 1947-54
Brown, Denys D., Northern Department, FO, 1948-49
Buhl, Vilhelm, Prime Minister of Denmark, May-November 1945
Butler, R. A., Under-Secretary of State for Foreign Affairs, 1938-41
Byrnes, James F., US Secretary of State, 1945-47
Cadogan, Sir Alexander M. G., PUS, FO, 1938-46; Permanent Representative to the United Nations, 1946-50
Churchill, Sir Winston, Prime Minister, 1940-45
Citrine, Sir Walter, General Secretary of the Trades Union Congress, 1925-46
Colban, Erik, Norwegian Minister (1934-1942), later Ambassador (1942-1946), London
Collier, Sir Laurence, Ambassador to the Norwegian Government in exile, 1942-45; British Ambassador, Oslo, 1945-50
Crawford, R. Stewart, Assistant Secretary, Control Office for Germany and Austria, 1946-47
Cripps, Sir R. Stafford, Chancellor of the Exchequer, 1947-50
Crossman, Richard, Labour MP, 1945-74

The Nordic Countries, 1944-1951

Crowe, Eric E., Counsellor, British Embassy, Oslo, 1948-51
Davidson, Alan E., Northern Department, FO, 1948-50
Denham, Captain Henry M., Naval Attaché, Stockholm, 1940-47
Dixon, Sir Pierson J., British Ambassador, Prague, 1948-50
Douglas, General Archibald, Chief of the Swedish Army, 1944-48
Eden, Rt. Hon. R. Anthony, Secretary of State for Foreign Affairs, 1940-1945
Elster, Torolf, Foreign Editor of *Arbeiderbladet*, 1945-46; editor of *Kontakt*, Norway, 1947-54
Enckell, Carl, Finnish Foreign Minister, 1944-50
Eriksen, Erik, Prime Minister of Denmark, 1950-53
Erlander, Tage F., Prime Minister of Sweden, 1946-69
Etherington-Smith, Raymond G. A., Northern Department, FO, 1947-52
Fagerholm, Karl-August, Speaker of the Finnish Diet, 1945-48; Prime Minister 1948-50
Falla, Paul S., Assistant, Northern Department, FO, 1949-51
Farquhar, Sir Harold L., British Ambassador, Stockholm, 1948-51
Federspiel, Per, Danish resistance leader; Minister for Special Affairs, 1945-47
Fog, Professor Mogens, Danish Minister for Special Affairs, May-November 1945
Frisch, Hartvig, Danish Minister of Education, 1947-50
Garner Smith, Colonel Kenneth J. G., Military Attaché, Oslo, 1945-47
Gartz, Åke, Finnish Minister of Trade and Industry, 1944-46; Foreign Minister, 1950-51
Gerhardsen, Einar, Prime Minister of Norway 1945-51
Gromyko, Andrey, Soviet Ambassador, Washington, 1943-46; Soviet Permanent Representative to the United Nations, 1946-48
Gundersen, Oscar C., Norwegian Minister of Justice, 1945-52
Günther, Christian, Swedish Foreign Minister, 1939-45
Gustav V, King of Sweden, 1907-50
Gustav VI, King of Sweden, 1950-73
Haakon VII, King of Norway, 1905-57
Hadow, Robert H., Counsellor, British Embassy, Washington, 1944-48
Hägglöf, Gunnar, Swedish Ambassador, London, 1948-67
Haigh, A. Anthony H., Northern Department, FO, 1943-45
Halford, Aubrey S., PS to the PUS, FO, 1946-49
Halifax, Edward Wood, First Earl of, Secretary of State for Foreign Affairs, 1938-40; British Ambassador, Washington, 1941-46
Hammarskjöld, Dag, Secretary-General, Swedish Foreign Ministry, 1949-51
Hankey, Hon Robert (Robin) M. A., Head of Northern Department, FO, 1946-49
Hansen, Hans C., Danish Minister of Finance, May-November 1945 and 1947-50
Hansen, Rasmus, Danish Minister of Defence, 1947-50
Hansson, Per Albin, Prime Minister of Sweden, 1936-46
Harrison, Geoffrey, Head of Northern Department, FO, 1949-51
Hauge, Jens Chr., Norwegian Minister of Defence, 1945-52
Hayter, William G., Head of Services Liaison Department, 1946-48; AUS, 1948-49
Hedtoft, Hans, Prime Minister of Denmark, 1947-50
Helo, Johan, Finnish Minister of Finance, 1944-45; Minister of Education 1945-46; Finnish Ambassador, Paris, 1946-56

List of Persons

Helset, Major-General Olaf, Commander in Chief of the Norwegian Army, 1946-48
Henderson, James T., British Embassy, Stockholm, 1946-49
Henderson, William W. (Lord Henderson), Joint Parliamentary Under Secretary of State, FO, 1948-51
Henniker-Major, John P. E. C., Assistant, European Recovery Department, FO, 1949-50
Heppel, Richard P., United Nations (Economic and Social) Department, FO, 1946-48
Hillilä, Karlo, Finnish Minister of the Interior, 1945-46; Minister of Supply, 1945-46
Hjalmarsson, Jarl, Chairman of the Swedish Conservative Party, 1950-61
Hollis, Major General Leslie. C., Secretary to the Chiefs of Staff Committee and senior Assistant Secretary to the War Cabinet, 1939-46; Deputy Secretary (Military) to the Cabinet, 1947-49
Hood, Viscount (Samuel), Reconstruction Department, FO, 1945-46
Howie, Commodore R. H., Senior British member of the Allied Control Commission, Finland, 1944-47
Hoyer Millar, Sir Derek R., Minister, British Embassy, Washington, 1948-50
Hull, Cordell, US Secretary of State, 1933-44
Hvass, Franz, Secretary-General, Danish Foreign Ministry, 1945-48
Hyndley, Viscount (John), Chairman of the National Coal Board, 1946-51
Inman, John, Labour Attaché, British Embassy, Oslo, 1946-49
Inverchapel, Lord *see* Kerr
Jebb, Sir H. M. Gladwyn, Acting Secretary-General United Nations, 1945-46; AUS, 1946-49; DUS, 1949-50, British Permanent Representative to the United Nations, 1950-54
Jellicoe, Earl (George), German Department, FO, 1947-48 (*see* Rushworth)
Jerram, Sir Cecil B., British Minister, later Ambassador (1947), Stockholm, 1945-48
Johnson, Herschel V., US Minister, Stockholm, 1941-46
Jung, General Helge V., Commander of the Swedish Armed Forces, 1944-51
Kallinen, Yrjö, Finnish Minister of Defence, 1946-48
Kekkonen, Urho, Finnish Minister of Justice, 1944-46; Deputy Speaker, 1946-48; Speaker, 1948-50; Prime Minister, 1950-53
Kenney, Christopher (Kit), Head of Norwegian Section, Political Intelligence Section, Ministry of Information, 1942-45; Press Attaché, British Embassy, Oslo, 1945-48
Kenney, Rowland, Adviser to the Norwegian Government in exile, 1942-45; Counsellor, British Embassy, Oslo, 1945-46
Kerr, Archibald J. K. Clark, British Ambassador, Moscow, 1942-46, created Lord Inverchapel, 1946, British Ambassador, Washington, 1946-48
Kinna, Peter F., APS to the Secretary of State for Foreign Affairs, 1947-51
Kirkpatrick, Sir Ivone A., AUS, 1945-48; DUS, 1948-49; PUS (German Section), FO, 1949-50; British High Commissioner for Germany, 1950-53
Kivimäki, Toivo M., Finnish Ambassador, Berlin, 1940-44. Sentenced to 5 years hard labour for war crimes, 1946.
Kivinen, Lauri, Director of Soteva, the Finnish War Reparations Commission, 1944-48
Kollontay, Aleksandra M., Soviet Minister, Sweden, 1930-45

Kraft, Ole Bjørn, Danish Minister of Defence, May-November 1945; Foreign Minister, 1950-53
Kristensen, Thorkil, Danish Minister of Finance, 1945-47 and 1950-53
Kukkonen, Antti, Finnish Minister of Education, 1940-43. Sentenced to 2 years hard labour for war crimes, 1946
Kuusinen, Otto W., Chairman of the Supreme Soviet of the Karelo-Finnish SSR, 1940-56
Labouchere, George P., First Secretary, British Legation, Stockholm, 1943-46
Lambert, Anthony E., Northern Department, FO, 1946-49, Counsellor, British Embassy, Stockholm, 1949-52
Lamming, G. N., Labour Attaché, Stockholm, 1945-48
Lange, Halvard M., Norwegian Foreign Minister, 1945-63
Langhelle, Nils, Norwegian Minister of Labour 1945-46; Minister of Transport and Communications, 1946-52
Ledward, Richard T. D., Consul, Helsinki, 1946-48
Leino, Yrjö, Member of Finnish Communist Party; Finnish Minister of Social Affairs, November 1944-April 1945; Minister of the Interior, April 1945-48
Lie, Haakon, Secretary of the Norwegian Labour Party, 1945-63
Lie, Trygve, Norwegian Foreign Minister, 1941-46, Secretary-General of the United Nations, 1946-1952
Linkomies, Edwin, Prime Minister of Finland, 1943-44. Sentenced to 5½ years hard labour for war crimes, 1946.
Lovett, Robert A., US Under-Secretary of State, 1947-49
Luukka, Eemil V., Finnish Minister of Agriculture, 1945-46
Mackenzie-Johnston, Henry B., Northern Department, FO, 1947-48
Mackenzie King, William L., Prime Minister of Canada, 1921-26, 1926-30 and 1935-48
Magill, Colonel J. H., British member of the Allied Control Commission, Finland, 1944-47
Malkin, Sir H. William, Legal Adviser, Foreign Office, 1929-45
Mallet, Sir Victor, British Minister, Stockholm, 1940-45
Makins, Sir Roger M., Minister, British Embassy, Washington, 1945-47; AUS, 1947-48; DUS, 1948-52
Mannerheim, Field-Marshal C. Gustaf E., President of Finland, 1944-46
Marshall, George C., US Secretary of State, 1947-49
Masaryk, Jan, Foreign Minister of the Czechoslovak Government in exile, 1940-45, and of the Czechoslovak Government, 1945-48
Mayhew, Christopher, Parliamentary Under Secretary of State, Foreign Office, 1946-50
McNeil, Hector, Minister of State, FO, 1946-50
Molotov, Vyacheslav, Commissar for Foreign Affairs, USSR, 1939-49
Montagu-Pollock, William H., Head of Cultural Relations Department, FO, 1946-47
Morrison, Herbert, Secretary of State for Foreign Affairs, March-October 1951
Møller, G. L. J. Christmas, Danish Foreign Minister, May-November 1945
Nielsen, Edgar E. M., British Embassy, Stockholm, 1942-45
Noble, Sir Andrew N., AUS, FO, 1949-51
Noel-Baker, Philip, Minister of State, FO, 1945-46; Secretary of State for Air, 1946-47, Secretary of State for Commonwealth Relations, 1947-50; Minister of Fuel and Power, 1950-51

List of Persons

Nordahl, Konrad, Leader of Norwegian trade union movement (*Landsorganisasjonen*), 1939-65
Nordenskiöld, Bengt, Commander in Chief, Swedish Air Force, 1942-54
Nygaardsvold, Johan, Prime Minister of Norway, 1935-45
Oftedal, Sven, Norwegian Minister of Social Affairs, 1945-48
Orlov, Pavel, Head of the Political Section, Allied Control Commission, 1944-45; Soviet Minister, Helsinki, 1945-47
Oxholm, Oscar O'N., Danish Ambassador, Oslo, 1939-40 and 1945-49
Paasikivi, Juho K., Prime Minister of Finland, 1944-46; President of Finland, 1946-56
Pakenham, Lord, Under-Secretary of State for War, 1946-47
Pekkala, Mauno, Finnish Minister of Defence, 1945-48; Prime Minister of Finland, 1946-48
Petersen, Harald, Danish Minister of Defence, 1945-47
Peterson, Sir Maurice D., British Ambassador, Moscow, 1946-49
Phillips, Morgan, Secretary, later General Secretary (1960) of the Labour Party, 1944-61
Prebensen, Per P., Secretary-General, Norwegian Foreign Ministry, 1945-46; Norwegian Ambassador, London, 1946-58
Pumphrey, John L., APS to the PUS, FO, 1946-47, APS to the Prime Minister, 1947-50
Prytz, Björn, Swedish Ambassador, London, 1938-47
Quisling, Vidkun A. L. J., Minister President of the German-appointed Norwegian National Government, 1942-45
Ramsay, Henrik, Finnish Foreign Minister, 1943-44. Sentenced to 2½ years hard labour for war crimes, 1946
Randall, Sir Alec W. G., British Minister, later Ambassador (1947), Copenhagen, 1945-52
Rangell, Jukka W., Prime Minister of Finland, 1941-43. Sentenced to 6 years hard labour for war crimes, 1946
Rasmussen, Gustav, Danish Foreign Minister, 1945-50
Reinikka, Tyko, Finnish Assistant Minister of Finance, 1943-44. Sentenced to 2 years hard labour for war crimes, 1946.
Reventlow, Count Eduard, Danish Minister, later Ambassador (1947), London, 1938-53
Roberts, Frank K., Minister, British Embassy, Moscow, 1945-48
Robertson, General Brian H, Deputy Military Governor Germany, 1945-48; Commander in Chief and Military Governor, Germany, 1948-49
Ronald, Sir Nigel B., Acting AUS, FO, 1942-47
Rose, E. Michael, First Secretary, British Embassy, Copenhagen, 1945-49
Rothnie, Alan K., Northern Department, FO, 1945-46
Rumbold, Sir Horace A. C., Head of Mutual Aid Department, FO, 1950-51
Ryder, Commander Robert E. D., VC, RN, Naval Attaché, British Embassy, Oslo, 1948-50
Ryti, Risto, Prime Minister of Finland, March-December 1940, President of Finland, 1940-44. Sentenced to 10 years hard labour for war crimes, 1946
Sargent, Sir Orme G., DUS, FO, 1939-46, PUS, FO, 1946-49
Savonenkov, Grigori M., Deputy Head, Allied Control Commission, Finland, 1944-48; Soviet Minister, Helsinki, 1948-51
Scavenius, Erik, Prime Minister of Denmark, 1942-43

Scott, Sir Oswald A., British Minister, Helsinki, 1947-51
Shepherd, Francis M., Political Representative, then Minister, Helsinki, 1944-47
Shepherd, Sir Edward H. G., British Minister, Reykjavik, 1943-47
Sihvo, Aarne, Commander in Chief, Finnish Defence Forces, 1946-53
Skaug, Arne, State Secretary, Norwegian Ministry of Foreign Affairs, 1947-49; Ambassador to the OEEC, 1949-55
Skog, Emil, Finnish Minister of Defence, 1948-50
Skylstad, Rasmus, Secretary-General, Norwegian Foreign Ministry, 1948-58
Sköld, Per Edvin, Swedish Minister of Defence, 1938-45; Minister of Finance, 1949-55
Söderhjelm, Johan O., Member of Swedish People's Party in Finland; Minister of Justice, 1939-40
Spaak, Paul-Henri, Prime Minister of Belgium, March 1946 and 1947-49; President of the United Nations General Assembly, 1947-49
Stalin, Joseph, General Secretary of the Central Committee of the Communist Party of the USSR, 1922-53
Stauning, Thorvald, Prime Minister of Denmark, 1924-26 and 1929-42
Steel, Christopher (Kit) E., Head of the Political Commission for the Allied Control Commission, Germany, 1945-47
Stefánsson, Stefán J., Prime Minister of Iceland, 1947-49
Steinþórsson, Steingrímur, Prime Minister of Iceland, 1950-53
Strang, Sir William, Political Adviser to C-in-C Germany, Berlin, 1945-47; Joint PUS (German Section), FO, 1947-1949, PUS, FO, 1949-53
Strömbäck, Helge, Vice-Admiral, Commander of the Swedish Navy, 1945-53
Sutton Pratt, Brigadier Reginald, Military Attaché, Stockholm, 1939-47
Svento, Reinhold, Finnish Assistant Foreign Minister, 1944-48
Tanner, Väinö, Prime Minister of Finland 1926-27; Foreign Minister, 1939-40. Sentenced to 5½ years hard labour for war crimes, 1946.
Talbot, Milo J. R. (Lord Talbot de Malahide, 1948), Northern Department, FO, 1947-49
Terboven, Josef A. H., Reichskommissar of Norway, 1940-45
Thomas, C. L., Labour Attaché, Helsinki, 1946 -51
Thorne, General Sir Andrew, Commander in Chief, Allied Forces in Norway, 1945
Thornton, Dr C. Grace, Second Secretary, British Legation Reykjavik, 1948-54
Thors, Ólafur, Prime Minister of Iceland, May-December 1942, 1944-47 and December 1949–March 1950; Foreign Minister May-December 1942 and 1944-47
Thorvardsson, Stefán, Icelandic Minister in London, 1944-50
Tomlinson, George, Minister of Education, 1947-51
Torp, Oscar F., Norwegian Minister of Defence, 1942-45; Minister of Supply and Reconstruction, 1945-48
Tranmæl, Martin, Editor of *Arbeiderbladet*, Norway, 1921-49
Truman, Harry S., President of the United States, 1945-53
Tuomioja, Sakari, Finnish Minister of Finance, 1944-45; Governor of the Bank of Finland, 1945-55
Törngren, Ralf J. G., Finnish Minister of Finance, 1945-48
Undén, Bo Östen, Swedish Foreign Minister, 1945-62
Vogt, Benjamin, Norwegian Minister, London, 1910-34
Vougt, Allan G. F., Swedish Minister of Defence, 1945-51

List of Persons

Vuori, Eero A., Finnish Minister of Labour, 1945; Finnish Minister, London 1945-52
Vyshinsky, Andrey, Deputy Commissar for Foreign Affairs of the USSR, 1946-49; Commissar for Foreign Affairs, 1949-53
Walsh, James M., First Secretary, Office of the Political Representative, Helsinki, 1945-46
Warbey, William N., Information Officer for the Norwegian Government in exile, 1942-45; Labour MP for Luton, 1945-50
Ward, John G., Reconstruction Department, FO, 1945-46
Wardrop, James C., First Secretary, British Embassy, Oslo, 1945-48
Warner, Christopher F. A., Head of Northern Department, FO, 1942-46, AUS, FO, 1946-1950
Warr, George M., Northern Department, FO, 1944-47
Warren, Avra, US Minister, Helsinki, 1947-50
Width, Trygve, Foreign Editor of *Morgenbladet*, Norway
Wied, Prince Victor zu, German Minister, Stockholm, 1933-43
Wigforss, Ernst J., Swedish Minister of Finance, 1936-49
Wilford, Kenneth M., APS to the Secretary of State for Foreign Affairs, 1949-51
Winant, John G., US Ambassador, London, 1941-46
Wold, Terje, Norwegian Labour politician and jurist; Minister of Justice, 1939-45
Wright, Michael R., British Ambassador, Oslo, 1950-55
Wærum, Ejnar, Head of Political-Economic Department, Danish Foreign Ministry
Wørm-Müller, Jacob S., Leader of the Norwegian Liberal party, 1945-52; delegate to the United Nations, 1946-51
Wuori *see* Vuori
Younger, Kenneth G., Minister of State, Foreign Office, 1950-51
Zaroubin, Georgi N., Soviet Ambassador, London, 1947-52
Zhdanov, Andrey, President of the Allied Control Commission, Finland, 1944-47
Zorin, Valerian A., Soviet Ambassador, Prague, 1945-47; Deputy Foreign Minister, 1947-55

DOCUMENT SUMMARIES

CHAPTER I

1944 –1945

	NAME	DATE	MAIN SUBJECT	PAGE
		1944		
1	SIR O. SARGENT DUS, Foreign Office	10 Mar.	Letter to Hollis (Cabinet Office) describes Norwegian Government's concerns about a possible Soviet occupation of Northern Norway.	1
2	MR EDEN Foreign Office	24 Sept.	Memorandum to War Cabinet discusses terms of armistice with Finland.	2
3	SIR A. CLARK KERR Moscow	20 Nov.	Letter to Eden reports that Molotov has suggested to the Norwegian Foreign Minister that sovereignty over Svalbard should be divided between Norway and the Soviet Union.	4
		1945		
4	SIR V. MALLET Stockholm No. 57	31 Jan.	Reports a conversation in which the Foreign Minister describes Swedish policy towards Russia and Germany in 1940-41.	6
5	MR SHEPHERD Helsinki No. 17	6 Feb.	Describes an evening with Zhdanov, head of the Allied Control Commission; discussion of Finnish history and fulfilment of the armistice terms.	7
6	MR WARR Northern Department, Foreign Office	25 Feb.	Minute to Haigh (Northern Department) comments on Sir V. Mallet's Annual Review for 1944 and assessing his judgement on Sweden's gradual move away from non-belligerency.	11
7	SIR O. SARGENT DUS, Foreign Office	7 Mar.	Minute to Northern Department covering Soviet reply to Norwegian Government's proposals regarding Svalbard and Bear Island, which the Norwegians regard as satisfactory.	12
8	TO LORD HALIFAX Washington Tel. No. 191 Saving	8 Mar.	Assesses the position of British forces in Iceland and long-term security interest there; requests that UK views be passed to State Department and their views sought, with a view to developing a common policy before the end of the war in Europe.	14

Document Summaries

	NAME	DATE	MAIN SUBJECT	PAGE
9	SIR O. SARGENT DUS, Foreign Office	9 May	Minute to Churchill describes allied intention to occupy Danish island of Bornholm and SHAEF's unexpected decision to inform the Russians beforehand.	16
10	SIR V. MALLET Stockholm No. 256	29 May	Reports a speech in which the Swedish Foreign Minister defended neutrality as the keystone of Swedish policy.	17
11	MR SHEPHERD Helsinki Tel. No. 219	8 Jun.	Reports that the Finnish Foreign Minister has assured him that a mutual assistance treaty with Russia is not on the agenda.	20
12	SIR V. MALLET Stockholm No. 295	17 Jun.	Valedictory despatch reviews Swedish foreign policy since his arrival in January 1940.	21
13	MR RANDALL Copenhagen Tel. No. 324	12 Jul.	Reports that the Danish Foreign Minister has asked whether it would be possible to link the ultimate withdrawal of British troops from Denmark with that of Soviet forces from Bornholm.	29
14	SIR J. ANDERSON Foreign Office Tel. No. 37 Saving	23 Jul.	Explains reasons for the reluctance of C-in-C Germany to allow the Danish Foreign Minister to visit the Danish minority in Schleswig.	31
15	SIR L. COLLIER Oslo No. 34	24 Jul.	Provides details of the Soviet response to the Norwegian proposals concerning Soviet demands about Svalbard and Bear Island.	32
16	MR SHEPHERD Helsinki No. 114	24 Jul.	Response to FO circular requesting information about the effect of the UK's external financial position on British foreign policy.	33
17	TO MR JERRAM Stockholm Tel. No. 1031	25 Jul.	Describes background to a joint British and US decision to approach Sweden with request for Government to institute controls over the exploitation of uranium deposits in Sweden.	35
18	MR HAIGH Northern Department, Foreign Office	25 Jul.	Letter to Allen (Terminal) encloses brief for British delegation at Potsdam on the possibility of a Soviet-Finnish alliance.	37
19	MR WARR, Northern Department, Foreign Office	28 Jul.	Minute to Warner (head of Northern Department) provides background briefing before a meeting with Shepherd, visiting from Helsinki.	39
20	MR WALSH Helsinki Tel. No. 328	7 Aug.	Reports that Soviet Union has announced its intention to establish diplomatic relations with Finland.	42

The Nordic Countries, 1944-1951

	NAME	DATE	MAIN SUBJECT	PAGE
21	TO MR BALFOUR Washington Tel. No. 8491	18 Aug.	Explains that UK cannot establish diplomatic relations with Finland until a peace treaty has been signed, but that there would be no objection to the establishment of quasi-diplomatic relations.	43
22	SIR O. SARGENT DUS, Foreign Office	28 Aug.	Record of meeting with Danish officials to discuss the treatment of the Danish minority in Schleswig.	43
23	TO MR RANDALL Copenhagen No. 148	28 Aug.	Meeting between Bevin and Danish Foreign Minister discussing position of Danish minority in Schleswig, Danish participation in occupation of Germany and withdrawal of British troops from the Faroe Islands.	45
24	TO SIR L. COLLIER Oslo No. 402	29 Aug.	Meeting between Bevin and Norwegian Foreign Minister discussing Norwegian military mission to Germany, whaling factories and the provision of equipment for Norwegian armed forces.	47
25	MR WARNER Northern Department, Foreign Office	5 Sept.	Minute to Sir O. Sargent comments on the Soviet intention to arrange a naval visit to Stockholm; supports a Swedish request for the British Navy to visit first.	49
26	MR BEVIN Foreign Office	8 Sept.	Memorandum to Cabinet Overseas Reconstruction Committee on 'The Problem of South Schleswig'. Concludes that there are insufficient grounds for a revision of the frontier, but that there would be no objections in principle to an exchange of population if that was acceptable to those concerned.	50
27	SIR O. SARGENT DUS, Foreign Office	14 Sept.	Letter to the Secretary, COS Committee, about the timing of the withdrawal of the majority of British troops from Denmark.	54
28	MR WARNER Northern Department, Foreign Office	23 Sept.	Letter to Hollis (Cabinet Office) informs him that Ministers will require time to consider American proposals to obtain bases in Iceland.	55
29	TO MR SHEPHERD Helsinki	25 Sept.	First official visit to the Foreign Office by Vuori, the Finnish political representative.	56
30	MR RANDALL Copenhagen Tel. No. 662	26 Sept.	Reports a further request from the Danish Foreign Minister for UK to fix a date for the withdrawal of military forces from Denmark.	57

Document Summaries

	NAME	DATE	MAIN SUBJECT	PAGE
31	MR SHEPHERD Helsinki No. 149	26 Sept.	Reports a meeting with Enckell, who raises concerns about the Peace Treaty, and hopes that there may be scope for some territorial readjustments.	57
32	NORTHERN DEPARTMENT Foreign Office	26 Sept.	Minute to Bevin on US desire for bases in Iceland; recommends that the State Department be advised to modify the basis on which they are planning to approach the Icelandic Government.	59
33	MR BEVIN Foreign Office	27 Sept.	Minute to Prime Minister seeks authority to propose to US Secretary of State that the US should request only a temporary lease of bases in Iceland, in view of concerns that a request for permanent facilities would give the Soviets a pretext for seeking similar facilities in Denmark and Norway.	60
34	LORD HALIFAX Washington Tel. No. 6859	14 Oct.	Reports that the US Chiefs of Staff are still considering Bevin's proposals on Iceland, though it is expected that they will prefer to keep to their original approach.	61
35	MR SHEPHERD Helsinki No. 171	17 Oct.	Comments on the consequences of Stalin's decision to extend by two years the time-limit for Finnish delivery of reparations.	63
36	MR ROBERTS Moscow Tel. No 4594	18 Oct.	Reports that Molotov has told the Norwegian Ambassador that it is time for USSR and Norway to resume conversations; assumes that this refers to the Soviet interest in Bear Island and Svalbard.	64
37	RECONSTRUCTION AND NORTHERN DEPARTMENTS Foreign Office	18 Oct.	Joint minute to Bevin about the US desire for bases in Iceland: considers that the Chiefs of Staff rather than State Department are determining policy and that they will not accept the British alternative proposal of a short-term lease.	65
38	MR SHEPHERD Helsinki	7 Nov.	Letter to Warner (Northern Department) describes an elk-shoot organised by the Minister of Agriculture.	67
39	LORD HALIFAX Washington Tel. No. 7470	8 Nov.	Provides details of US request for British assistance with its post-war military bases programme.	68
40	SIR L. COLLIER Oslo	15 Nov.	Letter to Sir O. Sargent discusses Norwegian Foreign Minister's concern that there 'was now a certain *malaise* in Anglo-Norwegian relations'.	70

	NAME	DATE	MAIN SUBJECT	PAGE
41	MR SHEPHERD Helsinki No. 197	24 Nov.	Comments on a paper by Magill of the Allied Control Commission recommending the adoption of a co-ordinated policy towards Scandinavia and Finland.	72
42	SIR W. STRANG Berlin Tel. No. 24 Saving	26 Nov.	Describes a meeting with representatives of the Danish minority in Kiel.	75
43	MR WARR Northern Department, Foreign Office	19 Dec.	Minute to Warner (Northern Department) comments on a press interview given by Danish Foreign Minister which suggests that there has been a change in attitude by the new Government towards the Russian presence on Bornholm and the withdrawal of British forces in Denmark.	76
44	TO MR RANDALL Copenhagen Tel. No. 640	23 Dec.	Describes a discussion with Danish Minister about the apparent change in Danish policy towards troop withdrawal: Reventlow is unable to explain his Government's position and will make enquiries.	78

CHAPTER II

1946 –1947

	NAME	DATE	MAIN SUBJECT	PAGE
		1946		
45	MR STEEL Berlin	10 Jan.	Letter to Warner highlights the danger of suggesting that German refugees in Germany will not have a vote, and the need to ensure that Randall understands the significance of this point.	80
46	MR RANDALL Copenhagen No. 11	11 Jan.	Draws attention to the 'small nation complex' in Danish relations with UK and anticipates that the new Danish Government may be more difficult to handle than its predecessor.	81
47	TO SIR L. COLLIER Oslo Tel. No 65	30 Jan.	Reports growing difficulties with the Norwegian Government over matters such as military equipment purchases; asks whether Collier thinks this may be due to increasing pressure from the Soviet Union.	82
48	TO MR REID BROWN Stockholm No. 30	31 Jan.	Encloses JIC paper on the disclosure of service information to the Swedish armed services, which recommends that Sweden should remain in Category C and so receive no classified information.	82

Document Summaries

	NAME	DATE	MAIN SUBJECT	PAGE
49	SIR L. COLLIER Oslo No. 23	2 Feb.	Reports that Lie has been replaced as Foreign Minister by Lange; provides details of Lange's background.	83
50	MR WARNER Northern Department, Foreign Office	2 Feb.	Letter to Collier comments on Lie's replacement by Lange and possibility of changes in Norwegian policy, including abandonment of western European co-operation and reluctance to continue with previously agreed military arrangements with Britain.	85
51	SIR L. COLLIER Northern Department, Foreign Office	12 Feb.	Reply to No. 50: considers that the Norwegians do not want to go back on their military understandings with the UK, but that joint defence arrangements with the Western powers are no longer practical politics as far as Norway is concerned.	87
52	MR SHEPHERD Helsinki Tel. No. 80	18 Feb.	Reports that the War Guilt Tribunal, due to announce sentences today, has adjourned; provides details of the sentences which it had proposed, and of a Soviet approach to Paasikivi urging longer sentences be given to all the accused.	90
53	MR WARNER Northern Department, Foreign Office	26 Feb.	Letter to Shepherd comments on No. 41; favours support for Finnish independence while not provoking a Soviet reaction.	91
54	MR JERRAM Stockholm No. 101 MR WARR Northern Department, Foreign Office	20 Mar.	Describes difficulties of carrying out instructions to seek removal of the few remaining anti-British officers in Swedish armed forces; proposes instead an approach to Undén. Warr supports this proposal.	92
55	SIR L. COLLIER Oslo No. 84	20 Mar.	Explains need to secure a better understanding of British policy by the Norwegian labour movement as a means of strengthening bilateral relations; outlines methods by which this can be achieved.	97
56	MR WALSH Helsinki No. 66	26 Mar.	Describes ceremony marking the retirement of President Mannerheim and explains the background to the election of Paasikivi as his successor.	100
57	MR WARNER AUS, Foreign Office SIR L. COLLIER Oslo	5 Apr.	Minute to Sargent, covering a minute by Collier proposing ways to deal with Norwegian difficulties in sending a full division to take part in the occupation of Germany.	102

xli

	NAME	DATE	MAIN SUBJECT	PAGE
58	MR WARR Northern Department, Foreign Office	10 Apr.	Report of a meeting considering the protection of British civil aviation interests when handing back Reykjavik airfield to the Icelandic Government.	104
59	TO MR WARDROP Oslo No. 181	19 Apr.	Instructions to invite Norwegian Government to send a mission to London to negotiate conditions for Norwegian military participation in the occupation of Germany.	106
60	MR SHEPHERD Helsinki No. 94	4 May	Describes a conversation with Finnish Foreign Minister reviewing relations with Soviet Union and expressing concerns about the Peace Treaty.	107
61	MR THOMAS Helsinki	20 May	Letter to Pickford (Ministry of Labour) gives personal impressions of the situation in Finland and of everyday life in Helsinki.	110
62	MR SHEPHERD Helsinki No. 106	21 May	Comments on Finnish fears of Soviet Russia, especially following the resignation of Mannerheim, and further apprehension about the Peace Treaty following the departure of a high-powered delegation to Moscow.	115
63	MR HANKEY Northern Department, Foreign Office	1 Jun.	Letter to Jerram refers to his concerns about apparent recent contradictions in UK policy towards Sweden, and reassures him that there has been no real change.	117
64	MR BEVIN Foreign Office	12 Jun.	Minute to Prime Minister asking whether he would be willing to meet Norwegian Ministers visiting London to conclude discussions about provision of equipment to the Norwegian armed forces and the supply of a Norwegian contingent to Germany.	118
65	MR RANDALL Copenhagen No. 264	24 Jun.	Provides an analysis of historical changes in Danish-Soviet relations, at a time when a Danish delegation is visiting Moscow to discuss trade matters.	119
66	SIR L. COLLIER Oslo No. 220	1 Jul.	Reports a speech by Norwegian Foreign Minister outlining the Norwegian policy of 'bridge-building' (i.e. between East and West).	124
67	MR JERRAM Stockholm	4 Jul.	Letter to Sargent comments on paper on 'The Soviet campaign against this country and our response to it' and assessing the limited extent of Communist influence in Sweden.	126

Document Summaries

	NAME	DATE	MAIN SUBJECT	PAGE
68	MR SHEPHERD Helsinki	16 Jul.	Letter to Hankey comments on Finnish-Soviet economic relations; emphasises that political considerations outweigh economic in the Soviet approach to Finnish matters.	129
69	SIR L. COLLIER Oslo	26 Jul.	Letter to Sargent comments on paper cited in No. 67 and proposes measures to counter Soviet influence in Norway.	131
70	MR SHEPHERD Helsinki	30 Jul.	Letter to Sargent comments on paper cited in No. 67: suggests encouraging the Finns to develop their democracy, and to avoid giving the Soviets a chance to complain about Finnish hostility to Russia.	133
71	MR WARR Northern Department, Foreign Office	27 Sept.	Minute to Hankey suggests a strong response to Danish reluctance to send a military contingent to Germany.	136
72	MR BEVIN Foreign Office	14 Oct.	Speech on conclusion of peace treaty with Finland.	137
73	SIR O. SARGENT PUS, Foreign Office	11 Nov.	Minute to Heads of Departments conveys Bevin's wish that arrangements should be made to give confidential briefings on foreign policy issues to Healey (International Secretary of the Labour Party).	138
74	MR SHEPHERD Helsinki No. 272	12 Nov.	Analyses Russian desire to integrate the Finnish economy with the Soviet Union, and describes the process by which this may be achieved; highlights the special position of Finnish industries which have been developed for reparations purposes.	139
75	TO MR RANDALL Copenhagen No. 459	20 Nov.	Record of conversation between McNeil and Danish Foreign Minister, who is disturbed about the deterioration in UK-Danish relations.	141
76	MR WARR Northern Department, Foreign Office	21 Nov.	Minute records first meeting at the War Office with a Danish military delegation, to discuss terms for the despatch of a Danish contingent to Germany.	142
77	CHANCERY Oslo	21 Nov.	Informs Northern Department of the arrangements made for the transport to Newcastle of two reindeer, which are being given to London Zoo by Gen. Dahl.	144

The Nordic Countries, 1944-1951

	NAME	DATE	MAIN SUBJECT	PAGE
78	MR MAYHEW Foreign Office	22 Nov.	Letter to Lord Pakenham (War Office) proposes a solution to the problem over finance which is preventing agreement with the Danes over terms for the supply of their contingent to Germany.	145
79	SIR L. COLLIER Oslo Tel. No 465	23 Nov.	Reports Lange's account of two recent conversations with Molotov, who had pressed for immediate negotiations on Svalbard; Lange undertakes to raise the matter in secret session in the *Storting*.	147
80	SIR L. COLLIER Oslo No. 416	26 Nov.	Provides a more detailed account of Lange's conversations with Molotov over Svalbard; comments on Lange's unwillingness to give ground and his readiness to consider making a public statement in due course.	147
81	MR BEVIN Foreign Office	3 Dec.	Minute to Prime Minister gives historical background to Molotov's recent discussion with Lange over Svalbard; notes that the Chiefs of Staff will be asked to reassess their view that the islands are of no strategic importance to the UK or Canada.	151
82	MR HANKEY Northern Department, Foreign Office	16 Dec.	Letter to Stapleton (Cabinet Office) requests Chiefs of Staff to reassess their view that there is no strategic objection to the establishment of Soviet bases on Svalbard.	152
		1947		
83	MR WARR Northern Department, Foreign Office	22 Jan.	Minute requests Bevin to speak frankly to Danish Minister about continuing problems with the provision of a Danish military contingent to Germany.	154
84	SIR L. COLLIER Oslo	24 Jan.	Letter to Hankey refers to Nos. 79 and 80; comments on the firmness of Lange's reaction to the Soviet approach over Svalbard.	155
85	MR HALFORD PS to PUS, Foreign Office	13 Feb.	Letter to Allen (Washington) concerning Danish plans to sell in the United States a diamond watch which had belonged to Eva Braun, and to divide the proceeds between the Danish *Frihedsfonden* and the British Special Forces Association.	157
86	MR SHEPHERD Helsinki No. 50	15 Feb.	Describes efforts of Legation staff and British Council in Finland to promote UK interests and policies.	158

Document Summaries

	NAME	DATE	MAIN SUBJECT	PAGE
87	SIR L. COLLIER Oslo Tel. No. 55	19 Feb.	Reports on the resolution on Svalbard, adopted by the *Storting* in secret session, declining to have any negotiation of a military character with a foreign power; states that Molotov has been informed of this decision.	164
88	MR WARR Northern Department, Foreign Office	22 Feb.	Minute to Jellicoe (German Department) expresses concern at the continued slowness of evacuation of German refugees from Denmark and the consequences thereof.	165
89	MR JERRAM Stockholm No. 70	11 Mar.	Submits annual report on political events in Sweden in 1946.	166
90	MR RANDALL Copenhagen No. 100E	13 Mar.	Comments on UK-Danish trade relations and their impact on the UK's external financial position.	170
91	MR SHEPHERD Helsinki No. 84	18 Mar.	Comments on UK-Finnish trade relations and their impact on the UK's external financial position.	173
92	NORTHERN DEPARTMENT, Foreign Office	20 Mar.	Brief for the UK Delegation in Moscow for a meeting to discuss Arctic bases, giving views on Iceland, Greenland and Svalbard.	175
93	JOINT PLANNING STAFF, Chiefs of Staff Committee	6 Jun.	Report on the strategic considerations involved in a common arrangement by Norway, Denmark and Sweden for the defence of Scandinavia.	178
94	MR RANDALL Copenhagen No. 208	20 Jun.	Reports on the possible impact on UK-Danish food price negotiations of the current adverse economic situation in Denmark.	182
95	MR SHEPHERD Helsinki No. 157	25 Jun.	Comments on an *Economist* article on the possible application to Finland of the methods recently applied by the Russians to Hungary.	184
96	MR HEALEY International Secretary, Labour Party	29 Aug.	Letter to Leskinen (Finnish Social Democratic Party) expresses concern about the possible political instability in Finland; invites him and party colleagues to visit UK in September.	187
97	MR RANDALL Copenhagen Tel. No. 352	12 Sept.	Comments on the cause and immediate likely consequences of the breakdown in the UK-Danish food price discussions.	188

The Nordic Countries, 1944-1951

	NAME	DATE	MAIN SUBJECT	PAGE
98	SIR C. JERRAM Stockholm No. 276	24 Sept.	Describes the background to the Swedish decision to raise status of the Legation to an Embassy, reports on his presentation of credentials to King Gustav and provides an account of the circumstances when one of his predecessors refused to yield precedence to the Danish Ambassador in 1654.	189
99	SIR L. COLLIER Oslo	29 Sept.	Extract from Annual Report on Heads of Foreign Missions in Norway, giving an assessment of the new Soviet Ambassador, Afanasiev.	192
100	TO MR SCOTT Helsinki Tel. No. 530	13 Nov.	Reports a conversation between Sargent and Finnish Minister, who has no information about the purpose of the visit of a large Finnish delegation to Moscow.	193
101	MR HANKEY Northern Department	14 Nov.	Letter to Jerram requests his views on whether the FO should reconsider its attitude towards publication of Prytz's telegram of 17 June 1940.	193
102	MR SCOTT Helsinki No. 288	24 Nov.	Reports that Enckell is unwilling to explain what happened when the Finnish delegation visited Moscow, but that Kallinen had left his Military and Air Attachés in no doubt that the subject of a military understanding had at least been raised there.	196
103	MR BEVIN Foreign Office	5 Dec.	Responds to a note from Reventlow, comments that the question of political recognition of the South Schleswig Association is now under review and explains the consequences which will follow if it is so recognised.	197
104	TO MR SCOTT Helsinki Tel. No. 569	16 Dec.	Reports an account by Swedish Ambassador which appears to confirm that a Finnish-Soviet political and military understanding was discussed in Moscow.	199
105	SIR L. COLLIER Oslo	27 Dec.	Letter to Hankey reports indications that Norway is beginning to move away from its policy of neutrality, starting to regard the Soviet Union as its enemy and taking measures accordingly.	199

Document Summaries

CHAPTER III

1948

	NAME	DATE	MAIN SUBJECT	PAGE
		1948		
106	SIR O. SARGENT PUS, Foreign Office	6 Jan.	Minute to Attlee covering a memorandum by the Overseas Negotiation Committee, proposing a compromise in the trade and financial negotiations with Denmark.	201
107	SIR L. COLLIER Oslo No. 8	15 Jan.	Reports a discussion with Norwegian Foreign Minister about Atlantic security, in which Lange expresses uncertainty about the US attitude in the event of war.	202
108	TO HM REPRESENTATIVES OVERSEAS Tel. No. 6 Saving	23 Jan.	Informs posts of Cabinet decision to establish an Information Research Department at FO to disseminate anti-Communist publicity.	204
109	MR BAXTER Reykjavik	26 Jan.	Letter to Bateman discusses Icelandic politics and Iceland's future relations with the United States.	206
110	MR MCNEIL Foreign Office	27 Jan.	Minute to Bevin reports conversation with Finnish Minister, who had asked whether the lack of mention of Finland in Bevin's Western Union speech implied a weakening of the British trade relationship with Finland.	209
111	TO SIR L. COLLIER Oslo Tel. No. 58	27 Jan.	Seeks comments on suggestion by Norwegian Minister of Defence that Norwegian troops should be withdrawn from Germany.	210
112	SIR C. JERRAM Stockholm Tel. No. 61	28 Jan.	Reports that Swedish Foreign Minister is most unwilling to express any opinion on Bevin's Western Union speech, though he has read it carefully.	211
113	MR RANDALL Copenhagen No. 49	3 Feb.	Reports reactions of Danish Foreign Minister to Bevin's Western Union speech; Rasmussen was interested in the policy but wished to consult his Scandinavian neighbours.	211
114	MR HANKEY Northern Department, Foreign Office	14 Feb.	Minute to Bateman summarises lack of progress in Scandinavian co-operation on moving towards closer association with the West.	213

The Nordic Countries, 1944-1951

	NAME	DATE	MAIN SUBJECT	PAGE
115	MR SCOTT Helsinki Tel. No. 89	27 Feb.	Reports that Stalin has written to the Finnish President proposing a pact of mutual assistance between Finland and the Soviet Union.	214
116	MR ETHERINGTON-SMITH Northern Department, Foreign Office	28 Feb.	Minute to Hankey reports on a meeting of the Chiefs of Staff Committee to discuss latest developments in Finland. Committee considered that a task force could be sent to the Baltic at short notice.	216
117	MR SCOTT Helsinki	2 Mar.	Letter to Hankey describes a range of Finnish ministerial reactions to Soviet proposal for a Mutual Assistance pact.	217
118	MR ETHERINGTON-SMITH Northern Department	4 Mar.	Minute to Hankey suggests that opinion in Finland is hardening against acceptance of the Soviet proposal for a pact.	218
119	TO MR SCOTT Helsinki Tel. No. 76	5 Mar.	Disagrees with US view that Finland should respond to Soviet pressure for a pact by reference to the United Nations.	219
120	SIR L. COLLIER Oslo Tel. No. 104	8 Mar.	Reports that the Norwegian Government has information from three different sources, indicating that they might soon be faced with a Soviet demand for a mutual assistance pact; Foreign Minister asks what help Norway could expect if she was attacked.	219
121	MR. HENDERSON Stockholm Tel. No. 178	10 Mar.	Concern of Swedish military that Sweden might have difficulty in obtaining military supplies from England in future.	220
122	LORD INVERCHAPEL Washington Tel. No. 1125	10 Mar.	Norwegian Government will soon raise with US the question of military assistance in the event of aggression; State Department wish to know outcome of Bevin's forthcoming meeting with Norwegian Foreign Minister in Paris.	221
123	TO LORD INVERCHAPEL Washington Tel. No. 2768	10 Mar.	Suggests that Norwegian apprehensions may be justified; instructs Ambassador to approach Marshall to discuss establishment of an Atlantic security system.	222
124	SIR L. COLLIER Oslo No. 74	12 Mar.	Reply to No. 108 outlines a series of measures to facilitate dissemination of anti-Communist propaganda in Norway.	223
125	LORD INVERCHAPEL Washington Tel. No. 1190	13 Mar.	State Department agree with the line Bevin proposes to take with Lange in Paris.	228

Document Summaries

	NAME	DATE	MAIN SUBJECT	PAGE
126	NORTHERN DEPARTMENT Foreign Office	13 Mar	Brief for Bevin before his meeting with Lange in Paris: suggests lines to take if Lange raises question of a possible Soviet threat to Norway.	228
127	TO SIR L. COLLIER Oslo No. 88	15 Mar.	Bevin has briefed Lange in Paris about his approach to the US to discuss the establishment of a system of Atlantic security, and about the US's positive response.	231
128	TO MR RANDALL Copenhagen No. 101	16 Mar.	Bevin has informed Rasmussen in Paris of his approach to the US on Atlantic security.	233
129	TO SIR C. JERRAM Stockholm No. 72	16 Mar.	Bevin has informed Undén in Paris that he is considering means by which the Brussels Pact could be extended in view of the indirect pressure being brought to bear on Norway.	236
130	MR SCOTT Helsinki No. 88	5 Apr.	Encloses memorandum comparing the situation in Czechoslovakia at the time of the Communist coup there, with current indications of Communist tactics in Finland.	239
131	SIR M. PETERSON Moscow Tel. No. 460	7 Apr.	Signature of Finnish-Soviet Treaty of Friendship, Co-operation and Mutual Assistance on 6 April.	242
132	CABINET CONCLUSIONS CM(48)27	8 Apr.	Finnish-Soviet Treaty has preserved Finland from Soviet interference in her internal affairs and treated her as a buffer state rather than a Soviet satellite.	243
133	MR SCOTT Helsinki Tel. No. 201	9 Apr.	President Paasikivi's assessment of Finnish-Soviet Treaty and his views on likely developments in Finnish politics	243
134	TO MR RANDALL Copenhagen No. 142	17 Apr.	Discussion with Rasmussen in Paris of Danish trade with Germany and Bevin's concerns about the high prices charged to the UK by Denmark for certain foodstuffs.	244
135	SIR L. COLLIER Oslo No. 110	21 Apr.	Reports a speech by Lange declaring that Norway would not enter into any pact with the Soviet Union, and welcoming both the Marshall Plan and the Bevin Plan (Western Union).	245
136	SIR L. COLLIER Oslo	22 Apr.	Letter to Hankey reports views of King Haakon on foreign policy issues, and his satisfaction with Lange's speech.	246

The Nordic Countries, 1944-1951

	NAME	DATE	MAIN SUBJECT	PAGE
137	MR SCOTT Helsinki No. 108	27 Apr.	Reply to No. 108 describes measures being taken in Finland to make anti-Communist publicity more effective.	248
138	SIR L. COLLIER Oslo No. 138	21 May	Reports on the visit by Churchill to Oslo, and the warm welcome he received.	249
139	MR KENNEY Oslo	26 May	Letter to Information Policy Department describes effective use of IRD material in Norwegian press.	250
140	MR WARNER AUS, Foreign Office	28 May	Reply to No. 124 describes measures taken to improve effectiveness of anti-Communist propaganda in Norway.	251
141	MR ETHERINGTON-SMITH Northern Department, Foreign Office	28 May	Minute to Sir O. Sargent before Bevin's meeting with Minister of Defence to discuss the supply of radar and other military equipment to Sweden.	252
142	MR BEVIN Foreign Office	7 Jun.	Speech to a Danish Parliamentary delegation visiting London.	254
143	MR SCOTT Helsinki No. 143	9 Jun.	Comments on Soviet decision to reduce Finnish reparations deliveries by 50%.	256
144	MR BATEMAN AUS, Foreign Office	12 Jun.	Minute to Bevin raises possibility of a more restrictive policy on the supply of arms to Sweden	258
145	MR TREVELYAN Economic Relations Department	16 Jul.	Letter to Rowan (Treasury) conveys Bevin's support for a suggestion that a Norwegian delegation should visit the UK to discuss closer economic collaboration.	259
146	SIR L. COLLIER Oslo Tel. No. 391	16 Sept.	*Storting* resolution that the 1935 decree imposing a new fishing limit should now be enforced.	260
147	SIR O. FRANKS Washington Tel. No. 4561	24 Sept.	US State Department have expressed concerns about British sales of fighter aircraft to Sweden and hope that Britain will adopt a more restrictive policy on arms sales in future.	260
148	MR HANKEY Northern Department, Foreign Office	30 Sept.	Memorandum on the relation of Sweden to Scandinavian co-operation and Atlantic and Western Union.	262
149	TO SIR O. FRANKS Washington Saving Tel. No. 1466	7 Oct.	Norwegian and Danish Foreign Ministers request postponement of any invitation to participate in a conference to discuss Atlantic security.	264

Document Summaries

	NAME	DATE	MAIN SUBJECT	PAGE
150	TO SIR O. FRANKS Washington Tel. No. 11146	9 Oct.	Meeting between Bevin and Marshall to discuss Atlantic security and prospects of encouraging Swedish involvement.	265
151	SIR C. JERRAM Stockholm Tel. No 570	13 Oct.	Refers to No. 150 and sets out the present Swedish attitude towards Scandinavian defence and Western Union.	266
152	MR HANKEY Northern Department, Foreign Office	22 Oct.	Record of FO meeting discussing Scandinavian adherence to an Atlantic security alliance and the tactics which Western powers should pursue to achieve that objective.	267
153	FOREIGN OFFICE MINUTE	27 Oct.	Agreed minute of discussions with Danish delegation on problems affecting the Danish-minded population in South Schleswig.	271
154	MR BEVIN Foreign Office CP(48)257	8 Nov.	Memorandum describing background to UK-Norwegian fisheries dispute and recommending that it should be referred to the International Court at The Hague.	273
155	SIR I. KIRKPATRICK DUS, Foreign Office	8 Nov.	Letter to Hoyer Millar (Washington) refers to No. 152 and concludes that decisions on further steps should await the outcome of current Scandinavian staff talks in Oslo.	274
156	MR JEBB AUS, Foreign Office	20 Nov.	Minute records discussion with Lange of Scandinavian defence negotiations and the Atlantic Pact.	275
157	MR FIGG Northern Department, Foreign Office	23 Nov.	Brief for a speech by Mayhew to a Swedish Parliamentary Delegation.	276
158	MR HANKEY Northern Department, Foreign Office	30 Nov.	Minute on Scandinavian defence negotiations; notes that Swedish opinion is cooling towards association with the West.	277
159	MR ETHERINGTON-SMITH Northern Department, Foreign Office	8 Dec.	Minute to Bevin on supply of arms to Sweden: recommends that Chiefs of Staff be asked to reconsider the problem and suggests that a more restrictive policy might now be desirable.	279
160	MR SCOTT Helsinki No. 274	15 Dec.	Reports on problems currently faced by the Finns in dealing with the Soviet Union, and Soviet complaints about Finnish behaviour.	281
161	MR FARQUHAR Stockholm Tel. No. 658	18 Dec.	Conversation with Foreign Minister about the supply of military equipment to Sweden.	283

The Nordic Countries, 1944-1951

	NAME	DATE	MAIN SUBJECT	PAGE
162	MR HANKEY Northern Department, Foreign Office	22 Dec.	Minute summarises developments concerning Scandinavia and the Atlantic Pact; notes that Swedish attitude remains unchanged despite the effect on arms supplies if Sweden does not join the Pact.	284

CHAPTER IV

1949 –1951

1949

163	MR HANKEY Northern Department	3 Jan.	Letter to Farquhar summarises FO views of the Swedish position on neutrality; agrees that it would be a mistake to put pressure on the Swedish Government.	287
164	MR HANKEY Northern Department	11 Jan.	Letter to Collier outlines Law Officers' opinions on fisheries dispute; these will be put to Cabinet for a decision on reference to International Court of Justice.	289
165	SIR L. COLLIER Oslo Tel. No. 11	12 Jan.	Reports on meeting of Scandinavian Prime Ministers at Karlstad and Swedish offer of arms to Norway.	290
166	MR HANKEY Northern Department, Foreign Office	13 Jan.	Minute to Bateman suggests that Norway and Denmark are impressed by the latest Swedish offer; proposes a series of interlocking pacts to buttress Scandinavia and provide the defence facilities the Western powers need.	291
167	MR FARQUHAR Stockholm	13 Jan.	Letter to Hankey suggests that Sweden is putting indirect pressure on Norway and Denmark, and is overselling itself as a military factor.	293
168	SIR L. COLLIER Oslo Tel. No. 23	14 Jan.	Reports Lange's view that there is no question of requesting postponement of the invitation to discuss the Atlantic Pact, though Norway and Denmark will put forward factors for special consideration.	296
169	TO MR FARQUHAR Stockholm Tel. No. 30	16 Jan.	Reports that Swedish Ambassador has been lobbying extensively to justify Swedish position; provides details of FO response.	297
170	SIR L. COLLIER Oslo Tel. No. 25 MR HANKEY Northern Department, Foreign Office	17 Jan.	Reports discussion with US Ambassador who sees no real change in Swedish policy and is concerned about Danish position; Hankey thinks that a system of interlocking pacts remains the best solution.	299

Document Summaries

	NAME	DATE	MAIN SUBJECT	PAGE
171	MR HANKEY Northern Department, Foreign Office	25 Jan.	Minute to Bateman reports that Swedish claims to satisfy defence requirements of all three Scandinavian countries have been disproved, and that Lange and Rasmussen will be discreetly informed.	301
172	MR HANKEY Northern Department, Foreign Office	25 Jan.	Letter to Collier comments on consequences of decision not to proceed with his proposal for a system of interlocking pacts.	302
173	MR HANKEY Northern Department, Foreign Office	26 Jan.	Minute to Bateman, for Sir O. Sargent, clarifies a report from Oslo of Hauge's apprehensions about Hankey's proposed system of interlocking pacts.	304
174	SIR L. COLLIER Oslo Tel. No. 51	31 Jan.	Reports a conversation with Secretary General of Foreign Ministry, who confirms there is no need to postpone the invitation to Norway to participate in discussion on the Atlantic Pact.	305
175	SIR L. COLLIER Oslo Tel. No. 59	1 Feb.	Reports Norwegian response to the recent Soviet approach, and Lange's intention to put questions to UK and US to help him deal with *Storting* and public opinion.	306
176	MR FARQUHAR Stockholm Tel. No. 42	1 Feb.	Reports that Air Attaché has been told by Swedes that if Norway joins the Atlantic Pact, Finland will place airfields at the disposal of the Russians.	308
177	TO MR FARQUHAR Stockholm No. 22	3 Feb.	Swedish Ambassador confirms that Sweden wishes any Scandinavian *bloc* to remain neutral, and prefers to keep Scandinavia outside the Atlantic Pact.	308
178	MR HANKEY Northern Department, Foreign Office	7 Feb.	Brief for Bevin on Atlantic Pact and Soviet note to Norway before his meeting with the Norwegian Ambassador.	309
179	TO SIR L. COLLIER Oslo No. 29	7 Feb.	Reports Bevin's discussion with Norwegian Ambassador of current state of negotiations for an Atlantic Pact.	312
180	TO SIR A. RANDALL Copenhagen No. 31	8 Feb.	Reports Bevin's meeting with Danish Ambassador, who explained Danish concerns about the loss of military supplies if they decide not to join the Atlantic Pact.	313
181	SIR O. FRANKS Washington Tel. No. 785	8 Feb.	Reports meeting with Acheson, who poses question whether Western interests are served better by Norwegian and Danish participation in Atlantic Pact, or by a neutral Scandinavian defence pact.	314

The Nordic Countries, 1944-1951

	NAME	DATE	MAIN SUBJECT	PAGE
182	MR BATEMAN SIR G. JEBB SIR O. SARGENT Foreign Office	9 Feb.	Minutes discuss No. 181 and favour Norwegian and Danish participation in Atlantic Pact despite COS preference for a Scandinavian defence pact.	316
183	FOREIGN OFFICE MINUTE	14 Feb.	Record of conversation with Norwegian Foreign Minister on latter's discussion with Acheson and terms on which Norway might join Atlantic Pact.	318
184	MR BEVIN Foreign Office	14 Feb.	Minute to Sir S. Cripps on Undén's attempts to persuade other Scandinavian countries to join a neutral *bloc* and lines to take should they meet at a forthcoming conference in Paris.	324
185	SIR L. COLLIER Oslo	23 Feb.	Letter to Hankey reports overwhelming support of Labour Party conference for Norwegian participation in Atlantic Pact.	325
186	MR ETHERINGTON-SMITH Northern Department, Foreign Office	3 Mar.	Minute to Hankey records discussion with Finnish Minister, who sought his views on Atlantic Pact discussions and doubted that Soviets would bring pressure to bear on Finland.	327
187	COUNT REVENTLOW Danish Embassy	7 Mar.	Letter to Sir I. Kirkpatrick acknowledges British assistance in resolving the problem of German refugees, who have now all left Denmark.	328
188	SIR A. RANDALL Copenhagen	8 Mar.	Letter to Hankey defends Danes against Norwegian allegations of 'defeatism'.	328
189	TO MR BAXTER Reykjavik No. 18	9 Mar.	Reports Icelandic concerns about Atlantic Pact negotiations.	329
190	SIR L. COLLIER Oslo	18 Mar.	Letter to Hankey refers to No. 188 and defends Norwegian criticisms of Denmark.	330
191	SIR A. RANDALL Copenhagen No. 97	30 Mar.	Discusses background to Danish decision to ratify signature of North Atlantic Treaty.	331
192	DR G. THORNTON Reykjavik No. 28	4 Apr.	Reports decision of *Althing* to approve Icelandic participation in North Atlantic Treaty and the Communist-inspired disturbances that followed.	334
193	TO MR CROWE Oslo No. 110	6 May	Discussion between Bevin and Lange of arrangements for implementation of North Atlantic Treaty.	337

Document Summaries

	NAME	DATE	MAIN SUBJECT	PAGE
194	MR HANKEY Northern Department, Foreign Office	9 May	Letter to Scott describes efforts of Soviet Ambassador to extract information from Finnish Minister on links between Finland and Brussels Treaty organisation.	338
195	SIR L. COLLIER Oslo	23 Jun.	Extract from Leading Personalities Report on Lange.	340
196	SIR A. CADOGAN New York Tel. No. 2164	13 Oct.	Forwards request from Icelandic UN delegation to IRD for anti-Communist material for use in forthcoming election campaign.	341
197	SIR A. RANDALL Copenhagen Tel. No. 318	29 Oct.	Reports sharp Danish press criticism of increase in British coal export prices; requests information and guidance.	341
198	MR FALLA Northern Department, Foreign Office	31 Oct.	Brief for Bevin before his meeting with Swedish Ambassador, who is expected to ask about the status of the supply of advanced radar equipment to Sweden.	342
199	MR HENNIKER-MAJOR Economic Recovery Department, Foreign Office	1 Nov.	Minute to Makins comments on a Norwegian proposal that UK should be associated with a Scandinavian regional grouping within the OEEC.	343
200	MR BEVIN, Foreign Office	7 Nov.	Minute to Attlee complains about lack of co-ordination and consultation before the Coal Board announced its decision to raise the price of coal exported to Denmark.	345
201	TO SIR L. COLLIER Oslo Tel. No. 727	20 Nov.	Reports Cripps's meeting with Scandinavian Foreign Ministers to discuss Scandinavian regional grouping within OEEC (No. 199.	345
		1950		
202	MR LAMBERT Stockholm No. 78	1 Mar.	Reports Swedish interest in, and reactions to, the British general election.	346
203	MR ETHERINGTON-SMITH Northern Department, Foreign Office	8 Mar.	Minute to Harrison reports that Finnish Minister has been put under more pressure to supply information to the Soviet Embassy, especially on the political situation in Scandinavia.	348
204	MR ETHERINGTON-SMITH Northern Department, Foreign Office	11 Apr.	Minute to Harrison reviews Scandinavian attitudes to North Atlantic Treaty, and concerns in Norway and Denmark about costs and the limitations of available assistance.	349

The Nordic Countries, 1944-1951

	NAME	DATE	MAIN SUBJECT	PAGE
205	MR SCOTT Helsinki No. 78	12 Apr.	Reviews economic and social developments in Finland during the last four years; highlights problems of reparations, rebuilding of foreign trade and inflation.	351
206	TO MR BEELEY Copenhagen No. 94	21 Apr.	Discussion with Danish Prime Minister of Denmark's economic problems following British devaluation and concerns about German rearmament.	354
207	SIR P. DIXON DUS, Foreign Office	10 Jul.	Discussion with Swedish Ambassador of the Council of Europe: the latter had commented positively on the Human Rights Commission.	355
208	MR BAXTER Reykjavik Tel. No. 70	15 Aug.	Describes Icelandic reluctance to improve their defence; suggests that Lange might be asked to take this up during a visit he will be making shortly.	355
209	MR BEVIN, Foreign Office	30 Aug.	Minute to Attlee expresses concern about the possible need, caused by supply shortages, to break the contract to supply coal to Denmark and Sweden.	356
210	MR HARRISON Northern Department	4 Sept.	Minute to Bevin reports an approach by Swedish Ambassador to discuss suspension of the supply of Vampire airframes to Sweden.	357
211	SIR H. FARQUHAR Stockholm	26 Oct.	Letter to Harrison reports assumptions which Swedish Defence Minister appears to have made about military supplies to Sweden in time of war and the difficulties which would be involved in providing clarification.	358
212	SIR L. COLLIER Oslo No. 281	22 Nov.	Valedictory despatch records his final impressions of Norway and UK-Norwegian relations after his long association with the country.	359
213	SIR H. RUMBOLD Mutual Aid Department, Foreign Office	1 Dec.	Minute to Northern Department expresses doubts about the value of UNISCAN meetings but notes the wider political advantages of the grouping.	364
		1951		
214	SIR R. MAKINS DUS, Foreign Office	13 Jan.	Minute to Strang records considerable importance attached by Hammarskjöld to UNISCAN.	365
215	MR HARRISON Northern Department, Foreign Office	15 Jan.	Replies to No. 211 that it would better not to say anything to the Swedes at this stage.	366

Document Summaries

	NAME	DATE	MAIN SUBJECT	PAGE
216	MR WILFORD APS to Foreign Secretary Foreign Office	2 Aug.	Minute to Barclay notes that four Cabinet Ministers will be holidaying in Norway in August.	367
217	TO MR LAMBERT Stockholm No. 170	6 Sept.	Reports meetings between Morrison and King Gustav VI and Prime Minister of Sweden.	368

MAP

THE NORDIC COUNTRIES AFTER THE SECOND WORLD WAR

From *The Scandinavian States and Finland: A Political and Economic Survey* (London and New York: Royal Institute of International Affairs, 1951).

CHAPTER I

1944-1945

No. 1
Letter from Sir O. Sargent to General Hollis (Cabinet Office),
10 March 1944
Most Secret (FO 371/43248, N1586/1586/30)

Dear Hollis,

I enclose copy of an *aide-mémoire* left with me on the 19th February by the Norwegian Minister for Foreign Affairs and the Norwegian Ambassador[1] on the subject of reports received by them regarding the combing out of German forces in northern Norway.[2] I was assured that the source of this information (which incidentally tallies generally with reports which we have received from SOE) was excellent and well known to, and trusted by, the Admiralty.

In communicating this *aide-mémoire*, M. Lie reverted to the subject of the Norwegian Government's desire (of which you are aware from Ronald's letter U6552/4214G of the 28th December last and connected correspondence)[2] that our military authorities should not confine their planning to Southern Norway but should provide for the occupation of Northern Norway if and when it was evacuated by the Germans. M. Lie contended that, if Northern Norway were left to fend for itself, this might very well mean that the Russians would break in and occupy the country indefinitely. The population in the north was so sparse that, in such an event, the occupying Russians might outnumber the Norwegians.

M. Lie had made similar representations to Warner of this Department on the 24th January basing himself on an article which had appeared in the *Sunday Times* the day before suggesting that the Soviet Union might be enabled to invade Norway from the north as a result of the Finnish capitulation. He was somewhat reassured by Warner's pointing out the physical difficulty of such an enterprise and the fact—of which M. Lie knew from our Secretary of State—that the Soviet Union had recognised that Norway lay within the Anglo-American military theatre.

I told M. Lie that the question of sending British detachments to the north of Norway was primarily one for the Chiefs of Staff and that in view of the major plans in which they were engaged, I thought it unlikely that they would be willing to consider at this juncture the earmarking of British forces for Northern Norway. I promised, however, that his representations would be brought to their attention.

[1] Trygve Lie and Erik Colban.
[2] Not printed.

I should be grateful if you would put this matter to the Chiefs of Staff and let me have some material for a reply to M. Lie.

In connexion with these Norwegian representations, we have been informed that on the 10th February, General Hansteen[3] wrote to the General Officer Commanding-in-Chief, Scottish Command,[4] urging that very serious consideration should be given to the possibility of an occupation of Trondheim and the Trondelag at an earlier date than is at present provided for in our plans for Norway. Owing to the difficulties of communication, General Hansteen considered that it would be difficult to keep effective control over South-Eastern Norway before the Trondelag had also been occupied. The moral effect of the presence of Allied troops in the south, for instance around Oslo, could not prevent 'incidents and disturbances' in the Trondheim area. General Hansteen also said that his Government attached importance to an earlier occupation of the Trondelag region for political reasons of the same kind as those which had made them anxious that British troops should be sent to Northern Norway.

We have been asked for guidance by our liaison officer at SHAEF as to what reply should be returned to General Hansteen's request. Perhaps you could also let me know the views of the Chiefs of Staff on this question.[5]

Yours sincerely,
(for Sir O. Sargent)
C.F.A. WARNER

---

[3] General Wilhelm Hansteen, Deputy Commander in Chief, Norwegian Armed Forces, 1944-45.
[4] General Sir Andrew Thorne.
[5] A draft was initially submitted for sending to Sir Frederick Bovenschen, Joint PUS, War Office. However, Warner decided that it would be better to put the issues raised by Lie directly to the Chiefs of Staff. He minuted that he did not think that the Foreign Office should try to influence the Chiefs of Staff as regards sending troops to Northern Norway by implying that they wished to provide reassurance to Lie, a consideration that had been mentioned in the draft letter to Sir F. Bovenschen. Lie attached considerable importance to the threat of a Russian occupation of Northern Norway: Warner noted on 25 February that after his meeting with Sargent on 19 February he had also raised it separately with the Secretary of State (FO 371/43428, N1586/1586/30G).

No. 2

Memorandum from Mr Eden to the War Cabinet, 24 September 1944
Secret (CAB 121/363)

Armistice with Finland

My colleagues will have seen the telegraphic correspondence with His Majesty's Ambassador at Moscow leading up to the conclusion of the armistice with Finland. But it may be convenient that I should make some comments upon it.

2. The armistice was signed on behalf of all the United Nations at war with Finland, i.e. besides the Soviet Union and this country, the Dominions and Czechoslovakia. The terms were communicated to the United States Government.

3. The main terms are, in most respects, those which were published and generally hailed as moderate when they were rejected by the Finns at an earlier stage. The conditions which were put to the Finns for acceptance before negotiations in Moscow could be opened were also published at the time, *viz.*, the rupture of relations with Germany and a provision that, if the Germans did not

comply with a demand that they should withdraw all their armed forces from Finland by the 15th September, they should be disarmed, and handed over to the Allies. Before negotiations had opened in Moscow, the Finns had received an assurance of Russian help in expelling the German forces from Northern Finland.

4. The Russians complicated matters by proposing to sign an immediate peace treaty. We pointed out that this was impossible and discussed with the Russians the possibility instead of embodying some of the long-term provisions in an agreement for preliminaries of peace. But in the end the Russians decided after all to conclude a single armistice agreement. The final peace treaty with Finland remains, therefore, to be concluded later. But the full extent of Russia's main demands on Finland are [sic] now fixed and known. This is, I consider, all to the good. Although they are not light, apprehensions fairly widely entertained in Scandinavia and elsewhere, such as that Finland would cease to exist as an independent nation, that under the heading of reparations practically the whole of Finnish man-power and economy might be conscripted for rehabilitation work in devastated Soviet territory, etc., are disposed of. The indemnity to be paid by Finland is, indeed, much lighter than that included in the earlier published demands; the amount has been reduced by half to 300 million dollars, and the period of payment has been extended by one year to six years. (This reduction is no doubt due to the view expressed by us earlier that the original Russian claim was very heavy and would seriously affect our prospects of getting important imports from there.)

5. As regards the territorial settlement, this save in one respect, follows the terms rejected by Finland earlier and accepted as moderate by world opinion at the time, viz., a return to the position under the 1940 treaty of peace between Finland and Russia and the cession of the Petsamo district. The addition is that Finland leases to Russia for fifty years territory at Porkkala-Ud on the south coast of Finland for a naval base in lieu of the thirty year lease of Hangö, which the Russians held under the 1940 peace treaty and which the Finns were most anxious to see terminated. My colleagues may have seen Stockholm telegram No. 1085 of the 18th September,[1] reporting that the Secretary General of the Swedish Foreign Office[2] is deeply depressed about this condition. I think his view is exaggerated. It is true that the area at Porkkala-Ud is larger than the Hangö leased area and that it runs to within 10 miles of Helsinki. But Helsinki would be just as much under a permanent threat from Russian bombers were there no base at Porkkala-Ud. The area is not commercially important, whereas Hangö was a very useful port and was also said to have considerable sentimental importance. The Chiefs of Staff saw no objection to the establishment of the Soviet base at Porkkala-Ud and the Russians insisted that, for military reasons, it was essential to them. The Russians (and we as their Allies) have suffered greatly since 1941 through the complete blocking of their Baltic fleet in the Gulf of Finland and it seemed to me extremely difficult in these circumstances to contest the Russian demand to safeguard themselves against Germany being able to repeat the process. Certainly to have done so would have made the worst possible impression on the Russians.

6. With the cession of Petsamo, the interests of the International Nickel Company of Canada in the Petsamo nickel mines (through their British subsidiary the Mond Nickel Company) will be taken over by the Soviet State, since of course no foreign company is allowed to operate in the Soviet Union. The Soviet

---

[1] Not printed.
[2] Erik Boheman.

Government, after suggesting that we should seek compensation from the Finns, have, I am glad to say, accepted the obligation to compensate the British interests involved and have offered a maximum of 20 million dollars. We are in touch with the Canadian Government, who have informed us that, although the International Nickel Company put their claim at 50 million dollars, they are prepared to accept 20 million dollars. We are discussing with the Canadian Government the further handling of this matter. My own view is that we should be ill-advised not to accept the Soviet offer immediately and so to avoid the possible risk that it would be withdrawn or that we should get into a difficult discussion with the Soviet Government in which they would ask for the company's claim to be substantiated in detail. I understand the Treasury view to be that the company are founding their claim on an abnormal basis, since they appear to be including a very large amount in prospective profits from the nickel mines. The actual amount of capital invested in the mines is only in the region of 6½ million dollars.

7. The other articles of the armistice require no special comment, I think. They are broadly on similar lines to the corresponding articles of the Roumanian armistice, except that the Finns are not required to declare war on Germany nor to use their army against Germany. In fact, there is no question of the Finns being co-belligerent like the Roumanians.

A.E.

No. 3

Letter from Sir A. Clark Kerr (Moscow) to Mr Eden, 20 November 1944
Top Secret and Personal (AP SCA 44/19, N8107/8107/G)[1]

My dear Anthony,

Soon after Trygve Lie's visit to Moscow, which seemed to have gone so well, I noticed something uncomfortable on the mind of my Norwegian colleague,[2] something gnawing at his kindly old bosom, which he wanted but did not dare to reveal to me. I felt pretty sure that it would come out sooner or later if I showed no interest and if I went on congratulating him on the happy achievements of Mr Lie and himself. Well, it did and this is it.

At the midnight goodbye talk at the Kremlin Molotov spoke of this country's need for security and of the unfairness of international conventions which had been concluded when the Soviet Union was down and out and to which it had only acceded with reluctance. For instance there was the Spitsbergen business which he thought, might well be reviewed. Bear Island, which was of no apparent use to Norway, would serve Russia well as an air base. Did it not command the entrance to the Barents Sea and therefore to the White Sea? And what about Spitsbergen itself? Russians had been digging coal there quite as long as Norwegians. Would not some kind of division of sovereignty be a good thing?

Mr Lie winced and showed some resistance, whereupon Molotov 'in almost threatening tone' remarked that it was always better to settle such matters amicably and not to have a row about them. Mr Lie might think it over.

[1] The original letter is in the Avon Papers at the University of Birmingham.
[2] Rolf Andvord.

When he got home Mr Lie did, and the result of his thinking was very painful. He told the Norwegian Ambassador that he would hug this dreadful story to himself until he could see you in London 'not at the Office but at your private house' and get your advice.[3] Meanwhile the Ambassador was to keep it closely to himself and above all not on any account to tell the British Ambassador. Well, as you see, somehow or other, the story has come to me and if Mr Lie ever heard that it had, the Norwegian Ambassador would most certainly get the sack. I was begged therefore not to telegraph it, and I promised not to do so. But I told the Ambassador that I would have to pass it on to you when I got to London and I am putting it down now while it is still fresh in my mind. I told him too that I felt sure that if it reached you from me before it reached you from Mr Lie, you would take it as completely fresh news when Mr Lie's turn came.

The Norwegian Ambassador has been doing some thinking about it, and in a letter to Mr Lie that will probably go in the aircraft which takes me to London he is advising that the Norwegian government should not reject Molotov's suggestion out of hand. They should rather declare their willingness to consider it, against some compensating rectification of frontiers roundabout Petsamo, when the time of the general settlement comes and when it is possible to consult in peace and quiet the signatories of the Spitsbergen convention.

He thinks that Bear Island, except as a meteorological station and a possible prison camp for Quislings, is of no use to Norway and might well become a Soviet airbase without any harm to Norway. Spitsbergen is a more difficult matter, but he does not see any dangers in some kind of division of sovereignty, or rather less than in a row with this country. Briefly, his advice is that Mr Lie should say to Molotov pretty quickly: 'We don't much like your idea, but if you are really bent upon it, we are ready to consider it and discuss it, and when the time comes, to put it to our fellow signatories and to our parliament.'

I much wonder what you will think of all this.[4]

Yours ever,
Archie

---

[3] Lie did raise the question with Eden shortly after his return to London, on 24 November. He did not inform the United States of this approach until July 1945: see FRUS 1945, Vol. V, pp. 91-92.

[4] Eden subsequently wrote to Churchill on 19 January 1945, describing the meeting between Lie and Molotov. He noted that the Norwegian Government had replied to Molotov, claiming that Russian economic interests were adequately safeguarded under the International Treaty of 1920 and suggesting that the two Governments should approach the other signatory powers with a view to securing their agreement to the Russian proposal. The Soviet Government responded that this did not go far enough to satisfy their wishes, and the Norwegians therefore proposed to tell them that they intended to inform the other interested Governments of the situation which had arisen. Lie remained anxious that the Soviet Government should not become aware that he had been briefing Eden (FO 371/47503, N502/90/30G). Churchill commented on 21 January: 'Surely await Peace Table' (FO 371/47503, N890/90/30G). After consideration of this question, the Chiefs of Staff concluded on 15 January 1945 that Russian possession of Spitsbergen would pose little threat either to Norway or to the UK (JP(44)321 (Final) of 15 January 1945, FO 371/47503, N1459/90/30G).

The Nordic Countries, 1944-1951

No. 4

Sir V. Mallet (Stockholm) to Mr Eden, 31 January 1945
No. 57 (FO 371/48041, N1421/1106/42)

Sir,

After dinner last night the Swedish Minister for Foreign Affairs and I drifted into a talk about the events of the last five years. Our conversation arose out of my asking him whether he thought there were any real grounds in the story being put around by the Russians and their friends here that it was really the Soviet Government which saved Sweden from invasion by Germany in 1940. Monsieur Günther said that it was true that in the spring of 1940 after the invasion of Norway the Soviet authorities had told the Swedish Government that they had warned the Germans to keep their hands off Sweden. Monsieur Günther had no reason to believe that this was not the case. Whether, however, it was this action by the Russians which really influenced Hitler, Monsieur Günther was much less certain. The Russian motives were of course quite obvious. During the first Russo-Finnish war it was urged by many Swedes, and of course by the British and French Governments, that Sweden ought to send several divisions to fight the Russians in Finland. The Swedish Government had all along held that this course would be utter folly because sooner or later Finland was bound to succumb to the enormous Russian superiority in manpower and armaments and a couple of Swedish divisions, or for that matter a couple of Allied divisions, would never suffice to turn the scale or even delay the decision for very long. Monsieur Günther had always felt that in refusing to allow the Allies facilities to pass through Northern Sweden to Finland the Swedes had rendered us a good service because they had prevented an armed clash between us and the Red Army which would have left us in more or less of a state of war in 1941 when Russia was attacked by Germany. I argued that of course there had been many quick changes during this war and that no doubt we should have found some way of making up our former quarrel with the Russians in order to fight the common enemy, Germany. Monsieur Günther went on to say that, while not imputing to the British and French the sole motive of wishing to occupy the Gällivare district and the iron ore mines, at the same time he believed that Swedish permission to us would merely have resulted in this and that our troops would never have got very much further towards Finland. This of course would have produced an intolerable situation for the Germans who throughout early 1940 had been impressing upon the Swedes that they intended to fight their enemies wherever they found them, that is to say, that if Allied troops were in Sweden the Germans would go after them. Obviously it was much against Russian interest to have the Germans anywhere in Sweden. After the war the Russians had taken Hangö from the Finns for the sole reason that they wanted to close the Gulf of Finland against the Germans. *A fortiori* they would not have wished to see the Germans installed on the Swedish coast in the Gulf of Bothnia.

The Germans on the other hand did not for the time being wish to pick a quarrel with the Russians because they intended as soon as the war in the West was settled in their favour to turn against Russia and attack her. It was much more for this reason than for fear of offending the Russians that Germany had not attacked Sweden in 1940. From the point of view of her strategy against the Allies, Germany had obtained what she wanted by seizing Norway and Denmark and she could afford to leave Sweden isolated, because she believed that the defeat of the

Western Powers would result in their making peace. The idea was that Germany would then attack Russia with Finland as an Ally and that Sweden, whose sympathy for Finland had been so strongly shown during the winter war, would join with Germany and Finland in this crusade against Bolshevism. Meanwhile Germany naturally did not wish to antagonize Sweden in any way, still less attack her, which would have upset the whole of this scheme. That the Germans firmly believed that at the right moment Sweden would cooperate with them was shown by the attitude of the German Minister, Prince zu Wied, when he visited Monsieur Günther on the day when Germany attacked Russia in 1941. He came to the Ministry for Foreign Affairs accompanied by two important Germans, one of whom I think Monsieur Günther described as a General. He entered Monsieur Günther's room smiling all over this face, grasped his hand for about two minutes and remarked that now at last the time had come when Sweden and Germany would march together as friends. He was subsequently extremely disillusioned at the coldness with which Monsieur Günther received these remarks. Monsieur Günther went on to give a rather feeble justification of his policy at the time in agreeing to the transit of one German division through Sweden to Finland. As far as I could understand him it was a case of sheer appeasement in order not to provoke the Germans to take violent measures. At the same time it was considered to be an act of friendship towards Finland whose Government had also asked the Swedes to allow this transit, rather than direct assistance to Germany. At that time Swedish sympathy for Finland was still very strong and anti-German feeling had not been fanned to its later intensity by the behaviour of the Gestapo in Norway, It was not until September 1941 that the first executions of trade unionists took place in Oslo. The very half-hearted amount of help which this transit constituted did not, as it turned out, satisfy the Germans although it did, in Monsieur Günther's opinion, ward off a very dangerous threat, and from that time onwards the Germans realized that they could never in any circumstances expect to find in Sweden an ally or even a co-belligerent.[1]

I have, etc.,
V.A.L. MALLET

[1] Northern Department minuting on this despatch expressed reservations about the views put forward by Günther. Ewart noted that while Günther had defended the Swedish policy of refusing facilities for the passage of British and French troops through Sweden to Finland, it was rather more difficult for him to explain the reasons for allowing a German division to pass through Sweden to Finland. Warr and Haigh also considered that Günther's arguments were inconsistent and unconvincing (FO 371/48041, N1421/1106/42).

No. 5

Mr Shepherd (Helsinki) to Mr Eden, 6 February 1945
No. 17 Confidential (FO 371/47369, N1600/33/56)

Sir,
I have the honour to report that I visited General Zhdanov at his request at 8 p.m. last night, accompanied by Captain Beale. The Colonel-General was attended

by Lieutenant-General Savonenkov,[1] M. Orlov, Colonel Vachitov and his Chief of Staff. After tracing the advances of the Russian armies on the large map of Europe in the Colonel-General's office (on which I noticed, as on the map at the Malmi airport, that only the Russian lines were marked and no indication of any Western Front was given) we sat down to talk. There was, as usual, a small table at right-angles to the General's desk but, possibly to mark the informality of the occasion, General Zhdanov sat at the table opposite and not at the desk. We started with a general and preliminary talk about Finland and the Finns and I rather miscalculated the duration of these necessary preliminaries because Orlov suggested that we should go into the next room to see a film before I had broached the question of the fulfilment of the armistice terms. I accordingly did so rather hurriedly and we talked on this matter for another half-hour. At the end of that time we went into the salon, which had been arranged for the showing of the films, the projector being hidden behind the sliding door of the adjoining dining room. General Zhdanov and I sat upon a sofa at one side of these doors flanked by Colonel Vachitov and Captain Beale. At the other side of the room were M. Orlov and General Savonenkov on a similar sofa, while the Chief of Staff was accommodated on a chair half-way down one side. The films shown were those I had sent to the Colonel-General consisting of a short film *V.1* another short called *The Common Cause*, and *Coastal Command*. The operator got the first and last of the seven reels of *Coastal Command* in their right order, but the rest were shown completely haphazard, so that the unfolding of the film was completely spoilt, and it was quite unintelligible so far as any connected story was concerned. After this performance we were treated to tea and tangerines, and then were shown a Russian newsreel and a two-reel film about the celebration of the anniversary of the Revolution. After that we had another glass of tea and continued talking for some time. I left a little before 12.30. I should not have stayed so long, but there were several subjects which I had hoped to mention before the cinema began. In view of the traditional absence of consideration for the feelings of their guests which the Russians are apt to show, I fear I felt a certain malicious pleasure in extending the obvious boredom of M. Orlov and General Savonenkov on their distant sofa while I persisted with the conversation.

2. As regards the Finns in general, very little that was fresh emerged. We agreed about the slowness of the Finns in any kind of action, their absorption in themselves and their ignorance of affairs outside their own country. The Colonel-General was inclined to consider that there was a definite core of Fascist influence in Finland, but thought that Fascism was now at such a low ebb that this core no longer had real importance. I pointed out that there was, nonetheless, a fairly widespread tendency, especially in certain classes, towards friendly feelings for Germany, as apart from Hitler Germany, for cultural reasons and because Germany had been the natural support for the traditional Finnish anti-Russian attitude. The Colonel-General agreed and considered that there was in fact a good deal of militarism in Finland rather on the German model, to which I replied that I rather doubted whether Finnish militarism was really comparable with that of Germany. The Finns had been for so many centuries a battleground between Sweden and Russia that they had been forced to be a military nation. The Colonel-General thought that there was something in that. We agreed that the Finns had no conception of the darker side of Germany or of the atrocities which had been

---

[1] Soviet Deputy President of the Allied Control Commission.

committed under the Hitler regime both before and during the war, and that the Finns could reasonably be accused of being deliberately blind to these matters. We also agreed that it was remarkable how little notice appeared to be taken by the Finns of the unreasonable devastation committed by the Germans in Rovaniemi and the north of Finland generally. I said that I considered it of great importance to do all that we could to enlighten the Finns on this subject and told him of the plans that the press attaché was working out for the dissemination of British books, films and propaganda generally. It was, however, going to be very difficult to bring the Finns into any realisation as to the kind of people with whom they had been collaborating during the war. I added that considering their history and the short time which they had had to create a working democracy, they had, on the whole, made a good and promising start. Colonel-General Zhdanov agreed to all these points and indicated that he was also of the opinion that the Finns were making progress towards democracy and would continue to do so. It may be remarked here that it was very difficult to get the Colonel-General to offer any definite opinions and it was necessary for me to attempt to formulate them for him and then get his views for or against. In the course of the conversation, I said that it had been brought to my notice from more than one source that although the Finns alleged that they knew Russia and the Russians very well, they were in fact very ignorant on the subject. I had been struck by the report of Mr. Waddams, the British clergyman who recently visited Finland and who had been with the Archbishop of York's mission to Moscow some time before. The Finnish clergy were completely ignorant of the progress in church matters in Russia since the Revolution and had been surprised and pleased to hear from Mr. Waddams what was going on. The Colonel-General rather surprised me by replying to this that he knew very little about church matters in Finland, though he understood that the Finns were, in the main, Protestant. I said that the influence of the Church in Finland was considerable and should not be under-estimated. I hoped that Mr. Waddams had been able to introduce a rather better atmosphere among them and I understood that the new Archbishop was a sensible and intelligent man. The Colonel-General interrupted to say that he had not seen a report of the Archbishop having made any exhortation to the clergy or the people, to which I replied that although that was, so far as I knew, the case, the influence of the clergy was in the main in the villages where the individual pastors had great influence. I hoped that our press attaché would be able to bring some enlightenment in this direction.

3. As regards the fulfilment of the armistice terms, the Colonel-General said that although the Finns had satisfactorily completed several of the terms, the picture was not completely satisfactory; it could be said to be speckled. He pointed to article 14 which concerns the return of munitions removed from Soviet territory to Finland and said that there were numerous small infractions of this article; some equipment was not being returned, some was in unsatisfactory condition, some had been hidden away. The Commission had also found a number of stores of hidden arms and munitions which, though individually quite small, added up to a considerable amount. They had also found that the Finns had been in fact smuggling out munitions by sea. The Swedish-Finnish frontier was badly patrolled and there was a good deal of illegal trading taking place across it. In general, there were too many signs of unwillingness to fulfil the armistice terms. I asked General Zhdanov whether by that he meant that persons in responsible positions were being obstructive or whether the obstruction came in the main from individuals of lesser importance. He said that he could not say that the Government were not doing their

best to carry out the terms of the armistice; a good deal of the obstruction came from small individuals, but some also came from people such as those who were responsible for the winding-up of organisations such as the *Skyddskår*.[2] I said that it seemed to me that, as regards article 14, the nature of the task was such that it was liable to take another six months to clear up and that from what I had heard, the amount of obstruction did not appear to be more than might be expected in the circumstances. To this the Colonel-General agreed, apparently without any difficulty.

4. The Colonel-General asked about the state of feeling of the Finns in current circumstances. I told him that they were terrified of the Russians during the first two months after the armistice and expected all kinds of horrors. There had been a state of considerable tension during that period but it had relaxed very considerably about the beginning of December. They had seen that the Control Commission had behaved very correctly and that the Russian attitude was in general friendly. They were, in fact, very surprised at this. I thought that the tension was progressively diminishing and that there was a universal desire to live on friendly terms with Soviet Russia. The difficulty was that the majority of Finns were so far only convinced of this with their heads and not yet with their hearts. That, in view of their history, would probably take a considerable time to achieve, but they had good memories of the earlier days of the Grand Duchy and I thought it would come in time. Here, also, the Colonel-General agreed and said that on his first arrival he had the impression that the Finns thought he had come with a regiment of tanks in one pocket and a squadron of aeroplanes in the other.

5. During the conversation I dwelt on the importance of dealing with the main German line of propaganda, which was that friendship and collaboration between Russia, Great Britain and the United States would not last, and I mentioned that I thought it would be a good thing if some occasion were taken from time to time for General Zhdanov and myself as well as Mr. Higgs to appear together in public. We were co-operating satisfactorily, but it would be a good thing for an occasional demonstration of solidarity to be brought home to the Finns. The Colonel-General thought that this was a good idea, but added that the Finns had frequent opportunities of seeing that there was no division of opinion in Finland between the three Powers. I managed also to bring up the question of the visits of British journalists, and mentioned that the legal difficulties which had existed when I spoke to him on the subject on the occasion of our previous meeting had now been overcome. It was possible, therefore, that other journalists would visit Finland. While I was introducing this subject I noticed that M. Orlov was beating a loud tattoo with his fingers on the back of his sofa, evidently with the intention of warning me off it. It seemed to me, however, that if there were any difficulty in the matter it would be better to have it out at once, and I therefore continued with it. The Colonel-General certainly looked somewhat embarrassed and said that he could take the matter up in Moscow: did I expect a visit from a delegation of journalists soon? I said that I did not expect a delegation, but there were a number of British journalists resident in Stockholm and it was likely that individuals would come over for a day or two from there in connexion with the elections as Swedish journalists were doing. I would try to let the commission know if and when journalists did come. The Colonel-General did not dissent. He soon afterwards

---

[2] In Finnish, *Suojeluskunta,* or civil guard, a paramilitary defence corps dating from the civil war of 1918.

asked me whether I had made the acquaintance of Finns such as Paasikivi, Pekkala, Svento, Hillila and other members of the Government, and I said I had. I had also had a long talk with Marshal Mannerheim, and in answer to a question by the Colonel-General, I told him that I thought that he was an impressive figure and a strong personality worthy of respect. To this the Colonel-General only replied that he was a remarkable man for his age: he had seen him since the armistice only three times.

6. General Zhdanov asked whether communications with the United Kingdom were satisfactory, and I said that we were hoping that a British aircraft would be allowed to come to Malmi aerodrome once a week with our mail and supplies. He had been good enough to grant permission for a single aircraft to come, but there had been some misunderstanding about this, and what we would like would be permission for a plane to come once a week. General Zhdanov said he hoped that this could be arranged but he was, I thought, rather non-committal. I said that, if necessary, the aircraft could go to Hyvinkää, but this was very inconvenient and we should greatly prefer, if it could be arranged, that the plane should come to Malmi.

7. As regards the recent statement of the Finnish Government on the question of war guilt on the part of leading politicians and others, the Colonel-General said he was pleased with this as a first step, though he did not appear very enthusiastic and thought it should have been taken long before. The Finns were very slow to realise the situation but he understood that this was their nature and he told me one or two stories to prove it.

8. The meeting was very friendly and pleasant and General Zhdanov was very unaffected. He is, however, curiously unimpressive for a man of his powerful position. There is, however, something of the unworldliness and even of the spiritual force of a high dignitary of the Catholic Church about him, in spite of his mediocre appearance.

9. I am sending a copy of this despatch to His Majesty's Ambassador at Moscow.

I have, etc.,
F.M. SHEPHERD

No. 6

Minute from Mr Warr to Mr Haigh, 25 February 1945
(FO 371/48015, N1856/14/42)

Sweden: Annual Review for 1944[1]

The report argues that the end of the Finnish War, by removing a hindrance to good relations with Russia, was calculated to encourage the Swedes to help the Allied cause more actively, and to put this into practical effect mainly by helping their neighbours. The result was that the Swedes gave all possible assistance to underground movements in Denmark and Norway, and also helped the transport of 'police troops' to Finnmark. But Sweden's growing willingness to help the allies was not merely expressed by increased sympathy with her neighbours: she was

---

[1] Not printed.

also willing to assist the Western allies in such matters as intelligence, recognition of the French Provisional Govt. and the release of interned allied airmen. In addition Sweden showed her increasing hostility to Germany during 1944 by her humanitarian efforts, and above all by growing firmness in her trade relations with Germany. A very clear account is given in Section II of the course of the negotiations during 1944 which ended in the complete stoppage of Swedish-German trade at the end of the year.

The argument therefore is that during 1944 Sweden leaned steadily further towards the allies and away from strict neutrality, driven to this course partly by the great improvement of the military position of the allies and partly by the growing evidence of Nazi brutality, particularly in Norway. This change was expressed by a growing desire to give all possible assistance, short of war, mainly to her neighbours, but also to the Western allies. But this gradual and happy development was cut into and interrupted by the question of the Swedish attitude to Russia. It emerges from the report that Sweden continued to mistrust Russian intentions throughout the year, and it does not seem that the evidence of the good behaviour of the Russians in Finland since the armistice did much, if anything, to reduce this mistrust. In view of this obstinate Swedish dislike of Russia, I think that it is a little misleading to say, in the second sentence of the report, 'at the end of 1944 Sweden's "non-belligerency" had almost become a fact'. Non-belligerency in the case of Spain implied sympathy with the aims of the axis. Sweden cannot be said to be in sympathy with the aims of the allies, while her whole outlook is coloured by fear and mistrust of Russia. It would be more accurate, I think, to say that during the year the military position of the allies improved so greatly that Sweden no longer feared an attack from Germany, and that with the removal of this threat Sweden took courage and began to help the victims of Nazi persecution in the neighbouring countries.

But apart from this slight overemphasis of pro-allied tendencies in Sweden, I think that the report contains an accurate and fair account of the events of 1944.

I hardly think we need thank.

G.C. WARR

No. 7

Minute from Sir O. Sargent to Northern Department, 7 March 1945
Top Secret (FO 371/47503, N2571/90/30)

M. Lie communicated today the attached copy of a telegram[1] from the Norwegian Minister in Moscow, which represents the answer to the Norwegian Government's reply to the Soviet Government's proposals regarding Spitzbergen and Bear Island.[2] M. Lie expressed himself as satisfied with this reply, which appeared to him reasonable. It was particularly satisfactory that the Soviet Government no longer called in question Norwegian sovereignty over these islands.

[1] See Enclosure.
[2] No. 3.

The Norwegian Government proposed to reply that they would be very glad to enter into negotiations with the Soviet Government as soon as they got back to Norway, but that they would find it difficult to start negotiations before they had been reorganised when Norway was liberated, and also as long as the Government were in exile they had no access to the documents, maps, etc., necessary to enable them to carry on in discussions. M. Lie feared, however, that the Soviet Government would insist upon immediate negotiations, in which case he expected that the Norwegian Government would have to agree.

I pointed out to M. Lie that in any case I did not see how the Soviet and Norwegian Governments could carry their negotiations very far, since such negotiations would involve fundamental modifications of the international Spitzbergen Convention. No Norwegian-Soviet agreement could therefore take effect until the other signatories to the Spitzbergen Convention had been consulted and had consented to the Spitzbergen Convention being replaced by some new instrument into which could be fitted the Norwegian-Soviet agreement now contemplated.

M. Lie agreed and said that if the Norwegian Government were compelled to start negotiations now, they would submit proposals to the Soviet government on the clear understanding that before coming into force they would have to be communicated for approval both to the other signatories of the Spitzbergen Convention and to the new Norwegian Government which will take office on the liberation of Norway.

Meanwhile M. Lie begged that we should not in any way reveal the fact that we knew of this exchange of views was proceeding between the Norwegian and Soviet Governments.[3]

O.G. SARGENT

Enclosure in No. 7

M. Molotov to M. Andvord, 29 January 1945

The Government of the USSR have studied with great attention the Norwegian statement conveyed to the People's Commissar for Foreign Affairs, M. V.M. Molotov, on the 25th of January this year by M. Andvord, to the effect that:

1. The Norwegian Government propose to negotiate on joint military Defence of the Islands of Spitzbergen and Bear Island, and

2. The Norwegian Government propose to consult the Allied Governments concerned about proposals worked out by the two Governments.

The Government of the USSR announce their agreement to the proposals submitted by the Norwegian Government and wish to propose on the basis mentioned above that negotiations should at the same time be carried out concerning the exploitation by the USSR and Norway of the coal and other

---

[3] Warr minuted on 11 March that Northern Department had originally proposed to inform Collier of the background of this question, and to instruct him to discover from Lie whether the Russians had replied. 'We now know from M. Lie that they have replied, and that they have made no unreasonable demands. It remains to be seen whether the Russians insist that negotiations should be started at once, and, if they do, whether the Norwegians are brave enough to insist on referring the proposals to all the signatories of the Spitzbergen Convention. I think that we can only wait and see what happens, and in the meantime not say anything to Sir. L. Collier' (FO 371/47503, N2571/90/30G).

resources on Spitzbergen, as well as concerning the necessity of cancelling the treaty of the 9th February, 1920.

No. 8

Mr Eden to Lord Halifax (Washington), 8 March 1945[1]
Tel. No. 191 Saving, Secret (FO 371/47481, N2117/1004/27)

Position of our forces in Iceland (C)[2] on and after general suspension of hostilities in Europe and related question of our long term security interest in Iceland have been under consideration here.

2. When Americans took over in Iceland in 1941 they promised 'to withdraw all their military forces, land, sea and air, immediately on conclusion of present war'. At the same time we promised to withdraw all our armed forces as soon as the United States forces were established in sufficient strength to ensure the defence of the country (Reykjavik telegram No. 143 of 27th June 1941).[3] When, in 1943, the Icelanders pointed out that we still had forces in Iceland, we replied that promise given by the United States in respect of withdrawal of United States forces applied no less to British forces (see my telegram No. 5468 of 24th November 1943).[3] United States Government and His Majesty's Government are therefore, if they are to fulfil these promises, bound to withdraw forces at conclusion of war. We presume United States Government will agree.

3. Admiralty will require facilities for operating from Iceland at least until all German warships including U-boats have been accounted for. Thereafter manpower shortage will probably dictate an early and complete withdrawal. These requirements should cause no political difficulties with Icelanders, as war clearly cannot be considered as concluded until all German warships have been disposed of. It is believed that United States position will be similar to our own, and we should welcome discussions through service channels in order to co-ordinate plans to withdraw in such a way as not to prejudice operational requirements mentioned above.

4. Similar considerations apply to RAF anti-U-boat forces. Air Ministry will however need to use airfields in Iceland for passage of aircraft of Transport Command throughout Japanese phase of war. They consider it likely that they will want to pass through about 200 aircraft per month. It would therefore be necessary from RAF point of view to retain military facilities in Iceland until end of war with Japan. Interpretation of promises referred to in paragraph 2 above is open to argument and it might be maintained that we were obliged to withdraw on termination of hostilities with Germany, in view of fact that when original United States promise, with which we later associated ourselves, was given, Japan was not at war, and the basis of our position in Iceland is defence against possible German attack. I am advised however that (a) there is little doubt that war with Japan is part of general war which began with hostilities with Germany and that therefore the 'conclusion of the present war' could be interpreted as meaning the conclusion of the war with Japan; (b) it is unlikely that state of war with Germany will be

---

[1] Repeated to Reykjavik.
[2] During the Second World War, by direction of Churchill, Iceland was known and recorded in British records as Iceland (C) to distinguish between Icelandic territory defended by Britain and that defended by the United States, and to avoid confusion with Ireland (Eire).
[3] Not printed.

legally terminated until some time after conclusion of actual hostilities. We thus have legal case for claiming right to use airfields after conclusion of hostilities with Germany. (Moreover Anglo-Icelandic agreement under which Reykjavik airfield reverts to Icelandic Government 'on conclusion of present war' was concluded after entry of Japan into war). It would however in our view be politically advisable to attempt to obtain Icelandic agreement to our having required facilities without stressing legal argument. It would of course greatly assist us if Americans were able to give us definite support, and we hope that they will be able to do so.

5. As regards our long term interest, Iceland has of course during this war assumed great importance from point of view of security of our sea communications in North Atlantic. It is almost certain that we shall desire after the war to be in a position to obtain certain naval and air facilities in Iceland should the need arise. United States Government will also, it is assumed, attach strategic importance to Iceland, and we should be glad of an expression of their views, however tentative, as to the part which Iceland should be called upon to play in the post-war security system.

6. If an international security organisation is set up on lines of Dumbarton Oaks scheme post-war security facilities would have to be obtained by agreement within its framework. As you know, scheme contemplates making of special security arrangements concerning bases and other facilities between individual member states. It also lays down that all members of the organisation should undertake to make available to the Security Council on its call and in accordance with a special agreement or agreements concluded among themselves, armed forces, facilities or assistance necessary for the purpose of maintaining international peace and security. If Iceland should join organisation, it is evident that she will have to make some contribution and that the 'facilities' which she could provide could only be in the form of some kind of bases. The Icelanders are likely to be difficult about this, but in the last resort it should be *possible* for the Security Council to say that, if the Icelanders entirely refused to agree to the provision of any bases for the use of the United Nations, Iceland was prejudicing the maintenance of international peace and security and to take action in accordance with the rules laid down in Ch. VIII B.[4]

7. If International Organisation is not formed or Iceland does not come into it powers interested would presumably at some stage approach Iceland Government for desired facilities either jointly or unilaterally. It will however probably prove best not to make any such approach until position of Iceland *vis-à-vis* international organisation is clear.

8. A further point that arises in connexion with withdrawal of our forces from Iceland is disposal of the installations erected there by British and United States

---

[4] Cadogan took issue with this last sentence of this paragraph, and wrote on the telegram: 'Surely this is pushing matters rather far. I shd. never have agreed to this if consulted. Iceland in such circumstances cd. probably be denied all the advantages of membership, but surely the Organisation cannot extract bases by force?' Following consultations between Jebb and Malkin, the Legal Adviser, the following correction was sent to Washington in place of this sentence on 12 March: 'The Icelanders are likely to be difficult about this and if they are it would not be possible, as we see it, for the Organisation to force them to provide bases. If however the same sort of situation arose as that in which we and the Americans were compelled by urgent strategical necessity to take the facilities which we required, the Charter might enable the Organisation to take such action as it considered necessary in the general interest of maintaining peace and security' (FO 371/47481, N2117/1004/27G).

authorities. Both Governments have already agreed with Icelanders that their respective airfields shall revert to Icelandic Government after the war. Arrangements have been made for disposal of surplus huts belonging to forces. Problem of naval base at Hvalffordur however still remains. The installations there have been constructed in part by us and in part by Americans. Americans must therefore have a say in question of their disposal and we should wish to keep in step with them. So far as we are concerned there is no objection in trying to obtain payment for immovable assets in a country like Iceland with which we have no mutual aid arrangements. In order to simplify speedy resumption of naval facilities should the necessity arise in the post-war period our policy should presumably be not to dismantle all these installations, but to leave them more or less intact and hand them over to the Icelandic Government whether against payment or not, with a view to their possible future use by British and United States Governments or United Nations in post-war period. In accordance however with our promises to Iceland we must relinquish control of base and hand it over to Icelanders on conclusion of hostilities under arrangement to be agreed between three Governments.

9. To sum up,
(a) we should as soon as possible after general suspension of European hostilities fulfil our promises to withdraw our forces from Iceland in co-ordination with United States,
(b) it will however be necessary to retain an RAF unit for Transport Command purposes throughout Japanese phase of war,
(c) the need may arise at short notice for some form of naval and air facilities in Iceland in post-war period,
(d) negotiations for such facilities should take place through machinery of future international organisation if Iceland is a party to it,
(e) control of naval base should be relinquished in accordance with (a) above but installations should be left with a view to possible future use.

10. Please inform State Department of our views on above lines and invite their views in order that an agreed policy may be reached before termination of hostilities in Europe. After your approach to the State Department and presuming that it meets with sympathetic response, further discussions on matters of detail could take place through service channels.[5]

[5] Commenting on these telegrams on 19 March Shepherd, the Minister in Iceland, referred to a conversation in August 1944 with the former Icelandic Foreign Minister, Thors, as the basis for assessing that Iceland would not object to the continued Allied use of airfields until after the end of the war with Japan (FO 371/47480/N3158/1004/27G). The State Department did not respond until 21 September. See No. 32.

No. 9

Minute from Sir O. Sargent to Mr Churchill, 9 May 1945
(FO 371/47223, N5097/9/15)

I think you should know the present situation as regards the Danish island of Bornholm, which lies in the Baltic considerably east of any other part of Danish territory.

2. On the 7th May Soviet aircraft flew over Bornholm, (which is on the Russian side of the bomb-line); they were fired at by the Germans; and they dropped bombs. We are told from Stockholm that, according to Danish military and naval intelligence service, Soviet planes again flew over Bornholm on the night of the 7th May and dropped leaflets urging the garrison commander to send a representative to Kolberg on the north German coast to negotiate surrender.

3. We yesterday instructed Mr. Steel, our political representative at SHAEF, to make it clear at SHAEF that we should be glad if they could arrange to take the surrender of the Germans in Bornholm, and that we saw no need to consult the Russians on this point.

4. SHAEF, however, without Mr. Steel's knowledge had already informed No. 30 Mission at Moscow that, at the request of the Danish authorities, they proposed to send a detachment to Bornholm to take the surrender of the Germans there and to arrange for the import of food; and had instructed No. 30 Mission to report urgently if such action conflicted with Soviet plans. We have told Mr. Steel that no opportunity should be missed of taking the surrender at Bornholm if the Russians do not reply soon. Bornholm is of particular interest to us, and to the Russians also, because a number of German U-boats are lying in the harbour of the island.[1]

O.G. SARGENT

---

[1] Churchill replied on 10 May 1945 'Good. Go ahead. Invoke my aid with the COS if needed' (FO 371/47223, N5244/9/15G). Sargent replied on the same date that they had learned from the Danes that five Soviet torpedo boats had entered Rønne harbour on Bornholm on the afternoon of 9 May, and that a Soviet Commission had gone ashore to discuss surrender with the German commander. He commented: 'It is therefore too late for us to accept the German surrender on Bornholm. We shall, however, watch matters closely, as it is possible that the Russians will be in no hurry to evacuate Bornholm' (FO 371/47223, N5244/9/15G). There were at this time approximately 20,000 Germans on Bornholm. By 14 May, some 18,000 of them had been evacuated. At that time, there were thought to be about 3,500 Soviet troops on the island. Sargent elaborated on his concerns on 26 May when he wrote to Hollis, the Secretary of the Chiefs of Staff Committee, to discuss the possibility that the Soviet Union had some idea of seeking permanent military facilities on Bornholm, 'to be fitted into the general scheme of security measures under the World Organisation'. He therefore sought an appreciation by the Chiefs of Staff of the strategic implications if that were to happen (FO 371/47224, N5682/9/15G).

No. 10

Sir V. Mallet (Stockholm) to Mr Eden, 29 May 1945
No. 256 Confidential (FO 371/48042, N7135/1106/42)

Sir,

I have the honour to report that on the 4th May, only a few days before Victory in Europe was proclaimed, the Swedish Minister for Foreign Affairs delivered a speech in the Concert Hall in Stockholm in which he made a reasoned defence of neutrality as a keystone of Swedish policy. The great events of the ensuing days overshadowed this speech which is, however, not without considerable interest.

2. M. Günther began his speech, a full translation of which is enclosed herein,[1] by asserting Sweden's desire to contribute to the consolidation of peace, but he

---

[1] Not printed.

offset these platonic phrases by expressing scepticism about the San Francisco Conference. He pointed out that Sweden, Denmark, Switzerland and Poland had not been invited, and that the invitations had in fact been based on ephemeral political considerations rather than upon the real ability of the nations concerned to further the high purposes of the conference, This was, in his opinion, hardly an auspicious start since the object of the conference was to construct a peace organisation which would brave the storms of centuries rather than to solve the immediate problem of the Great Powers. He did not deny that the new League of Nations might contribute to the preservation of peace, but considered that it could never guarantee it, since, in the future as hitherto, the peace of the world depended upon the relations between the Great Powers who would not surrender control of their policy to an international body.

3. In these circumstances, M. Günther continued, the small nations must pursue a very independent course designed to serve the double purpose of preventing their being drawn into future wars and at the same time contributing to peace. It was frequently alleged that neutrality once and for all had proved its inefficacy as a policy for the small Powers, but while there were many cases which pointed in this direction, there were others—such as Sweden and Switzerland—which suggested a different conclusion. It was clear, therefore, that one could not generalise as to the merits or demerits of any particular foreign policy for any and every nation. There were reasons to believe, however, that Sweden could best contribute to the preservation of world peace by remaining outside *blocs* and alliances of the Great Powers, for in any such alliances she would constitute an advanced outpost of a kind which would inevitably strain the relations between the Great Powers concerned. It was sometimes alleged that a small State could only hope to preserve its existence by relying upon the support of a Great Power, but in fact Sweden's geographical position was such that she could not be effectively defended by anyone but herself. Her own defences could not indeed resist attack by a Great Power, but she could at least avoid becoming a military vacuum. Swedish policy should be designed to convince every Great Power that it need never fear an attack by another Great Power through Swedish territory.

4. Having thus established to his own satisfaction the wisdom of armed neutrality as an objective of Swedish foreign policy, M. Günther went on to argue that such a policy was not egoistic nor did it involve isolation. There was no nation more anxious than Sweden to co-operate with the other nations of the world to establish peace, and if an organisation was established for this purpose Sweden could not fail to participate and to accept such obligations as other members were willing to undertake. These obligations would include the duty to bring armed force to bear upon any disturber of the peace, and this duty was one from which Sweden should not shrink. If, however, a conflict arose among the Great Powers and disrupted the peace organisation then Sweden should not let herself be drawn in.

5. M. Günther concluded his speech with some general remarks upon the question of Nordic co-operation. Finland was in a special position, but he did not despair of her adopting a policy which would find understanding in the north. Although Norway and Denmark were at present little tempted by the idea of neutrality, M. Günther found it hard to believe that they would not by degrees adopt the same line of thought as Sweden. In the absence of pressure from a powerful Germany, the position of these three Scandinavian countries would be more identical than ever before, and it would be remarkable if this did not result in

the three countries adopting similar views on foreign policy. If this occurred, the third principle of Swedish policy would be co-operation with the other Nordic countries. Before the war, Nordic co-operation had not embraced co-operation in the defensive sphere, but in the future such co-operation might be of great practical value on condition that all concerned were in agreement as to the purpose of the defence in question.

6. It is always irritating to hear a Swede speak of neutrality as if it were some remarkable achievement or discovery of Swedish statesmanship which all the world should admire. Undoubtedly also there is in M. Günther's speech some element of self-justification for past conduct and possibly a tinge of injured pride that no Swedish delegate was invited to San Francisco. On the other hand it would be too superficial a view to interpret the speech as being inspired solely by such sentiments. With the collapse of Germany as a European Power Sweden sees the balance of power in Europe upset. In 1918 the collapse of Germany had been preceded by the collapse of Russia and Sweden emerged from the war surrounded by small independent States in a world where the Western Powers alone counted. When Germany once again became the strongest military Power in Europe there was, however, as far as Sweden was concerned, a balance of power between Germany and Russia which enabled Sweden to preserve her independence without hitching her wagon to any star in the political firmament. Today what was once Germany is a vacuum, and the question of how the balance of power will adjust itself between East and West is, as I have pointed out in my despatch No. 249 of 26th May,[1] a matter which causes Sweden some nervousness. While naturally hoping that the concord and collaboration which has existed between the United States and the Western Powers on the one hand and the Soviet Union on the other will continue in the making of the peace and after, the Swedes feel that this is by no means certain and in conformity with the Swedish habit of always suspecting the worst they probably fear armed conflict between the democratic Powers and the Soviet Union as sooner or later inevitable.

7. M. Günther's speech is possibly, therefore, to be regarded as the Swedish Government's proposals on how they consider the uncertainties of the future are to be met. Sweden as a small Power could certainly play but a very small part in a third world war, but at the same time her geographical position is such that there is a *prima facie* case for supposing that Sweden should be able to remain outside the conflict. There is, however, a chink in this armour of neutrality. If Sweden's neighbours, Denmark and Norway, threw in their lot with the Atlantic Powers, either by formal alliances or by participation in some regional security pact, Swedish neutrality might not merely be threatened but Sweden herself might become the battleground of the next war, the Western Powers seeking to strike at Russia from their bases in Norway and Denmark across Swedish territory and the Soviet Union seeking to expel the Western Powers from these bases likewise across Swedish territory and to obtain the Lapland ore mines. It may well be that M. Günther had this very danger in mind when he said that Sweden could at least avoid becoming a military vacuum and that Swedish policy should be designed to convince every great Power that it never need fear an attack by another great Power through Swedish territory. The Minister for Foreign Affairs is a wise enough statesman, however, to know that it was not only the Germans who excused their invasion of neutral countries on the grounds that they feared attack from their enemies, and that a country may be invaded because its neighbour wishes to attack its enemy from more advantageous bases. It must, therefore, be a

further object of Swedish policy that Sweden's neighbours should pursue a policy of neutrality similar to the Swedish. That in my opinion is the explanation of M. Günther's concluding remarks reported in paragraph 5 above. Whether or not Denmark and Norway will, as he hopes, adopt the same line of thought as Sweden remains to be seen. On the answer, however, depends the whole future of inter-Scandinavian relations and, indeed, the whole concept of Scandinavia as a political expression. If Norway and Denmark refuse to follow in Sweden's wake, the consequences may be of far-reaching and fundamental importance.[2]

A copy of this despatch is being sent to His Majesty's Chargé d'Affaires at Copenhagen, His Majesty's Embassy at Oslo and the British Political Representative at Helsingfors.

I have, etc.,
(for Sir V. Mallet)
G. LABOUCHERE

[2] Günther's speech, setting out the position on neutrality which Sweden was to maintain during the immediate post-war period, provoked some lively minuting in Northern Department. Haigh observed that it showed that Sweden would accept an invitation to participate in what was still called the World Organisation and would assume military obligations in that connection, that Sweden would in no circumstances take part in a Western Security Bloc or any such regional grouping and that Sweden would use her powers of persuasion to the utmost to prevent Norway and Denmark from taking part in a Western Security Bloc. He continued: 'It is to this last point above to which I would in particular draw attention. Had we organised a Western Security Bloc before the end of hostilities with Germany, there would have been every chance of getting the Norwegians and (on liberation) the Danes to join. Were we to set about organising such a regional grouping now, the chances would still be favourable. But as time passes, and the memory of our joint fight against the Germans grows fainter in Norwegian and Danish minds, I incline to share M. Günther's view that the Swedish view of neutrality will begin once more to commend itself to the Norwegians and the Danes' (FO 371/48042, N7135/1106/42).

No. 11

Mr Shepherd (Helsinki) to Mr Eden, 8 June 1945, 5.06 p.m.

Tel. No. 219 Important, Top Secret (FO 371/47408, N6630/1131/56)

Your telegram No. 207.[1]

Please see my telegram No. 196 paragraph 1(b) and paragraph 2.[2]

2. In conversation with the Minister for Foreign Affairs today I referred to press reports of a treaty of Mutual Assistance between Finland and Russia. M. Svento said that he could tell me that this 'was not on the agenda'. He himself had not spoken with the Russians on the subject. There were no doubt people who had had their personal opinion that such an agreement was desirable.

3. It is clear from the manner in which he spoke that some such agreement is in a preliminary stage of discussion but has not yet come before the Cabinet. The secret report referred to in your telegram under reference is strengthened by recent

[1] Not printed.
[2] Not printed. This telegram contained Shepherd's first report of press rumours about discussions of a treaty of mutual assistance between Finland and the Soviet Union, which were linked to the signature in April of a similar treaty between the Soviet Union and Yugoslavia (FO 371/47408, N5728/1131/56).

information that defences west of Porkkala are being strengthened and by press reports to the effect that the Russians had insisted that Finnish armed forces should not be reduced below strength provided for in the Armistice. On the other hand Vice Chairman of the Commission told the Head of the British element on June 5th that they were not interested in the question whether or not Finnish forces should be reduced further. Clauses in postal agreement referred to in paragraph 4 of my despatch No. 71 may have some significance in this connexion.[3]

4. Significant point in the secret report is provision of putting Russian troops into Finland in the event of a tense situation arising. It is natural that the Russians should wish to provide against a repetition of the situation in 1941 when German troops came to Finland in preparation for attack on Russia. One must presume however that the Finns would not agree to this clause being left so dangerously vague, but would insist on a definition of a 'tense situation' as being an international situation likely to lead to war or some similar specific restriction.[4]

---

[3] Not printed.
[4] Warr minuted on 12 June there was nothing very conclusive in this, and it did not appear that discussion of any alliance had reached an advanced stage, at least in Helsingfors. However, rumours of a possible treaty continued to circulate in greater detail over the next few weeks and began to cause greater concern in the Foreign Office, such that a brief was prepared for the British delegation at Potsdam (FO 371/47408, N6630/1131/56G). See No. 18.

No. 12

Sir V. Mallet (Stockholm) to Mr Eden, 17 June 1945
No. 295 Confidential (FO 371/48042, N7460/1106/42)

Sir,

On the eve of my departure from Sweden it seems appropriate to attempt to review the events of the last five and a half years. Swedish foreign policy has throughout the war, of course, been guided by external events outside her control and her outward attitude towards the belligerents has cautiously followed the developments of the war in Europe. Four phases can be defined: (1) the early period before the 9th April 1940, when Germany had overrun Poland but Norway and Denmark were still free and Swedish communications with the western world were still almost unhindered; (2) the period from the 9th April 1940, when Denmark and Norway were invaded, until the 22nd June 1941, when Germany attacked Russia; (3) the period from the 22nd June 1941, until D-day, the 6th June 1944; (4) the final phase until Victory Day in Europe.

2. During period (1) British policy aimed principally at restricting by economic warfare methods the extent of Sweden's trade with Germany and especially the export of Swedish iron ore. In the late autumn of 1939 the Anglo-Swedish War Trade Agreement was signed in London, whereby Sweden undertook not to exceed the 'normal trade' exports to Germany of 1938 and to place on a secret list certain Swedish products the export of which to Germany and her allies would be forbidden. It should be noted that from the outset of the war the Swedish Government had already forbidden the export to all belligerents of arms and war material as defined in the Geneva Convention. At the time of the signature of the War Trade Agreement another agreement, known as the Carlsson-Mounsey

Agreement, was signed whereby a large amount of Swedish tonnage was chartered to the United Kingdom.

3. During this period the first Finnish 'Winter' war took place. His Majesty's Government and the French Government bent all their endeavours to persuade Sweden to do more to help Finland against the Soviet Union and latterly to allow the transit of a few British and French brigades through Sweden (and Norway) to assist the Finns in their struggle against the Russians. In case this might expose Sweden to a violent reaction by Germany, the Allies were prepared to afford extensive military help to Norway and Sweden and to start immediate staff conversations. The Swedish Government refused these suggestions for two reasons, one of which they would not openly have admitted, namely, their grave suspicion that the Allied troops intended to occupy the Lapland ore mines on their way to Finland and to remain there; the other reason, openly given, was that the troops would be insufficient in numbers and could not arrive in time to help the Finns and that their arrival would merely embroil Sweden with the Germans and force the Germans to make a battleground of Scandinavia. Of late the Swedish Government has often made great play with their refusal of these transits on the ground that had they permitted them Great Britain and Russia would have found themselves at war.

4. The second period was one of intense alarm in Sweden. The Swedes had been watching for several weeks the accumulation of German ships and troops in the Baltic ports and they received from secret sources inside Germany information which convinced them that Denmark and very probably Norway also were to be the objects of an attack by Germany in the spring. A few days before the event the Swedish legation at Berlin obtained information which they considered absolutely authentic and passed it on to the Danish and Norwegian Legations in Berlin. The Swedish Government took other steps to warn the Norwegians, including the despatch of M. Boheman, the Secretary-General at the Ministry for Foreign Affairs, to Oslo on a special mission. Both the Danish and Norwegian Governments pooh-poohed the information. After the 9th April Sweden was still quite unprepared to defend her own long and vulnerable coastline and, although she has often been blamed for not having quixotically gone to the assistance of her Nordic neighbours, there is no doubt that the Swedish army was in no shape to take the field outside its own frontiers. Moreover, the Swedish Air Force was quite negligible and half the anti-aircraft guns and ammunition for the defence of Stockholm and other cities had been sent to Finland during the Winter War. Had the campaign in Norway gone better from the Allied point of view and in particular had British troops succeeded in the first few days in capturing Trondheim and advancing towards the Swedish frontier, it is possible that the Swedes might have reconsidered their policy of neutrality. Even if they had not done so, it seems unlikely that Germany would have refrained for many weeks from entering Sweden in order to be able to send reinforcements through this country to Norway. As things turned out, the Germans won a swift and easy victory in Norway and thereafter preferred to turn their attention westwards rather than to waste troops and energy upon a campaign in Sweden. Some time after the 9th April the Swedish Government had, indeed, received a somewhat reassuring hint from the Soviet Minister to the effect that the Soviet Government had made clear to Berlin their interest that Sweden should be left alone by Germany. Mme. Kollontay has since been heard to say that it was during a visit to Berlin on the 24th December, 1939, that M. Molotov told Ribbentrop that while he gave Germany *carte blanche* to go

ahead with her plans for attacking Norway and Denmark in the spring, the Soviet Government would consider an attack on Sweden as contrary to the spirit of the German-Soviet Alliance. Mme. Kollontay even claimed that M. Molotov's action was the result of her own prompting. It is therefore quite possible that Sweden owes her escape to the action of Russia at this critical time. After the fall of France there was, nevertheless, again a serious danger that Germany might decide to absorb Sweden into her continental system. It is believed here that certain elements in the German General Staff urged such a course on Hitler but that he was overpersuaded by certain of the pro-Swedish elements in the party, such as Göring. The German Government were apparently receiving reports from their legation in Stockholm about that time to the effect that Swedish opinion, which had been greatly impressed by the might of German arms, was so fanatically anti-Russian that Sweden, far from ever turning towards the Allies, would certainly take active sides with Germany in the event of a clash between Germany and the Soviet Union. I have heard it said that the notorious arch-Nazi, Sven Hedin, may unwittingly have rendered great services to his country by having during his frequent visits to Germany succeeded in convincing Hitler and others of this point of view. Moreover, the Swedes had indulged in a fair amount of appeasement to Germany. Immediately after the Norwegian campaign had closed with the departure of the Norwegian Government to England, the Swedish Government had yielded to strong pressure in agreeing to the so-called 'leave' transit of German troops between Norway and Germany. This in fact meant that the Swedish railways could be used for giving every soldier in Norway a spell of home leave in Germany at least once a year by travelling back and forth over the Swedish railways. A good deal of war material, foodstuffs and oil also transited the country in this way. His Majesty's Government naturally protested and the Swedish Government attempted to find some justification in international law. The transits continued for three years before Sweden felt strong enough to stop them. It is, however, perhaps more remarkable that having gone thus far on the road of appeasement the Swedish Government should have had the nerve to refuse many other German demands for transits of various kinds. On looking back I am driven to the conclusion that the Swedish Government had remarkably steady nerves during this dangerous period of 1940-41. In December 1940 there arrived a large contingent of German journalists, headed by the notorious Paul Schmidt of the Wilhelmstrasse[1], in order to conduct a propaganda tour to Sweden, which was inaugurated at a dinner given to them by the Swedish Government, by the Germans making speeches on the subject of the New Europe. The Swedes, although very perturbed at what this high-powered propaganda might portend, expressed themselves as quite unconvinced on the subject of a New Europe whereby they would in future be debarred from free trade with their old customers across the North Sea and the Atlantic. I now believe that this propaganda tour was very carefully timed in order to soften up Swedish public opinion for the day when Germany was ready to attack Russia.

5. The prelude to the third phase in Swedish policy occurred when M. Jacob Wallenberg[2] informed his Government some time in June that he was convinced that Germany intended to attack Russia on the 20th June 1941. M. Wallenberg, who as a well-known international banker had many business friends in Germany

---

[1] German Foreign Office press spokesman,
[2] Jacob Wallenberg, then Chairman of the Skandinaviska Enskilda Bank, played a central role in trade negotiations with the Germans during the Second World War.

and is also chairman of the Swedish Match Company, had in Berlin as local managers of the company certain Swedes who were both well informed and in touch with high circles. They had personal contact with Gördeler, the mayor of Leipzig, who in turn was on terms of the closest friendship with General Beck. General Beck, although in disgrace with Hitler, was still very friendly with many of the highest German generals and was kept accurately informed of the plans of the general staff. So accurate did this source of information prove that M. Wallenberg was able to inform his Government early in June that Germany would attack Russia on the 20th June 1941. I understand that this was the date originally fixed and that at the last minute a postponement of forty-eight hours actually took place. This, incidentally, was how M. Boheman was able to inform Sir Stafford Cripps and me in the course of the latter's passage through Sweden in June 1941 that he was absolutely convinced that this attack on Russia was about to take place.

6. On the 22nd June 1941, Prince Victor zu Wied, the elderly and stupid German Minister, called upon the Swedish Minister for Foreign Affairs and with the demeanour of a cat which had swallowed ten canaries, wrung M. Günther warmly by the hand and remarked: 'Now at last Sweden and Germany will be friends!' M. Günther, according to his own account to me, met this remark with a look of incomprehension, whereupon the Prince remarked that surely now that Germany was at war with Bolshevik Russia, Sweden's hereditary enemy, there could be no question of Sweden not assisting Germany and Finland. M. Günther strongly demurred and the Prince left in a very crestfallen mood. The German Government were reported to be furious at Sweden's 'treachery', and the Swedish Government became highly alarmed. Under severe pressure and at the request of the Finnish Government, who were put up to this by the Germans, the Swedish Government eventually agreed to the transit of not more than one German division through Sweden to Finland. They also allowed German transport ships to pass through territorial waters. Beyond this they refused to go. This act of appeasement was most properly met with strong protests from His Majesty's Government, but it was a question of whether, if the Swedes had been absolutely intransigent, Germany might not have turned upon them. The Swedish situation looked distinctly bad from our point of view, because here was yet another step on the fatal downward path, and I certainly wondered whether the Swedes in their mood of the moment would have the nerve ever to put the brake on. On the other hand, the Germans had undoubtedly expected that Sweden would allow unlimited transits and probably air bases and other advantages, commercial and financial; and the sharp attacks on Sweden in the German press reflected the disgust and disappointment of the Nazi chiefs. Then, as the German campaign in Russia dragged on into the winter, the Swedes began to feel more cheerful and public opinion held that the best thing would be to let dog eat dog until both were so weakened as to be no longer strong enough to threaten Sweden. About December M. Jacob Wallenberg, through his usual source, learnt that Hitler was preparing to attack Sweden in the spring of 1942 and that the German General Staff were already far advanced with their plans for this operation. On receiving this information the Swedish Government began to make earnest preparations for a rapid mobilisation in the spring. By February, however, M. Wallenberg had learnt that after all Hitler had decided not to attack Sweden as early as the spring of 1942, the reason being that the campaign in front of Moscow had met with the most unexpectedly formidable defence. General Beck and Herr Gördeler, the latter of whom, I think, visited Sweden about this time and saw M. Wallenberg, reported

that the whole German transport system in Russia was in a state of complete chaos. Hitler had relied upon his weather prophets and astrologers who had assured him that the winter would be a mild one, whereas it turned out to be the most severe for a hundred years. On the strength of this information M. Wallenberg tells me that he was absolutely convinced and endeavoured to convince his Government that the danger was past for some time to come, but they did not entirely believe him. In February 1942 the Berlin Legation obtained from their sources, which consisted of contacts between their military attaché and certain pro-Swedish members of the German General Staff, information very similar to that which M. Wallenberg had obtained in December, namely, that Sweden was to be attacked in the spring. M. Wallenberg, having checked up with his source, again told his Government that he was convinced that the reports from the legation were a hangover of the decision taken some months before but since cancelled. Nevertheless, in February 1942 the Swedish Government called up a large number of troops to the colours and undertook a partial mobilisation. There was great alarm in the country and it is still believed in many quarters in Sweden that the spring of 1942 was the most dangerous period of all and that Sweden's mobilisation was the thing which deterred the Germans from attacking them. King Gustaf himself appears to have sent some kind of message to Hitler about this time, probably to the effect that if Sweden were attacked she would defend herself. M. Boheman has recently publicly declared that February 1942 was the danger period and that the warning then received from sources in Germany enabled Sweden to mobilise in time and thus induce Hitler to believe that the Swedish operation would prove too costly. The truth may well be, however, that the danger had already passed before the mobilisation took place and that Sweden had once more been saved by Russia. General Douglas, the present Commander-in-Chief of the Swedish Army, told me not long ago that he never believed that Sweden was in any danger after Christmas 1941. I suppose he was referring to the above information. Certain it is that thereafter Germany's commitments to Russia became more and more immense and with the growing strength of America to turn the scale the risk to Sweden steadily diminished. Nevertheless even after Stalingrad there were times when the Swedish Government felt a certain nervousness. Talk of invasion in Europe was in the air and who could tell whether Norway might not once more become an active theatre of war? It was always felt that in such an event Germany would have no alternative but to insist at least upon the use of Swedish railways and airfields, and by this time the Swedish Government had sufficiently recovered their nerve to be determined not to yield to such demands. After the landings in North Africa this determination crystallised into a desire to return as soon as it could safely be done to the path of stricter neutrality and public opinion clamoured aloud for the cessation of troop transits to Norway.

7. Public opinion was by now indeed aroused through the increasing degree of persecution against the Norwegians by Terboven and Quisling and by the execution of trade unionists and patriots, the deportation of school teachers and the oppression of the clergy. Thus it came about that our war trade negotiations in the summer of 1943 were successful in greatly reducing the quantity of exports from Sweden to Germany, while the troop transits both of men and material, which had become increasingly odious to the Swedish public, were stopped at the end of the summer. The Swedish Government would probably have acted some months earlier but for the fact that they set great store by what had come to be known as the Gothenburg safe-conduct traffic. This was a system whereby five Swedish

merchant ships a month were allowed by both belligerents to leave Gothenburg for ports in North and South America carrying with them a certain amount of such merchandise as the Germans considered harmless and bringing back such goods as the Allied controls would permit them to obtain and transport. Oil and rubber were the prime requirements for the Swedish defence forces and until certain reserves of these were safely in Sweden the Swedish Government did not wish to challenge Germany in such a way as to provoke her to refuse further safe-conducts. Meanwhile, a crisis in the relations between Great Britain and Sweden had already occurred at the New Year of 1943, when the British Ministry of Supply desired to send out of the port of Gothenburg to the United Kingdom on a hazardous secret voyage two Norwegian ships, the *Dicto* and the *Lionel*, which had been demise-chartered to the Ministry of War Transport and loaded with ball-bearings and special steels. There had been much litigation on the subject of these ships during the previous year, when the Germans had tried to prevent us from enjoying the charter, but finally the Swedish courts pronounced in our favour. The trouble about the *Dicto* and the *Lionel* was that the Swedish Government were afraid of what the Germans would do in revenge if the Swedes allowed these ships to sail. There had been an incident in the spring of 1942 when these ships had attempted to break the Skagerak blockade, had returned to Gothenburg and been caught with smuggled arms on board which had led to a violent protest by the Germans and a consequent Swedish promise or at least a half-promise that they would not be allowed to depart. The Swedes were convinced from what the Germans were saying to them that the Gothenburg safe-conduct traffic would immediately be stopped by the Germans the moment the ships left Gothenburg. Eventually the Swedish Government agreed that they should be free to leave the moment after two large tankers had arrived with important cargoes of oil from America for the Swedish defence forces. It eventually turned out that for operational reasons the voyage of the *Dicto* and the *Lionel* was put off as being too risky, even though the ships had on board cargoes so precious that we had informed the Swedish Government that they were absolutely vital for our war effort. The ships eventually sailed on the night of the 23rd May, 1945! Nevertheless, although from this fact it might be deduced that our strong action culminating in an ultimatum that we ourselves would close the safe-conduct traffic if the Swedes did not give way had in the end been a wasted endeavour, I believe that the pressure then applied had the effect of making the Swedish Government for the first time declare themselves as no longer afraid to act against German pressure and as favouring the Allied cause as far as circumstances would allow them. I remarked not long ago to M. Günther that I believed that this dispute and the Swedish Government's favourable decision had indeed proved a turning point in our relations. After reflection he was inclined to agree with me.

8. A further serious argument with the Swedish Government arose in the spring of 1944 on the subject of the export of ball-bearings to Germany. By our war trade agreement of August 1943, in which the Americans participated, Sweden had been permitted to export to Germany during 1944 a considerably reduced quantity of ball-bearings. At the time the agreement was made presumably the British and American Governments felt that this was the best bargain they could get. On the strength of it the Swedes had made their usual annual trade agreement with Germany in December 1943, and had fixed the quantity of ball-bearings to be exported at the limit stipulated in their agreement with us. By the spring of 1944 it was apparent that Swedish ball-bearings were playing an important part in

maintaining the German output of aircraft, tanks and other machinery of war. The United States Government felt particularly strongly about this and together with His Majesty's government began to put strong pressure on the Swedes to stop all exports of ball-bearings to Germany. The Swedish Government argued that having made their agreement with the German Government within the framework of their previous agreement with us, they were not prepared to break their pledged word. As a way out of the deadlock it was finally decided to put pressure on the Swedish ball-bearing company (SKF), which had valuable assets in the United States of America and which also required the goodwill of the Allies in the postwar period. A mission arrived from America, heralded by an unfortunate press campaign against Sweden. This mission was assisted by the Ministry of Supply member of my staff, and they eventually reached a satisfactory agreement with the company after a long and arduous struggle. The company was to be indemnified for its losses and the Germans were to get a very small trickle of ball-bearings until the autumn of 1944, whereafter the delivery of the remaining quota for the year was to be allowed to go forth to Germany. At the time it was presumably thought that by the autumn our campaign in Germany would have progressed further than it actually did, so that in the end fresh pressure had to be brought to bear and a fresh agreement made in October whereby all exports of ball-bearings to Germany ceased for the duration of the war.

9. The ball-bearing dispute culminated during the opening days of what I have described in paragraph 1 as the fourth phase. On the 6th June the Allies landed in Normandy, and so immense was the feeling of relief throughout Sweden that from this time forth the Swedish Government ceased seriously to believe that Germany would attack Sweden in any circumstances except if the Allies were to land in Norway. The fact that the landing had taken place in such strength in France disposed the Swedish Government to believe that we were unlikely to undertake a large-scale landing in Norway as well, and their relief was therefore all the greater. From that time forward the Swedes became increasingly co-operative. In many secret ways they rendered us important help. V-bombs had been observed to fall in certain parts of Sweden and with the willing and secret co-operation of the Swedish Minister for Foreign Affairs and certain members of the Defence Staff and Air Staff, our experts were allowed to examine them in July, and even to transport the fragments of these infernal machines by air to the United Kingdom for further examination. Already in 1943 the Norwegian Government had been allowed to enrol in a so-called 'police corps' several thousand young refugees in Sweden who were placed in secret camps and given a thorough military training with modern weapons against the day when the Norwegian Government might wish them to enter their own country. After the events of August 1943 in Denmark, Sweden received many thousand Danish refugees, mainly Jews, and a Danish 'police force' was also organised. This training was now intensified and Swedish officers were appointed to advise on various details. Several hundred interned British and American airmen were released on the flimsiest of pretexts. Increasingly favourable facilities were granted for Allied 'courier' aircraft. Relief to Norway increased very rapidly and many of our intelligence and propaganda activities upon which the Swedish police had previously frowned were now almost openly connived at. By the end of the year the number of refugees in Sweden numbered nearly 200,000, including many Finnish children. The Finnish armistice with Russia was a great relief to the Swedes, who then once more felt free to help that impoverished country. War trade negotiations with Great Britain and America

The Nordic Countries, 1944-1951

in the autumn of 1944 resulted in the Swedish Government agreeing to cease all exports to Germany as from the 1st January 1945, and this agreement was rigidly put into force in spite of the fact that it entailed, as might have been anticipated, the final cessation of the Gothenburg safe-conduct traffic. Sweden had thus voluntarily, although admittedly under strong pressure, entirely cut herself off from foreign trade, including the importation of coal and coke, for an indefinite period which at the time seemed quite likely to last fort the best part of a year. In doing so she was certainly the only neutral to go so far. Others had access to markets outside German control, but Sweden had not.

10. During the very last phase of the war there was much discussion whether Sweden should mobilise fully in order to send her troops into Norway and/or Denmark in case the Germans in those countries decided to make a last stand there. Although strongly pressed by the Norwegian Government, the Swedish Government preferred to adopt a waiting policy until such time as the situation became clearer. The Swedish Government were anxious not to lay themselves open to an accusation of having precipitated the destruction of Norwegian cities and industries. Nevertheless, I felt sure that if SHAEF had eventually decided to back the Norwegian request strongly and had arranged staff co-operation and air support, the Swedish Government would eventually have been prepared to play their part after the collapse in Germany itself. The Swedish Prime Minister told me only last week that this was indeed the innermost determination of his Government and that although the public were less prepared for the plunge the Government could easily have worked upon opinion.

11. Sweden's record, therefore, during the war is that of a country large in area, thinly populated and inadequately prepared for defence, which found itself isolated for five years from the outside world by the German armed forces. Thanks to her skilful adaptation of various forest products to many fresh uses her internal economy did not suffer in the way that was expected and indeed the Stockholm shops are probably now the best stocked in the world. She certainly traded with Germany, but she would have preferred to trade with the west. She certainly exported to Germany much iron ore, ball-bearings, timber and machinery which helped the German war effort. On the other hand, she kept her war trade agreements with us, even in the worst period after the fall of France, and the record of Sweden's dealings with the Ministry of Economic Warfare is, I think, not by any means a dishonourable one. M. Hansson, the Swedish Prime Minister, recently told me that even during the worst period after Dunkirk his Government were always determined that if ever they were forced to take sides in the war they would, without hesitation, choose that of the Allies. Public opinion, which was never pro-Nazi, would have supported the Government in resisting German aggression, although certain small and old-fashioned cliques were then and even later remained pro-German in the sense that they continued to insist upon the existence of the 'other Germany'. But even in 1940 the German press was complaining that 'Sweden's heart remained unregenerate'. The Swedish press, hampered during the more dangerous years by a rather mild censorship, was always more outspoken than any other neutral press, except perhaps the Swiss, and for the last eighteen months all restraint was relaxed and almost the whole press poured withering scorn and hatred upon all things Nazi. Films which were banned in Dublin and elsewhere were shown in Stockholm, although some of our finest propaganda films were considered too hot to handle. As the war progressed the Swedes more and more took to heart the lessons that their Norwegian and Danish

cousins were learning and reacted in a manner which did credit to their conscience. Thus Sweden has come through intact and with a remarkably fine industrial system and a large merchant navy. She lost 253 vessels, totalling nearly a million tons, and 1,357 lives in the ships chartered to the United Kingdom under the agreement made in 1939, but she has replaced the ships from her own shipyards. The people, who from their own character and from the constant neutrality sermons of their politicians suffer from a certain smugness and complacency which at times can be irritating, have nevertheless got a strong social sense of duty towards their less fortunate neighbours and will, I feel sure, wish to play with becoming modesty their proper part in assisting the reconstruction of Europe.

12. Sweden will always be nervous of the great strength of Russia, which is now deployed along the whole eastern coast of the Baltic and no longer has the counterpoise of a strong Germany. Swedish policy, therefore, while endeavouring to keep on friendly terms with the Soviet Union, will tend towards the closest possible relationship with Norway and Denmark and will resent any attempt by Russia to counteract such a tendency. Sweden's need for foreign trade will drive her more towards western markets now that Germany is no longer available for large scale trading. She will seek close ties with the United States of America, but her people's genuine admiration and affection for Great Britain, immensely increased by the British achievement during the war, afford us a real opportunity not only for the closest political and cultural relations but also for a valuable market for our exports.

13. I am sending copies of this despatch to His Majesty's Ambassador in Oslo, His Majesty's Minister in Copenhagen and His Majesty's representative in Helsingfors.[3]

I have, etc.,

V.A.L. MALLET

[3] This valedictory despatch did not attract significant comment in the Foreign Office, perhaps because Northern Department had already expressed their views on a number of occasions on the question of Swedish neutrality during the war. However, in a minute which was seen in the Department by his successor in Stockholm, Cecil Jerram, Haigh noted that the Swedes had a very sympathetic apologist in Sir V. Mallet (FO 371/48042, N7460/1106/42).

No. 13

Mr Randall (Copenhagen) to Mr Eden, 12 July 1945, 7.58 a.m.[1]
Tel. No. 324 Secret (FO 371/47225, N8589/9/15)

Withdrawal from Denmark has at no time been discussed with the Danish Government but yesterday Danish Minister for Foreign Affairs[2] referring to the dissolution of SHAEF asked me whether I thought it possible to establish a relation between the ultimate withdrawal of British forces and that of Russian forces from Bornholm and what I thought of the possibility of arriving at an understanding on the subject at the forthcoming conference of the Big Three. In regard to the latter I

[1] This document has also been printed in DBPO Series I, Vol. I, No. 104.
[2] John Christmas Møller.

gave him no encouragement and on the former I said it depended on what functions the respective forces still had to perform, and what exactly the term withdrawal comprised; for example mine sweeping which was of as much importance to the Danes as to anybody, might necessitate a fairly long stay by certain British forces. I also had in mind, although I did not mention it, the possibility that continued presence here of British air or military or naval mission might be so interpreted by the Russians as to justify their remaining in Bornholm indefinitely.

2. Danish Minister for Foreign Affairs made it clear that he would very much like His Majesty's Government to assist the Danish Government in taking the initiative with the Russians. I did not respond to this, but [?observed] perhaps we might know more about Bornholm after Admiral Holt and General Dewing[3] had paid their informal visit to the Governor. I added, in reply to suggestion that I might go to Bornholm, that as there were no British residents there I did not think that the visit by me at the present juncture would be justifiable or advisable.

3. On the assumption that the Russian stay in Bornholm will be determined by their own interpretation of their interests, I think it would be a mistake to allow the Danish Government to use the withdrawal of our forces as a lever. In their eagerness to get the Russians out, they might be led to press for termination of activities by our military naval or air services here, which are as much in Danish interests as our own. The case might be altered if we could reach understanding with the Russians, and Danes about synchronising withdrawal of fighting units, but the plain truth is, I think, that the Danish Government is prepared to accept the unostentatious presence of the British here for a long time, but does not, despite the excessively cordial remarks made by the Minister for Foreign Affairs on various occasions, want any Russians at all in Bornholm and wishes anyone but himself to ask them how much longer they propose to stay.[4]

[3] Vice-Admiral Holt was British Flag Office, Denmark. Major-General Dewing was British member of the SHAEF Mission to Denmark.

[4] The Foreign Office reply (telegram No. 232 of 22 July) explained that it had not been the intention to raise the question of Bornholm with the Russians during the conference at Potsdam. If the Russians were to do so, the British response would be that 'we are already withdrawing our forces and propose to continue to do so as and when their tasks are completed and that we assume that the Russians will do likewise'. It concluded that if the Danish Government wished to find out when the Russians proposed to leave Bornholm, they should surely ask them directly. It expressed a preference that the withdrawal of both forces should be decided independently and on purely military grounds, though acknowledged a willingness to consider simultaneous withdrawal if this were judged necessary on purely political grounds (FO 371/47225, N8589/9/15).

No. 14

Sir J. Anderson to Mr Randall (Copenhagen), 23 July 1945[1]
Tel. No. 37 Saving (FO 371/47273, N8996/1866/15)

My telegram No. 100 of 21st July to Political Adviser to Commander-in-Chief, Germany (repeated to you as my telegram No. 229).[2]

The following background, for your own information, may help to explain reluctance of Commander-in-Chief, Germany, to permit visit of Mr. Christmas Møller.[3]

2. The so-called Danish minority in South Schleswig, though of Danish origin, consists of German citizens. Our policy is not to differentiate between German citizens on grounds of race and to break completely with the policy followed after the last war of establishing minority rights. This means that, unless our policy is revised, we cannot admit any Danish right to intervene in the affairs of the Danish minority in South Schleswig.

3. There are however other possible solutions such as:

(*a*) the reincorporation of South Schleswig into Denmark, and

(*b*) an exchange of populations between the Danish and German minorities on either side of the present frontier.

Responsible Danish spokesmen have made repeated declarations against a revision of the frontier. We have not so far received any proposals from the Danes for an exchange of populations.

4. The problem is being studied here. But it cannot be considered in isolation, since a decision in respect of the Danish minority would have repercussions upon other minorities, e.g. the Slovene population in the British zone of Austria. It may therefore be some time before our minds are clear on the subject. Meanwhile, it is important not to create precedents which would prompt e.g. Marshal Tito to claim the right to visit the Slovene minority in Carinthia, even for such personal conversations as Mr. Christmas Møller wishes to have with the leaders of the Danish minority in South Schleswig.

5. I am afraid there is little in the above which will help you in calming down the Danish Government. But you will perhaps be able to impress upon them that we cannot be rushed into giving privileged treatment to a section of the German citizens in our zone of occupation on the grounds of their Danish origin, in view of the tremendous political problems which we have to face in our zone and of the

---

[1] Repeated to Office of Political Adviser to Commander-in-Chief Germany, No. 88 Saving. Anderson was in charge of the Foreign Office during Eden's absence at the Potsdam Conference. This document has also been published in DBPO Series I, Vol. I, No. 374.

[2] Not printed.

[3] In his telegram No. 374 of 21 July, Randall had challenged the reluctance of the Commander-in-Chief Germany to allow a short visit by Christmas Møller. In addition to visiting the Danish minority there, he wanted to go to Flensburg to visit the grave of his son, who had been killed there while serving in the Grenadier Guards in April 1945. Randall had explained that Christmas Møller did not expect entertainment, would make no speeches and would remain only two or three hours. Randall did not consider that such a visit would set a precedent and argued that a refusal would cause considerable embarrassment (FO 371/47273, N8996/1866/15). It was subsequently agreed that a visit by Christmas Møller to Flensburg could be permitted. This telegram was cleared by Sargent, who directed that a paper on possible methods of dealing with the Danish minority problem should be prepared for the Overseas Reconstruction Committee. This was submitted by Bevin on 8 September. (No. 26.) These exchanges reflected the complexity of the problems represented by Schleswig-Holstein, which were not resolved until the autumn of 1948.

precedents which would thereby be created in respect of other minorities who would claim similar privileges. While we cannot admit that the Danish Government have any *locus standi* in pleading for special treatment for any group of German citizens in our zone, we shall nevertheless be glad to examine any proposals which they may care to put forward for dealing with the problem of South Schleswig.

No. 15

Sir L. Collier (Oslo) to Mr Eden, 24 July 1945.
No. 34 Top Secret (FO 371/47503, N9713/90/30G)

Sir,

With reference to my telegram No. 123 of July 20th,[1] and to previous correspondence relative to Soviet demands concerning Spitzbergen and Bear Island, I have the honour to transmit to you herewith copies of a note on this subject delivered by the Norwegian Ambassador at Moscow to the Soviet Commissar for Foreign Affairs on March 31st last,[1] together with the draft of a joint declaration to be made by the Norwegian and Soviet Governments before negotiating detailed arrangements for the defence of the Islands, which M. Andvord communicated to M. Molotov on April 9th last.[2] These documents were given to me yesterday by the Norwegian Minister for Foreign Affairs in pursuance of the undertaking reported in the last paragraph of my telegram No. 192 of July 4th.[1] (As you will now see, the statement in the second paragraph of that telegram that the offer of negotiations on this basis had been made to M. Molotov at San Francisco, was not correct: what happened there, as M. Lie has now explained to me, was that M. Molotov, who had returned no reply to M. Andvord's communication, was asked whether he agreed to the proposed joint declaration, and remarked that he would deal with this matter when he had returned to Moscow.)

2. The account which M. Lie has given me of the previous history of this question corresponds with that in your despatch No. 292 (N8052/90/G) of July 16th,[1] which I have now received. (With reference, however, to M. Molotov's assertion, reported in the second paragraph of that despatch, that Bear Island 'had originally been Russian', I understand that, though there had been a Russian claim to the Island, it had never been recognised as Russian territory). The further history of the matter is that it was raised with M. Molotov at San Francisco, with the result reported above, and with the further result that M. Hambro, who had to be made aware of it, since he was a member of the Norwegian delegation there, insisted that it should be laid before the *Storting* on the Government's return to Norway, whether or not there had been any further developments by that time. At M.

---

[1] Not printed.
[2] Collier, who was then still unaware of Molotov's approach over Spitsbergen of November 1944 (No. 3), had reported on 4 July that Lie had told him that he had given the *Storting* in secret session an account of the Russian demands over Spitsbergen and Bear Island. The Foreign Office decided that he needed to be briefed, and sent him a detailed account of the background on 16 July. They also asked Collier to consult Lie to establish whether he still wanted Britain to treat this as a very secret subject, because the Norwegians had brought this up with the Americans at Potsdam (FO 371/47503, N8052/90/30G; FRUS 1945, Vol. V, pp. 91-97). Collier replied in his telegram No.123 of 20 July that Lie had no objection to this (FO 371/47503, N8976/90/30G).

Hambro's insistence, too, it was decided to include a reference to it in the confidential statement on the background of foreign affairs which was made to leading journalists after the secret session of the *Storting*, in accordance with the usual practice of the Norwegian Government, with the result that the editor-in-chief of *Aftenposten* has already spoken of it in some agitation to the Press Attaché to this Embassy, and it will inevitably become common knowledge among informed circles in Oslo.

3. My United States colleague, to whom M. Lie has given another copy of these documents, has no information to show why the matter was raised with Sir A. Cadogan at Potsdam, as reported in your telegram No. 114 of July 19th:[3] he presumes that the delegation merely wish to be prepared in case the matter should be raised from the Soviet side, but he also presumes that it will be so raised in the fairly near future, in connexion with the questions of the control of entrances to the Black Sea and to the Baltic, to which it has a certain affinity, since in each case the Soviet interest is ostensibly in safeguarding the approaches to Soviet ports and the communications between these ports and the open sea. He is considering the advisability of sending a copy of the documents to Potsdam direct by air, in view of his distance from Washington; but in the absence of any indication that the Soviet delegation have raised the matter, or are likely to raise it in the immediate future, I am proceeding on the assumption that it will be sufficient for me to report to London by despatch. If the matter is in fact raised from the Soviet side, I presume that M. Lie will at once be invited to Potsdam.[4]

I have, etc.,
L. COLLIER

[3] Not printed.
[4] Ewart noted on 3 September that Lie had recently told Sargent that he had briefed Bevin on the status of the Russian demands during a meeting on 29 August. It appeared that there had been no further developments (FO 371/47503, N11276/90/30G).

No. 16

Mr Shepherd (Helsinki) to Mr Eden, 24 July 1945[1]
No. 114 Confidential (FO 371/47393, N9908/356/56)

Sir,

I have not so far made any comments on the Foreign Office secret circular despatch of the 30th March regarding the effect of our external financial position on our foreign policy.[2] This is partly because (*a*) as pointed out in paragraph 17 of the circular, Finland is one of those Scandinavian countries where the maintenance of flourishing trade relations should present no difficulty, (*b*) partly because the direction of Finnish foreign trade and the general economic situation of the country are still somewhat uncertain, (*c*) but also, and perhaps mainly, because the attitude we may propose towards Finland must depend to an appreciable extent on our

[1] This document has also been printed in DBPO Series I, Vol. I, No. 396. For a discussion of the UK's financial problems at this time, see DBPO, Series I, Vol. III, No. 1, note 4.
[2] Not printed.

policy with regard to the Scandinavian States in general with special reference to Russia.

2. As regards the first consideration, there seems every reason to hope that economic relations with Finland will not only regain their pre-war characteristic but will develop in a manner favourable to us. We bought before the war 45 per cent of Finland's total exports but Finnish imports from the United Kingdom were only 19 per cent. We are likely to be in the market when normal trade conditions return for similar quantities of Finnish forest and agricultural products and while abnormal postwar conditions prevail our demand for anything Finland can supply is likely to be exceptionally high. Finland, like other European countries affected by the war, is in need of raw materials and machinery in order to build up her worn-out and war-damaged industries; while for the next two years she will be requiring more than normal imports of foodstuffs during the period required to rehabilitate the land, which is short of fertiliser, and to carry through the necessary reallocation of arable land to accommodate the refugees from Karelia.[3] Finnish imports from Germany before the war amounted to 17 per cent of the total, and it seems likely that this figure will fall to little over zero and will give us the opportunity to replace Germany in the Finnish market. There may be some competition from the United States, but the Finnish capacity for earning dollars is small and we should find Finland a valuable unit of the sterling area. The only fly in this ointment is the Soviet Union. There was comparatively little trade with Russia before the war, partly owing to difficulties connected with the Soviet organisation, partly owing to a strong disinclination on the part of the Finns to allow business with Russia to assume large proportions. This attitude completely changed as a result of the defeat of Finland and even without a strong Communist party there would be great inducement from a political point of view to the development of trade between Finland and Russia. This inducement will undoubtedly be strengthened by the influence of the Communist party, which is indeed likely to do everything it can to diminish Finnish trade with the west in order to strengthen Finnish dependence on Russia and emphasise the necessity for Finland to regard herself as definitely and permanently coming within the Russian sphere. The development of this trade is rather difficult to forecast. During the immediate years ahead Russia will probably require timber products which she would not normally import, especially paper, of which her manufactures, even in peace time, were comparatively small. At the present time, the Finns are giving Russia all they can in addition to reparations deliveries and deliveries under article 14 of the armistice, in return for foodstuffs and raw materials. There is also a strong possibility that the Finnish army will in the not very distant future be reorganised and rearmed on the Russian model and with Russian weapons. It is certain, therefore, that we shall find Russia a strong trade competitor.

3. The development of Finland as a medium of good trade relations depends, of course, on her weathering the economic storms which still beset her. Reparations and restitution deliveries are burdensome and there is a general decrease in the average production of individuals which I believe is characteristic of post-war periods. The financial situation, while not entirely out of hand, is precarious, and while interim rates of exchange which involve sterling and the dollar have been fixed in Finland itself, the effective value of the Finnmark is a matter for

---

[3] In the aftermath of the Finnish cession of the Karelian Isthmus to the Soviet Union by the peace of 12 March 1940.

speculation. It is certainly decreasing fairly quickly. The internal price level is rising rapidly and wages are rising as well, so that the spiral of inflation is proceeding, if not unchecked, with only occasional touches of the brake. In spite of efforts to curtail it, the black market still flourishes and is likely to continue to flourish until the volume of consumer goods is sufficient to absorb surplus purchasing power. Labour conditions are also unstable, partly owing to price difficulties, partly owing to political subversion, and partly owing to difficult relations between employers and employees, a branch of the social structure in which Finland appears to have been curiously backward, in spite of her social progressiveness in some other respects.

4. The extent to which official support of resumption of trade relations with Finland will be required depends to a considerable extent on the policy which we propose to adopt with regard not only to Finland, but to Scandinavia as a whole. There is presumably no doubt that we shall do our utmost to retain and improve our interests in the other Scandinavian countries but Finland is in an intermediate position. She is definitely in the Russian defensive sphere and it is a matter for consideration whether, after a certain point, British interests in Finland would not invoke counter-measures by Soviet Russia which might not only nullify our own efforts but might even have the opposite effect. It is possible that Russia may wish to use Finland as an outlet to the west and that efforts on our part to develop Finnish cultural interests in Britain would not be unpalatable to the Russians. It is certain, however, that there would be strong Russian reaction to a situation in which Finnish relations with the west would be strong enough to keep alive anti-Russian feeling to an extent where Finland might become a dangerous or even inconvenient neighbour.[4]

I have, etc.,

F.M. SHEPHERD

[4] Minuting in Northern Department and Economic Relations Department fully agreed with Shepherd's assessment that Russia would be the vital consideration so far as Finland's relations with the outside world, both economic and political, were concerned. Warr (Northern Department) also noted the strong possibility that the Finnish Army might be recast on the Russian model, observing that this was being considered in relation to the draft Peace Treaty (FO 371/47408, N9908/356/56).

No. 17

Sir J. Anderson to Mr Jerram (Stockholm), 25 July 1945, 4.20 p.m.
Tel. No. 1031 Top Secret, Personal (CAB 126/82)

1. In connexion with a TOP SECRET defence project in which the United States and United Kingdom Governments co-operate closely, it has become necessary to ask the Swedish Government to institute a measure of control over the uranium deposits in her territory.[1]

[1] It was decided to make this approach to the Swedish Government following a meeting on 18 July 1945, which was chaired by the Chancellor of the Exchequer and attended by John G. Winant and Herschel Johnson, US Ambassador in London and Minister in Stockholm respectively (CAB 126/82). See also DBPO, Series I, Vol. II, No. 186.

2. The two Governments have been experimenting in the use of uranium for military purposes and the experiments have shown that the material has definite military value, though this can only be exploited by nations with vast industrial capacity. The two Governments are therefore making every effort to secure control of sources of uranium in the interests of world peace.

3. The existence of uranium in Swedish deposits of kolm and in oil shale has long been known, but only lately have the quantities and accessibility of the material been at all closely assessed. His Majesty's Government recently sponsored a visit to Sweden by Dr. Davidson of the Geological Survey to discuss recent progress in geophysics in Sweden and other matters of interest to geologists. Secret arrangements had previously been made with Mr. Bengt Walstad of the Svenska Diamantbergborrnings A/B to co-operate with Dr. Davidson in collecting samples of information about the deposits. This investigation has established that there is a very large quantity of workable uranium ore in two fields, in Västergötland and Närke, the former being much the largest and practically untouched, whilst the latter is worked by the Swedish Admiralty for oil.

4. It is proposed that the Swedish Government should be immediately informed in general terms of the interest of the two Governments, and of the significance of the material for world peace and asked to agree:

(*a*) to institute effective control of its uranium-bearing deposits for a long period of years.

(*b*) to prevent export of such materials except with the consent of the two Governments.

(*c*) to give the two Governments first refusal of the uranium content of the materials.

5. In consideration of an undertaking of this kind by the Government of Sweden, the two Governments would be prepared to purchase a reasonable quantity of the material, bearing in mind the rate at which the deposits can be worked economically.

6. By agreement with Her Majesty's Government, Mr. Herschel Johnson, United States Minister in Stockholm, has been instructed by his Government to speak to the Swedish Foreign Minister on behalf of the two Governments, asking the Swedish Government to enter into negotiations. Mr. Johnson will report to Mr. Winant the Swedish Government's reaction and if the latter is favourable, actual negotiations will be conducted jointly by the two Governments with representatives of the Swedish Government either in London or in Stockholm as may seem best. Mr. Johnson has been told that you are being informed.

7. The nature of the recent investigation, and in particular the part played by Mr. Bengt Walstad will not, at any rate for the present, be disclosed to the Swedish Government, who will merely be told that it is believed that considerable quantities of uranium can be recovered in fields which can be developed easily. More detailed disclosure will no doubt be necessary as detailed negotiations develop.

8. No action is necessary on your part at this stage but it was felt that you should be made aware of the proposed negotiations in view of their probable importance to Anglo-Swedish relations. Until otherwise informed you should keep this matter strictly to yourself (repeat strictly to yourself). Mr. Johnson is being asked to let you know the result of his first approach to the Swedish Foreign Minister.[2]

---

[2] A minute to the Prime Minister of 22 September 1945 explained that it had been established that the two fields in Southern Sweden probably contained about 80,000 tons of uranium oxide, which could be obtained without great difficulty. The negotiations with the Swedish Government had been

complicated, partly because the Americans had dropped atomic bombs in Japan which had made Sweden nervous of the possible political consequences of any undertaking to provide supplies exclusively to Britain and the United States. A solution was eventually reached whereby Sweden undertook to introduce legislation forbidding the exploitation of any uranium-bearing material without the permission of the Government, and forbidding any export of such material (CAB 126/82).

No. 18

Letter from Mr Haigh to Mr Allen (Terminal),[1] 25 July 1945
Secret (FO 371/47408, N8592/1131/56)

[No salutation on this copy]
I enclose a brief about the question of a Soviet-Finnish alliance.

You will see from paragraph 11 that you are asked to discuss with the Americans the desirability of taking this up with the Russians.

Enclosure in No. 18

Soviet-Finnish Alliance

In the course of the discussions between the Secretary of State and Marshal Stalin in Moscow in 1941, Stalin said that there should be in the future an alliance between the Soviet Union and Finland giving the former the right to maintain naval and military bases on Finnish territories.[2]

2. In his telegram No. 196 of the 21st May 1945 Mr. Shepherd reported that there had been some discussion in the press about the question of a treaty of mutual assistance between Finland and the Soviet Union.[3] He was, however, unable to find any definite indications that anything of this sort was contemplated.

3. A secret report dated 1st July stated that negotiations for a defensive alliance were being conducted between the Finns and the Russians in Helsinki.[3] The treaty would among other things give the Russians the right to put Russian troops into Finland in the event of a tense situation arising. As from the date of signing the treaty the Finnish Army would be permitted to be maintained at its peacetime strength.

4. In his telegram No. 219 of the 8th June Mr. Shepherd reported that the Finnish Minister for Foreign Affairs had informed him that a treaty of mutual assistance with Russia was 'not on the agenda'.[4] He himself had not spoken with the Russians on the subject. Mr. Shepherd commented that it was clear from the manner in which he spoke that some such agreement was in a preliminary stage of discussion but had not yet come forward for the Cabinet.

5. In his telegram No. 280 of the 13th July Mr. Shepherd reported that the Finnish Minister for Foreign Affairs had told him that the question of a military agreement with Russia was still not on the agenda.[3] Colonel-General Zhdanov had

---

[1] See also DBPO, Series I, Vol. I, No. 396 (Calendar). 'Terminal' was the official designation for the Potsdam Conference.
[2] Eden reported on these discussions to the War Cabinet in a memorandum of 5 January 1942 (PREM 3/394/3).
[3] Not printed.
[4] No. 11.

been in Helsinki recently for a few days and there had been a question of the Finnish Prime Minister asking for an interview in order, apparently, to raise this matter. It had however been decided to leave the initiative to Colonel-General Zhdanov. Mr. Shepherd deduces that the matter appears to have been progressing, though it is evidently still in its preliminary stages. The Russians may however have a draft agreement ready which the Finns would in practice have little opportunity of amending.

6. Such an alliance would be in accordance with the present policy of the Russians, who have been concluding bilateral treaties of alliance with the countries within their sphere. They have made such alliances with the three minor Slav countries and are reported to be about to make Roumania into an 'Ally'.

7. The Charter of the World Organisation blesses 'regional arrangements' in general terms as agencies to help in preserving the peace, provided that the terms of such agencies and their activities are consistent with the purposes and principles of the United Nations. The principles laid down in the Charter for members of the World Organisation include the 'sovereign equality of all its members' and refraining from the threat of force against the territorial integrity or political independence of any State. Though the Russians might have some difficulty in squaring the arrangements imposed on Finland with these principles, they will certainly expect all their alliances with Eastern European countries to be accepted as legitimate arrangements under the Charter.

8. The Soviet Government are not likely to be deterred from making a treaty of alliance with Finland by the fact that she is still technically an enemy, nor is it likely that we should have much opportunity for comment before the signature of an alliance.

9. It is for consideration whether we should attempt to dissuade the Soviet Government from concluding a treaty of alliance with Finland, since such a treaty would be likely to give them control of Finland's foreign and defence policies. It is clear that the Soviet Government will not again permit Finland to conduct an anti-Soviet foreign policy, with or without a treaty. It is equally clear that, in the event of trouble, neither we nor anyone else could prevent the Soviet Government from using any part of Finland as a military base. A Soviet-Finnish treaty of alliance would be unlikely to do more than confirm the actual state of affairs.

10. Should the Soviet Government conclude a treaty of alliance with Finland, it might be desirable to consider (after we had ourselves made a peace treaty with Finland) proposing the admission of Finland to the World Organisation, with a view to bringing Finland a little out of the Russian orbit and into the wider community of nations. By the very fact of having concluded a treaty of alliance with Finland, the Soviet Government would be in a weak position to oppose the admission of Finland into the World Organisation.

11. The British delegation at Terminal may wish to discuss with the American delegation the desirability of asking the Russians whether they are contemplating a treaty of alliance with Finland, and whether they will discuss the matter with us in advance of concluding such a treaty. (We should presumably point out that such a treaty should not be made until peace had been concluded between the Finns and all countries at war with her.)

12. Hitherto the Soviet Government have only concluded treaties of alliance with the three Allied Slav countries, i.e. Poland, Czechoslovakia and Yugoslavia. If they now conclude one with one ex-enemy country, namely Finland, we may soon expect this to be followed by similar treaties of alliance with Roumania,

Bulgaria and Hungary. There is every indication that the Russians have this in mind. Having secured governments to their liking in these countries, the Russians have now suggested the resumption of diplomatic relations, and they will not stop at anything to ensure that these countries remain firmly under their control. The conclusion of Russian treaties of alliance with Finland, Roumania, Bulgaria and Hungary would have a most depressing effect on the limitrophe Allied countries, such as Norway and Greece, who would be alarmed at the strength of the new combination of alliances with Soviet Russia as the centre piece.[5] The Greeks have for some time past made it clear that they would like to enter into a formal alliance with us, and we might expect an immediate request for such an alliance if not only Yugoslavia but also Bulgaria were to ally themselves with Moscow. The disadvantages of aligning Europe into two camps are obvious. But if the Soviet Government proceed with their plans, there would be even greater disadvantage in our merely watching without doing anything to put heart into our friends who live on the border of this Russian system of alliances. Although we may feel that formal treaties with these distant countries add little to their actual strength, the psychological effect on the countries concerned would be considerable in that the existence of a treaty would make them feel less isolated and more certain of our support.[6]

[No signature on this copy]

[5] Warr, Northern Department, suggested on 20 August that if Finland was to sign such a treaty with the Soviet Union, it might be desirable for Britain to make a similar alliance with Norway. Ward, Reconstruction Department, noted that Bevin considered that an understanding or treaty with France should come first, adding that Lie was due to visit London shortly and might raise this himself. He suggested that a brief should accordingly be prepared for Bevin. However, Lie did not bring the subject up (FO 371/47408, N8592/1131/56G). See No. 29.

[6] In the event, this subject was not raised with either the Americans or the Russians at Potsdam. Sargent requested that a copy of the brief should be sent to Helsinki and Moscow, with a note explaining the background and asking both posts to watch the situation and report any developments. These instructions were also to be sent to Oslo. This was done by Warner on 8 September (FO 371/47408, N8592/1131/56G). Roberts replied from Moscow on 5 October, reporting that the Embassy had heard nothing which bore out this possibility. Neither had the American Embassy (FO 371/47408, N13744/1131/56G).

No. 19

Minute from Mr Warr to Mr Warner, 28 July 1945
(FO 371/47412, N9686/1743/56)

Finland

Mr. Shepherd is coming home for consultation and will be here on the 30th July. Colonel Magill of the Control Commission will be here at the same time: Captain Howie has despatched him to this country on the ground that the situation in Finland is 'such' that he considers it essential to send an officer to London for consultation. Mr. Caplan[1] is also here. The following note of the state of affairs in Finland may be useful for our consultations with Mr. Shepherd, and possibly with the other two persons named where necessary.

[1] Ministry of Supply.

2. The Finnish internal political situation presents no particular problems at present. It has been very fully and well reported by Mr. Shepherd and I do not think there is anything which we need to ask him to add. The situation in Finland is, however, dominated by the attitude of the Soviet Union, and on this question of Russo-Finnish relations I think we should certainly ask Mr. Shepherd for his opinion and for his forecast of the future to supplement his reports on the subject. In his most recent report dated 18th July, Mr. Shepherd says that the Finns seem to be recovering some of their independence of spirit and to be indulging in some criticism of Russia.[2] At the same time, he considers that there is less tension among the Finns in their feelings towards Russia. I think we might ask Mr. Shepherd to elaborate his thesis and to say in particular whether there are any signs that Finnish apathy is wearing off, and whether there is likelihood that the Russians will continue to treat the Finns with their present patience. On another aspect of Russo-Finnish relations there is the rumour that a Soviet-Finnish alliance is in the offing. We have briefed Terminal on this subject, in particular suggesting that the British delegation may wish to discuss with the American delegation the desirability of asking the Russians whether they are contemplating a treaty of alliance with Finland, and whether they will discuss the matter with us in advance of concluding such a treaty. We also said in the brief that we should presumably point out that such a treaty should not be made until peace had been concluded between Finland and all the countries at war with her. I do not think there is anything here about which we need consult Mr. Shepherd. We should, however, inform him of what we have done.

3. Mr. Shepherd in his most recent despatch, above referred to, says that 'what the Finns are really looking for is a peace treaty'. The draft of a peace treaty is in the process of being prepared here. Mr. Shepherd has provided us with the information we asked for about it, and in particular has reported on the fulfilment of the Armistice terms, and has done what he can to provide us with a list of the treaties to which Finland but not His Majesty's Government is a party. At this end the next step is for us to consult the Chiefs of Staff about the military aspects of the draft treaty. Perhaps Mr. Shepherd might be willing to meet Lord Hood[3] and myself in order that we may tell him in more detail what is happening and ask for any advice he may wish to give.

4. The reason why the Finns are so anxious for a peace treaty is, of course, in order that they may get rid of the Control Commission. This attitude of the Finns is quite understandable, although our information up to date is that the Control Commission have confined themselves to seeing that the terms of the Armistice are carried out. We might ask Mr. Shepherd to confirm whether the Control Commission have in fact confined themselves to their proper sphere.[4]

5. Our element of the Control Commission certainly considers that our Russian colleagues have not interfered in Finnish affairs beyond what is required by the Armistice terms. They have just been confronted with a set of Russian proposals for certain 'adjustments' in the Armistice terms upon the conclusion of hostilities in Europe. Similar proposals have been made in respect of the Balkan satellites,

---

[2] Not printed.
[3] Reconstruction Department.
[4] In a minute of 9 August recording the outcome of the meeting, Warr noted that Shepherd's conclusion was that apart from certain incidents (such as the arrest of some White Russians by the Finns at the instigation of the Soviet element of the Control Commission) the Control Commission had in general confined itself to its proper sphere (FO 371/47412, N9686/1743/56).

and the question is being discussed at Terminal. Mr. Shepherd's opinion is that these modifications amount to very little in practice as regards Finland.

6. At the same time, the President of the Control Commission has explained to our element of the Control Commission that the end of the war with Germany called for certain changes in the application of the Armistice Agreement. These proposed changes fall under three heads:

(*i*) The Russians will still retain control over the Malmi airfield for the needs of the Control Commission, although Article III of the Armistice terms would appear to indicate that such airfields would be returned to the Finns after the end of hostilities against Germany. It appears, however, that in a later interview with Colonel-General Zhdanov, Captain Howie has obtained some satisfaction on the point in which we are interested, namely, the right to have a regular air courier service once a week from Stockholm. He says he has forwarded details of this plan in a weekly report sent by bag. It has not yet arrived. We can consider this question further when the report reaches us.

(*ii*) Much more serious is the question of the substitution of the word 'Soviet' for 'Ally' in paragraph 2 of the Annex to Article III of the Armistice terms, the effect of which is only to permit Russian ships to use Finnish ports. On being pressed by Captain Howie, Colonel-General Zhdanov has agreed to add in the words 'and British merchant ships'. This is, however, not sufficient, and instructions are being sent to our Element of the Control Commission to return to the charge and insist as a matter of principle that the original wording of the Armistice terms be reinstated.

(*iii*) In spite of paragraph 2 of the Annex to Article V of the Armistice terms, neutral diplomatic missions are still not going to be allowed cypher and bag facilities. We should take up this breach of the Armistice terms, but perhaps should first ask Mr. Shepherd's advice on the question of whether it would be advisable to go into action with the Russians on behalf of the neutrals.

7. Finally, we might ask Mr. Shepherd's opinion about our Element of the Control Commission, and whether they are, as we assume, upholding British prestige *vis-à-vis* the Finns now that they can have not much work to do over the fulfilment of the Armistice terms. We should also consult Mr. Shepherd about the guidance for which Captain Howie has asked about how far he should subordinate his views to those of Colonel-General Zhdanov, and whether he should be firm on certain occasions. Captain Howie has since reported that in the absence of guidance from us he is continuing his policy of 'appeasement'.[5]

8. There are certain other subjects on which we might ask Mr. Shepherd's advice:

(*i*) The economic side has been covered in a separate minute of a conversation I had with Mr. Caplan. Mr. Shepherd has reported that from a political point of view he is in favour of providing the Finns with all the goods we promised them as against timber, and of maintaining the quantity of our supplies to them although they are in fact sending us less than the contract quantities of timber.

(*ii*) Has Mr. Shepherd adequate staff, particularly on ciphering and shorthand-typing? I have seen complaints from Helsingfors that they are short of both these branches.

(*iii*) Mr. Shepherd was very keen, as we are, that the British Council should

---

[5] Warr recorded that Howie had been given separate instructions on military channels that 'we do not mean to stand any nonsense' (FO 371/47412, N9686/1743/56).

operate actively in Finland. In view of the long delay in starting we should ask him, I think, whether he is satisfied with the present arrangements.

(*iv*) Finally, we should ask him whether he is receiving adequate reports from Mr. Bosley,[6] and whether the arrangements made for communicating these reports to the Russians are working satisfactorily.

G.C. WARR

[6] R.W. Bosley was working as an Information Officer in the Embassy in Helsinki at this time.

No. 20

Mr Walsh (Helsinki) to Mr Bevin, 7 August 1945
Tel. No. 328 (FO 371/47408, N9992/1131/56)

It was disclosed on Finnish radio last night (August 6th) that Colonel General Zhdanov had addressed a note to the Finnish Prime Minister stating Russia's intention of establishing diplomatic relations with Finland.[1]

2. I am unable to see Orlov about this as he is away and not expected back for ten days. It is likely however that Captain Howie will receive a copy of note in the near future.

3. Finnish Ministry of Foreign Affairs has unofficially confirmed receipt of note but is obviously not anxious to give any details at present. Announcement on the radio was apparently an indiscretion due to leakage and today's press carries no report of the matter.

4. I gained the impression in conversation with head of Political Department of Ministry of Foreign Affairs that note may be no more than official intimation of terms of Terminal communiqué and that it is not specific as to the date or procedure.[2]

[1] For previous correspondence on this subject, see DBPO, Series I, Vol. I, No. 39
[2] Bevin wrote on this telegram: 'How will this affect us?' Northern Department replied that it would be good for Finnish morale if Britain were to follow the Russian lead, pointing out that failure to do so might also be prejudicial to British commercial interests in Finland. Treaty Department emphasised that it would not be possible to establish full diplomatic relations with Finland until a peace treaty had been signed, and it was therefore concluded that representatives could be exchanged who would have the personal rank of Minister, but who would not be given extraterritorial rights. This would be similar to the arrangement which had been made in Italy. On being informed that the American Embassy were also going to propose a resumption of diplomatic relations to the Finnish Government, Cadogan suggested synchronising the UK's announcement with theirs, or at least giving them warning of the date proposed by the British Government (FO 371/47408, N9992/1131/56). See No. 21 and FRUS 1945, Vol. V, pp. 554-55.

No. 21

Mr Bevin to Mr Balfour (Washington) 18 August 1945, 12.40 a.m.[1]
Tel. No. 8491 Confidential, Important (FO 371/47399, N10827/55/56)

Helsingfors telegram No. 328 [of 7th August: Resumption of diplomatic relations between the USSR and Finland].[2]

It was decided at the Berlin Conference that the Council of Foreign Ministers should undertake the task of preparing peace treaties with (among other countries) Finland. Moreover, 'the three Governments agree to examine each separately in the near future, in the light of the conditions then prevailing, the establishment of diplomatic relations with Finland (Roumania, Bulgaria and Hungary) to the extent possible prior to the conclusion of peace treaties with these countries'.

2. Constitutional considerations make it impossible for The King to resume diplomatic relations with the Head of a State with which His Majesty is still technically at war. Diplomatic relations cannot therefore be resumed with Finland until a treaty of peace has been signed.

3. But there is no constitutional objection to the establishment of quasi-diplomatic relations with the Finnish Government on the model of our present relations with the Italian Government. Moreover, His Majesty's Government in the United Kingdom see no political objection to the establishment of such quasi-diplomatic relations with the Finnish Government, since they are satisfied that the Finnish Government are a true democratic Government and that they enjoy the support of a majority in the Diet freely elected subsequent to the signature of the Finnish Armistice.

4. His Majesty's Government have accordingly decided to invite the Finnish Government to appoint a political representative in the United Kingdom, to whom they may accord the personal rank of Minister; and to request the Finnish Government to regard the British political representative in Finland as having the personal rank of Minister in Helsingfors. There would be no presentation of credentials on either side.[3]

5. Please inform the United States Government/Soviet Government of the foregoing.

[1] Repeated to Moscow and Helsinki.
[2] No. 20.
[3] FO telegram No. 287 to Helsinki, sent simultaneously with this telegram on 18 August, instructed Shepherd to inform the Finnish Government of this decision (FO 371/47399, N10827/550/56).

No. 22

Record of a meeting between Sir O. Sargent and M. Hvass and M. Rasmussen,[1] **28 August 1945**
(FO 371/47274, N11254/1866/15)

1. I saw M. Hvass and M. Rasmussen this afternoon.

[1] Franz Hvass and Gustav Rasmussen were respectively the Secretary-General designate of the Danish Foreign Ministry and the Danish Chargé d'Affaires in London.

2. M. Hvass quickly got on to the subject of the Schleswig 'minority', and I explained to him as gently as I could the fact that we did not wish to repeat on this occasion the mistake the peacemakers made in 1919, when they laid down that special rights and privileges should be secured to racial minorities, and thereby recognised that the country with whom the racial minority was connected had the right to defend the interests of the minority.

3. M. Hvass tried to draw a distinction between political interest and cultural interests, but I pointed out that it was very difficult to separate one from the other in practice. If the Danish Government, as I understood, did not wish to alter their present frontier with Germany in Germany, their remedy lay in exchanging the Danish minority in Germany against the German minority in Denmark. Was this not desirable in Denmark's own interest? M. Hvass did not think so, and argued that it would be difficult to uproot the Danish minority in Germany which had lived so long in Schleswig, although the Danish Government were anxious to get rid of some of their own Germans in Denmark. He also seemed to hint that it might, for political reasons, be quite convenient for Denmark to maintain the Danish minority, though I could not quite make out what was in his mind.

4. I pointed out to M. Hvass that in any case the matter was more or less academic at present as long as Schleswig was under British military occupation, for naturally the British military authorities would not interfere with any of the cultural rights which the Danish 'minority' were already enjoying and which indeed they had enjoyed even during the Nazi regime. It would be time enough to consider the position again when Schleswig was handed back to the German Government under a purely German administration.

5. Eventually it emerged that what was at the present moment worrying the Danish Government was the fact that the local populace on each side of the German-Danish frontier were not allowed to move backwards and forwards as they were in the habit of doing in normal times. Thus, members of the German minority had been in the habit of visiting friends and relations in Denmark, and similarly, the Danes used to visit friends and relations among the Danish minority in Schleswig. This intercourse was at present stopped. I said that this no doubt was due to difficulties of transport and accommodation, but I was prepared to bring the matter to the attention of Sir William Strang[2] to see whether the present restrictions might not to a certain extent be relaxed[3].

[2] Political Adviser to Commander in Chief, Germany.
[3] Clarke, Northern Department, minuted on 1 September that 'We should make it clear that, though we do not admit the right of the Danish Government to interest themselves in the minority, we wish to avoid friction with the Danes and unfavourable comparisons between the Military Government and the German regime and that we should therefore wish the minority to be accorded the privileges to which they were previously accustomed' (FO 371/44274, N11254/1866/15). In a subsequent letter of 28 September, Randall took issue with the principle that Britain could not admit the right of the Danish Government to intervene on behalf of the Danish minority in Schleswig. He cited examples where he considered that such a right had been conceded, concluding that the problem of the Danish minority was unique and should be treated independently. Warner disagreed. In a reply to Randall on 19 October he wrote that 'Our point is briefly that we admit to no obligation to do anything for the Danes, even to listen to their requests in respect of the minority in South Schleswig; but we mean in practice to be reasonable, while reserving to ourselves a right to determine where we draw the line. There is, we think, something in the distinction between the official and the unofficial. So long as Christmas Møller raises these matters unofficially we see no objection to your accepting any reasonable requests and passing them on. If we are approached unofficially we may find it necessary to remind the Danes of our principle of not admitting their

6. In this connexion, M. Hvass suggested that it might be useful if the Danish Government were allowed to appoint a liaison officer to be attached to British headquarters at Flensburg. I said that this also was a question which I would put to Sir. W. Strang.

7. Lastly, M. Hvass drew my attention to an announcement issued by the Allied Control Commission in Berlin on the 20th August (see notice in *The Times* of the 21st August attached), to the effect that the Control Commission had decided that the Danish and Netherlands Governments should be invited to appoint representatives in Berlin with the Control Commission. The Danish Government had questioned Brigadier Crowe at Copenhagen about this announcement, but had so far received no further information. I promised to look into the matter and to let the Danish Legation know what the position was.

O.G. SARGENT

'right to approach us. We hope that it will not be too difficult in practice to maintain this line' (FO 371/44274, N13370/1866/15).

No. 23

Mr Bevin to Mr Randall (Copenhagen), 28 August 1945[1]
No. 148 Secret (FO 371/47226, N11265/5934/15)

Sir,

The Danish Minister for Foreign Affairs called upon me on the 28th August, accompanied by M. Hvass, the Secretary-General designate of the Danish Ministry for Foreign Affairs, and by the Danish Chargé d'Affaires. I understand that the purpose of M. Christmas Møller's visit to this country is partly personal and partly concerned with the affairs of the Danish community in London.

2. After conveying to me the good wishes of the Danish Prime Minister, M. Christmas Møller informed me of the interest of the Danish Government in the future of the Kiel Canal. The decisions on this matter would no doubt be taken by the Great Powers; but the Danish Government would be glad of an opportunity of giving their view upon any proposals for the future of the Kiel Canal before these were finally adopted. I asked whether the Danish Government would like us to fill in the Canal. M. Christmas Møller had no comment on this suggestion, but thought that, in present conditions of warfare, the strategic importance of the Canal must be very small. I agreed that it was certainly less important than it had been.

3. The interest of the Danish Government arose out of the presence in South Schleswig of a Danish minority numbering between 12,000 and 15,000 persons. The Danish Government had no wish for any revision of the present Danish-German frontier; they thought that the incorporation of German territory into Denmark would create undesirable problems for the future.

4. While not wishing to claim any political interest in the Danish minority, the Danish Government did, however, take a keen cultural interest in them, and were concerned with their general welfare. They hoped, therefore, that they might be allowed to advise the British occupation authorities on the treatment of the Danish minority, in view of their long experience of the subject. M. Christmas Møller

[1] This document has also been printed in DBPO Series I, Vol. V, No. 19.

drew attention in particular to the influx into South Schleswig of some 300,000 refugees from Eastern Germany (quite apart from the 300,000 German refugees in Denmark itself). The presence of these refugees made living conditions very difficult for the inhabitants, and M. Christmas Møller asked whether they could be removed. I replied that we were doing our best to deal with this problem.

5. The Danish Government hoped that, by the beginning of April 1946, 10,000 Danish troops would be ready to join the ranks of the British Army and participate in the occupation of the British Zone of Germany.[2] M. Christmas Møller considered it of political importance that these Danish troops should not be employed in South Schleswig, but should be sent to some other part of the British Zone. I undertook to bring this consideration to the notice of the Chiefs of Staff.

6. Turning to the British occupation of the Faroe Islands, M. Christmas Møller said that our action in occupying these Islands has been greatly appreciated by the Islanders themselves and by Danish officials there. He understood that the majority of our forces had now left the Islands but that the meteorological station still remained, manned by a small number of our troops. There was one point in this connexion which M. Christmas Møller wished to put to me very confidentially. The Russian forces that had liberated Bornholm would probably not leave until the British forces left the Faroe Islands. When British forces landed on the Islands in April 1940, Mr. Churchill undertook that they would be handed back to Denmark at the end of the war. M. Christmas Møller urged that the remaining British forces should be withdrawn at an early date, and the Faroe Islands then formally handed back to Denmark, preferably with some ceremony. This example would be useful to the Danish Government in connexion with the presence of Russian troops in Bornholm. If we had any requirements in connexion with a meteorological station in the Faroes, the Danish Government would be very glad to run these themselves for our benefit.[3]

7. M. Christmas Møller then talked of trade relations between the United Kingdom and Denmark. He started by complaining that travel between the two countries was excessively difficult; it was only possible for three or four Danish officials to make the journey every week, and the interests of Anglo-Danish trade required far greater facilities. He asked that permission might be given for a Danish air service to start between the two countries at the earliest possible moment.

---

[2] Christmas Møller had first taken the initiative and mentioned this figure during a meeting with Randall on 11 June 1945, as he reported in his despatch No. 12 of that date. The papers do not make clear to what extent this figure had been agreed with the Danish Minister of Defence or the Cabinet. The Foreign Office responded enthusiastically to this offer and welcomed the prospect of a Danish contingent to share in the occupation of Germany, as long as it was properly trained and equipped (FO 371/47301, N7292/5732/15).

[3] Sargent wrote to Hollis on 30 August, recalling that at their meeting on 29 May the Chiefs of Staff had agreed to the early withdrawal of the garrison from the Faroe Islands and that this had largely happened with the exception of those troops manning the Loran meteorological station. He repeated the points made by Christmas Møller, stressed that Bevin wished to try to help the Danes get the Russians out of Bornholm and that he wanted this issue to be settled before a meeting of Foreign Ministers on 10 September. He therefore asked the Chiefs of Staff to consider Christmas Møller's proposals as a matter of urgency (FO 371/47259, N11539/507/15). Soon afterwards Christmas Møller extended his request to include all British troops in Denmark, requiring a further letter from Sargent to the Chiefs of Staff (FO 371/47226, N12914/9/15). (See No. 30.) There were reservations about an immediate handover of the Loran station to the Danes, and it was agreed on 6 October that as a temporary measure British troops would continue to run the station, but on a civilian basis (FO 371/47259, N13473/507/15).

8. Denmark was anxious to re-establish quickly the pre-war trade between the two countries. Her most important shortage was coal; her apparatus of production was intact, and could be put into production as soon as coal was available. Apart from coal, Denmark was short of machine tools, printing machinery, and rubber. Denmark did not wish to obtain her requirements from the United States, for the United States were not a market for Danish exports and any purchases which Denmark made in the United States would not lead to continuing trade.

9. I spoke to M. Christmas Møller of our well-known difficulties in starting up production for export again, which depended on getting our men home from the Far East, releasing men in the forces, and absorbing them into civilian employment. I added that we were pressing on urgently with the resumption of our export trade. While I held out no hope in respect of coal and printing machinery, I said that I thought we should probably be able to make machine tools available to Denmark, and that the cessation of hostilities in the Far East would probably relieve the rubber position very shortly.

10. M. Christmas Møller told me of the willingness of the Danish Government to provide Danish ships at Danish expense to help us get our men home from the Far East. He also told me how the Danish Government had cut down food consumption in Denmark at the end of the hostilities in order to make as much food available for export to those who needed it.

11. I undertook to give careful consideration to all the points raised by M. Christmas Møller and to let him have replies to them at the earliest possible moment.

I am, etc.,
ERNEST BEVIN

No. 24

Mr Bevin to Sir L. Collier (Oslo), 29 August 1945[1]
No. 402 Secret (FO 371/47528, N11314/716/30)

Sir,

The Norwegian Minister for Foreign Affairs came to see me today and spoke on the following subjects:

2. *Norwegian Military Mission to Germany.* M. Lie told me that the Norwegian Government had instructed their representatives in London, Washington, Paris and Moscow to inform the Governments to which they were accredited of the desire of the Norwegian Government to despatch a military mission to each of the four zones of occupation in Germany. This mission, which would be headed by General Steffens, would be charged with the task of investigating the condition of Norwegian interests in Germany. The Norwegian Government was being pressed on this subject by Norwegian concerns which had interests in Germany; and M. Lie would be grateful if early and favourable consideration could be given to these requests. I promised to expedite consideration of these requests.

3. *Reparations.* The Norwegian Government have been shown by the Soviet Government the text of a Polish-Soviet Agreement dated the 18th August relative

---

[1] This document has also been printed in DBPO Series I, Vol. V, No. 20.

to reparations. The Norwegian Government would be glad if an agreement on similar lines could be made between Norway and the United Kingdom.

4. *Whaling Factories.* It had been the understanding of the Norwegian Government that the attitude of Her Majesty's Government was that the disposal of any whaling factories captured from the Germans or the Japanese should be made between Great Britain and Norway alone, as being the principal whaling nations. Three German whaling factories had been found: the *Walther Rau*, *Unitas*, *Wikinger*. The Norwegian Government had now learned that two of these, the *Unitas* and *Wikinger* had been taken over by the United Kingdom. This action had been taken without prior consultation with the Norwegian Government; and M. Lie felt that the British authorities had acted unfairly in doing this. The Norwegian Government considered that they were entitled to one of these whaling factories (M. Lie mentioned either *Unitas* or the *Walther Rau*); they would have no objection to the United Kingdom receiving the other two. I told M. Lie that we were not certain that we could gain acceptance among the Great Powers for the allocation of a German whaling factory separately from the allocation of German shipping as a whole; this was a disputed point. I would, however, take note of the attitude of the Norwegian Government, and study whether it would be possible to meet their wishes.

5. *Dollars.* One of the subjects which M. Lie had wished to raise with me was the desire of the Norwegian Government to obtain a sum of approximately 1 million dollars per month for the next years in respect of insurance on shipping which had been sunk during the war. The Norwegian Merchant Navy had been built in many countries; and the Norwegian Government were anxious to commission replacements in many countries also. The insurance money was, however, available to them only in sterling. It was only fair that part of this money should be converted by us into dollars. In view, however, of the sudden termination of Lend-Lease supplies to this country from the United States, M. Lie realised that our dollar position was now extremely grave; and in the circumstances he would not press this request at the moment. He reserved the right, however, to revert to the matter later when the situation became clearer. I thanked him for his understanding of our difficulties, and for the forbearance of the Norwegian Government in this respect.

6. *Anglo-Norwegian Mutual Aid Agreement.* This agreement, concluded between the Norwegian Ministry of Finance and His Majesty's Treasury on the 4th October, 1944, was now due to terminate on the 8th November, 1945, six months after the German surrender. M. Lie felt that this choice of date had been governed by the expectation that British troops would have been withdrawn from Norway by then. As it was, however, some British troops were likely to remain in Norway until the end of the year; and in the circumstances the Norwegian Government were anxious that the Mutual Aid Agreement should remain in force until the end of the year also. I said that this seemed to me a very reasonable suggestion, to which I would give immediate consideration.

M. Lie took this opportunity of paying a very generous tribute to the work in Norway of General Sir Andrew Thorne and of the British staff officers as a whole, and of the behaviour of all British troops in Norway. But for one incident in Bergen, to which the Norwegian Government did not attach importance, the British troops had behaved in an exemplary fashion. As for General Thorne, he had maintained thoroughly harmonious relations with the Norwegian Government, and had shown himself a good combination of politician and soldier. M. Lie then quoted some figures to show the magnitude of the task which General Thorne and his staff were successfully discharging in removing prisoners of war and displaced persons from Norway; this showed moreover that General Thorne was obtaining full support from the United Kingdom authorities in obtaining transport for this purpose; I expressed my gratitude to M. Lie for this generous tribute.

7. *Equipment for Three Norwegian Divisions.* M. Lie mentioned the desire of the Norwegian Government to obtain German material for the training of Norwegian forces pending their re-equipment with British material. He then turned to the question of purchasing British material for these forces. Norway was anxious to obtain the complete equipment of three divisions. But the price asked was £12 million, a sum which was quite beyond Norway's means. I told M. Lie that I did not think we were asking an excessive price for the material which the Norwegian Government required. Our military authorities were anxious to open early discussion with the Norwegian military authorities on the whole matter of the re-equipment of the Norwegian Armed Forces; and we hoped that a Norwegian military delegation would arrive here at an early date to open these discussions. When this delegation arrived, I thought that they would find our authorities not unreasonable. I handed to M. Lie an *aide-mémoire* in confirmation of my remarks on this subject.[2]

I am, etc.,
ERNEST BEVIN

[2] Several of the issues raised by Lie during this conversation were not readily resolved to Norwegian satisfaction. See for example No 40, in which Collier reported to Sargent a conversation where Lie complained about the manner in which it was proposed to dispose of the German whaling fleet. On the matters raised here, the Foreign Office decided that it was not willing to negotiate a reparations agreement with the Norwegian Government and the request for an extension of the Anglo-Norwegian Mutual Aid Agreement was refused after it was determined that this would result in a significant financial loss to Britain (FO 371/47528, N16026/716/30).

No. 25

Minute from Mr Warner to Sir O. Sargent, 5 September 1945
(FO 371/48035, N11547/570/42)

Naval Visits to Sweden

The head of the Swedish Navy[1] has informed our Naval Attaché at Stockholm that the Soviet Naval Attaché has just requested permission for Soviet warships to pay a visit to Stockholm, probably on some date in September, and that the Swedes have approved the proposal though 'without relish', and the Swedish Admiral enquired whether it might be possible for the British Navy to pay the first post-war visit by a belligerent country to Sweden.

2. The Admiralty asked our views and we told them that we would be in favour of getting in first. The Admiralty told us an early visit could be arranged.

3. We later received a telegram (No. 1302) from His Majesty's Minister in Stockholm saying that 'it would not seem desirable even if it were practicable to try to get in before the Russians'.[2] We replied that the preliminary view here and in

[1] Vice-Admiral Helge Strömbäck.
[2] Not printed.

the Admiralty had been in favour of getting in first and asked for a further explanation of Mr. Jerram's view.

4. He has now telegraphed: 'The chiefs of the Swedish armed forces are somewhat naturally apt to presuppose in their conversation that we are as apprehensive of the Soviet Union as they are.

5. This is a danger that has constantly to be guarded against and in the specific instance dealt with in my telegram No. 1302 it would clearly be unadvisable (whatever His Majesty's Government's views may be of the desirability of keeping pace with or ahead of Soviet moves such as naval visits and so on) to enter at the present juncture into even the shadow of a conspiracy of this nature with Sweden'.[3]

6. It seems to me that His Majesty's Minister is being too subtle and that we should encourage the Admiralty to arrange a visit as soon as possible.

7. The attitude of the Swedish Navy during the war was not satisfactory, and in April Mr. Cavendish Bentinck suggested that there might be a danger that Germany might transfer her naval secrets to Sweden for safe keeping and asked the Admiralty whether they had any plans for converting the Swedish Navy. We have received no reply from the Admiralty and have been awaiting Mr. Jerram's views after discussion with his Service Attaché.

8. The new Swedish head of the Navy is well reported of by our Naval Attaché and the point has been made that the Swedish Navy's attitude during the war might have been different if it had not been rather neglected by our Navy before the war.

9. This seems to me an additional reason for responding to the Swedish Admiral's hint and getting our naval visit in before the Russians.

?Inform Admiralty accordingly and explain to Mr. Jerram our reasons for disagreeing with him.[4]

C.F.A. WARNER

[3] Stockholm 1308 of 3 September 1945.
[4] The Foreign Office was not willing to accept the cautious line proposed by Jerram. Noting the admission in his telegram No.1308 that British neglect of the Swedish armed forces had proved disastrous during the war, Cadogan replied on 7 September that a visit by the Fleet would be bound to be good for relations between the two navies. Britain should be careful not to line up with Sweden against Russia as a matter of general policy in naval matters, but 'we think that this little conspiracy to get our visit in first is in a different category and comparatively innocent'. It was therefore decided that the advantage lay in responding to Admiral Strömbäck's hint and the Admiralty were told to arrange an early visit to Sweden (FO 371/48035, N11547/570/42).

No. 26

Memorandum from Mr Bevin to the Cabinet Overseas Reconstruction Committee, 8 September 1945
Secret (CAB 121/361)

The Problem of South Schleswig
Memorandum by the Secretary of State for Foreign Affairs

I circulate for the consideration of the Overseas Reconstruction Committee a paper (Annex) prepared in the Foreign Office on the problem of South Schleswig.

The present Danish-German frontier was fixed as a result of a plebiscite in 1920. The Danish Government have made it clear that they do not propose to seek a revision of the frontier. There is, however, some agitation among the residents in South Schleswig for incorporation into Denmark.

The conclusions of the paper are briefly as follows:

1. There are no sufficient grounds for a revision of the frontier and no encouragement should, therefore, be given to agitation among the residents in South Schleswig in favour of revision.

2. There would be practical difficulties in the way of an exchange of populations, but there would be no objection in principle to this course if proposals acceptable to those concerned should be put forward.

3. During the period of military government, we cannot admit the right of the Danish Government to approach us on behalf of German citizens of Danish origin. On the other hand we can, as an internal matter, ensure so far as possible that such German citizens are accorded the privileges to which they have been accustomed.

If these conclusions are approved by the Committee, I propose to communicate the annexed paper to Sir W. Strang and His Majesty's Minister in Copenhagen for their guidance.[1]

Enclosure in No. 26

ANNEX

The problem of South Schleswig

Historical

1. In 1864, after the war between Denmark on the one hand and Prussia and Austria on the other, the King of Denmark ceded his rights in the Duchies of Schleswig and Holstein to Prussia and Austria. By the Treaty of Prague of 1866 between Austria and Prussia, Austria surrendered her share in the duchies to Prussia.

2. The Treaty of Versailles stipulated that the frontier between Germany and Denmark should be fixed by a plebiscite. The area of Schleswig, in which there was a considerable Danish minority, was divided into two zones. The first, the predominantly Danish area of North Schleswig, was to be treated as a unity; its future was to be decided by a simple majority of votes. In the second, the Southern, zone votes were to be counted parish by parish and the frontier drawn in accordance with the result. Voting took place in 1920, after the ratification of the Peace Treaty. In Zone 1 74 per cent of the votes cast were for union with Denmark. In Zone 2 the result was a conclusive victory for Germany in practically all parishes. The new frontier was drawn in accordance with the results of the plebiscite, Denmark receiving all Zone 1 but none of Zone 2, and has remained unchanged ever since.

The German minority in South Jutland

3. It is difficult to estimate the number of 'Germans' in the territory north of the present frontier. In 1920 some 25,000 of the inhabitants of this territory voted for union with Germany. In 1939 the Schleswig (German minority) Party polled some 15,000 votes in the election to the Danish Parliament. The total number of

---

[1] The paper was discussed at the Cabinet Overseas Reconstruction Committee meeting ORC (45) 6th meeting on 4 October. Bevin commented that he had discussed it with the Danish Minister of Foreign Affairs, who had agreed that the problem should not be reopened: the Danish Government had no wish for any revision of the present Danish-German frontier (see No. 23.) The paper was approved.

'German-minded' persons has been estimated at 30,000. The Danish administration of South Jutland since 1920 has been characterised by liberality towards the minority, who have been allowed every facility for attending German schools, etc. Certain of the activities of the minority, particularly after the advent of Nazism, have aroused concern in Denmark, and the disloyalty of many of the members of the minority to the country during the occupation has resulted in some bitterness of feeling towards them.

The Danish minority in South Schleswig

4. In 1920 some 12,800 voters (out of nearly 65,000 votes cast) in this area favoured union with Denmark. The numbers of those 'of Danish outlook' has been estimated as 12,000 to 15,000. Official German statistics, however, in 1935, gave the number of Danish-speaking persons as only 5,000, though this is certainly an under-estimate. The Danish minority have on the whole been fairly well treated by the Germans and have been allowed their own schools, etc., even under Nazism.

Views of the Danes

5. The 1939-45 war, ending with the surrender of Germany, has resulted in the reopening of the frontier question. In the latter months of the occupation there was much discussion of it in Danish resistance circles, and an extension of the frontier southwards was advocated by some, particularly members of the small nationalist party *Dansk Samling*. There is no doubt, however, that these views were not shared by the great majority of Danes.

6. The views of the Danish Government formed on the liberation of Denmark were expressed by the Danish Prime Minister's speech of the 9th May in which he said: 'The Government standing firm on the basis of national self-determination are of the opinion that the Danish frontier remains firm. The totally changed conditions at the end of the war mean that the question of the Danish minority south of the border as well as of the position of the German minority in Denmark must be considered.' The Danish Minister for Foreign Affairs has repeatedly expressed himself against any annexation of German territory. M. Hedtoft Hansen, a prominent Social Democrat minister, has stated that there is today no frontier problem for Denmark. These views are in accordance with the traditional Danish policy of keeping Denmark a 'national State' and refusing to have more than the minimum non-Danish elements within the country's boundaries.

Revision of frontier

7. A new frontier line could only be decided upon on one of the following grounds: (*a*) historical (*b*) strategic (*c*) ethnological or linguistic (*d*) self-determination. These will be examined in turn in the following paragraph.

8. (*a*) a return to the pre-1864 frontier would mean the inclusion in Denmark not only of South Schleswig, whose predominantly German character was proved by the 1920 plebiscite, but also of Holstein, the population of which is indisputably of German character. Such a course would certainly cause trouble in the future and the Danes would undoubtedly refuse such a gift if it were offered them.

(*b*) In the conditions of modern warfare it is unlikely that any new frontier would have any substantial strategic advantages over the present one.

(*c*) It would almost certainly be impracticable to draw a better frontier than the present one on an ethnological or linguistic basis owing to the mixed character of the population in the border district.

(*d*) The 1920 settlement was conducted on the principle of self-determination and was generally recognised as satisfactory. A new plebiscite in German

Schleswig, at any rate if it took place in the near future, might well mean that in addition to the 'Danes' of South Schleswig a large [?number] of Germans would, for reasons of material advantage, vote for inclusion in Denmark. This would be an unsatisfactory state of affairs and would not be welcomed by the Danes.

9. In view of the above considerations and of the attitude of the Danish Government (see paragraph 6 above) no encouragement should be given to agitation in favour of a revision of the frontier.

Exchange of Populations

10. There would be serious difficulties in the way of any exchange of populations. The Danish minority in South Schleswig are mainly farmers attached to their land and do not want to move. There is, moreover, no clear cut division between 'Danes' and 'Germans' in the frontier regions. The same applies to the German minority of south Jutland.

11. There is some feeling among the Danes that some of the German minority should be expelled on account of their pro-German attitude during the war and to avoid trouble in future, but it is unlikely that any drastic measures will be proposed. While an exchange of populations is probably impracticable there would be no objection in principle to this course if the Danish Government should put forward reasonable proposals acceptable to those concerned. The problems does not, however, appear to be of sufficient magnitude to justify such a solution.

A Danish Mandate

12. It is occasionally suggested that some form of Danish mandate should be established over the regions south of the frontier. Mr. Steel reported on the 20th July that a petition was being organised in Flensborg in favour of a Danish mandate in South Schleswig to be followed by attachment to the Danish Crown. The Danish Minister for Foreign Affairs has informed Mr. Randall that he considers this an impossible plan; its advocates merely disguised their real aim, the eventual attachment of South Schleswig to Denmark; it was, therefore, contrary to the policy of the Danish Government.

13. Mr Christmas Møller, in a memorandum communicated to the Secretary of State on the 11th April 1945, said, 'If the victorious Powers wish the Kiel Canal to be situated in non-German territory, Denmark must hold the view that a separate Canal State must be created. This Canal State must be in no way connected with the Danish State. Denmark would also prefer to avoid the task of administration of a State of this kind, but it is not likely that Denmark would wish to refuse obligations which it might seem unnatural for her to undertake.'

Treatment of the Danish Minority

14. Presuming that the frontier remains unaltered and that there is no exchange of populations, the Danish minority in South Schleswig will wish their minority privileges to be maintained, and the Danish Government will wish to interest themselves in the minority's welfare. Inasmuch as our policy is not to differentiate between German citizens on grounds of race and to break completely with the policy followed after the last war of establishing minority rights, we cannot admit any right of the Danish Government to approach us on behalf of German citizens of Danish origin. On the other hand, we can as an internal matter ensure so far as possible that Germans of Danish origin in the British zone in Germany are accorded during our occupation the privileges to which they were accustomed before our occupation (for example, they should be allowed to retain their schools). If we do not do this, there will be strong feeling in Denmark that we compare

unfavourably with the Germans in this respect. If Danish forces are introduced into the British zone, it would be preferable that they should be stationed in some other area than South Schleswig.

15. The above refers of course only to German citizens of Danish origin and not to Danish nationals, in whose welfare the Danish Government have every right to be interested.[2]

ERNEST BEVIN

[2] The general election in Denmark in October 1945 led to the formation of a Venstre Party minority Government. Christmas Møller told Randall that he thought that his party had lost seats through their, or perhaps his, attitude to the problem. In telegram No. 803 of 7 November, Randall predicted that this outcome would mean that the South Schleswig question would remain open, and the Foreign Office anticipated that it might be necessary to reconsider its policy in the light of the change of Government (FO 371/47275, N15340/1688/15).

No. 27

Letter from Sir O. Sargent to General Hollis (Cabinet Office), 14 September 1945
Secret (FO 371/47226, N12065/9/15)

[No salutation on this copy]

1. I refer to Copenhagen telegram No. 607 of the 11th September,[1] from which you will see that the Danish Minister for Foreign Affairs wishes to be given a date, even if only approximate, for the withdrawal of our forces from Denmark, in order that he may use this with the Russians when he raises the question of Russian withdrawal from Bornholm during his forthcoming visit to Moscow. He leaves Denmark on 15th September.

2. You will see from Copenhagen telegram No. 608,[1] that the United States Minister is recommending to his Government that he should be authorised to give a time limit of, say, 60 days after which all United States forces would either be withdrawn or brought under the control of his service attachés, and that our Minister suggests that he might be authorised to do likewise, with a longer time limit.

3. My Secretary of State is anxious that we should do what we can to help the Danes in getting the Russians out of Bornholm, and we should like to be able to tell Mr. Christmas Møller that our forces in Denmark will be withdrawn at a definite date, the sooner the better, so that the Russians will then have no excuse for staying on in Bornholm.

4. We were under the impression that our forces would all be withdrawn by mid-October, and are rather surprised that Randall should have suggested six months hence as a possible date for final withdrawal. I hope there will be no unnecessary delay in withdrawing our forces as soon as their tasks are completed or can be handed over to Danish agencies.

5. As regards any service personnel whom it may be necessary to keep on after the main body of forces has left, it might help the Danes with the Russians if such personnel could be differentiated so far as possible in status etc. from the forces who went in to take the German surrender, and if it could be made clear in any way

[1] Not printed.

possible that they are there only for certain specific purposes under special arrangements agreed with the Danes.

6. We should be grateful if the Chiefs of Staff would consider the question of the withdrawal of our forces from Denmark in the light of the political considerations I have mentioned above and advise us as soon as possible as to how we should reply to Randall's telegrams.

O.G. SARGENT

No. 28

Letter from Mr Warner to General Hollis (Cabinet Office), 23 September 1945
Top Secret (FO 371/47481, N12597/1004/27)

My dear Hollis,

With reference to Sargent's letter of the 18th September[1] and my letter N12597/1004/G of the 21st September about the American proposals to secure bases in Iceland,[2] we think we shall have to send a telegram to Washington asking the Embassy to warn the State Department that the matter raises issues of such importance that we must ask for time for its consideration by Ministers.

2. Our preliminary view is that, while there will obviously be great advantages for us in the establishment of American bases in Iceland, all arrangements for maintaining peace, including the provision of 'facilities' (which includes bases) should, according to Article 43 of the Charter of the United Nations Organisation, be made on the basis of special agreements between individual States and the Security Council as a body. The American proposal if proceeded with would suggest a complete lack of confidence in the proposed procedure under the Charter, and might give the Russians an excuse for trying to get similar bases elsewhere by direct pressure on the countries concerned. It looks as if Ministers will have to consider whether any practical advantages of getting the Americans established in Iceland outweigh these considerations.

3. You will have seen from Sargent's letter referred to above that Byrnes spoke to our Secretary of State about sending us a list of the bases the Americans had in mind. When the Chiefs of Staff consider this matter, we should be grateful for their advice as to whether we should take the line with the Americans that we should like to see this list and consider the question of bases as a whole before giving

---

[1] Not printed, but see DBPO, Series I, Vol. III, No. 48, note 1. In this letter, Sargent informed Hollis that the US Secretary of State James Byrnes had told Bevin at Chequers on 15 September that the American Government were becoming convinced of the need to maintain bases in Iceland and Greenland, and sought the views of the Chiefs of Staff on the military implications of this (FO 371/47481, N12432/1004/27G). For subsequent correspondence, see DBPO, Series I, Vol. III, No. 48 (Annex and Calendar).

[2] Not printed. This referred to Washington tel. No. 6329 of 21 September, describing the State Department's reply to the *aide-mémoire* sent by the Embassy, based on FO tel. No. 191 Saving of 8 March (No. 8). The American Government intended to ask the Icelandic Government for a long-term lease of a naval base, and two air bases, and proposed to approach the Soviet Government formally to explain their intention. In response, the Embassy asked the State Department to wait until British Ministers had considered their proposal, before approaching the Soviet Government (FO 371/47481, N12597/1004/27G).

them our views on this isolated proposal regarding Iceland. This point is one which should be covered in any interim telegram we send to Washington asking for further time for consideration, so we should be glad of the Chiefs of Staff's advice upon it at the earliest possible moment.

C.F.A. WARNER

No. 29

Mr Bevin to Mr Shepherd (Helsinki), 25 September 1945
Confidential (FO 371/47370, N13421/33/56)

Sir,

The Finnish political representative paid his first official visit to the Foreign Office today, and was received by Mr. Warner.

2. After an exchange of courtesies, M. Vuori showed interest in the discussion, which he had seen from the press are taking place in the Council of Foreign Ministers, on the Finnish Peace Treaty. He explained first of all that the Karelians, who had been displaced from their homes by the cession of Finnish Karelia to the Soviet Union, were hopeful that a rectification of the frontier in Finland's favour could be obtained in the peace treaty. The Finnish Government were less hopeful of this, but he wished to enquire what were the possibilities. Mr. Warner said that, if M. Vuori were to write to him on this matter, we should, of course, give him a considered reply; he could not, however, hold out any hope that the request would meet with a favourable response, unless M. Vuori was able to say that a similar approach had been made to the Soviet Government and been sympathetically entertained. M. Vuori said that this was not the case. Mr. Warner said he felt that the Finnish Government would probably have to resign themselves to the fact that the frontiers had been settled by the armistice.

3. M. Vuori then asked whether he could be told anything of the course of the discussions on the Finnish treaty in the Council of Foreign Ministers. Mr. Warner told him, for his own confidential information, that he could say no more than that the discussions had been concerned with the general substance of what was to go into the Finnish and other peace treaties, but that the drafting stage had not yet been reached. There was, however, so far as we were aware, no particular reason to anticipate that the Finnish Government would be confronted with any surprises. There were some matters which must be treated on similar lines in the various peace treaties: there was thus a certain inter-connexion between them which might delay the drafting of the Finnish treaty.

4. Finally, M. Vuori asked whether the Finnish Government would merely be presented with a treaty for signature, or would they be given an opportunity of discussing it at any stage. Mr. Warner said that this was a matter of procedure which, so far as he knew, had not even been discussed yet, so it was impossible for him to give M. Vuori any guidance on it.

5. I am sending a copy of this despatch to His Majesty's Ambassador, Moscow.

I am, etc.,
ERNEST BEVIN

No. 30

Mr Randall (Copenhagen) to Mr Bevin, 26 September 1945, 2.10 p.m.
Tel. No. 662 (FO 371/47226, N12914/9/15)

My telegram No. 608.[1]

Minister for Foreign Affairs again asked me yesterday whether I could not fix a date by which all our forces would either be withdrawn from Denmark or brought under diplomatic cover. I repeated that they would leave as soon as they had completed the tasks for which they had originally come to Denmark, but that I could not at present give a precise date: it would probably have to be different for each of the three services.

2. Mr. Christmas Møller again emphasised that it would be helpful if I could say something definite on this subject and hold out a prospect of the Danes themselves carrying out the necessary duties which retain considerable British forces here. He added that it was no lack of appreciation for the wonderful British effort and valuable services; it was only that he had no lever to get the Russians out of Bornholm with the least possible delay.[2]

[1] Not printed.
[2] Bevin wrote on this telegram: 'Could the Danes do this for us. I do not want our troops kept there if they can be brought home. EB' (FO 371/47226, N12914/9/15).

No. 31

Mr Shepherd (Helsinki) to Mr Bevin, 26 September 1945
No. 149 Confidential (FO 371/47370, N13353/33/56)

Sir,

I have the honour to report that I called on the Minister for Foreign Affairs on the 22nd September. M. Enckell began the conversation by very cordially expressing his pleasure that I had returned to Finland with the rank of minister, and that it had been possible to send M. Vuori in the same capacity to London. He added that he had discussed with Mr. Walsh at some length the constitutional difficulty which stood in the way of formal resumption of diplomatic relations and said that he quite understood this and that indeed the British observance of tradition was a stabilising factor in present times.

2. M. Enckell went on to say that there was a certain amount of disquietude in Finland regarding the Peace Treaty. There had been conflicting reports in the press about differences of view in London between Russia and Great Britain and it had been said that no Finnish delegation would go to London to discuss this question. Perhaps I knew more about this than they did in Helsinki and could tell him something about it. I explained for his confidential information that the procedure was that the Russians had circulated their views on the Finnish Peace Treaty and the British delegation had in the same manner circulated their own. As soon as agreement had been come to on the general form of the treaty, it would be passed to a drafting committee and it was clear that until the drafting committee had finished their work there could be no question of our discussing the treaty with the Finns.

3. It would appear that the Finns have jumped to the conclusion that the Finnish Peace Treaty would be concluded during the course of the present conversations in London and that they are consequently apprehensive at any delay in case this may portend some developments ominous for Finland. I have attempted to dispel this impression in conversation with M. Enckell and M. Svento and also in a press interview today.

4. M. Svento, whom I visited on the 24th September, said that there was some hope in Finnish circles that there might be some territorial readjustments in the treaty. These circles hoped that it would be possible to recover, in exchange for other territory, some parts of Karelia so that the strong desires of many Karelian refugees to return to their lands might be satisfied. He himself was extremely doubtful whether any representations of this kind would be agreed to by the Russians, especially since the Russian policy had always been to secure Karelia for defensive purposes. In reply to a question, he said that this matter had not been taken up with the Russians, but he asked me what the procedure would be in case the Finns wished to put forward their views in connexion with the Peace Treaty. I said that the best way for them to get information about this was to get M. Vuori to enquire from the Foreign Office what procedure the Finnish Government should adopt in this matter. M. Svento said that they had already asked M. Vuori to make such a request. In connexion with the desire of the Karelians to return to their lands, I enquired whether there had been any development of the movement which had been talked about some three months ago, when it was suggested that many Karelians would like to return to a Soviet Karelia, if they could get their land back. M. Svento said that he had heard of no movement of this kind but certain persons had unofficially put forward a memorandum, which they had given to the Russians, suggesting that parts of Karelia should be returned to Finland on condition that Finnish military forces should be kept at a distance and that the Soviets should be allowed certain military strong points for defensive purposes. He understood that the Russians had been displeased about this memorandum and that there was very little likelihood of it being adopted. It had been entirely unofficial, and the Government had only known about it on receiving a copy of the memorandum itself. There were, in addition, two questions which were troubling the Government and which they were afraid might hold up the conclusion of a Treaty of Peace. These were the war guilt question and the matter of arms dumps. The Russians had sent a note to the Finnish Government regarding the war guilt question, and in it had characterised the Finnish proposals as farcical. I asked him specifically whether this note had come from the Control Commission or from the Russians and he said the latter.[1] As regards the arms dumps, this had been shown to be a good deal more widespread than it had at first been thought, and was undoubtedly a serious matter. The organisers had been in touch with both Germany and Japan before the collapse of both those two countries and also with other foreign countries.

I have, etc.,
F.M. SHEPHERD

---

[1] Warr minuted on 15 October: 'The memorandum referred to . . . is news to us. The result of its presentation at least serves to confirm that the Russians are not thinking of ceding any territory to the Finns on any condition in the Peace Treaty' (FO 371/47370, N13353/33/56).

No. 32

Minute from Northern Department to Mr Bevin, 26 September 1945
(FO 371/47482, N12927/1004/27G)

American desire for bases in Iceland

The attempt made by Mr. Byrnes, at the request of the Secretary of State, to prevent the US Chargé d'Affaires at Moscow from presenting to the Soviet Government a note on the American desire for post-war bases in Iceland was unsuccessful, for the note had already been presented.[1]

2. The formal position is that the US Government have notified HM Government and the Soviet Government that the US Government intend to propose to the Government of Iceland the conclusion of an arrangement which would provide the United States with sea and air base facilities in Iceland, adding that 'If and when Iceland becomes a member of the United Nations, the US Government for its part would be prepared to give sympathetic consideration to a request from the Icelandic Government that the military facilities mentioned . . .[2] above be made available to the Security Council, on its call, in fulfilling the undertakings which the Icelandic Government would assume under the Charter' (i.e. to provide its contribution to the maintenance of international peace and security).

3. The Chiefs of Staff have concluded that on balance the military advantage lies in not resisting the American desire for bases in Iceland. They consider, however, that we should ask the Americans for an assurance that their presence in Iceland would not under any circumstances (e.g. in the event of the US remaining neutral when we were at war) be allowed to compromise the security of our Northern Atlantic communications. They also wish us to ask the Americans to agree to diversionary and emergency landing rights in their landing fields for British Service aircraft.

4. From the political point of view the assumption by the United States of responsibility for the defence of bases so close to the UK would be very welcome *if* this could be achieved without harm to the present World Organisation. But unfortunately the American method of procedure does not fulfil this proviso. If the Americans proceed to conclude a bilateral agreement with the Icelandic Government, this will provide a dangerous precedent for the Russians, who are likely to seek analogous facilities from the Danish Government (e.g. in Bornholm) and from the Norwegian Government. The US Government would, by their action in Iceland, be prevented from protesting against such Soviet action; and so should we, if we told the Icelandic Government that we approved the American proposal, as the Americans have asked us to do in the event of the Icelandic Government consulting us.

5. This would get us straight back to the worst form of power politics and armed neutrality. An American agreement with Iceland for the provision of bases would in fact appear as a vote of no confidence in the procedure laid down in the Charter of the World Organisation.

6. Our best course, therefore, would probably be to inform the US Government that we fully sympathise with their desire for bases in Iceland, and shall be very

---

[1] See No. 28 and DBPO, Series I, Vol. III, No. 48.
[2] Ellipsis in original.

glad to see them installed there, subject to the requests formulated by the Chiefs of Staff in paragraph 3 above. But we consider that the method proposed by them, envisaging as it does a bilateral agreement between the US and Icelandic Governments, strikes a blow at the procedure envisaged in Article 43 of the Charter of the World Organisation, whereby such facilities as those required by the US Government in Iceland should be provided on the basis of special agreements between individual States and the Security Council as a body. We should therefore like to suggest that the US Government should limit themselves, in their forthcoming negotiations with the Icelandic Government, to staking out a claim for the facilities which they require. These facilities for the US Government might then be included in the security agreement which Iceland will make with the Security Council when, as is to be hoped, Iceland is shortly admitted to the United Nations Organisation. The US Government could if they wished put their proposals before the Security Council at its first meeting; and HM Government for their part would be very glad to support these proposals.

7. It could at the same time be made plain to the US Government that our suggestions for a modification of the procedure proposed by them were aimed solely at avoiding an apparent vote of no confidence in the United Nations Organisation and the provision to the Soviet Government of an excuse for negotiating bilateral agreements for Soviet bases in e.g. Danish or Norwegian territory.

No. 33

Minute from Mr Bevin to Mr Attlee, 27 September 1945[1]
(FO 371/47482, N12927/1004/27)

American desire for bases in Iceland

The United States Government have officially notified His Majesty's Government and the Soviet Government that they intend to propose to the Government of Iceland the conclusion of an arrangement which would give the United States forces permanent sea and air bases in Iceland, subject to the proviso that when Iceland becomes a member of the United Nations, the United States Government would give sympathetic consideration to a request from the Icelandic Government that these military facilities should be made available to the Security Council as Iceland's contribution to the maintenance of international peace and security.

2. When I first heard of the matter I persuaded Mr. Byrnes to try to defer the presentation of the American note to the Soviet Government, as I feared its effect upon the Council of Foreign Ministers and upon the chances of the security system for which the Charter provides.[2] But this was too late.

3. I have now considered what action we should take in these circumstances. The Chiefs of Staff have advised that on balance the military advantage lies in not resisting the American desire for bases in Iceland, subject to our obtaining an assurance that in no circumstances would the presence of United States forces in Iceland be allowed to compromise the security of our own communications in the

---

[1] This document has also been printed in DBPO Series I, Vol. III, No. 48.
[2] Bevin's letter to Byrnes of 28 September is printed as an Annex to the document cited in note 1 above.

North Atlantic (e.g. in the event of the United States remaining neutral when we were at war).

4. From the point of view of our political relations with the United States, I feel sure that we ought to welcome their assumption of responsibility for the defence of Iceland. But there is obviously a serious risk that the American proposal will give the Soviet Government a pretext for seeking similar bilateral arrangements with Denmark and Norway. The Russians already occupy the Danish island of Bornholm and this American proposal may induce them to stay in Northern Norway. We might thus get straight back to the worst form of power politics and armed neutrality. The chance of organising world security on an international basis through the Security Council would be gravely prejudiced and the relevant provisions of the Charter might remain a dead letter.

5. However, we can now only make the best of the difficult situation created by this precipitate American action. In my view the proper course would be for the Americans to put their demands in Iceland in the form of a request for a temporary lease of the bases, pending the coming into force of the security procedure laid down in the Charter and the admission of Iceland to the United Nations.

6. I have put my idea in the form of a suggestion to Mr. Byrnes in the attached draft letter. In view of our unfortunate experience in the past with leakages from the State Department into the American press I have confined the letter to the point about the effect on the United Nations Organisation. I would propose to supplement the letter by informing Mr. Byrnes orally (*i*) that His Majesty's Government would, for their part, be glad to see United States forces permanently established in Iceland (subject to the Chiefs of Staffs' proviso mentioned in paragraph 3 above); and (*ii*) that my suggestion in the letter is intended not only to avoid an apparent vote of no confidence in the United Nations Organisation but also to deny to the Soviet Government an excuse for demanding Russian bases in Denmark and Norway, both of whom are already members of the United Nations Organisation.

7. The Chiefs of Staff Committee have concurred in the draft letter to Mr. Byrnes, on the understanding that it would be supplemented by oral explanations as suggested above.

8. I should be grateful to know whether you approve of my proposed action.

ERNEST BEVIN

PS The report to the Cabinet will be my letter to Byrnes.

No. 34

Lord Halifax (Washington) to Mr Bevin, 14 October 1945, 7.12 p.m.[1]
Tel. No. 6859 Secret (FO 371/47482, N13886/1004/27)

Your telegram No. 10261.[2]
State Department say that proposal put forward in your letter to Byrnes about Iceland (C) is still being considered by American Chiefs of Staff.[3] The

---
[1] Repeated to Reykjavik and Moscow.
[2] Not printed, but see DBPO, Series I, Vol. III, No. 90 (Calendar) for related correspondence.

considerations you put forward had been subject of long and anxious debate before the United States Government decided to act. The United States Government had been reluctant to contemplate a procedure under which their desire for long term leased bases in Iceland would be subject to decision by Security Council with the Soviet Union participating. On the other hand they were anxious to avoid prejudicing or damaging in any way the working of the United Nations Organisation and provisions of the Charter. With this in mind they had inserted paragraph 4 of their memorandum of September 24th (see my telegram No. 6330).[2] They admit that this may amount to attempting to square a circle by an optical illusion but they had been at a loss to find a better way round the difficulty. They had purposely timed their approach to come after San Francisco (so as not to prejudice discussions there), and before first meeting of the United Nations Organisation as further method of minimising any adverse effect on authority of the United Nations Organisation. The State Department add that they are giving careful consideration to your views [?as] they feel the force but clearly anticipate that American Chiefs of Staff will judge that balance of power lies in adhering to their present course of action and that their views would prevail.

2. State Department further say that they are still discussing with American Chiefs of Staff British request made in your oral communication to Dunn but have not (repeat not) yet received their final views. Meanwhile State Department are preoccupied with the question of form in which assurances might be given to us (if Chiefs of Staff agree). They are anxious to avoid adopting form of a treaty (which would have to be ratified by the Senate) or of an executive agreement which would probably have to become public. They are now thinking of an oral communication of which a record would be kept on the file. It would help me to learn whether you would regard this as satisfactory. I am in constant touch with the State Department in the matter.

3. With reference to paragraph 3 of your telegram State Department have received enquiries both from United Press and from Swedish Minister at Washington. They are confining themselves at present to saying the whole question of future bases which the United States Government may desire is under constant review by the State Department and Service Departments but that they have nothing to say at present on any aspect of the matter. They add that what they may say further will depend on the nature of press reports which may come from Iceland or elsewhere. They promise to keep us informed and if possible to let us know beforehand should they decide to say more.[4]

---

[3] The Foreign Office was already aware, from Reykjavik tel. No. 153 of 6 October, that the US Minister had approached the Icelandic Government with a proposal for a long-term lease (FO 371/47482, N13531/1004/27G).

[4] Bevin minuted on this telegram: 'I must have Depts. views on this.' For the response see No. 37.

No. 35

Mr Shepherd (Helsinki) to Mr Bevin, 17 October 1945
No. 171 Confidential (FO 371/47408, N14508/1131/56)

Sir,
The decision, announced by Generalissimo Stalin to the Finnish Minister of Education on the 8th October, to extend by two years the time-limit for the delivery of reparations gives rise to a number of speculations. It may be that the Russians had in mind that, since concession had recently been made to Roumania and Hungary, something should be done for Finland also. It may have been in the nature of a hint to the world in general, and perhaps Sweden in particular, that Soviet Russia is not an entirely unreasonable country, and it may have been partly intended to estop later Finnish requests for reduction of total quantities or reconsideration of the price-level fixed last December. It may also have been influenced by the thought that supplying countries like the United States and ourselves would not be disposed to release to the Finns materials destined to supply demands of too rapacious a nature. But though any or all of these considerations may have been present in the minds of the Russians, it seems most probable that the concession represents a genuine appreciation of the difficulty of the Finnish position, and of the efforts made by the Finns to comply with the reparations Agreement.

2. The first year's deliveries, it is true, fell short by about 2 million dollars of the specific programme, thus exposing the Finns to penalties for non-delivery. But the total of deliveries amounted, in fact, almost exactly to the required 50 million dollars, since some of the following year's products were delivered early. The Russians have, indeed, been somewhat harsh in enforcing penalties where inability to deliver was due to circumstances, such as the Swedish metal strike, outside Finnish control. They have, in addition, been apt to strain the interpretation of the agreement to an extent which has led the Finns to keep a 'B' account (with a view to subsequent payment) of deliveries which they have been compelled to make but which they do not consider could properly be demanded by the Russians under the agreement.

3. The *Soteva*, the Finnish organisation set up to deal with reparation deliveries to Russia, has, however, earned praises from the Russians, and the chairman, M. Kivinen, has been more energetic and sensible in handling very difficult problems which have often aroused the opposition and obstinacy of Finnish suppliers. I think that the Russians who have dealt with *Soteva* have recognised, not only the very great difficulties which the Finns would have had in coping with the Russian demands for 1946, but also the honesty and willingness of M. Kivinen and his colleagues to do their utmost to fulfil their obligations. If this judgement of Russian motives is correct, it confirms the many indications that Finland is being nursed as a model Russian protégé.

4. M. Stalin, according to press reports, also informed M. Helo that, after reparation deliveries were completed, Russia would continue to take Finnish imports to three or four time the value of the annual exports on reparations account. This might be construed to mean that Russia would practically monopolise Finnish export trade, which before the war amounted to little more than four or five times the 50 million dollars of annual reparations. The remark, however, while confirming the likelihood that Russian trade with Finland will be

encouraged, was probably intended to calm fears, which had often been expressed, that the expansion of Finnish engineering industries entailed by manufactures for reparations will lead to difficulty and unemployment once deliveries have been completed. M. Stalin's assurance that Russia will continue to buy from these industries will be welcomes by all those concerned.

5. It is a curious example of Russian methods that the Finnish delegation (which was of an educational and cultural character only) had already reached Leningrad on its way home when it was recalled to Moscow to be received by Generalissimo Stalin. Far from indicating any irritation at this imperious and, one would have thought, somewhat inconvenient summons, the members of the delegation expressed the utmost delight, and described their audience in terms of quite absurdly sycophantic reverence and awe.

6. I am sending a copy of this despatch to his Majesty's Ambassador at Moscow.[1]

I have, etc.,

F.M. SHEPHERD

[1] Northern Department found it difficult to understand why the Soviet Government should have decided to extend the reparations period. They concluded that the main reason was possibly the fact that the Russians had too much on their hands and did not want to have to deal with a breakdown in the Finnish economy. They also found it peculiar that Stalin himself should have informed the Finns of this decision, and that he had chosen to do so to a cultural delegation led by the Minister of Education. They interpreted this as a further sign of the great importance which the Russians attributed to cultural propaganda in Finland, assessing that they hoped to win the country over by persuasion rather than by overt political or economic pressure (Minute by Warr, 26 October 1945, FO 371/47408, N14508/1141/56). In a subsequent despatch of 29 October, Shepherd commented on Finnish reactions to Stalin's decision, quoting Hella Vuolijoki, a member of the delegation: 'It is also a reflection of the Finnish mentality that she regretted volubly that Stalin's suggestion of a longer period for the delivery of reparations should have been made suddenly to a cultural delegation: if they had known more about the matter and had not been taken unawares, she thought, they could have asked for, and obtained, more. This regret is shared by other members of the delegation who apparently thought that they had brought Stalin to a soft and generous mood of which more advantage might have been taken' (FO 371/47408, N15193/1131/56).

No. 36

Mr Roberts (Moscow) to Mr Bevin, 18 October 1945, 3.45 p.m.[1]
Tel. No. 4594 Top Secret (FO 371/47503, N14133/90/30)

Shortly after his return from London Molotov told the Norwegian Ambassador at a party that it was time they resumed their conversations. The Ambassador has no doubt that Molotov has in mind the Soviet interest in Bear Island and Spitzbergen. So far Molotov has not followed the matter up and the Ambassador is not himself responding to Molotov's hint although he has to raise some time one or two questions concerning fishing rights etc. which arise from the change of frontiers in the Petsamo region.[2]

[1] Repeated to Oslo.
[2] The Norwegian Ambassador in Moscow also informed the American Ambassador of Molotov's approach (FRUS 1945, Vol. V, p. 99).

No. 37

**Joint minute from Reconstruction and Northern Departments to Mr Bevin,
18 October 1945**
(FO 371/47483, N14664/1004/27)

American Desire for Bases in Iceland
Request for Comments on Washington Telegram No. 6859[1]

This telegram tends to confirm our impression that the US Joint Chiefs of Staff have the upper hand of the State Department and are determined to get what they consider essential for the future security of America, although this may well jeopardise the system of international security for which the United Nations Charter provides. This means that the US Government have been planning to sidestep the Charter by getting and holding their bases by bilateral lease. When the Charter system got going, the Americans would be established and, as the Secretary of State observed when we first heard of the American proposal, 'possession is nine-tenths of the law'.

2. It is pretty clear that the Americans are not going to accept our alternative suggestion of a short-term lease pending the entry into force of the Charter system. They made their demand to Iceland for a long-term lease on 1st October (several days after the Secretary of State made our alternative proposal to Mr. Byrnes), and it has already leaked out through the Scandinavian press that the USA desire to retain these bases. The Russian press has so far confined itself to carrying the press leakages, and the Soviet Government, although officially informed by the Americans of their approach to the Icelandic Government, have not so far expressed any view.

3. We have received strong hints from prominent personalities in Iceland that the Icelandic Government desire the views of His Majesty's Government before making up their minds on the American demand.[2] The Secretary of State may wish to put the issues before the Cabinet so that our view can be given to the Icelandic Government at the proper moment and we may be able to handle the situation as it develops. The question for decision is really whether we back the United States in their policy of trying to secure their position here and now by bilateral arrangements with the Icelandic Government, or whether we insist upon the point of view put to Mr. Byrnes, that *long-term* arrangements for bases in Iceland should be made strictly in accordance with the Charter system.

4. The Chiefs of Staff have agreed with the Foreign Office that the vital interests of the United Kingdom would be served by the retention of American forces in permanent bases in Iceland. On the other hand, it is a main objective of His Majesty's Government to make a success of the United Nations Organisation, and we cannot escape from the fact that the American haste to secure their position in Iceland (and also in the Azores, and in certain British and other Allied territories in the Pacific) in advance of the entry into force of the Charter system, may, by antagonising the Russians and minimising the role of the United Nations Organisation, destroy the whole Charter system of international security before it has been given a chance. If the United Nations Organisation fails as the overriding

---

[1] No. 34. See also DBPO, Series I, Vol. III, No. 90.
[2] Reykjavik tel. No. 160 of 14 October reported a series of informal approaches by Icelanders from all political parties, except the Communists, though there had not at this stage been any formal approach from the Government (FO 371/47482, N13884/1004/27G).

body for international security, the experience of the League of Nations suggests that it will sooner or later break down altogether.

5. The choice before His Majesty's Government is a very difficult one. But the decisive consideration is perhaps the fact that the Americans have already committed themselves to the demand for a long-term lease and it is most unlikely that they will now be ready to amend this by adopting our alternative proposal.

6. It is suggested, therefore, that our present policy might be as follows:

(i) Not to press the Americans to revise their demand on the Icelandic Government, but of course to welcome their substituting a short-term demand if they should spontaneously decide to do so, for example as a result of Icelandic or Russian reactions to their long-term demand.

(ii) Not to volunteer our observations to the Icelandic Government, but to authorise HM Minister at Reykjavik to respond to enquiries from the Icelandic authorities regarding our attitude by speaking on the following lines:

'This war has shown that the presence of American forces in the North Atlantic area is essential for the security of that area. We therefore welcome the proposal that American forces should continue to occupy bases in Iceland. We naturally assume that such occupation will be brought in due course under the international security system provided for in the United Nations Charter. In the meantime it would seem natural for an arrangement to be made direct between the Icelandic and US Governments.'

(iii) To reconsider out attitude in the event of the Russians taking up an openly hostile attitude to the American initiative, or demanding as a counter-part long-term lease of bases in Denmark or Northern Norway. In such circumstances it might well be necessary for His Majesty's Government to come forward as 'mediators', with the proposal which the Secretary of State put to Mr. Byrnes, i.e. the Americans to have a short-term lease of bases in Iceland pending the entry into force of the Charter system of security and the admission of Iceland to the United Nations. We could then presumably encourage the Danes and Norwegians (as the case may be) both of whom are members of the United Nations Organisation to invoke the Security Council procedure in response to any Russian demands and refuse to negotiate bilaterally.[3]

7. As for the separate point on which Lord Halifax asks for guidance in paragraph 2 of the telegram (namely in what form the assurances for which we have asked should be given to us), our view (in which the CoS have concurred) is that it would be better to receive these assurances in writing, but that in the last resort we should agree to accept them orally provided they were duly recorded in the files of the State Department.

---

[3] Bevin accepted this advice, and incorporated it into a memorandum to the Cabinet of 30 October. (DBPO, Series I, Vol. III, No. 90). He noted that the Icelandic Government had now formally asked for an expression of British views before deciding how to respond to the US proposal, and that he had authorised Shepherd to respond in the terms suggested in paragraph 6(*ii*) above.

No. 38

Letter from Mr Shepherd (Helsinki) to Mr Warner, 7 November 1945
(FO 371/47368, N15863/21/56)

Dear Christopher,

For various reasons I think it better to send you a background letter this week rather than attempt a number of despatches.

2. I went off on the weekend of October 27th for an elk-shoot organised by the Minister of Agriculture, Luukka, an almost inarticulate and peasant-like Finn. Four other Ministers were present including Pekkala, Leino and Kekkonen, Minister of Justice. Bosley came with me and Magill was also present as the guest of Kivinen, the Chairman of *Soteva*, the Finnish commission for reparations. These two speak very good Finnish and this was a great help as it was a purely Finnish party, no Fenno-Swedes being present. The only other foreigner was the French Commercial Attaché. The shoot was very well organised but rather strenuous; we got up at six and walked long distances through thick and marshy forest, which was very heavy going, and got back at three o'clock in the afternoon. After having a Finnish bath followed by an extremely short plunge in the lake, the other end of which was already frozen, I went to my room to find it furnished with an unopened bottle of whisky, a very touching attention in view of the shortage of whisky in Finland. I was able to get hold of three of the Ministers and the Public Prosecutor and we polished off a large proportion of the bottle before dining at five. By nine o'clock I was too weary to compete further with the language difficulties and went to bed, leaving Bosley and Magill to carry on until about eleven o'clock, by which time they had sworn brotherhood with all the Ministers and had culled a certain amount of information. We had two further drives the following morning without result and came home in the early evening. It was, on the whole, a very useful and enjoyable experience but elk shooting would be more amusing if one had better expectation of seeing something to shoot at after half an hour of chilly immobility in a marshy forest.

3. You will have seen by telegram that Mannerheim has now gone off to Portugal to convalesce. He is certainly very tired but I am not very sure what else is the matter with him. The official explanation is stomach ulcer but I have also been told that there is something wrong with his throat and I hear that the domestic report in his own household is that he has never actually taken to his bed at all. In any case the Russians seem determined to treat his departure as being caused by genuine illness, although there is little doubt that the imminence of the trials of war responsibles is at least part of the reason for his departure. There seems considerable doubt as to whether or not there will be a Governmental re-shuffle. It is officially denied and nobody seems to know what shape a reshuffle would take if there were one.

4. As you will have seen the Government has now decided to prosecute eight persons as war responsibles and it is a little Gilbertian to note that, as I have reported by telegram, the Communists appear to have taken a more moderate line than the rest of the Cabinet. I do not think that the Public Prosecutor will have a very easy passage, but the Government are determined that something must be done with the accused though the legal grounds for their prosecution seem to me to leave a good field for the defence. The trials should come off within a week or two.

5. The Government seem also rather anxious to conduct a commercial purge at the same time and have asked unofficially for the ideas of the Americans and ourselves as to what persons ought to vacate prominent positions. I have taken the line that we do not wish to intervene in Finnish internal affairs, but Bosley has taken advantage of the friendships made at the elk-shoot to give to one or two Ministers the names of people like von Fieandt[1] and von Frenckell[2] who are known to have been unnecessarily pro-German and anti-British during the war. Hulley[3] is taking the same line. I shall probably send you a telegram on this point.

6. I am very grateful for your prompt help about Reuter's visa[4] and the departure of Grundy. The latter has now arrived and is tackling the various British Council problems with energy and I hope that results will soon accrue.[5]

7. I have had to send an SOS by telegram on the question of staff since the accumulation of work is now beyond the capacity of the Chancery staff to cope with. I very much hope Personnel Department will be able to come to our assistance in the very near future. The lack of staff is in fact one reason why I am condensing things into this personal letter.

8. This is the anniversary of the Soviet Revolution and I am now to suffer the application of what vodka and champagne I am unable to avoid.

Yours ever,
Frank Shepherd

---

[1] Rainer von Feiandt was an official without party affiliation who was later Prime Minister of Finland 1957-58.
[2] Erik von Frenckell was a politician and member of the Swedish party.
[3] Benjamin Hulley was the American chargé d'affaires.
[4] Professor Ole Reuter was the President of the Finnish-British Society, Helsinki.
[5] J.B.C. Grundy was head of the British Council in Finland from 1945 to 1949. His experiences are described in his memoirs, *Life's Five Windows* (London, 1968), pp. 159-76.

No. 39

Lord Halifax (Washington) to Mr Bevin, 8 November 1945, 5.54 p.m.
Tel. No. 7470 Top Secret (FO800/469)[1]

My immediately preceding telegram.[2]
Following is text of memorandum enclosed in Byrnes' letter November 7th.
[Begins]
Mr. Byrnes spoke to Mr. Bevin on one or two occasions while he was in London about the post-war military bases programme of the United States suggesting it will be recalled that the United States Government informed the British and Soviet Governments of its proposed approach to Icelandic Government in regard to post-war bases before official negotiations were opened with Iceland (C). At that time Mr. Bevin sent a letter to Mr. Byrnes expressing the hope that no action would be taken indicating a lack of confidence in the United Nations Organisation just at the time it was getting under way. Mr. Byrnes replied in a note stating that far from regarding its action in Iceland as indicating a lack of

---

[1] This was one of three telegrams concerning US proposals on bases of which copies were sent by Bevin to Churchill (then Leader of the Opposition) in a personal letter of 12 November. Churchill's reply of 13 November is printed in DBPO, Series I, Vol. III, No. 102. See also *ibid.*, No. 135.
[2] Not printed.

1944-1945

confidence in the United Nations Organisation, the United States Government feels that its proposed action will reinforce and strengthen the organisation. The United States proposals to Iceland visualise that bases operated by the United States in Iceland will be made available to the Security Council on its call if Icelandic Government is agreeable to doing so.

Mr. Byrnes has visualised that in the course of the next few months there may well result a number of agreements between the United States and United Kingdom Governments growing out of the present conversations. He attaches a very real importance to a satisfactory agreement between the United States and the United Kingdom in regard to post-war bases. He feels that negotiations looking to such an agreement should be undertaken at once.

The things which the United States Government wishes the United Kingdom Government to do for the United States in connexion with its post-war base programme are as follows:

1. The United States Government desires an assurance that the British Government will support and assist the Government of the United States of America in negotiations between the United States Government and Iceland and Portugal on the other in regard to post-war base requirements in those countries. The United Kingdom has been informed in some detail in connexion with United States desiderata in Iceland. It is expected that the United Kingdom Government will be informed in detail in the next few days in regard to rights which the United States Government desires to obtain in the Azores and Cape Verde Islands.

2. There is enclosed a list of places in territories administered by the United Kingdom, Australia or New Zealand where the United States Government wishes to obtain long term military base rights. Included in this list are two places, one under a mandate administered by the Australian Government and the other under a mandate administered by the New Zealand Government. The United States Government has not yet informed the Australian and New Zealand Governments of its desire to obtain base rights in these places and it requests that the British Government not inform those Governments until the British Government has checked informally with the United States Government and has learned that the latter has informed Australia and New Zealand. Similarly, the French Government has not yet been informed about our desire to obtain based rights in Espirito Santo and it is requested that the British Government not inform the French Government until the United States Government has itself taken up this question with the French Government. It will be observed that three places on this list Canton Island, Funafuti and Christmas Island, are places over which sovereignty is claimed by both the United States and United Kingdom Governments, and which are also dealt with under numbered paragraph 4 of this *aide-mémoire*.[3]

Mr. Byrnes believes that the provision of bases mentioned above will contribute materially to the effectiveness of the United Nations Organisation in maintaining peace. It is anticipated that in drafting the contemplated agreements for furnishing military facilities to the Security Council of the United Nations Organisation, these and other United States bases, along with existing and projected ones of all member nations of the Council, would be considered in determining the availability of bases for carrying out such enforcement

---

[3] See note 3 below.

measures as may be directed by the Security Council.

3. The British Government will recall that over a considerable number of years there has been correspondence between the Governments of the United States and the United Kingdom in regard to territorial claims to the Pacific Islands.[4]

[4] The rest of this document has not been printed. In it, the USA also sought British assistance and co-operation in establishing its claim to sovereignty over more than 25 islands or groups of islands in the Pacific where claims were disputed with the UK, New Zealand, Australia and France, as well as its rights to bases in 10 further sites, mainly in the Pacific but also in the South Atlantic.

No. 40

Letter from Sir L. Collier (Oslo) to Sir O. Sargent, 15 November 1945
(FO 371/47528, N16016/716/30)

Dear Sargent,

I know that you are not as a rule directly concerned with matters such as the forthcoming whaling conference; but I should be grateful if you would look at my despatch No. 142 of today's date[1] reporting a conversation with Lie on that subject, since Lie particularly asked that you and the Secretary of State should be informed of what he had to say.

This was the first time since our arrival here that Lie has come anywhere to 'making a scene' with me, although, as you will remember, he used to make them fairly frequently when we were in London and they were usually a sign that his own position with his Cabinet colleagues was becoming difficult. This time he spoke 'more in sorrow than in anger'; but that did not prevent him from saying a good many things which, if I were to report them literally, would sound distinctly rude. He seemed to realise this at the end of the conversation, for he asked me to put his arguments in my own words, since his command of English was not good enough to enable him to be sure that he had said things in the right way.

What Lie wanted the Secretary of State to realise—and what I think he genuinely believes—is that, in spite of the good work done by Thorne,[2] which he fully acknowledged, there was now a certain *malaise* in Anglo-Norwegian relations, due partly to causes for which we were not to blame, such as the comparatively unsatisfactory nature, from the Norwegian point of view, of the recent Payments Agreement (which he knew was due to our own financial difficulties, but which it was difficult to make the Norwegian business public understand), and the agitation against the destruction of German war material (where again he had been doing his best to explain the true facts to a somewhat sceptical public), but also to affairs such as those of the removal of German fishing vessels from Norwegian ports, which had seriously upset the Norwegian Parliament, because the export of fish to Germany had been an important item in Norwegian pre-war trade, and of the Mutual Aid Agreement, where his request to the Secretary of State had been turned down, apparently because the British Treasury thought it would lose them a few pounds, although Thorne has testified in his report to the generous treatment accorded to him by the Norwegian authorities in supply matters, and lastly this affair of the whalers. He had hoped, after his visit

[1] Not printed.
[2] General Sir Andrew Thorne, Commander-in-Chief, Allied Forces in Norway, 1945.

to the Secretary of State, that Anglo-Norwegian relations would be improved by the settlement of a number of outstanding questions; but how many of the requests which he then made had been dealt with satisfactorily, or dealt with at all? He was hearing on all sides that the British bureaucracy was worse than it had ever been during the war; and, though a Labour man himself, he feared that the advent of a Labour Government had not improved either its efficiency or its manners. Finally, he threatened to pay a further personal visit to London.

All this, of course, need not be taken *au pied de la lettre*; but, as I have indicated above, I think it is a sign that Lie's colleagues are accusing him of letting himself be trodden on by the British, and it is also, clearly, a sign that Norwegian *amour propre* has been hurt and is up in arms. In our present position it is so much easier to satisfy *amour propre* than to satisfy the material requests of foreign Governments that I am frankly at a loss to understand why the Ministry of Agriculture and Fisheries, who are primarily concerned with these whaling questions, should have departed from their previous policy of consulting the Norwegians in advance before taking any steps about whaling conference, etc. My Dutch colleague, to whom, as reported in my despatch, Lie has also spoken on the whaling question, and, I gather, with equal vehemence, tells me that he himself recommended to his Government a preliminary approach to the Norwegians and was told that it was unnecessary because the British would be sure to have made one themselves.

I do not suggest that there is much we can do now in this matter, except to try to prevent the Americans and the Russians from collaring German whaling ships and to let the Norwegians have one of these ships if we possibly can, and perhaps also to urge the authorities in the British zone of Germany to bring to an early and favourable conclusion the negotiations for the purchase of fish which they are now conducting with Norwegian interests; but I do feel that we shall need to be more careful over such matters in future. As Lie said to me today, 'Norway ought really to be one of the easiest countries in the world for you to attach to your side; but you must pay some regard to our vital economic interests such as shipping, whaling and fishing, and, above all, you must consider our feelings. We do not like to lose our money because we simply can't afford to lose it, and we like even less to be treated without consideration, because we are touchy people. You may think this touchiness absurd if you like, but you must reckon with it because it is there and I can't alter it.'[3]

Yours ever,
L. COLLIER

---

[3] Collier visited London shortly afterwards and discussed this problem with Warner, head of Northern Department. A minute by Warr of 8 December showed that Collier was anxious to be able to provide some satisfaction to the Norwegian Government over this issue. He explained that the Norwegians did not understand why Britain and America should be in a position to secure German whalers while Norway, which had a much greater interest in whaling, should be given none (FO 371/47528, N16026/716/30).

No. 41

Mr Shepherd (Helsinki) to Mr Bevin, 24 November 1945
No. 197 Top Secret (FO 371/47450, N17623/10928/63G)

Sir,
I have the honour to transmit herewith a copy of a paper on the subject of British policy in Scandinavia prepared by Colonel J.H. Magill the Military member of the British element of the Allied Control Commission.[1] This paper has already been submitted to the War Office by the Head of the British Element, with copies for the Admiralty, Air Ministry and Foreign Office.

2. As will be seen from paragraph 1 of the paper, it constitutes a plea for the adoption of a co-ordinated policy towards Scandinavia as a whole, comprising Norway, Sweden, Denmark and Finland. I have read the report through carefully and find myself in agreement with it, and especially with certain paragraphs to which attention is drawn below.

3. The first paragraph of the paper, however, gives rise to the question of whether Finland can in fact be regarded as forming part of Scandinavia. This question seems to me to be capable of a dual answer. From the strategic point of view Finland forms part of the Russian defensive system and no amount of solidarity with the Scandinavian States would enable her to be used as a western defensive outpost. Under the terms of the Armistice Agreement, which are likely to be perpetuated in the Peace Treaty, Finnish armaments are confined to the peace time scale before 1939. In case of international tension, it is certain that Soviet Russia would not permit Finland to be a place of assembly for potentially hostile forces, as was the case in 1941. It is in some ways remarkable that Russia contented herself in 1940 with a frontier adjustment designed to strengthen the defences of Leningrad together with a base at Hangö which in the event turned out to be useless. Russia was no doubt precluded from re-acting against the arrival of German troops in Finland in 1941 (of which she must certainly have been aware) by her anxiety to avoid precipitating a conflict with Germany, or giving Germany a *casus belli* which might have alienated Western sympathies with Russia. It is in the last degree unlikely that Finland will for a third time be allowed to constitute a potential threat to the Russian western flank. Even if the Finnish army decided to resist by force any Russian attempt at a defensive occupation of Finland, they would very soon be overwhelmed. Their armaments would no longer be adequate, and the Russian base at Porkkala would be too imminent a threat to the capital which might well be bombarded from there with naval guns. Any such resistance will in any case probably be provided against fairly soon after the signature of a peace treaty by a military alliance which would automatically place Finnish forces on the side of Russia in case of another war. Certainly the present Finnish Government has repeatedly given assurances that it will not adopt a foreign policy hostile to that of Russia. The Scandinavian military vacuum referred to by Colonel Magill in paragraph 5 of his paper will therefore undoubtedly be filled as regards Finland by Russia, and Finland including the Åland Islands should accordingly be excluded from Scandinavia so far as military considerations are concerned.

---

[1] Not printed. The despatch was dated 30 October 1945. In submitting it to Captain Howie, Magill noted that he had been prompted to write it as a result of his contact with Russian officers over the previous twelve months, as well as by his visits to other Scandinavian countries during the same period (FO 371/47450, N17623/10928/63G).

4. While Russian military domination of Finland is inevitable, there are I think good grounds for resisting so far as possible too strong a domination in other respects. So long as the spirit of independence is preserved and fostered in Finland there will be a sense of solidarity with the rest of Scandinavia, and so long as this sense of solidarity remains, Finland will be a doubtful ally of Russia and a belt of resistance against Russian attempts at penetration in the other Scandinavian countries. It would be to our advantage therefore, even from the strategic point of view, to encourage not only Finnish independence but also the western form of democracy in Finland, Finnish cultural relations with Scandinavia and Western Europe, and Finnish affinity with Scandinavia in general. For these reasons, I believe that Finland should be treated as part of Scandinavia on all planes other than the military plane.

5. In paragraph 16 of his paper, Colonel Magill speaks of the undermining of the will to self-defence by a feeling of isolation and states that the spirit of independence could be kept alive by a conviction among Finns that the subjection or absorption of their country would meet with opposition from other powers. This is undoubtedly true. There has been during the past year some danger that Finland would sink into a state of apathy through the feeling of helplessness which the imminent might of Russia inspires. Native resilience has to a large extent overcome this apathy. But not entirely, and any sudden hardening of Fenno-Russian relations might well cause a relapse. The revival of international criticism of Soviet Russia has accordingly been instinctively welcomed in Finland, not merely with the normal *schadenfreude* that might be expected, but as affording Finland some hope that a stand for independence might receive at least some sympathetic or moral support from the west. Unfortunately there is far too strong a tendency to exaggerate Russo-occidental antiphony into a prospect of future war, and this has developed almost into wishful thinking. While a reaction from servility to Russia is healthy and desirable, such exaggerations, if pushed too far, would be likely to lead to political complications, and possibly worse. Fortunately, Finnish expression of opinion or aspiration in this regard has so far been kept within bounds and both the Government and the press have persistently discouraged speculation about a rift between Russia and Western powers.

6. In paragraph 21 Colonel Magill refers to the importance of filling up the gap in Scandinavian psychology left by the temporary annihilation of Germany, and points out the importance of demonstrating that we have the power as well as the will to support Scandinavian independence. This is in my opinion a most important point. It would be a great mistake on our part to allow our sense of the power of the United States and Russia to prevent us from emphasising the greatness of our people or the power of our Empire, both absolutely and comparatively.

7. Colonel Magill has added two appendices to his report, and I venture to offer the following observations on them.

8. In paragraph 4 of Appendix A he refers to the present dominating position of Russia on the Baltic. It will be recalled that Russia has already staked a claim to exclusive responsibility for the defence of the Eastern Baltic coastline, including the coast of Finland. (see paragraph 2 of Moscow tel. No. 3869 to the Foreign Office).[2]

9. In paragraph 7 Colonel Magill mentions among other things the affinity of Communist Russia with Peter the Great. There is perhaps no point in labouring this

---

[2] Not printed.

affinity which the Russians themselves have not hesitated to underline. But the new 'window on Europe' is on a different scale of architecture from that of its predecessor, and free access for Russia to the Atlantic may now be regarded by the Russians as of equal importance with free access to the Baltic in the former age. If so, Russian interest in the Sound, to say nothing of the Dardanelles, the Suez Canal and the Straits of Gibraltar will inevitably clash with the paramount interest of Great Britain on her Empire routes and with our interest in free access to the Baltic from without.

10. In paragraph 8 Colonel Magill draws attention to the hostile or at least carping attitude of Finnish Communism towards the west. This attitude is of practical interest to the United Kingdom, since any preponderance of Communist influence in the Finnish Government may be expected to result in obstacles in trade with the west. A sign of this was discernible in the sensitiveness of the Finnish Cabinet in the spring of this year to the ratification of timber contracts with Great Britain without making certain that there were no Russian objections. Fortunately, the Communist Party in Finland would appear at the moment to be if anything losing rather than gaining ground, though I would hesitate to prophesy as to its future potentialities.

11. As regards Appendix B, I would only remark that in the propagation of the idea that England is finished and the British Empire doomed we have a form of propaganda which it is incumbent upon us to counter, not only by the example of the next few years but by our own propaganda in the immediate future. This is important both from the point of view of providing correct information, and from the point of view of fostering confidence in the power of Western Europe, without which Scandinavia will become increasingly sensitive to Russian influence.[3]

I have, etc.,
F.M. SHEPHERD

---

[3] Commenting on Shepherd's letter and Magill's paper in a minute of 3 February, Warr agreed with Shepherd's observation that whereas Finland should from a military point of view be considered as being within the Russian orbit she was in all other ways a part of Scandinavia, and that 'as a part of Scandinavia she has strong political, commercial and cultural affinities with Britain, which we should try by all means to foster. But we shall have difficulties in doing so while the communists remain in their present strong position. As Mr Shepherd points out, the influence of the communists seems to be slightly on the decline, and if this tendency persists we shall be presented with increasingly great opportunities of extending our connexions with Finland. But this is all based on the assumption that the present lenient attitude of the Russians towards Finland will continue, and on this there is no certainty whatever' (FO 371/47450, N17623/10928/56G). Warner replied to this letter on 26 February: see No. 53.

No. 42

Sir W. Strang (Political Adviser to Commander in Chief Germany, Berlin) to Mr Bevin, 26 November 1945, 4.25 p.m.[1]
Tel. No. 24 Saving (FO 371/47275, N16272/1866/15)

Your telegram No. 229 Saving to Lubbecke.[2]
As proposed during his recent visit to the Foreign Office,[3] Mr. Steel went to 8 Corps Headquarters on November 15th and accompanied General Barker when the latter received representatives of the Danish minority at Kiel. In effect those selected turned out to be all Danish citizens, which somewhat reinforces the suggestion of the large part which the Danish Government is taking in minority affairs. The names were: Herr Thygesen, a secretary of the Danish Foreign Office and now serving with the minority movement in Flensburg; Herr Hansen, superintendent of the Danish minority schools; and Lieutenant Colonel Tousieng, Liaison Officer with Headquarters British Troops at Flensburg.

2. General Barker opened the proceedings by saying that he had arranged the meeting in order that Mr. Steel might make clear certain points in regard to the position of the minority which appeared to be in doubt, and asked the Danes to put forward questions. They replied that they had none to ask. The general then produced one of the recent pamphlets full of demands and said that he would accordingly have to bring up the questions himself. This broke the ice and a general discussion ensued. The following are the chief points.

3. Mr. Steel made it clear at the outset that the minority were from the political point of view German citizens. Political activity in Germany at the present moment was under strict control by the Allied Government and it was not our intention in the present difficult circumstances to permit agitation of any kind. Political activities by the Danish minority must therefore be limited to those permitted to ordinary German citizens. On the cultural side on the other hand we were willing to grant them the privileges which they had enjoyed under the former German governments but these privileges were a matter of grace and must not be abused.

4. The discussion then turned to the matter of Danish schools. It was made clear to the Danes that these must not be used as an instrument of proselytisation. The Danes are now educating some 2,000 children as against an immediate pre-war 500 and a maximum pre-war of 1,000. It has proved impossible to limit these

---

[1] Copied to Copenhagen.
[2] Not printed.
[3] There remained differences of view between the Foreign Office, the Embassy in Copenhagen and the British military authorities in Germany. Steel wrote to Randall on 26 October, explaining the attitude of the Military Government towards the Danish-minded minority in South Schleswig: 'The Military Government have a monumental job to do without the constant intervention of a noisy minority whose sacrifices for the Allied cause are conspicuous by their absence. The 7,000 Danes in South Schleswig are, I daresay, less comfortable than they have been in the past, but their discomfort is probably not so acute even now as that of many other Allies further south in their own countries. At any rate, the latest pretensions of Herr Thygesen to move to and fro across the frontier fostering this movement are really a little absurd, and I agreed with the Northern Department when I was last in London that once the elections are over I should go up and talk to him and his associates rather straight. The talking will be on the lines of the Foreign Office paper of September 8th . . . It is not intended to do this until after the Danish elections, so as to avoid whatever is said being dragged into them, but clearly something must be done, and I am afraid that, having made so much capital out of the fuss, the Danish Government will not pass on to their dupes the salutary remarks which you have been making to them' (FO 371/47275, N14921/1866/15).

schools to Danish speaking children in view of Danish contention that Nazi repression was responsible for their not knowing the language. It was eventually agreed that a working party of the Military Government should take the evidence of the Danes and fix the categories of parents whose children might attend the schools. Schools for those children would then be provided within existing possibilities of accommodation.

5. The next matter raised was participation of the Danish party in the forthcoming municipal (*Kreis*) elections at Flensburg and elsewhere. The Danes contended that this party had always taken part in the elections and participated in municipal administration as they are now doing (this is true). While we do not want to let this become the thin end of the wedge, I do not think we can resist this request. Mr. Steel said the matter must be referred to you. I think we should agree, while seeing that the party's activities are restricted to local matters. Please let me know your views as soon as possible so that I may advise out Chief of Staff.

6. The next point was Danish complaints of the number of East Prussian officials appointed in Schleswig. Mr. Steel said that the number of Prussian officials in Schleswig was about 30 out of more than 800. Many of the 30 were not refugees. We had had to get rid of a great many Nazis and fill their places with the best available men. It was our policy to employ local talent where possible, but failing local talent we would take the best men for the job. Moreover the influx from the East was not a temporary phenomenon but a consequence of the sins of the German community. Many more Germans would be coming to the West, and Schleswig would have to take a large permanent share of refugees.

7. The Danes then asked for improved facilities for correspondence and official minority visits to Denmark. It was agreed that this would be taken up sympathetically.

8. Finally the Danes raised the question of a German language newspaper for Danes. Mr. Steel made it quite clear that the Danes were lucky to have a Danish newspaper and that a German one would not be permitted. Even the German parties had not yet got newspapers. Furthermore, a German language newspaper for Danes could not be considered as otherwise than an instrument of political propaganda, which would be most unwise for them to start as we would not tolerate it.

9. At the conclusion of the meeting General Barker told Mr. Hansen that he would not allow him to distribute pamphlets on the Danish minority to British troops as this was exactly the kind of one-sided propaganda to which we objected.

10. While the British points were firmly made and the Danes were in a rather submissive mood, the interview was quite friendly and General Barker considered that it had done a good deal to clear the air.

No. 43

Minute from Mr Warr to Mr Warner, 19 December 1945[1]
(FO 371/47227, N17162/9/15)

This interview shows that the present Danish Government, formed on the 8th November, takes a different attitude from that of the previous Government over

---

[1] This document has also been printed in DBPO Series I, Vol. V, No. 101.

Bornholm.[2] Mr. Christmas Møller, when he was Foreign Minister, continually pressed that we should accelerate the withdrawal of our troops from Denmark in order that he might have a lever with the Soviet Government to get the Russians out of Bornholm. We did our best to meet the Danes about withdrawing our troops but have no evidence that the Danish Government ever protested to the Russians about the continued presence of Russian troops in Bornholm, though at one point Mr. Christmas Møller said that he would speak to the Soviet Minister. We do not know whether he ever did so but as he raised the question of the retention of our Air Disarmament Wing in Denmark it is clear that he was worried.

The present Minister for Foreign Affairs, however, has given no sign that he minds the Russians remaining in Bornholm and since he took office he has never once raised the question of the presence of our troops in Denmark. Moreover, he was quite content when told that the Air Disarmament Wing might have to stay on until next March instead of leaving in November as the Danes had previously been informed.

We did our best to satisfy the wishes of the previous Danish Government about the withdrawal of our troops and now, apart from the Air Disarmament Wing, there only remains in Denmark a British Military Mission which is there at the desire of the Danes to assist in the training of their Army. The only remaining British troops in Denmark are therefore either performing an essential technical task or helping the Danes. They are there for essentially different reasons from the Russians on Bornholm. This being so, the Foreign Minister is quite unjustified in saying that the 'Danish Government regarded the presence of Russians in Bornholm in exactly the same light as that of the British and Americans in other parts of Denmark'.

As regards the Americans, M. Rasmussen must be referring only to Greenland as there are no American troops in Denmark proper. A copy of the 1941 Cordell Hull-Kaufmann Agreement is attached.[3] Article 10 shows that the bases in Greenland afforded to the American Government are to be given up when 'it is agreed that the present dangers to the peace and security of the American continent have passed' and after consultation between the two Governments. We have not heard that there has been any such consultation. It is peculiar that M. Rasmussen should mention this agreement implying that the Americans were in Greenland for the same reason as the Russians in Bornholm.

I think we should ask Mr. Randall for his comments on this peculiar statement of M. Rasmussen's with particular reference to the point about British troops and about Greenland. We might ask Mr. Randall to repeat his reply to Moscow so that the Delegation there may be aware of the latest position, in case the question of the withdrawal of Russian troops from Bornholm is raised at the Conference.[4] We might give our comments to the Delegation now but the bags are very uncertain

---

[2] In his telegram No. 148 Saving, of 14 December, Randall summarised an interview in which the newly appointed Danish Foreign Minister, Gustav Rasmussen, had stated that the Danish Government regarded the presence of the Russians in Bornholm in the same light as they did that of British and American forces in other parts of Denmark.

[3] Not printed.

[4] Warner minuted on 19 December that just before he left for Moscow, Cadogan had asked whether the delegation should raise the question of Bornholm. Warner had replied that it might well be mentioned if the general question of the withdrawal of Allied troops was discussed in connection with the Soviet suggestion that the withdrawal of British troops from Greece should be put on the agenda (FO 371/47227, N17162/9/15).

and we shall have therefore to telegraph. I hardly think it is worth doing this before we have Mr. Randall's views.

Draft telegram submitted.[5]

[5] Before this telegram was sent, the issue was discussed with the Danish Minister, who had fortuitously visited the Foreign Office. See No. 44.

No. 44

Mr Bevin to Mr Randall (Copenhagen), 23 December 1945, 10.56 p.m.[1]
Tel. No. 640 Important (FO 371/47227, N17432/9/15)

Your telegram No. 925 (of 22nd December: Bornholm).[2]

Before this telegram was received, opportunity of visit by Danish Minister[3] was taken to tell him informally that we felt that we did not altogether understand the outlook behind statements of Minister for Foreign Affairs reported in your telegram No. 148 Saving and to enquire if he could explain it.

2. It was pointed out to Minister that we had understood the aim of Mr. Christmas Møller in consulting His Majesty's Government about the early withdrawal of our troops had been to use our withdrawal as a lever to secure simultaneous or at least early withdrawal of Russian troops in Bornholm. In order to help Danish Government, we had arranged to leave at the earliest possible moment leaving only missions charged with specific tasks, who could be represented by Danish Government as on a completely different basis from Russian troops in Bornholm. When the matter had been discussed with the present Danish Minister for Foreign Affairs he had, according to our understanding, actually preferred that our bomb disposal party should remain until their task was finished although we had been prepared to leave task to Danes under minimum RAF supervision and assistance.

3. In interview recorded in your telegram No. 148 Saving, however, Danish Minister for Foreign Affairs appeared almost to have gone out of his way to assimilate our remaining Service missions in Denmark with Russian troops in Bornholm. Moreover, he had brought in the question of the Americans in Greenland.

4. It was clearly desirable that we should understand aim and outlook of present Danish Government in the matter, if only in order, if possible, to take account of it supposing some form of public statement at any time had to be made here on the matter. Moreover, His Majesty's Government from their own point of view, would certainly not subscribe to the theory that military training mission provided at request of Danes, and bomb disposal mission which was remaining on under the circumstances described above, were in any way in analogous position to Russian troops in Bornholm.[4]

[1] Repeated Saving to Stockholm, Oslo, Reykjavik, Washington and Moscow.
[2] Not printed.
[3] Count Eduard Reventlow.
[4] At this time, as Warner wrote separately to Rumbold in Moscow, there were 63 all ranks in the British military mission, 30 in the RAF bomb disposal unit and some 30 naval personnel, against an estimated 5-6,000 Soviet troops in Bornholm.

5. Danish Minister was unable to explain his Government's standpoint in the matter and said he would enquire. He was told we had no desire to make much of the matter nor were we complaining, but only seeking elucidation.

6. In point of fact, we find it extremely hard to understand how it could be anything but disadvantageous to Danes to draw parallel between our military training mission, whose stay will presumably be prolonged, and Russian troops in Bornholm.

7. Comments on your telegram under reference will be sent later.

CHAPTER II

1946-1947

No. 45

Letter from Mr Steel (Control Commission for Germany, Berlin) to Mr Warner, 10 January 1946
(FO 371/55748, C695/688/18)

Dear Christopher,

I have just got back from leave and have seen FO despatch to Copenhagen No. 334 (N16272/1866/15) of December 7th.[1]

I feel I must bring to your attention the extreme danger, as it appears here, of suggesting that German refugees in Germany will not have a vote. *All* Germans are to blame for the war and the E. Prussians who have suffered infinitely more than the Schleswigers (who have not suffered) were in fact far less Nazi than the latter who had the highest percentage of party members to population in Germany.[2] You must take it and help us to get into Alec Randall's head that, thanks to the Potsdam Agreement about the Eastern frontiers, these Germans are here to stay and will have to have votes. Otherwise our talk about democracy is greater ----s [*sic*] than we can afford to advertise so obviously. I really was very disturbed by your despatch. It may encourage these Danes no end I fear.[3]

Yours ever,
C.E. STEEL

---

[1] Not printed.
[2] In telegram No. 46 Saving of 24 December 1945, Steel wrote that according to recently investigated statistics the density of Nazi party members in Schleswig-Holstein (4.58 per cent) was the highest per head of population of any province in Germany.
[3] In an earlier exchange with the Foreign Office, Steel had sent telegram No. 60 of 20 July 1945, in which he recommended refusal of a Danish Government proposal to send a Danish subject to Flensburg to take over the job of general secretary of the Danish minority movement in South Schleswig. This and telegram No. 48 of 18 July, recommending refusal of Møller's request to visit Flensburg, were shown to Eden, who minuted to Cadogan: 'Doesn't Steel seem rather anti-Dane in these telegrams?'

No. 46

Mr Randall (Copenhagen) to Mr Bevin, 11 January 1946
No. 11 (FO 371/56126, N669/394/15)

Sir,

From the time of taking up my post here I have drawn attention to the influence of the 'small nation complex' in Danish relations with Great Britain, and have suggested that we should as far as possible see that any suggestion of patronage in those relations should be avoided, that, too, no impression should be allowed to form that Denmark was in 'Britain's pocket', and, finally, that any offer on Denmark's part to assist us should be welcomed wherever practicable. On the whole there have been few departures from this policy and remarkably little Danish complaint about our attitude. Lately, however, a certain spirit of criticism has been observed, and in general I think we must expect the present Danish Government to be rather more difficult to handle than its predecessor. There have been public suggestions that we are indifferent to long-term Danish interests in South Slesvig, that we have allowed the Danish accumulation of sterling to grow to excessive proportions, that the food-prices to which the previous Danish Government agreed are kept down while the prices of British exports to Denmark are increased out of all proportion. Two private criticisms to add to this collection are, first that we are pressing the Danes with exceptional severity over the liquidation of German commercial and financial interests here, and that we have excluded Denmark from the alternating presidency of the section of the Minesweeping Commission which is to have its seat in Copenhagen.

2. These criticisms have been dealt with separately and it has been shown that the Danish complaints are usually unjustified or exaggerated. This despatch is merely intended to invite attention to the general psychological and political aspect, and point out that there is in Denmark an immense fund of admiration for and community of thought and interest with Great Britain, but that it must not be drawn upon too complacently, and that due account must be taken of Denmark's desire not to prejudice her position with Russia or a re-awakened Germany. This kind of theme is developed at greater length in an article in the Resistance paper *Information* for January 3rd. This paper has of late been unreasonably critical of our policy in Slesvig-Holstein, and in other ways rather tiresome, but I think the article may be taken as a fair reflection of instructed Danish opinion on Anglo-Danish relations, and I therefore have the honour to transmit a full translation with this despatch.[1]

I have, etc.,
A.W.G. RANDALL

[1] Not printed. Commenting on this article on 18 January Rothnie, Northern Department, made a comparison with an interview given by Foreign Minister Rasmussen to *Berlingske Tidende* on 6 January which was more moderate and conciliatory than the article in *Information*, and which he considered to be at least as representative of Danish views.

No. 47

Mr Bevin to Sir L. Collier (Oslo), 30 January 1946, 11.55 p.m.
Tel. No. 65 Important (FO 371/56293, N882/539/30)

My despatch No. 22 of 18th January: interview with M. Lie.[1]

Norwegian Minister for Foreign Affairs informed us on 24th January that he much regretted he had been unable to persuade his Government to send Minister of Defence to this country to complete arrangements for supply of equipment by His Majesty's Government for Norwegian armed forces. He said Norwegian Government and people had developed pacifist outlook and were disinclined to interest themselves in national defence or to spend money thereon. He had not even been able to obtain financial authority for purchase of British military aircraft arranged last autumn. M. Lie said that he intended to press his Government really hard on equipment question on his return to Norway and hoped to arrange visit here by Minister of Defence. But he regretted to say that public opinion in Norway had become very pacifist and had quite 'forgotten 1940'.

2. General Berg[2] has told War Office confidentially that he is meeting political difficulties over fulfilment of undertaking to supply division for British zone in Germany.

3. I am somewhat disturbed by these signs that Norwegian Government may have changed their minds about establishing close links between our two countries on Service matters. It occurs to me that this may be due to fear of, or even pressure from Soviet Union. I shall be glad of your views on this point.

4. We understand from Norwegian Embassy some time ago that Defence Estimates were likely to come before *Storting* soon after they met. It would of course be most regrettable if they did not contain adequate provision for purchase of equipment from us. I shall seek opportunity of discovering from M. Lie whether he was able to influence his Government favourably in this matter while in Norway and how matters stand regarding Norwegian division for Germany. Please telegraph any information you may have on both matters and take any action at your end which may seem appropriate.

[1] Not printed.
[2] Lt.-Gen. Ole Berg, Chief of the Norwegian Defence Staff.

No. 48

Mr Bevin to Mr Reid Brown (Stockholm), 31 January 1946
No. 30 Top Secret (FO 371/56941, N78/78/42G)

Sir,

I transmit to you herewith a copy of a paper prepared by the Joint Intelligence Sub-Committee of the Chiefs of Staff Committee regarding the policy of His Majesty's Government concerning the disclosure of Service information to the Swedish Services.[1]

2. The policy laid down in this paper has been considered by the Deputy Chiefs of Staff Committee and has been in general approved by them. But they have

[1] Not printed.

decided that Sweden should remain in Category C and not be raised to Category B; which means that no classified information will be given to Sweden but that Norway and Denmark, who are in Category B, will receive information up to and including 'confidential'. It has, however, been agreed that the Air Ministry and the Ministry of Aircraft Production in consultation with the Foreign Office may at their discretion disclose information in respect of aircraft and equipment for sale to Sweden up to and including information classified as confidential.

3. Your Service Attachés will shortly receive instructions from their respective Departments concerning this policy. You will observe from paragraph 13(*b*) of the enclosed paper,[1] that you are to coordinate its execution bearing in mind the importance (*a*) of ensuring that the Soviet authorities do not gain the impression that the British service authorities are making anti-Russian plans with the Swedes and (*b*) of using the available information to secure the abandonment of what is understood to be the present habit of the Swedish Service authorities of refusing to impart any information of value to your Service Attachés. Furthermore, it is desirable that you and your Attachés should make the best use you can of Swedish requests for information and equipment to weaken the position, and if possible secure the removal, of the anti-British officers in positions of importance in the Swedish Armed Forces. To this end there will be no objection, if you should think fit to do so, to an intimation being made to the appropriate Swedish authorities to the effect that more confidential information cannot be made available since certain senior Swedish Service officers hardly appear worthy of our confidence.

4. I should be glad to learn, after you have discussed this matter with your Service Attachés, how you are proposing to handle it.

I am, etc.,
ERNEST BEVIN

No. 49

Sir L. Collier (Oslo) to Mr Bevin, 2 February 1946
No. 23 Confidential (FO 371/56302, N2083/345/30)

Sir,
As foreshadowed in my telegram No. 58 of January 31st last[1], it has now been announced that Mr Lie's successor as Norwegian Minister for Foreign Affairs is M. Halvard Lange.[2]

2. M. Lange, the son of the late Christian Lange, a well-known pacifist who was Norwegian delegate to the League of Nations Assembly and Nobel Prize winner in 1921, is forty-three years of age. He studied at Geneva and in Norway, and in 1923 became Assistant Secretary of the Fellowship of Reconciliation, a pacifist organisation in London. Thereafter he travelled widely in Europe, where he studied social and political questions, including the Polish minority problem. In 1926 he took a course in economic history at Geneva and in the following year studied at the London School of Economics under Professor Laski. On his return to Norway

---

[1] Not printed.
[2] Collier's despatch crossed with a letter from Warner, also of 2 February (No. 50), which asked about the Norwegian attitude to Britain and to Russia, and how this might be affected by Lie's departure as Foreign Minister.

he joined the Labour Party, in which he soon made a name for himself. He took up teaching as a profession and in 1939 he was appointed headmaster of the new Sørmarka High School.

3. On the German invasion of Norway, M. Lange escaped to Stockholm, where he was instructed to organise the movement of volunteers to North Norway. When the Allied forces withdrew from Norway he returned to Oslo and was there arrested and imprisoned for a year. In 1941 he was released on parole; but he was re-arrested the next year on the suspicion, which was not unfounded, of being in close touch with the Home Front leadership. After six months in solitary confinement he was transferred to Sachsenhausen, where he made the acquaintance of his future colleagues, MM. Gerhardsen, Oftedal and Langhelle.

4. M. Lange has a reputation not only in Norway but also abroad as a writer on political and sociological subjects. His works include the histories of the Norwegian Trade Union organisation and the Labour Party, and he contributed the Scandinavian section of the British publication 'Organised Labour in Four Continents'. He has also made a considerable name for himself as a journalist (he was recently regarded as the most likely successor to M. Tranmæl as editor of *Arbeiderbladet*), his articles inspiring respect for his objectivity and knowledge of his subjects. His pacifist background might have occasioned some misgivings if the position of Norwegian Minister for Foreign Affairs permitted the play of natural predilections; but in present circumstances that is out of the question. The Prime Minister, indeed, recently told the Counsellor of H.M. Embassy that the personality of the Minister for Foreign Affairs was of little consequence, since the lines on which Norwegian foreign policy must proceed were already established;[3] and this has been emphasised by *Arbeiderbladet*, the Government organ in a leading article published on February 1st under the heading 'Clear Lines', from which I enclose a translation of certain extracts,[1] declaring that there can and will be no change, either in foreign policy or in defence measures.

5. The Norwegian press uniformly approves M. Lange's appointment, doubtless reflecting the attitude of the public as a whole in view of the new Minister's reputation and popularity. The public, however, is not now so deeply interested in foreign affairs, as might have been indicated by a reading of the press, which devotes much space to reports from London and constantly declares that Norway must play a worthy part in the work of the United Nations organisation; and, as will be seen from the enclosed extract from the Counsellor's report of his conversation with the Prime Minister at which the latter made the remark quoted above,[1] M. Gerhardsen, for his part, is not sorry that this should be so. M. Gerhardsen, as M. Lie remarked to me last year (please see my despatch No. 33 of July 24th, 1945)[1] is himself rather an extreme example of Norwegian *insouciance* in these matters: but there is no doubt that even those Norwegian circles which are genuinely concerned about them tend to feel subconsciously that it is of no use for the inhabitants of a country like Norway to trouble their heads over developments in world politics, still less to attempt to influence them. In the great quarrel between the Soviet Union and the West, which Norwegians see sharpening almost every day, their sympathies (except for those of the small Communist minority) are with the West; but they fear the Russians and have no great confidence in the power of Great Britain or the readiness of the United States to protect them against

---

[3] Kenney had expressed concerns about the risk of Norway becoming isolated, and had concluded from Gerhardsen's response that he had not yet had the time and experience to develop an international outlook.

the consequences of Russian displeasure. Hence a natural tendency to say with Candide that '*il faut cultiver notre jardin*'. Only the most far-seeing realise that, if the crash comes, they are not likely to be allowed to cultivate their garden in peace and should therefore lose no time in making military and diplomatic preparation for that eventuality.

6. Since writing the above, I have heard the King of Norway, at an audience granted me this morning in another connexion, state of Norwegian opinion: people wanted, said His Majesty, 'to bury their heads in the snow' and he feared that the government, now that M. Lie had left it, would be difficult to keep on the right lines. He and M. Lie had understood each other; now, however, he would be dealing with new men of no experience and would have to start afresh with the education of his Ministers. His Majesty referred in this connexion to the question of equipment for the Army, discussed in my telegram No. 60 of today's date,[1] which, he said, was one of the reasons why M. Lie had paid his recent flying visit to Oslo: the Prime Minister's attitude in this matter was to leave it to the *Storting*, and it was true that no definite financial commitment could be made without the *Storting*'s approval, but, as he had pointed out to M. Gerhardsen, the Government could, and should, decide now what recommendation to make to the *Storting* and how strongly to make it. As for M. Lange, His Majesty, to the best of his knowledge, had never met him; but he had known his father, 'a terrible pacifist', and he could only hope that the son's experience in Sachsenhausen had taught him that it took more that one party's goodwill to keep the peace.[4]

7. I am sending copies of this despatch to H. M. Ministers at Copenhagen and Stockholm.

I have, etc.,
L. COLLIER

[4] Initial Foreign Office views of Lange were not positive. Warr wrote: 'I don't think we can expect much from M. Lange in educating the Norwegians to take a greater interest in the outside world.' Warner added: 'It will be no good our trying to rush Norway or to expect from her *spectacular* manifestations of alignment with this country. We must try to build up practical links with the Norwegians in the field of military equipment and inconspicuously keep our end up in the field of publicity.' Sargent added: 'We may still live to regret M. Lie' (FO 371/56302, N2083/345/30). However, it did not take long before some of the reservations about Lange began to be dispersed. On 25 February, Collier reported a conversation between Rowland Kenney and Lange, where Kenney detected no signs of pacifism (as he had been led to expect by Torp) and concluded: 'I was most favourably impressed by M. Lange . . . I believe that he is a man of much wider vision than most of his colleagues and that, if he can 'catch up' on world affairs, he will do very well indeed' (FO 371/56302, N3266/1345/30). See also No. 195.

No. 50

Letter from Mr Warner to Sir L. Collier (Oslo), 2 February 1946
Confidential (FO 371/56302, N1602/345/30)

Dear Collier,

We have been wondering about the present Norwegian attitude to ourselves and to Russia and how this may be affected by M. Lie's departure from the Ministry for Foreign Affairs, and I have been instructed to write this letter asking for your views. On the surface, at any rate, Lie has appeared to be rather in the Russian pocket during the proceedings in the Assembly. Apart from the fact that he was the

Russian candidate for the Presidency of the Assembly and their second string for the Secretary-Generalship (their first string was Simic, the Yugoslav), Lie's general speech on behalf of Norway in the opening debate of the General Assembly appeared very much the speech of one of the Slav *bloc*. He made all the stock points: he was against all political questions being raised at this session, he was pro Great Power hegemony, anti-*blocs* (except Nordic co-operation) and dragged in the Fascist bogey at the end of his speech. I have it on Berg's authority confidentially that this last point was omitted in the draft prepared by the Delegation jointly and was put in at Lie's personal insistence.

Simultaneously, we find the signs, mentioned in our telegram No. 65,[1] that the Norwegians are receding from the arrangements made with us for co-operation in military matters.

Our Delegation to the Assembly have got the impression that the Russians were using on Lie a mixed policy of pressure and prizes. I got the impression in my two very confidential talks with Berg that Lie was being pretty secretive within his own delegation.

We have naturally therefore been trying to analyse the situation. It is not easy to reach any conclusion. It has been pointed out to me that the Norwegians were pro Great Power hegemony at San Francisco; and one might reasonably argue that the motive for their anti-*bloc* remarks was not only that Norway cannot afford to come out in an anti-Russian sense on any matter on which the Russians have expressed their views so forcibly, but also that Lie has reached a similar conclusion to the one reached here, namely that in working for Western European co-operation, you will get further if you concentrate on quietly establishing practical links in specific directions (e.g. military and economic) and avoid more spectacular arrangements and publicity.

As regards the Presidency and Secretary-Generalship, it is clear from what I have heard and you have reported that Lie was looking around for some job which would take him to a larger scene than that of Oslo. I had heard from several different sources and in a definite form the story that he was thinking of succeeding Colban as Ambassador here for this reason. He was of course, too, a very natural person for the Russians to think of as a rival candidate to Spaak. Once he knew that they were thinking of running him for the Secretary-Generalship, he would not have been human in the circumstances (including one of the highest salaries in the world) if he had not adjusted his behaviour accordingly.

We should very much like to know from you therefore first whether you regard the present Norwegian Government, out of fear of Russia or for whatever other reason, as having become either subservient to Russia or determined to maintain a rigidly middle position between Russia and western Europe and therefore to abandon any special policy of western European co-operation; secondly how you read Lie's own attitude and what you think it is likely to be *vis-à-vis* Russia and ourselves in his new capacity (Wuori, the Finnish representative here, expressed the unsolicited view the other day that he wanted the Secretary-Generalship but that he would recover his balance when he got to the east coast of the United States); thirdly, whether Lie's leaving the Norwegian Government is likely to loosen the Norwegian links with this country or the contrary.

As regards the signs that the Norwegians do not wish to proceed with the military arrangements with us, one should note that Lie has certainly purported in

---

[1] No. 47.

conversation with the Secretary of State and Sargent to be most anxious to get the equipment arrangements agreed and budgeted for and to be most disappointed that he could not get the Minister of Defence over here. Moreover, Berg, in talking to me expressed a strong opinion in an altogether different connexion that the Norwegian Government were pursuing a very foolish financial policy, especially in spending so much money on the armed forces on top of a most expensive insurance programme (Berg went on to say how unpopular the military were making themselves by maintaining unnecessarily large headquarters, throwing their weight around generally and retaining for their use goods such as motor cars confiscated from Norwegians by the Germans.) It may then well be that the Norwegian motive is mainly financial, although Lie curiously enough did not use this line of defence, but spoke as recorded in our telegram[2] of the Norwegians having completely forgotten 1940 and having reverted to pacifism.

C.F.A. WARNER

No. 51

Letter from Sir L. Collier (Oslo) to Mr Warner, 12 February 1946
Confidential (FO 371/56302, N2485/345/30)

Dear Warner,

I think the best way of answering your letter of February 2nd[1] about the Norwegian attitude towards ourselves and the Russians is to deal in turn with the three subjects which it raises, *viz.* the Norwegian Government's general policy, the question of equipment for the Norwegian forces, and Lie's personal attitude, and then to discuss the connexion between them, which I do not believe to be very close or direct.

2. My view of the Norwegian Government's foreign policy and the motives for it are really summarized in my despatch No. 23 of February 2nd,[2] about the appointment of Lie's successor, Halvard Lange: the Government are, I believe anxious to avoid even the appearance of taking sides in the quarrel between Russia and the West, because they are afraid of the Russians and because, as I have reported in that despatch, most Norwegians 'now tend to feel subconsciously that it is of no use for the inhabitants of a country like Norway to trouble their heads over developments in world politics, still less to attempt to influence them'. This means, in effect, that they are, as you suggest, 'determined to maintain a rigidly middle position between Russia and Western Europe', in the sense that they will not take any *new* step which the Russians might regard as a commitment towards the West (I underline the word 'new' because, as you will see later, I do not think they are going back on their military understandings with us); and their policy is sufficiently rigid for the Prime Minister to be able to say that the personality of the Minister for Foreign Affairs is of little consequence. I suspect (though I have no positive evidence for the suspicion) that this was the main reason why Lie hankered after a new job: he was safe enough as Minister for Foreign Affairs but he could take no initiative, and he had begun to despair of being able to carry

[1] No. 50.
[2] No. 49.

through that policy of western collaboration on which, I am convinced, he had genuinely set his heart when he was in London during the war.

3. The crux of the matter, as I see it, is that, as I reported in my despatch No. 23, Norwegians in general 'have no great confidence in the power of Great Britain or the readiness of the United States to protect them against the consequences of Russian displeasure. Hence a natural tendency to say with Candide: "*Il faut cultiver notre jardin*"'. They see that the Swedes got away with neutrality in the last war, they fail to realise, or have forgotten, by how narrow a margin that was achieved, and they hope they may have a similar escape in the next world crisis. Lie, when he was in London with me, foresaw that Norwegian opinion would develop on these lines, even without the incentive of an Anglo-Russian dispute; and for this reason, as I reported at the time, he was always urging that we should work out our plans for the joint use of bases etc. before the end of the war. We were not able, however, to make him any concrete proposals, and every month of peace that went by made it less likely that he could get such proposals accepted by his colleagues or by the Norwegian Parliament. As things are, I fear that the original idea of joint defence arrangements between the Western Powers is no longer practical politics as far as Norway is concerned. I do not know what else we have in mind: you refer, I see, to possible economic arrangements, but even these would be looked at askance here if they could be represented as directed against either the Russians or the Americans, as would seem almost inevitable if they were to be of much use from our point of view. Moreover, the creation of UNO and the acceptance of the doctrine that it must be relied upon for Norway's defence, which is the official propaganda line against isolationists like Dr Scharffenberg[3] (see my despatch No. 29 of February 5th),[4] makes it difficult, at this stage at least, to maintain openly that something more is required for Norway's safety.

4. This however, need not, and in my view does not, imply that the Norwegian Government want to back out of their agreement to take their military supplies from us, to have their forces trained on British lines, and to send a detachment to take part in the occupation of Germany. These are all undertakings of long standing, to which even the Russians have never dared to object; and we have assurances from the Minister of Defence to the Military Attaché, from Torp (formerly Defence Minister, and still a member of the Cabinet as Minister of Supply) to Kenney, and from the new MFA to me, that the three of them, Hauge, Torp and Lange, will all stand by the principle of these undertakings and do their best to get the *Storting* to sanction the expenditure involved. As reported in my telegram No. 60 of February 2nd,[4] I am convinced, and so is the Military Attaché, that the reason why the Norwegians have not yet committed themselves on the question of military equipment is genuinely financial, though their reluctance to spend money on the army is doubtless intensified by their disillusionment with the international outlook and consequent desire to concentrate on internal reforms described in my despatch No. 23. Those who, like the present Prime Minister, are more interested in such reforms than in defence questions, tend, consciously or subconsciously, to use the financial argument, and the connected constitutional argument that nothing can be done without *Storting* approval, as an excuse for delaying a decision (see, for example, paragraph 6 of my despatch No. 23); and I have been wondering whether we could not force their hand by proposing a

---

[3] Johan Scharffenberg was regarded as an isolationist who argued against membership of the UN, and later of NATO.
[4] Not printed.

provisional agreement, subject to confirmation by the *Storting*, under which that part of the equipment, as least, which is now in Norway could be handed over 'on approval', so to speak. It would be difficult for the Norwegian Government to find a plausible reason for rejecting such a proposal; and once they had accepted it, they would be obliged to put the utmost pressure on the *Storting* to ratify it, if only for the practical reason that it would be very inconvenient to have to hand the equipment back again.

5. Lastly, as regards Lie himself, I doubt if his departure from the Government at this juncture will make much difference in practice. I believe him still to be at heart a 'westerner' and an anglophile; and as he would certainly have supported Hauge and Torp in pushing through the *Storting* any agreement reached about military equipment, his loss is to be regretted on that score, though it is probably not fatal, even there. For the rest, however, I doubt that we shall see much difference here: the Cabinet as a whole will be even less ready than it was before to take any but a negative decision on a question of foreign affairs, since, as King Haakon said to me, Lie was the one man in it who had any real education in such matters, but even Lie could hardly have induced it to deviate to any appreciable extent from the strictly 'neutral' line now followed. I do not think that Lie is really under Russian influence, though you in London will have had better opportunities than I for judging his present sentiments; but he has always known very well which side his bread is buttered and I suspect that Wuori is right in prophesying that he will 'suffer a sea change' when he gets to America. Apart from his personal ambitions, however, Lie has had Norwegian interests to consider; and according to what he told me when I last saw him here on January 29th, his final decision to allow his name to be put forward for the chairmanship of the London meeting of the UNO was taken when the Russians intimated that his refusal to stand might disturb Russian-Norwegian relations. (There is always, for example, Spitsbergen, over which the Russians have been lying suspiciously low of late). Lie, in short, is affected by fear of Russia in the same way as most of his countrymen; and that, I think, is the main explanation of his actions. It also explains, in my view, why his departure from the Ministry for Foreign Affairs here, though I regret it, will probably not make much difference to present Norwegian policy. Even those Norwegians who would like to see that policy changed—and there are some, mainly in the 'bourgeois' parties—have no hope of changing it, as will be seen from the following extract from Kit Kenney's record of a conversation with Width, the editor of the Conservative *Morgenbladet:*

> 'Width . . .[5] considered that, unless a great change took place in the course of events, Norway would now lapse into passivity so far as international policy (and particularly any move to strengthen political or military ties with Great Britain or other western countries) is concerned. Width remarked that he and his friends hoped to see some form of post-war Western alliance, to include Norway, but even should Britain and the U.S. be prepared to revive this idea any support from Norway would, in his view, be out of the question now. Width remarked that the Norwegian Government's fear of incurring Russian accusations of attempting to form a Western *Bloc* is now so great that we must expect it to abstain from any constructive action and initiative which may draw Russian criticism. In fact, Width said, he expects that the near future will hold a reversion to the neutral and isolationist atmosphere in Norway which

[5] Ellipsis in original.

characterised the pre-war years, with Russia constituting the overshadowing factor instead of Germany. He added by way of conclusion that we must expect a difficult time in Norway, with increasing criticism of British and U.S. policies.'

Similar remarks have been made to Rowland Kenney by old Benjamin Vogt, the former Minister in London; and though the views of both Width and Vogt are coloured by their Right-wing politics, they are borne out by those of other circles, as far as the present situation is concerned. The position might perhaps be different if, in the future, the prospect of a final breach with Russia became so imminent that we decided to offer Norway (as we offered Poland and Roumania in 1939) the choice between complete isolation and a definite alliance with us; but it has not yet come to that yet.[6]

Yours ever,
L. COLLIER

[6] Warner accepted Collier's views about developments in Norwegian foreign policy and concluded that there was nothing which could be done at that stage, other than to maintain publicity and to make such arrangements as were possible in the field of the armed forces and the economic sphere to cultivate mutual interests and links. He wondered whether it might be possible to make some inconspicuous arrangements to help the Norwegian military with training (FO 371/556302, N2485/1345/30).

No. 52

Mr Shepherd (Helsinki) to Mr Bevin, 18 February 1946, 5.02 p.m.
Tel. No. 80 Immediate (FO 371/56182, N2208/271/56)

War Guilt Tribunal which should have given sentence today adjourned until 21st February.

2. I learn from a very reliable source that the following sentences were proposed:

Ryti	8 years	Ramsay	2 ½ years
Rangell	5 years	Kukkonen	2 years
Tanner	3 ½ years	Reinikka	2 years
Linkomies	3 years	Kivimäki	Acquitted

3. I understand that the Vice Chairman of the ACC sent for the Finnish Prime Minister yesterday and presented him with a vote from the ACC urging that the first 5 persons should receive sentences from between 5 to 10 years and that the remaining three should receive 'appropriate sentences' which was understood to imply two to three years.

4. The Government is holding a Cabinet meeting tonight. The Russians did not (repeat not) consult or inform the British element before taking the action referred to in paragraph 3. Captain Howie is seeing the Vice Chairman this evening in order to protest.

5. If my information about the sentences proposed by the Finns is correct these are obviously excessively lenient in view of the importance of the issues involved. If those concerned are adjudged guilty in any degree of the crimes for which they were charged it seems to me irresponsible and even provocative to give such light

sentences. The Russians suggestions are unexpectedly moderate.[1] I propose to find an opportunity of conveying the sense of this paragraph to the Finnish Government as my personal view while disclaiming any desire to interfere in the course of justice, but I shall await the result of Captain Howie's talk with Savonenkov before doing so.[2]

[1] Warner agreed, commenting that the Finns would be making a great mistake, and provoking the Russians who were still behaving very mildly towards them, if they were to hand out such mild sentences (FO 371/56182, N2208/271/56).
[2] In a telegram of 19 February, Shepherd reported that Savonenkov had apologised to Howie for the failure to consult, explaining that time had been very short. Shepherd had spoken to Enckell to emphasise his hope that the Russian ideas on sentences would be adopted since this was a matter of great importance to Russo-Finnish relations (FO 371/56182, N2231/271/56). Significantly heavier sentences were subsequently imposed on nearly all of the accused (FO 371/56182, N2990/271/56).

No. 53

Letter from Mr Warner to Mr Shepherd (Helsinki), 26 February 1946
Top Secret (FO 371/47450, N17623/10928/56G)

My dear Frank,

We have read with much interest your despatch No. 197 of the 24th November last about Magill's paper on the subject of Foreign Policy in Scandinavia.[1]

We agree generally with your despatch. As regards the point made in paragraph 4, we are naturally in favour of publicity in Finland for things British, the British way of life and forms of democracy, of Trades Unionists and the Cooperative Movement etc. I gather that there have been very few visits to Finland so far by Trade Unionists and Cooperatives. It would I think be a good plan to encourage visits of this kind. If you agree perhaps you could discuss with Thomas[2] how such visits could best be arranged.

As regards Finnish independence and the gap left in Scandinavian psychology by the annihilation of Germany (paragraphs 4 and 6 of your despatch) I think that we should *assume* and encourage Finnish independence; but it is perhaps rather a question of not discouraging Finnish affinity with the rest of Scandinavia rather than encouraging it, since anything in the nature of a Scandinavian *bloc* or of overt Finnish participation, at the present time at least, in Scandinavian affairs, must be regarded as ruled out by fear of Russia.

As regards emphasising that we have the power as well as the will to support Scandinavian independence it seems to us that while we should obviously not be self-deprecatory, it would perhaps be better to let the Finns look to the United Nations Organisation to support their independence rather than to this country individually. There would be no objection to you letting it be known discreetly that His Majesty's Government look forward to Finnish membership of UNO after the signature of the peace treaty. At Potsdam it was of course agreed that the conclusion of peace treaties with recognised democratic governments in Bulgaria, Hungary, Finland and Roumania would enable the Governments of the USSR, United States and Great Britain to support applications from them for membership of UNO.

[1] No. 41.
[2] C.L. Thomas was the Labour Attaché in Helsinki.

But in all this we must be careful not to provoke a Russian reaction upon the Finns (which we should be powerless to prevent) or too rash a demonstration of independence from the Finns (which would bring about their own punishment from the Russians). Finland has got off lightly so far and if as you say the Communist party seem to be losing rather than gaining ground, this shows that the Russians have not wished to see to it that the Communists' position is strengthened. The Russian attitude would probably be reversed if they considered we were attempting to challenge their influence in Finland. Moreover we understand that the Finnish War Guilt Trials have provoked a good deal of internal discussion and that the situation created by Mannerheim's indecision about resigning the Presidency is also causing internal uncertainty. All this tends to make a position of delicate balance in Finland, which in all the circumstances is getting on about as well as could be expected. This delicate situation could perhaps be easily upset for the worse if we seemed suddenly to have decided to play a stronger hand in Finland, especially so soon after the open Anglo-Soviet clashes in the Security Council which will themselves no doubt have caused reactions in Finland.

Yours ever,
C.F.A. WARNER

No. 54

Mr Jerram (Stockholm) to Mr Bevin, 6 March 1946, with minute by Mr Warr of 20 March 1946
No. 101 Top Secret (FO 371/56941, N3331/78/42)

Sir,

In your despatch Top Secret No. 30 (N78/78/G) of January 31st[1] you instructed me (*a*) to co-ordinate the execution of the policy for the disclosure to Sweden of Service information as approved by the Deputy Chiefs of Staff Committee and (*b*) to make the best possible use of Swedish requests for information and equipment to weaken the position, and if possible secure the removal, of the anti-British officers in positions of importance in the Swedish Armed Forces. You further informed me that my Service Attachés would shortly receive instructions from their respective Departments concerning this policy.

2. I am confronted at the outset by two difficulties. First, only my Air Attaché has as yet received instructions from his Department for the putting of this policy into effect. The question of co-ordination can hardly be fully considered until all Service Attachés have received their detailed instructions. In the second place the expression 'anti-British officers in positions of importance in the Swedish Armed Forces' is in the opinion of my Service Attachés somewhat misleading. Both in your despatch and in the enclosure thereto the suggestion is made that we would wish to secure the removal of these officers. Some comment on this suggestion seems necessary at the outset at the risk of covering ground which has already been traversed.

[1] No. 48.

3. 'German sympathisers' in the Armed Forces of Sweden are due to two main causes:

(*a*) German wooing of Sweden during the inter-war years; Germany had Service Attachés resident at this post; we had not until 1939. The close contact maintained by Germany produced a great admiration for German military methods. Evidence of the influence of such contact can be found in the fact that the Swedish Air Force showed a considerably higher degree of pro-British sympathy during the war than the other Services; this is undoubtedly due to their far closer contact with Great Britain in the years before the war.

(*b*) The need by Sweden of a strong Germany as a protection against the hereditary bogey, Russia.

4. These 'German sympathies' were for the most part pro-Nazi only by reason of the fact that the Nazi Party had succeeded in turning a weak Germany, who was nothing of a protection against Russia, into a strong Germany. German totalitarian strength was pitted against Russian totalitarian strength as previously German Imperial strength had been pitted against Russian Imperial strength. The argument that the pro-German sympathy of the Swedish Armed Forces was not pre-eminently pro-Nazi is supported by the fact that such sympathies were still more in evidence during the 1914-1918 war.

5. My Service Attachés are unanimously of the opinion that few, if any, senior officers now serving in the Swedish Armed Forces can be dubbed 'anti-British'. The expression of admiration for Germany during the war was by no means confined to highly placed officers and Swedes of the extreme Right. Moreover it is noteworthy that the present Social-Democrat Minister of Defence[2] was one of the most outspoken apologists for Germany during the war. The utter destruction of Germany had left no obvious buffer against Russia, who by her virtual control of Finland is back again on the frontier of Sweden with apparently more immediate designs than Imperialist Russia.

6. After full discussion with my Service Attachés, whose views coincided almost entirely, I asked them to let me have their recommendations on measures that might be taken to implement a more vigorous policy of weaning the Swedish Forces from their German sympathies and imbuing them with sympathy towards ourselves, bearing in mind the question of Russian susceptibilities, and considering whether drastic or milder measures could better be employed. I enclose (enclosures A, B and C) the memoranda handed to me by the Naval, Military and Air Attachés respectively.[3] It will be seen that they are in essence in agreement as to the policy that should be pursued, though, whereas the Military and Air Attachés are in favour of promoting Sweden to Category B in matters of Service information, the Naval Attaché feels that nothing would be gained from any immediate change in this direction. In general the Service Attachés are of opinion, I cannot judge with what accuracy, that information of a confidential nature supplied to Norway and Denmark can readily be obtained from those countries by Sweden.

7. All three Service Attachés are opposed to any attempt to secure the removal of particular pro-German officers. They state (*a*) that the really bad ones have already gone and (*b*) that pro-German sympathy in the forces has been of a nature that cannot be removed by truncation. After searching carefully for the origin of the impression that has prevailed in the Foreign Office that some of the officers of

---

[2] Allan Vougt.
[3] Not printed.

this Legation were in favour of pursuing a policy of trying to secure the removal of such officers, I believe this to have been based on personal recommendations made whilst the war was still in progress or in a spirit of very natural immediate post-war dudgeon, when German sympathisers (particularly in the Navy) were still in command. Since shortly after my arrival here my Service Attachés have been basing themselves upon the recommendations made in my telegram No. 1308 of September 3rd, with which they were in entire agreement.[3] Nevertheless I feel myself that the question of pro-German sympathisers as distinct from pro-German sympathies should not be entirely ignored and I revert to this matter in paragraph 9 below.

8. It remains then to consider, apart from the recommendations made by the Service Attachés in the enclosures to this despatch, how far previous pro-German sympathies, now wandering in a sort of Limbo, can be eradicated and given a different bias; and how our policy can best be brought home to the Swedes. The enclosure to your despatch under reference makes it clear that Sweden is almost as important to us as Norway and Denmark. The question of our future relations with Sweden cannot be left entirely to an eventual common membership of the United Nations Organisation. You might feel it desirable that I should have some conversation with Monsieur Undén on this matter and I have tried in the next paragraph to suggest the lines my language might take.

9. 'We feel that although you have a Social-Democratic Government very much like our own, with much the same aspirations, your Armed Forces are still largely under the influence of the residue of a long-standing admiration for German might, and in the control of some who clearly showed sympathy with our enemies during the war. We should not therefore be able to help feeling some hesitation at frankly sharing with you technical information and so on which has reached a very high standard in Great Britain and on which our ability to rid the world of insufferable Nazi tyranny so largely depended. Every approach to us by your Armed Forces for such information or for confidential equipment will be considered on its merits, but the above consideration must necessarily weigh with us in making our decision. As far as we ourselves can, we want to do our best to inspire a feeling of mutual confidence between our respective Armed Forces. For this purpose we shall continue to retain Service Attachés at this post; it will be remembered that we had none resident here before the war. But up to now we have, particularly as regards the Army and the Navy, found that your people give us little or no information or facilities. We should wish to see a change in this direction. We do not wish to indulge in recriminations, but we do feel that there are persons in high command in whom we find it difficult to place complete confidence. Doubtless time and the natural process of retirement will eliminate these; and the Swedish Government may itself feel it expedient to reduce the influence of those with the old-time German complex. As Sweden is always likely to be a Democratic country, we want to see a strong Sweden capable of looking after herself and taking a full share in the preservation of world security. Our interest in Europe is, or should be, identical.'

10. Some of the above would no doubt require more careful wording, but, as my Soviet colleague has himself recently made the complaint to me that the Swedish Armed Forces are still full of German sympathisers, Russia could not properly object to the main burden of such language. As Russophobia was the main basis of the pro-Germanism of this or that Swedish officer a specific attempt for their elimination would certainly suit the Russian book. But should Monsieur Undén in

fact ask me to specify the officers to whom we object, I should propose to reply that pro-Germanism in the Forces has been notorious, that we are making no complaints, recriminations or representations, but simply wish to create that feeling of confidence which has been lacking. Should he press me, I could in the last resort retort by confronting him with some of the remarks made during the war by his own Minister of Defence, adding that I had no wish at all to attack Monsieur Vougt and was merely giving him an example of the sort of thing that was being felt and said in Sweden at that time; that remarks and acts that gave countenance to and helped our enemy during the war still rankled at home; and that it was precisely my wish to remove this feeling that had induced me to speak frankly to him on the matter.

11. The 'German sympathies' in the Swedish Armed Forces can in fact be eliminated only if something else is provided in their stead. And pure sympathy is not enough; there must be a feeling of strength behind it. We can, and should, supply the sympathy by carrying out as far as possible the recommendations made by my Service Attachés for far closer contact than we maintained before the war. If we can supplement this by technical and material assistance to as high a degree as possible, so much the better.

12. Given the desirability of a strong Sweden in the interests of world security, it might conceivably be felt that that objective could be more safely pursued through United States assistance than through our own. I make no reference here to the too obvious commercial consideration. However this may be, unless Sweden can acquire some degree of confidence through a higher standard of preparedness, it would seem that she must either (*a*) pin her whole faith to the UNO, (*b*) concede more and more to Russia should Russia feel it necessary to push her Finnish bastions still further East, or (*c*) hope for the revival of some kind of anti-Comintern Pact, either on a recrudescence of Nazism (only a small minority would desire this), or on a Social-Democratic basis for which there might be wide support were it not that Sweden's proximity to the Soviet Union renders her so terribly vulnerable.

13. Since I drafted the above, the recommendations to the Foreign Minister by the Commander-in-Chief of the Swedish Armed Forces on the question of Sweden's joining the UNO have appeared in the press (see my Saving Telegram No. 13 of today).[3] May I ask that these recommendations, and the considerations on which they are based, be read in conjunction with this despatch.

I have, etc.,
C.B. JERRAM

Minute from Warr to Hankey and Warner, 20 March 1946

The points which emerge from this despatch are:

(1) Our policy of trying to extirpate individual pro-Germans from the Swedish armed forces is not going to work. All three service attachés and Mr Jerram are agreed on this point. I think therefore that we shall have to revise the conclusion 13(*b*)(*ii*) of the JIC paper,[3] and remove the reference to pro-Germans. We originally asked for it to be put in as a result of a conversation between Mr Warner and our Naval Attaché on 6th November 1945 (please see my minute in

N11547/570/42 dated 6th November . . .).[4] Para 7 of this despatch and the NA's report enclosed now shows that Captain Denham has completely reversed what he then said. I see no alternative but to accept this change of mind. But this is no reason why we should not complain of the admiration for Germany which is generally felt in the Swedish services: I think that the action suggested by Mr Jerram in para. 9 is right and we ought to approve his plan to speak to Mr Undén on the lines he proposes.[5]

(2) Mr Jerram points out that only his AA has received instructions about our new policy. Mr Mayall[6] tells me that there was a misunderstanding in our despatch and that the Service Depts never intended to send instructions to the Attachés. I should have thought that as our new policy involves a fresh departure in the relations between the Swedish armed forces and our own, it was absolutely essential for all the Service Attachés to be independently instructed. They would then know how to deal with specific proposals from the Swedes, and be clear what line they should take in conversation with Swedish officers. Only in cases of doubt would they refer for advice to the Minister, he being responsible for co-ordination. At present there is all too great a tendency for the Service Attachés to pursue their own separate policies as regards relations with Sweden. Moreover the Service Depts themselves are apt to go off on their own lines, as Mr Jerram points out in N3662/78/G.[4] Actually the Bofors incident to which he refers was the fault of the Ministry of Supply, but they have now been warned not to fail to warn us in advance if there are any further visits to Sweden. Though it is hardly necessary to get instructions sent to the Service Attachés before our policy is revised as proposed in (1), I think that we must be quite certain that instructions are sent afterwards.

(3) Mr Jerram points out that his despatch should be considered in the light of General Jung's recommendations (see the attached copy of Stockholm tel. No. 13 Saving).[4] The general tenor of these recommendations and in particular the marked passage on page 3 of the tel. show that, even if Sweden joins UNO she will maintain herself in a neutral defensive position, and at all costs avoid getting involved in any conflict between East and West. It is therefore perfectly clear that we shall not succeed in weaning Sweden into our strategic orbit and that in her relations with us she will always have one eye on Russia. This consideration does not seem to me to apply to quite the same extent to Denmark and Norway and I think therefore that there is a good case for revising that part of our policy (especially paras 9 and 10 of the JIC paper) which says that Scandinavia should be treated as a strategic whole.

(4) The MA and the AA argue that Sweden should be raised from Category C to Category B as regards the disclosure of service information (in point of fact in air matters Sweden has been so raised). Mr Jerram points out that there may not

---

[4] Not printed, though see No. 25.
[5] In early 1946, consideration by the Foreign Office of this sensitive subject had been complicated by a recommendation from Brigadier Sutton Pratt, the Military Attaché in Stockholm, to the War Office that the nomination of Major Francke to be the Swedish Military Attaché in London should be turned down because of his alleged wartime Nazi connections. Sutton Pratt had not consulted Jerram before making this recommendation, and after being required to make further enquiries he changed his mind, found that there was no substance to the allegations about Major Francke and agreed that the nomination should go ahead. Incidents such as this may for a time have encouraged an exaggerated view in the Foreign Office of the seriousness of the extent of pro-German sentiment among the Swedish military (FO 371/56941, N2098/78/42G and N3110/78/42G).
[6] Services Liaison Department.

be much point in treating Sweden less favourably than Norway or Denmark, on the ground that the relations between those 3 countries being so close, Sweden would easily be able to obtain from the other two any of the secrets we had given them. It seems to me that this argument ignores the practical point that we want to treat Norway and Denmark, our allies, more favourably than neutral Sweden. It is another matter whether to do so would harm our strategic interests. Personally I should have thought that in view of the considerations put forward in (3) above no amount of information disclosed to the Swedes would make any difference to their attitude, and that therefore there is no point in treating them favourably.

(5) Finally, the MA and NA recommend certain exchanges between the Swedish army and our own. I think that our attitude to these proposals should be to favour those which are a means of encouraging the Swedish services to be pro-British, and to discourage any attempts at strategic planning with the Swedes.

To sum up, I suggest we should

(*a*) approve the line proposed in para. 9 of Mr Jerram's despatch. Perhaps we should do so by tel. as his letter within shows that he will be meeting the Crown Prince and General Douglas on 28th March. We could further inform him that further instructions will follow about revising the policy in the light of this despatch.[7]

(*b*) revise the JIC paper for the reasons given in (1) and (3) above, but without raising Sweden to Category B.

(*c*) make sure after this revision that all 3 Service Depts send instructions to their attachés.

G.C. WARR

[7] Warr minuted further on 4 April that Warner had agreed that the Foreign Office should drop the idea of extirpating pro-Germans from the Swedish armed forces. Further, in those circumstances he thought that it would be logical to make no further reference to the subject and had decided to drop the suggestion that Jerram should raise the subject with Undén as he had proposed: 'this would merely draw attention to a grievance which we were not prepared to insist on the Swedes remedying'. In a despatch of 11 May, the Foreign Office formally notified Jerram of the reversal of the policy of trying to secure the removal of officers considered to be unfriendly who were in positions of importance in the Swedish armed forces, though it maintained the idea of using every available opportunity to strengthen the position of friendly elements as far as possible (FO 371/56941, N5019/78/42G).

No. 55

Sir L. Collier (Oslo) to Mr Bevin, 20 March 1946
No. 84 (FO 371/56284, N4417/219/30)

Sir,

My attention has lately been drawn on several occasions to the need for securing a better understanding of British policy by the Norwegian Labour movement; and this problem seems to me and to my staff of such importance that I venture to submit the following appreciation of the position, with suggestions for dealing with it.

2. The Norwegian Labour movement now occupies a dominating position in the country's political life, a position unlikely to be shaken in the foreseeable future. In

the *Storting*, as reported in my despatch No. 128 of December 2nd last, the Labour Party has a majority of one vote over all the other parties combined; and as the Communist fraction, which is about one-seventh of its size, usually votes with it against the other parties, it has a comfortable working majority.[1] The opposition is split into four parties, the largest of which, the Conservative, is only one-third the size of the Labour Party, and the general attitude of these parties shows that they do not really regard themselves as potential rulers of Norway. The Labour Party on the other hand, has both confidence in its own abilities and an unusual sense of responsibility; and there is reason to think that its strength in the country is, if anything, on the increase. The latest figures of party membership are the highest ever recorded, and the Trade Unions, which had already become strong in the years before the war, have shown a further increase in membership since the liberation. The Trade Union movement has a strong central organisation, which takes a positive and active part in politics, and the Unions are regularly consulted on all matters connected with the Government's economic policy.

3. In British-Norwegian relations, therefore, the attitude of the Labour movement is, on the Norwegian side, a major factor. Although in spirit and policy it probably resembles the British Labour movement more nearly than does any other Labour movement in Europe, knowledge of British affairs and understanding of British policy appears to be less among its members than among other sections of the community. The mental outlook of the rank and file in the movement, and even of some of its leading personalities, is largely coloured by the Social Democratic propaganda of the past century, in which Britain was depicted as an Imperialist power abroad and at home a country characterised by aristocracy on the one hand and slums on the other (neither being regarded by the average Norwegian as the mark of a self-respecting community); and more recently it has been affected by the Party's close affiliations with German socialism in the decade following the first world war, and with communism in the 'radical' period of M. Tranmæl's leadership.[2] Comparatively little is known of the progressive aspects of British life, of British social services and the progress made in Britain between the wars in such matters as housing, or even of the British Trade Union and Labour movements. In correspondence with this lack of knowledge about Britain there is a widespread belief in Russia as the true workers' State; and this pro-Russian bias affects much wider sections of the population than those from which the Communist Party recruits its relatively few adherents. The Labour organ *Arbeiderbladet*, for example, though engaged in prolonged and bitter controversy with the Communists on internal policy, as reported in my despatch No. 78 of March 14th, is printing articles by one of its chief contributors, M. Elster, which invariably support the Russian as against the British thesis in any disputed question of foreign affairs.[1]

4. Among the Labour leadership, however, and to a lesser extent in the rank and file, there is an influential section, consisting largely of Norwegians who lived in Britain (or America) during the war, which is much more aware of the actual conditions in Britain and has in general a more international and less provincial outlook.[3] This section of Labour opinion is anxious to see relations with Britain

---

[1] Not printed.
[2] The Norwegian Labour Party had affiliated to the Comintern between 1919 and 1923.
[3] Both Konrad Nordahl, the president of LO from 1939 to 1965, and Haakon Lie, the secretary of the Norwegian Labour Party from 1945 to 1963, had spent most of the war in London. Among

developed in all possible ways—through the supply of information to the press, the exchange of delegations from educational and other organisations of the Labour movement, the increase of facilities for the study of British social developments and the expansion of contacts between those concerned with such matters in the two countries. It desires this development both because, realising the affinities between the two movements, it hopes thereby to forward united Labour action on an international basis, and also because it wishes to set up a focus of interest to counter the pro-Russian inclinations mentioned above; and I am given to understand that it is formulating definite schemes for that purpose.

5. It would seem obviously desirable that this tendency should be encouraged from the British side. In an international crisis the British cause could probably count upon the sympathy of nearly all non-Labour circles in Norway; but among Labour supporters—and these are in the majority—the position is more doubtful, the sympathy of such circles being likely at best to be half-hearted and tinged with misgivings. The situation, however, is due to ignorance rather than to ill-will, and could, I believe, be much altered with a sustained effort from the British side, combined with assistance from the friendly section of Norwegian Labour. An opportunity for now making a beginning with this work of conversion has now been provided by the action of the Federation (*Landsorganisasjon*) of Norwegian Trades Unions in inviting the TUC to send delegates to their annual conference in May next. The President of the Federation, M. Konrad Nordahl, has told a member of my staff that this is not a merely formal invitation but that the presence of a British delegation would be greatly appreciated: he added that the Norwegian Federation would like to send delegates to the annual conference of the TUC and that Norwegian Unions more generally were anxious to exchange delegates with their British counterparts for the annual conferences of each. I venture to suggest that it is to the interest of HM Government to encourage the acceptance of such invitations, and that on this occasion the TUC might be recommended to respond favourably to M. Nordahl's approach. The Press Attaché to HM Legation has already recommended similar proposals for a visit to Great Britain by a delegation from the Norwegian Iron and Metalworkers' Union and a visit to Norway by a group of British workers under the auspices of the Workers' Educational Association. A further suggestion which has been made to me in this connexion, and which I have the honour to submit for your consideration, is that a Member of Parliament in the confidence of the Government, but not actually holding an official position, should visit Norway for the purpose of giving private talks to gatherings of Norwegian Labour leaders on the situation in Britain and the aims of British policy abroad. I have reason to believe that it would be possible to organise such meetings, addresses to which would be much more effective than public lectures or statements to the press.[4] In any case, I submit that early consideration should be given to the possibility of taking action on these or similar lines, if we

---

other prominent Norwegians Erik Brofoss, Minister of Finance from 1945-47, also worked in London from 1942-45 in the Ministries of Finance and Supply.

[4] The Minister of State, Hector McNeil, suggested that William Warbey (who had worked as an Information Officer for the Norwegian government in exile during the war) should visit Norway, but the Embassy pointed out that he held extreme views on Franco's government in Spain and he did not go on this occasion (FO 371/56284, N4417/219/30). However, several other delegations of Labour MPs did visit Norway during this period.

are not to find the state of Norwegian opinion in the next world crisis as unsatisfactory, from the British point of view, as it was in 1939.[5]

> I have, etc.,
> L. COLLIER

[5] Bevin wrote on 23 April to Walter Citrine, General Secretary of the TUC, to emphasise the value of a visit by a TUC delegation to the LO congress (FO 371/56284, N4417/219/30). Citrine responded positively and the TUC was represented at the congress (FO 371/56284, N6470/219/30).

No. 56

Mr Walsh (Helsinki) to Mr Bevin, 26 March 1946
No. 66 Confidential (FO 371/56174, N4419/226/56)

Sir,

The essential facts regarding the resignation on the 3rd March of Baron Mannerheim, Marshal of Finland, from his position as President of the Finnish Republic, and the subsequent election of President Paasikivi were reported in Mr Shepherd's telegrams Nos. 102 and 115.[1]

2. President Mannerheim's resignation marked the close of an eventful period in the history of Finland, and it may be reckoned not the least of his services to his country that he was probably the only figure of sufficient stature to lead the people through defeat and armistice (and the severe psychological revaluation of the national position which that has entailed), while preserving to them something of a sense of national pride and continuity. Though his precise influence on pre-war policy and events remains obscure, and has indeed been brought into question by recent revelations of the excessively active part played therein by the High Command, he is, nevertheless, widely credited with having exercised a restraining influence during the winter war and with having, at a relatively early stage of the second war, been ready to support a peace policy. The conclusion of the war responsibility trials saw the fulfilment of the last of the 'temporary' terms of the Armistice Agreement and permitted him to feel free, under the stress of ill-health, to retire from office. He thus passed from the public scene, 'full of years and honours', and incomparably the most eminent figure which Finland, in its period of independence, has produced.

3. A dignified ceremony of farewell took place when the Cabinet made its official call at the Presidential Palace on the 8th March, M. Paasikivi, as Prime Minister, read the following short address:

'Mr President, Marshal of Finland,

Since you, Mr President, because of impaired health, are now leaving the high office of President of the Republic, an office that you, upon the unanimous wishes of the people, accepted at so eventful a moment, permit the Council of State to convey to you its appreciation for the trust you have reposed in it and for the spirit of collaboration you have always evinced.

Immediately upon assumption of the presidency, you were faced with difficult tasks and you have since that time had to make weighty decisions and to solve

[1] Not printed.

difficult problems. We appreciate the support that you, in the capacity of President of the Republic, have given us during a time that has been of such great significance to Finland, especially in the field of foreign relations. We also wish to express to you our thanks for the kindness you have shown us personally. And to our expressions of gratitude we add the sincere wishes that you, Mr President, Marshal of Finland, may long enjoy health and rest after your arduous labours.'

To which the President replied:

'Mr Prime Minister, Ministers,

I beg you, Mr Prime Minister, to accept my sincere thanks for the kind words which you have just addressed to me and I beg all the Members of the State Council to accept my thanks for calling upon me here today.

My incumbency, which has now come to a close, has been comparatively short, but during that time much has happened in the world at large and here at home. The war that has shaken humanity has ended and the nations of the world have begun to rebuild what has been destroyed and to establish a basis for collaboration among the peoples.

For my own part I rejoice in the fact that, as head of State, I have been able to contribute towards disengaging my country from the war and achieving the armistice in the autumn of 1944, and I rejoice that I have been able to participate in the task of overcoming many difficulties that seemed insuperable and in lightening the heavy burdens that have been placed upon our people.

I am fully aware of the fact that, in these circumstances, the work of the Cabinet and your work, in particular, Mr Prime Minister, has been unusually exacting and difficult. As our ways now part, it is from the heart that I speak when I request you, Mr Prime Minister, and the Council of State as a whole, to accept my sincere thanks for this work and for what each one of you has accomplished for the benefit of his country. And I wish you success in removing the deep traces that are a heritage of the war, and it is my most devout wish that our people will soon have their long-desired peace in order that, independent, they may continue with their work of creating a secure and happy future for the country.'

4. The usual method of presidential election was clearly inappropriate in view of the need of urgent action and of the fundamental changes of political strength since the election of 'electors' took place. Two alternative methods were available: the new President could be elected by the Diet, as was done in the case of the first President in 1919, or special legislation nominating a particular person would be passed, as in August 1944. A Bill, introduced by the Government, providing for election by the Diet, was passed through all its stages between the 5th and the 8th March, and the Diet on the 9th March, proceeded to the election of Premier J K Paasikivi by 159 out of a total of 184 votes cast. Fourteen votes, possibly cast by Progressives (who were the only party to oppose the Government Bill in the first place) were given to former President Ståhlberg.[2] The outsider could only remark a characteristic lack of purpose in these votes, since it was never in doubt that M. Paasikivi would be elected by an overwhelming majority. M. Ståhlberg, by reason of his age, would not have been a suitable holder of the office in these strenuous times and, indeed, he had not, as far as it is known, shown any willingness or desire to accept it. Eleven voting papers were left blank. On the 11th March M.

---

[2] Kaarlo Ståhlberg was the first President of Finland from 1919-25.

Paasikivi was officially inducted for a term which will expire on the 1st March 1950.

5. The new President did not come new to the functions of his office, for, owing to President Mannerheim's failing health, he had, as Prime Minister, been to all intents and purposes Acting President since the middle of 1945. The double work was undoubtedly beginning to tell on him and although his loss in Council will be greatly felt, it is probable that he will continue, in an advisory capacity, to exercise considerable influence on policy and he will in some ways be the better able to 'con the ship' as a result of his liberation from the details of daily politics and administration.

6. M. Paasikivi is a man of 75 years who can look back on a varied career. After leaving the university with a degree of MA he subsequently obtained a Doctorate of Laws and then entered journalism and politics. In 1908 he became Minister of Finance, but he retired from politics in 1914 to become manager of the Kansallis Osake Bank, which post he held until 1934. This did not prevent him from undertaking special political missions, such as membership of the delegation which visited the Scandinavian countries in 1917 to announce Finland's independence, and in 1918 he re-entered politics to become head of the Government. In 1936 he was appointed Finnish Minister to Stockholm, when he was recalled in the autumn of 1939 to proceed to Moscow to negotiate the territorial demands which Russia was then making. He was Minister without portfolio during the winter war and after the peace went to Moscow as Minister until shortly before the outbreak of the second war. In February 1944 he was entrusted with the task of making peace feelers through the Soviet Legation in Stockholm, and in March of the same year he was again in Moscow engaged on an abortive attempt to obtain an armistice. In November 1944 he formed the first post-armistice Government, which he has led with skill and success (especially when measured against the fears of what might have followed upon failure) until his election to the presidency on the 9th March 1946.

I have, etc.,
J.M. WALSH

No. 57

Minute from Mr Warner to Sir O. Sargent, 5 April 1946, covering minute by Sir L. Collier of 4 April 1946
(FO 371/56294, N4921/539/30)

Norwegian Armed Forces

You will remember the brief which the Northern Department put up for the Defence Committee Meeting on the question of the Norwegian and Danish armed forces, in which it was suggested that the Norwegian Government would not be able to provide a full division for our zone in Germany, that there were also financial difficulties, and that in negotiations with the Norwegians we should take account of these considerations and should bear in mind the over-riding importance of securing a long-term link-up with the Norwegian army.[1]

---

[1] Not printed.

You will see from the attached minutes of the Defence Committee meeting that we have been instructed, on the contrary, to insist with the Norwegians that they should supply the full division and pay all the expenses.[1]

I attach a minute by Sir L. Collier, who is over here for consultation and leave, bearing out the Department's view and suggesting that we may endanger the long-term link-up with the Norwegian army altogether.

I am trying to arrange for Sir L. Collier to see the Secretary of State in any case, and if so he will mention the matter; but if he does not, you may care to send this to the Secretary of State and suggest that we should modify our approach to the Norwegians to take account of the considerations which Sir L. Collier mentions.[2]

C.F.A. WARNER

Minute by Sir L. Collier, 4 April 1946

When I called yesterday at the Foreign Office on my arrival from Oslo on leave of absence, I was shown the minutes of the Cabinet Defence Committee indicating that the Norwegian Government are to be pressed to send to Germany the whole force of one division, which was originally to have been their contribution to the Army of Occupation, and to pay for all of its equipment.

I venture to support the view which, I understand, has already been put to the War Office by my Military Attaché, Colonel Garner Smith, that the Norwegian Government, having with great difficulty secured Parliamentary approval for the despatch of a force of 4,000 men, will not be moved from this position by any British representations. Nor can they be induced to increase the global sum voted for expenditure on the three defence forces, which has apparently been estimated on the assumption that, while they are prepared to pay the price asked for the British naval and air equipment offered them, they will be able to compromise on the sum demanded for the British Army equipment, possibly through some scheme of 'lend-lease' for the equipment required in Germany.

The Norwegian Government, on the other hand, might reasonably be expected to advance the date proposed for sending the 4,000 men to Germany. It is my considered opinion, however, which is shared by Mr Rowland Kenney, with his unrivalled knowledge of Norwegian politics that, apart from this concession and a compromise on the question of payment for equipment to be used in Germany, nothing else could be extracted from them and that, by attempting to extract it, we should run the risk of losing our long term objective, the linking up of Norwegian with British defence measures, which is presumably of much greater importance to us than securing an extra 4,000 Norwegians in Germany. The Norwegian Ministers for Foreign Affairs and Defence, as well as M. Lie, have impressed upon me that the Government have no intention of buying military equipment from more than one foreign source—either they buy it from us or they will buy it from, say, the Swedes, who are known to be ready and able to offer it; and I cannot exclude the

---

[2] Hankey minuted to Warner that the Secretary of State had been receptive to the argument put forward by Collier, and was thinking of raising the issue with the Prime Minister. Warner instructed a written brief to be prepared, also covering Denmark, which Allen (Northern Department) cleared with the War Office. The War Office supported the principles raised by Collier, and on Denmark thought it best to arrange to get the contingent there as soon as possible, leaving questions such as the duration of its stay, until later. Instructions, which went some way to meeting anticipated Norwegian objections, were subsequently sent to Oslo on 19 April. See No. 59.

possibility that, being obstinate people, as we all know, they might decide to give up altogether their attempt to equip their army (though not necessarily their navy and air force) from British sources, if we require them to pay a total price (including the cost of equipment in Germany) which is more than has been voted. They cannot now go back to their Parliament for a further vote, while we for our part could hardly reduce still further the very generous terms we have offered for naval and air equipment; and there will thus be a deadlock over army equipment if, as I believe, the total figure voted does not allow for the purchase outright of the equipment to be used in Germany.

The continuance of such a deadlock would expose us, moreover, to a further danger. So far the Norwegian Government, though notoriously frightened of the Russians, have been willing to ignore the possibility that the Soviet government might show themselves seriously displeased at the plans for providing British training and equipment for the Norwegian forces; but that possibility is always in the background, and I would not like to say what would happen if the Soviet Government thought it worthwhile to start, say, a press campaign against British influence in the Norwegian Army. I submit therefore that we have every reason for getting a definite agreement on army equipment as soon as possible, even at a cost of some sacrifices: otherwise we may lose everything through holding out for more than we can expect to get.

L. COLLIER

No. 58

Record by Mr Warr of a Meeting held on 10 April 1946
(FO 371/71479, N1775/1652/27)

Airfields in Iceland
1. A meeting, attended by Mr Shepherd the Minister in Reykjavik, was held by Mr Hankey on 10 April to consider the questions of the British airfield in Iceland and the American request for bases. Mr Jones, Ministry of Civil Aviation, Mr J. G. Ward, Mr Warr and Mr Wright were also present.

Reykjavik Airfield
2. It was explained that in accordance with our exchange of notes with the Icelandic Government of October 1944, we were bound to hand back to the Icelandic Government after the end of hostilities the airfield we occupied during the war. We were now in the process of withdrawing and after the end of April the only RAF personnel remaining would be there only for the purpose of care and maintenance. Mr Shepherd drew attention to the likelihood that now that we had handed back the airfield to the Icelandic Government the Russians would at once obtain concessions from the Icelanders for the use of the airfield. This was particularly likely to occur in that the Icelandic Minister of Communications and the head of the Icelandic Ministry of Civil Aviation were both Communists. Moreover, the Soviet Minister had an inflated staff, many of whom were experts in civil aviation matters who could, if desired, be immediately used to operate facilities on an airfield. Mr Hankey stressed the importance from the political point of view of our getting the rights we needed for ourselves and actually exercising them before the Russians got civil aviation rights. Otherwise experience showed

that the Russians would push us off our airfield whatever our theoretical rights might be. The meeting then considered whether our position was sufficiently safeguarded by the exchange of notes of October 1944, and decided that although we would thereby acquire most-favoured-nation rights when we vacated the airfield, the only watertight way of ensuring that the Russians did not get concessions before ourselves was for ourselves to operate a service to and from the airfield. Mr Jones explained that Reykjavik aerodrome was not required as a regular port of call on trunk routes. Nor had BOAC a plan to operate terminal services to Iceland. It was therefore unlikely that with the ending of the RAF service to Iceland there would be any British civil air service to replace it, at any rate not for the present. Mr Shepherd said that it was important both from the commercial and political points of view to have a regular air service between this country and Iceland so that the Icelanders, who had at present plenty of capital available for purchases in this country, could easily journey to and fro. The existing sea routes were slow and precarious, and without a regular air route Mr Shepherd feared that we should both lose business custom and the goodwill of the Icelanders which had been of importance to us in the war and might be of great value in any future emergency.

3. The meeting then discussed the various possible methods of arranging for a British air line to operate regularly to Iceland. It having been agreed that there was not sufficient justification to press the BOAC to operate such a service if, as apparently was the case, it would mean that a service would thereby be withdrawn from another route in Europe, the suggestion was made that an Icelandic company, in which British aircraft, personnel and technical assistance would participate, might be encouraged to run a service. Mr Jones undertook to explore the views of the Ministry of Civil Aviation and to provide the Foreign Office with a note of their views about the proposal as soon s possible. When it had been received, Mr Shepherd would discuss the suggestions made in it informally with the Icelandic Minister in London and the head of the Icelandic Air Company, who was now in this country. The suggestion was also made that we might urge the section of the Ministry of Supply responsible for the sale of British aircraft abroad, (the name of Mr Haynes was mentioned) as well as the Board of Trade, to release British aircraft to Iceland.

US bases in Iceland

4. We have learnt from Washington that in the advice of the US Minister in Reykjavik, the US Government proposes to defer any approach to the Icelandic Government for bases until after the Icelandic elections in June. The US Minister considered that after the elections an approach to the Icelandic Government would be much more likely to receive a favourable response than before. Mr Shepherd was asked whether he would endorse this view. He replied that he felt that it was a most unfavourable time to broach this matter before the elections as all the political parties were then in the habit of ventilating their grievances, and an approach to the Icelanders would in these circumstances be publicly and vigorously opposed, by not only the Communists but also probably by all the other political parties except the Conservatives. After the elections there was a strong likelihood of the Communists being in a weaker position than they were at present and therefore of the Icelandic Government being less likely to oppose an American request for bases. But without knowing how the different Icelandic Ministries would be allocated between the parties he could not forecast with any certainty

how the Icelandic Government would react to any American approach after the elections.

G.C. WARR

No. 59

Mr Bevin to Mr Wardrop (Oslo), 19 April 1946
No. 181 (FO 371/56294, N4921/539/30)

Sir,
I have had under consideration Sir Laurence Collier's despatch No. 63 of the 1st March enclosing a translation of an *aide-mémoire* handed to him by the Norwegian Minister for Foreign Affairs on the subject of the provision of a Norwegian contingent of 4,000 men for occupation duties in Germany.[1]

2. This matter has now been fully considered and I shall be glad if you will convey to the Norwegian Government in whatever manner you consider appropriate the views of His Majesty's Government along the following lines.

3. His Majesty's Government are grateful for the assurance that the Norwegian Government, subject to the agreement of the *Storting*, are willing to provide a contingent for occupation duties in the British zone of Germany, as has been contemplated in previous discussions. They look forward to entering upon the more detailed negotiations proposed by the Norwegian Government regarding the conditions for this Norwegian contingent's participation in the occupation of Germany. They wish to propose for this purpose that a suitable Norwegian Mission should come to London at the earliest possible date. They would be gratified if it were found possible for this Mission to be led by the Norwegian Minister of Defence or some other member of the Government.

4. His Majesty's Government attach the utmost importance to the participation of other European powers in the occupation of Germany, which constitutes a European problem affecting the security of all. His Majesty's Government feel fully entitled to ask the Norwegian Government to bear a fully proportionate share of the burden. They had expected that it would be possible for the Norwegian Government to provide one division. Their offer of British equipment for the Norwegian armed forces and the plans of the British Military authorities in Germany have in fact been based on such an expectation. His Majesty's Government still trust that the Norwegian Government will feel able to reconsider the matter and will at least supply a larger contingent than that of 4,000 men at present suggested. In this connexion it is understood that the Soviet authorities in Berlin have now expressed their willingness to accept immediately in the Soviet zone of Germany the German prisoners of war who have hitherto been held in Norway and that the necessary transport arrangements for their early transfer are already being made. This should materially assist the Norwegian Government in overcoming the manpower difficulties to which they referred in their *aide-mémoire* enclosed in your despatch under reference.

5. His Majesty's Government also feel entitled to ask the Norwegian Government to bear their share of the burden of the cost of the occupation of

[1] Not printed.

Germany. While they will be glad to do all in their power to meet the Norwegian Government's requirements of equipment both for the contingent for Germany and for the rest of their armed forces, they much regret that they will not be able to supply this equipment free of cost, They will however be glad to discuss the matter in detail with the Norwegian mission visiting London. As regards the maintenance of the Norwegian troops in Germany the Norwegian authorities will be entitled to billets, office accommodation, coal, firewood, electric light, water, German civilian servants and other items of German origin at no cost to the Norwegian government and at German expense. In addition the Norwegian forces will be allowed the free use of the German railways and no payment will be expected for any German transport requisitioned by them. The Norwegian military authorities will also be able to use German land for training purposes at no cost to the Norwegian Government.

6. His Majesty's Government are ready to discuss all these questions in a broad and friendly spirit with a Norwegian Mission in London and feel confident that it will be possible to reach an agreement that is acceptable to both sides.

I am, etc.,
ERNEST BEVIN

No. 60

Mr Shepherd (Helsinki) to Mr Bevin, 4 May 1946
No. 94 Confidential (FO 371/56179, N6144/232/56)

Sir,

I have the honour to report that I had a conversation lasting nearly two hours this morning with the Minister for Foreign Affairs, during which M. Enckell surveyed the position in which Finland finds herself with regard to Russia.

2. Referring to the recent Finnish delegation to Moscow, M. Enckell proceeded to deplore the hapless position of Finland in anything that had to do with the Peace Treaty. Although it had been stated that Finland would be permitted to put forward her views, there was no point in disguising the fact that the treaty would, in fact, be a dictated one. Finland had lost two wars, and however disastrous the consequences might be, she would have to make the best of them. The procedure of peace-making was that the draft treaties would be submitted for the observations of the twenty-one United Nations (some of which, M. Enckell remarked in parenthesis, could scarcely be said to have played a decisive part in the war—what, for instance, had Brazil done?). The Finnish Government did not consider it consonant with the country's dignity to appear in a mendicant role to ask for help from these twenty-one assorted nations. In fact, the war in which Finland had been engaged was actually a Fenno-Russian war, and the fact that England had found it necessary to declare war had been due to the clumsiness of the then Finnish Government—Russia had been the only real enemy.

3. In making peace the only real problems were consequently those between Finland and Russia. It had been, in fact, frequently asked in private conversations by Russians what interest Great Britain could really have in Finland. M. Enckell had suggested to his Government after considerable thought that the best course for Finland would be to discuss direct with Russia those points which directly

concerned Finland and Russia only, and to discuss with Great Britain any points in which the latter were interested. The recent delegation to Moscow had adopted this procedure.

4. M. Enckell then embarked on one of his inevitable historical disquisitions, but on this occasion he was more relevant and less discursive than usual. He recalled the success which had attended the policy of the Tsar Alexander I[1] immediately after the annexation of Finland in creating friendliness and loyalty to Russia in a country which had for centuries been accustomed to wage war against her. Mutual respect had grown up between Finland and Russia, and Finnish officers who had fought on the side of Sweden were content to join the Russian army. The oppressive Russification period which set in at the beginning of the present century had aroused considerable interest in Europe. An ex-Tsarist Foreign Minister had told M. Enckell very soon after the Russian revolution that if the Tsar's Government had imagined that Europe would have taken the interest in Finnish affairs that was in fact taken, they would never have dirtied their hands with the Russification policy. The development of Finnish democracy and the industrial progress of the country since its independence had further aroused the interest of Europe, and this had been demonstrated during the 1939 Russo-Finnish war. Finland's only hope of alleviation of her present situation lay in the interest and sympathy of Europe, for which she was precluded from asking. It was a fact that if there had been no 1939 there would have been no 1941, but in view of Finland's situation *vis-à-vis* Russia, she could not mention the 1939 war. The Finnish Prime Minister had asked M. Enckell whether he would head the delegation to Paris if one were sent, but what, M. Enckell enquired, could he say if he did go to Paris? Finland's case was in the hands of the United Nations, but he was afraid that the complexity of the important affairs which the Foreign Ministers would have to decide would mean that they would have little time to study the affairs of Finland and that country's case might go by default in view of these considerations and the preponderating influence of Russia in Finnish affairs.

5. The question of frontier adjustment, M. Enckell went on, had been raised at Moscow, but M. Stalin had stated definitely that the frontiers had now been fixed and could not be altered. At the same time the Russians had indicated that they were anxious that displaced Karelians should return to their former homes as Russian citizens. M. Enckell found this curious and asked what the reason could be. It was not a very new attitude. At the time of the armistice the Russians had insisted that no steps could be taken by the Finns to remove the inhabitants of Karelia and that they should be notified that they could remain. By that time, however, the vast majority had left and gone into Finland. The Communists (not the Russians) had raised the matter, in the form of a question in the Diet, during the previous session as to why the Karelians had not been invited by the Finnish Government to remain at that time. Owing to an oversight the question had not been replied to, but it had been repeated in the present session by a list of seventeen members, the previous question having only had the backing of ten. The Government had been able to justify themselves, but why had the question been raised now?

6. This led M. Enckell on to further remarks on the Karelian question. At the time of the Russian revolution it had been said that the new Russia trusted Finland and wished to realise the centuries-old Finnish dream of a greater Finland. A

---

[1] Tsar of Russia 1801-25.

proposed frontier was accordingly tentatively suggested which would include all-Finnish-speaking populations and would have moved the entire Finnish frontier many miles further east. The project was revived on the outbreak of the winter war, when Kuusinen was put forward as puppet President of Finland.[2] The Russians had hoped that the whole affair would be over in a couple of weeks, but when the war had become a serious reality, the project had been dropped. It had, however, been said in Communist circles that Greater Finland must come from the east and not from the west. There was surely some significance in the fact that Kuusinen had been retained as President of what was now called the Fenno-Karelian Republic, which had been erected into one of the sixteen constituent republics of the USSR. It was also significant that a large portrait of Kuusinen had been carried by the Communists in the May Day procession. It had always been the desire of Russia to incorporate the Northern Karelian territories and to reach out round the north of Scandinavia.

7. M. Enckell then went on to refer to the Russian demand for about 3,700 milliards of Finnmarks in payment, among other things of war material received by Finland from the Germans but not paid for. The Finnish Government had pointed out that, in view of the devastation caused by the Germans in Lapland, they did not consider that they owed the Germans anything, but the Russians would not consider this view and had demanded payment. Was it the intention of Russia, in spite of the Atlantic Charter, to upset the Finnish economy and to stage penetration from the east under the renewed leadership of Kuusinen, under cover of the resultant confusion and economic distress? In this connexion he had heard from Paris that influential international circles there had been given to understand that Fenno-Russian relations had deteriorated. During the May Day celebrations in Helsinki, some students had sung a ribald song while the procession was passing, and some irresponsible persons had thrown some kind of firework or smoke bomb from a roof among the crowd. The Russian Chargé d'Affaires had delivered a sharply worded protest completely out of proportion to the very minor incidents reported. He feared that M. Orlov was intriguing in Paris with the object of distracting the sympathy of the powers from Finland by suggesting that in spite of previous Russian acknowledgements the conduct of Finland was not, in fact, satisfactory. This in order to secure a peace treaty suited to Russian desires.

8. The consequence of all this was that Finland was obliged to strain every nerve to avoid giving Russia any occasion for interference in her affairs. M. Enckell lamented the fact that the entire existence of Finland as an independent nation had been coloured by fear of Russia. There had never been any doubt that Finland was in the Russian sphere of influence. It was true that before the war the Finnish position had been that, as an independent country, she would resist with her forces any attack from without. In 1938 the Russians had admitted that they trusted the Finns to defend themselves if attacked, but had said that they were not strong enough to do so successfully. They had requested permission to make arrangements to support Finland if necessary, and it was Finnish intransigence on this point which had led to the winter war. M. Enckell had no doubt that it was perfectly logical and inevitable that there should be some agreement with Russia

---

[2] Otto Kuusinen was leader of the January 1918 revolution in Finland which created the short-lived Finnish Socialist Workers' Republic. After its defeat he fled to Moscow and helped to form the Finnish Communist Party. He was declared head of the puppet Finnish Democratic Republic at the beginning of the Winter War in November 1939, and was subsequently Chairman of the Supreme Soviet of the Karelo-Finnish SSR from 1940 to 1956.

that in the case of attack from the west Russian forces would come to Finland's assistance.

9. M. Enckell said that he did not wish to have any secrets from me and he had therefore told me his views in confidence. I propose to comment on them in a later despatch.[3]

10. I am sending copies of this despatch to His Majesty's Minister at Stockholm and His Majesty's Chargé d'Affaires at Moscow.[4]

I have, etc.,
F.M. SHEPHERD

[3] No. 62.
[4] Warr commented that the key to the situation was an economic one. For the first year after the war it had been thought that Russia had been showing no particular interest in Finland and would allow her to restart her pre-war trade which was predominantly with the West. Latterly there had been signs that Russia was going to object to such trade and would require all Finnish exports for herself. Finland was apprehensive that such economic dependence on Russia would result in her being drawn into the Russian political orbit also. Hankey subsequently wrote to Shepherd to ask for his views about Finnish-Soviet economic relations (FO 371/56180, N6147/232/56). For Shepherd's reply see No. 68.

No. 61

Letter from Mr Thomas (Helsinki) to Mr Pickford (Ministry of Labour), 20 May 1946[1]
(FO 371/47399, N630/550/56)

Dear Pickford,

It occurs to me that it might be useful to let you have a few background impressions of Finland. I have had it in mind to do this for some little time, but I have waited until now in order that I should not be making any unduly hasty judgements. I think perhaps it is more appropriate to send this in the form of a letter than as a formal report, as it is intended to be not so much a report but rather a background against which other reports may be read.

The first impression one gets of Helsingfors, which is to a large extent typical of Finland, is one of general shabbiness. One is of course used to shabbiness in London, but the shabbiness here is of a different kind altogether and is probably enhanced by the gloom of the people. There is an air of despondency of which one cannot fail to be conscious: this is characteristic not only of the people but of the place.

The condition of the streets here during the winter was almost indescribable. It is natural to expect snow and ice, but one is entitled to expect too that some effort will be made to mitigate the worst effects. Here, however, roads and pavements were covered with a thick layer of ice throughout the winter and, apart from half-hearted attempts to throw sand down here and there, no effort was made to provide for personal safety. The result was that walking about was usually a real adventure: there was the greatest possible difficulty in keeping one's feet. Traffic skidded wildly, and hospitals and doctors had to deal with hundreds of broken limbs daily.

[1] Pickford forwarded a copy of this letter to Northern Department on 25 May 1946.

1946-1947

I am told that before the war conditions were very different: that the streets were kept reasonably clean and that it was possible to walk in complete safety.

Social customs I found rather bewildering at first. It is usual, as in some other countries, for men to raise their hats on meeting male acquaintances and to bow to females. This excessive politeness, however, is not indicative of a high standard of courtesy. The man who raises his hat to a male friend will a moment later unhesitatingly shove aside any person of either sex or any age who chances to obstruct his free passage. A little courtesy one misses is the holding open of doors for a person following. Anyone passing through a swing door here simply lets it go without a thought for any other person, and men never give way to women with whom they are not acquainted. When my wife slipped and fell in the street breaking her wrist, no-one offered to assist her although the accident occurred at a quite busy crossing, and several people actually walked past her while she lay on the ground.

The Finns are naturally a gloomy people, but one has the feeling that the gloom today is much deeper than normal and there seems to be little inclination to snap out of it. Typical of the general deterioration are the taxi cabs. Taxis are very few and far between and those that are running are in a really shocking condition. They are filthy inside and out; upholstery is torn, windows are frequently boarded up, and one often sees rope used to keep doors in position.

The Finns, or many of them, are filled with self-pity. They do not seem to be able to realise that, while their situation is bad, their country has not been a battlefield and they have had very little damage indeed except, of course, in Lapland, where there was wholesale burning by the retreating Germans after the armistice. There is practically no industrial damage at all. The Finns generally do not realise how they have escaped in comparison with many other countries, and that many countries on the allied side are in far worse shape than Finland. As far as I can gather Finland was never mobilised on anything like the scale with which we were familiar in war-time Britain. There was some direction of labour, but it seems to have been a punitive measure rather than an essential concomitant of total war. Direction always meant work at heavy and uncongenial tasks under direct supervision, and was used by employers as a threat to control recalcitrant workers.

Finland's most serious losses are the cession to Russia of Karelia, Petsamo and Porkkala, and the disruption of communications. The taking by the Russians of Porkkala has cut the main line between Helsingfors and Åbo, and now communication between these two towns has to follow a very circuitous route and takes roughly twice as long as formerly. In addition, the loss of Karelia has involved the loss of the Saimaa Canal which carried an enormous volume of timber traffic to the sea. The Finns are hoping that the Peace Treaty may give them the right to use the Saimaa Canal again and may also contain some concession regarding the railway through the Porkkala district.

One finds on all hands a tendency to look at the British as a counter to the Russians, and it is very curious that they seem to think that they have a right to demand help from Britain. I have on more than once occasion been told that the British should not have allowed the Russians to take places like Porkkala or to demand reparations from Finland. It frequently needs all one's tact to avoid being drawn into a discussion on these topics.

The Finnish press is, quite naturally, strongly pro-Russian, and even those organs of the press which represent the right wing point of view are never critical of the Soviet Union. This, however, does not in my judgement reflect popular opinion. The Finns do not like the Russians: they have never liked them, and this dislike has nothing to do with political ideology. At the present time this historical dislike is coupled with some degree of fear.

Housing conditions in Helsingfors are just deplorable. There is a regulation, which is very strictly enforced, by which a Finnish family is allowed one room only. People who have more than one room are forced to take homeless people into their houses on the basis of one family per room. The housing shortage in Helsingfors arises not only from the fact that there have been no building operations since the outbreak of the war, but also from the enormous influx of people who have been transferred from Karelia and Porkkala. I do not know the exact figure of evacuees from these two places but it certainly runs into many many thousands.

A further point worthy of mention is that the population of Helsingfors lives almost entirely in flats, the majority of which are centrally heated. In an effort to save wood, heating is limited and wood is rationed. The boilers for central heating are permitted to be fired up for two hours per day when the temperature is zero, and for a longer period in accordance with a sliding scale as the temperature falls. Hot water for baths, etc. is very rarely permitted. On the day I arrived here (22nd December) there was hot water. Since then there has been hot water on two occasions only. One may say that there are virtually no hot baths in Finland.

Rations are inadequate and of very poor quality. In general, the country people fare better than towns-people.

Finland is a country of substitutes. People eat and drink things that are just substitutes for something else. One of the things one misses here is a tea-shop. One cannot go into a shop in Finland and have a cup of tea or even a cup of coffee for that matter: all one would get would be a cup of coffee substitute without sugar or milk. Apart from the general inadequacy of the rations, there is no sort of guarantee that even the rationed quantities of goods would be available.

One of the most serious shortages in Helsingfors is milk. Before the armistice the great bulk of the milk supply of Helsingfors came from Porkkala, and to a lesser degree from Karelia. With these two territories in Russian hands, milk is no longer available from these sources. The result is that the milk ration is very small indeed and milkless days are frequent. March was the worst month, during which there were eighteen milkless days. Here again the position is accentuated by the great increase of population.

I remarked some time ago on the almost complete absence of cats in Helsingfors and I was told that the explanation was that they had all been eaten. One sees occasionally rabbits exposed for sale, and sometimes these 'rabbits' have long tails, but even so they are bought for food.

The black market of course is universal. Discussing this question with members of the Government and others I am told, quite rightly, that people could not live if it were not for the black market. The possible increase in rations which would result from the elimination of the black market is variously estimated at from 40 to 100 percent. The failure to eliminate or even control black market operations is explained by the fact that 60 percent of the population of Finland are engaged in agriculture, and it is notoriously difficult to control the distribution of produce from such a large number of individual farms. There is, of course, an element of truth in this but I still have the feeling that the Government have not made any serious effort to deal with this question. In particular, while it may be difficult to control farmers, there should be no difficulty in controlling imports: and it is a fact that there can be obtained on the black market all kinds of goods, such as coffee, tea, saccharine, and many other commodities which are not produced in Finland. I feel quite sure that if the Government were really in earnest in the matter, black market trading in imports could be reduced to a very considerable extent.

Clothing is in very short supply and the quality is poorer than anything I have ever seen or imagined. Here again substitutes are very much in evidence. Shoes have paper uppers and wooden soles: the so-called cloth is made largely of wood fibre: sheets, pillow cases, towels, are all made of paper. I do not know what the socks are made of, but it is probably wood. Clothing, of course, is rationed like other commodities, but the possession of a clothing ration card is not sufficient to enable one to purchase clothing. One must have in addition a licence, to obtain which it is necessary to prove need. Here again, however, the black market is rampant. I am told that it is possible to buy a very good suit for anything from Fmks 30,000 upwards. There are at present more goods appearing in the shop windows but they are still of poor quality. There has recently been a new issue of clothing coupons, but it is understood that the total number of coupons issued represents 50 per cent more goods than those actually available.

The Finnmark is grossly overvalued at 540 to the £1, and there are rumours of impending devaluation in relation to foreign currencies. At a Finnish-Swedish fair held recently in Helsingfors it was remarked that the prices being asked for goods were greatly in excess of those being charged for the same goods in other countries. An example is a Singer sewing machine, for which the price asked in Finnmarks was just seven times the Finnmark equivalent of the number of *kroner* required to purchase the same machine in Sweden.

There is considerable apprehension at the present time regarding the dangers of further inflation. Wage demands are increasing, and I am informed that there are now seventy such demands awaiting settlement. While the workers are agitating for higher wages, farmers are pursuing a campaign to secure higher prices. The Government is dependent on a liaison between Agrarians and Communists and, as one may well imagine, the Agrarians exact a pretty stiff price in return for their support. The Communists are playing a very curious game at the moment. Officially they are opposed to wage increases in view of the general economic situation, but in the country they seem to be behind a good deal of the agitation.

There seems to be a curious unwillingness to work. Hours in general here are 8 a.m. to 4 p.m. with 12 public holidays a year, and under a recent enactment 12 days holiday with pay annually with 18 days annually after five years' service with the same employer. The unwillingness to work seems to be due to a variety of causes: the knowledge that a large amount of production will go as reparations to Russia; a feeling (usually quite unjustified) that whatever is produced will be taken by the Russians, and a general war weariness.

There is no doubt that the only remedy for the present position lies in an increased availability of consumer goods. To furnish this there is a need for increased exports to finance the import of raw materials and finished articles. The Finns expressed the feeling of hopelessness twelve months ago when they said that production was limited to 60 per cent of capacity on account of the shortage of raw materials and, in particular, the shortage of coal. To compensate for the lack of coal, wood had to be used, and this very seriously curtailed the amount of wood available for export. To get coal and raw materials they must export wood; they could not do this because they had to use wood in place of coal, and thus they find themselves in a cleft stick. The position has, however, very greatly improved since then with foreign credits, etc. and supplies of coal and raw materials coming in steadily.

The division of labour between the sexes here is in some respects different from British custom. In addition to the usual tasks performed by women, it is also customary for women to be employed on quite heavy manual labour and on many jobs normally performed by men in Britain. For instance, snow shovelling, breaking up ice in the streets with pickaxes, general builder's labourers' work, house painting and decorating, gardening in public gardens, heavy portering and quite heavy goods delivery, heavy factory labouring and factory work involving a good deal of strength and stamina. At one factory where houses are being prefabricated I saw women engaged on a job which consisted of driving in 6" nails. I was told that women are always preferred to men on this kind of work as their output is higher.

Drunkenness is very prevalent, and I would venture the opinion that drink is a major social evil in Finland. The average Finn sees nothing reprehensible in intoxication: in fact he goes to a party with the expectation and intention of getting drunk. The tragedy is that so many young people habitually drink to excess. It is rather shocking to see numbers of boys and girls in their teens staggering along the streets in an advanced state of inebriation. This is even more disturbing by reason of the nature of the drink consumed. Very little beer is drunk—Finnish beer is not worth drinking anyway. It is the colour of light ale, but the resemblance to beer ends in the colour. It is almost tasteless, and I fancy that the only evil results that could accrue from excessive consumption would be disturbance in the stomach. Almost the only drink available is locally distilled spirit—wood alcohol—and in my opinion it is little better than poison. On the rare occasions when I have been unable to avoid *jalovinna*—so-called Finnish brandy, and the most popular drink—I have had the impression that my throat was being seared.

One rather pathetic feature of Finland, or at any rate of Helsingfors, is the disposition to 'dress up'. People seem to seize every possible opportunity to wear evening dress. No matter if there be very little to eat, and what there is be of poor quality or substitute, it pleases the Finn to sit down to it in a dress suit. Pathetic is the only word I know to describe this particular phenomenon. I suppose it is a form of escapism, but one could hope that there were a greater accent on the essentials and less regard for the trimmings. I have found the Finns most hospitable. Their food is poor and insufficient, but they are always ready and even anxious to show goodwill by sharing it with a stranger, observing the strict forms all the time.

Despite the pressure of war and post-war conditions, families of any standing still have domestic servants, and on visiting Finns one finds that there is still a parlour maid to assist with one's clothes, maids to wait at table and, I understand, cooks in the kitchen even though the table itself is very bare. They like to put on a sweet course for strangers but this is almost invariably porridge without sugar or milk. On the rare occasions when sugar is available, it is explained with great gusto and pride that it was obtained in the black market.

I have not encountered anywhere in Finland any of that sense of urgency with which we are familiar in Britain. So many people seem to be afflicted with a kind of fatalism accompanied by a tendency to expect Britain or America to help them out of their troubles. There is much talk in the press of the need for Finland to save itself, but this seems to find little echo in the hearts of the people.

You will gather from all this that the position is very interesting indeed. I would not like to venture a prediction of the course of events, but at a later date I will send you a further narrative on these lines.

Yours sincerely,
C.L. THOMAS

No. 62

Mr Shepherd (Helsinki) to Mr Bevin, 21 May 1946
No. 106 Confidential (FO 371/56180, N6750/232/56)

Sir,
In my despatch No. 94 of the 4th May I have had the honour to report the views of the Minister for Foreign Affairs on Russian policy towards Finland.[1] It will be remembered that M. Enckell appeared to have come to the conclusion that Soviet Russia intended, by means of reparations and other exactions, such as the demand for the payment to Soviet Russia of sums due to Germany for war material, to imperil the Finnish economy to a point where internal unrest would supervene and give to the Communists the opportunity of assuming control; and that Russia would use such a situation to engineer some kind of amalgamation of Finland proper with the Fenno-Karelian Republic with the object of incorporating the resultant area into the Soviet Union. M. Enckell's references to the happy results arising from the benevolent attitude of Russia under Alexander I at the time of the annexation of Finland as a Grand Duchy appear to be meant to point a contrast between Russian magnanimity in the earlier period and the friendship for Russia which arose as a result, and the anti-Soviet feeling which undoubtedly exists in Finland in consequence of the less generous behaviour of Soviet Russia since the armistice.

2. This is the first time that M. Enckell has permitted himself to give expression to criticism and fears of Soviet Russia, but I have the feeling that his remarks to me are not merely the result of the obvious differences which have arisen during recent months between the Soviet Union and Great Britain. His synthesis has rather the appearance of having been recently erected, and I am not altogether sure that they represent considered views or that they will not be modified in the future. However this may be, the course of recent events has certainly had the effect of crystallising to some extent the Finnish fears of Soviet Russia which have been hitherto, though deep enough, difficult to formulate during the tense period since 1944.

3. There are several factors which seem to have now led to a period in Finnish affairs which is characterised not so much by tension as by depression. The disappearance of Marshal Mannerheim from the presidency of the country has certainly had a strong psychological effect. The Marshal was undoubtedly a personification of Finnish independence, a rigid and unfailing symbol which has been conspicuous in Finnish affairs ever since the achievement of her independence. There is little doubt that his departure has signified for the Finnish people in general the removal of the greatest barrier to a possible overwhelming

---
[1] No. 60.

tide of Soviet influence in Finland. However respected and, indeed, venerated M. Paasikivi may be, he is not identified with the defence of Finnish independence against Soviet Russia in the same way as the Marshal. On the other hand, his own disappearance from the Cabinet, together with the departure of men like MM. Gartz, Kekkonen and Hillila,[2] has left a Government of which little is known and which gives the impression of being somewhat deficient in backbone. The new Government has had a very short time in which to show its paces, but it does, I think, give the impression of being more content than its predecessor to devote its attention somewhat submissively and predominantly to Fenno-Russian relations. The general effect of the resignation of Marshal Mannerheim and the formation of a new Government, therefore, has been to diminish to some extent the confidence of the country in the conduct of its struggle for continued independence.

4. This loss of tone has been to some extent increased by the visit of a powerful delegation to Moscow, and a feeling that the interest of Soviet Russia in the drafting of the peace treaty with Finland is so predominant that little is to be expected from the fact that Great Britain was also a signatory of the Armistice and will have a hand in the drafting of the treaty. It seems to be true that the delegation which went to Moscow in April left Helsinki with some trepidation as to what far-reaching demands might be made upon them. I have been given to understand, indeed, that it was the apprehension that demands of far-reaching importance would be made that led the Government to include in its delegation representatives of as many parties as possible, so that there should be the widest possible organ for consideration of those demands when they came. Although there was considerable relief that nothing dramatic emerged from the Moscow meeting, there was, nevertheless, great disappointment that Generalissimo Stalin categorically refused to consider any rectification of the frontiers, some modifications of which have always been hoped for by the Finns, although they have never had the slightest reason for thinking that their hopes would be fulfilled.

5. The Finnish capacity for distrust of Soviet Russia found expression in the suspicious way in which the public received the news that Moscow had abjured further deliveries on restitution account under article 14 of the Armistice, and they derived a certain morbid satisfaction in the announcement soon afterwards that the Russians were demanding payment for war materials supplied by Germany to an amount roughly equal to the relaxations under article 14. This blow, indeed, came at a time when there was (as, indeed, there still is) considerable fear of inflation. Costs of production have been increasing to such an extent that, according to the business community, the prices arranged in several barter agreements which the Finnish Government have made with different countries are no longer adequate to preserve a balance between receipts and deliveries, so that the barter agreements themselves are likely to be a heavy charge on the Finnish State, whether or not individual producers are called upon to bear a proportion of the loss. It has also been remarked that the currency circulation, which has been deliberately cut down by the Government by means of the calling-in of the note issued at the end of the year, has returned to almost exactly the same figure before the re-issue was made.

6. The demand for the resignation of the Governor of Nyland Province, on which I reported in my despatch No. 100 of the 14th May,[3] together with the removal of several of the senior officers in the Criminal Police, have suggested not

---

[2] Ministers of Trade and Industry, Justice and Supply respectively.
[3] Not printed.

so much a purge of pro-Fascist undesirable elements as the opening moves in a campaign on the part of the Communist Minister of the Interior[4] to increase his control over the internal affairs of the country. Nor has the sharp Russian reaction to the comparatively trivial incidents on May Day done anything to calm the general uneasiness.

7. I think that all these factors coming together have created a mood of pessimism of which M. Enckell's synthesis is an example. There is, I think, little doubt that Russian pressure through the Minister of the Interior is increasing, but I do not, at present, see any indications of a desire on the part of the Soviet Union to do anything more than consolidate its gains in Finland so far as that can be done in legitimate ways.[5]

8. I am sending a copy of this despatch to His Majesty's Ambassador in Moscow and to His Majesty's Minister at Stockholm.

I have, etc.,
F.M. SHEPHERD

[4] Yrjö Leino.
[5] Northern Department did not find these views gave much cause for concern. Hankey observed: 'I am not sure there is much in this, but the Soviet authorities do seem to have turned the screw slightly' (FO 371/56180, N6750/232/56).

No. 63

Letter from Mr Hankey to Mr Jerram (Stockholm), 1 June 1946
Personal and Confidential (FO 371/56941, N6731/78/42)

[No salutation on this copy]
Many thanks for your two letters of 16th May about our policy to Sweden.[1] I am so sorry that you have been left with the feeling that you lacked guidance.

I do not think that there has been any real change in our policy to Sweden, but there have of course been 'nuances' as the general situation has changed.

Thus it has in the last six months become apparent that the Union of Soviet Socialist Republics instead of being our friend and ally as we should have hoped, is out to make difficulties for us everywhere. Perhaps this is why we tend to judge countries on the Soviet periphery a little bit more by their desire to be independent and to decide their relations with us for themselves and not in accordance with Soviet pressure, and are slightly less interested than we were in the purely local significance of their past attitude to the Germans. We shall take a much closer interest in Norway and Denmark than in Sweden because they are allies, are closer to us and of somewhat greater direct strategic importance. Thus our attitude to Sweden will still be cooler. However, while the last thing we want to do is to pep the Swedes up to take an anti-Soviet line, still less to expose them to any charge of ganging up with us against the USSR, we are definitely interested in promoting in Sweden a healthy intention to protect their own independence. A corollary to this

[1] Not printed. Jerram had sought guidance because he saw a contradiction between the policy of adopting a reserved attitude towards Sweden, on which he had been briefed before leaving London, and recent developments, including several ministerial visits, which appeared to him to imply that Sweden was now going to be treated with greater favour (FO371/56941, N6731/78/42).

is that we have, as you know, now given permission for Sweden to be treated so far as the supply of confidential service equipment is concerned, on the same footing as Norway and Denmark. Moreover we have abandoned the idea of trying to get the Swedes to extirpate pro-Germans from their armed forces. (I am afraid the minutes of the discussions on this were not at all enlightening. We sent you pretty well all there was in our despatch about it.)

At the same time we are quite glad that contacts should be resumed between British and Swedes because it will show the Swedes how particularly inappropriate is the prevailing communist propaganda designation 'Reactionary' as applied to post-war Britain. Therefore we do not discourage intending visitors to Sweden such as the Minister of Agriculture[2] and others. Incidentally, as you will now have heard, the Lord Chancellor[3] is not going to Sweden after all.

I do not think, though, that any very great political significance should be attached to the stream of visitors. It is really quite spontaneous and we have in any case not much control over it. Most of them go to Sweden on some excuse for a holiday in a country not racked by war or else for some specific technical purpose such as the study of Swedish hospitals etc. Their simultaneous arrival just now is no doubt partly explained by the fact that they prefer for obvious reasons to go to Sweden in the spring and summer rather than the winter; and people are now able to travel for the first time for six years. I think 'soup-ticket brigade' is no bad description. We shall not cut down this innocent traffic to please the Russians. Let them send some Russians to see what other countries look like!

I hope the foregoing will explain the situation to you, but if it is still not clear, please do not hesitate to let me know.

Yours ever,
R.M.A. HANKEY

[2] Tom Williams.
[3] Lord Jowitt.

No. 64

Minute from Mr Bevin to Mr Attlee, 12 June 1946
(FO 371/56294, N7364/539/30)

Prime Minister

As you will see from the attached telegram,[1] the Norwegian Minister of Defence[2] and the Minister of Finance[3] are coming to this country on about the 24th June to conclude the discussions, which have been in progress for many months with our Service Departments, about the provision of British equipment for the Norwegian Armed Forces and the supply of a Norwegian contingent to assist in the occupation of Germany.

2. I would have liked to see the Ministers of Defence and Finance myself at a preliminary meeting before the technical discussions start. But, as you know, I shall almost certainly be away at the time, and I am therefore writing to ask

[1] Oslo telegram No. 268 of 5 June (FO371/56294, N7364/539/30).
[2] Jens Chr. Hauge.
[3] Erik Brofoss.

whether, as Minister of Defence, you yourself would be prepared to meet them instead. If, as I greatly hope, you felt able to do so, I would arrange for you to be sent a brief note on the position for your guidance during the interview. I would only like to say now that I attach importance to the maintenance of a link between the Norwegian Armed Forces and our own, and consider that the supply of British equipment to them would be very valuable from this point of view. It is also important, if only because of the manpower situation in Germany, that the Norwegians should send a contingent there as soon as possible. The Norwegians are unwilling at present to send more than 4,000 men, whereas we need a whole division, and there are also financial and other difficulties which will be explained in the brief which will reach you very shortly.

3. Another reason why it would be a good thing if you could spare the time to see these two Norwegian Ministers, is that it is the first time since Lie left the Norwegian Government that Norwegian Ministers have been over here and we are told on all hands that Norway, including the present Government, is completely preoccupied with its own affairs and out of touch with the foreign affairs situation. I am sure you could do much to let in some badly needed daylight.[4]

ERNEST BEVIN

[4] Attlee replied on 12 June: 'I agree.' The Norwegian delegation came earlier than initially planned, and met Attlee on 21 June. He subsequently entertained them at Chequers on 23 June. Full records of this meeting are in PREM 8/297 and FO 371/56295, N8081/539/30. A shorter account is contained in telegram No. 372 of 25 June to Oslo (FO 371/56294, N7845/539/30). A compromise agreement was reached, which involved a Norwegian commitment to send 4,000 troops to Germany for two years, and to pay a capitation rate to cover most expenses (including hiring charges for certain British equipment), the details of which remained to be worked out. A price of £6,600,000 was also agreed for the Norwegian purchase of British equipment for all three armed services.

No. 65

Mr Randall (Copenhagen) to Mr Bevin, 24 June 1946
No. 264 Confidential (FO 371/56108, N8277/62/15)

Sir,

It may seem a little hazardous to attempt to assess Denmark's present relations with Soviet Russia at a moment when, after one or two abortive beginnings, a large and important Danish delegation is in Moscow engaged in discussions regarding mutual trade, and possibly other aspects of Russo-Danish relations which have so far not been revealed. So far, however, there seems no reason to think that political questions have been raised or that Denmark's fundamental position will be modified, so that a sketch of the background against which the negotiations are being carried out may be of some interest.

2. Between 1914 and 1939 Russia was not a primary element in Danish foreign policy. In contrast to the position in the Napoleonic wars the Baltic was not in 1914 regarded as of vital positive importance to either group of belligerents, and Denmark's action, under German pressure, in mining the Little and Great Belts and the Sound merely met with sympathetic understanding on the part of Great Britain and Russian acquiescence. Denmark was allowed to bar a junction between the western and eastern Allies and otherwise pursue a neutral policy to her profit.

Thereafter came the Bolshevik revolution and the prolonged exclusion of Russia from effective participation in European affairs. The first, with the German revolution, had a decided influence on Danish domestic politics; it strongly stimulated the movement for social reform—the eight hour day was legalised in 1919—and a Social Democratic Government—with small but essential Radical support—took the place of the Venstre or Agrarian Government (the same party as in power at present) which, it is interesting to note, in 1923 concluded a commercial treaty in spite of its Conservative supporters.

3. By the time the Socialist-Radical Government under M. Stauning had started its long reign in 1929 Dano-Russian relations had settled down into uneventful normality. Danish economy was bound up to a very great extent with the United Kingdom; this was not challenged from the East which, indeed, was to prove a serious rival to Denmark as an agricultural exporter; but it was challenged increasingly from Germany, who, after the Ottawa Agreements, stepped in as a taker of Danish products and pushed her way into the Danish market which British industry had so largely dominated. Meanwhile, politically, Denmark pursued a 'League policy', favoured Russian claims to equality with the West, and generally took the same line as countries whose Socialist Parties adhered to the Second International, that is, marked friendliness to Moscow in foreign policy, firm opposition to Communist infiltration into the trades unions. In the late thirties this infiltration had begun to make its presence felt, particularly in the Seamen's Union, but the Communist Party was at no time in a position to challenge Social Democratic predominance in Parliament or trade union organisation generally. Correct diplomatic relations between Moscow and Copenhagen were able to persist alongside the freest criticism of Russia in the Danish press—a contrast to the reticence which later came to be shown in regard to German National Socialism. There is no doubt that the great bulk of the Danish nation after 1933 detested both the German and the Russian political systems, but felt obliged to pay more attention to the nearer danger as well as to the increasingly important German market.

4. To this precarious but not altogether unprofitable state of equilibrium the Russo-German Pact of August 1939 came as a severe shock. The comfortable international home in which Denmark had lived as a modest but honoured member had been practically wrecked when Germany left the League, but now the balance between East and West on which she had come to base her security was shattered also; moreover, her defensive forces had been reduced to a negligible quantity, and she had no common policy with the other northern nations.

5. To continue the story would be to re-tell the tale of Danish politics under the German occupation. The Danish Communists in 1939 followed the Moscow directive; for them the western Allies were merely engaged in an 'imperialist war'. A more reserved attitude was taken up when Germany invaded Denmark, but, as a rejoinder to the Communist taunt against the Socialist Government who failed to resist the invader, the latter party can still find some choice quotations of Russian-inspired Communist attacks on the western Allies, even after April 1940, which are difficult to explain away. With the German invasion of Russia the Communist line, as everywhere, was shifted overnight, and individual Communists later played a brave and successful part in the underground and Resistance movements. Their party had been suppressed, the Government of M. Scavenius had adhered to the anti-Comintern Pact, and a small volunteer corps, 'Frikorps Danmark', had been permitted to serve on the German eastern front. It was a weak policy, but Denmark

is for geographical and other reasons perhaps the weakest nation, materially speaking, in Europe. The more vigorous spirits, therefore, bided their time and prepared for resistance at an opportune moment. Their policy, their direction and their material support were from the first sought and obtained from the western Allies, mainly British. Russia was too heavily engaged, or otherwise not in a position to furnish the instruments by which the small but skilful and disciplined Danish Resistance movement gave, at critical moments, valuable service to the western Allies, so redeeming the honour of their country, and justifying its eventual inclusion among the Allied nations.

6. Resistance was not dominated by any one political party; its members cooperated on the pure basis of patriotism, and bound themselves to a spirit of comradeliness which still persists. Possibly for this reason Resistance was at first regarded with some coolness by the Russians; it did not, in any case, come under strong Communist influence as in other countries, and has never developed as a united party. Contact with Moscow, which was maintained through the Russian Ambassador in Stockholm, produced occasional Russian criticisms of the 'old politicians', even those who had been opposed to Denmark's adherence to the Anti-Comintern Pact. When Germany's complete defeat was near Russian approval was sought and obtained for a 'shadow Government', half of whom were 'old politicians', on the understanding that the other half of the posts should be held by resistance nominees. It was thus that the Communist Party, freed from its ban, was allowed two places in the first Government after liberation and that diplomatic relations were renewed with Moscow, the adherence to the Anti-Comintern Pact being regarded as abrogated. Although, by their spectacular entry into Denmark on the 4th May 1945, the British and Americans were regarded as the primary liberators, due tribute was paid by Denmark to the immense Russian share in the Allied triumph, and every effort was made to live down the unhappy reputation which the Danish Government during the war had gained in Moscow.

7. In the weeks and months that followed only two developments troubled Dano-Russian relations, the Russian occupation of the Danish island of Bornholm, from which the Russians expelled the German garrison after a heavy bombardment which rendered several hundreds of people homeless, and the presence of some quarter of a million German refugees whose return to the eastern zones the Russians refused to facilitate. The second problem persists, but eventually the first problem was overcome; the Russians on the 5th April 1946, left Bornholm with no other condition than that the Danes alone would take their place.[1] Their real motives are generally assumed in Denmark to be that they (*a*) had assured themselves that there was no strategic value in retaining the island; (*b*) wished to make a gesture in connexion with the widespread criticism of their action in Persia; (*c*) were reducing their military commitments at unnecessary points. The prolonged Russian occupation of Bornholm occasioned much official anxiety which every official effort was made to conceal. Sometimes this took a form for which the Danes privately apologised to me—namely, public comparison made

---

[1] In telegram No. 152 of 12 March, Randall reported a conversation with Rasmussen, who described a meeting with Vyshinsky in which he had pointed out that British troops had practically completed their withdrawal from Denmark and emphasised that Denmark was ready and able to assume control of Bornholm itself. The Soviet government later replied by asking the Danish government if they really would be ready to take over full responsibility and control without the slightest foreign support or intervention. Rasmussen provided this assurance (FO 371/56107, N3382/62/15).

even by Cabinet Ministers between the Russian occupation of Bornholm (known to be about 5,000 men) and the British 'occupation' of all Denmark (known to have been reduced to a few hundreds engaged on real tasks). This kind of make-believe, which deceived no one, continued until its only plausible justification—its success in convincing the Russians of the entire innocence of British designs and helping the decision to evacuate the island—was accomplished. The whole episode illustrated the Danes' fear that the Russians would permanently occupy their territory and, in any case, regard Denmark as being 'in Britain's pocket'.

8. In the first weeks after liberation Denmark felt that the realisation of the United Nations might protect them against the necessity for taking sides, but, as differences between the East and the West became wider and deeper, the more acute became their apprehension. I am convinced that a direction was given to the press to 'play down' any Danish connexion with the potential conflict between East and West. The fullest and often most sensational publicity was given to the polemics in London and Washington, but there was, for example, practically no notice of the report that Marshal Stalin had raised with you, Sir, the question of the Great Belt and the Sound;[2] equally little comment was made on the statement by Marshal Göring in his defence at Nuremberg that M. Molotov has sought Germany's agreement to a special arrangement over the Great Belt.

9. Now and then an unofficial speaker would express the unspoken fears of all thoughtful political observers. From the Swedish press was taken the watchword of Scandinavia as a 'no man's land', or 'political vacuum between East and West'. The phrase was used amongst others by the Socialist leader Hedtoft, who showed his sensitiveness as a Dane to the problem by opposing the idea of any resurrection of the Socialist International on the ground that Denmark could not afford to provoke Moscow. Later on, in May last, two articles by the *Observer's* diplomatic correspondent written after a tour of Scandinavia, which spoke of Denmark's grave embarrassment at realising that she held the key to the Baltic, were quoted by Copenhagen papers as bringing into the open a dilemma which Denmark had hitherto tried to banish from their minds.

10. Apart from an enquiry through the Danish Minister in London, the Danish Ministry for Foreign Affairs showed no perturbation over the report after Marshal Stalin's intervention mentioned above, and remained apparently quite content with the general brief confirmation which Count Reventlow received from the Foreign Office. Later on M. Rasmussen told me that he thought the Great Belt and Sound quite natural and unobjectionable, provided it had no conditions attached to it, in other words, was not coupled with a demand for bases. Their equanimity was not shared by all the Foreign Minister's colleagues, still less by Danish service chiefs. They gave the opinion, in private, that American demands on Iceland, the Americans' presence in Greenland, even the British hold on Heligoland, would eventually lead Denmark into trouble with Moscow, whose suspicions, as M. Rasmussen more than once told me during his negotiations over Bornholm, seemed to be unlimited. Apart from the Moscow wireless, which now and again prodded the Danes with accusations of tolerating Nazis or fostering reaction, the Danish Communist Party revealed itself as more and more the obedient

---

[2] The two busiest straits between the Baltic and the Kattegat. Stalin's approach to Bevin had also been the subject of an *aide-mémoire* to the US Secretary of State of 14 January 1946, asking the United States to consider how best to pursue a common line in any future discussion on the subject. For this document and subsequent British and American correspondence, see FRUS 1946, Vol. V, pp. 394-98.

mouthpiece of Moscow. It may here be noted that this development was of comparatively slow growth. At the liberation Danish Communists, such as the intellectual Professor Mogens Fog, showed themselves to be Danes first and Stalinist Communists afterwards. There was, in the Danish Communist press, a generous acknowledgement of the British contribution to victory, and Communist interest was concentrated on domestic policy. I met and spoke with a number of the Communist leaders in the weeks and months after the liberation and found them personally friendly and reasonable in their view of British interests. But this independence gradually changed. Reports began to appear—such as that the British intended to use the Danish volunteers to fight the Indonesians—which could only be designed to create anti-British prejudices in Danish minds. A member of the staff of the Communist organ *Land og Folk*, invited last month to London by the Foreign Office Information Department, confessed to my press attaché that he felt ashamed of the anti-British line taken by his paper. This guidance from Moscow was amusingly illustrated a little later when a leader in the same paper was completely contradicted two days afterwards after a line had been given by Moscow radio. There was no doubt, in fact, that the Danish Communist Party had become almost if not quite as much an agent in Russian foreign policy as Communist Parties elsewhere, and would oppose, for example, any marked rapprochement between the northern nations, or the latter and the West generally, as dictated by the Kremlin.

11. This is something with which British interests must reckon. M. Christmas Møller, Foreign Minister after the liberation, once told me that he did not think he would be accepted in Moscow as negotiator, as he was regarded as being too pro-British. He was proved right. The Danish Communist newspaper's attack on Dano-British commercial relations illustrated Russian resentment at what was regarded as the privileged British position in Danish foreign trade. This was an argument which appealed to many non-Communists. Thus even the English-educated and western-minded Minister for Special Affairs in the present Government, M. Per Federspiel, has argued against excessive commercial connexion between Denmark and the West, and probably the majority of the Danes concerned would genuinely like to see a large exchange of goods with Russia; some would not find unwelcome the opportunity of playing the United Kingdom off against Russia and *vice versa*, in the matter of prices. Most realise that the East cannot provide the secure long-term market for Danish agricultural exports that is offered by Great Britain, but as long as Germany is out of the running, Russia provides the only counter-weight, the only means of avoiding that putting of all the eggs in one basket which Danes regard as making their economy so precarious. This has a political counterpart. It is unnecessary to emphasise that after the liberation and particularly with the accession of the present Danish Government, traditionally partial to Danish interests in Slesvig, the latter issue has become dominant. In this, unfortunately, British administration in the British Zone is implicated, and there are many Danes who think that they might get a better hearing for their case if they interested the Russians in it. The possibility of even the Danish Government pursuing this in the near future cannot be excluded as I draft the present despatch, and it is unnecessary for me here to dwell on the political consequences of any serious and active Russian championship of the Danish nationalist cause. I fear there may later be opportunities for me to invite more attention to this subject.

12. To sum up, the complete eclipse of Germany as a factor in European politics, commerce and culture left a gap in the Danish mind. It took some time for

Danes to appreciate the fact that for some years at least Russian power would be able, or at least might attempt, to take Germany's place, or rather the place Hitler coveted. The older Danes were reluctant to face this; the Social Democrats' dream was of the revival of a largely German-dominated Second International; in default of this they preferred to look to the United Kingdom for leadership and a working alternative to the Russian form of communism. The younger people, and older men, too, among the intellectuals felt that more attention would have to be paid to the Russian language and Russian culture. Finally, the exporters, with all their pronounced anti-Communism in domestic politics, felt that Russia would prove a good secondary market and supplier of certain essential imports, and free them from a dependence on the West, especially the United Kingdom. All Danes, however, whatever their western sympathies, hope that somehow, by skill or luck, they will be able to escape making a choice between East and West. From all of this the practical moral to be drawn is, I think, that we should encourage and pay due regard to Danish independence, and avoid anything which may enable Russia, with some plausibility, to point to Denmark as a 'British dependency'. The more skilfully we do this, the more effectively shall we be able to co-operate with Denmark in promoting those western political and social ideas which are an essential part of the Danish way of life, and of which, in Europe, Great Britain is looked upon here as the only strong defender.[3]

13. I am sending copies of this despatch to His Majesty's representatives at Stockholm, Oslo, Moscow and Berlin.

I have, etc.,

A.W.G. RANDALL

[3] Hankey minuted on this despatch on 2 July: 'We will have to follow a policy of "softly catch monkey" if we are going to arrange any real defence link with Denmark.'

No. 66

Sir L. Collier (Oslo) to Mr Bevin, 1 July 1946
No. 220 (FO 371/56302, N8703/1345/30)

Sir,

With reference to my despatch No. 155 of May 14th last[1] and to previous correspondence regarding the attitude of the Norwegian Government and public towards questions of foreign policy, I have the honour to report that on June 20th last the Minister for Foreign Affairs delivered a speech to an 'association of northern youth leaders' (from Norway, Sweden, Denmark and Finland), in the course of which he declared that Norway had a co-operative and active part to play in international affairs and must fulfil her obligations—military, economic and social—to the United Nations, and that the Northern Countries as a whole, far from isolating themselves from the rest of the world, must play a similar part. 'We can seek—and we must seek with all our strength—to build a bridge between east and west: we must retain the trust of all parties and must not join any 'power *bloc*', but we must build our whole policy on loyal and active membership of the United Nations'. The speech formed the text for a leading article in the government organ *Arbeiderbladet* on June 22nd, which repeated the above sentiments in more

[1] Not printed.

emphatic language, declaring that 'the worst danger is that Europe may be divided into two *blocs*, a western and an eastern *bloc*.[1] If this should happen, Norway must hold herself outside both *blocs*. We must in that case adopt a mediatory and neutral attitude. The Northern countries must, as the Foreign Minister said, see it as their task to build a bridge between East and West'.

2. When I called on M. Lange in connexion with the proposed telecommunications conference in the United States, as reported in my telegram No. 298 of June 27th last,[1] I took the opportunity to ask His Excellency whether the leading article in *Arbeiderbladet* was to be regarded as an expression of Government policy, and observed that, since he had given me to understand on previous occasions that he was under no illusions as to the real aims of Soviet policy, I had not expected him to say anything which might be interpreted as encouraging Norwegian public opinion to think that the conflict between East and West was 'six of one and half a dozen of the other' and that it was possible for Norway to act as a neutral mediator: I quoted the Frenchman who in 1938 had said of Mr Chamberlain's efforts to mediate between Hitler and his intended victims that they were mediation *entre le loup et l'agneau* and enquired what other sort of mediation could be contemplated in the present situation. His Excellency, who took my remarks in very good part, declared that the leading article in *Arbeiderbladet* had been in no way inspired and that his speech had not been intended as a major political pronouncement: he intimated, indeed, that he had only said what a Norwegian representative was expected to say on these 'Nordic' occasions, and that he himself had little belief in the possibility of successful mediation between the Soviet Union and the Western Powers by Norway or by the northern countries as a whole. He agreed that, if the Paris Conference broke down, the Norwegian public would require to be educated in a different direction; and his only defence (which he did not make very strongly) was that it was too soon to take a different line and difficult to take no line at all when one had to say something on the topic.

3. This attitude is, I fear, typical of M. Lange. He is an attractive character of wider culture and greater personal integrity than his predecessor, and he impresses all who come into contact with him both by the extent of his knowledge of foreign affairs and the soundness of his judgements of them; but he is not a strong man in the political sense of the term, and I fear that he will never do much to counter the isolationist trends in public opinion. In the opinion, however, of competent observers, such as the Foreign Editor of *Morgenbladet*, the development of events is itself doing much to destroy belief in the possibility, if not the desirability, of isolation for Norway; and if His Majesty's Government were to decide to use all the evidence in their possession for a public exposure of Soviet aims and methods, the effect on Norwegian opinion might well be considerable, if not decisive.[2]

---

[2] The Foreign Office was not encouraged by Lange's speech. Hankey minuted: 'If this is going to be the attitude of the Norwegian Govt. and people, we are unlikely to succeed in making any defence link with them, other than the supply of arms.' Warner added: 'It is, I am afraid, inevitable and natural that the Scandinavian countries should take up a "natural" or "straddling" attitude in public. The most we can hope for is that they shd. not in practical affairs carry any appeasement of the Soviet Union so far as to become satellites—to the detriment of their own real interests in defence and economic matters, and of ours. But even in public speeches, spokesmen of small nations shd. not talk nonsense about "mediating" between great powers or "building bridges" between them. The Russians once (very properly) "bit" a Czech spokesman—I think it was M. Masaryk—for using such a fatuous expression' (FO 371/56302, N8703/1345/30).

4. I am sending copies of this despatch to His Majesty's Ministers at Copenhagen and Stockholm.

I have, etc.,

L. COLLIER

No. 67

Mr Jerram (Stockholm) to Sir O. Sargent, 4 July 1946
Top Secret (FO 371/56785, N9160/140/38)

Dear Sargent,

On the day I received your letter N7905/140/G of June 21st[1] I had marked the following passage in the leading article of a prominent Stockholm paper:

'The totalitarian parties have resuscitated the total lie, wherein the choice between truth and untruth is dictated solely in the light of political ends. If the lie seems more suitable it is used; it is accepted . . .[2] The democratic Swedish press, since the end of the war, has shown the greatest moderation in commenting on the great Powers' policy and their mutual relations. Insofar as criticism has been forthcoming it has been mild and discreet. An immense body of Swedish opinion probably feels anxiety regarding Soviet Russia's marked expansionist tendency, but observes moderation because it is hoped that good relations can be arranged between the Allied great Powers. The Communist press on the other hand is pursuing quite a different policy. It is unjustly and violently attacking the Western Powers, who are depicted as scoundrels and bandits with evil designs on the Soviet Union. Any one who fails unreservedly to acclaim Russia's policy is accused of Russophobia and incitement to war. It is difficult to imagine a more perfect form of mendacious sabotage. The Communist party is the only one of any importance which can justly be accused of conducting a policy of opportunism not only towards Russia but also Germany. As long as the Russo-German pact remained in force, from August 1939 to June 1941, Communism disassociated itself entirely from the national and democratic lines in Sweden's policy. When Germany occupied Norway the Western Powers were blamed by the Communist press, and the Norwegian people were urged to lay down their arms. Until June 1941 the world war was described as an imperialistic war; only after Germany's invasion of Russia was it converted into a war between Fascism and the forces of liberty.'

2. In Sweden the Communist menace is not immediately acute, and the picture presented in Warner's paper is fully recognised. Of the 'threats we have to guard against', detailed in para. 16 of the enclosure to your letter, (*a*), (*c*) and (*d*) do not apply here and (*f*) is already largely insured against by a number of factors ranging

---

[1] Not printed. The letter covered a memorandum by Warner entitled 'The Soviet campaign against this country and our response to it', printed in DBPO, Series I, Vol. VI, No. 88, which contained a series of recommendations for actions both in Britain and abroad, which had not yet been approved by Ministers. Sargent sought comments from certain selected missions (which included all five Nordic posts) so as to facilitate consideration of the policies which Warner suggested. The paper also marked the first stage in a process which led to the establishment of Information Research Department in 1948 (FO 371/56784, N7905/ 140/38G). For replies from Oslo and Helsinki see Nos. 69 and 70.

[2] Ellipsis in original.

from an identity of interests and political outlook to the personality of our Foreign Secretary.[3]

3. But first it will be useful to give a picture of the position in Sweden. Sweden is enjoying political and economic conditions that are as settled and favourable as anywhere in the world at the present time. She has, like Britain, a Social Democratic Government with a parliamentary majority, which has plenty of opportunities for making political deals (as it has done in the past) with the Agrarians, Liberals or even the Conservatives, without seeking aid from the Communist Party.

4. The Swedish Communist Party is in no way a rival to the Social Democratic Party. Its membership is less than 50,000 while that of the Social-Democratic Party is between four and five hundred thousand. In the *Riksdag* Lower Chamber (230 seats) the Communists have 15 and the Social Democratic Party 115. In the Upper Chamber (150 seats) the Communists have 2 seats and the Social Democratic Party 83 seats. In Sweden the Communist Party is playing the role of 'goader' to the Social Democratic Party and not that of challenger. There has never been a Communist member of a Swedish Government.

5. During the war the Swedish Communists succeeded in extending their influence partly by aggravating domestic grievances, e.g. the wage ceiling, and partly by reflecting the glory of Russian military victories. In particular they worked assiduously to increase their influence in the Trade Union Movement, more particularly in the Metal Workers Union, the largest and most powerful of the Swedish unions. Various circumstances, mostly of a purely domestic and internal character, gave them some success; and last year they were able to organise a big engineering strike in defiance of the union leaders. Since then, however, their ability to keep their position in the industrial field has been patchy. Competent trade union officials who have been travelling the country say that while in Stockholm, Gothenburg and Malmö, the Communists are possibly retaining their power, the same is not true of the provinces.

6. In these circumstances our field for a defensive-offensive anti-Communist campaign in Sweden would be rather narrow. There is no likelihood of a Communist Government being established in Sweden, and, while the Communists are possibly still in a position to cause some labour trouble, their efforts in this respect are counter-balanced by the industrial boom and demand for labour, which is putting the workers in a very strong position to get wage increases without employing the strike weapon or other extreme forms of industrial action.

7. To get back to the points in para. 16 of the enclosure to your letter, which arise for consideration in Sweden. These are:

(*b*) the weakening of the influence of elements friendly to us in this country,

(*e*) Soviet attempts to divide us from those who share our basic political conceptions and

(*f*) Soviet attempts to discredit us as weak and reactionary.

8. I do not think I can do better for a start than give the views of my Labour Attaché on these three points. So far as I have discussed the matter of your letter only with my Labour Attaché, who is by far the best informed member of my staff;

---

[3] These threats were: '(*a*) The establishment of communist governments in countries where a hostile influence threatens our vital interests,' (*c*) 'The creation of troubled conditions where we are responsible for or interested in peace and prosperity (including, of course, our own colonies and India),' (*d*) 'Soviet blocking of schemes for restoring settled conditions in countries outsider her own sphere,' (*f*) 'Soviet attempts to discredit us as weak and reactionary.'

no one else has seen it. (I cannot too strongly endorse the value attached by the Foreign Secretary to the appointment in these days of Labour Attachés, judging at any rate by my experience here.) Lamming, my Labour Attaché, writes in a minute to me:

'Under point (*b*) falls the question of Communist influence in the Trade Union movement. I have often heard complaints in this country (and in the other Scandinavian countries) that the British Trades Union Congress did far too little to build up close personal relations with the European Trade Union centres. My experience here suggests that it would be of the utmost value to us if no opportunity were missed in the future of strengthening the relations between the manual and non-manual workers' federations in Sweden on the one hand and the TUC on the other.

Under points (*e*) and (*f*) I think the advantage should be taken of the fact that Britain has a Labour Government to stress with unwearying repetition that Britain has a Social Democracy which can and does work., Admittedly this line is directed chiefly to those who are either Social Democrats or who support and sympathise with Social Democracy in Sweden. But they are relatively such a large number and the Social Democratic Party has such a dominating position in Swedish politics, that any arguments we can produce to demonstrate the success of reformist Labour in Britain will buttress up the big stabilising factor in Swedish politics as well. It cannot be forgotten that although the Communist Party is not in a position to challenge the Social Democratic Party for power in Sweden as in several other countries, it makes the Social Democratic Party its chief target of attack, just as it regards the Social Democratic Party ranks as its chief source of potential recruits.'

9. I do not know that, *mutatis mutandis*, the position would be very different if we had a Conservative Government in either or both of these countries. The whole question is principally one of moral support and countenance. Both countries seem likely for a long time to come to enjoy Governments of a moderate persuasion, and the countenance that could be given to Sweden by a Conservative Government at home, even if there were still a Social Democratic Government here, and the moral support afforded to an anti-Communist Sweden by the social and political success of such a Government need not, one would imagine, be less than that afforded by any other British Government of a non-Communist persuasion.

10. I should add that the Swedish Social Democratic Party has taken a very firm line, on the British model, against co-operation or amalgamation with the Communists.

11. The point that needs constant watching is (*e*) *viz.* Soviet attempts to divide us from those who share our basic political conceptions. Sweden as a whole in all her ranks and classes can be regarded in fact as sharing our basic political conceptions. But Sweden is very near the Soviet Union and Soviet wooing of her, both politically and economically, might easily be dictated by hostility to ourselves as well as in her own more immediate interests. We are watching in this connection the present negotiations for a commercial treaty between the two countries, though the dowry of the Swedish lass probably makes her less attractive than the maid of Denmark.

12. Of course the best insurance we have is to enrol Sweden in the UNO as soon as possible. She 'talks the same language' as we do and association with ourselves in UNO should give her just that moral support that might one day fail her if left too long alone in an area to which Russia might redirect her attention at any time.

As you know the Swedish Government has been authorised by a unanimous *Riksdag* to 'take the necessary measures for the affiliation of Sweden to the United Nations when it considers the time opportune'. We might well consider whether we can usefully do anything to hasten the opportune moment for Sweden's entry. The moral support Sweden might give us in UNO could well be valuable; and the moral support Sweden herself would derive from membership of a team might too prove of great value to ourselves.

Yours ever,
C.B. JERRAM

No. 68

Letter from Mr Shepherd (Helsinki) to Mr Hankey, 16 July 1946
(FO 371/56180, N6750/232/56)

Dear Hankey,
I apologise for taking so long over your letter (No. 6147/232/56) of 28th May about Fenno-Soviet economic relations.[1] I realise that the questions which you have under consideration go deep and I doubt whether, with the data at our disposal, we can do more than scratch the surface. However, I offer the following comments in the hope that they may assist you in piecing together one corner of your picture of the Soviet Union's economic intentions.

2. In the first place, political considerations clearly outweigh the economic in the Soviet approach to Finnish matters. The strategic stake which the Soviet Union has in Finland means political prudence in the face of the Finns' historic antagonism, and political prudence means reluctance to shove the Finnish economy around. To make the Finnish economy subservient to Russian needs under the fourth Five Year Plan would require a good deal of shoving, as the main Finnish and Soviet exportable surpluses naturally and normally compete with each other and are by no means complementary. Thus, Finland can hardly be expected to be as adaptable as, for example, Poland, whose textile manufactures correspond to a substantial Russian demand. My general view, therefore, is that any commitments of Finnish exports to the Soviet Union, such as would obviously be in excess of the latter's needs and which might seriously obstruct Western trade, would entail political repercussions here that, in their present mood, the Soviet authorities prefer to avoid.

3. As evidence of this comparative reasonableness, I quote the views that my Soviet colleague gave me the other day on the subject of German assets in Finland arising from the supply of arms and provisions during the war for which the Finns have not paid. These amount to some 3.7 milliard Finnmarks and their transfer to the Soviet Union might place the Finns in an awkward position if the Soviet Government insisted on the transfer taking place immediately. M. Orlov told me that this was a question on which the Soviet and Finnish economists must come to some agreement which would be capable of fulfilment. He admitted that fulfilment might be a matter of several years. He also admitted that two years was too short a time in which to expect any change of heart in Finland *vis-à-vis* Russia. If a change

---
[1] Not printed.

of heart is what the Russians really want, they will have to go about it in a very cautious and long-term manner.

4. The waiving of restitution deliveries coincided accidentally with the taking over of German assets. I do not think that there was any deliberate connection. As regards the new trade agreement, the Finnish authorities are satisfied that this is the best agreement that they have ever had and they do not anticipate that it will have any long-term effect upon the goods which Finland can export to the West and, in particular, to Great Britain. The goods supplied by the Soviet Union are confined to Finnish necessities; they do not even include such luxuries as radio parts which formed part of the Fenno-Dutch agreement. The Russian undertaking to supply 100,000 tons of cereals was not a gift, but was part of an exchange of which the values were equated. The prices are generally considered fair. The Finnish authorities anticipate that, after the cessation of reparation payments, their exports to the Soviet Union will be mainly in the nature of metal products, ships, etc.

5. I do not by all this mean to exclude completely any Russian desire to absorb Finnish economy, only that so far they have by their actions shown that they do not contemplate unilateral or immediate steps in that direction. There is however a definite feeling growing up in extreme left circles that Finland should and in any case will have to orientate her economy more and more towards the East, and this has led in the past to reluctance to re-establish too heavy trade commitments with the West. But circumstances have been too strong to prevent trade exchanges with Sweden, Denmark, France, Belgium, Holland, etc. and it will be up to us as well as these countries to keep this going against the tendency referred to above, which will certainly be backed by Russia.

6. You will have noticed the Reparations Agreement provides for quantities of manufactured goods which the Finns have never made, or never made on any scale, in the past. This means the building up of what are referred to here as 'Reparations Industries' and the Russians have made it clear that they realise this since the proportion of reparations to be paid in such goods is small at first and rises in later years when the new industries can be expected to get going. It was for these industries especially that Stalin has promised a continued market after the reparations period and indeed the Finns will be dependent almost certainly on Russia for an outlet if they are not to abandon them entirely. This seems to me to represent quite possibly the extent to which the Russians feel that they can get a long-term grip on Finnish economy in view of the non-complementary nature of Finnish and Russian products referred to in paragraph 2.[2]

Yours ever,
F.M. SHEPHERD

[2] Hankey observed to Warner that Shepherd's letter confirmed that the Soviet Government were pursuing the same moderate line in economic as in political matters—but that they were getting some strong cards in their hands (FO 371/56180, N9491/232/56). Northern Department continued to be concerned about signs which might indicate that Russia and the extreme left in Finland wanted to increase Finnish-Russian trade at the expense of trade with the West. See for example No. 74.

No. 69

Letter from Sir L. Collier (Oslo) to Sir O. Sargent, 26 July 1946
Top Secret and Personal (FO 371/56786, N9817/140/38)

Dear Sargent,

Your letter N7905/140/G of June 21st[1] was very welcome to me, since I had long been wondering what we were going to do to counter the Russian campaign against the British Government and everything British which is proceeding in Norway as everywhere else; and having discussed it with Wardrop, the First Secretary and Head of Chancery, Kit Kenney, the Press Attaché, and [. . .][2] who is in touch with 'C's' friends,[3] I can now give you our considered views on it.

In Norway, as you know, there is no immediate danger of the Government coming under Soviet control or direct Soviet influence. Relations between the Labour Government and Labour Party, on the one hand, and the local Communist party on the other, are bad and not improving; and if the Government should show signs of adopting a pro-Russian and anti-British attitude on any specific question, this will be due not to sympathy with Russian policy, but simply to fear of the consequences of incurring Russian displeasure. The only remedy for that, of course, is to convince them that such displeasure can safely be risked; and until we do that (and we can hardly do it at present) it would be worse than useless to attempt to put any pressure on them to alter the general lines of their policy. As my despatches will show, I have on occasion suggested to the Minister for Foreign Affairs that he and his colleagues should try to educate the public in the realities of the international situation or at least not mislead it by public utterance of studied 'neutrality' and woolly optimism; but I have had little success, though everyone with whom I talk professes to have no illusions as to the real position. As regards keeping a watch on Communist activities within the country, including those of the Soviet Embassy, the authorities need no encouraging. The Intelligence Service and the Police are aware of what is going on and [. . .][4] is in close touch with them. Moreover, we have bound the Norwegian government and the armed forces to our side, more closely than they perhaps realise, by the recent agreement for the supply of British military equipment. The question, therefore, is almost exclusively one of propaganda to the public.

Here there is certainly a great deal to be done. Although, as I have said, the Government and the Labour Party leadership are on bad terms with the Communist Party, the average Norwegian Labour voter is accustomed to collaboration with the Communists on local councils etc. and there is considerable Communist influence in some of the Trade Unions. The Labour press, moreover, particularly the Oslo paper *Arbeiderbladet,* which is the chief Government organ, is full of talk about friendship with Russia and of articles presenting Russian policy in the most favourable light possible, while British policy often comes in for criticism on the old 'anti-imperialist' grounds. The Labour voter, therefore has at present only a confused idea of the international issues now at stake, when he thinks of them at all

---

[1] Not printed. See No. 67, note 1.
[2] A phrase is here omitted.
[3] The phrase "'C''s friends" was a reference to SIS's contacts in Norway. For an account of SIS's activities in post-war Scandinavia, see Keith Jeffery, *MI6: The history of the Secret Intelligence Service 1909-49* (London: Bloomsbury, 2010), Chapter 20.
[4] A phrase is here omitted.

(which is probably not very often), and it is on him that we must concentrate: he represents the dominant force in the country and everyone to the Right of him is already anti-Communist, while the more educated classes, to judge from conversations with intellectual and commercial leaders and what is written in the non-Labour press, have now formed a fairly clear and accurate idea of Soviet policy and methods.

Detailed recommendations on the methods by which propaganda could reach the rank and file of the Labour party, and the Norwegian public in general, have been put forward in Kenney's last Quarterly report (a copy of which was enclosed in my letter to Warner of July 9th)[5] and in the reply to the request for comments on the proposed reorganisation of the Information Service which was given in my despatch No. 191 of December 27th, 1945;[5] and these methods would still be suitable if the content of the propaganda became more specifically anti-Russian, as proposed. As regards the content, however, I must make one recommendation which I consider of the greatest importance—and which, I find, is also emphasised by Kenney after quite independent consideration of the problem—*viz.* that we should concentrate on bringing home to the Norwegians, and still more on inducing friendly Norwegians to bring home to their own public, the *moral* issue involved in the present struggle against the domination of Europe and perhaps of the world by a Power which both preaches and practices the doctrine that the Soviet system is above morality, that, as the medieval Church proclaimed, 'faith need not be kept with heretics', and that a crime is not a crime if it advances the interests of Communism and the Soviet State. It is this, rather than the political or economic doctrines of Communism or the territorial and political claims of Russia, which is so repugnant to the average Norwegian, as it is to the average Englishman, and which has already caused the same revulsion of feeling among educated Left Wing sympathisers in Oslo as it has in London in such men as Bertrand Russell, Gollancz and Kingsley Martin; and there is every reason to believe, from what is known of the effect produced here by the similar German philosophy and methods in the first as well as in the second World War, that the reaction of the average Norwegian workman would be the same if he could once be convinced of the facts. If propaganda on these lines is combined with a positive policy of making Britain known to Norway, which would deal with the last item in paragraph 16 of Warner's memorandum, 'Soviet attempts to discredit us as weak and reactionary', it should stand as good a chance of effecting that definite orientation in our direction of the mass of Norwegian public opinion which is now lacking but is essential if Norway is to be of any use to us when the conflict in Europe really warms up. One of the best means of disseminating information about British conditions and ideals is of course the exchange of visits, particularly by Trade Union delegates etc; and, as Northern Department know, we have been trying to arrange a number of such visits. Our chief difficulty has been the lack of transport, since shipping services to and from Norway are expensive and usually booked up. It has been suggested that this difficulty might be overcome if the Admiralty would let us have one of the small ships which they are now selling for a song to avoid having to break up and which we could use (perhaps under the name of the Ambassador's barge) for carrying across the North Sea anyone who could be described as a guest of His Majesty's Government. This, of course, is not the place to go into the details of such a proposal, but I will supply these if I can be

---

[5] Not printed.

given any hope that the scheme might be thought worth discussing. (It may seem a little alarming at first sight; but the more I think of the position the more convinced I am that anything is worth considering which will enables more representatives of Norwegian working class opinion to visit Great Britain.)

What I recommend, therefore, is in essentials a campaign of information, showing both what the Russians are really doing and what we are really doing, to be conducted, not as a rule directly, but indirectly, by means of visits, of discreet 'whispering campaigns' and above all of press articles—not so much articles handed out to the press by the Embassy as articles in the British press which would be syndicated in some Norwegian papers and commented on in the others. Some such articles are already appearing, and it is for London to see to it that there are more of them and of a strong tone—and also to see to it that the London commentators are supplied with all the available material. (I mention this last point because I have seen a great deal of invaluable material in Foreign Office print, such as accounts of the horrifying conditions in Jugoslavia or Poland, for example, which has not yet been made public, although it could easily be dished out by the News Department in an impersonal form and would have a tremendous effect on public opinion if released. We can hardly expect Norwegians to speak out about conditions which the British Government largely conceals from its own public.)

I have said enough, I hope, to show that I am in entire agreement with the suggestions in Warner's paper as far as they are applicable to Norway, and to indicate how far they are applicable and how they could be put into practice. It seems hardly necessary to enter into further detail until the Cabinet have decided to adopt the proposed policy: if and when they do I could send Kit Kenney over to discuss ways and means, since in Norwegian conditions these would be almost entirely a matter for his section of the Embassy.[6]

Yours ever,
L. COLLIER

---

[6] Hankey agreed with all the proposals put forward by Collier—apart from his suggestion for an Ambassador's barge, which Hankey thought would probably be ruled out on the grounds of cost. He observed to Kirkpatrick that the penultimate paragraph highlighted a central theme: 'We are not educating our own people adequately.' Kirkpatrick agreed that the lack of proper publicity at home was hampering Britain's efforts (FO371/56786, N9817/140/38G).

No. 70

Letter from Mr Shepherd (Helsinki) to Sir O. Sargent, 30 July 1946
Top Secret and Confidential (FO 371/56786, N10077/140/38)

Dear Sargent,

I must apologise for the delay in replying to your Top Secret and personal letter of June 22nd (N7905/140/G).[1] A good deal of the time has been taken up in resisting the temptation to comment on the first part of Warner's paper rather than to confine myself, as I am now doing, to the limited comments and suggestions asked for in para. 2 of your letter. I think perhaps I may yield to the temptation to comment further later on since such comments can do no other harm than to waste

---

[1] Not printed. See No. 67, note 1.

a little time, while they may possibly contain some point of interest as coming from a Russian limitrophe country.

Before proceeding to comment on the methods to be adopted for an anti-communist campaign in this country, may I suggest that it would be ill-advised to initiate a campaign which would set out to expose communism as totalitarianism, as suggested in para. 18 of the paper. Presumably we, in England, are prepared to tolerate the propagation by legitimate means of communism as a political theory while we object strongly to the methods which are normally adopted by communists in furthering their aims. In other words, should we not be careful to emphasise that our campaign is directed against the totalitarian methods of communists rather than against the basic theory which they wish to spread?

So far as Finland is concerned, the passing, to a great extent, of the period of prostration which followed the armistice, together with the developments of disagreement between Russia and the West, has led to a situation where there is a growing feeling that, while friendship with Russia must be cultivated, servility should be avoided. This feeling has found expression in the Diet recently where objection to the development of communist police methods was expressed in the refusal of a special police supplementary vote for the Ministry of the Interior. At the same time there are signs that the Centre and Right Wing parties, which have naturally kept very much in the background since the Armistice, are beginning to feel that the time will shortly come when they will be able to resume some part in affairs. Simultaneously with all this, the extreme leftist press has definitely got into the habit not only of publishing extravagant adulation of the Soviet Union, but also of criticising the Western Powers on the lines made familiar from the Moscow press. It can therefore be said that the Finnish position is analogous to the general world position in that the gap between Russia and the West has reached a point where a decision should be taken whether or not we should actively support the renascent anti-communist movement.

We have in Finland hitherto taken the line, at first, during the war, of complete co-operation with the Russians, and later, of impressing upon the Finns that they must continue to cultivate close and friendly relations with Russia in their own national interests. It is clear that this latter line must continue and we must therefore, whatever action we decide to take, make a distinction between exposing totalitarian communistic methods and advocating hostility to Russia. That the Finns themselves are quite aware of their delicate position is illustrated by the recent vacillation of the Social Democratic Party which, at its Congress, refused to co-operate with the Communists and, a few weeks afterwards, reversed this decision and invited the Communist Party to co-operate on social though not in political maters.

The way is open for us to encourage the Finns to proceed with the development of their own sturdy democracy and to avoid becoming tainted with the totalitarian methods which the Communists would like to introduce. I have, indeed, already for some time past adopted this attitude and have told the Finns who suggest that they are at the mercy of the Communists that, so long as they are true to their own form of democracy which has been so successful during the period of independence as well as before, they will be in a position to preserve their independence. One method of carrying out the policy referred to in the Foreign Office paper would accordingly be to intensify this movement towards confirming the Finns in confidence in their own form of democracy and in encouraging them to defend it. This method is probably the best which can be adopted in the press because it can give very little offence to the Russians while the Finns themselves would be able to pursue such a campaign without allowing themselves to be overwhelmed by their endemic fear of Russia. We shall have to be careful, however, to avoid encouraging those circles which are tainted with Fascism so far as to engender a danger of a strong swing to the Right.

As regards para. 19 of the FO paper, the difficulty in attacking and exposing in Finland the myths which the Soviet Government are trying to create in justification of their policy lies in that fear of Russia to which I have just alluded. It is possible that this fear may dissipate after the Peace Treaty, to a certain limited extent, but it would be unwise to immediately exploit a state of peace by a series of anti-Soviet articles, even if the Finns could find the courage and the authorities would allot the paper. Here again, I agree that steps should be taken to expose these myths but that can best be done verbally. I could, in conjunction with members of my staff, work out a programme to be adopted to this end. This programme would, of course, include positive propaganda about the true situation in the British Empire, which the Russians so persistently misrepresent and this aspect of the campaign, together with the activities of the British Council, could obviously be publicised in print.

Whatever methods are taken to counter Soviet propaganda and communist methods in Finland, will have to be adjusted to the varying local situation in such a manner that the Soviet Government is not given an opportunity of complaining about Finnish hostility to Russia and, as noted above, it will always be necessary for us to insist that the Finnish policy must be one of friendship to Soviet Russia while we support Finland in resistance to undesirable Soviet propaganda and infiltration.

Fortunately circumstances have obliged the Russians to connive at barter trade agreements with Western countries, if only to secure a continuation of Finnish economy and the payment of reparations. The West has in consequence already a certain vested interest in Finland, so that opposition to too decided a trade orientation towards Russia is likely to be strong.[2]

Yours sincerely,
F.M SHEPHERD

---

[2] Hankey commented: 'This is a wise letter. We must not make the Finns think we can help them if, by opposing Soviet wishes too obstinately, they get themselves into trouble.' Warner thought that Shepherd's paragraph 2 raised a general point which should be noted for discussion by the Russia Committee. Kirkpatrick disagreed, asserting that Britain should object to the totalitarian character of Communism, because experience showed that such a character was wicked, corrupting and eventually aggressive. 'But I imagine that the Finns know more about the character of Soviet Russia than we do, and so I am disposed to agree with the general thesis that we should direct our efforts towards explaining ourselves'. Warner's proposal was therefore dropped (FO 371/56786, N10077/140/38G). The Russia Committee had been established in April 1946 following a recommendation from Frank Roberts, the Minister in Moscow, that a group should be created within the Foreign Office to study Soviet activities and to co-ordinate a global response. See DBPO, Series I, Vol. VI, No. 82.

No. 71

Minute from Mr Warr to Mr Hankey, 27 September 1946
(FO 371/56089, N12283/3/15)

The Danes show signs of being quite intolerable over this question.[1] It is particularly monstrous that, having a much closer interest in Germany than Norway has, they should appear to be unwilling to send any troops to Germany, whereas the Norwegians are sending 4,000.[2]

The Danes give as their chief excuse the continued presence of the German refugees in Denmark.[3] The position is that of the original 200,000, there has been agreement in Berlin to receive into the different zones a total of just under 40,000. Of this 40,000, we are taking between 9,000 and 10,000 in our zone (i.e. those who previously lived there). The other zones are also taking at least a proportion of those who lived there up to a total of 30,000. The fate of the remaining 160,000 is in complete abeyance. Apparently, so Mr Crawford, Control Office, tells me, the Russians in Berlin have shown complete ignorance of Stalin's 'offer' to take 100,000 in the Russian zone provided the other zones received between them the remaining half, and have stolidly refused to act on the basis of it. I suggested that we might take up the question in Moscow. Mr Crawford replied that this would be useless, because whatever happened the authorities of our zone refused to receive more than the 10,000 for the moment: and the Americans could not take any more either. In any case the problem of German refugees returning to Germany would have to be considered as a whole (there were for instance some Germans in Yougoslavia whom the Yougoslav Government were anxious to get rid of) and however strong the Danish case might be (and is) it could not be considered in isolation. The upshot is that the problem is in abeyance till next spring and that the Danes have got to keep 160,000 refugees throughout the winter.

---

[1] Rose, Chargé d'Affaires in Copenhagen, had reported in a despatch of 24 September that Hvass had informed him that, although no final decision had been taken, he thought that the Danish government would conclude that they would be unable to supply any contingent until the German refugees had been removed from Denmark (FO 371/56089, N12283/3/15).

[2] The Danish government had attempted to draw a parallel with the size and provision of the Norwegian contingent as early as May 1946. See, for example, Randall's despatch of 6 May 1946. Northern Department made clear at that time that it did not consider that this example was analogous (FO 371/56086, N6056/3/15).

[3] Rasmussen had sounded out Randall as early as December 1945 about whether a Danish division was still required for the occupation of Germany. He had cited potential costs and hinted at parliamentary difficulties as potential problems. During a subsequent conversation shortly afterwards, he had explained that there would also be unforeseen demands on Danish manpower to guard German refugees and also, perhaps, for a possible Danish garrison on Bornholm. Randall commented that these explanations seemed lame and he felt that Rasmussen was conscious of the fact (telegram No. 156 of 31 December 1945, FO 371/56086, N3/3/15).

So we can't help the Danes over their refugees for the moment. But we can I think try and bully them a bit over their unsatisfactory attitude over the contingent. Mr Randall returns early next week and I suggest we should instruct him by tel. to reinforce Mr Rose's arguments and in particular to say that Denmark appears to be unwilling, although she has a greater interest in Germany than Norway, to do even as much as Norway about providing a contingent.

?tel. on the above lines to Copenhagen.[4]

G.C. WARR

[4] Rose's despatch of 24 September was discussed with Randall, who was visiting London. It was agreed that on his return he would urge the Danish government to send a technical delegation to London as soon as possible (FO371/56089, N12475/3/15).

No. 72

Speech by Mr Bevin at the Plenary Session of the Paris Peace Conference, 14 October 1946
(FO 371/56189, N13133/303/56)

The draft peace treaty with Finland has been agreed by the commissions concerned and is now submitted to the plenary session of the conference.

When the armistice with Finland was concluded by the Soviet Government, British Government and Finnish Government on the 19th September 1944, it was intended that the eventual peace treaty should reproduce, broadly speaking, those terms of the armistice which were not of a transient character. This has been done. In general I think my Soviet colleague would agree with me that the Finnish Government has loyally fulfilled the terms of the armistice and that they are carrying out satisfactorily those of their obligations which still remain in force. I hope and believe that when this treaty is signed Finland can look forward to better times though the tasks of reconstruction are, I know, imposing many hardships and difficulties.

Finland will resume her independence as a sovereign State and we look forward to taking up our former relations of friendship and confidence very much where we left off. It is a source of satisfaction to the British people to see again a free, vigorous and truly democratic Finland whose progressive and enlightened policy and institutions before the war aroused keen admiration in my country as elsewhere in the world. Now that the errors of the war are behind us my Government will be glad to welcome Finland back into the comity of peace-loving nations of which I feel sure she will again be a widely respected member.

With the conclusion of this last of the five peace treaties I may perhaps be permitted to say two words on the work accomplished by the conference as a whole. What did this Paris Peace Conference set out to do? In our preoccupation with the particular subjects which have filled our debates we may have lost sight of the general aims of this gathering. There have been three or four subjects which have taken up long hours and much discussion. Attention has naturally been focused on them, but we should also remember the constructive side of our work. Remember that this conference assembled with the object of considering the drafts of the five treaties laid before it by the Council of Foreign Ministers and of sending back the drafts with its recommendations to the Council. The conference has accomplished this task and accomplished it well. The difficult and often contentious problems raised by the treaties have been debated and sifted. The views of all including the ex-enemies have been patiently heard and duly weighed.

We now look forward to the final drafting of the treaties in New York. We shall be fortified in our work if we recall the successful as well as the difficult in the work already done. I can only hope that our work may lead to lasting peace and economic recovery and that at last the people may feel that they live and move and have their being in absolute security.

No. 73

Minute from Sir O. Sargent to FO Heads of Department, 11 November 1946
Strictly Confidential (FO 371/56705, N14905/14905/G)

The Minister of State and Parliamentary Under-Secretary are in constant personal contact with Mr D. Healey, Head of the Foreign Department of the Labour Party.

2. Mr Healey would be glad to receive, on a confidential basis, any information about foreign affairs which Mr McNeil and Mr Mayhew care to put at his disposal, and the Secretary of State is anxious that Mr Healey should be kept as well informed as possible.

3. Heads of Department should pass to Mr Heppel, for Mr Mayhew's consideration, any papers which they think could usefully be shown to Mr Healey, whether papers for his general background information on the international situation or papers on current questions of importance—particularly, of course, those which are exciting public attention. Information from secret sources would not be suitable for this purpose; apart from this, papers otherwise suitable for showing to Mr Healey need not be ruled out because of the sources of information contained therein; but if the papers are for any reason of especially confidential nature, attention should be drawn to this in passing them to Mr Heppel, in order that, if Mr Mayhew decides to show the papers to Mr Healey, he may draw his attention to the point.

4. There frequently arise matters in which the Labour Party's Central Office can assist the Foreign Office, e.g. in arranging suitable contacts among the Labour Party for foreign representatives here or foreign visitors of importance, arranging for action to be taken by the Labour Party with their contacts in Socialist Parties abroad, etc. In many cases Mr Healey will be the right person to approach and such matters should be brought to Mr Mayhew's attention.

5. This matter should be treated as strictly confidential and must not be mentioned to persons outside the FO.[1]

O.G. SARGENT

[1] The minute was drafted by Warner. Both the Foreign Office and the Labour Party gained from the closeness of the relationship which Bevin encouraged by this means. For example, Healey visited Oslo in October 1947 at the instigation of Kenney, who wished to counteract the influence of a visit by Konni Zilliacus, a left-wing Labour MP who had been very critical of Bevin (Wardrop despatch, 22 November 1947, FO 371/66061, N13645/4718/30). Separately, the Foreign Office asked Mallet, Ambassador in Rome, to make arrangements to look after Phillips and Healey during a visit they were making to assist with the strengthening of the moderate wing of the Italian Socialist Movement (FO tel. No. 599 of 11 March to Rome, FO 800/494). Such assistance was sought on a number of occasions when senior Labour Party officials were travelling in Europe on similar business.

No. 74

Mr Shepherd (Helsinki) to Mr Attlee,[1] **12 November 1946**
No. 272 Confidential (FO 371/56181, N14796/232/56)

Russian desire to integrate Finnish economy with the Soviet Union

Sir,
In his letter to me of 17th October[2] Mr Hankey adverted to a point which has on several occasions been referred to in communications from this legation, namely, the desire evinced by Soviet Russia and by the extreme Left in Finland to increase Fenno-Soviet trade at the expense of commerce with the Western Powers, and the special position of Finnish industries, which have had to be developed exclusively for reparations purposes.

2. There is no reason to doubt that Soviet Russia would like to integrate Finnish economy to the greatest possible extent with that of the Soviet Union, and that this desire is shared at least by the Communist party in this country. It has never been adopted as an official policy of the Government, and any attempt to do so would certainly arouse a storm of protest. All the political parties as far leftward as the Social Democratic Party are jealous of the preservation of the freedom of trade and have every objection to Soviet economic domination. The Social Unity party has so far acquiesced in this attitude, but I have some doubts whether they would find themselves strong enough to resist Russian pressure to expand and go on expanding trade with the Soviet Union at the expense of the West. The extreme Left press, in the direction of which the Social Unity Party are supposed to have a share, loses no opportunity of airing the Communist line that too much dependence on trade with the West would submit Finnish economy to participation in the dangers of crisis and inflation, which are said to afflict Western countries but not the Soviet Union.

3. The Russian campaign in the same direction has three phases:
(*a*) The design of reparations payments.
(*b*) The conclusion of a series of barter agreements which assure to the Finns commodities, such as foodstuffs, which they find the greatest difficulty in obtaining elsewhere at present. These agreements will, in the aggregate, provide a formidable weapon for those who wish to paint the Soviet Union as the benefactor and natural supplier of Finland in times of stress.
(*c*) The preservation in Finland of German assets. Nothing has been done about these yet, and it may, of course, be doing the Russians an injustice to suggest that they propose to use this debt as a hold over the Finns, but the fact remains that any attempt to force the Finns to transfer the value of these assets in any manner whatever would have a disastrous effect on Finnish economy.

4. As regards the design of Finnish reparations deliveries, the essential particulars have already been supplied from this legation. The commercial coun-

---

[1] The Prime Minister was in charge of the Foreign Office in Bevin's absence.
[2] Not printed. Hankey's letter crossed with a letter of 15 October from Chancery Helsinki, which reported some further points of concern—in particular, that Russia was bringing pressure to bear on the Finns not to sell timber to Britain, using the argument that Britain could not export the primary need of the Finns, which was coal which Russia could provide (FO371/56181, N13378/232/56). Shepherd's conversation with the Governor of the Bank of Finland, reported in paragraph 6 below, may have provided some reassurance on this point. Barclay, Northern Department, observed that there were some hopeful signs here that Finland would not become economically bound to Russia.

sellor has now completed a memorandum on this subject, which is transmitted herewith.[3] It seems to me to cover the ground admirably, and I would not attempt to propose to summarise it here. It will be noted that the value in gold dollars at 1938 prices, plus 10 per cent or 15 per cent as the case may be, of annual deliveries from specially developed reparations industries amount to 14 million dollars. The dollar value of Finnish exports in 1938 was $187 million. Allowing for a reduction of 15 percent in Finland's total industrial capacity due to the cession of territory to Russia, total export capacity may be placed at about $160 million at the same price level, so that reparations industries would involve less than 10 per cent of the Finnish export potential. M. Stalin has on more than one occasion assured Finnish representatives that, after reparations have been paid, Soviet Russia will continue to provide a market for the products of these industries.

5. It is, I think, relevant in this connexion to consider the direction of Finnish trade during the latest period when commerce with Russia was a practical possibility. After the declaration of Finnish independence in 1918 and the emergence of the Soviet Government, trade between Finland and Russia practically ceased, and it is therefore necessary to go back to the period before 1918, when Finland was an autonomous Grand Duchy forming part of the Russian Empire. The commercial secretariat has prepared a memorandum with graphs on Fenno-Russian trade for the years 1900-1920, which I transmit herewith and which I think is of interest in showing what was then possible in the normal development of trade between the two countries.[3] It is, of course, true that present and past conditions do not correspond and that the main development of the Finnish woodworking industries and agriculture took place after independence, while Russian industry has also been developed. Since Finland and Russia are contiguous States, however, some natural development of trade between them is to be expected quite apart from any more or less sinister politico-economic developments.

6. In conclusion I may perhaps add two observations. The Governor of the Bank of Finland said, in a conversation which I had with him recently, that he was not perturbed at the probable developments in Fenno-Russian trade. On the exporting side he did not foresee very great Russian demands for timber and timber products after the reparation period, nor was he unduly worried about the future of the reparations industries. As regards the latter, I think he was merely being opportunist, since he added 'a lot may happen before 1952'. On the importing side he pointed out that the commodities which Finland was now importing from Soviet Russia were in the main those such as cereals, which she would hope in due course to supply by her own exertions as she had done up to the outbreak of war. He did not consider, in fact, that the economy of the two countries was so constituted that a preponderating proportion of Finnish external trade would be absorbed between them. The other point is the growing dissatisfaction of both employers and workers with Russian methods, especially with such matters as the last-minute alterations of specifications and fussy inspections. Unless the Russians alter their methods the production of goods for the Soviet Union will be unpopular, a point not without importance in view of the obstinacy of the Finnish character.[4]

[3] Not printed.
[4] In a despatch of 18 December, Shepherd reported details of a new agreement for the exchange of goods between Finland and the Soviet Union. Deakin (Economic Intelligence Department) commented that it appeared that the value of Finnish-Soviet trade in 1947 would be slightly less than that in 1946, and that the level of Finnish exports to the Soviet Union from January to

7. For reference purposes I enclose a single copy of despatch O.T. B. No. 247 of 7th November regarding Finnish external trade in 1946, copies of which have also been sent to the Economic Intelligence Department of the Foreign Office.[3]

8. I am sending a copy of this despatch to the Economic Relations and Treaties Department of the Board of Trade.

I have, etc.
F.M. SHEPHERD

September 1946 was only 23.6 per cent of total free exports by value, compared with 24.8 per cent exported to Britain and roughly 40 per cent exported to the rest of Western Europe and the United States (FO371/56181, N16386/232/56).

No. 75

Mr Attlee to Mr Randall (Copenhagen), 20 November 1946
No. 459 Confidential (FO 371/56127, N15022/394/15)

Sir,

I transmit to you herewith a record of the conversation between the Minister of State and the Danish Minister for Foreign Affairs, M. Rasmussen, on 20th November, when M. Rasmussen was passing through London on his way to New York. I also enclose the texts of three memoranda which M. Rasmussen left at the same time and which are being separately examined in the Foreign Office.[1]

I am, etc.,
C.R. ATTLEE

Enclosure in No. 75
Record of Conversation between the Minister of State and M. Rasmussen (Danish Foreign Minister) on 20th November 1946

The Danish Foreign Minister came to see me, and left the following *aide-mémoires* on German warships, the Danish-minded people in South Schleswig, and the Danish refugee problem. In addition he raised the subject of facilities for the Danish Government to present their point of view on the German draft treaty. I told him that although we could not yet see what we considered to be the appropriate stage, at that stage we would uphold the right of the Danish Government to make their case. The Foreign Minister seemed very relieved, and admitted that they have been in slight doubt as to whether we would be of this view following their last note.

He also spoke briefly on the resumption of the Anglo-Danish trade talks, and said that he hoped that politically we could appreciate their case, which was that the Danish people would be asked to find extra taxation to subsidise the export of food to Britain which they, the Danish people, would be asked to forego from their existing dietry.

I did not elaborate the point, but said that I hoped equally he would appreciate our political difficulties, particularly in relation to our New Zealand prices.

He reverted to the subject of the provision of equipment for the Danish occupying forces in Germany. I told him that we had, of course, considered that, in

---
[1] Not printed.

our previous agreement about equipment, we had covered the equipment which the Danish forces would need for occupation. I added that this seemed to me a matter of substantial political importance, and that, apart from their financial difficulties, they should also consider the loss of political prestige which they would incur from refusing to take a share in the occupation in conformity with their dignity and status.

I also introduced the subject of the pending Danish-Russian civil aviation talks, and told him that I feared the consequences of making a type of agreement with Russia which so far no other Western European Power had agreed to.

He told me that they were going to put first to the Russians the hope of a clear reciprocity in Moscow-Copenhagen flights. That if this proved impossible, they would then press for Danish planes flying to and from Copenhagen to Memel, and Russian planes to and from Moscow to Memel, and that it would only be at the third stage that they would discuss at all the possibility of Danish flights being from Copenhagen to Memel and Russian flight being from Moscow to Copenhagen. I pressed our argument very firmly upon him, and I think he was a bit shaken.

As he was leaving, in a very friendly and personal fashion, the Minister said that he was disturbed by the deterioration of Anglo-Danish relationships.[2] He cited as causes particularly the refugee, food and equipment questions. He added that he thought that our willingness to uphold the Danish right to make representations on the draft treaty would help a little. He also thought that if it were possible to make some small German naval vessels available that this would be a substantial contribution, and I am most anxious that this point should be pursued. Although it is not my business, I find it difficult to believe, with the sustained reduction in our naval manpower, that it is impossible to make available some of these vessels for which the Danes are asking.

The whole talk, which lasted about an hour, was sustained at a reasonable and very friendly level.

HECTOR McNEIL

---

[2] Randall had raised similar concerns on this subject on several occasions. In a private letter to Warner of 4 July, he had drawn attention to the imbalance of ministerial visits between Britain and Denmark (there had been almost no senior British visitors to Denmark during the previous twelve months) and had suggested measures for putting this right (FO 371/56109, N8829/63/15). He had also sent a despatch to Bevin on 20 August which highlighted much the same causes as those adumbrated by Rasmussen to McNeil, though he also concluded that the British media and recent British visitors had failed to pay sufficient interest in, or respect to, Denmark (FO 371/56127, N10751/394/15).

No. 76

Minute from Mr Warr to Mr Hankey, 21 November 1946
(FO 371/56089, N15027/3/15)

I attended the first meeting with the Danish Military Delegation at the War Office yesterday to discuss the terms on which a Danish contingent would be despatched to the British zone of Germany. The meeting lasted nearly all day and went exhaustively into all details with which I need not bother you. But I think you should know the main points which emerged. It was clear throughout that nothing the Danish Delegation has said could commit the Danish Government in advance but they were quite clear about the limits beyond which their Government would in no circumstances agree.

The Delegation appeared to be willing to provide a force of not more than 4,000 men to be ready in Germany by the 15th April next, to be relieved every six months and to stay there two years, or longer if necessary. The contingent would be located in an area to be decided by the Commander-in-Chief, Germany, and on the understanding that they should not be sent to South Schleswig. The Danish Government would provide them with food and would also pay the officers and men.

So far the Danish proposals were satisfactory, although the War Office had rather hoped to secure a contingent of 10,000 instead of 4,000. But when it came to the cost of the equipment a complete deadlock was immediately reached. The Danes said that they wanted the equipment for the contingent (valued by the War Office at £3,500,000) to be provided on loan. The Danish Delegation pointed out that the Danish Government had not yet decided whether British equipment would be suitable for their army and would like to give it a trial during the period when the contingent would be in Germany. If the Danish Government decided at the end of this period that the equipment was suitable they would buy it, or part of it, at its value then. They would return what they did not want to this country. The Financial Branch of the War Office argued that most, if not all, the equipment was in Denmark already and had been provided on the clear understanding that the Danes would pay for it; that if the Danes got the equipment on loan they would be obtaining much better terms than the Belgians and Norwegians whose contingents were helping to occupy Germany; and that the Treasury would in any case not agree to the price being lowered. The Danish Delegation admitted the force of these arguments but said that it would be quite impossible for the current Danish minority government to convince their Parliament that the expenditure of £3,500,000 was in present circumstances justified. They were afraid that if we did not meet their terms the only effect would be that the contingent would not go to Germany.

There is some force in the Danish arguments. At the same time it is alarming from the long-term strategic and political point of view that they should be thinking of equipping their army from other sources than our own. It would be greatly to our disadvantage if they did so and I think we should try to tempt them to take our equipment if we can. I suggested privately to the financial expert at the meeting, Major-General Hicks, that a solution might be a capitation rate on the Norwegian model. The Norwegians have agreed to pay the sum of 10 shillings per man in Germany per day and in return to receive all arms and equipment, food and clothing etc. without cost to themselves. While the troops are being trained in Norway to go to Germany the Norwegians will pay for similar services, 6/- per man per day. The equipment will remain throughout the property of HMG. At the same time the Norwegian Government agreed to purchase from HMG certain naval, military and air equipment. Major-General Hicks said that it would be impossible to apply a similar system to the Danes who, unlike the Norwegians, were providing their own food and certain other services while the Norwegians wanted everything from us. Moreover, the Danes were not purchasing any military equipment from us.

Later in the discussions, however, it became clear that the Danes would purchase at least some of the equipment with which we had provided them for use by their metropolitan army. Moreover, they have agreed to buy from us £450,000 worth of RAF aeroplanes and equipment as a nucleus for their air force. They have also purchased one submarine and are negotiating to buy two others and some more naval craft. On this basis, I think we might try and induce the War Office to accept a capitation rate in the Danish case which would admittedly be different from the Norwegian capitation rate but which it should not surely be impossible for the WO to work out. If we do not propose some such solution, I am convinced that the delegation will return to Denmark after a further meeting tomorrow reporting complete disagreement on finance. I very much doubt if we should get the Danish Government to budge and the only result will be that we shall not only get no contingent for Germany but also run the risk of not equipping their army and so losing a valuable political and possibly strategic link with Denmark. The only alternative is to allow the Delegation to return and report a deadlock and then to take Mr Randall's advice about how to get out of it. But I think that if we did this we would risk not only the Danish Government making a firm agreement with, say, Sweden to purchase arms from there, thus losing all, by delay.

After discussion with Mr Hankey I attach a draft to Major John Freeman at the War Office, which Major Mayhew might be willing to sign, which we hope might induce the War Office to yield and suggest a capitation rate at the meeting with the Danes tomorrow at 11.00am. If necessary, this meeting could be postponed: the Danes are perfectly willing to stay a few days longer.[1]

Draft submitted.

G.C. WARR

PS Since drafting this, I have had lunch with the chief Danish Delegate. It was quite clears from my conversation with him that we should not secure any basis of agreement on finance, if we did not go some way to meet them.

[1] Hankey agreed with this approach, and approved the draft for Mayhew to send (see No. 78). He commented: 'We have warned the W.O. and they (Staff Duties branch *not* Finance!) are substantially in agreement.'

No. 77

Chancery (Oslo) to Northern Department, 21 November 1946
(FO 371/56318, N15192/4929/30)

Dear Department,

Will you please refer to our correspondence about the reindeer, ending with Hankey's letter to the ambassador, N13568/4929/30 of October 26th?[1]

Cumming[2] and General Dahl have now completed the necessary arrangements between them. The latter is obtaining the veterinary certificate required by the

[1] Not printed. The background to this unusual story is that General Dahl, the Commanding Officer of the Northern Norway Military District, had heard that the only reindeer in London Zoo had died, and offered to provide a mating pair as replacements, an offer which was gratefully accepted by London Zoo. The arrangements took some time to conclude; General Dahl, not unreasonably, was unwilling also to pay for the costs of transportation so the Zoo agreed to meet the expenses involved. The animals eventually had to be shipped in winter in a pen on the open deck of a trawler from Alta to Bergen, and thence to Newcastle.

[2] Commander A. P. Cumming was the British consul in Tromsø.

Ministry of Agriculture, and is providing a keeper in the person of his own Lappish batman (who, incidentally, will travel in his own national costume).

The party will leave Alta on or about December 1st with the necessary ration of moss, and should reach Newcastle on SS *Jupiter* on December 23rd.

In passing this information to the Zoological Society would you please ask them to have the animals met at Newcastle on the date mentioned, and also to look after the batman, Kristian Eriksen, during the two days which he will have to spend there before the boat returns to Norway? As General Dahl says: 'he would be delighted to have a look around such a big city, his most enormous experience in that way so far is Tromsø', and we should be grateful, therefore, if someone could be spared to take him in hand.

We agree with Cumming in regarding December 23rd as a very seasonal date for the party's arrival, and, like him, 'we should like to hear the comments of the Geordie stevedores when they unload Father Christmas complete'. We are sending copies of this letter to Cumming and Vorley.[3] The latter will be seeing to it that the animals are safely transhipped at Bergen and will confirm their expected time of arrival at Newcastle by telegram.

Yours ever,
CHANCERY

[3] N. Vorley was the British consul in Bergen.

No. 78

Letter from Mr Mayhew to Lord Pakenham (Parliamentary Under-Secretary, War Office), 22 November 1946
Immediate (FO 371/56089, N15027/3/15)

[No salutation on this copy]

May I ask your advice and invoke your aid about the question of the despatch of a Danish contingent to help occupy the British zone of Germany which is, at present, under discussion at the War Office with a Danish Military Delegation?

Although the discussions have not been concluded, I am informed that it seems likely that they will break down on a question of finance. There has been some advance on the Danish side. The Danish Delegation now say that their Government are likely to be willing to provide a contingent of 4,000 men for service in the British zone. But they wish the arms and equipment for their contingent in Germany to be provided and paid for entirely by HMG; and as regards the rest of their army at home, while there are signs that they might be willing to buy and pay for some of the arms and equipment from us, they wish to remain free to purchase most of this elsewhere if they so decide and meanwhile to keep what they have received from us on loan. The Departments of the War Office concerned are unable to accept this condition which, they point out, would give the Danish contingent more favourable treatment than that accorded to the Norwegian and Belgian Governments, both of whom have agreed to help to occupy the British zone. The Belgians agreed to buy all their equipment. The Norwegians bought the equipment for their armed forces at home and borrowed the arms and equipment for their contingent in Germany, paying us a capitation rate in return.

Admittedly, the Danish proposals are disappointing. But I think we must face the fact that if we do not reach agreement with them, we shall not only fail to secure the contingent for Germany, but also lead the Danish Government to purchase equipment for their army from other sources than Great Britain. We understand they have this under consideration. The Danes say they wish to try out our equipment in Germany which will give them an opportunity of deciding whether it is suitable for their needs or not; if they decide that it is suitable they will purchase it.

It would be highly unfortunate if the Danish army were eventually to be equipped from other sources, as we should lose a valuable political and possibly a strategic, link with Denmark to the preservation of which we attach particular importance. Moreover, opinion in the Scandinavian countries is tending to drift more and more into a 'neutral' position and if we let the Danish delegation go away without any sort of agreement. I feel sure we shall have much difficulty in getting negotiations going again or in reaching any result. They would be only too glad to elude the question. In the hope therefore of resolving the present deadlock, I put forward for your consideration the following suggestion.

It strikes us that we should be able to settle this case in the same way as we settled the Norwegian case, i.e. by arranging to supply arms and equipment in return for a capitation rate for each man. Admittedly, the case of the Norwegians is not the same as that of the Danes who, unlike the Norwegians are providing food and certain other services for their troops in Germany. But I think it should be possible to work out a lower capitation rate which will cover the equipment which the Danes want, and the very fact that the circumstances for the Norwegians are different will protect us against embarrassing comparisons being made about the size of this capitation rate. Another possible objection is that whereas in the agreement with the Norwegians over the capitation rate, it was at the same time stipulated that they should buy certain naval, military and air equipment from us, we may not be able to make a similar stipulation in the Danish case. But we at least have the fact that the Danish Government have bought and are paying for the nucleus of their air force and are beginning to do the same for their navy. Moreover, as I have said, there are signs that they might be persuaded to buy some British equipment for their metropolitan army.

The War Office must of course judge how best to handle these negotiations. But I should like to press the War Office to explore the possibility of proposing some agreement to the Danes along lines similar to what we did for the Norwegians so as to meet their point of having the equipment so to speak on approval and also preserve, so far as we can, the link between their army and ours. I understand that a meeting is to be held on November 22nd at 11 a.m. and I hope that at any rate the negotiations will not be allowed to break down until this question has been more thoroughly gone into.[1]

C.P. MAYHEW

---

[1] The War Office accepted the arguments put forward by the Foreign Office, and an agreement was subsequently worked out whereby the equipment would be loaned to Denmark at an annual charge of 20 per cent of the selling price, which would be deducted from the selling price if, at the end of the occupation period, Denmark wished to buy any of the equipment. The Danish delegation made clear that the agreement was subject to approval by the Government and by Parliament. In a despatch of 17 December, Randall was instructed to impress upon the Danish Government that the UK regarded it as of primary importance that they should signify their agreement at an early date (FO 371/56089, N15486/3/15).

No. 79

Sir L. Collier (Oslo) to Mr Bevin, 23 November 1946, 2.30 p.m.[1]
Tel. No. 465 Secret (FO 371/56287, N15059/220/30)

Hankey's letter of November 2nd about Spitsbergen.[2]
Norwegian Minister of Foreign Affairs gave me today account of two conversations which he had had with M. Molotov just before leaving New York. M. Molotov pressed for immediate negotiations on basis of draft agreement enclosed in my despatch No. 31 July 24th[3] but with several important amendments most of which seemed unacceptable. M. Lange promised to lay the whole matter before the *Storting* in secret session but emphasised that any agreement must receive assent first, of all signatories of Spitsbergen and then of, UNO Security Council.

2. Matter will now be discussed in secret first in Foreign Affairs Committee *Storting* and then in full house probably at beginning of December. Meanwhile Norwegian Ambassador at Washington has been instructed to give full account of Soviet proposals to United States Secretary of State. They are also known to M. Prebensen who was present at my interview with Minister for Foreign Affairs and leaves for London November 29th. Norwegian Government are considering whether it is possible or desirable to maintain secrecy any longer but will not decide this until after secret session of *Storting*.[4]

[1] Copied to Washington, Moscow and the UK Delegation to the UN.
[2] Not printed. Molotov had raised Spitzbergen again with Lie during the latter's visit to Moscow in July 1946, when he had already been UN Secretary-General for some months. The British Embassy in Moscow reported that Lie had been irritated to have been treated as a Norwegian personality (FO 371/56287, N9677/220/30). At this stage the Norwegian Government had not yet made any public announcement about Soviet demands. Lange informed the Americans of Molotov's approach on 11 December. (FRUS 1947, Vol. III, pp. 1003-04).
[3] Not printed.
[4] A full account of this meeting is contained in No. 80.

No. 80

Sir L. Collier (Oslo) to Mr Attlee, 26 November 1946
No. 416 Secret (FO 371/56287, N15346/220/30)

Sir,
I have the honour to report, in amplification of my telegram No. 465 of November 23rd,[1] that the Norwegian Minister of Foreign Affairs, who had returned from New York on November 20th, asked me to call upon him on the morning of November 23rd, when I found him with M. Prebensen, Secretary-General of the Ministry of Foreign Affairs and Ambassador designate in London, both appearing much preoccupied and surrounded by documents relating, as it proved, to the Soviet demands regarding Spitsbergen. M. Lange then gave me a full account of recent developments in this matter, summarised in my telegram under reference. As I had no opportunity of taking notes I may not be able to record it accurately in detail, but it was to the following general effect.

[1] No. 79.

2. M. Molotov had told M. Lange in Paris that he now wished to proceed with discussions on joint defence measures in Spitsbergen which he had begun with M. Lie, and when M. Lange explained that he had not come prepared for such discussions, had intimated rather vaguely that he might bring the matter up in New York. M. Lange (if I understood him aright, which is perhaps doubtful in view of the terms of Mr Hankey's letter to me of November 2nd)[2] had mentioned this conversation to you at the time, asking whether, in your opinion, M. Molotov's move might not be connected with the question of United States bases on Iceland, to which you had replied that since the requirements of the United States Government in that matter had now been reduced to very small proportions, it would afford the Soviet Government but a poor excuse for pressing the Spitsbergen question, and it might be hoped, therefore, that nothing further would come of M. Molotov's approach. Nothing indeed was said to M. Lange at New York until just before his departure, when M. Molotov had two interviews with him of an hour each, the second on the morning of his last day in New York. He had asked to see you on the afternoon of that day in order to give you an account of the conversations, but was told that you had engagements for every hour of that time; and for the same reason the United States Secretary of State had found it impossible to see him. He had accordingly arranged for the Norwegian Ambassador at Washington to give a full account of the interview to Mr Byrnes at the same time as he described them to me and this, he believed, had now been done.

3. M. Molotov had begun the first interview by saying that the Soviet Government desired to take up the Spitsbergen question again on the basis of the draft joint declaration handed to them by the Norwegian Ambassador at Moscow on April 9th, 1945 (a copy of which was enclosed in my despatch No. 31 of July 24th in that year),[3] which, however, would require considerable amplification and amendment. In the first place it referred to the 'archipelago of Spitsbergen (Svalbard)', which did not include Bear Island; was this omission of Bear Island a slip or intentional? M. Lange replied that it was intentional: Bear Island had no harbour and could not possibly be used for military purposes, and its inclusion in a military agreement would not only be pointless but might arouse suspicion of Soviet motives. M. Molotov grumbled but did not press the point.

4. M. Molotov then tried to argue that the establishment of the United Nations Security Council had made it unnecessary to consult the signatories to the Spitsbergen Treaty of 1920; and when M. Lange showed that this contention had no legal basis, he first maintained that the Soviet Government had never recognised the treaty and then, when it was proved to him that they had done so (*de facto* in 1924 and formally in 1935), declared that, in any case, it had been signed at a time when the position of the Soviet Union was very different from what it was now, and so was not necessarily binding upon them—a remarkable interpretation of the doctrine of *rebus sic stantibus*. In particular, said M. Molotov, it was not reasonable that all the governments which had signed it, and only those governments, should have the right to concern themselves with Spitsbergen in these days: not only ex-enemies, as proposed in the joint declaration, but also some 'neutrals' ought to be excluded from discussions on the future of the islands, while some other countries ought now to be included, such as Finland—a particularly

[2] See No. 79, note 2.
[3] Not printed.

surprising suggestion to M. Lange, who remarked to me (although he does not seem to have said as much to M. Molotov) that the Soviet Union had taken great care in the Peace Treaty with that country, to deprive her of her previous access to the Arctic Sea. M. Molotov's most serious objection, however, was to the stipulation in the draft declaration that all permanent defence installations should be situated on land belonging to or expropriated by the Norwegian Government. It was not clear what he wished to substitute for this stipulation, but presumably he had in mind the establishment of permanent Soviet military bases on the lines of the United States bases in the West Indies.

5. Finally, M. Molotov declared that joint defence measures were not enough: there should be joint economic exploitation as well, and the Spitsbergen Treaty should be amended to permit Soviet mining interests to be treated differently from those of the other signatory Powers. M. Lange pointed out that joint defence measures were one thing and special economic concessions were quite another, that the Soviet Government already had a large coal mining concession (the Grumant mines) which they had not yet begun to work again after the dismantling of all the Spitsbergen mines during the war (they have, in fact just announced the despatch of a large expedition to restart the mines, at what M. Prebensen regards as a suspiciously late season of the year), and that in any case they had, according to their own public declarations, ample coal resources inside the Soviet Union, the development of which would occupy all their energies for many years to come; but M. Molotov insisted that his Government expected to have a greater share in the economic exploitation of Spitsbergen, saying 'there is enough for us both'.

6. M. Lange, although much taken aback at these proposals, declared finally that he would submit the whole matter to the *Storting* when he returned to Norway; but he made it plain that there could be no negotiations of any sort until the *Storting* had decided what their basis could be, that it would not be likely to reach a decision in time for negotiations to begin before January next at the earliest, and that any agreement reached as a result of such negotiations must receive the assent, first of all the signatories of the Spitsbergen Treaty and then of the Security Council of the United Nations.

7. M. Lange will now make a statement in the course of the present week to the Foreign Affairs Committee of the *Storting*, which will lead to further discussions by the whole *Storting* in secret session at the beginning of next month. The *Storting*, he says, will receive a severe shock, and it will be very difficult to keep the matter secret any longer: indeed, he is himself inclined to think that it will be to the advantage of the Norwegian Government to make a public statement of their attitude as soon as possible after the secret session. That attitude, he expects, will be that they are prepared to negotiate on the basis of the draft declaration as it now stands but not otherwise, that the negotiations must be confined to defence and must not involve economic concessions, and above all, that the Spitsbergen Treaty is valid and that all non-enemy signatories thereto, as well as the Security Council of the United Nations, must assent to any change in its terms. He still hopes, however, that they may be able to avoid any negotiations at all, and he will do all he can to bring about a situation in which the Soviet Government will decide that it is not to their interest to enter into them.

8. In making this declaration of his intentions His Excellency spoke with unwonted firmness; and I had the impression from his manner that M. Molotov's demands had come as an unpleasant surprise not only to the Norwegian Government as a whole, but in particular to him in person. He had apparently

hoped that the comparative favour shown to Norway in the Soviet press, and Soviet official utterances during the present year indicated approval of his own very discreet and cautious policy in matters affecting Soviet interests, and that this, combined with the preoccupations of the Soviet Government elsewhere, would have induced them to leave Norway alone; and at the end of our interview he indulged in some speculation on the reasons for the present Soviet move, which he was still inclined to connect with United States activities in Iceland and perhaps also in Greenland, although he admitted, when I pointed it out, that this would not explain the demand for economic concessions and that if it were intended to justify the Soviet demands to world opinion by a comparison with the United States requirements of Iceland, the former should logically have been made public at a time when the Icelandic question was still actual, whereas it is now almost forgotten and there is in any event, as you appear to have pointed out at Paris, a glaring disproportion between the two cases. I suggested to him that previous experience of Soviet methods pointed to the simpler explanation that whenever the Soviet Government were held up in one direction in their attempts to expand Soviet influence, as they were now held up at the Dardanelles, in Persia and in China, they reverted to, and intensified, previous attempts at expansion in other directions, such as Spitsbergen in this case: there was also the further possibility that the development of V weapons had been such as to make Spitsbergen of special value as a base for such weapons directed against the North American continent. (I understand from the Military Attaché to His Majesty's Embassy that the Canadian authorities are interested in this possibility, although I have not discussed the matter with the Canadian Minister here and shall not do so without further instructions.)[4] Even in present conditions it might not be impossible for such a base to be established on the site of the Soviet mining concession in Spitsbergen, since I understand that this is isolated from the other mining settlements and since the exiguous Norwegian military and police forces on the islands have probably neither the means nor the wish to conduct investigations there. I believe, indeed, that they seldom or never visited the place before the war and knew next to nothing of what went on there, nor did they have any contact with the miners, who were all imported from the Soviet Union.[5]

9. I am sending copies of this despatch to His Majesty's Ambassadors at Washington and Moscow and to the Permanent United Kingdom representative to the United Nations.

I have, etc.,
L. COLLIER

[4] Warner recommended that the Canadian government should be informed of this point.
[5] Warner observed that Lange's attitude was excellent. He agreed that publicity would probably be useful. He decided that Attlee should be briefed, and submitted a draft to Sargent on 30 November (FO 371/56287, N15346/220/30G): see No. 81.

No. 81

Minute from Mr Bevin to Mr Attlee, 3 December 1946
PM/46/224 (FO 371/56287, N15059/220/30G)

Sir,
The following account will serve to explain the background to Oslo telegram No. 465 about Spitsbergen attached about which I understand you have asked.[1]

2. The sovereignty of Spitsbergen and Bear Island was conferred on Norway by a Treaty of 1920, signed by Great Britain, Denmark, France, Italy, Japan, Norway and Sweden. By Article 9 of the same Treaty, the islands were demilitarised. The Soviet Union adhered in 1935. In 1944 the Soviet Government proposed to the Norwegian Government that, in order to safeguard Russian economic and strategic interests, Spitsbergen be placed under a condominium of Norway and USSR and that Bear Island be given to the Soviet Union.

3. The Norwegian Government in March 1945, put forward counter-proposals that Spitsbergen and Bear Island should remain under Norwegian sovereignty; that the Norwegian and Soviet Governments should negotiate on the joint military defence of the islands, that defence measures should be 'in accord with the arrangements which may be made by an international security organisation, of which both parties are members'; that the abrogation of the Treaty of 1920 can only be affected by agreement with the signatories of the Treaty of 1920, excluding ex-enemies.

4. The Soviet Government, who appeared to accept these counter-proposals as a basis for negotiation, now wish to make certain amendments which the Norwegian Government do not appear willing to accept. We do not yet know just what the amendments consist of.

5. The Americans seemed last year to take the view that a request for strategic facilities in Spitsbergen and Bear Island should be made to the United Nations Organisation. But they have not, so far as we know, formulated their final view, and were consulting the US Chiefs of Staff.

6. Our own Chiefs of Staff, when consulted early in 1945, considered that the islands are of no strategic interest to ourselves and that our attitude to the Russian-Norwegian negotiations can therefore be governed by political considerations alone. We have told the Norwegian Government that in our view any Norwegian-Soviet agreement on this subject would necessarily involve fundamental modifications of the status of Spitsbergen and would therefore require the prior consent of the signatories of the Treaty of 1920. This view has been adopted by the Norwegian Government, as you will see from the attached telegram.[2]

7. It seems clear that the Russians have strategic considerations chiefly in mind in making their approach to the Norwegians about Spitsbergen. We are again consulting the Chiefs of Staff to make sure they still adhere to the view that the islands are of no strategic interest to ourselves (or Canada).[3] We propose to discuss the question with Monsieur Prebensen, the new Norwegian ambassador, when he

---
[1] No. 79.
[2] Not printed.
[3] No. 80.

arrives here shortly, and we shall also need to discuss the question with the Americans.[4]

ERNEST BEVIN

[4] The view of the US Joint Chiefs of Staff was that Spitsbergen, 'in the hands of an aggressive Soviet Russia, would have an offensive potential against the United States, but not sufficient from the purely military point of view to justify military action by the United States to prevent a measure of Soviet control'. The Secretaries of War and of the Navy added that 'agreement to any substantial Soviet demands with respect to Bear Island and the Spitsbergen Archipelago would "seriously impair the overall security interests of the United States"' (FRUS 1947, Vol. III, pp. 1012-13). This opinion was sent to Marshall on 4 February 1947.

No. 82

Letter from Mr Hankey to Group Captain Stapleton (Cabinet Office), 16 December 1946
Top Secret (FO 371/56287, N15346/220/G)

Dear Stapleton,

Early in 1945 we referred to the Chiefs of Staff the question of the demands which the Soviet Government had been making for concession in the Norwegian islands of Spitsbergen and Bear Island. The sovereignty of these islands, as you may remember, was conferred upon Norway by a Treaty of 1920 signed by Great Britain, Denmark, France, Italy, Japan, Norway and Sweden. The Soviet Union adhered to it in 1935. By the same treaty the islands were demilitarised. The Soviet Government had proposed late in 1944 to the Norwegian Government that in order to safeguard Russian economic and strategic interests, Spitsbergen should be placed under a condominium of Norway and the USSR, and that Bear Island should be given to the Soviet Union.

2. The Joint Planning Staff prepared a paper on this subject (reference JP(44) (321) of the 15th January 1945) which was approved by the Chiefs of Staff.[1] One of its conclusions was that the Chiefs of Staff saw no strategic objections to the Russians establishing bases in Spitsbergen (it was considered unlikely that any bases could be established in Bear Island).

3. The Chiefs of Staff should be aware of what has happened since that time, in case in the light of developments they may wish to modify the views contained in the JPS paper referred to above. In March 1945 the Norwegian Government put forward counter-proposals to the Soviet Government which the latter appeared to accept in principle. These proposals are explained in detail in the enclosed copy of Sir Laurence Collier's despatch No. 321 of the 24th July 1945 and the memorandum contained in it.[1] In brief, these proposals are:

(1) that Spitsbergen and Bear Island should remain under Norwegian sovereignty;

(2) that the Norwegian and Soviet Government should negotiate on the joint military defence of the islands;

(3) that any defence measures should be made in accord with any arrangements which may be made by an international security organisation of which both are

[1] Not printed.

members (this phrase was presumably used because UNO was not yet in existence);

(4) that the abrogation of the Treaty of 1920 can only be effected by those signatories of the Treaty of 1920 who are not ex-enemy.

4. These counter-proposals have now been modified, as you will see from Oslo telegram No. 465[2] and Oslo despatch No. 416,[3] copies of which are enclosed. You will observe that though we had previously thought that Bear Island was included in the plan for joint Russo-Norwegian defence measures, the Norwegians now want Bear Island kept out of the discussions and that M. Molotov 'did not press the point'.

5. In the face of these renewed Russian demands, the Norwegians seem to be showing very considerable firmness and have adopted the advice which we have given them, taking the line with the Russians that no alteration in the status of Spitsbergen can be effected except with the concurrence of those signatories of the Treaty of 1920 who are not ex-enemies and of the Security Council of the United Nations. The Norwegian Government do not intend to pursue the matter with the Soviet Government until after a secret session of the Norwegian Parliament.

6. The Norwegian Government have kept the United States Government informed of the revised proposals for concessions in Spitsbergen. The United States Government's reaction when they first heard of the matter last year was that a request for strategic facilities in these islands should be made through the United Nations Organisation rather than by direct negotiation between the Soviet and Norwegian Governments. But the United States Government have not so far as we know formulated any final view. We heard last year that they were consulting the United States Chiefs of Staff. We do not know what the outcome was.

7. It is now clear that while the Soviet Government have dropped their demand for a condominium they want military facilities, and economic rights to exploit the coal, in Spitsbergen. As regards the military facilities, it emerges from Sir Laurence Collier's despatch No. 416 (paragraph 8) that the Canadian authorities are showing interest in the potential use of Spitsbergen as a site for V weapons aimed at the North American continent. I do not know how much there is in this.

8. We should be grateful if you would inform the Chiefs of Staff of these developments and enquire whether in the light of the changed situation since 1945, they still adhere to the view expressed in JP(44)(321) of the 15th January 1945 that there is no strategic objection to the establishment of Russian bases in Spitsbergen.[1] If objection is now seen, would it extend to economic concessions on the ground that V weapon sites might be established therein without becoming known. We propose that the United State Government and Canadian Government should be consulted when we have received the Chiefs of Staff's views.

Yours sincerely,
R.M.A. HANKEY

[2] No. 79.
[3] No. 80.

No. 83

Minute from Mr Warr to Mr Bevin, 22 January 1947
(FO 371/65854, N895/121/15)

Secretary of State
We are having great difficulty in persuading the Danish Government to reach a decision about despatching a Danish contingent to help occupy the British zone of Germany. The War Office are keen to have this contingent because of our acute manpower shortage in Germany. From a political point of view we want the Danes to send the contingent because its presence in Germany would, as regards manpower from the political point of view, check the present Danish tendency to lapse into a mood of passive indifference to the affairs of the outside world, would be a means of achieving our aim of preserving the ties formed during the war between the Danes and ourselves, and would help to ensure that the Danes continue to look to us for advice and help in Service matters. All efforts to induce the Danish Government to make up their mind having so far failed, it is suggested that the only hope now of hastening a decision would be for the Secretary of State to send for the Minister and speak to him frankly.[1]

2. *The background*
In May, 1945, the then Danish Minister for Foreign Affairs offered to send a Danish contingent of 10,000 men to help occupy Germany. We never received a formal confirmation of this offer from the Danish Government but we left them in no doubt that we expected them to abide by it and to pay the cost of equipping the contingent. The Danish Government said that they were willing in principle to provide the contingent but stressed that various difficulties had arisen since the original offer was made. The essence of these difficulties was their shortage of money and manpower. The shortage of manpower was aggravated by the presence in Denmark of 200,000 German refugees, the guarding of whom tied up a considerable number of the available Danish troops. In an attempt to clinch matters we asked the Danish Government to send a small technical military delegation to discuss in detail with the War Office exactly what we wanted them to do and how much it would cost. The Delegation came in November 1946 on the understanding that any agreement they might reach was provisional only and was subject to the approval of their Government. Provisional agreement was duly reached but only after substantial concessions both as regards the size of the contingent and the cost of its equipment had been made on our side. The essence of this agreement was that the Danish Government would provide 4,000 men to be ready for Germany in April. The contingent would remain in Germany for two years. The cost of their equipment would be met by a hiring arrangement by which the Danes would pay an annual charge of 20% of the selling price thus enabling the Danish Government to make up their minds whether the equipment was suitable to the needs of their Army or not and buy it at the end of the occupation period if they wanted to do so. The Danish Delegation undertook to submit these proposals to their Government,

---

[1] Randall had reported (tel. No. 139 of 21 January, also on N895/121/15) that he had not received an answer from the Danish Foreign Ministry to a request for information within the promised timescale. Northern Department decided that the best solution was to ask Bevin to make representations to the Danish Ambassador. In the event, Bevin was ill and Warner therefore spoke to Reventlow on the lines of this brief on 24 January.

and to urge that a decision be reached with the least possible delay. We explained that we were fully aware of the Danish difficulties particularly over the refugees, and that we were doing our best to help them though we did not think that the existence of these difficulties should present any insuperable obstacle to the provision of the contingent. In spite of repeated approaches to the Danish Minister for Foreign Affairs by HM Minister in Copenhagen, we have not yet received any indication of the Danish Government's views. Matters are now getting urgent because the War Office point out that if they do not receive a reply by the 1st February, when the authorities in Germany plan the allocation of manpower for April, it will be extremely difficult to guarantee to fit in the Danish Contingent at the time and place proposed.

3. In speaking to the Danish Minister, the Secretary of State might make use of the following arguments:

(1) We regard the Danes as Allies and expect them to shoulder the responsibility of all Allies to help in the solution of problems, like the occupation of Germany, which result from our common victory.

(2) We do not see why the Danish Government should lag behind other European Allies in this respect. The Belgians have four Brigades in Germany. The Norwegians, with a smaller population than Denmark and a less close interest in Germany, have agreed to provide 4,000 men who are already on their way to Germany.

(3) The serious delays in receiving the Danish Government's decision are proving embarrassing to our military authorities who have to plan well in advance how to dispose their available manpower in Germany.

(4) From their own point of view the Danish Government should surely realise that they are here being presented with an opportunity, which is most unlikely ever to recur, of learning about British methods of military administration. Such lessons cannot fail to be of value to the Danish Army of the future.[2]

G.C. WARR

[2] The Danish Parliament approved the despatch of a Danish contingent to Germany on 22 May 1947.

No. 84

Letter from Sir L. Collier (Oslo) to Mr Hankey, 24 January 1947
Secret (FO 371/66021, N122468/30G)

Dear Hankey,

You will have gather from my telegram No. 31 of January 22nd[1] that I have had a very full and frank discussion about Spitsbergen with the Norwegian Minister for Foreign Affairs. If we had a proper bag service I would have sent a much shorter telegram and followed it up with a despatch; but I thought it unsafe to risk leaving the Secretary of State in ignorance of any important point in the conversation for as long as ten days or a fortnight, which might have been the result of adopting that course. There is now no need for a despatch as well as a telegram; but it is difficult to give the whole picture in a telegram, however lengthy, and I am therefore

[1] Not printed.

writing this letter to cover those further points in which I think Northern Department might be interested.

The doubts of Lange's firmness expressed in my despatch No. 441[1] were subsequently strengthened by what I heard from other sources, such as the American Ambassador,[2] who had called on him a week before I did, without instructions but, as he said, to tell him how the matter appeared 'to a plain guy' (and he is a very plain guy), and John Sanness,[3] a journalist normally well informed and in very close touch with Lange, who had talked to Inman, the Press Reader, and afterwards to Littler, Kenney's assistant. Mr Bay's impression was that Lange was relying on the signatories to the Spitsbergen Treaty and/or the Security Council to pull his chestnuts out of the fire for him, while Sanness was convinced that if the Russians pressed him hard enough he would acquiesce in their demands, and seemed to think it quite natural that he should do so. I therefore quite expected to find, when I saw him on January 21st, that he had at the very least advised the *Storting* to stand by the offer of 1945,[4] and was agreeably surprised to discover that, on the contrary, he was recommending a line which involved its withdrawal. He implied, indeed, that he was not only firmer in the matter than Lie had been, but also firmer than some of his colleagues in the present Cabinet: he said that when he had first taken office he knew nothing of the previous history of the question, not having been a member of the *Storting* when it was debated in secret in 1945, and had been horrified to read the draft protocol and to find how far Lie had committed himself. 'My first thought', he said, 'was: "How could any Norwegian Foreign Minister have agreed to this, and how can I get us out of it?"' and he has since told the Canadian Minister that he objects to any agreement of that sort with the Russians, however anodyne, because it would look like linking Norway up with the Eastern *bloc*—which is perhaps the real Russian objective. He confirmed what I had previously heard from Professor Worm-Müller,[5] that Nygaardsvold[6] had been angry with Lie when he learned what had happened at Moscow in 1944 and had wished to repudiate the whole negotiation but had been over-ruled by the rest of the Cabinet, led by Terje Wold,[7] who comes from the North of Norway and could not forget that there were Russian troops at Kirkenes. (It was Wold, he said, who as Chairman of the Foreign Affairs Committee, a post which he still holds, had been largely responsible for persuading the *Storting* in 1945 to approve the protocol.) As for the members of the present Cabinet, it seems evident, from the way in which they are now proceeding, that some of them, at least, must be a bit wobbly: they have put no Government proposal before the *Storting*, but have let Lange suggest a line of policy to it on his own authority and, as he specifically told me, are waiting to see what happens in the next secret debate before taking any decision.

As regards publicity, Lange said that the Norwegian Embassy in London, whom he had asked to find out who was responsible for the *Times* leakage, had reported that the source was in Norway but not at Oslo.[8] I think this means that the ultimate

---

[2] Charles Bay.
[3] Foreign editor of *Arbeiderbladet*.
[4] No. 7.
[5] Member of the Norwegian Government in exile, 1942-45.
[6] Prime Minister of Norway, 1935-45.
[7] Minister of Justice, 1939-45.
[8] FRUS 1947, Vol. III, p. 1006, note 2, states that 'Responsibility for the leak in newspapers was admitted by the London correspondent of the Oslo *Arbeiderbladet*, who informed the (London) *Times*.'

source was one of the Foreign Affairs Committee of the *Storting*: Lange said, indeed, that he had been expecting the news to break ever since he had made his report to the Committee and was even rather surprised that it had not broken earlier still. As indicated in my telegram, I suspect that those responsible for the leakage, knowing that the *Storting* was due to take a decision on the whole question this month and fearing that, as it would be taken in secret session and with only such knowledge of the facts as the Government chose to communicate, it might not be firm enough, acted at what they thought was the psychological moment—and, I am bound to say, with very satisfactory results from their point of view. The sensation here has been very considerable—much greater, indeed, than has been allowed to appear in public, and if the Government want the support of public opinion in standing firm, they can certainly have it. It is even believed in some circles (including several of my colleagues) that they themselves instigated the leakage in order to secure such support; but this is clearly disproved by Lange's attitude and his language to me.

Throughout this business, indeed, Lange seems to have been unduly apprehensive of the consequences of telling the truth to the public (who even now, of course, know nothing like the whole truth: for example, they do not know what the Russians originally demanded in 1944[9] nor what Molotov demanded at New York);[10] and he is still afraid of Russian reaction, for he begged me, at the end of our interview, to bear in mind the importance of keeping his plans secret until the communication had been made to the Russians. In this respect, however, he is no worse than Lie was, and in general I begin to think that he may not compare so unfavourably with his predecessor. He is as frank with me as Lie used to be, and is, of course, a more cultivated man; and it now looks to me as if he was 'celebrated, cultivated and under-rated', like the Duke of Plaza-Toro. I am still not quite sure on the last point: there are matters, such as the Churchill visit and his prevarication to the Turkish minister, which require some explanation; but if he gets away with this Spitsbergen business he will certainly have deserved well of his country.

Yours ever,
L. COLLIER

[9] No. 3.
[10] No. 79.

No. 85

Letter from Mr Halford to Mr Allen (Washington), 13 February 1947
Confidential (FO 371/65889, N2232/2232/15)

[No salutation on this copy]

Shortly after the capitulation of Germany, a SCI (Special Counter Intelligence) team, partly composed of British officers of SOE and partly of Danes, obtained possession of a platinum and diamond watch, originally the property of Eva Braun, which was a gift to her from Hitler, and apparently bears an inscription to this effect. The actual finding of the watch was done by the Danes, and it is now in the possession of the Danish Military Authorities. At the time it was found, it was agreed that the watch should later be sold, and the proceeds divided in equal parts between the Danish *Frihedsfonden* and the (British) Special Forces Association Provident Fund of 8, Herbert Crescent, SW1.

After some discussion in Copenhagen, the Danes have decided to send the watch to the United States and to sell it there to the highest bidder. I am informed that the Danish Military Attaché in Washington is being instructed to deliver the British half of the proceeds to the British Embassy. I think you should be forewarned that you may be approached in this connexion.

I gather that Danish title to this watch is based on the view, shared by our military authorities, that it is 'legitimate loot', and that there is no likelihood of the Danish claim to possession being contested.[1] Unless you see objection I should be grateful if you would accept the money, when the time comes for it to be handed over, as a gift to the Special Forces Association Provident Fund, and forward it to me for delivery to the recipients.[2]

[No signature on this copy]

[1] An opinion had been sought from Sir William Beckett, the Foreign Office Legal Adviser, to confirm that this view was correct.
[2] No document has been found recording the response from the Embassy in Washington to this request.

No. 86

Mr Shepherd (Helsinki) to Mr Bevin, 15 February 1947
No. 50 Confidential (FO 371/65910, N2330/3/56)

British Policy in Finland: Activities of Legation Staff and British Council
Sir,

In view of the signature of the Finnish Peace Treaty, I feel that, insofar as British policy in Finland finds expression and support by means of the activities of the members of the legation staff and of the British Council, it may be of some interest if I comment on those activities during the period since the armistice.

2. I should define present British policy in Finland thus:

(*a*) To supervise by means of the British element of the Control Commission the carrying out of the terms of the armistice.

(*b*) To encourage, and as far as possible secure, the continued political and economic independence of Finland; and for this purpose to encourage relations with the West in general and discourage undue subordination to the USSR.

(*c*) To encourage Fenno-British trade with particular regard to the United Kingdom imports of timber and timber products, and United Kingdom exports of manufactured and semi-manufactured goods.

(*d*) To reinstate friendly relations between the Finnish and British Governments and peoples by means of expanding cultural and business relations.

3. As regards (*a*), the reports of the British element of the Allied Control Commission will have shown the progress of this particular task. If I may be allowed to comment, I should say that it has been a comparatively easy task, to the extent that the Russians have set themselves to avoid imposing major infringements of the armistice terms, so that there has been little ground for dispute. The Russians have, however, consistently kept the British element in ignorance of what was going on, so far as they were able to do so, while never hesitating to emphasise the Allied character of the commission in connexion with

any interventions unpalatable to the Finns. But while the conduct of the Russians cannot be said to have been either frank or co-operative, and while they have undoubtedly been harsh and over-bearing towards the Finns, and even unjust in their interpretations of matters of detail, the British element have found little ground for serious complaint against their Allies, nor have the Finns found the Russian methods such as to justify even unofficial hints to the British element that they should apply a moderating influence.

4. The task as regards the Finns has not involved many complications. The determination of a considerable number of Finns, including numerous officers and men of the army, to make provision to resist any Russian attempt at military occupation, led to concealment of arms and other conspiracies at the time of the armistice and soon after it, and these conspiracies have led to action by the Finnish Government as well as activity by the Control Commission. Otherwise the Finns have fulfilled the armistice terms in such a manner as to leave comparatively little ground for intervention by the commission.

5. As regards (b), it would be too optimistic to say that, even though she has been spared an army of occupation, Finland has made good her independence. She is still a country under an armistice regimen, and the struggle for independence has scarcely yet begun. But the deep gloom and acute apprehension of the immediately post-armistice period has at least given place to hope strongly impregnated with incredulity. The Russians have frequently expressed their desire to right the wrongs suffered by Finland under the Czars and have repeatedly said that Finnish independence will be respected; and they have given earnests of their sincerity in the markedly better treatment that they have accorded to Finland in comparison with other ex-satellite countries. But they have never hesitated to give harsh expression to their displeasure with Finland for having joined in the German attack with an eye to sharing the spoils of the victors, and have been careful to check any signs of resurgence based upon impenitence. But of whatever complex of reasons their attitude is composed, they have undoubtedly afforded the Finns a reasonable possibility of working their passage and thus restored life to the germs of independence which were so nearly stifled two years ago.

6. There is no doubt that the Finnish Government and people looked on the British Political and Military Missions on their arrival much as a drowning man is supposed to regard a substantial straw. And though they were not justified in their expectations that we should promptly interpose ourselves as barriers between themselves and the Russians, the mere presence of the two missions has had an incalculable effect on Finnish morale. In these circumstances it has been a task of some delicacy to avoid, so to speak, disappointing our public, while refraining from any actions of policy which might lead the Russians to react by turning the screw to teach the Finns who was the real master. The British element of the Control Commission have wisely confined themselves carefully to their duties in connexion with the armistice, and while gradually increasing friendly contact with the Finns, have never let it be forgotten that they are in fact an element of an Allied body. So far as I am personally concerned I was fortunate in being able, within a short time of my arrival, to demonstrate that we wished to resume, as far as circumstances permitted, friendly trading relations with the prominent Finnish exporters with whom we had had so much to do before the war. The arrival of a timber mission from the United Kingdom in January 1945 gave me an opportunity of giving a dinner party which not only initiated the resumption of those relations, but was understood as a gesture of British sympathy and support for Finland. I did

not think it desirable to make these relations too intimate since the persons concerned, though mainly very pro-British, were anti-Russian and the objects of suspicion by our Allies, but the development of trade made it possible for the counsellor (commercial) to re-establish confidential relations when he arrived.

7. The complexion of the political parties varied from pro-Nazi on the Right to Communist on the Left. There were, in fact, few actual pro-Nazis, but there was a widespread and well-rooted friendship for Germany as a country. Combined with it was a historic and bitter hatred of Russia which was not confined to hatred of Bolshevism or Czarism, but had the quality of dislike and fear of Russian domination, founded on hard experience. This hostility to Russia penetrated further to the Left than did friendship for Germany, and the ranks of the Social Democratic Party were themselves split by the identification of their leader, Mr Tanner, with Russophobia. In consequence the Russophilism of the extreme Left had a supplementary intensity due to the sense of being in a righteous and now ascendant minority, an intensity that was also reinforced in many cases by prison sentences.

8. The Government was necessarily formed from the Russophil elements, so far as this was possible. But since these were in a minority, the Cabinet contained members of the Right, or Tanner, wing of the Social Democratic Party and, in addition to the Communists and the Radical Left, a proportion of Agrarians whose parliamentary representation was equally as strong as the other two groups, but whose war record was certainly not tinged with sympathy for Soviet Russia.

9. It was evident not only that the future of Finland depended on good relations with Soviet Russia, but that it was of the greatest importance that these relations should be shown to be good. In an ex-satellite country it was clearly desirable that the British and Russian representatives should show a united front as far as possible, especially in view of the apparent Finnish conviction that the role of the British representative should be that of a mediator between Russians and Finns. We need at the same time to conserve Finnish friendship and respect.

10. It did not take long to convince the Finns that neither of our missions had arrived in order to secure modifications of the armistice terms, but, as I have already mentioned, the very presence of the British representatives had a moral effect which can scarcely be exaggerated, since it gave the Finns a conviction that they could at least count on justice within the terms of the armistice agreement. Since our arrival this mission and myself especially have received a degree of pictorial and other publicity which is certainly more a measure of that conviction than of any intrinsic merit. It was a method of publicising a welcome gleam of hope for salvation.

11. My staff and I lost no opportunity, however, of emphasising that the future of Finland must be built upon friendship with Soviet Russia, and that the United Kingdom has a treaty of alliance and friendship with that country to which we attached great importance. I did what I properly could to support and encourage the Finnish Government in their policy of fulfilment of the armistice terms and of demonstrating their determination to make possible a period of genuine friendship with Soviet Russia, while deprecating any unnecessary servility. This task was fortunately made easier by two important factors—the behaviour of the Russians themselves and the common sense of the Finnish people. The Russians have neither exasperated the Finns by a policy of unbearable bullying, nor attempted to excite anti-British feeling, as they have done in other countries, though the extreme Left press has been consistently unfriendly and occasionally obstreperous. The

Finnish people for their part have behaved with most admirable restraint. Anti-Russian feeling is still extremely strong throughout the country, especially away from Helsinki and this is illustrated by the widespread nature of the preparations for what would have been the useless resistance to military occupation which were revealed by the arms dumps conspiracy. Yet apart from the shooting of a Russian officer very soon after the Armistice there has not been a single major anti-Russian incident since September 1944. Even the excitement aroused on May Day by a provocative Communist procession, in which a portrait of Otto Kuusinen was displayed, led to only extremely minor demonstrations, which were regarded with quite unnecessary sensitiveness by the Russian authorities.

12. It is noteworthy that when the Russian members of the Control Commission arrived they did not immediately interfere with freedom of movement between Finland and Sweden, or with the freedom of the press. They took no measures even to keep themselves informed of the identities of persons travelling between the two countries, and it was only in March 1945, when Great Britain showed signs of wanting to inaugurate air services with Finland, that they placed a ban on external flying. Communication by boat was never interfered with. On the other hand, to judge by the early exchanges which I had with Colonel-General Zhdanov when I insisted on freedom of entry for British journalists, and the close control exercised on a party of foreign correspondents from Moscow, there was some doubt in the Russian mind whether the iron curtain should be kept entirely away from the Finnish scene. In the event, it has merely thrown a shadow, and this is, I feel sure, due to the satisfactory development of the Finnish situation, especially in the light of the two important factors I have mentioned. I think that the legation has been able to apply stabilising correctives here and there by maintaining good relations with the Russians, and by discreet advice and other action. I have been able, I think, to stiffen the Finns when they have had doubts whether they should stand out against yielding too privileged a position to their own Communist Party, and have done what I could to impress on them that their best hope of independence is to maintain, in conjunction with a friendly attitude to Soviet Russia, the sturdy democracy which has been a characteristic of the people throughout their recent history. On the other hand it has been possible to restrain them on occasion from impolitic expressions of nationalism which might have adversely affected their future relations with their Eastern neighbour. At the same time I have frequently been able to emphasise that we regarded it as important that Finland should maintain substantial trade and cultural relations with the West.

13. Trade relations were successfully inaugurated by the timber and pulp mission which came to Finland in January 1945. The investigations made at that time by Mr Caplan of the Ministry of Supply, showed that timber supplies for the United Kingdom were dependent on the import into Finland of a variety of material. An emergency import programme was, not without difficulty, arranged under the auspices of the British Government, and this opened the way for private trading. In 1946 the percentages of imports and exports for the most important countries were as follows:

The Nordic Countries, 1944-1951

Country	Exports	Imports
United Kingdom	26.7	21.3
Soviet Union	20.6	21.2
Denmark	11.0	10.3
Sweden	9.3	10.0
Belgium	7.2	5.7
United States	6.9	19.5

These figures which have been attained in the main by the enterprise of private concerns are, I think, remarkable when it is considered that Finnish trade with all other countries has been carried on by means of barter agreements, and in the case of the United States, partly by loans. They reflect credit on the energy of British exporters, helped by hard work on the part of the commercial counsellor and his staff in re-establishing and maturing friendly contacts with Finnish business men, and in bringing Finnish and British suppliers and customers in contact with each other. The important trade relations with the United Kingdom, combined with those which have been developed with other western European States and transatlantic countries, have gone a long way towards settling the pattern of the future economy of Finland. The extreme Left journals have regarded this tendency with distaste, since they appear to support a complete reintegration of Finnish economy with that of Russia, regardless of the natural channels of demand and supply, and their displeasure is evidence of the importance to Finland of western trade, not only for the sake of her economic health, but also as some kind of guarantee of continued independence.

14. Cultural and business relations between Finland and the United Kingdom have been developed quietly but successfully. The Russians made something of a splash with their cultural propaganda soon after the armistice. There were visits by the Red Army choir and by a folk dancing troupe, together with other musical performances, while the Finnish-Soviet Union Society was launched, if not literally with a flourish of trumpets, at any rate, with chords from the symphony orchestra. The membership was rapidly brought up to a high figure, but the society devoted too much of its activities to political propaganda, and degenerated more into a meeting ground for the extreme Left than an organ for the genuine cultivation of human relationships. The Finnish-British Society on the other hand achieved a more or less spontaneous resurrection under the guiding hand of Professor Reuter, and became a centre for the learning and practice of the British language, as well as a vehicle for lectures and social intercourse. The Helsinki membership, in spite of some reluctance to pay subscriptions, is now about 1,500 and similar but not subsidiary societies have sprung up on a smaller scale all over Finland. There are now about thirty of them in the provinces and seven smaller Anglophil societies in the capital. The organisation of these societies leaves something to be desired and the 1946-47 session in Helsinki has scarcely fulfilled expectations, though the meetings, which take place every three or four weeks, attract an audience of between 200 and 300. I had the pleasure of launching both the Helsinki and Turku societies by giving lectures in November and December 1944, and was impressed by the evident relief and enthusiasm with which the renewal of contacts with Britain were welcomed. It may be mentioned in passing that the Finnish-British Societies are self-supporting, whereas the Finnish-Soviet

Union Society receives a subsidy of 3 million Finmarks, and recently asked for 7 million Finmarks more, which was refused by the Diet.[1]

15. The information section of the legation has had to be built up from the beginning, and the press attaché has had to work hard to secure the necessary contacts with the Finnish press. The press is in many respects amateurish and somewhat unworthy of the general level of progress in the country. Finland is really a western European backwater, and eddies from the affairs of Europe pass almost unnoticed into it, drift sluggishly round and pass out again without much disturbing what might be called the pond life in the middle. Hence it has been necessary to aerate the Finnish consciousness of external affairs by actively pumping in suitable information. A certain amount of method seems now to have been induced, but the level of editorial comment is remarkably low compared with, for instance, the Swedish press. It is true that the press has been affected by the general gloom and apathy of the post-armistice period, and that the necessity to placate the censorship and avoid anything hurtful to Russian sensitiveness has been a severe handicap. Perhaps the quality of Finnish expression on international matters may improve when peace has been concluded, but a good deal must still depend on the quality of Finnish thought. All we can do is to maintain the quality of the information we supply.

16. The British Council, like the press section, suffered from birth pangs due to lack of staff, accommodation and equipment. It has now got into its stride and is doing very useful work, especially perhaps in the sphere of instruction in English. This is particularly important at present since a change over is taking place from German to English as the first language in schools. The British Council and the Finnish-British Society co-operate in this matter, though unfortunately not without jealousies and friction.

17. I have been particularly pleased with the success of the new venture as far as Finland is concerned of appointing a labour attaché. Finland's industrial development between the wars outstripped the development of social organisation. There were some points of resemblance between the Finnish and British industrial revolutions; labour welfare and conditions became very largely a matter of patriarchal provision by the big employers. Sweating and slum conditions never appeared, but there has nevertheless been a good deal of ground to make up. Mr Thomas[2] has rather stolen the Soviet thunder in this respect since he has been able to give information and explanation of what has been done in Britain by agreement between employers and workers and by Government action. These expositions have shown a state of affairs far more palatable to Finnish industry in general than the totalitarian methods of Soviet Russia. It has also been possible for the labour attaché to organise contacts with Left-wing and social welfare circles which the legation has never before been able to reach, and there is evidence that this development is much appreciated.

18. To sum up what I fear is a rather rambling despatch, the method which I have adopted, and encouraged my staff to adopt, in carrying out the policy referred to in paragraph 2 of this despatch, has been to exert a maximum of influence with a minimum of display. Too much prominence on the part of this mission would probably have encouraged the Finnish tendency to intransigence without being of material help, while the Russians would have corrected the balance by increased

---

[1] For an account of the work of a member of the British Council with the Finnish-British Society of Kajaani, see Diana Ashcroft, *Journey to Finland* (London: Frederick Muller Ltd., 1952).

[2] C.L. Thomas, Labour Attaché.

harshness. On the other hand too great an apparent indifference would have deprived the Finns of significant comfort at a time when the Russian shadow was felt to be most menacing. I think we can claim to have established respect for the watchful interest of the mission and appreciation for the practical help which we have been able to afford. Many Finns would have preferred us to be less modest and politically less encouraging towards the Left, but on the whole I am satisfied that the methods we have striven to pursue have been sound and trust that they have at least not aroused disapproval at home.

19. The fact that events in Finland have appeared to pursue a comparatively even course has certainly not meant that the Armistice period has been free from strain for the personnel of the British element and the political mission, and I am much indebted to the members of both missions for their assistance and support in the business of steering a level course between the real and imaginary troubles that have been frequent enough in the last two and a half years.[3]

I have, etc.,
F.M. SHEPHERD

[3] Northern Department commented very positively on this despatch. Warner noted that Shepherd's personal position stood very high, and that he was surprised and delighted to learn that Britain stood first in commercial exchanges with Finland. Hankey suggested that McNeil should show the despatch to Healey at the Labour Party (FO 371/65910, N2330/3/56).

No. 87

Sir L. Collier (Oslo) to Mr Bevin, 19 February 1947, 4.59 p.m.[1]
Tel. No. 55 Important, Secret, Light[2] (FO 371/66021, N2237/68/30G)

My telegram No.52. Spitsbergen.

Norwegian Minister for Foreign Affairs who has returned to work for a week, told me today that *Storting* in secret session on February 15th had adopted resolution (he gave me translation which I am forwarding by bag) which he had communicated to Mr Molotov in a personal letter brought by M. Koht (a junior official in Ministry of Foreign Affairs, not State Secretary as described in Moscow telegram No. 436)[3] and delivered on February 17th to Mr Novikoff in Mr Molotov's absence.

2. Resolution points out draft protocol was submitted in war conditions which have now given place to situation in which United Nations Organisation is in existence and has passed disarmament resolution at Soviet initiative. Protocol is therefore no longer appropriate and 'negotiations of a military character with any single foreign power concerning the defence of a region under Norwegian sovereignty would be contrary to foreign policy which the Government in concert with the *Storting* have pursued since liberation'. Nevertheless in view of assistance given to Norway by Soviet Russia which has particular economic interests in Spitsbergen, it is agreed that discussions 'should be continued in other respects to

[1] Repeated to Washington and Moscow.
[2] 'Light' was a codeword introduced in August 1946 to ensure that higher authority in the FO saw certain telegrams. The system proved less than satisfactory and was discontinued in January 1950.
[3] Not printed.

prepare the way for a revision of Spitsbergen treaty to make it more satisfactory', and that ex-enemy states should be excluded from any eventual negotiations with other signatory powers (Minister for Foreign Affairs realises that Italy cannot legally be excluded but is leaving it to Russians to find out).

3. Minister for Foreign Affairs has heard nothing so far in reply to his communication, which he made by letter as there have been no official negotiations since 1945. Letter however had stated that the position of the Norwegian Government must now be made plain to the public, and a statement would shortly be issued, giving text of resolution with an explanatory extract from his report to *Storting*. When this had been done and he had made statement on Spain (on which I am reporting separately by despatch) he would leave for some six weeks as Secretary General had stated.[4]

[4] The Soviet Union never replied to this note. In reply to an enquiry by the US Chargé d'Affaires in May 1948, Lange 'indicated that he considered the subject "dead" at least for the time being' (FRUS 1947, Vol. III, p. 1018).

No. 88

Minute from Mr Warr to Mr Jellicoe (German Department), 22 February 1947
(FO 371/65885, N2682/122/15)

Please see the attached letter from the Control Office to me of the 22 February.[1]

I cannot think why the COGA[2] have only just got around to dealing with General Robertson's letter which I see is dated January 7th. So far as the German refugees in Denmark are concerned that letter is not quite up to date. Out of the total of 200,000 German refugees in Denmark, the three Western zones of Germany had, according to our information, agreed to take 36,000. The Russian zone had agreed to take 15,000. This meant that the Soviet Govt were not even beginning to implement Stalin's offer to the Danish Govt. to take half of the total number of refugees into the Soviet zone, provided the 3 Western zones received between them the remaining half. The Danish Govt. took this up in Moscow and we gave them support (please see the attached copy of tel. No. 4125 to Moscow).[3] Sir M. Peterson then wrote a letter to Molotov, the answer to which we have now received and which is contained in Moscow tel. No. 446 (copy attached).[1] It will be seen that the Russians have moved a step forward and have at least sent instructions to the Russians in Berlin, and are showing signs of implementing Stalin's offer, though without mentioning it.

But even if we do get some advance from the Russians in Berlin, I think that progress will be too slow if the question is allowed to drag on quadripartite in the Control Council and General Robertson's letter bears this out. We owe it to the Danes to make a more determined effort to get rid of their refugees and we have often told them that, though we do not bear the prime responsibility, we will make

[1] Not printed.
[2] Control Office for Germany and Austria
[3] Not printed. This telegram also commented that the refugees were a heavy financial burden on Denmark, that the guarding of them placed a considerable strain on the small reserves of Danish manpower, and that the Foreign Office had every sympathy with the desire of the Danes to be rid of the refugees.

every effort to help them. The latest occasion was when they made it a condition of their providing a contingent to serve in Germany that the refugees would be removed within the next few months. In our official note in reply we used the following words: 'HMG will exert their utmost efforts to secure their (the refugees') early and total removal.' (For a fuller quotation from our note please see para 2 of tel. No. 76 to Copenhagen in N1623/121/15.)[3] The only way, I suggest, that we are likely to get any progress in this matter is by taking it up at the Moscow Conference and there urging the French and the Russians to take more in their zones. But this Danish problem cannot obviously be taken up in isolation but only as a part of the problem of which General Robertson outlines the picture.

The first thing to do I think is to discover whether or not the Russians have evaded their commitments under Potsdam to take refugees from Poland. I believe that this is being explored. If the Russians turn out to have evaded their commitments then we have a clear case for arguing with them that they should take a larger proportion of the Germans from Denmark than would fall to their share under Stalin's offer. Until we know what the exact position is with regard to the Germans from Poland I do not think that there is much point in the meeting with COGA suggested in the attached letter. In any case I think that the problem is more for German Dept. than Northern Dept. to co-ordinate. No doubt a meeting with COGA will be necessary sometime, but I propose to tell Mr Irving[4] that we do not propose to have it until we have discussed the question further here.

[4] Of COGA.

No. 89

Mr Jerram (Stockholm) to Mr Attlee,[1] 11 March 1947
No. 70 (FO 371/66513, N3288/3288/42)

Sir,
I have the honour to submit herewith the enclosed report on political events in Sweden for the year 1946.

2. I am indebted to Mr Henderson[2] and to Mr Nielsen[3] for the bulk of the work entailed in the compilation of this report.

3. I am sending copies of this despatch to His Majesty's representatives at Oslo, Copenhagen and Helsingfors.

I have etc.,
C.B. JERRAM

Enclosure in No. 89

The year 1946 has been described by a leading Swedish newspaper as 'the first year of war', by which it meant the first full twelve month period in which party politics again held sway. The period of unity under a coalition Government is definitely over.

[1] The Prime Minister was in charge of the Foreign Office in Bevin's absence.
[2] First Secretary, British Embassy, Stockholm.
[3] Honorary Attaché, later First Secretary, British Embassy, Stockholm.

2. The outstanding event of the year was undoubtedly the death of the Prime Minister, Per Albin Hansson. More than any man he typified for his own countrymen the Sweden of the middle way and the policy which, with a pliancy perhaps distasteful in retrospect, was nevertheless successful in keeping Sweden out of the war and on tolerably good terms with the victors. His sudden decease left a problem of succession which was somewhat surprisingly solved by a compromise in the person of Monsieur Erlander, who seems however to have got into his stride with confidence and ease.

3. It is too early to judge whether Monsieur Erlander will content himself with the Per Albin policy of swimming with the tide, or whether he will strike out for himself. The inheritance to which he succeeded was not altogether an easy one. While still assured of a majority in the *Riksdag*, the Social Democratic Party had received a nasty jolt in the municipal elections (losing seats to both the Liberals and Communists) which had been fought on a national rather than a parochial basis. The Social Democrats had resisted all attempts on the part of the Communists to form a common front, and the attitude of Monsieur Erlander has so far shown no signs of weakening on this point.

4. During the earlier part of the year the attacks on the Liberal and Conservative parties had been directed largely against the principles of planned economy, though with little success. While steadily pursuing its programme of social legislation, which was indeed largely non-controversial, the Government refrained from any drastic measures of socialisation and at the end of the year reports had still to be received from the commissions appointed to examine such questions as the socialisation of insurance and the oil trade. Nor did the appreciation of the *krona* in the early summer meet with substantial criticism, though its effect on the controlled prices fixed for forest products caused some discontent in business circles. Towards the end of the year, the fear of inflation was marked, and to deal effectively with this will not be the least of the problems vexing the Government.

5. While the Social Democrat party were faced during the year with a succession problem, the monarchy was relieved of any such anxiety by the birth in April of a great-grandson to King Gustaf, and the public rejoicing at this event served to emphasise the stability of the Crown.

6. Throughout the year a spirit of 'De-nazification' was manifest and Swedes of all shades of opinion appeared anxious to demonstrate that they were 'good democrats', at times to an almost ludicrous extent. The various pots missed no opportunities of calling the kettles black and the dusty files of newspapers of the early war years were ransacked for compromising utterances. The witch-hunt was directed especially against members of the armed forces, but Per Albin Hansson with characteristic ingenuity contrived a temporary lightning conductor in the shape of the so-called 'Purge Board', with its somewhat vague and general powers of investigation into the antecedents of candidates for promotion. The inadequate recruitment of long-service officers and NCOs also gave rise to much concern, a problem which was unsolved at the end of the year.

7. In the field of Foreign Affairs the most important event was the adherence of Sweden to the United Nations with the responsibilities which this implies. On several occasions during the year both the Prime Minister and the Swedish Ministry of Foreign Affairs emphasised the fact that Sweden would not become a member of any *bloc*, an attitude confirmed at the session of the UNO after her election, where her vote was awarded in the various Committees sometimes in line with the Anglo-American and sometimes with the Soviet point of view.

8. The Swedish attitude towards Russia remains something of a riddle. At the beginning of the year she was still faced with the liquidation of the Balt affair which had caused such a storm in the closing months of 1945, but the repatriation of the ex-*Wehrmacht* Balts was finally carried through and the agitation died down; it had however served as a reminder that it would not take much to revive the anti-Russian feeling which is ever latent in the average Swede, at any rate of the middle and upper classes, and which had been stimulated, until the signature of the trade treaty with Russia, by violent anti-Swedish propaganda from Moscow. Anti-Russian sentiments found further expression in the agitation against the treaty, which was nevertheless eventually passed after a controversial debate by a unanimous vote of the *Riksdag*. Newspaper and *Riksdag* critics alike were however at pains to emphasise that their strictures were levelled at the purely commercial aspects of the agreement, and that all parties were agreed as to the desirability for improved relations with the Soviet; but these assurances rang somewhat hollow. The fear that a horde of Russian 'inspectors' will seize the opportunity for commercial and other espionage is already being voiced. Immediately after having concluded the Trade and Payments Agreement with the USSR, Sweden began trade negotiations with the East European States under Russian influence.

9. The situation in Finland has been watched with anxiety, and the slightest sign of a relaxation of the Russian grip on that country welcomed, but it is clear that Finland has been written off by Sweden as a member of the Nordic community. The sentimental interest however remains, and Finnish children have been maintained in Swedish homes on a wide scale.

10. The death of Per Albin Hansson, deeply regretted as it is, may perhaps contribute towards the better understanding between Sweden and Norway which is gradually developing. The late Prime Minister possessed a singular knack of irritating Norwegian opinion by his public utterances in justification of Swedish wartime policy. The White Books dealing with policy during the war, promised by both Governments, had not been published by the end of the year, though the selection of documents and their simultaneous publication in both countries had been agreed in principle. The Swedes have welcomed any approach by the Norwegians in the sphere of military training, and the training of Norwegian cadets at the Swedish military academy has made for good will.

11. Relations with Denmark have been uniformly cordial even though the bond of a government of the same political persuasion has not existed, as in the case of Norway. Sweden has kept a watchful eye on developments in the South Slesvig question but has been careful not to express an opinion. While the connection with Iceland has not been intimate, the abandonment of the idea of the cession of air bases in that country to the United States of America was obviously welcome to Sweden.

12. The acquisition by Poland of part of the East Prussian littoral has obviously increased her importance as a Baltic power, and though Sweden's dealings with Poland have been largely confined to the commercial field, she is clearly anxious to stand well with that country, whatever the complexion of its government, as it is the main source of Swedish coal supplies.

13. As remarked earlier in this report, the Swedes have been desperately anxious to demonstrate that they have shaken off every trace of Nazism, and on the whole there has been little sign of the sympathy campaign on behalf of Germany. The Nuremberg criminals were generally adjudged to have deserved their fate, and a movement to receive German children in Sweden has not met with great support.

This has not prevented the Swedes from passing criticism on the shortcomings of the occupying powers, but on the whole Britain has enjoyed a favourable press.

14. Spain is sufficiently remote and the trade connection with that country sufficiently small to allow full play to the agitation of the Swedish left wing circles for a breach with Franco, though the Government have consistently refused to be stampeded into any premature action: the new Swedish Minister to Spain, however, appointed in 1945, was never allowed by his Government to proceed. It seems likely that in any debate on the subject in UNO Sweden will be found on the side advocating a tough line with Franco.

15. With the other European powers, no political problems arise as far as Sweden is concerned: she has been mindful of her commercial interests, however, and concluded trade agreements with a number of them.

16. Asia may be said to lie largely outside Sweden's sphere of interests, but in Africa she has made the most of such opportunities as are offered by Ethiopia as a field for Swedish administrators. Whether they will meet with disappointment in the future remains to be seen.

17. The importance of the United States of America in world affairs and her determination not to disassociate herself from European politics have duly impressed Sweden, but it may be doubted whether the influence of America is as strong in Sweden today as it was a year ago. American press references to Sweden are apt to be ill-informed, and the American objections to the Russia-Sweden trade agreement caused resentment—even amongst many Swedish opponents of the agreement. The designs which the United States of America were thought to harbour on Iceland and Greenland caused apprehension in Sweden and some doubt is felt as to the lasting commercial prosperity of the United States of America.

18. On the other hand Sweden is eager to secure a share of the market in South America, and by the despatch both of a trade mission under the leadership of Prince Bertil[4] and of the cruiser *Gotland* on an extensive cruise in American waters has kept the Swedish flag well to the fore. These efforts are ably supplemented by the development of the Swedish civil air lines which now have direct and regular routes to the majority of European capitals, to both North and South America and also to Abyssinia, and Iran.

19. The keynote of Swedish foreign policy is the avoidance of risk. It is fear, rather than affection, which makes her lean towards Russia, though not so far as to jeopardise irretrievably her connections with the Western Powers. She is still at heart solidly democratic in the western sense: her natural instinct is to play the leading role, if not to assume the active leadership, among the Scandinavian peoples: but she will make no move which may offend a Russia which looms dangerously large now that Finland can hardly be recognised as a buffer state and Norway possesses a land frontier with the USSR. She has joined UNO without exaggerated hopes or fears, largely because her prestige demanded it, but with the reflection that if a clash between the Great Powers should occur she can once more take refuge in neutrality.

[4] Third son of King Gustav VI.

No. 90

Mr Randall (Copenhagen) to Mr Bevin, 13 March 1947
No. 100E Confidential (FO 371/65858, N5341/274/15)

External Financial Position of the United Kingdom
Anglo-Danish Trade Relations

Sir,

The following are my comments on your circular despatch No. 028 of 12th February:[1]

Before the war the United Kingdom was Denmark's best customer and Denmark was the United Kingdom's third best customer in Europe. The United Kingdom could then pay in goods for rather less than half of what Denmark sent. The balance was made up largely of sterling which Denmark could use for purchases in countries with which her balance of trade was unfavourable and for the service of loans and so on. The United Kingdom has once more become Denmark's best customer and Denmark today has risen to be the United Kingdom's best customer outside the British Empire. But the balance of payments position has changed so radically that the United Kingdom has a favourable trade balance of something like £40 million, or, in other words, is holding the equivalent of that sum in inconvertible *kroner*. In addition, out of regard for our long tradition of commercial and financial friendship with Denmark, we have undertaken to do out best to supply 'hard currency' for Denmark's essential purchases outside the sterling area, and we have carried out this undertaking in spite of our all too rapidly dwindling stock of dollars.

2. After the United Kingdom, Germany was up to 1939 Denmark's largest supplier of manufactured goods besides being the principal supplier of some raw materials and some semi-manufactured goods. Germany was also Denmark's prime secondary market and Denmark is exercised to find a successor to her both as market and supplier. At present, apart from trade with the United Kingdom, Denmark's external trade is controlled by a series of short-term trade agreements supported by clearing arrangements. Denmark is therefore in the position of having an unfavourable trade balance with the United Kingdom; being almost entirely dependent on the United Kingdom for hard currency for essential purposes in the extra-European areas; and of being unable to earn balances with any of the other countries with whom she trades. It is, however, true that Denmark can call for the settlement of her outstanding balances (understood to be between 40 million and 60 million *kroner* at the moment) with Russia in gold or dollars when it exceeds 2 million *kroner* (not quite 'at any time'—paragraph 118 of the appendix to the survey), but Denmark has so far shown no sign of exercising her right—either through fear of giving offence or from the desire to obtain from Russia raw materials (both industrial and agricultural) rather than dollars or gold so long as we are willing to furnish the former. The pre-war picture was quite different. Denmark was able to use her sterling balance to liquidate her unfavourable trade balance with Germany and other countries as well as to service her loans with the United States and others.

3. I may remark in passing that the reference in paragraph 124 of the Survey of the Overseas Economic Situation (January 1947)[1] to Denmark's strong bargaining

---

[1] Not printed.

position in relation to various continental buyers needs some qualification. I think that it is due to the fact that we pre-empt high proportions of Denmark's exportable surplus of butter, bacon, and eggs, that Denmark is able to sell what is left at 'fancy' prices to other markets. The Danes maintain that the Russians offered to buy much larger quantities of butter and the Poles much larger quantities of bacon than Denmark could offer. In the first case it was bluff—the Russians could not handle larger quantities and really wanted only enough for Leningrad. And, if they had thrown us over, would the Danes have had the courage to ask for settlement in gold or dollars? In the second case, Denmark has had to undertake to grant her goods on credit to Poland, under the compelling necessity of obtaining Polish coal.

4. Danish economy is centred on agriculture which, in living memory, is directed towards the United Kingdom. The intensive agriculture of Denmark, the most economic having regard to the area and soil to be exploited, produces butter, bacon, and eggs, as primary products, meat (old cows), fat pork, and so on as ancillaries. The United Kingdom used to take 100,000 to 110,000 tons of butter from Denmark before the war and there is no other market or group of markets that can take and pay for over a period anything like this quantity. Danish bacon has long been developed to suit the English taste. The United Kingdom took 60 percent of the exportable surplus of Danish eggs before the war and what is said above of butter applies to eggs. If therefore Denmark chose to re-orientate her economy, as has been threatened or at least hinted by her farming interests because of the alleged inadequate prices paid by the United Kingdom for her chief products, she would have:

(1) To convert her dairy industry from producing high-fat content milk to the maximum instead of optimum milk yield and sell the proceeds as cheese or preserved milk in the world's markets.

(2) To convert her pig industry from the comparatively light-weight bacon pigs to the heavy-weight lard pigs.

(3) To reduce her poultry population and put out of business thousands of farmers who regard poultry as their livelihood or, at least, the bread and butter of their farms, or to convert the eggs into manufactures and compete on the world's markets.

A revolution of this kind would bring in its train all the hardships that revolutions carry and it is hard to conceive of a Danish Government seriously considering it.

5. If, on the assets side, Danish economy has changed only secondarily as a result of the war, on the liabilities side there has been a primary change. Before the war Denmark drew from the United Kingdom up to 80 percent of her needs of coal and coke. Now and for some years to come our supplies of these will be negligible and Denmark must look to Germany for them if she is to be able to pay for any considerable proportion in goods. As noted above, Denmark had before the war an adverse trade balance with Germany, which was accounted for in part by political pressure and by the differential exchange systems operated by Nazi Germany; partly by the operation of cartels; and partly by the fact that Germany produced the fertilisers and raw and semi-manufactured iron and steel that Denmark needed.

6. I take it that there is no doubt, if we hope to raise the present low standard of life in the United Kingdom, we shall for many years to come need all the butter, bacon and eggs that Denmark can supply at competitive prices. In view of our worsened capital position as the result of the war, we shall have to raise our proportion of exports to Denmark above the less than 50 per cent of our imports from Denmark ruling before the war. If we are to do so without coal figuring

among our exports, it will be at the expense of Germany and, in connexion with the annex to the survey, it is interesting to note that Germany supplied:

	Per cent
Chemicals	61.8
Dyestuffs	60
Iron and steel goods	60.9
Machinery and apparatus	57.3
Iron and steel, raw materials and semi-manufactures	53.1
Minerals of glass and products thereof	50

of Danish requirements, whilst we supplied:

	Per cent
Coal, coke, etc.,	70.3
Yarns and threads	60
Piece-goods	60

and more than 30 per cent of Danish requirements other than those supplied by Germany mentioned above.

7. Germany was, then, supplying commodities with increasing percentage shares of world trade, whilst we were supplying those with constant or falling shares of world trade. Owing to our own needs, we cannot for some time take Germany's place as supplier to Denmark of iron and steel raw materials and semi-manufactures. But it seems that we can capture some of this former German market for chemicals, dyestuffs, manufactures of iron and steel, machinery and apparatus, and optical and precision instruments.

8. However much we may be compelled to direct our exports to the Western Hemisphere for the time being, I doubt if we can afford over a long term, on either economic or political grounds, to neglect Denmark, our third best customer in Europe, representing a constant and safe £25 million (pre-war values) a year of our exports. At the same time, the world is (and we are) so short of foodstuffs that it must pay us to encourage Danish production to the utmost and secure as high a proportion of it as possible. Finally, it would be highly prejudicial to our interests for an economic revolution to occur in Denmark.

9. Denmark is, in miniature, in the same position as we are. She has a dead weight of hard currency debts; an adverse sterling balance which she has undertaken to stabilise at least during the current year at about £40 million, but her ability to fulfil this undertaking and revive her agriculture and industry to pre-war level is doubtful; at the moment Denmark has no ability to earn to any substantial extent hard currency or sterling elsewhere, a restoration of Germany or a development of Russian industry and raw material export to a degree sufficient to benefit Denmark both being ruled out. In spite, therefore, of our much greater difficulties, I think—and paragraphs 2 (c) and (d) of your despatch under reference appear to support this—that we should do all we can to help Denmark out of her difficulties during the next five years or, if we cannot do enough, to press others (i.e. the United States) to assist. The long-term result of the latter course will be that Denmark will use her sterling balance less in liquidating her adverse sterling

balance than in servicing a larger dollar loan. With the delay to be foreseen in the recovery of Germany as a large purchaser, and therefore as Denmark's secondary market and supplier, I would conclude that we are in the strong position of being able to insist on our position as Denmark's chief market and chief supplier, and urge on her the necessity of retaining our goodwill and devoting her production to our needs primarily. The means of doing this must, in view of Denmark's 'small State' psychology, be carefully chosen and tactfully exercised, but, if properly presented, the case for treating the United Kingdom and Denmark as complementary on the economic plane should have no great difficulty in securing acceptance, in spite of the reiterated Communist propaganda that Denmark is 'in Britain's pocket' and that a vast and profitable market exists in Soviet Russia.

I have, etc.,
A.W.G. RANDALL

No. 91

Mr Shepherd (Helsinki) to Mr Attlee, 18 March 1947
No. 84 (FO 371/65926, N5877/365/56)

Sir,

With reference to paragraph 4 of Foreign Office circular despatch No. 028 of February 12th,[1] I venture to offer the following observations regarding the position of Anglo-Finnish trade in the general picture of the external financial position of the United Kingdom.

2. Finland is a country whose currency I suppose would come under the heading of both soft and inconvertible, and trade with her has disadvantages which are surpassed by the advantage that she is an important supplier of timber and timber products. Before the war we bought a large quantity of timber from Finland, and in spite of efforts which culminated in a 'British Week' at Helsinki, we were unable to bring our exports into any sort of alignment with our purchases from this country. This situation shows signs of returning in the post-war period and it is exaggerated at the present time by the necessity we are in of buying as much timber as we can get hold of while at the same time we are unable to compete with Finnish demands for British exports. It is especially unfortunate that for the first time in the history of our trade relations with this country it would be practicable to achieve a balance of trade just at the moment when our production is insufficient to take advantage of the fact. In this connection, it seemed to me curious that whereas we have agreed to take a certain amount of token exports from Finland, we have made no arrangements for retaining the interest of importers in the Finnish market by arranging for a complementary token supply of British manufactured goods to Finland. This is all the more regrettable since there is a tendency on the part of British firms to neglect to make provisional arrangements with Finnish importers on the grounds that there is nothing they can at present offer to Finland. Instances have indeed occurred where the neglect of British firms to make some kind of provision arrangement for the future has led to Finnish concerns, which would

---
[1] Not printed.

have preferred to trade with England, to make arrangements with foreign importers.

3. The Finns have attempted to solve their difficulties by concluding bilateral agreements with most European countries but they look to the United States for a great many of their most important requirements. The United States is in a position to fulfil these requirements but only through the machinery of dollar loans. The general result is that the Finns need dollars and are receiving sterling.[2] When the convertibility of current receipts comes into effect in July next, the Finnish import trade is therefore likely to become a drain on our own dollar resources. This is likely to take place in spite of the loans already made by the United States since these do not cover all Finnish requirements.

4. It may be of interest to refer in this connection to what are called reparations industries, that is to say industries which are being built up in Finland in order to comply with that part of Russian reparations demands which calls for deliveries of engineering products. These demands greatly exceeded the normal capacity of Finland to produce and the industries have therefore had to be enlarged or created. It is understood that at least seven milliard Finmarks have been invested in such industries. Generalissimo Stalin has on more than one occasion promised the Finns that after the reparations period Russia will absorb the products of these industries, but it remains to be seen whether Russia will wish to continue to absorb such products unless the Finnish industries concerned show themselves capable of producing materials which are competitive with the world market prices. If the Russians are exigent on the matter of price or if they do not fulfil their promise to absorb the output of these industries, the Finns will be faced with the alternatives of either liquidating the industries or of finding some means of protecting them. These contingencies have apparently already occurred to the Finns, since there is at present a proposal on the part of the communists that the government should take powers to take over excess profits which it is thought are now being made by the timber industries, with the object of assisting the reparations industries. The extent of any help which the reparations industries could obtain from such arrangement would depend on the extent to which the costs of production of Finnish timber fall short of the world market price for timber products. There is, I believe, some reason to think that at the present time the Finnish industries are in fact making high profits.

I have, etc.,
F.M. SHEPHERD

[2] Economic Intelligence Department observed on 1 April that Finnish conversions of sterling would need watching: 'If in fact, as a result of Finland's large favourable trade balance with us, they are excessive, it may be necessary from a purely financial point of view to increase the availability of British exports to Finland, so as to reduce the outflow of sterling' (FO 371/65926, N5877/365/56).

No. 92

Brief for UK Delegation at a Moscow Meeting on Arctic Bases, 20 March 1947
Secret (FO 371/65972, N3447/3447/63G)

Arctic Bases

Iceland
In an exchange of messages at the time when United States forces first went into Iceland in July 1941, the United States Government undertook to remove their forces from Iceland at the end of the war and by the beginning of 1946 they had fulfilled this obligation, except in the case of an air base, comprising a number of airfields, at Keflavik. Evidently hoping to get their rights in this base prolonged, they approached the Icelandic Government in October 1945 on the subject of a permanent base. We were anxious from our own strategic point of view to see the Americans permanently established in a base in Iceland and we gave them support in their endeavours. In return we wanted to secure certain rights for ourselves in connexion with any facilities which the Americans might obtain. We wanted in particular to be sure that in no circumstances would the presence of United States forces in Iceland be allowed to compromise the security of British communications in the North Atlantic, and to reserve the right, in case we were ever engaged in a war in which the United States of America was neutral, to claim to participate in the bases which the United States might obtain.

2. Meeting with strong opposition from Icelandic public opinion, press and parliament, the United States Government decided not to pursue their request for a permanent base, Instead they made an agreement with the Icelandic Government on the 7th October 1946, by which Keflavik was handed over to the Icelandic Government, but the agreement, however, also stipulated (paragraph 4) that 'Keflavik airport will continue to be available for use by aircraft operated by or on behalf of the Government of the United States in connexion with the fulfilment of United States obligations to maintain control agencies in Germany'. We gave support to the United States Government in their negotiations with the Icelandic Government over this agreement.

3. We have learned from our embassy in Washington that the United States Government intend to rest content for the present with these temporary transit rights in Iceland, but that if they decide later to ask the Icelandic Government for more extensive facilities they would inform His Majesty's Government. We thought, and the Chiefs of Staff agreed, that in those circumstances it was not necessary to pursue further with the State Department the question of securing the rights for ourselves which we had wanted when the Americans were asking for a permanent base.

4. It does not seem necessary for us to revert to the matter with the Americans unless it should become evident that they are seeking to turn their present temporary transit rights into something more permanent. In which case we should require to re-examine with the Chiefs of Staff the question of what facilities we should want for ourselves in connexion with the rights which the United States Government might obtain.

Greenland
An agreement concluded between the Danish minister in Washington and Mr Cordell Hull on the 9th April 1941 stipulated that the United States Government

should have the right to construct bases in Greenland in order to prevent Greenland being used as a 'point of aggression against the nations of the American continent'. Article 10 stipulates that the agreement 'shall remain in force until it is agreed that the present dangers to the peace and security of the American continent have passed. At that time the modification or termination of the Agreement will be the subject of consultation between the Government of the United States of America and the Government of Denmark. After due consultation has taken place, each party shall have the right to give the other party notice of its intention to terminate the Agreement, and it is hereby agreed that at the expiration of 12 months after such notice shall have been received by either party from the other that this Agreement shall cease to be in force.'

2. The Danish Government evidently consider that, the danger to the American continent having passed, the 1941 Agreement should be terminated and have made proposals to the United States Government to this end. At a press conference on the 5th February the Danish Foreign Minister said that there had been discussions with the Americans which should be regarded as preliminary to negotiations about the Treaty. We do not know exactly what the United States Government have said in reply but we have the assurance of the State Department that no definite proposals have been made. But the Americans almost certainly want a permanent settlement of this question and a suggestion in the American press that the United States should buy Greenland from Denmark may give a hint of what the United States Government have in mind. The suggestion has been indignantly repudiated from the Danish side.

3. We are not directly concerned in this question which is one for settlement between the United States and Danish Governments but, from the point of view of the defence of the Western hemisphere and especially as Canada is so closely involved, we should be in favour of such a permanent arrangement, although in face of Soviet objections we might not wish to indicate this publicly. In their propaganda the Russians have been quoting the continued presence of Americans in Greenland (and their facilities in Iceland) as one proof that the United States Government are buying [*sic*: ?trying] for aggressive purposes to get control of the Arctic.

Spitsbergen

A Treaty of 1920 assigned the sovereignty of Spitsbergen and Bear Island to Norway, and Article 9 stipulated that the islands be demilitarised. The Treaty was signed by Great Britain, the Dominions, the United States of America, Denmark, France, Italy, Japan, Norway, the Netherlands and Sweden. The Union of Soviet Socialist Republics did not sign the Treaty at the time because the Soviet Government were not then recognised, but they adhered to it formally in 1935.

2. In 1944 the Soviet Government proposed that, on grounds of safeguarding Russian economic and strategic interests, Spitsbergen should be placed under a condominium of Norway and the Union of Soviet Socialist Republics and that Bear Island which had originally been Russian should be returned to the Soviet Union. In 1945 negotiations took place and a basis for discussion was agreed between the two governments. This basis for discussion (sometimes called draft protocol) as modified subsequently, laid down that both Spitsbergen and Bear Island should remain under Norwegian sovereignty, that the two governments should negotiate on the joint military defence of Spitsbergen, that the defence measures should be in accordance with arrangements made by the Security Council and that any alteration of the Treaty of 1920 be subsequently effected by

agreement with the signatories. M. Molotov pressed the Norwegian Minister for Foreign Affairs, when they were both in New York in November 1946, for immediate negotiations on the basis of the draft protocol of 1945. The Norwegian Minister for Foreign Affairs replied that the Norwegian Parliament must first be consulted. This consultation is now complete and the Soviet Government have been informed that the draft protocol occurred in war conditions which have now given place to a situation in which the United Nations is in existence and has passed a disarmament resolution on Soviet initiative. The protocol of 1945 was therefore no longer appropriate and 'negotiations of a military character with any single foreign power would be contrary to the foreign policy' which the Norwegian Government have pursued since the liberation. But the Norwegian Government added that they were prepared to initiate discussions to prepare the way for a revision of the 1920 Treaty 'in other respects', which is presumably a reference to the economic clauses of the Treaty.

3. The Norwegian Government have kept us closely informed since 1944 and on more than one occasion in 1945 we told them that we trusted that they would not agree with the Soviet Government to take any measures which would alter the demilitarised status of Spitsbergen and that in our view such changes could only be effected with the concurrence of the signatories of the Treaty. We also in 1945 drew the attention of the Norwegian Government to their obligations under Article 43 of the Charter.

4. We have been in consultation with the Chiefs of Staff about the strategic aspect of the question. Their conclusion is that they confirm the view they expressed in 1945 that no strategic threat to the United Kingdom is likely to develop from Spitsbergen. But they also point out that, in view of recent developments in long-range weapons, the acquisition by the Union of Soviet Socialist Republics of military rights in Spitsbergen might prejudice the strategic interests of Canada and the United States of America and that it would thus have a bearing on the overall defence of the British Commonwealth and the United States of America. From this point of view the Chiefs of Staff consider that there would be advantage in supporting Canada and the United States of America in any action they may think fit to take to ensure that the demilitarisation of Spitsbergen continues. The Chiefs of Staff consider that what matters most is that no military installations should be erected by the Soviet Government on Spitsbergen.

5. His Majesty's Ambassador in Oslo has on instructions now expressed the hope that the Norwegians will not agree anything with the Russians prior to consultation with the other signatories of the Treaty. We are not mentioning this time the point about Article 43 of the Charter. While the Norwegian Government are free to make use of this point in their discussions with the Soviet Government it seems wise for us to refrain from bringing it forward at present, because, among other reasons, it might be quoted against us in our endeavours to secure military rights in Iraq or Egypt and might also be used against the Americans in a similar way. Finally Sir Laurence Collier has been authorised to reveal that we are consulting the United States and Canadian Governments.

6. We have heard that the preliminary view of the United States Government is that they doubt whether they should take any action in advance of a formal approach which will presumably be made to the signatories of the 1920 Treaty. The State Department think that it might ultimately be necessary to make concessions to the Soviet Government over this question so as not to risk prejudicing their own negotiations for bases elsewhere but they say it should be

clearly stated that such concessions in no way constitute a precedent as regards the Dardanelles. The State Department express the wish for close consultation with us on this matter and they state that their policy will not be finally formulated until General Marshall has thoroughly investigated the whole question.

7. We are informing the United States and Canadian Governments of the gist of the Chiefs of Staff's conclusions and our instructions to the Ambassador in Oslo and have invited their comments. But now that we know that the Norwegian attitude is satisfactory, it does not seem necessary for us to broach this question with the Americans again.

No. 93

Report by the Joint Planning Staff of the Chiefs of Staff Committee, 4 June 1947
JP(47)56 (Final) Top Secret (FO 371/65961, N6750/127/63G)

Scandinavian Defence—Strategic Considerations

In anticipation of instructions we have examined a letter from the Foreign Office on the strategic considerations involved in the question of a common arrangement by Norway, Denmark and Sweden for the defence of Scandinavia.[1]

Scandinavian discussions

2. In their letter the Foreign Office state there have been indications that Service Departments in Norway, Denmark and Sweden are considering the question of common defence between the three countries and even that there have been discussions between them, though these have probably been on a technical level only and have not proceeded far.

It appears that the initiative in this matter has come from the Danish Naval Staff. The Danish Naval Commander-in-Chief has talked with his opposite numbers, both in Norway and in Sweden and, in company with the Danish Army Commander, he has had discussions with the Swedish Defence Staff.

So far as is known these talks have been on a purely exploratory basis and there has been up to now no question of making anything in the shape of formal common defence plans. It is believed, however, that discussion has covered common training arrangements and the possibility of Denmark obtaining munitions from Swedish factories preferably on models standardised with Great Britain. It is understood, too, that the practicability of setting up Swedish armaments shadow factories in Norway and Denmark, has been discussed.

3. The Foreign Office state that the Danish Naval Authorities, although they have informed the British Naval Attaché confidentially of what is going on, have not asked for British views other than whether we should agree to Swedish factories producing British arms under licence. The Danish Naval Commander-in-Chief is now in this country and has taken the opportunity of discussing Scandinavian defence.

4. The Foreign Office ask for the views of the Chiefs of Staff on the strategic implications of a possible Scandinavian *bloc*.

---

[1] Hankey had written to the Chiefs of Staff on 24 April, asking for their views of the strategic considerations involved in a common arrangement by Norway, Denmark and Sweden for the defence of Scandinavia (FO 371/65961, N3398/127/63G). This paper was sent to Hankey on 10 June 1947.

Strategic Value of Scandinavia

5. By virtue of their geographical position, Norway, Sweden and Denmark would assume great strategic importance in a war between the Western Powers and Russia. Both sides would gain considerable advantage by occupying these countries and would, therefore, at the least, be anxious to deny them to the enemy.

6. The value of Scandinavia to the Western Powers would be:

(*a*) We would have advanced air bases which would halve the distance to Moscow. We would also be very favourably placed for rocket and air attacks on Russian communications with Western Europe.

(*b*) Our early warning system would be very greatly improved. We would, moreover, be well placed far forward on the direct air route between Western Russia and the industrial east of the North American continent.

(*c*) We would be well placed to cover naval and air operations in northern waters and the Baltic.

(*d*) Additional manpower and valuable raw materials would be available to assist our war effort.

7. The value of Scandinavia to Russia would be:

(*a*) She would gain control of the exits from the Baltic to the North Sea.

(*b*) She would gain control of the western seaboard of Norway, from which she could operate naval forces to attack British coastal and north Atlantic communications.

(*c*) She would acquire additional air bases from which to strike at the UK, particularly the northern part, and our sea communications.

(*d*) She would obtain a useful advance of her early warning system, particularly on the direct route from USA to Western Russia.

(*e*) She would obtain additional raw materials and industries.

8. We regard the integrity of Scandinavia in the event of war with Russia as almost as important as the integrity of France, Holland and Belgium. This integrity, important to us at all times, would be particularly important in the early stages of a war with Russia. Separately the three countries would fall an easy prey to aggression. As a *bloc* their power of resistance would be somewhat increased and the effort required to overcome this resistance would be an additional drain on Russian resources and, by its delaying effect on Russian progress into Western Europe in the initial stages of hostilities, might have far reaching effects on the course of the war.

Possibilities of forming a Scandinavian bloc

9. The three Scandinavian countries are small and do not possess powerful armed forces. Sweden has a highly developed, though specialised, armament industry which could be expanded to supply most of her needs as well as those of Norway and Denmark whose industries are negligible. Indigenous production alone, however, could not possibly give a scale or standard of equipment approaching that of a great power.

10. The three countries themselves are not entirely in accord with one another. A traditional suspicion exists between Norway and Sweden and to a lesser extent between Denmark and Sweden. There is recent evidence, however, that this suspicion might be overcome, particularly by the services of the three countries.

11. As regards their foreign policies, all three countries have strong sympathies with the west, but situated as they are between east and west, they have no choice but to seek good relations with the Soviet Union, while maintaining their friendly attitude towards us. This policy of balance applies particularly to Sweden, but the

latest information shows that Swedish Service Departments, particularly the Air Force, are strongly in favour of a western outlook. On this critical point therefore, the opinion of the Foreign Office is decisively confirmed.

It appears that the Scandinavians fear possible Russian aggression, if not for motives of territorial expansion, then at least to make use of their countries in a future war against the western powers. Many members of the armed forces, and even perhaps of the Governments, believe that a Scandinavian *bloc* would assist them to withstand Russia, but they are deterred from taking any steps through fear of what the Russian reaction might be.

12. The co-ordination of defence between all three Scandinavian countries would be a practicable proposition provided that the traditional mistrust between certain of the countries, to which we have already referred, was overcome. We understand that this could be achieved.

13. There is, however, some doubt if the Governments of the three countries would be politically bold enough to create a *bloc*, because of their fear of Russian reactions. It seems, therefore, that it would only be possible to bring about its formation under cover of secrecy.

In our view the danger of Russian reactions can be overemphasised and we feel that the Russians would do little more than offer objections and threats. Moreover, the open creation of a Scandinavian *bloc* might have some slight deterrent effect upon Russian expansionism.

Nevertheless it is better to have a covert *bloc* than no *bloc* at all. We suggest, therefore, that the Scandinavians should be encouraged to begin on a secret basis if they themselves feel it is impossible to proceed openly.

14. The Scandinavian countries would reap some advantages, from a purely military point of view, as a result of the co-ordination of their manpower and resources. The practical and moral value of this co-ordination would be seriously decreased if one of the three countries stood out, especially if this country were Sweden.

In spite of the advantages gained by co-ordination the combined strength of the three countries would be unable, unless supported from elsewhere, to resist Russian aggression, although it might act as some slight deterrent. The Scandinavian countries realise this and are therefore unlikely to be willing to set up a common defence organisation unless they receive specific guarantees of immediate and effective support, including military aid, from the western powers in the event of war.[2]

British backing

Military aid

15. As already stated, the Scandinavian countries realise that their united efforts will not be sufficient to withstand a Russian attack, and they therefore want some sort of assurance that if they undertake a co-ordination of defence there will be enough help from outside to make it worthwhile.

16. While we cannot on any grounds give any sort of guarantee or promise of military aid, we think the formation of a Scandinavian *bloc* creates possibilities of such great strategic advantages that we ought not to let the opportunity slip by making a damping and disheartening reply.

17. Moreover, at first sight it seems to us that it would be no easy task for the Russians to overrun Norway and Sweden: geographical and climatic conditions in

---

[2] Hankey sidelined this last sentence and annotated it '*Voilà*'.

general would favour the defence. It might be that an effective defence of these two countries or at least a valuable and perhaps decisive delay in Russian plans for an advance into Western Europe, could be achieved with support from British or US air forces and carrier forces.

The problem of the defence of Denmark is a much more difficult one and the chances of success depend upon the situation in the rest of Europe. The problem would of course be simplified if an association of Western European Powers—France, Belgium and the Netherlands—were also in being, and could be relied upon to support a Scandinavian *bloc* in an equal resistance to Russian aggression.

18. All this requires a further examination, and we suggest that we should put in hand a full investigation of the potentialities of a Scandinavian and a Western European *bloc* in war against Russia. Although this examination would have to be based on a number of rather doubtful assumptions, we think it should show the measure of outside assistance which either *bloc* would require, and we could then judge the likelihood of our being able to provide it.

Supply of Arms

19. Though the supply of arms would be put forward as a normal trade agreement, the provision of similar types of military equipment to the Scandinavian countries would, in fact, be a method of furthering a Scandinavian *bloc*. We are unlikely, however, to be able to supply from our own production the full requirements of all three countries. The next best method would be that Sweden with a healthy armaments industry of her own should manufacture British arms under licence.

We appreciate that any equipment used in Sweden would be seen by Russian agents and samples removed to Russia, but with the exception of certain arms on the secret list together with the industrial processes connected with the manufacture of certain weapons not on the secret list, there is no valid security objection to the manufacture under licence of British arms in Scandinavia.

In addition to the arms reserved for security reasons we understand that there are certain other specialised items which we would wish to exclude in order that we may maintain our war potential at a desirable level.

Conclusions

20. We conclude that:

(*a*) We should encourage the greatest possible measure of co-ordination in matters of defence between Norway, Sweden and Denmark.

(*b*) We should put in hand an examination of the potentialities of both a Scandinavian and a Western European *bloc*, to enable us to judge whether we can give more practical encouragement to a Scandinavian *bloc*.

Recommendations

21. We recommend that:

(*a*) A copy of this paper be forwarded to the Foreign Office as an expression of the views of the Chiefs of Staff.

(*b*) The Joint Planning Staff should be instructed to put in hand an examination on the lines suggested in paragraph 18 above.

(*c*) Copies of this paper should be made available to the Canadian Liaison Officers in the UK for transmission to the Chiefs of Staff, and to the UK Liaison

Staff in Ottawa for their information.[3]

J. F. STEVENS
G. H. MILLS
R. H. BARRY

[3] In subsequent minuting to Jebb and Sargent, Northern Department observed that the chances of getting Scandinavian Governments to agree to an overt co-ordination of defence arrangements would be slender. Since the question could not be tackled on a political level, they concluded that it would be best to inform the Scandinavian service authorities of British views. The Danes were known to be awaiting these, and it would also be easy to inform the Norwegians. However, they were less certain about how to approach the Swedes. After further consideration, the Foreign Office therefore decided to instruct Randall to approach the Danes and to inform them of the British position, though without offering any further advice on how to proceed. They also asked Collier and Jerram for their views on whether the Norwegian and Swedish Governments were likely to be aware of these inter-service discussions (despatch to Randall, 5 August 1947, FO 371/65961, N6750/127/63G).

No. 94

Mr Randall (Copenhagen) to Mr Bevin, 20 June 1947
No. 208 (FO 471/1, N7343/1096/15)

Economic Situation in Denmark:
Possible Effect on Anglo-Danish Food Price Negotiation

Sir,
I have the honour to report that the political situation in Denmark is at present dominated by the long drawn out typesetters' strike, which is more and more being resolved into a controversy between the Social Democrats and the Communists—and the economic outlook. Of the first it is unnecessary to say anything here, as it has been dealt with at length in other despatches. But the second may affect the future of the Government, and the Anglo-Danish food price negotiations which are due to open next month, and deserve describing in some detail.

2. On my return from leave several days ago I was struck by the astonishing and unprecedented agitation among Danes over a shortage of food. The loud protests in the Socialist and Communist daily papers, the only ones appearing normally in the capital, were accompanied by street demonstrations, and by refusals, mainly by the shipyard workers, to work overtime as long as the Government failed to afford working people sufficient fats and meat and, above all, potatoes, which have been practically unobtainable for some weeks past. There was substance in these complaints. Meat is now beyond the means of most working-class households, and a serious drain even on the better off; so are most vegetables; the combined butter and margarine ration of 250 gr. a week is, in the practical absence of any other fat, regarded as totally inadequate, at least for a manual worker. For the lower-paid families there remain plentiful eggs but at 30 øre each—bread, and unlimited, but expensive, cheese, and still more expensive fish. To the British housewife this would not appear at all a dismal prospect, and the mimeographed Government paper has pointed out, no doubt with justice, that Denmark is still the best fed country in Europe, with a daily calorie consumption of 2,900 calories, compared with Sweden at 300 less, or Britain at 600 less, or Finland, at 900 less a day. Within certain limits, food consumption comparisons are largely a matter of habit

and relative standards, and to the Danes, as heavy consumers of fats and meat, unaccustomed to adaptability in diet and plentifully supplied even under the German occupation, a severe drop in meat supplies, or even a moderate reduction in the fat ration, appears as a severe deprivation for which someone must be blamed. And, of course, it has been excellent material for the Left parties, who have, more especially the Communists, unduly exaggerated and generalised the hardships, however genuine they may be in the poorer families. The danger is that increased attention will be drawn—it has already been drawn in the Communist papers—to the fact that the foodstuffs of which there is such a pronounced shortage have been shipped in large quantities to the United Kingdom at alleged unremunerative prices, against which Britain is said to have sent Denmark expensive luxuries, refusing to supply the coal and cotton yarn, the iron and steel which Denmark so sorely needs.

3. The Government reply to the charges of incompetence and neglect of working-class interests has been to the effect, not only that Denmark is still better fed than any other country in a continent of want, but that the shortage of feeding-stuffs which are the basis of Danish agriculture has caused serious under-production and a drop in agricultural export of some fifty percent as compared with 1939. To the responsible representations of the trades unions, promises have been given that potatoes will be transported from Sweden and a meat rationing scheme is to come into force on 1st July. The Minister of Supply, M. Axel Christiansen, who now generally figures as the Government spokesman, has explained that Denmark must export food to obtain other essential supplies; that lard for example, must go abroad—at the price of 6 *kr.* a kilo, he added, as compared with 4.50 received for butter—in order to obtain indispensable Finnish timber. In the same speech the Minister dwelt on the great difficulty of carrying through the fair distribution of meat in a country in which some 200,000 persons have facilities for home slaughtering. Nevertheless, with goodwill from all classes, it is hoped that with rationing all households will get an allowance at a reasonable price.

4. While, therefore, on the one hand anxious to lighten the picture, on the other—the foreign trade side—the Government seems to wish to intensify the gloom of the prospects for the next few months. On 14th June an official statement was issued to the effect that the anticipated increase in Denmark's industrial exports during the current year, of about 50 million *kroner*, would be offset by a drop in agricultural exports, owing to the severe winter, below the figure anticipated in the trade balance plan. Denmark must also face the necessity of importing bread-corn and making certain unexpected purchases of goods under bilateral agreements. The conclusion was that the foreign currency would not be sufficient to avert a further limitation of imports.

5. In subsequent public speeches the Minister of Supply elaborated these points. Speaking at Vejle on 16th June he said that, as Denmark's debt to Britain had to be reduced to 35 million sterling by the New Year, the position until then would be difficult; he added, however, that if only Britain would consent to recognise Danish agricultural exports as current business instead of debt-repayment, 'it might be possible slightly to loosen the iron ring'—a possible pointer to Denmark's case in the coming discussions. To the trades union representations mentioned above, he observed that, unless the required balance could be obtained, a reductions of rations must be made, and the Government organ has already stated that this 'cut' will amount to 5 gr. of butter a day, the enforcement of margarine purchases, an

unspecified reduction in the sugar ration and, in any case, no provision this year of extra sugar for jam making.

6. It is this prospect which caused a prominent Dane last night to observe to me, after a sumptuous dinner, that at last Denmark was preparing to 'take it'! Yet it would be a mistake to treat the matter as a joke. There is the possibility that the meat-rationing may send prices sky-high (they are already excessive, the cost of meat in restaurants being, I would estimate, double the comparable prices ruling in London); there is the distant but serious shadow of wage agreements to be negotiated next March; there is the extreme Left parties' interest in darkening the picture; and, finally, there is the virtual certainty that the Government's plain speaking and the alleged unfavourable development of the import and export plan will be used to exclude British goods and justify a number of unacceptable demands in the food negotiations with His Majesty's Government in a few weeks time. Unfortunately, it is on this last that the Communists and the farmers, for differing reasons, make common cause, and we shall be hard put to it, in my opinion, to avoid a considerable share of the blame for Denmark's difficulties, now and in the coming months.[1]

I have, etc.,
A.W.G. RANDALL

[1] See also No. 97.

No. 95

Mr Shepherd (Helsinki) to Mr Bevin, 25 June 1947
No. 157 Confidential (FO 371/65917, N7625/158/56)

Sir,

I notice that the confidential supplement to the *Economist* has printed an interesting article on the possible application to Finland of the methods recently applied by the Russians to Hungary,[1] and that Mr Eden has suggested in the House of Commons that Finland may be high up on the Russian list for similar treatment.

2. The *Economist* article accurately summarises Finnish apprehensions on the subject. Given the geographical and historical associations of Finland, it was inevitable that precisely such speculations should emerge. Finland is physically helpless and morally cowed according to normal strategic and political standards, and there is theoretically scarcely any limit to the exactions which Russia could make. But the situation is not simple and an enumeration of the main factors in it may be of interest.

3. Factors leading towards a determined Russian campaign to secure complete domination over Finland may be summarised as follows:

(*a*) In spite of post-war treatment which is certainly lenient by comparison with other countries and which the Russians themselves probably regard as intrinsically lenient, there has been little sign of any increased friendliness towards the Soviet Union by the bulk of the Finnish population. Finnish feelings have been exemplified in:

[1] Not printed. The article 'Windmill Tilting in Finland' was published in the *Economist* of 15 May 1947.

(1) Evident lack of sympathy with the war responsibility trials, and the leniency of the sentences by Russian and Balkan standards.

(2) Evident sympathy with the aims of the arms dump conspirators, whose aim of guerrilla warfare in case of Russian occupation was (and I think still is) sanctioned by a large proportion of the population.[2]

(3) Private and unguarded conversation throughout the country.

(b) After the first reaction against the Nazi orientation, it has become evident that this did not entail a disposition to enter the Communist camp. The move leftwards went only so far as to tolerate a rather more extreme left Administration (out of fear of Russia) than public opinion seemed to warrant. In proportion as the post-war tension subsided, impatience with undue influence by the Left has increased. This has been exemplified by:

(1) Suspicion and vigilance in connexion with the State police and constant criticism of the Minister of the Interior.[3]

(2) Agitation against Communist methods, such as street demonstrations.

(3) Centre and Right complaints that a policy of friendship with Soviet Russia is not exclusive to the Communists and extreme Left.

(4) The abortive attempt this spring to secure a new Government less subservient to the Communists.

(c) There has been a very evident desire to insure against economic domination by Russia. This is exemplified in:

(1) Resumption of trade with the United Kingdom, United States and other Western countries.

(2) Loans from America.

(3) Finnish resistance to demands for Russian participation in Finnish industry in connexion with the handing over of German assets.

(d) There has been a marked intention to maintain cultural as well as economic ties with the West and particularly with Scandinavia. There have been innumerable exchanges of visits of all kinds, except foreign political.

4. All these factors make it clear that Finland has no intention of subsiding gently behind any sort of Russian curtain. Although there is a genuine realisation that a policy of friendship with Soviet Russia is essential for the present, there is little doubt that the Finns would once again be seriously tempted if the rift between East and West developed, and if there were a reasonable chance of effective Western support. The Russians, in fact, have very little reason to conclude that they can count on any sort of loyalty from the Finns, or that the Finns would not make a similar decision to that of 1941 if comparable conditions were to be created.

5. But probably the most important factor in Russo-Finnish relations is the attitude of the Scandinavian countries. So long as Russia is satisfied that Norway and Denmark especially can be relied on not to become bases of operations against the Soviet Union, she can afford to be content with rather less than the drastically organised form of security which she has striven for in South-Eastern Europe. A courageous and independent Western orientation on the part of Scandinavia might well lead the Russians to incur the risks and the odium of action of one kind or another to secure a complaisant Finland.

---

[2] See Nos. 31 and 86.
[3] Yrjö Leino.

6. The factors which have hitherto acted in restraint of such action are indicated below. The Russians would, I think, have to be convinced of the necessity of a complete change of policy in this part of the world before these factors ceased to guide their actions.

7. Prominent Russians from Stalin down have stated that it is the desire of the Soviet Union to compensate Finland for the wrongs done her by the Tsars. This can only refer to the so-called Russification policy. While there is no need to doubt the sincerity of these protestations, it remains true that the characteristics of the Russification policy were the obstinate resistance of the Finns and the interest aroused in the outside world. These same factors were prominent during the opening period of the winter war, when the puppet Kuusinen Government failed so remarkably to make any impression on the Finnish people, and when the outside world, acting through the League of Nations, expressed so strongly its disapproval of the Russian attack. It is a case of twice bitten twice shy.

8. The Russians attach some importance to reparations and are therefore likely to be careful about any action which would interfere with deliveries. This is perhaps a comparatively minor matter and they might well consider the advantages of a bellicose Communist opposition in disintegrating Finnish economy and making her more amenable to pressure. But they can have few illusions about the solid and stubborn hatred which pressure would induce, or about the practical difficulties which would ensue. Exile to Siberia of actual and potential anti-Soviet elements, as in the Baltic States, would mean the practical depopulation of the country.

9. Short of drastic action, the Russians are likely to continue the treatment of *'Douches Écossaises'*[4] so as to keep Finnish morale low. It must have been a satisfaction to them to observe the nervous reaction here to events in Hungary, and they are likely to apply further cold showers as occasion may demand. I am still of the opinion that I have held for some time now, that the sturdy Finnish democracy can defend itself and the independence of the country so long as Finnish politicians not only retain their courage, but are prepared to adapt their tactics to the situation. Unfortunately Finnish politicians are not remarkable for their ability to guide or curb their followers, and the least that can be expected is the continuation of an uneasy period of tensions and *détente* for some time to come. The recent failure of the Centre and Right to secure a reconstruction of the Government should satisfy the Russians for the immediate future.

I am sending a copy of this despatch to His Majesty's Ambassador at Moscow and His Majesty's Minister at Stockholm.

I have, etc.,
F. M. SHEPHERD

[4] A shower which alternates between hot and cold water, i.e. quite a shock.

No. 96

Letter from Mr Healey to M. Leskinen,[1] 29 August 1947
Strictly Confidential (FO 371/65910, N10315/3/56)

My dear Leskinen,

I think you know me well enough not to require an apology for a letter which might seem impertinent to people with a more diplomatic training.

The fact is, we are very disturbed here by recent events from Finland. I understand that since the Trade Union elections the Communists have become increasingly provocative, making it almost impossible for the Social Democrats to maintain even the appearance of friendly relations with them; from what I hear, everyone expects s fresh governmental crisis in the near future.[2]

You know that my knowledge of the situation in Finland is limited to my too infrequent contacts with yourself and Varjonen[3], the newspapers, and any first hand information which Englishmen returned from Finland can give me. So it is not for me to try to influence your party's reaction to events. But I must tell you that we feel here that it is of the greatest importance that the political situation should remain stable in Finland during the next few months. We have evidence to suggest that the Soviet Union is preparing to ratify all the 'satellite' peace treaties in the immediate future. As soon as Finland is an independent sovereign state again the perspectives for your party will be completely altered. It is therefore essential that you should give the Russians no reason or excuse, either for delaying ratification of the Finnish treaty, or for pursuing direct action by force against Finnish democracy in anticipation of early ratification.

It is obviously impossible to discuss the issues at length in a letter. Do you think there is any chance of yourself and some other party members visiting England in September? We should be very glad indeed to see you. The Consultative Committee on September 26th might provide an excuse;[4] I do not think it would be wise to make it an official fraternal delegation to the Labour Party in view of the extreme sensitivity of Russian suspicions nowadays.

Do not feel too depressed by the news you read of the British economic crisis. As you know, the crisis has in fact existed fundamentally for two years already, and many of us in the party feel that the Government's determination to tackle it at last in a serious way is the most encouraging thing that has happened since Labour took office.

---

[1] Väinö Leskinen was the Secretary of the Finnish Social Democratic Party. He later occupied a series of ministerial posts, including Social Affairs, the Interior, Trade and Industry, Social Welfare and Foreign Affairs.

[2] Ledward's despatch of 27 August, enclosing a memorandum from the Labour Attaché, Thomas, described the extent of Communist influence in the trades unions and concluded that if they took a decision not to resort to force, then Communist prospects would progressively deteriorate (FO 371/65930, N10194/640/56). Healey wrote this letter after discussing the internal situation in Finland with Hankey, with the aim of supporting British interests by encouraging the avoidance of another ministerial crisis in Finland: Leskinen was regarded as 'one of the hotheads'. Healey added the postscript at Hankey's request. Hankey forwarded the letter to Ledward on 2 September for transmission to Leskinen (FO 371/65910, N10315/3/56).

[3] Unto Varjonen was a member of the Social Democratic Party and assistant Minister of Finance 1949-50.

[4] The Consultative Committee of COMISCO, the Committee of the International Socialist Conference 1947-51, which preceded the Socialist International established in 1951.

I hope most sincerely that you or some of your comrades will find it possible to visit us during the coming weeks. If not, perhaps we shall meet in Warsaw in October.

>With best wishes,
>Yours ever,
>DENIS HEALEY

PS Since finishing this letter, the Supreme Soviet have ratified the peace treaties. But I feel that the caution I suggested is no less necessary, at least during the next three months, until the instrument of ratification is deposited.[5]

---

[5] Ledward replied by telegram on 4 September saying that he would deliver Healey's letter to Leskinen, though he doubted that it would have much effect beyond showing that the Labour party were keeping an avuncular eye on developments (FO 371/65910, N10377/3/56).

No. 97

Mr Randall (Copenhagen) to Mr Bevin, 12 September 1947, 3.07 p.m.
Tel. No. 352 Immediate (FO 371/65847, N10637/9/15)

Reasons for suspension (as the press calls it this morning) of Anglo-Danish food discussions will be reported by Mr Feaveryear[1] in detail on his return to London today. Briefly the position is that the Danish Government have yielded to farmers' pressure to be allowed to make their own bargain with us and now to open negotiations with third countries. Farmers asked far too excessive prices for butter and bacon and between these prices and our counter offers, although the latter were equal to prices which Danish Government at present guarantee farmers, the gap was so large that Danish Government were unable or unwilling to impose price even approaching what we would have accepted.

In view of greatly diminished Danish production it may be possible for farmers to dispose of the whole of the exportable surplus of butter and bacon for the next six months and I cannot think that the Danish Government, even though a farmers' Government, would have allowed this freedom of trade had not farmers persuaded them that there were acceptable offers from third countries principally Russia who has offered one hundred thousands tons of rye to be paid for in butter and who, I suspect, is the country who, the farmers alleged, is offering dollars for pork.

Political consequences of considerable diversion of exports to the east if farmers can effect it may be unfortunate for time being: certainly the communists would represent it as a Russian diplomatic victory and the beginning of the liberation of Denmark from 'British stranglehold'. Danes may well be disillusioned eventually over both prices and supplies but temporary setback to Anglo-Danish relations—despite very friendly atmosphere which Mr Feaveryear and his colleagues maintained throughout—seems to me to be unavoidable under our present financial conditions. There can, I think, be no doubt that Minister for Foreign Affairs and Minister of Finance are privately perturbed by the Government's adventurous policy (former described it as 'taking a risk'); and commercial and industrial circles are thoroughly alarmed by loss of Danish purchasing power in the British

---

[1] Albert Feaveryear, DUS, Ministry of Food.

market. It is to be hoped that they will this time visit their dissatisfaction on the farmers, since the terms of our offers when published, should amply justify us in the eyes of Danish industry, both employers and workers. But the political situation here is at present fluid with a fairly even balance for a coalition with Conservatives and Radicals, at the price of the Prime Minister's concentration on South Schleswig and general elections. In view of this I suggest door to resumption of talks be kept open until expiry of agreement. This would involve agreeing with the Danish Government's terms of report on the negotiations and until draft which Feaveryear will prepare has been approved I recommend that public comment be confined to regret, emphasis on unfortunate reduction in Danish exportable surplus and hint of short-sighted Danish farmers' abandonment of old and tried customer who in return for Danish goods had given such vital assistance to Danish economy since 1945. It seems to me important not (repeat not) to bring into prominence heavy Danish dependence on us for dollars and essential imports. These serious implications of Danish Government's decision have gone deep enough into the consciousness of informed opinion here and I think it would be best to let facts speak for themselves at least until after question of Wærum's visit to London has been decided.[2] Telegram on this will follow.

Tone of press this morning is markedly restrained and somewhat apprehensive.[3]

[2] Hankey minuted on 16 September that Wærum's visit had been postponed.
[3] Commenting on this telegram, Hankey judged that the food negotiations had broken down because the Danish Government had left it to the farmers. He concluded that much the best solution would be if Danish concern culminated in some sort of political crisis and in a change of government, because the current government was weak and subject to pressure by the farmers— though he emphasised that the Foreign Office should be careful to avoid a situation where it could be suggested that it favoured a change of government or were anxious to bring one about.

No. 98

Sir C. Jerram (Stockholm) to Mr Bevin, 24 September 1947
No. 276 (FO 371/ 66501, N11641/810/42)

Sir,
The raising of this Mission to the status of Embassy was in this wise.

2. In November 1946 I was informed confidentially in the Foreign Ministry that an approach had been made to Sweden by the Americans for the raising of their respective missions to the status of Embassy. Similar representations had been made simultaneously by the Americans in Denmark. The Swedes did not receive the suggestion with any great enthusiasm, and in February of this year I was told by my United States colleague that the Swedish Government had given a negative answer, not being prepared, they said, to choose four or five countries for a change in the form of representation, which was not in accordance with previous practice. I was told soon afterwards however by the Foreign Minister that the matter was still being considered, but it was not until July that we were approached by the Swedes with the information that the Swedish Government were prepared to exchange Ambassadors with HMG if the latter so desired. They were, they said, making this proposal in the first place to the permanent members of the Security Council and in addition Norway and Denmark. They admitted that this was a change of view since the matter was first mooted but that, as we knew, the

initiative had not originally come from Sweden. It was explained that the Chinese Minister would retain the rank of doyen but that the Danish Minister would be given the position of second senior ambassador as the Danish Queen was a Swedish princess. The subsequent order would follow the present order of seniority. On this I made no comment, not knowing the date on which the *agrément* for a British Ambassador might be sought or granted, nor whether I should in fact myself be selected for the post. Times too have changed since Whitelocke, appointed by Cromwell as Ambassador to Queen Christina of Sweden in 1653, resolutely refused to give the *pas* to the Danish Ambassador, to whom he was in fact junior in date of appointment, claiming that the Lord Protector of England, Scotland and Ireland was a greater personage than any sovereign on earth however *sacré*. I enclose with this despatch an extract from Whitelocke's memoirs recounting his dispute with the Grand Master of the Ceremonies on the subject: it makes interesting reading.[1]

---

[1] An extract from *A Journal of the Swedish Embassy in the years 1653 and 1654* by Ambassador Bulstrode Whitelocke was attached as an enclosure to this document:

April 8, 1654
The master of ceremonies came to Whitelocke from the Queen, to desire his company that evening at a masque; and they had this discourse.
Whitelocke: Present my thanks to Her Majesty, and tell her that I will wait upon her.
Master of Ceremonies: What would your Excellence expect in matter of precedence, as in case you should meet with any other ambassador at the masque?
Whitelocke: I shall expect that which belongs to me as Ambassador from the Commonwealth of England, Scotland and Ireland; and I know of no other ambassador now in this Court besides myself, except the Ambassador of the King of Denmark, who, I suppose, hath no thoughts of precedence before the English Ambassador, who is resolved not to give it to him if he should expect it.
Master of Ceremonies: Perhaps it may be insisted on, that he of Denmark is an ambassador of an anointed King, and you are only ambassador to the Protector—a new name and not *sacré*.
Whitelocke: Whosoever shall insist on that distinction will be mistaken, and I understand no difference of power between king and protector, or anointed or not anointed; and ambassadors are the same public ministers to a protector or commonwealth as to a prince or sultan.
Master of Ceremonies: There hath always been a difference observed between the public ministers of kings and of commonwealth, or princes or inferior titles.
Whitelocke: The title of Protector, as to a sovereign title, hath not yet been determined in the world as to superiority or inferiority to other titles; but I am sure that the nation of England hath ever been determined superior to that of Denmark. I represent the nations of England, Scotland and Ireland, and the Protector, who is chief of them; and the honour of these nations ought to be in the same consideration now as it has been formerly, and I must not suffer any diminution of that honour by my person to please any whatsoever.
Master of Ceremonies: I shall propose an expedient to you, that you may take your place as you come; he who comes first, the first place, and he who comes last, the last place.
Whitelocke: I shall hardly take a place below the Danish Ambassador, though I come into the room after him.
Master of Ceremonies: But when you come into the room and find the Danish Ambassador set, you cannot help it, though he have the upper place.
Whitelocke: I shall endeavour to help it, rather than sit below the Danish Ambassador.
Master of Ceremonies: I presume you will not use force in the Queen's presence.
Whitelocke: Master, it is impossible for me, if it were in the presence of all the queens and kings in Christendom, to forbear to use any means to hinder the dishonour of my nation in my person.
Master of Ceremonies: I believe the Danish Ambassador would not be so high as you are.
Whitelocke: There is no reason why he should: he knows his nation never pretended to have the precedence of England, and you, being master of the ceremonies, cannot be ignorant of it.
Master of Ceremonies: I confess that your nation always had the precedence of Denmark when you were under a king.

3. The Chinese and Danish Ministers presented their Letters to His Majesty King Gustaf on September 20th. I and the Norwegian Minister (in that order) presented our Letters on September 22nd. On September 19th, according to tradition, the Grand Master of Ceremonies called upon me in uniform to bid me welcome to Sweden on behalf of His Majesty. I received him together with my staff, all in uniform. I thought that I could hardly better the terms in which Whitelocke had received the Grand Master of Ceremonies on a similar occasion in 1653, and therefore asked Count von Rosen to convey to His Royal Master my humble thanks for His Majesty's gracious message, adding that His Majesty did me great honour in sending so distinguished an officer of his court to bid me welcome. I did not however follow Whitelocke in presenting the Grand Master of the Ceremonies with 'an English beaver hat, with a gold hatband and a pair of rich English gloves: at which the Master seemed offended saying that Ambassadors used to send their better presents to the Master of Ceremonies; but being desired to try if the gloves would fit him, he found thereby 40 twenty shilling pieces of English gold, and thereby much satisfaction in the present'. After a glass of champagne and the usual toasts, I attended the Grand Master to his coach. Whitelocke throughout his stay in Sweden, with the ardour of a Puritan, rather churlishly refused to drink toasts, though strongly advised by the Grand Master to conform to the practice of the country.

4. The arrangements for my audience with His Majesty were carried out with the very greatest ceremony. The royal 'glass coach' as it is called, was sent to fetch me with six horses, outriders and coachmen all in the royal livery. Other carriages were provided for members of my staff. At the Palace a royal salute was given by a Guard of Honour mounted in the Fore Court and at the foot of the Great Staircase I was met by the Grand Master of the Court and some fifty gentlemen-in-waiting in court dress. Led by these gentlemen and followed by my staff, I proceeded up three flights of stairs, lined by Troopers of the First Royal Horse Guards, dressed in the uniform of Charles XI and by Guardsmen of the Royal Svea Lifeguards dressed in blue tunics and bearskins. On the first floor was mounted a Colour Party of the Royal Svea Lifeguards with the full Regimental Colour and Band. I passed through the anterooms full of uniformed court officials and was shown into a private audience with His Majesty. The King, as usual, showed a keen interest in current affairs. He admitted that he was growing old in body, though not in mind. I congratulated him on the success he is having in this season's elk shooting. His Majesty replied that it was largely luck, as he could only see out of one eye. King

Whitelocke: I should never give it from them though they were under a constable.
Master of Ceremonies: If you insist upon it, the Danish Ambassador must be uninvited again, for I perceive that the two of you must not meet.
Whitelocke: I suppose the gentleman would not expect precedence of me.
Master of Ceremonies: I can assure you he doth.
Whitelocke: I can assure you he shall never have it, if I can help it. But I pray, Master, tell me whether her Majesty takes notice of this question of precedence, or did she wish to confer with me about it?
Master of Ceremonies: The Queen commanded me to speak with you about it, hoping that the question might be so composed that she might have the company of you both at her entertainment.
Whitelocke: I shall stay at home rather than interrupt her Majesty's pleasures, which I should do by meeting the Danish Ambassador, to whom I shall not give precedence, unless he be stronger than I.
Master of Ceremonies: The Queen makes this masque chiefly for your Excellency's entertainment, therefore you must not be absent, but rather the Danish Ambassador must be uninvited; and I shall presently go about it.
[The Danish Ambassador did not appear.]

Gustaf expressed himself strongly about the lack of co-operation shown by the Russians. Other subjects of conversation were the wedding of Princess Elizabeth and the success of Lord Mountbatten in India.[2] On leaving His Majesty I presented members of my staff, after which the procession was re-formed and I returned to my Embassy in the coach.

5. France has not yet requested an *agrément* for an Ambassador: the Soviet Minister is away; and Mr Dreyfus, my American colleague, has, to his great disappointment, not been appointed Ambassador to Sweden by his Government. Instead the US Government have asked for *agrément* as Ambassador for Mr H. Freeman Matthews, who is expected to arrive here at the end of October. Mr Dreyfus is at no pains to hide his opinion that he has been very shabbily treated by the State Department.

I have, etc.,
C.B. JERRAM

[2] *Footnote in original:* 'It is amusing to see that Whitelocke in his audience with Queen Christiana was more concerned with Her Majesty's soul than with her body. He reproved her on several occasions for her lack of rigour in observance of the Lord's Day, and reminded her of her duty to put down drinking and swearing in the Swedish Army. Her Majesty apparently took all this in good part, though Whitelocke's puritanical zeal seems to have had the wrong effect, for three months after he left Queen Christiana embraced the Catholic religion. Whitelocke did unbend enough on one occasion to dance with the Queen at her request.'

No. 99

Mr Collier (Oslo) to Mr Bevin, 29 September 1947 (extract)
(FO 491/1, N11559/98/30)

Heads of Foreign Missions in Norway

M. Kuznetsov, having suddenly been recalled to Moscow for reasons hitherto unexplained but believed to be connected with the Spitsbergen crisis, was replaced by his counsellor, M. Sergei Alekseevich Afanasiev, who, accompanied by a retinue of no less than sixteen members of his staff, presented his credentials as ambassador on 8th July 1947. He speaks fluent French and German, although he does not admit to any English, and has a more polished but less attractive appearance than his predecessor. I understand that he is a person of some standing in the Soviet hierarchy, having been assistant personal secretary to M. Molotov, and that he played an important part at the Potsdam Conference. He is generally believed to have been the real master of the Soviet embassy in M. Kuznetsov's day, and the Norwegian authorities are still wondering uneasily why so important a personage was ever sent to Norway. He is married.

I have, etc.,
L. COLLIER

No. 100

Mr Bevin to Mr Scott (Helsinki), 13 November 1947, 10.35 a.m.[1]
Tel. No. 530 Secret (FO 371/65930, N12972/640/56)

Your telegram No. 35 Saving of November 4th: Finnish delegation to Moscow.[2]
In conversation with the Finnish Minister on the 10th November, Sir O. Sargent enquired what the latter considered would be the meaning of this visit and said he hoped we would be kept informed if the visit meant that the Finnish Government were going to enter into some political agreement with the Soviet Government.

2. Mr Wuori said that he had no information about the visit. He would however hazard a guess that the Finnish Government might have decided that it would be better for them to take the initiative in proposing political negotiations with the Soviet Government rather than to wait for such negotiations to be forced upon them. Mr Wuori thought it probable that in that case the discussions might turn on the size of the Finnish army. He said that the Bourgeois parties were anxious to keep the army as small as possible but that the Communists wished to have a large army which could collaborate with the Red Army in case of need.

3. Sir Orme Sargent warned the Minister that if there were any question of interpreting or modifying the terms of the Peace Treaty including of course the limitation of the size of the Finnish army to a total strength of 34,400 personnel, it was essential that His Majesty's Government should be brought into the discussions from the outset as they were also signatories of the Peace Treaty. Mr Wuori said that he recognised this.

4. I should be glad of any further information you or His Majesty's Ambassador in Moscow may be able to obtain.[3]

---

[1] Repeated to Moscow.

[2] Not printed. The telegram reported that the Secretary General of the Finnish Foreign Ministry had told Scott that the delegation going to Moscow was a large one because of the need to include representatives from a range of political parties. He did not consider that there were any items of really major importance on the agenda.

[3] Neither Moscow nor Helsinki was initially able to provide any detailed reporting in response to this request. On 14 November, Scott reported by telegram that the Minister of Defence had told him that he and the small body of Ministers left behind knew very little of what had been going on in Moscow, and he thought that no major questions had come up for discussion. He thought that there might be a possibility that the Soviet authorities would put forward some plan for a military understanding but that there was nothing to indicate that any such suggestion had actually been made (FO371/65931, N13076/640/56).

No. 101

Letter from Mr Hankey to Mr Jerram (Stockholm), 14 November 1947
Secret (FO 371/66493, N12976/199/42)

Dear Jerram,

Since we received your telegram No. 677 of the 11th October[1] and Chancery letter 114/14/47 of the 13th October, we have given some thought to the question

---

[1] This reported that the magazine *Allt* had published an article entitled 'When England thought of giving up'.

whether we should not reconsider our attitude towards publication of Prytz's famous telegram to his Government on the 17th June, 1940, about his conversation that day with the Parliamentary Under-Secretary of State.[2]

2. It appears from the correspondence that after Günther publicly referred to this telegram at a dinner held by the Swedish Institute for Foreign Affairs on the 31st October 1944 (Mallet's despatch No. 689 of the 18th November, 1944, of which I enclose a copy in case your file has been destroyed), Warner wrote to Mallet (our reference No. 7869/1586/G) of the 28th December 1944) suggesting that if the impression created by this 'revelation' had not been dispelled by Günther's subsequent *démenti* and other developments, it might be desirable to issue some statement indicating that Mallet had taken action with the Swedish Government on the 19th June 1940, to dispel any misapprehension as to our attitude. When Warner wrote, the war in Europe was not yet over and we felt that our stout-heartedness when we stood alone in 1940 was such a tremendous asset that we should not let any doubts be cast on it. Mallet, however, replied in a letter No. 71/1/45 of the 18th January, 1945, to the effect that as the excitement in the Swedish press had died down, he thought it would be better to let sleeping dogs lie. He also mentioned as considerations in favour of this policy the embarrassment which publication would cause to Lord Halifax and Butler, the gift which it would be for British and American gossip-writers and the poor showing which Butler's vague recollection of the conversation as reported in our telegram No. 531 of the 20th June, 1940, to Stockholm, would make if published beside Prytz's much more circumstantial account. We therefore allowed the idea to drop and when the Swedish Legation formally asked our permission to publish Prytz's telegram and the connected correspondence, we refused (see correspondence enclosed in Foreign Office printed letter despatch No. L5139/2728/402 of the 22nd November 1946).

3. Circumstances have, however, in our view changed since then. For one thing, the story is clearly not dead. It does not appear to have been taken up in the American press or here, but that is quite probably only a question of time. The telegram itself has now been referred to openly in an official Swedish publication (your telegram No. 127 of the 18th February last) and your telegram No. 677 of the 11th October shows that the actual text has now got out. We feel, therefore, that publication should not do us any real harm and that if we were to publish at the same time our own exchange of telegrams with Mallet, this would, despite the weakness of our telegram No. 531 referred to above, definitely strengthen our position and make misrepresentation less likely in the future. There might be a sudden flash of publicity but the embers would after that quickly burn out.

4. I should be grateful for your views on the subject. Clearly any action we might take with a view to publication would have to be in concert with the Swedish Government. As they themselves proposed to publish Prytz's telegram and the connected correspondence last year, they are unlikely to demur now about that and they could not reasonably object to our publishing our own correspondence at the same time.

5. If you agree that it would be desirable to publish the documents with Swedish approval, the question arises as to how this would best be done. The more usual procedure would be to lay the papers before Parliament in reply to an inspired

---

[2] None of the correspondence referred to in this letter has been printed. Prytz's telegram of 17 June 1940 described a conversation with Mr R.A. Butler, and included a greeting to Prytz from Halifax, the Foreign Secretary, which included the comment that 'common sense not bravado would determine the British Government's policy'.

question in the House. We should, of course, only lay the British documents. The Swedes would no doubt publish theirs separately. It might however be argued that, with a view to avoiding controversy and in the hope of killing the matter once and for all, we should get the Swedish Government to go as far as possible with us in making the disclosure. In that case we might possibly adopt the exceptional procedure of issuing simultaneously in London and Stockholm a joint statement by the two Governments together which would cover both series of telegrams.

6. I enclose a draft statement giving the sort of thing we have in mind if the second method of publication referred to above were adopted. This contains both the Swedish and British telegrams in logical sequence, as far as this is possible. We have, however, deliberately omitted the Swedish memorandum B.4. which was enclosed in the Swedish Legation's note of the 16th July, 1946. As this really adds little to the story and as its publication would more or less compel us to publish on our side Mallet's despatch No. 689 of the 18th November, 1944, I feel we should do our best to avoid this for two reasons. The first is that Monsieur Boheman would be embarrassed by the statement in paragraph 3 of the despatch that he had admitted in a private conversation with Mallet that the decision to allow transit facilities to German troops was taken in principle the day before Prytz's famous telegram was received, i.e. on June 16th, 1940, and that it had no serious effect on Swedish policy. The second reason is that publication of this despatch (and this does not apply to the other correspondence) would directly raise the issue of the responsibility of Prytz's telegram for the transit decision. It is clear that it is in order to try and justify their attitude on this question that the Swedes continue to raise the ghost of the Butler conversation in the hope of laying at least a part of the blame on us. Boheman's admission to Mallet shows this to be unjust but I doubt if we have any interest in refuting the Swedish allegations as such now. Our only interest, as we see it, is to clear up the reputation of the British Government in June, 1940, and the more we can avoid hurting Swedish susceptibility in doing so, the less likely it is that there will be a violent come-back from the Swedes. For these reasons we suggest that it should be put to the Swedes that B.4. should not be published on the ground that it is superfluous.

7. Before any approach is made to the Swedes we should have to get Butler's authority for publication of this correspondence. We consulted him before we agreed to the publication of the other Swedish correspondence enclosed in the legation's note of the 6th July, and he replied that he was ready to leave to our discretion the question of suppressing Prytz's record of the conversation on 17th June. We, nevertheless, feel that we ought to consult him again. When we get your views about all this we must also consult higher authority here, so this is only a preliminary sounding.[3]

---

[3] In a reply of 29 November, Jerram commented that the only valid grounds for reconsidering publication of the 'Prytz telegram' would either be the national interest or strict historical accuracy. He observed: 'Butler's and Prytz's respective versions of the interview differ so radically that they are difficult to reconcile, but Prytz's is very circumstantial and Butler's defence is admittedly weak. The world would be left to draw its own conclusions which might not be wholly favourable to Butler. You in any case wish to suppress the only piece of evidence which effectively shows up the Swedish Government, namely Boheman's admission to Mallet that the Swedish Government had made up its mind *before* the receipt of Prytz's telegram.' He concluded that to issue a joint communiqué would only serve to throw a spotlight on a matter which was at present attracting little notice. Replying on 15 December, Warner accepted these arguments, though he thought that it would be prudent to hint to the Swedes that we might feel obliged to publish the correspondence if there were a revival of the story in the Swedish media (FO 371/66493, N14272/199/42)

8. One final small point. You will notice there is a corrupt group in the enclosed version of Mallet's telegram No. 748 of the 20th June, 1940. If you still have the original text, could you kindly give us the correct rendering?

Yours ever,
R.M.A. HANKEY

No. 102

Mr Scott (Helsinki) to Mr Bevin, 24 November 1947
No. 288 Secret (FO 371/65931, N13817/640/56)

Sir,
I have the honour to inform you with reference to my despatch No. 284 of the 18th November,[1] that I saw Mr Enckell by appointment today in the hope that, having unburdened himself to the Foreign Affairs Committee of the Diet, he would feel at liberty to tell me something more about what happened during his stay in Moscow. I cannot say that he told me very much that I did not know already.

2. I told him that I had naturally read all the newspapers had to say and realised that he had said that the delegation were not authorised to discuss such matters as a defensive alliance, but I should, I said, feel happier if I could give my Government the Minister for Foreign Affairs' assurance that nothing has passed at Moscow which could in any way prejudice the interests of His Majesty's Government under the Peace Treaty.

3. Mr Enckell did not give me a direct reply but said that, as stated in the papers the Delegation had had no authority to discuss such a thing as a defensive alliance. He then went on to say that away back in 1945 at a time when the Soviet Government had discussed a form of defensive pact with Czechoslovakia, similar discussions had been conducted here most secretly by President Paasikivi, who was at that time Prime Minister. Nothing positive had been decided then nor were they now in a position to come to any positive arrangement even if they desired to do so. This meagre information was wrapped up in an almost unbroken flow of conversation and left me with the impression that Mr Enckell was once again anxious to evade the issue.

4. This afternoon the Military and Air Attachés had a conversation with the Minister of Defence, which left them with the conviction that whatever had actually been done, the question of a military understanding had at least been raised in Moscow, for Mr Kallinen was clearly much concerned at what had been taking place there and both he and the Commander-in-Chief had been in conference with the President of the Republic this morning.

5. It is clear that there is also uneasiness among the editors of the Helsinki press who, it would seem, do not realise sufficiently the truth of Mr Enckell's comment to me this morning that a military understanding could really be of little importance, for it would be of no material value except in case of war, and if there should be war between east and west, none would really be necessary for the Soviet authorities would be bound to take immediate steps to secure for themselves positions of control from Archangel to Tromsø.

[1] Not printed.

6. To sum up, Mr Enckell has not specifically denied that a military pact was discussed in Moscow, and he has confirmed that the question had been raised previously. Mr Kallinen, without committing himself to a definite statement, has left my Service Attachés in no doubt that such a pact was discussed in Moscow and is now causing the government anxiety. While therefore I cannot quote any specific statement by any particular Minister, I find it difficult to avoid the conclusion that the question of a military pact was raised in Moscow and is now being discussed here.[2]

7. I have sent copies of this despatch to His Majesty's Representatives in Moscow, Stockholm and Oslo.

I have, etc.,
O. SCOTT

[2] Northern Department (Talbot) concluded on 4 December that this despatch provided fairly conclusive evidence that the question of a Finnish-Soviet Treaty of Mutual Assistance was raised during the visit of Finnish ministers to Moscow. Hankey wrote that a pact at such a time between Finland and the Soviet Union would be inopportune, and that 'we should do some wrecking'. Warner added that he had just heard of a possible explanation from the Swedish Ambassador, Boheman (FO 371/65931, N13817/640/56). See No. 104.

No. 103

Mr Bevin to Count Reventlow, Danish Ambassador, 5 December 1947
(FO371/64290, C14204/86/18)

South Schleswig

Your Excellency,

I have the honour to state that His Majesty's Government has given careful consideration to the note, No. 434/47,[1] which your Excellency was good enough to address to me on 7th July last, coupled with the note, No. 445/47, of 10th July last,[1] addressed to me by M. Eickhoff,[2] concerning the position in South Schleswig.

2. The principal subject dealt with in these notes was the status of the South Schleswig Association. I had hoped that the concessions made by the British authorities in Germany to the association in response to the views of the Danish Government would have satisfied all the legitimate aspirations of the association and their supporters in Denmark. It seemed, indeed, that the association enjoyed a particularly privileged position insofar as they were allowed, for all practical purposes, the same rights of political action as a German political party, while at the same time maintaining their intimate connexion with Denmark and receiving important material assistance from Denmark. The association are, however, still dissatisfied with this position and wish to be recognised as a German political party, having the same rights as other German parties. It is not clear whether they realise that German political parties have responsibilities, obligations and limitations as well as rights and privileges. It would, for instance, no doubt be recognised by the Danish Government to be quite improper for a political party in

[1] Not printed.
[2] Johann Eickhoff, Counsellor, Danish Embassy.

Germany in present conditions to advocate the transfer of a part of German territory to another country or the creation of a new, independent territory in what is now German territory. It would also be improper, or, at least, most embarrassing, for such a party to have the kind of close and continuous relations with officials or nationals outside Germany's borders that the South Schleswig Association have hitherto enjoyed.

3. The Regional Commissioner for Schleswig-Holstein has, however, been instructed to inform the South Schleswig Association that the question of their political recognition is being reviewed, subject to their political programme being acceptable. In order to assist this consideration the association are, therefore, being requested to produce a political programme covering generally the same points as are covered by the political programmes of the existing parties in the British Zone of Germany, together with any specific points they may wish to include.

4. The Regional Commissioner is also being instructed to make it clear that if the South Schleswig Association are recognised as a political party, they would at the same time have to accept exactly the same responsibilities, obligations and limitations as are incurred by other German political parties. If they are to be recognised on an equality with these parties they could not, for example, retain their present intimate connexion with persons and organisations outside the German borders or continue to receive special assistance from outside sources. The immediate practical effects of this condition would be twofold: (1) persons of Danish nationality could no longer belong to the South Schleswig Association as officers, or as committee members; (2) gifts of food etc., could no longer be sent to the association from Denmark except on the same terms as they may be sent to other associations of German nationals. This would mean that any gifts consigned to the association or any related organisation would have to be distributed throughout Schleswig-Holstein in accordance with the greatest need so as not to involve preferential treatment for a particular party.

5. If an arrangement on the above lines was introduced it would follow that the South Schleswig Association would be authorised to use their present supply of newsprint in such a manner as they thought fit, i.e. to publish a German newspaper as well as, or instead of, a Danish newspaper provided this did not involve the use of extra newsprint.

6. With regard to section 3 of your Excellency's note of 7th July regarding the presence of refugees in Schleswig-Holstein, I regret that I have nothing to add to my previous statements on this subject.

7. With regard to paragraph 3 of your Excellency's note, in which reference is made to educational arrangements in South Schleswig, I have the honour to enclose herewith a copy of certain new regulations[1] on this subject which have recently been issued by the Government of Land Schleswig-Holstein. I think these regulations will be found to deal satisfactorily with the point on which you expressed concern, namely, the right of members of the Danish-minded minority to place their children in schools of their own choice.

I am, etc. ,
ERNEST BEVIN

No. 104

Mr Bevin to Mr Scott (Helsinki), 16 December 1947, 6.50 a.m.[1]
Tel. No. 569 Important, Secret (FO 371/65931, N14297/640/56)

Your despatch No. 288 of November 24th: Reported Soviet approach to Finns for military pact.[2]

The Swedish Ambassador told Mr C.F.A. Warner on December 10th that although he had not got definite confirmation, it looked to him pretty certain that question of a Finnish-Soviet political and military understanding had arisen during Moscow visit in following manner. Finnish Prime Minister had, he believed, referred in course of effusive speech (which might perhaps be referred to in Moscow telegram No. 2395 of November 6th)[2] to desirability of drawing closer the ties between Finland and USSR not only in economic but also in political terms. Remark had been immediately taken up by Molotov who suggested military as well as political understanding. Remainder of Finnish delegation were filled with consternation and President was furious. Mr Boheman said that what he knew of Mr Pekkala, whom he described as a fellow-traveller, made this story quite possible. It appeared to fit with publicity line taken by Finnish Government that no *negotiations* on Defence Pact had taken place. But Molotov would be able to claim that Finns had taken initiative. According to Swedish Ambassador Finns were of course very anxious to wriggle out of this most unfortunate dilemma.

2. See my immediately following telegram.[3]

---

[1] Repeated to Moscow.
[2] Not printed.
[3] Not printed. This telegram (No. 570 of 16 December) recorded Warner's conversation with Vuori, when the former expressed concerns about this development, which he presumed the Finnish Government would resist to the best of their ability. Vuori, about to return to Finland on leave, said that he would pass on these views to President Paasikivi. Scott replied by telegram on 23 December that he had seen both Enckell and Vuori (who had met President Paasikivi) and had the impression that Boheman's story was substantially true. Vuori said that he had done all he could to emphasise the serious view which the British government would take if the Finnish government gave the Soviets any encouragement (FO 371/65931, N41297/640/56G).

No. 105

Letter from Sir L. Collier (Oslo) to Mr Hankey, 27 December 1947
Top Secret (FO 371/71485, N34/34/20)

Dear Hankey,

Since I wrote my letter of December 11th[1] about developments in Norwegian foreign policy, I have had two items of news which confirm and amplify what I told you then.

In the first place, the Minister of Defence has followed up his statement to me, reported in that letter, by a speech at a farewell dinner to Garner-Smith[2] on December 19th, in the presence of the Commander-in-Chief of the Army and Air

---

[1] Not printed.
[2] British Military Attaché.

Force and other representatives of the defence forces, in which he declared, in a manner which left no doubt that it was a political pronouncement, that the time had come for Norway to choose one of the three courses, eastward, westward and neutral, open to her in world affairs, and that she was choosing association with Great Britain, her old ally in peace as well as war. At the same dinner, General Helset, the Commander-in Chief of the Army, told Garner-Smith that he had asked the Prime Minister direct for considerable increases in next year's army vote and threatened to resign if they were not forthcoming; and he added, in this connexion, that Brofoss wanted to build up industry behind the defence forces before reconstructing these, and that he had pointed out to the Prime Minister that there was no point in this, since Norway could not hold out for more than six weeks without help from abroad.

The second, and even more instructive item is the information [. . .][3] from an absolutely reliable source, that Lange, Hauge and Gundersen, the Minister of Justice, have held a meeting to discuss the coordination of anti-Russian and anti-Communist measures, presumably with reference to Communist preparations for sabotage and other forms of violent action in an international emergency, of which there is now a good deal of evidence [. . .][3] but it is clear that the Norwegian Government are now convinced that they must regard Russia as their enemy and take measures accordingly, and also that Gundersen, whatever he may have been in the past (and I have now heard from more than one source that he was never really pro-Eastern), is now as much alive to the situation as any of his colleagues. He has, indeed, given definite instructions to the police to give us and the Americans 'most favoured nation treatment' in intelligence matters [. . .][3]

Yours ever,
L. COLLIER

---

[3] A phrase is here omitted.

CHAPTER III

1948

No. 106

Minute from Sir O. Sargent to Mr Attlee,[1] 6 January 1948
(FO 371/71366, N10637/9/15)

Prime Minister

Danish Trade and Financial Negotiations. Statement of Problem.

A memorandum prepared by the Overseas Negotiation Committee (ON(48)10) on negotiations with Denmark is attached.[2] It has been submitted by the Chairman to the Chancellor of the Exchequer and members of the Committee representing the other departments concerned are asked to bring the memorandum to the attention of other Ministers. The Chancellor has approved the memorandum and considers that it is not necessary to bring it before Cabinet.

2. The last Danish negotiations broke down primarily on the question of the prices of bacon and butter. The Ministry of Food have proposed to import as their 1948 programme butter to the value of £16.7m, bacon to the value of £4.4m and other miscellaneous products to the value of £26.5m. The existing rations of 7 oz. of fats and 1 oz. of bacon per week can be maintained in 1948 without any supplies of butter or bacon from Denmark. It is essential to limit dollar rations to the minimum, particularly since the dollar forecast made recently is like to be considerably exceeded as a result of the negotiations in relation to Canada, Germany and Egypt. The Danes will be likely to want to sell their butter and bacon at inflated prices in view of the prices which they have been getting recently from other countries for small amounts of these commodities.

3. We propose to make it clear to the Danes that our present alternative source of butter i.e. New Zealand and Australia, does not cost us dollars; that we doubt whether the Danes will be able to maintain their high prices, and that there can be no question of a dollar ration or a guarantee of scarce commodities, with the possible exception of coal. Since the bacon and butter are not essential to us, we do not propose to adopt exceptional measures in the way of guaranteed supplies, prices etc., which would form a precedent for other negotiations. We shall not mind if we get no butter; but we shall make more efforts to get some bacon, since the difficulty about the price is not so great and since if we do not take bacon this year, the pigs will be killed and we shall not be able to revive the trade quickly. The maximum prices which we propose

---
[1] The Prime Minister was in charge of the Foreign Office in Bevin's absence.
[2] Not printed.

to offer are 310s. a cwt. for butter and 220s a cwt. for bacon, these prices being applicable to five year contracts providing for minimum quantities. This goes some way to meet the Danes on prices; but at the same time takes account of the adverse reactions which may be expected from the Dominions if we pay to the Danes very much larger prices than we pay to them for the same commodities. It is considered impracticable to attempt any scheme of differential prices. The difficulties are set out in Annex 3 attached to the paper.

4. The Committee therefore request authority for the negotiators to proceed on the lines suggested above, and in particular that they should be empowered to say that we do not propose to take butter at the cost of dollars or of guarantees of scarce commodities, other than coal.

Recommendation

5. The Foreign Office recommend that the proposals of the Committee should be accepted.

Argument

We are anxious to do all that we can to strengthen the present Danish Government, which is weak, and the credit of which is likely to be affected by the course of these negotiations, and the effect of them upon the Danish farmers. It is also unfortunate that our commercial links with Denmark should be weakened at a time when we are trying to draw Denmark closer to us. In the long run this development can only have an adverse effect upon our interests. Nevertheless, the Foreign Office do not consider that these political considerations should outweigh the supply and financial considerations involved when deciding the lines on which these negotiations should be conducted.[3]

O.G. SARGENT

[3] Attlee wrote on 7 January that he agreed with the Foreign Office recommendation (FO 371/71366, N282/61/15).

No. 107

Sir L. Collier (Oslo) to Mr Attlee, 15 January 1948
No. 8 Secret (FO 371/71449, N637/637/63)

Sir,

I have the honour to report that on receipt of your despatch No. 431 (UN 5532/9/78) of December 24th last[1] (which did not arrive until last week owing to the disorganisation of the bag service) I arranged to see the Norwegian Foreign Minister for Foreign Affairs on January 12th and conveyed to him the message from the Minister of State contained in the eighth and ninth paragraphs thereof.[2]

[1] Not printed.
[2] In a minute of 1 December 1947, McNeil recorded that Lange had approached him in New York and asked whether, before the next Assembly, 'it would be possible to arrange some device which would permit the United Kingdom, the Scandinavian powers and the Western European powers with reliable labour majorities to have pre-Assembly discussions'. This would enable them to go on the offensive. He had suggested a fishing conference as a cover for such a meeting: Western Department supported the idea in principle but had reservations about a fisheries conference as the ostensible reason for a meeting. They were also unsure about the wisdom of including only other Western European countries with large labour majorities. In the despatch of 24 December, the Foreign Office instructed Collier to

2. Mr Lange's reaction to this message was all that could have been desired. He agreed at once that there were obvious objections to using a fishing conference as cover for discussions on general policy and remarked spontaneously that the organisation to be set up under the European Recovery Programme[3] would seem preferable for this purpose, (from which it seems quite clear that he expects the three Scandinavian governments to acquiesce in the establishment of that body); and he then proceeded to explain his present position and future plans along the following lines.

3. M. Lange said that he had been awaiting Mr McNeil's reply before broaching this matter to his Cabinet colleagues but did not expect any trouble from them, since every informed person in Norway now realised that a combined stand must be made against Soviet tactics if the United Nations were not to break up and Soviet aggression be allowed a free field in Europe. He fully confirmed the change in Norwegian opinion reported in my letters to Mr Hankey of December 11th and 27th last,[1] saying that the whole Norwegian delegation at New York had returned to Norway convinced that 'the Russians were impossible', and drawing attention to the change in tone now evident in the Norwegian press (as reported in the letter of December 1st last from the Chancery of His Majesty's embassy to the Northern Department of the Foreign Office)[1] which, he observed, had extended even to the writings of M. Torolf Elster (the Kingsley Martin[4] of Norway). The next step, he continued, would be to consult the Swedish and Danish Governments; and here he feared that there might be trouble from M. Undén, though he thought that he could probably bring him round, particularly now that the Swedish socialists had agreed to discuss party policy in London with the other Western socialists. After that he might wish to consult Mr McNeil on what to do next; and in that connexion he at first jibbed a little at the idea of bringing in the French Government, though he finally admitted, when I pressed him on the point, that their inclusion was necessary from the British point of view.

4. I then ventured to make a point which seemed to me of some importance in view of the attitude of the Minister of Defence[5] reported in the fourth paragraph of my letter to Mr Hankey of December 11th last, and of the information since received from an officer in close touch with him to the effect that the three alternatives to which he had referred in the speech reported in my further letter to Mr Hankey of December 27th last,[1] were not Eastward, Westward and neutral, but neutral, pro-American and pro-British. I said that I hoped that it was realised in Norway that in present circumstances a Western European policy could not be different in essentials from United States policy, and that the hard facts of a situation created through no fault of ours, but by Soviet aggression, left no room for Western Europe to manoeuvre between the Soviet Union and the United States in the manner advocated, for example, by Mr Crossman, MP. To this M. Lange entirely agreed, saying that M. Hauge's attitude which he had discussed with him, was a matter of tactics only. They both held that Norway, and Western Europe as a whole, must join with the United States to uphold the values of western civilisation, (I have since learned, indeed, that the Secretary-General of the Ministry for Foreign Affairs, M. Andvord, has said as

---

say that they welcomed Lange's idea, as it could contribute to securing better results at the next Assembly. They suggested that the details could be worked out nearer the time, and said that they would welcome any further ideas which Lange might have (FO 371/71449, UN5532/9/78).

[3] The European Recovery Programme (ERP), also known as the Marshall Plan, had been launched following Secretary of State George C. Marshall's speech at Harvard University on 5 June 1947.

[4] Editor of the *New Statesman* from 1930 to 1960.

[5] Hankey annotated this: 'i.e. one of the main protagonists of aligning Norway with the West.'

much to the Counsellor of the United States Embassy); and the consultations which he envisaged would themselves be preliminary to an understanding with the United States authorities on a joint policy—in short, we would first talk among ourselves, then talk with the Americans and finally both talk very firmly with the Russians; but the Americans did not fully understand the European point of view, particularly in economic matters, and it was essential to put it before them with the greatest possible authority, so as to prevent them from saying or doing things which would make it more difficult for the European rank and file, particularly in the Labour parties, to avoid being misled by Soviet propaganda against them. It was, indeed, the need for avoiding trouble with a still largely uninstructed public opinion which explained much which His Majesty's Government might not have found palatable in Norwegian policy: 'our aims', he said with emphasis, 'are the same as yours, but we have to proceed so as to avoid creating any more of a "fifth column" here than can be helped'. (He seemed to take it for granted that some fifth column would be created in any case.)

5. M. Lange then referred to another question which is perhaps the fundamental reason for his government's attitude. 'Our position would be easier', he said, 'if we were sure that the American strategists did not intend to "write off" Scandinavia in the event of a conflict. To judge from recent statements by President Truman and others, they do not intend to "write off" Italy, but we have reason to believe that they have written off Spitsbergen, and in general we know nothing of their military plans'. I evaded further discussion of this subject, which might have produced awkward enquiries into British military plans; but it is evidently at the back of the minds of M. Lange, M. Hauge and their colleagues and will remain an inhibiting influence on the Norwegian Government so long as they are uncertain what, if any, Anglo-American plans exist for dealing with an eventual Soviet invasion, of which, it is clear, they now envisage the possibility.[6]

6. I am sending copies of this despatch to His Majesty's representatives at Washington, Paris, Brussels, The Hague, Stockholm, Copenhagen and Reykjavik, and to the United Kingdom Delegation to the United Nations.

I have, etc.,
L. COLLIER

[6] Hankey sidelined this paragraph and annotated it '*Voilà*'.

No. 108

Mr Bevin to HM Representatives Overseas, 23 January 1948[1]
Tel. No. 6 Saving, Secret (FO 1110/1, PR1/1/913G)

His Majesty's Government have decided that the developing Communist threat to the whole fabric of Western civilisation compels us to adopt a new publicity policy designed primarily to give a lead and support the truly democratic elements in Western Europe, which are anti-Communist and, at the same time, genuinely

[1] This telegram was addressed to embassies in Europe, the Middle East, North and South America and the Far East. A separate telegram, No. 11 Saving of 23 January, was sent to embassies in Eastern Europe and to Moscow, making clear that it was not expected that they would be able to carry on active anti-Communist propaganda locally.

progressive and reformist, in withstanding the inroads of Communism.[2] This new policy will also require special application in the Middle East and possibly in certain Far Eastern countries such as India, Pakistan, Burma, Ceylon, Malaya, Indonesia and Indo-China.

2. The following will be the broad directive on which the new policy will be based:

(*a*) We should advertise our principles as offering the best and most efficient way of life. We should attack, by comparison, the principles and practice of Communism, and also the inefficiency, social injustice and moral weakness of unrestrained capitalism. We must not, however, attack or appear to be attacking any member of the Commonwealth or the United States.

(*b*) Our main target should be the broad masses of workers and peasants in Europe and the Middle East. We should, therefore, use the arguments most likely to appeal to them. First amongst these is the argument that, compared with 'Social Democratic' countries, such as Britain, Sweden and New Zealand, the standard of life (wages, food, housing, etc.) for the ordinary people is extremely low in the Soviet Union, where 'privilege for the few' is a growing phenomenon. Russia's pretence to be a 'Workers' Paradise' is a gigantic hoax. We can fairly ask why the Communists, if life under Communist rule is so enviable, should shut themselves off so completely. 'Social Democracy', on the other hand, gives higher standards for the masses and protects them against privilege and exploitation whether Capitalist or Communist.

(*c*) Equally important is that we should stress the civil liberties issue, pointing to the many analogies between Hitlerite and Communist systems. We cannot hope successfully to repel Communism only by disparaging it on material grounds, and must add a positive appeal to Democratic and Christian principles, remembering the strength of Christian sentiment in Europe. We must put forward a positive rival ideology, which, in fact, has its basis in the value of civil liberty and human rights. Examples should be given in order to show what the loss of civil liberties and human rights means in practice. This is especially necessary in countries where the loss of these rights and liberties has never been experienced and therefore is not appreciated.

(*d*) We should represent Communism and the foreign policy of Communist countries as a hindrance to international co-operation and world peace. We should expose the immorality, militancy and destructiveness of Communist foreign policy, and diplomatic methods, their manoeuvres to divide and impoverish Western European countries and to exploit their control of Europe's main food producing areas. We should represent the satellite countries as 'Russia's new colonial empire', serving Russia's strategic and economic interests at the cost of the freedom and living standards of the Eastern European peoples. The myth that the Russians never break treaties should be exposed, and Communism portrayed as the stalking-horse of Russian imperialism.

(*e*) Finally, we should disseminate clear and cogent answers to Russian misrepresentations about Britain. We should not make the mistake of allowing ourselves to be drawn into concentrating our whole energy in dealing with those subjects which are selected for debate by Russian propaganda. On the other hand we must see to it that our friends in Europe and elsewhere are armed with the facts

---

[2] This telegram was based on a paper entitled 'Future Foreign Publicity Policy' (CP(48) 8) which had been submitted by Bevin to Cabinet on 4 January and had been approved. It provided the directive for the establishment of Information Research Department (IRD), which assumed responsibility for the implementation of this policy. See also *IRD History Note*.

and the answers to Russian propaganda. If we do not provide this ammunition, they will not get it from any other source.

3. An additional Information Department will be established in the Foreign Office to collate information concerning Communist policy, activities and propaganda, to prepare the material of our long-term anti-Communist publicity for dissemination through His Majesty's Missions and the Information Services abroad, to prepare quick replies to Communist propaganda attacks and to brief Government spokesmen at home and at conferences abroad on the Communist propaganda lines and replies thereto. It is proposed that the material should include a periodical issue in foreign editions only of a publication containing information, facts and figures useful to our active anti-Communist friends abroad. It will be of great importance that you should ensure personally that the anti-Communist material provided is digested and disseminated as fully as possible, not only by your Information staff, but by every member of your Mission.

5. [sic] The preparatory steps for conducting the new offensive anti-Communist publicity policy will necessarily take time. You should not, therefore, initiate any general change to the new policy in your local publicity pending further instructions. You will, however have observed that the Prime Minister, in his broadcast of January 3rd, adopted the new line and it will be appropriate to adopt it also on specific occasions and in regard to specific matters from now on. On these occasions I shall send special instructions to the Missions concerned or the line will be indicated in Intels. or in the London Press Service.

6. In the meanwhile I shall be glad of any observations and suggestions regarding the carrying out of the new policy in your country likely to be useful to me in making the necessary preparations e.g. as regards (*a*) the methods and media of dissemination likely to be most fruitful, (*b*) the character of the material required, (*c*) probable effects upon the work of your Information staff.[3]

7. You should also furnish me from now on with any intelligence and material likely to be of value for anti-Communist publicity, both such as would, when made widely known, expose, damage and help to defeat the Communists and their policies and activities and such as would encourage anti-Communists by illustrating the frauds, deficiencies and drawbacks of communism and the superiority of the policies and way of life of those who share our beliefs.

[3] For replies see Nos. 124 and 137.

No. 109

Letter from Mr Baxter (Reykjavik) to Mr Bateman, 26 January 1948
Confidential (FO 3712/71479, N1775/1652/27)

My dear Charles,

Christopher Warner, in his letter N14907/1160/27 of the 31st December,[1] has asked me to address to you any further semi-official letters about the political situation here. I should like therefore in the first place to send you personally my congratulations on your new appointment, which I hope you will find a pleasant change after your long period of duty at Mexico City. Anyway, whatever the

[1] Not printed.

disadvantages of being back in the turmoil of European politics, the work will at least be most interesting and important.

Since December 20th, the date of my last letter to Christopher Warner,[1] the outstanding event here has been the entry into force of the Government's new deflationary measures for dealing with the high cost of living. These measures were duly approved by the *Althing* before the Christmas recess, and became operative as from the New Year. Thus there has been, as from January 1st, a reduction in the cost of living bonus on wages, accompanied by a consequential reduction in the controlled prices of local produce.

It is interesting that the reduction in the bonus should have been accepted by the workers, admittedly with some grumbling, but without more serious troubles. There have, as yet, been no strikes, in spite of the strong Communist hold over the Trade Unions. No doubt the Government had deliberately timed their new measures to coincide with the Christmas and New Year holidays, when people are thinking of other things, and political activities are at their lowest ebb. Other reasons for the absence of strikes was that the sacrifices demanded of the Icelandic wage-earners were really very small (probably too small to have much effect upon the economic crisis), that they were partially set off by a perceptible though very small reduction in prices, and that the Government's measures were not of course confined to reducing the worker's [sic] pay, but required similar sacrifices from all sections of the community. In any case it is evident, from the smooth passage of the Government's plans, that the necessity for doing something to remedy the country's economic position is widely recognised.

I should perhaps add that the Foreign Minister tells me that in his opinion the Communists will almost certainly organise a series of strikes during the next few months. It is important, he thinks, that these strikes should not be too successful: the Communist party must not be allowed to get away with the argument that they alone can, by strikes and political action, still obtain improvements in the working man's conditions of life, in spite of the economic crisis which is causing the other parties to enact reductions in his pay.

The surprisingly good winter herring-fishing, which long before mid-December had broken all records, has continued throughout January. More than twenty German trawlers have now called at Reykjavik to take away herrings to the British-American zone, in accordance with the recent agreement. But by far the largest quantities of herrings are being shipped to the herring-oil factories on the North Coast. The herring-oil now being produced is being reserved as an important bargaining asset in the forthcoming fish negotiations with ourselves and the Russians.

Communist propaganda seems for the time being almost to have dropped the agitation about Keflavik airfield. It has lately switched to a new theme, namely, the folly of the Government in trying to market Iceland's fish mainly in Great Britain and Germany, both of which countries have trawlers of their own and catch their own fish to an increasing extent, and are thus, from Iceland's point of view, diminishing markets; whereas, it is argued, the Government would do much better to market Iceland's fish in the countries of Eastern Europe, where there will always be an almost unlimited demand. This is of course merely a preparation for the coming fish negotiations with Britain and Russia. The Government are very much alive to the dangers of becoming too dependent economically on Soviet Russia and her satellites. There is no need for us to stress the point.

I will close this letter by attempting to answer the question you put to me in Christopher Warner's letter N12678/1160/27 of the 15th December,[1] about Iceland's future relations with the Americans.

It is difficult to be very categorical about a hypothetical situation which may arise at some time in the future when conditions are very different from those existing at present. But personally I would not agree without considerable qualification to the thesis that, if Iceland were to be in desperate need of American economic help, she would be bound to accept in return *any* political conditions that the Americans might wish to impose. I doubt whether such conditions as would, in Icelandic eyes, deprive the country of its independence and liberty would stand any chance of acceptance. National sentiment here is very strong, stronger than in many other countries.

The Americans, of all people, ought to be able to appreciate the strength of this feeling, and no doubt will make every endeavour to draw up their conditions in such a way as not to antagonise the Icelanders. With care and tact, and provided that they do not try deliberately to override Icelandic public opinion, they should be able to obtain a good deal. They will probably not find the Icelanders entirely unresponsive, if treated in the right manner; unless of course the Communists happen to be in power.

If, however, the Americans ask too much, the Icelandic Government of the day (if non-Communist) will presumably point out that neither they, nor any other non-Communist Government, could possibly accept such terms, in opposition to Icelandic public opinion; and that if the Americans insisted there might be a landslide in favour of the Communists, which would not be in American interests.

I do not think that, even in that case, the Icelanders would willingly throw in their lot with the Russians. They would, most of them, be even more apprehensive of a threat to their independence from that quarter. But a Communist Government here would certainly do a lot of harm to American interests.

There is, even at the present moment, some danger of the Communists returning to power as a component part of a coalition Government. After all, they formed a part of a coalition Government just over a year ago. As the economic crisis develops, there may be a movement in favour of the formation of a National Government to include the Communists as well as the other main parties. The inclusion of the Communists might be expected to eliminate the likelihood of strikes, which would be so disastrous at a time when all the national energy must be concentrated on economic recovery. This political regrouping would be preceded by negotiations between the parties, and might result in a compromise whereby the Communists would be given power to deal with the situation at Keflavik. It is this possibility, I think, that is worrying the Americans.

At present there is no sign that the Icelandic Government want American economic assistance. A few days ago I drew the attention of the Permanent Under-Secretary in the Ministry for Foreign Affairs to certain conflicting reports which had appeared in the press regarding the assistance which Iceland was expecting to receive under the European Recovery Programme. He told me that all the Icelandic Government had done up to date was to furnish certain factual information in reply to the enquiries addressed to all the participating countries. They had not said that they wanted any American assistance. Nor had they said that they did not want American assistance. In general, however, he could tell me that the Icelandic Government were not so much interested in the possibility of obtaining direct assistance for themselves, as in the possibility of supplying some of the needs of other European countries, e.g. by exporting fish to them, under the Marshall plan.[2]

Yours sincerely,
C.W. BAXTER

[2] Replying to Baxter on 2 March, Bateman noted the advances made by the Communists in Central Europe, and expressed concerns about the possible inclusion of Communists in the Government in Iceland. He encouraged Baxter to find ways of drawing the attention of his Icelandic contacts, especially in the press, to the dangers involved (FO 371/71479, N1755/1652/27).

No. 110

Minute from Mr McNeil to Mr Bevin, 27 January 1948
(FO 371/71421A, N1292/588/56)

The Finnish Minister asked me if Mr Bevin's speech by its total omission of any reference to the Finnish position meant that the Finnish trade relationship with our country would be weaker or given a lesser priority by reason of this decision to develop Western European associations.[1]

I told him on the contrary that the Secretary of State had considered carefully whether he should make any reference to the peculiar position of Finland and that he had only decided to say nothing because he thought that anything he had to say would only embarrass our Finnish friends. I said that he could be quite assured we understood very clearly the importance to Finland, as well as to ourselves, of our trade relationship and that they could be certain that they would be given no less consideration in the future than they had in the past. I told him that in relation to Finland and the Scandinavian countries the Secretary of State had thought that rather than make any political approach the wisest approach was to hope that as Western European relations developed, and as the Marshall Plan as we hoped succeeded, the ties between us would be firmer.

The Finnish Minister said that this had been his own interpretation, but he knew that his Government would be glad to be re-assured on this point.

I asked him if there had been any developments in the Russian pressure on his country. He told me that at first sight the replacement of the Russian Minister at Helsinki by a Russian officer who had previously been a Control Authority [*sic*] in Helsinki, had been translated gloomily by his Government. However, he said that this Foreign Minister, who had known the new Russian Minister in the occupation days, was now not nearly so pessimistic. His Foreign Minister thinks that this new Soviet Minister is by no means an unreasonable fellow nor so badly disposed towards Finland.

He said that one of the results of the recent Anglo-Soviet trade pact had been to take the steam out of the communist campaign inside Finland against the Anglo-Finnish trade relationship, and that there had been a noticeable slowing up in this propaganda.[2]

[1] Bevin's speech proposing the formation of a Western Union was delivered in the House of Commons on 22 January 1948: *Parl. Debs., 5th ser., H. of C.*, vol. 446, cols. 383-409.
[2] Bevin commented on this record 'There are many ways I think in which we can develop trade with Finland. We used to do a good trade with them in flour. I do not know what our position is now, but we used to get an enormous lot of pulp back from them. It is one of the great connections both for the pulp

He told me that as far as he could gather in his recent visit home, the elections were not now likely to take place before July. As indications went, opinion seemed to agree that the communists would lose further ground. However, he said that his Prime Minister did not think that whether the communists won or lost ground would make much difference. Whatever the result he feared the communists would retain the important offices.

H. McNEIL

and the egg trade and would help to keep the Finnish line going. I suppose that the Minister of Food is not in a position to do much yet, but it ought to be kept in mind' (FO 371/71421A, N1292/588/56).

No. 111

Mr Bevin to Sir L. Collier (Oslo), 27 January 1948, 8.55 p.m.[1]
Tel. No. 58 Top Secret (FO 371/71494, N949/949/30)

Minister of Defence has received letter from Norwegian Minister of Defence[2] suggesting that Norwegian troops in Germany should be withdrawn. He is proposing to reply strongly but in friendly terms opposing such withdrawal

(*a*) on practical ground that this would form a precedent for withdrawal of other Allied troops who together form one quarter of our occupation forces in Germany, and

(*b*) on wider issue that this would imply a breach in Anglo-Norwegian solidarity forged during the war and have a proportionately bad effect on Anglo-Norwegian relation.

2. My immediate reaction is full agreement with general lines of proposed reply, but before it is finally approved I should be grateful for your urgent views as to what may be motive for Norwegian suggestion.[3]

[1] Repeated for information to Copenhagen and Berlin
[2] Jens Chr. Hauge.
[3] Collier replied on 28 January that he was not quite sure what lay behind Hauge's approach, but that he entirely agreed with the proposed reply (FO 371/71494, N1001/949/30G). In a further telegram of 29 January Collier reported that he had subsequently spoken to Lange, who referred to parliamentary difficulties and said that 'he had warned Hauge that he would get a dusty answer' (FO 371/71494, N1060/949/30G). The Foreign Office wrote to the War Office on 2 February, agreeing with the proposed draft and concluding that 'rather confused parliamentary considerations, resulting from public anxiety over the international situation are probably all that is at the back of it. . . . However, it looks as though the Norwegian Foreign Minister will do his best to see that we hear no more of the matter' (FO 371/71494, N1001/949/30G).

No. 112

Sir C. Jerram (Stockholm) to Mr Bevin, 28 January 1948, 7.35 p.m.
Tel. No. 61 Important, Secret, Light (FO 371/71724, N1009/577/42)

Swedish Foreign Minister is most unwilling to express any opinion about Mr Bevin's speech.[1] He tells me that he had read it carefully. To others he has added that it lacks detail and he does not fully understand its implications. It would do no good and might do harm if I were to press him. But I feel that it would be most valuable if I were authorised to give him, simply *à titre d'information,* the detailed propositions that have been made to Benelux.[2]

2. In addition informed official sources whom I do not wish to quote tell me that Undén will in fact in his speech at Foreign Affairs debate on 4th February come out in favour of the Marshall Plan and express anti-Communist views but that he will carefully avoid giving any indication of this beforehand and is most anxious not to be pressed. Then there is to be a meeting of the three Scandinavian Prime Ministers at Stockholm on 9th February and of the three Foreign Ministers at Oslo on 23rd February when a common line may well be adopted.

3. In press reports from London it is suggested that His Majesty's Government will make no approach to Scandinavia until Scandinavian statesmen have themselves shown where they stand. It would be a pity to give Sweden an opportunity to stand aside on the pretext that she was without information and I therefore hope that I may be authorised to approach M. Undén at least in an informatory fashion as a presumably 'kindred soul'.[3]

[1] See No. 110, note 1.
[2] Northern Department observed that Jerram's conclusion was premature: no negotiations had been started with any of the Benelux countries.
[3] As a result of a misunderstanding about the wishes of Bevin, who had been travelling, it did not prove possible to provide Jerram with any instructions before Undén made his speech. Hankey commented that it seemed doubtful whether it would have altered what he said, as it corresponded to his previous line. In a subsequent letter to Jerram he added that he thought that there was little doubt that Undén was not inclined to identify Sweden too closely with any western union which might come about (FO 371/71723, N1009/577/42).

No. 113

Mr Randall (Copenhagen) to Mr Bevin, 3 February 1948
No. 49 Restricted (FO 371/71367, N4688/61/15)

Sir,
Today I found an opportunity of speaking to the Danish Minister for Foreign Affairs about the speech which you, Sir, delivered on 22nd January on the subject of a Western union. Mr Rasmussen told me that he had received a report from the Danish Ambassador in London on the lines of your telegram No. 60 of 29th January,[1] and fully appreciated the motives and basis of your declarations. I said that I had no instructions, that your speech was a statement of principles and a constructive programme and that practical measures would take some time to work out, but that I supposed that I might before very long be able to discuss the question with him in

[1] Not printed.

more precise detail. Meanwhile, after referring to your disclaimer of any intention of using the smaller Powers to make difficulties for the Greater, I emphasised the main purpose you had in mind, the reuniting of a Europe whose unity had certainly not been broken by us, and said that, for the Northern countries, the most immediate fact seemed to me to be their practical support of the Marshall Plan. This, I remarked, could not be called a '*bloc*'

2. Mr Rasmussen, who did not rise to this sidelong reference to his Prime Minister's recent declaration against Denmark's entering either a Western or Eastern '*bloc*', said that Denmark was much interested in the future of the policy you had described, but would have to consult her Northern neighbours. Here, he said, in confidence, he expected it would be somewhat more difficult going with the Swedes than it had been; they could not forget their neutrality during the war. The chief thing was that the Marshall Plan countries should go on, aside from politics, with their share with determination and without any reservations; Denmark was ready to continue her unreserved support and co-operation, but he feared that if any political motives or alignments appeared to be coming out of the Plan, the Swedes might try to introduce the reservations they had wished to formulate at the outset.[2] I said that I very much hoped this would not be so, and said we appreciated the influential part which Denmark had played in getting the plan accepted and the Marshall organisation in working order.

3. I then remarked that, as no doubt the Minister knew much better than I, the Russians always despised weakness and lack of decision; it was best to deal with them frankly and even with brutal candour at times. In this connexion, I said, I had been very glad to see—since we were included in the charge made by the Moscow *Red Star* of making Denmark a base for Anglo-Saxon imperialism—that the Danish Prime Minister had made such a prompt and vigorous rejoinder; I knew that this would have been appreciated by my Government. The Minister said that the *Red Star* had made itself ridiculous, but in such matters he thought that the Russians were apt to be wanting in intelligence.

4. Finally, at the end of a long informal talk which I do not think necessary to reproduce in full, the Minister emphasised that the forthcoming meeting of the Norwegian, Swedish and Danish Prime Ministers in Stockholm was concerned more with their roles of Socialist Party chairmen, but that he had no doubt that other questions of common interest to the three countries would be informally discussed, and these discussions would be continued at the more formal Foreign Ministers' conference to be held in Oslo later this month.

5. My general impression from the talk I have summarised above was that Mr Rasmussen and probably most of the present Government at heart approve entirely of the line taken in your speech, but that they are nervous of being brought to the point of making any public declaration and still more taking any practical step which goes beyond the present participation in the Marshall Plan and the well-known lines of Scandinavian co-operation. To this extent the anticipated Swedish lead in the direction of neutrality, while at heart and in private discussion disapproved, may well be taken as an opportune excuse to do nothing more, or at least to go very slowly. Denmark, as the Minister remarked when commenting on the *Red Star* article, is only

---

[2] In his telegram No. 40, also of 3 February, Randall had commented on an earlier statement by Hedtoft about Denmark's attitude to a European *bloc*. He concluded that it would be wise not to expect, and still more not to press for, any explicit adherence to Western Union. Hankey fully agreed with this, observing that it would be necessary 'to handle the Scandinavians most carefully' (FO 371/71370, N1284/240/15G).

too conscious of her utter defencelessness, and I feel that it will need some solid assurance from both ourselves and the Americans if the Danish Government are to be persuaded to adopt a more forward policy. They will certainly be receptive to all theories of European union and declarations regarding the ethical and spiritual value of Western civilisation, but an advance by us to practical political suggestions is certain to lead to embarrassing counter-questions. The position will no doubt become clearer when the practical developments in the Benelux countries are known. The only two things, however, that Denmark seems honestly at present to wish to pursue with vigour, are the practical working out of her share in the Marshall Plan and the study of a Northern Customs Union. I do not think the present Danish Government, or any of the parties, with one possible exception, will want to go further. The possible solitary exception is the Conservative Party, traditionally concerned with the question of defence which their spokesman, Mr Ole Bjørn Kraft, former Defence Minister, has just raised in forthright and even alarmist terms. But even they, much reduced in influence by the recent elections, could not hope to sway the *Rigsdag* towards a public declaration of defensive solidarity with the West.[3]

6. I am sending copies of this despatch to His Majesty's Ambassadors at Oslo and Stockholm.

I have, etc.,
A.W.G. RANDALL

PS The conclusions in the latter part of the foregoing despatch are borne out by the declaration of the Danish Prime Minister at a public meeting held in the evening of February 3rd and reported in my telegram No. 42 of 4th February[1] to the effect that Denmark's co-operation in the Marshall Plan or with her Northern neighbours in measures of European reconstruction have nothing to do with the formation of any '*bloc*'.

[3] Mackenzie-Johnston commented that it was very evident that the Danish attitude to Western Union was stopping short of politics, and that Randall's despatch was merely evidence of that. Hankey added that it looked unlikely that the Russians would frighten the Danes off the Marshall Plan. Bateman pointed out that the benefits of the Marshall Plan were too tangible (FO 371/71370, N1496/240/15).

No. 114

Minute from Mr Hankey to Mr Bateman, 14 February 1948
(FO 371/71724, N1676/577/42)

Until the Swedish Foreign Minister made his speech in the *Riksdag* a fortnight ago, it appeared that the Scandinavian countries were gradually moving towards some closer association with the West, as well as some measure of unity among themselves. Subsequent events, of which the latest are reported in the attached telegrams,[1] have shown that these hopes are premature and that the present state of affairs shows little improvement on the position as it existed at the beginning of the year.

It is of course the Swedish attitude which has mainly been responsible for this lack of progress. Monsieur Undén has resolutely refused to hold out any hope of a closer political alignment of Sweden with the West. While affirming Sweden's wholehearted support for the Marshall Plan, he has repeated with tedious frequency, but undeniable emphasis, her refusal to participate in any political or military *bloc*. He has also made a quite unjustified suggestion that attempts had been made in foreign (and therefore, by implication, British) quarters to influence Swedish policy. It is true that Monsieur Undén has not completely turned his back on any kind of participation in Western Union. He has said that he is prepared to consider the Secretary of State's proposals and that Sweden will be ready to associate herself with them on the understanding that they are 'mainly' economic, i.e. fulfilment of the Marshall Plan. But that does not really get us much further than we were before.

On the contrary, it appears that some ground has actually been lost both as regards relations with the West and Scandinavian solidarity. Telegrams from Stockholm and Oslo show that the recent Foreign Ministers' [sic] meeting[1] was split on the question of Western Union; Norway and Iceland being in favour of more active participation, and Denmark inclined to side with Norway, while Sweden refused to move. It has, at the same time, been learned that the Swedish Minister of Defence will not, after all, be going to Oslo and that the Swedish-Norwegian defence talks have come to a standstill. It has also become known that the Swedish Commander-in-Chief, General Jung, has cancelled his proposed visit to England this spring.

It cannot therefore be said that the prospects for the Foreign Ministers' Meeting in Oslo in just over a week's time (February 23rd) are at all promising: while there is a possibility that a serious divergence may develop on a major question of policy. It certainly appears unlikely, on present information, that the Swedes will change their attitude in the near future. Indeed, I have the impression that the increasingly unforthcoming line which Monsieur Undén is taking in his recent utterances is largely the result of the support which the Swedish press and public opinion gave to his *Riksdag* speech. This may account for Monsieur Erlander's statement, reported in Stockholm telegram No. 104 (Flag C),[2] that the Swedish Government is willing to be led by public opinion. Meanwhile the Swedish-Norwegian defence talks are apparently in abeyance, the Swedish Government having reportedly been unaware of, and subsequently disapproved, the action taken by their Service representatives.[3]

R.M.A. HANKEY

[1] This was annotated ?'Prime Ministers'.
[2] Not printed.
[3] Bateman minuted to Sargent that when the Swedish Ambassador had been to see him recently, he had made a half-hearted apology for Undén's Norrköping speech, adding that it did not read so badly in the original Swedish. 'This showed that Undén had not tried to convey the impression of pressure from us. I said that perhaps the less said, the better' (FO 371/71723, N1676/577/42).

No. 115

Mr Scott (Helsinki) to Mr Bevin, 27 February 1948, 12.43 p.m.[1]
Tel. No. 89 Top Secret (FO 371/71405, N2258/83/56)

Pact of Mutual Assistance between Finland and Soviet Union.
The Minister for Foreign Affairs took the opportunity of my seeing him this morning to tell me in the strictest confidence that the President of the Republic had yesterday received a letter from Stalin.

[1] Repeated to Moscow.

2. In this Stalin stressed the similarity of Finland's position with that of Roumania and Hungary and had indicated the desirability of her following the example of these countries in negotiating with the USSR a pact of mutual assistance against German aggression. Negotiations Stalin suggested could be conducted in Moscow or if the Finnish Government preferred, in Helsingfors.

3. The President of the Republic, Mr Enckell said, had summoned the Parliamentary leaders of political parties in the Diet to a conference this evening at 1700 hours.

4. He added Savonenkov [2] had recently invited him *en tête à tête* and sounded him as to the reception likely to be given to this proposal. Enckell said that he had taken the line hitherto adopted in regard to the defence pact that, with a Parliament whose term would expire very shortly, the moment was not favourable.

5. He then asked whether in the event of Finland negotiating such a pact this would necessarily interfere with the exchanges with and financial assistance from the United Kingdom and the United States.

6. I replied as I had indicated to him earlier in connexion with the defence pact talks such an alliance must to some extent prejudice Finland's relations with the United Kingdom and that we could hardly be expected to conduct our mutual trade on the same basis as hitherto.

7. He agreed with me that such a pact would have no practical value for the USSR and that it could be of prestige upkeep only. I then stressed that with the example of Roumania and Hungary and recent developments in Czechoslovakia before us the whole process of surrendering one's independence was clear, and that it would seem that once he Communists had secured the Ministry of the Interior the process was but a matter of time. By 'stalling' I said he had already gained two or three months and I urged that the Finnish Government should adhere to these tactics. To this the Minister for Foreign Affairs replied he feared Finland would then be exposed to actual provocations: these, I assured him, would occur if the Russians felt there was any advantage to be gained whether Finland signed an agreement with the USSR or not, adding that once Finland set her foot on this slippery slope the subsequent loss of her independence seemed inevitable. I doubt if we can count on Enckell to resist for his foot seems to be already on this slope.

8. From what he said it was clear that he thought it improbable that what took place at this afternoon's meeting would remain secret for long.[3]

---

[2] Formerly Deputy Head of the Allied Control Commission, newly appointed Soviet Minister to Finland.

[3] This telegram led to considerable minuting and discussion in the Foreign Office and with the Chiefs of Staff. Bateman wondered whether it would be possible to refer the issue to the Security Council, but it was eventually concluded that there were insufficient grounds to take this step. Explicit guidance on this point was sent on 5 March, after it became apparent that the State Department was considering the possibility of such a reference. (See No. 119.) It was decided that Scott should be told to encourage the Finns to resist as long as they could, and to the best of their ability. It was also agreed that Anglo-Finnish trade should be treated as a separate issue, and that Scott was to be told to avoid discussion of the subject until he had received instructions which would follow later.

No. 116

Minute from Mr Etherington-Smith to Mr Hankey, 28 February 1948
Top Secret (FO 371/71447, N3331/78/42)

I attended a meeting of the Chiefs of Staff Committee this morning to discuss the latest developments in Finland.

2. The meeting had before it a copy of Helsinki telegram No. 89 of February 27th[1] together with a draft letter to the Foreign Office setting forth the views of the Chiefs of Staff. Briefly, these were that it was only a matter of time before Finland fell completely under Russian domination like the other Russian satellites and that, although the Chiefs of Staff had written off Finland long ago from the military point of view, they attach great importance to maintaining the position in the other Scandinavian countries. With this end in view they felt that we should immediately consider making a suitable gesture to bolster up Scandinavian morale and that this should be done by sending a Naval and Air task force to the Baltic, which would visit suitable Scandinavian ports at the invitation of the countries concerned. The Admiralty had considered the matter urgently and they were prepared to provide a fully balanced task force for this purpose at three days' notice. It was also proposed that the Americans should if possible be induced to participate in this demonstration.

3. I told the meeting that I thought that it was too early to decide on a step of this kind. In the first place we did not yet know the exact implications of the latest Russian move in Finland or, indeed, to what extent the Finns would accede to Russian demands. Moreover, a gesture of the kind proposed at the present stage might well have the opposite effect to what was intended.[2] Certainly in Finland it might provoke the Russians to going much further than they intended to go at present and would inevitably make it more difficult for the Finns to resist Russian pressure. All our efforts at present were concentrated on holding the situation as far as possible in Finland, for if Finland were swallowed up this might have a very intimidating effect on the other Scandinavian countries. I therefore felt that at the present stage it would be unwise to make this gesture, since it might only lead to an intensification of Russian pressure.

4. The meeting nevertheless felt that the Secretary of State would like to know that a task force of the size indicated could be sent out at short notice and it was agreed that a letter should be sent to the Foreign Office setting forth the views of the Chiefs of Staff in the sense explained above.[3]

R.G.A. ETHERINGTON-SMITH

[1] No. 115.
[2] Hankey annotated this 'Yes'.
[3] In a minute of 28 February, Sargent advised Bevin that a visit to the Baltic would risk converting the warning to a provocation, that any deployment should be limited to the Atlantic seaboard, and that the Americans should not be involved, though 'we could not discourage them from making a similar demonstration later if they wanted to'. Roberts minuted later on 28 February that Bevin had discussed this with the Minister of Defence, who had agreed that a demonstration in the Baltic was not desirable at present. It was decided to seek advice from the Ambassadors in Copenhagen, Oslo and Stockholm before proceeding further (FO 371/71447, N2471/516/63G).

1948

No. 117

Letter from Mr Scott (Helsinki) to Mr Hankey, 2 March 1948
Secret (FO 371/71406, N2850/83/56)

My dear Robin,
I hope that our telegrams about the Mutual Aid Pact and my despatch,[1] which goes in the same bag as this letter, will have given you enough information as to the more important developments following Joe's gesture[2] but perhaps I can add a little local atmosphere which may be of interest though it would not warrant a telegram or a despatch.

First of all, I have reluctantly reached the conclusion, towards which I have been moving for some time, that the Russians have now worn down poor old 'Uncle Charles' (Enckell) and that for our purposes we must reckon that he will hold that the line of least resistance is identified with the interests of his country. Avra Warren[3] (as Hadow[4] foretold in a letter he wrote to me when he heard of his appointment) seems to be a very good friend and he has come to the same conclusion. The President on the other hand is disposed to take a tougher line and when pressed by Uncle Charles to send an encouraging reply to Stalin's invitation to sign up, refused to go further than a quite formal interim reply (copy of which accompanied my despatch).

When Savonenkov was invited to come and receive this on Saturday morning from the President he appears to have sent a very off-hand reply to the effect that he was busy and wasn't sure if he could go. In the event he went down to the Castle and was given the reply at 2 p.m. on Saturday. I do not think that there have been any further exchanges since.

Matters have been delayed, quite fortunately, by the fact that the Prime Minister, Mauno Pekkala, who has been incapacitated by another drinking bout, only came to just in time to attend yesterday's meeting of the cabinet. He is now so drink sodden that he too may be counted out. As a setoff to this I'm told that the Minister of the Interior (Leino) has been taking to *Wein* and *Weib* in a big way and I have no doubt that he has let himself go in *Gesang*, *'Stalin, Stalin über Alles'*, for he must feel that he's winning a signal victory!

I have been told that the Government, realising their sorry plight, may seek a vote of confidence on a quite minor issue and some of them would welcome a defeat which would allow them to offer their resignation. If such a *dénouement* could give the President an opportunity to exchange his Communist Minister of the Interior for someone less pernicious that really would be a gain, but it would be expecting a bit too much!

I went to the Diet this afternoon with Bosley as my *cicerone*: only formal business was being transacted and within half an hour the session was adjourned but as we were leaving the building we ran into old Kallinen, who accepted Bosley's offer of a lift. When we dropped him at his door he asked us to come in and, as he seemed to want us to do so, we accepted. From his conversation it was clear that he, whatever happened, would oppose negotiations and he expected that seven other Ministers would line up with him: of six uncertainties he expected Enckell to favour negotiating, Svento he seemed to think would be 6 to 5 against and of the remaining

---
[1] Not printed.
[2] See No. 115.
[3] American Minister, Helsinki.
[4] Counsellor, British Embassy, Washington.

four two would probably be for and two against negotiations. The four Communist Ministers would, of course, favour negotiating. We discussed the pros and cons of a Pact and I said that His Majesty's Government were following developments with the closest attention adding that while I was not in a position to say anything officially as to the view they would take, I felt personally that the Finnish Government could not be wrong if they played for time for in no case could their longer term prospects be improved by their concluding a Pact. In Kallinen we have the staunchest of friends and we could count on his giving the right orders to the army though it is less certain that Sihvo, the Commander in Chief, would loyally give effect to them.

Yours ever,
O.A. SCOTT

No. 118

Minute from Mr Etherington-Smith to Mr Hankey, 4 March 1948

(FO 371/71405, N2524/83/56)

Attached is the latest telegram from Mr Scott on the situation in Finland at N2524,[1] together with a secret report which we have just received on the same subject in CX.21095.[1]

The two reports are to some extent contradictory, since the secret report indicates that feeling among Finnish political leaders is turning in favour of negotiation (this impression was also conveyed in the previous telegram from Helsinki No. 105 Flag C),[1] whereas Mr Scott in his Tel. No. 106[2] reports that a majority of the Cabinet are known to favour rejection. I think it is clear however that Mr Scott's telegram represents the latest position and that opinion has hardened against acceptance of the Russian proposal. A definite decision still remains to be taken, but it now seems possible that the Finns may refuse to negotiate at all.

Paragraph 5 of Mr Scott's telegram reports the possibility that a new Government may be formed without the Communists. I should have thought that it would be rather risky for the Finns to take such a step at the present moment, as it might provoke the Russians to take violent retaliatory measures. But they may feel it is essential to get the Communists out of the Government in order to prevent trouble arising through their control of the Ministry of the Interior if Russia should invoke Article 8 of the Peace Treaty (this is the familiar clause dealing with the suppression of Fascist organisations and of propaganda hostile to the Soviet Union). It is thought that if a change of Government does occur M. Fagerholm[2] might become Prime Minister. He would not be an ideal choice for this post, but there is no other candidate.[3]

R.G.A. ETHERINGTON-SMITH

[1] Not printed.
[2] Not printed. In a marginal note, Hankey described Fagerholm as a 'prominent right-wing Social Democrat and Speaker of the Diet since 1945'. He became Prime Minister in July 1948.
[3] Bateman commented 'It seems that the non-Communists may be in danger of doing just what the Communists want, *viz.* giving grounds for alleging that there is a plot afoot. If so, it is a pity that they have not digested the lesson of Czechoslovakia and the other satellites' (FO 371/71405, N2524/83/56G).

No. 119

Mr Bevin to Mr Scott (Helsinki), 5 March 1948, 11.50 p.m.[1]
Tel. No 76 Immediate, Top Secret (FO 371/71406, N2851/83/56G)

My telegrams 69 and 70 [proposed Soviet-Finnish pact].[2]

The instructions sent to your United States colleague envisage the possibility of a reference to the United Nations only in the event of Finland's independence and territorial integrity coming under a definite menace of armed force. This presupposes the existence of a dispute which has *not* in fact yet arisen, since the Soviet Government have done no more than propose the conclusion of a mutual aid pact.

2. In my view, it will be very dangerous for the Finnish Government to consider reference to the United Nations unless and until they become convinced, as a result of actual discussions, that the Soviet Government contemplate action which might in the words of Article 34 of the Charter lead to international friction or give rise to a dispute. Any premature action on their part might lead to their being non-suited at the Security Council and might well provoke the Soviet Government to retaliate by indulging in economic and other reprisals and generally to exercise the very kind of pressure which the Finnish Government must hope to evade. You should therefore refuse to discuss this matter pending further instructions.

3. Meanwhile, I see no objection to your seeing the President as suggested in your telegram No. 105[2] if you consider that any useful purpose will be served. You might explain my reading of the present Soviet proposals as set out in paragraph 2 of my telegram No. 72,[2] the sole aim of your talk being to persuade the President to ensure caution in the discussions, in view of the equivocal nature of the present Soviet proposals. Your remarks should remain confidential.

[1] Copied to Washington and Paris.
[2] Not printed.

No. 120

Sir L. Collier (Oslo) to Mr Bevin, 8 March 1948, 10.23 p.m.[1]
Tel. No. 104 Most Immediate, Top Secret (PREM 8/788)

Helsingfors telegram No. 120: Soviet pact moves.

Norwegian Minister for Foreign Affairs sent for me this evening to tell me that he had just told my United States colleague[2] that the Norwegian Government had information from three different sources, Moscow, Helsingfors and Warsaw indicating that they might be faced with Soviet demand for a pact as soon as, or even before, Soviet-Finnish pact was concluded. Cabinet would discuss this tonight but refusal was a foregone conclusion whatever the consequences.

2. Nevertheless, the Norwegian Government would like to know what help Norway could expect if attacked; theoretically she was practically defenceless, even if troops were recalled from [?Germany] which was not desired. He was accordingly putting the question to the United States Government and His Majesty's Government,

[1] Repeated for information to Stockholm, Helsinki, Moscow and Washington.
[2] The US Ambassador's report is cited but not printed in FRUS 1948, Vol. III, p. 44.

though he realised that, as I pointed out, there could hardly be a separate British view on such a matter.

3. Minister for Foreign Affairs added that, although refusal was certain, the terms of the reply might be . . .[3] The Prime Minister thought for example that working-class opinion could best be rallied round the government if reply stated that Norway would not enter into any pacts. I pointed out that this might be all the Soviet Government wanted since it would preclude adherence to the Bevin Plan. Could not the reply be confined to statement that Soviet request would not be considered? He said that he himself was anxious to avoid anything which would prevent adherence to the Bevin Plan of Norway and ultimately of Sweden and Denmark too, but here again the question of military help was relevant. The Swedes would certainly expect it. Their present attitude was quite negative and he had even had difficulty in persuading the Swedish Minister for Foreign Affairs to come to Paris. Soviet Government were stated not to contemplate any demands on Sweden. They were confident, with Norway once controlled, she would do whatever they wanted.

4. Minister for Foreign Affairs expressed strong desire to discuss the whole question with you at Paris. He would be there by the evening of March 14th at the latest and would be at your disposal from his arrival.[4]

---

[3] The text is here uncertain.

[4] It was during this period that Collier sought permission from the Foreign Office to discuss with the Norwegians planning for the evacuation of British subjects in Norway. They declined to give him authority to do so, despite the fact that the US Embassy had already made a similar approach to the Norwegian authorities, because they did not wish to do anything which might damage Norwegian morale. This decision was only changed more than six months later in September 1948, after Collier informed Northern Department that a Norwegian general, Beichmann, had approached the Americans to discuss their detailed requirements for evacuation (correspondence in FO 371/71491).

No. 121

Mr Henderson (Stockholm) to Mr Bevin, 10 March 1948, 6.35 p.m.
Tel. No. 178 Secret (FO 371/71716, N2948/9/42)

Following from Air Attaché to Air Ministry.
AX32 March 10th.[1]

Yesterday the Commander-in-Chief of the Swedish Air Force and Chief of the Swedish Air Force Board both asked me to visit them. They were considerably alarmed by a suggestion received from the Swedish Air Attaché in London that Sweden might have some difficulty in the future of obtaining military supplies from England. The Swedish Air Attaché said that he felt that the British were alarmed by the close proximity of the Russian influence in Finland and by . . .[2] on the part of Swedish politicians. He gave as an example his recent application for certain parts of new Swedish J.29 jet aircraft to be tested in Farnborough which had been turned down. He was under the impression that the undertakings had been quite acceptable to our technicians but had been refused at the last minute by ACAS(I).[3]

General Nordenskiöld was very outspoken on the matter and told me that the Minister of Defence and the whole of the Defence staff were now exceedingly

---

[1] Not printed.
[2] The text is here uncertain.
[3] Assistant Chief of Air Staff (Intelligence).

worried about general defence of Sweden and that he hoped that at this critical moment England would not withhold material from them. He was particularly worried about General Söderberg's[4] visit to England on March 13th (see my AX30 March 10th).[1]

It would, he said, be extremely bad for Sweden if after committing herself to British aircraft she were unable to obtain further supplies.

General Nordenskiöld tried to impress on me the fact that the Swedish Minister for Foreign Affairs was doing no more than playing at politics and that he sincerely hoped that modern radar equipment would not be withheld on grounds of Security. In reply I told him that as far as I was aware Great Britain's attitude towards Sweden had not altered and if some special request had been turned down there were no doubt good reasons. However, I promised to pass on his fears and said that I hoped that there would be no difficulty in the purchase of further Vampire frames nor in the matter of photo reconnaissance Spitfires. These again would be subject to our production and demand. The Commander-in-Chief asked that I treat the matter of the Swedish Air Attaché's letter as confidential, so request that on no account is this matter taken up direct with von Arbin.[5]

[4] General Nils Söderberg was responsible for administration in the Swedish Air Force.
[5] Swedish Air Attaché in London.

No. 122

Lord Inverchapel (Washington) to Mr Bevin, 10 March 1948, 10.35 p.m.[1]
Tel. No. 1125 Important, Top Secret (PREM 8/788)

Oslo telegram No. 104.[2] *Possible Soviet demand for a defence pact with Norway.*

United States Ambassador at Oslo has reported to State Department that Norwegian Minister for Foreign Affairs told him that Norwegian Government would shortly have to raise with the United States Government the question of military assistance in the event of aggression. The State Department are thus faced with the necessity of giving a reply, but they are in some perplexity as to how they will answer when the question is put to them. They will, therefore, be most grateful to receive, in due course, any information you can give them about your forthcoming conversation in Paris with M. Lange.[3]

[1] Repeated to Oslo.
[2] No. 120.
[3] Bevin noted: 'This is not very helpful.'

No. 123

Mr Bevin to Lord Inverchapel (Washington), 10 March 1948, 11.15 p.m.[1]
Tel. No. 2768 Top Secret (PREM 8/788)

Oslo telegram No. 104.[2]

I fear that there is ground for Norwegian apprehensions, and that we shall in fact be shortly confronted by Soviet demands on Norway. As a first step I think we should instruct our representatives in Oslo to do their best to infuse some courage into the Norwegian Government. They could point out that Turkey and Persia have successfully resisted Soviet demands and that Norway would be ill-advised to put her foot on the slippery slope by sacrificing her right to conclude pacts with whomsoever she chooses. They could add that if Norway requires outside support to maintain her independence, she is much more likely to get it by showing resolution rather than by temporising.

2. I fear, however, that we cannot be sure that such language will suffice to induce the Norwegian Government to hold out. Nor can we afford at this moment to risk a Norwegian defection which would involve the appearance of Russia on the Atlantic and the collapse of the whole Scandinavian system. This would in turn prejudice our chance of calling any halt to the relentless advance of Russia into Western Europe.

3. We may thus shortly be confronted by two serious threats, the strategic threat involved by the extension of the Russian sphere of influence to the Atlantic and the political threat to destroy all our efforts to build up a Western Union. In this situation only a bold move can avert the danger. Moreover the pace set by Russia in Czechoslovakia, then Finland and now Norway, tells us that there is no time to lose.

4. I have for some time been turning over in my mind how best to tackle a problem which has now been brought to a head by the impending Russian move on Norway. I think that the most effective course would be to take very early steps before Norway goes under, to conclude under Article 51 of the Charter a regional Atlantic approaches pact of mutual assistance in which all the countries directly threatened by a Russian move to the Atlantic could participate, for example the United States, United Kingdom, Canada, Eire, Iceland, Norway, Denmark, Portugal, France and Spain, when it has a democratic regime.

5. I gave long and careful thought to the question of inviting the Scandinavian countries to join with the United States, France and Benelux in the system now being negotiated in Brussels. I came to the conclusion however that this would be a mistake since France and the United Kingdom with the Benelux countries could not by themselves defend Scandinavia against pressure. Nor was there quite the same outlook from France and the Benelux countries as from the Scandinavian countries in regard to the whole problem of Atlantic security. Therefore I decided against approaching the Scandinavian states at this juncture and kept our co-operation with them entirely on the ERP plane. Now however the issue has been raised of pressure against Norway which might lead to the encirclement of Sweden, and we must therefore devise practical schemes to meet this danger. The most practical course in my view is to work for the following three systems:

(1) the United Kingdom-France-Benelux system with United States backing;
(2) a scheme of Atlantic security with which the United States would be even more

---

[1] This telegram and subsequent exchanges on the subject were not copied to Oslo.
[2] No. 120.

closely concerned;

(3) a Mediterranean security system which would particularly affect Italy;

We are pressing ahead for the first system, but in view of the threat to Norway the Atlantic security system is now even more important and urgent.

6. I am convinced therefore that we should study without any delay the establishment of such an Atlantic security system, so that if the threat to Norway should develop we could at once inspire the necessary confidence to consolidate the West against Soviet infiltration, and at the same time inspire the Soviet government with sufficient respect for the West to remove temptation from them and so ensure a long period of peace. The alternative is to repeat our experience with Hitler and to witness helplessly the slow deterioration of our position until we are forced in much less favourable circumstances to resort to war in order to defend our lives and liberty. We can turn the whole world away from war if the rest of the nations outside the Soviet system become really organised and in turn save Russia itself.

7. Please put all these considerations to Secretary of State and suggest that as a preliminary we should very secretly explore my proposal.[3] I suggest that we might repeat the procedure so successfully adopted in regard to the Middle East.

8. We are making a similar approach to Mr Mackenzie King through our High Commissioner in Ottawa and we hope that Mr Marshall will agree to Canada taking part in these talks if they wish.

9. I do not want to alarm the United States by requiring an immediate answer. But I rely on you to do your best to impress on them the gravity of the situation and the need for urgent action to meet it. For your own information I shall be in a difficulty if I can say nothing to the Norwegian Minister for Foreign Affairs in Paris on March 15th, who has asked to see me, probably about this threat to Norway.[4]

---

[3] The British Embassy accordingly transmitted an *aide-mémoire* to the State Department on 11 March (FRUS 1948, Vol. III, pp. 46-48).

[4] Bevin cleared the draft of this telegram with Attlee, who agreed, subject to minor amendments concerning the intention to make a parallel approach to the Canadian Prime Minister, Mackenzie King.

No. 124

Sir L. Collier (Oslo) to Mr Bevin, 12 March 1948
No. 74 Secret (FO 1110/3, PR 97/1/913G)

Sir,

I have given careful consideration, in consultation with the Press Attaché to His Majesty's Embassy and other appropriate members of my staff, to your circular telegram No. 6 of January 23rd[1] last outlining the alterations made by His Majesty's Government in their information policy regarding Communism; and I now have the honour to submit the following comments thereon.

2. As will be clear from my despatch No. 65 of March 3rd[2] Norwegian opinion of Communist policies and methods has recently passed a turning point and will henceforth be wide awake to the threat which confronts the Norwegian way of life. It might consequently be assumed that the anti-Communist front should now be the

---

[1] No. 108.
[2] Not printed.

main preoccupation of British information work here; but in fact this would be dangerously to oversimplify and underestimate the problems with which such work is confronted in Norway.

3. As a people the Norwegians are tenacious of their established opinions, slow to accept new views, independent-minded and consciously wedded to their ideal of objectivity, with a sturdy reliance on the merits of their own judgement. Failing that, they may accept the views of a fellow-Norwegian; but for foreign views they have little use, unless they can assimilate them unconsciously and then regard them as Norwegian. It follows that the recent change of opinion concerning Communism and Russian policies must be given time to consolidate itself, and that any overt or pushful attempt to influence Norwegian opinion will excite hostility, and that our endeavour should be to make available the true facts of the situation without seeming to wish either to hurry, to excite, or to influence our public.

4. Our best means of assisting the consolidation of the present Norwegian revulsion against Communism is to expand the flow of factual and reliable news about conditions in Communist-dominated areas and about the aims and methods of international Communism, and to let such information speak for itself. (I would instance the extract from the Communist resolution of 1920 quoted in your INTEL. No. 90 of February 27th last,[2] which was immediately given prominence on the front page of Norway's main newspaper *Aftenposten* on March 6th.) Several proposals for increasing such a flow of news are outlined below in the seventh paragraph of this despatch; but, as will be evident from the preceding paragraph, the Norwegian public prefers that news and information should derive from trustworthy Norwegian sources, or be transmitted by responsible Norwegians, or—at the very least—originate from recognisedly responsible sources abroad. Observations from anonymous 'official spokesmen', for instance, make no more than a superficial impression, whereas statements in parliament by members of His Majesty's Government—and particularly by yourself—will, as a rule, be accepted as honest evidence.

5. Such measures, however, should be regarded as short-term tactics rather than long-term strategy; and our information policy must be based, as hitherto, on the axiom that the most potent argument against Communism is convincing evidence of the vitality and consolidation of Western democracy. Specifically anti-Communist activates should proceed unobtrusively against the background of a sustained effort to depict the inexorable forward march of democratic processes, measures and reforms in the Western democracies in general, and the United Kingdom and British Commonwealth in particular.

6. Opinion in Norway, however, as in other countries, is not homogeneous; and it is relevant to consider which elements therein are the targets at which our efforts should primarily be directed. With isolated exceptions, the Norwegian Government, the administrative officials and the *bourgeoisie* are already anti-Communist and merely need continuing confirmation of their beliefs. The majority of the organised Labour movement, as such, is by tradition hostile to Communism and has recently been driven by Russian policies and methods to take an open stand against these. The Prime Minister—who is also the chief figure of the Labour movement—has called for an ideological war on native Communists and has evoked a unanimous response. There remain, however, three groups which are either undecided in their allegiance or definitely pro-Russian:

(*a*) a dwindling element of left-wing radicals and intellectuals;

(*b*) a section of the trades unions and other Labour organisations, consisting mainly of middle-aged workers who have been educated along Marxist and 'anti-imperialist' lines and are reluctant to relinquish their belief in Russia as the workers' friend and 'capitalist' states as their enemies; and

(c) the Communists.

Nothing, of course, can influence the hard core of the Communist movement, while the Communist waverers are already under moral and political pressure from the Labour Party and the Trades Unions. There are, however, considerable possibilities for influencing the two former categories, by some of the methods indicated in the following paragraph.

7. The means by which specifically anti-Communist matter can be brought before the Norwegian public are—roughly in order of operational merit—as follows:-

(a) influencing Norwegian press correspondents abroad, particularly those in London. MM. Kildal, Nerdrum, Buraas, Thorstad and Martinsen should be cultivated personally and be permitted to benefit from Foreign Office reports on conditions in Communist-dominated countries. (I venture to repeat in this connexion the suggestion made in the penultimate paragraph of my letter to Sir O. Sargent of July 26th 1946, that more of this should be made public.)[3]

(b) intensifying the existing relationship between the British and Norwegian Labour Parties, and, to a lesser extent, between the British and Norwegian trade union movements. The British and Norwegian organisations are on cordial terms, but there is far too little traffic between them; and a greater interchange of visits by lecturers, Trade Union delegations, study groups and so forth would yield valuable results.

(c) using the British press. His Majesty's Embassy distributes 900 copies of British newspapers per week to the Norwegian press, which, as a result, has come to depend in a considerable measure on the British press for opinion and news. In this connexion, it is hardly necessary to emphasise the regrettable effects of such severe newsprint rationing as now exists in Britain: the foreign news coverage of the press has suffered greatly from the ensuing space shortage, and I venture to suggest that it might be worth while for His Majesty's Government to offer a slight increase in newsprint allocations to newspapers willing to increase that coverage.

(d) utilising the information services of the Norwegian Labour Party and other political parties and of the Norwegian trades union movement, and the Norwegian press. His Majesty's Embassy is already in close relations with these agencies, and through them it can procure the dissemination of the right kind of anti-Communist material.

(e) producing a periodical in Norwegian designed to keep the Norwegian Labour movement informed of labour, industrial and political affairs in Britain and the Commonwealth. (In this connexion, please see my despatch No. 174 of June 26th last.)[2]

(f) utilising the Norwegian and Home Service broadcasts of the BBC.

(g) official statements in Parliament reinforced by the personal approach to Norwegian correspondents recommended at (a) above.

8. I would venture to lay particular stress on the need for expanding personal relationships between the British and Norwegian Labour movements. As indicated in the sixth paragraph of this despatch, our principal target in Norway should be certain diffused elements of the Labour movement, and no one can better influence such elements than the representatives of the British workers; but by Scandinavian

---

[3] No. 69.

standards the information side of the British Labour movement, particularly in the international field, is distressingly inadequate.

9. The general character of the material needed will be evident from what has been said in the fourth and fifth paragraphs of this despatch. The material must be factual and strictly accurate, and capable of standing the test of comparison with news from reliable sources on the Continent. It must be presented soberly and with a complete absence of emotional enthusiasm. It should set out, not so much to attack, as to explain the errors of Communism and the Communists, and to show where these last, as believers in Socialism, have gone wrong. At all costs, the 'black' of wartime memory, in which anything was permissible so long as it 'smeared' the enemy, must be avoided. Since belief in human rights and liberties, and in democratic processes, is fundamental to the Norwegian outlook, details of the rooting-out of democracy in Czechoslovakia are therefore the best immediate antidote to Communism in Norway; but in the long run it is equally important to convince Norwegians that such rights and liberties are deepening their roots in Britain and the Commonwealth, in the United States of America, and in Western Europe, and are spreading elsewhere in the non-Communist world. It is also important to deal with the tendency hitherto common in Norway, to excuse the present oppressive regimes in the Balkans on the score of the 'revolutionary situation' and by the argument that the old regimes were far from democratic: here it should not be difficult to show, by producing the full evidence in the possession of His Majesty's Government, that, by the touchstones of democracy accepted in Norway and Britain, human rights and liberties have now sunk to a lower ebb in the Balkans than they had ever reached since the end of Turkish rule.

10. Sooner or later the bases of Marxist theory will have to be tackled—first, the fundamental Marxist fallacy of the increasing poverty and exploitation of the workers, and then the doctrine that the workers' revolution is not safe until it has conquered the world, a doctrine which is bound to end in military imperialism, as well as the glorification of dictatorship, rejection of civil rights, and incitement to conquest and oppression in the writings of Lenin and Stalin. Such work, however, should be done by Norwegians themselves as part of their own domestic political propaganda, our part being confined to furnishing some of the ammunition.

11. I am aware that the difficulties of producing material of the sort indicated in the two preceding paragraphs are great, and that the dangers of disseminating the wrong sort of material unsuited to Norwegian conditions, are even greater. Should the Norwegians come to feel that our approach is alien, or that our presentation of news implies political or social ends different from their own, their goodwill will be lost; but, on the other hand, official information agencies in Britain must of necessity be omni-directional in their output, and risk pleasing no one through trying to please everyone. It would be inappropriate in this despatch to suggest a solution to that dilemma; but I would emphasise that if, in terms of your telegram, 'our main target should be the workers and peasants of Europe and the Middle East' (a target, incidentally, presenting as heterogeneous a complex of social and political opinions as humanity has to offer) and if 'we should use the arguments most likely to appeal to them', then as much of the work as possible should be done through agencies capable of understanding the problems and preoccupations of the various groups which make up the target, such as the British Labour movement at home and the information officers of various missions abroad, and these agencies must be given wide discretion in the choice of news and views to be presented.

12. Further, it is important that the anti-Communist Labour front in Norway should be consolidated and strengthened by being fully informed of developments on the

anti-Communist Labour front elsewhere. While Great Britain and the United States maintain considerable and effective information services (and it goes without saying that a measure of co-ordination of policies and activities between the two, both in the field and at the base, would greatly strengthen the anti-Communist front), most of the Western European countries and the Dominions possess no such apparatus; and failing a vigorous and effective information agency within the European Labour movement, a case might be made for such work to be undertaken by the official British information services, perhaps through the vehicle of a daily publication similar to the 'EH Digest' produced by the Political Intelligence Department during the war. As a corollary, it would be necessary to improve the arrangements for collecting and collating information about developments on the anti-Communist front; for instance, news of the attitudes of students in the United States, the Dominions, the United Kingdom and Western Europe towards the International Union of Students and the World Federation of Democratic Youth would have been useful and effective during the recent debate in Scandinavia which led to the rupture of relations with the federation.

13. As indicated in paragraph 7(*a*) above, I feel that better publicity use should be made of Foreign Office information, particularly from Russia and the Communist-dominated countries of Eastern Europe. The Foreign Office Confidential Print contains a mass of informative but not necessarily secret matter of this type; and the memorandum of the Anglo-Egyptian dispute produced by Information Policy Department last year (J2128/12/16 of May 9th last)[2] shows what can be done when such intelligence is worked up into a publishable form.

14. The suggestions put forward in the seventh paragraph of this despatch envisage, in general, a more efficient utilisation of existing channels of information rather than the establishment of new ones and would not involve any serious increase of staff in the Press Section of His Majesty's Embassy. I must point out, however, that the Section is at present working under heavy disadvantages owing to the transfer and non-replacement of the Second Secretary (Information) and the consequent burdening of the Information Secretary with more detailed work than one officer can manage. It will be evident, therefore, that no progress can be made in implementing the new policy until a new Second Secretary (Information) has begun work; and in view of the present directives it would seem more important than ever that he should be (as I have suggested in my letter to Mrs Atkins of January 14th last)[2] of a type and able to fraternise with Norwegian journalists and Labour representatives at the working level. The question will then arise of finding a translator/editor for the publication proposed in 7 (*e*) above. Inasmuch as both the editor/translator and the Second Secretary will need clerical assistance, and as the usefulness of the Press Section Library and Archives has suffered considerably as a result of the reduction of staff imposed on the Section a year ago, it would be necessary to engage a local shorthand-typist (with knowledge of English and Norwegian) who could then at the same time assist in the Library.

I have etc.,
L. COLLIER

No. 125

Lord Inverchapel (Washington) to Mr Bevin, 13 March 1948, 1.12 p.m.
Tel. No. 1190 Most Immediate, Top Secret, Light (PREM 8/788)

Your telegram No. 2870.[1] *Advice to Norwegian Government.*

State Department would see no objection to your speaking to the Norwegian Foreign Minister in Paris on the lines proposed in paragraph 1 of your telegram No. 2768.[2]

2. State Department have instructed United States Ambassador at Oslo to inform M. Lange immediately that United States Government are giving urgent consideration to this whole question. He is to add that if a Soviet demand is made, it is imperative that the Norwegian Government resist resolutely. Recent events in Czechoslovakia and elsewhere have shown that this is the only possible course. Turkey and Persia have successfully resisted Soviet pressure in the past and United States Government have supported them in their firm stand.

3. The United States Ambassador at Oslo is also being told that the United States Government are in consultation with His Majesty's Government and he is instructed to concert his action with His Majesty's Ambassador.[3]

4. State Department hope that His Majesty's Ambassador may receive immediate parallel instructions.

5. They inform us in confidence that they had thought of adding to their instructions to United States Ambassador something to the effect that, if the Norwegian Government wished for United States support, they must understand that they could secure it only by making a firm stand and that American willingness to help them would be directly proportional to the resolution shown by the Norwegian Government. But Mr Marshall and Mr Lovett had both left Washington before it had been possible to clear these instructions with them, and in their absence it was decided to limit the instructions to the line summarized in paragraph 2 above.

---

[1] Not printed. This telegram reminded the Embassy that Bevin was shortly to see Lange in Paris, and of his wish to learn the views of the State Department before that meeting.
[2] No. 123.
[3] These instructions were conveyed to the American Ambassador in Oslo on 12 March (FRUS 1948, Vol. III, pp. 51-52).

No. 126

Brief for Mr Bevin before a meeting with M. Lange in Paris, 13 March 1948
(FO 371/71504, N3337/2710/30G)

Secretary of State

Norway

The Norwegian Government have recently become alarmed by reports that the Soviet Government would shortly propose to Norway the negotiation of a treaty similar to that which has been offered to Finland.

2. The Norwegian Government appear determined to refuse a Pact, but the Prime Minister is reported (by the Minister for Foreign Affairs) to be in favour of replying to any Soviet approach, that Norway would not enter *any* Pacts. His Majesty's Chargé

d'Affaires in Stockholm now gives it as his opinion that the Swedish Government would only support a Norwegian refusal if it were given in those terms.

3. Meanwhile, M. Hauge, the Norwegian Defence Minister, has been over to London and seen the Minister of Defence. He asked for an informal staff appreciation of a number of points concerning Scandinavian defence which would involve an indication of the help we would be ready to give Norway if attacked. Mr Alexander told M. Hauge that the Chiefs of Staff were already studying strategic questions in relation to Scandinavia, and promised to extend this review to cover the specific points the Norwegians had in mind. The Norwegians have also approached the United States Government.

4. As regards the possibility of a threat to Norwegian independence from within, a suggestion has recently been made that the Communists in Norway are stronger than is generally supposed and may be preparing to carry out a *coup* whenever they think the time is ripe. The Norwegian Ambassador in London has expressed grave concern at this suggestion and has privately admitted that his Government would not be able to lay their hands on all the Communists in Norway should an emergency overtake them. The position is now being carefully studied, but such information as we have at present, based largely on reports from Top Secret sources, does not suggest that there is any immediate cause for alarm in this respect: the Norwegian authorities are at least alive to the Communist danger. Briefly, our information shows that the Communists, who as a result of the part they played in the Norwegian resistance movement held a position of some importance at the end of the war, have since been steadily losing ground in the country; that although there are Communist minorities in all the trade unions, the Labour Party has the situation there well in hand; and that there is no reason to believe that there has been any infiltration of the armed forces and police or in mines, shipyards and the like. There is thus no possibility of the Communist party achieving power by legal means or of their bringing off a *coup* without external aid. At the same time the fact that the Communists dispose of considerable quantities of weapons and ammunition held by partisan groups during the war, would undoubtedly make it possible for them to carry out certain sabotage operations should they wish to do so. But it is thought unlikely that they would take such action except as part of a general Communist offensive, since it would only consolidate opinion against them and would give the Government valid grounds for taking repressive measures against them. In a land of such sparse communications, trained saboteurs would of course be able to attain a certain measure of success. In the event of a major crisis, therefore, Communist action would be likely to be directed against isolated measures of sabotage and disruption rather than any attempt to obtain power by political means.

5. His Majesty's Ambassador in Oslo reports that the Communist *coup* in Czechoslovakia has shocked Norwegian opinion more than any similar event since the war and that Norwegians are beginning for the first time to realise the full implications of Soviet and Communist policy. There is, too, a general realisation that Norwegian Communists are ready to give unflinching obedience to any directives from Moscow. This trend of opinion received expression in a speech made by the Prime Minister on February 29th when, after a categorical condemnation of the events in Czechoslovakia, he declared that 'what threatens the freedom and independence of the Norwegian people is the danger always represented by the Communist Party. The most important task . . . is to reduce as far as possible the size and influence of the Communist Party'. He did, however, go on to say that 'we must not create any spirit of intolerant violence against them . . . The Norwegian Communists will continue to

enjoy all democratic rights . . . We shall fight against the Communists with democratic means and mental weapons'.[1]

6. The Norwegian Minister for Foreign Affairs has expressed a strong desire to discuss the question of a possible Soviet threat to Norway with the Secretary of State in Paris. If he does so, there are three main points which the Secretary of State may like to make.

(*a*) It would, in our view, be a great mistake for the Norwegian Government to qualify their refusal of a Soviet offer of a Pact by saying that they will not join *any* Pact. Such a statement might gravely prejudice their chances of securing effective help from us in the event of a threat to Norway. They stand a much better chance of maintaining their independence by a firm attitude *vis-à-vis* the Russians—as the experience of the Turks and Persians has shown—than by hedging, in the hope of securing Swedish support, which may not in any case prove very effective.

(*b*) Strategic problems concerning the defence of Scandinavia are already being discussed in London in connexion with our own plans for the whole Western area. Norway's special problems are being taken into account in this study.

(*c*) Meanwhile, Norway may be threatened by a more immediate menace in the form of Communist attempts at infiltration and intimidation. We are doing all we can to strengthen the military defence of the West. But only the Norwegian Government themselves can overcome the enemy within the gates. It would therefore be a great help to us to feel that the Norwegian Government has the situation well in hand.

7. The Norwegian Minister for Foreign Affairs may broach the question of an appeal by Norway to the United Nations in the event of a Russian threat to her independence and territorial integrity. This possibility was canvassed in the case of Finland. The US Government were believed to be willing to support a Finnish appeal but in our view the case could hardly be taken to the Security Council unless the Russians committed or at least threatened an act of aggression, and they have certainly not done this in the case of Finland. The same would presumably apply if the Soviet government were to offer to negotiate a treaty with Norway.

8. The Norwegian Minister for Foreign Affairs may also make an appeal for help in strengthening the Norwegian armed forces. Since the end of the war we have already supplied equipment to the Norwegians for two divisions and the brigade group in Germany, together with one year's maintenance. The total value of this equipment amounts to over £4 million and the Norwegians are only paying some £2 ½ million for it. We are also supplying them with four 'Vampire' aircraft and have given them an option on 20-25 more. We are doing our best to supply certain additional material but unfortunately the supply position in this country is very tight, and in particular we shall probably not be able to deliver in the course of this year more than two of the seventeen radar sets which the Norwegians have ordered.

[1] Ellipses in original.

No. 127

Mr Bevin to Sir L. Collier (Oslo), 15 March 1948
No. 88 Top Secret (FO 371/71485, N3492/34/30)

Sir,

The Norwegian Minister for Foreign Affairs called on me in Paris this morning at his request to discuss the position of Norway.[1]

2. I asked M. Lange how things were in Norway. He replied that economically they were not so bad, but they were now having to increase their military budget by 50 percent, which would cause some difficulties. I asked him about the position of the Communists. He told me that they were between 11 per cent and 12 per cent of the electorate before the Czech crisis, which had harmed the Communist cause. Although the Communists had some influence in the trade unions, they had no influence whatever in the Trade Union Congress.

3. I warned M. Lange of the trouble the Communists could cause by having cells in factories, and similar methods. I thought it most important that his Government should see that they themselves and the Norwegian trade unions took this danger really seriously.

4. The Minister then referred to his recent conversation with you, and I replied that I would come straight to the point, which was the danger of an approach to Norway from the Soviet Union for a treaty. M. Lange told me that there had been nothing definite yet, but there had been what looked like calculated leaks from Poland and Finland. I told M. Lange that I did not like the situation, and I had immediately got in touch with the United States Government. I felt very strongly that it was no use the United States making exhortations to stand firm unless they were ready to give support. Therefore I had not felt able to give any strong advice to Finland since we could not back it up. Norway, however, with its position in the Atlantic, was a very different matter. I had therefore communicated with the United States and told them that we must consider what we should do if the Soviet war of nerves translated into action. I could tell the Minister very secretly that I had made the following three proposals to the United States Administration:

(1) That we should work for a United Kingdom-France-Benelux system with United States backing.

(2) That we should work out a scheme of Atlantic security from Spitsbergen to Gibraltar and the Azores consistent with Article 51 of UNO with which the United States would be even more closely concerned and to which she would in fact be a party.

(3) That we should work out a Mediterranean security system affecting Italy, Turkey, etc.,

I could now tell him in absolute secrecy, which I must beg him to respect, that I had had a favourable reply from the State Department and also from the Canadian Government and that there were to be staff talks in the very near future in Washington to consider a practical plan. This would certainly not stop at words. I had felt that the United States would respond psychologically more rapidly to an approach concerning the Atlantic than to one concerning only Western Europe. I added that I was anxious to have M. Lange's views on my Atlantic proposal.

---

[1] Bevin was in Paris to attend a conference of countries participating in the Marshall Plan.

5. M. Lange said that you had asked him about the Norwegian attitude to Western Union. He had replied that in Norway there was a very strong body of opinion in favour. He was not, however, at all confident that public opinion in Sweden and Denmark was similarly favourable. He thought I should discuss the matter with the Swedish and Danish Ministers for Foreign Affairs. When I asked M. Lange whether he had in mind Western Union only or the Atlantic system which I had outlined, he replied that his remarks applied to the former. As regards the suggested Atlantic system, there would no doubt be strong inhibitions on the part of both Sweden and Denmark and he did not feel certain about the reaction of parts of the Norwegian Labour Movement. I told him that in our discussions with the United States we would consider whether it was advisable to invite Scandinavia into the Western Union system or, indeed, any system of pacts. It might be better to give a guarantee to the Scandinavian States and then leave it to Norway, Sweden and Denmark, fortified by this guarantee, to turn down any approach they might receive from the Soviet Union.

6. M. Lange told me very secretly that he and his Swedish and Danish colleagues were in absolute agreement that, even if the United Kingdom and United States response to the recent Norwegian approach had been negative, and he was very glad that it had not been, they would still refuse any Russian suggestion for a pact. This applied to Sweden and Denmark, as well as to Norway. But the Swedes and the Danes unfortunately still had their neutrality complex and their Foreign Ministers did not feel that they could swing public opinion in their countries in favour of a Western pact. M. Lange was less worried about Norwegian reactions. But he thought it important not to frighten away the Swedes and the Danes by forcing the pace. I told M. Lange that in my speech on 22nd January I had carefully avoided mentioning Scandinavia for this very reason. M. Lange said that he was grateful for this. He felt it most important to keep the backing of the Labour Movement in Norway and Scandinavia, generally. The Labour Movement was rather critical of America and it was therefore important not to give the appearance of siding with America against the Soviet Union. I told M. Lange I was satisfied with this, provided we knew that the Norwegians would resist any Soviet pressure or an internal *coup*. We would work out plans to come and help if either of these dangers arose.

7. I then told M. Lange that I had agreed with M. Bidault that the headquarters of the CEEC should be in Paris because:

(1) I thought it better not to put it in a small country which might be accused of giving way to American pressure;

(2) I wanted to give back to France her feeling of national confidence and self-respect; and

(3) I also had in mind that in my Atlantic security system I would be going far beyond France.

8. I then told M. Lange that I felt we were just in time to save the world from war or further troubles, provided we stuck together. M. Lange mentioned that he had discussed with you what reasons would be given to the Norwegian public for the Norwegian Government turning down any Soviet proposals. The Norwegian Prime Minister felt that perhaps the best line would be to reply that Norway would not join in any pacts other than the United Nations Charter. You had, however, suggested that perhaps this was what the Russians wanted in order to tie the hands of Norway. When M. Lange asked me for my views on this, I said I would prefer to wait a little and see what developed out of our secret conversations with the Americans. We might decide not to ask Norway to join in any pact in the certain knowledge that Norway and the other Scandinavian countries would resist pressure. But I felt it most important that

Norway should agree to conduct secret military talks with us so that we should know what facilities, etc., were available if we had to come to her assistance. M. Lange agreed with this, but once again mentioned that he thought it important not to do anything which might split Scandinavia. I said I only wanted to have proper military plans so that Norway should not be at the mercy of improvised last-minute measures as she was in 1940. I asked him whether he thought there would be any objection to a statement by the United States President guaranteeing to come to the assistance of the Scandinavian countries if they were attacked. M. Lange replied that he would be glad to have such a statement. In fact he would be happy merely to know where he stood, one way or the other. But he repeated again that he wanted me to discuss the matter with the Swedish and Danish Foreign Ministers as he thought they might be hesitant even over a statement by the United States President.

9. I concluded the conversation by impressing upon M. Lange the need for getting the Norwegian security services and the trade unions to prevent any danger of Communist control through cells in factories and suddenly organised *coups*.

I am, etc.,
ERNEST BEVIN

No. 128

Mr Bevin to Mr Randall (Copenhagen), 16 March 1948
No. 101 Top Secret (FO 371/71371, N3245/302/15G)

Conversation with the Danish Minister for Foreign Affairs

Sir,

The Danish Minister for Foreign Affairs called on me this morning in Paris to continue a brief conversation I had had with him at a dinner given by M. Bidault last night.

2. I told M. Rasmussen that I was not so much concerned about the danger of Soviet aggression in terms of actual war, as of the Soviet Union pushing out their defensive system further, for example into Scandinavia, by pressing the defence pacts or by internal Communist pressure and *coups*. I asked M. Rasmussen what the position of the Communists was in Denmark. He told me that before the October elections they had had eighteen seats out of a total of 149, but they had come down to nine at the last elections. The general position of the Communists was certainly weakening and public opinion was cautious and very much on its guard against them. All other parties were united in their determination to stop Communist infiltration. But there was still considerable Communist influence in labour circles and there had been a Communist attempt to interfere in negotiations between representatives of labour and employers. He hoped, however, that agreement would be reached without strikes. I told M. Rasmussen that the present Cominform method was an adaptation of the old Communist technique of action committees with cells in factories. The bulk of the workers, who had little sympathy with the Communists, tended to remain on strike out of solidarity. The French had had to take energetic measures to deal with this situation.

3. M. Rasmussen told me he had received indirect and unconfirmed information from his representative in Prague about a fortnight ago to the effect that there had recently been a Cominform meeting in Milan at which it had been stated that

Denmark was the next country on the list after Czechoslovakia. He had not, however, taken this report too seriously since in all the circumstances Italy or France seemed more likely. I replied that I agreed that the concentration at present was on Italy, but that the Communists were clever tacticians and it was as well to be on one's guard lest they might strike somewhere else.

4. M. Rasmussen then referred to the rumour of Soviet pressure on Norway for a non-aggression pact. I asked him what Denmark would do if she received a similar approach. He replied that they would certainly refuse to consider such a suggestion, even if it related not so much to a treaty as to a simple non-aggression undertaking given by a Great Power to a small country. Even an innocent pact of this character might lead on to further demands.

5. I then asked M. Rasmussen what Denmark's attitude was towards the West. He replied that she was very much in favour of closer economic organisation within the framework of the Marshall Plan or beyond it. He had stated this many times. There was great interest and strong feeling in Denmark on this subject and the public mood wished to go as far as possible in harmony with the Western Powers short of a military alliance. He thought, however, that it might not be very wise at the moment for the Western Powers to offer Denmark an alliance. But a good deal depended upon the actual situation and the degree of assistance which Denmark might expect in case of need. He remembered that Mr Churchill had said in February 1940, that Britain hoped to be able to help Norway effectively, whereas she could not help Denmark.

6. I told M. Rasmussen that I was aware of the possible threat to Norway and I had been in consultation with the United States Government. I had in mind that we should consider giving assurance to the Scandinavian countries that if Soviet pressure were brought to bear on them and was resisted we would assist them. I did not like asking the Scandinavian countries to join in pacts of a military character unless we were clearly in a position to defend them effectively. I wondered, however, whether a unilateral statement from the President of the United States undertaking to support the Scandinavian countries against Soviet pressure would have a good or a bad influence in Denmark. M. Rasmussen replied at once that it would have an excellent effect in Denmark. He had had the same idea himself and had mentioned it in a private conversation with the United States Ambassador at Copenhagen. He thought that a statement of this kind would deter the Soviet Union more than anything else. If, however, Denmark joined in a military alliance with the Benelux countries, France and even with the United Kingdom, this would not be enough for Danish security. Denmark would still be in the front line and her position would be even more dangerous. I told M. Rasmussen that I sympathised with this view. I had deduced from our conversation that the Brussels Treaty was not suitable for the Scandinavian countries. If, however, we could work out an Atlantic Security system to which the Scandinavian countries need not formally be parties, but would be protected by a unilateral statement, e.g. from the President of the United States, that would be a more hopeful approach.

7. I told M. Rasmussen for his very secret personal information that I was already discussing with Mr Marshall the regional defence of the Atlantic from Gibraltar to Spitzbergen. M. Rasmussen said that this was a great conception. The idea, however, was a new one to him and to his Government. After reference to the great cost of modern armaments and the consequent necessity for co-operation between peaceful Powers I concluded that if we acted on the lines I had indicated I was convinced that we could look forward to a long term of peace. Otherwise, we should inevitably drift into war. This was the vital year and we must ensure that there were no more Soviet

coups as in Czechoslovakia. M. Rasmussen agreed with me. He said that there was considerable anxiety in Norway, which had a common frontier with the Soviet Union, and also in Denmark, which was now only too close to zones of Soviet influence. He did not, however, himself think that the Soviet Union was planning to start a new war.

8. I impressed upon M. Rasmussen that even if we did not have a formal alliance we must be able to discuss military matters secretly with Denmark, and indeed we had discussed certain military questions with them already in the post-war years. It was, however, essential that we should be able to hold such discussions confident that there would be no danger of leakages to the Russians. I drew attention to the statement made yesterday by the Prime Minister about overhauling our security to prevent Communist infiltration, for example, into Government Departments and atomic research. We felt that our own security measures needed overhauling and we were very ready to discuss this particular problem with Danish experts if M. Rasmussen thought this would be useful. M. Rasmussen told me confidentially that the Government had already held a very private conference with high police officials and discussed measures to be taken to prevent Communist infiltration.

9. I then told M. Rasmussen that I was very glad that in his speech at the Committee on European Economic Co-operation Conference yesterday he had raised the question of dollar payments for German exports. I thought it most important that we should persuade the Americans to abandon this insistence upon dollars or gold which was embarrassing not only for the Germans, but the other European countries. I wanted to get the Finance Ministers of Europe together under the umbrella of the Committee on European Economic Co-operation and I had kept this in mind when referring in my own speech yesterday to clearing arrangements. I had not, however, wanted to say too much for fear of frightening some people. We should certainly have a dollar deficit for the next four years, and possibly afterwards, but if European harvests were good and we kept up our coal production things might get better. Fortunately the Ruhr production was up and with this coal and our own British coal we should be able to prevent the Russians at any moment bringing pressure to bear on any individual country through the refusal of Polish coal. I did not wish to harm trade with Poland and was indeed trying to increase our own, but we must all make ourselves independent of possible Soviet pressure.

10. M. Rasmussen welcomed this, pointing out that he was very glad to have secured 870,000 tons of coal from the United Kingdom under the recent coal agreement. Denmark had taken 6 million tons of coal and coke a year before the war, of which 85 per cent had come from the United Kingdom. I went on to say that I was very anxious to encourage Danish trade with Germany, which was badly in need of Danish food. M. Rasmussen told me that the Danes were beginning trade negotiations in Frankfurt next week and particularly wanted to sell fish and offal, but prospects were not very encouraging. I replied that a way must be found and I undertook to get in touch with Sir W. Strang and General Robertson with a view to seeing what could be done.

11. I then reverted to the general international situation. I told M. Rasmussen that I had purposely left all mention of Scandinavia out of my speech on 22nd January to avoid embarrassing the Scandinavian Powers with Russia.[1] I also had in mind even then the conception which I had outlined to him of an Atlantic security system. Meanwhile, however, the Benelux Treaty provided us with a hard core for the

---

[1] See No. 108, note 1.

consolidation of Western Europe. M. Rasmussen agreed that this had been the right approach.

12. Before leaving, M. Rasmussen said that he wished to speak to me again about the question of German refugees in Denmark. There were still 60,000 there. He had spoken to M. Bidault about this. The French had been generous and had already taken 30,000 into their zone. He hoped they would take more. Clearly they could not take all the 60,000, who were unfortunately mainly elderly people, children or women. There were very few workers and young men among this last 60,000. They were, however, well fed and equipped and they would not therefore be such a burden as they might otherwise have been upon any country taking them. Danish representatives were going to discuss the matter in London with the Foreign Office next week. He did not wish to ask the United Kingdom, who had already done so much in this connexion, to take all the 60,000 but he hoped each of the Occupying Powers might be persuaded to take 15,000. In reply to a remark of mine M. Rasmussen explained that Denmark did not want to keep these people in the country as they did not want to risk a mixture of German blood in a population which was not so numerous.

I am, etc.,
ERNEST BEVIN

No. 129

Mr Bevin to Sir C. Jerram (Stockholm), 16 March 1948
No. 72 Top Secret (FO 371/71724, N3244/577/42G)

Sir,
The Swedish Minister for Foreign Affairs called on me in Paris this morning for a general conversation. He said he had no special question for me but he would like to hear my views on the present international situation.

2. I told M. Undén that it was very difficult to be dogmatic. I was convinced that, as far as issues of peace and war were concerned, Russia was still the old Russia with whom it was possible to come to some kind of settlement as we had been able to do after the Napoleonic wars. But there was a great danger that dogmatic Communist ideology might drive Russia into war almost against her will. For example, Soviet pressure might go so far against Scandinavia that Russia would find herself in serious difficulties. This general impression had been confirmed as early as December 1945 when I was in Moscow.[1] Difficulties arose there over Persia. I had never opposed a straightforward oil concession to the Soviet Union similar to our own oil concession in Southern Persia. I thought I had reached agreement with Stalin about Persia but on the last night things broke down. The Russians then broke their Treaty with Persia and ourselves, undermined the Persian Government and used the Tudeh Party in Southern Persia to undermine our own position there. We had sent a brigade to the Persian Gulf and Russia at once drew back. We had had a similar story in Greece, where Russian pressure on the Aegean was long-standing, and also in Turkey. There was a mixture of the ideological drive, of the Russian obsession with security and of old Russian diplomatic methods. The danger was that one of these elements might drive the

---

[1] For the Moscow meeting of Foreign Ministers in December 1945, see DBPO, Series I, Vol. II, Chapter III.

Russians to stick their heads out further than was safe. In Czechoslovakia we had not been able to take effective action. But if the Russians took any risks in Italy that would mean very great danger. So would further support for General Marcos[2] or the renewal of pressure against Turkey and Persia.

3. Turning to Scandinavia I said that the situation seemed to me a little alarming. We Northern democracies tended to be tolerant and placid. But we had to investigate urgently how far the Communists had infiltrated into factories with action committees, etc. M. Undén at once assured me that Sweden was very much alive to this danger. I told him that after Mr Marshall's Harvard speech I had hoped that this was an opportunity to bring Russia really into European co-operation. At first M. Molotov seemed ready to participate but the withdrawal of the Soviet Delegation from Paris followed shortly afterwards and I knew at once that there had been a major development in Soviet policy and that we must expect strong pressure at many points. M. Undén said that he did not think that the Soviet Union intended to push matters so far as war. I agreed that this was not the Soviet intention, but until the rest of the world was really well organised Russian pressure would continue. If, however, the Soviet Union could be faced with a solid front, then I felt that peace could be assured for a very long time. Power was the only thing which the Russians really recognised.

4. M. Undén told me that he would like to give me an explanation of Swedish policy. He agreed that it was a wise move for as many countries as possible to keep together in a united front. But Swedish policy must be determined by her geographical situation. After the war Sweden had willingly entered the United Nations Organisation, but it had been decided that, if there were a split between the Great Powers and rival *blocs* were formed, Sweden would try to keep outside these *blocs*. Although Sweden's neutrality policy in the war had at times been criticised, by himself among others, on the whole there were no differences among the Swedes about the correctness of this policy. It had been to the benefit not only of Sweden, but also of the Western Powers that she had not been occupied by Germany. He recalled the Soviet representations to Germany in July 1940 about respecting Swedish neutrality, and the Nazi-Soviet documents recently published by the State Department showed that M. Molotov had repeated these declarations at Berlin in November 1940.[3] Sweden felt that, if she entered any sort of military *bloc*, and, for example, committed herself to the Western Powers, she would be regarded by the suspicious Russians as having opened her frontiers to the West for Allied military preparations on her territory aimed against the Soviet Union. This would damage Sweden's peacetime relations with Russia, and, if war should come, the Soviet Union would immediately occupy Sweden to deny to the Western Powers what she would regard as a potential base. Therefore for geographical reasons it was in the Swedish interest, and was not contrary to the interests of the Western Powers that Sweden should maintain her policy of neutrality. There was practical unity about this in Sweden. Of course, Sweden would strengthen her military forces as far as possible and she would resist any Soviet pressure. Ideologically she was in the camp of the democracies and there could be no question of concealing her opinions on this point. But she would not enter any military alliance. M. Undén went on to remind me of the Swedish efforts to normalise Swedish relations with the Soviet Union since the war. In many Swedish circles there was a good deal of anti-Russian feeling for historical reasons. Swedish

---

[2] General Markos Vafiades was a Communist who was the Prime Minister and War Minister of the Provisional Democratic Government in Greece from December 1947 to February 1949..

[3] *Nazi-Soviet Relations, 1939-1941: Documents from the Archives of the German Foreign Office* (US State Department, Washington, DC, 1948).

papers often spoke very frankly in criticising Russia. However, a trade agreement which had been based upon a proposal from the Russian side during the war had done some good. Recent events in Czechoslovakia and Finland had very much upset Swedish public opinion. The strong public and press reactions would be noted by the Russians who, with their suspicious minds, would conclude that the Swedish Government's policy to normalise relations so far as possible with the Soviet Union was not sincere. However, the Swedish Government felt that they must continue along the same path. But the Soviet Union knew that Sweden would resist if they insisted upon treating Sweden as an enemy. After all, the present crisis might well pass and international relations become better. Sweden would not then wish to have incurred Soviet suspicions, which would take a long time to remove, by having appeared to enter the so-called anti-Russian camp now.

5. I told M. Undén that I had purposely left all mention of Scandinavia out of my speech on 22nd January[4] because I realised the position and wished to avoid bringing further Soviet pressure down on the Scandinavian countries. M. Undén said that he had noted this. He was sorry that his own statement at the time had been misrepresented as a reply to my speech. This had not been his intention. There had been longstanding arrangements for a debate on foreign affairs and he was dealing with the purely internal position and with suggestions voiced in the Swedish press that Sweden should choose sides in the present world crisis. He had referred very briefly to my remarks about the European Recovery Programme but he had not had my speech in mind at all when talking about Swedish military commitments.

6. I then told M. Undén that we now had to decide whether we were to extend the circle of the Brussels Pact in the light of the indirect pressure now being brought to bear on Norway. I asked what Sweden would do if she were approached by the Soviet Union for such a pact. He replied that Sweden would refuse without any hesitation. I went on to ask whether it would embarrass Scandinavia, and Sweden in particular, if the United States Government, without inviting the Scandinavian countries to join in anything like a military *bloc*, stated that Scandinavian security was a matter of direct concern to the United States. M. Undén replied that he did not think that this would be at all embarrassing, although he would prefer any such American statement to be couched in general terms: for example, in the framework of a declaration that America could not allow the Soviet system to advance further than the present Soviet-controlled Eastern *bloc*.

7. I told M. Undén that for the three years during which I had been Foreign Secretary I had tried to avoid this situation of rival *blocs* arising. But we could not allow the Russians to continue to play a cat and mouse game with the rest of Europe. Nor could we allow her to go on behaving as if the United Kingdom and other European countries were of no account. M. Undén asked whether we could speak frankly to the Soviet Union through diplomatic channels instead of public speeches and show her clearly that she could go so far and no further. I said that I agreed that it was worth considering whether we should not make such a frank communication and that I agreed that it was better not to make public statements if possible. He would notice that I had avoided any reference to Russia in my speech at the Committee on European Economic Co-operation yesterday. I was sure that everything would come right provided that the Western world organised itself. M. Undén then told me that he had suggested to the Norwegian Foreign Minister that M. Lange might warn Russia privately now, i.e. before any proposal for a pact came from the Russians, that such a

---

[4] See No. 108, note 1.

proposal would be rejected. I replied that I thought this was worth consideration. Concluding the conversation, I told M. Undén that I thought that the Russian policy was partly guided by fear, although there was, in fact, no American or British plan aimed against Russia. Russia had treated us all very badly since the war but it was still possible that she might, faced with a well-organised Western world, go back into her shell. I was afraid only of matters drifting on. It was better that Russia should know clearly where we stood and I would certainly consider the advisability of making some statement to the Soviet Government privately through diplomatic channels.[5]

I am, etc.,
ERNEST BEVIN

[5] Hankey and Bateman both thought that there would be considerable advantages to be gained from a joint approach with the Americans to serve a warning to the Russians. Hankey thought that the Russians were at risk of miscalculating the degree of disturbance in Western countries, such as Italy, which could easily lead to war. Bateman thought that the approach should be made to Stalin, and not to Molotov. Sargent disagreed. He did not see an occasion when such a warning could be delivered without dangerous repercussions. 'If we wait until the Atlantic Pact is signed it will be too late for the Italian elections, and if the warning is given before the Italian elections it would look as though we (and the United States) were declaring a protectorate over Italy. The best warning we can give to Stalin is the fact that we are giving practical effect to the Western Union by the Brussels Treaty, the setting up of ERP and the eventual signature, I hope, of the Atlantic Pact. . . . This does not of course preclude the suggested broadcast by the Secretary of State in which he would in effect 'report progress on the plans originally outlined in his speech of January 22nd. Nor do I see any objection to M. Lange warning the Soviet Government privately (as suggested by M. Undén) to the effect that the Norwegian Government would reject any proposal for a treaty with the Soviet Union.' Bevin agreed with Sargent (FO 371/71724, N3244/577/42G).

No. 130

Mr Scott (Helsinki) to Mr Bevin, 5 April 1948
No. 88 Confidential (FO 371/71409, N4233/100/56)

Sir,
The comparison between the situation in Czechoslovakia at the time of the Communist *coup d'état* and that in Finland at the present moment has been made freely and frequently in the British press. I have the honour to enclose a memorandum in which an attempt is made to analyse the position here and such indications as we have of Communist tactics in Finland in comparison with those described in the enclosure to Mr Dixon's despatch No. 46 of March 6th.[1]

I am sending copies of this despatch to His Majesty's Representatives at Moscow, Prague, Stockholm, Oslo and Copenhagen.

I have, etc.,
O.A. SCOTT

[1] Not printed. In this despatch, Dixon had drawn attention to the differences between the situation in Czechoslovakia and Finland. In a comment on Scott's despatch, Dixon wrote to Bateman on 16 April to explain the sort of indications which should cause concern (FO371/71410, N4667/100/56).

Enclosure in No. 130

1. *Disposition of Communists and their opponents.*

While the Finnish communist movement has not the popular backing which the Czechoslovak communists gained from the part they played in the resistance movement, the communist *bloc* are nonetheless in control of 25% of the seats in the Diet. This represented the strength of the communists and fellow-travellers in 1945 and may be taken to be about 20% more than the actual communist strength in the country today.

Until free general elections are held, (they are due in July) the communists and Folk Democrat fellow-travellers are likely to retain control of the offices of:

(*i*) Prime Minister.
(*ii*) Minister of the Interior.
(*iii*) Assistant Minister for Foreign Affairs. (He has recently shewn a tendency to revert to the Social Democrat party.)
(*iv*) Minister of Supply. (He has also an Agrarian colleague.)
(*v*) The Minister for Social Affairs is an Agrarian but he has also a communist colleague.
(*vi*) Head of the State Radio.
(*vii*) Governor of Helsinki province.
(*viii*) Minister of Education. (M. Kilpi is nominally a Social Democrat but may secede to the Folk Democrats at any moment and his main administrative subordinate is a fellow-traveller.)

There are thus few aspects of the administration of the state which the communists cannot at least supervise.

In the Council of the trade union movement the communists are in a minority to the Social Democrats of 6 to 8.

While the pressure which can be brought to bear upon state policy in Finland is thus very great the Finnish government is not at present wholly dominated by the communists. The fact that the remaining 75% of the elected representatives of the people in the Diet are anti-communist makes it necessary for more than half of the ministerial posts to be held by Social Democrats, Agrarians and members of the Swedish party. Thus, the communists could not obtain complete control over the government unless a number of these ministers resigned.

Even so, the President is resolutely opposed to a domination of the government by communists or any other procedure likely to impair Finland's national independence or the free operation of the constitution. He is, therefore, the main obstacle confronting the communists. He is old, but physically and morally tough.

The Defence Forces are in the last resort at the disposal of the President, but the Minister of Defence is a Social Democrat and known to be resolutely opposed to communist domination. Communism has made little headway in the armed forces.

Except in those Ministries where communist ministers have established themselves, there has been little attempt to infiltrate communists into the civil service. The civil service has indeed been the object of constant communist attack as 'a stronghold of reaction' and its organisation was recently tested in a civil servants' strike which was carried through in defiance of the threats of the Prime Minister and other Folk Democrat Ministers. In the Ministry of the Interior, however, and also to a certain extent in the Ministries of Supply, Education and Social Affairs there has been a limited infiltration, sufficient one must assume to enable the foundation of action committees such as were used in the *coup d'état* in Prague.

Though the main body of the Finnish Police are capably and energetically led and could be counted on to resist communism, the Mobile Police (1600) have been penetrated and the State Police (500) effectively communised and could be relied upon to play a leading part in a communist *coup*.

2. *Object of a coup at this juncture.*

If a *coup* were attempted, its aim would be to obtain complete control of the State before elections could be freely held in July, and to prevent the expression of the will of the people in elections of any description or through their representatives in Parliament. Timing would of course be dictated from Moscow; success of the Czech *coup* may increase the desire of the Soviet authorities to make the attempt. The only object in delaying a *coup* might be (*a*) fear of failure, (*b*) desire to cultivate sense of false security among other Scandinavians.

A *coup*, to be effective, would demand wholesale arrests of members of parliament, of members of the cabinet and the virtual arrest of the President. To be effective it would also mean widespread arrests among trade unionists, civil servants and private citizens—notably judges, the press, financiers and industrialists.

Control in the capital would not alone be effective for it will be recalled that in 1918 members of the government withdrew to Vaasa at the time of the communist *coup d'état* and continued the government from there until the capital was freed.

3. *Possibilities of preventing a coup.*

A frontal assault with all members of the government still in office would be a most difficult achievement, unless the Finnish communists had some assurance of active military intervention by the Soviet Union. To bring it about it would be necessary to immobilise the defence forces by intimidating the Minister of Defence and Commander-in-Chief and to make such a display of force as to render such active resistance movements as have already been organised ineffective.

The position would be easier if as in the case of Czechoslovakia, the non-communist ministers were to resign voluntarily from the government and the President were to be obliged to call upon one of the leaders of the communist *bloc*, as the largest group in the government coalition, (the communist *bloc* command 51 seats in the Diet as opposed to the Agrarians' 49 and the Social Democrats' 48) to form a temporary government until elections could be held. Such a position might be brought about by the refusal of the Social Democrat and Agrarian Diet groups to accept terms for a pact with which the communist *bloc* were in agreement. It is probable that the President sees this difficulty and is therefore doing everything possible to prevent such a state of affairs from arising. So far communist pressure upon the delegation in Moscow has not been great enough to cause difficulty, but it must always be reckoned that the Russians may be playing for time until their organisation within Finland is sufficiently complete to make a *coup* effective.

The recent appointment of three new counsellors to the Soviet Legation in Helsinki, headed by M.A.N. Feodorov, who was formerly NKVD representative on the Control Commission, may be taken to be the equivalent of the visit of M. Zorin[2] to Prague. The arrival of these people lends force, as did also the appointment of General Savonenkov, to the efforts of the Finnish communists to intimidate their opponents by threats of individual victimisation after 'A free Finland has been established'. These threats are now being made particularly against Social Democrats who are actively opposed to communist control of the trade union movement, and in the communist

---

[2] Soviet Deputy Foreign Minister.

press against the civil servants, the judicature and the right wing press and party organisations.

While the possibilities of a *coup* may be diminished by the non-communist ministers firmly resolving to remain in office until free elections can be held, this will be insufficient unless steps are taken to oppose force with force, notably (*i*) to counteract attempts by action committees to seize control in the Ministries and (*ii*) to prevent any attempt at coercing or removing the President. The first of these counter measures might be achieved by the formation of 'security cells' ('defence committees' as they are called in France) prepared to resort to force against the action committees. The second should be secured unless there is defection on the part of the Palace guard and the army in the event of a clash of force. It would later be necessary for the President personally to order the arrest of the communist ministers and other leaders of the *coup*; at the time of writing it is hard to see whence he would derive the shock-troops necessary for this purpose.

4. *Conclusion*

It would seem therefore that events in Czechoslovakia have at last opened the eyes of many to the dangers of a communist *coup* being attempted here even though the conditions which favoured the communists in Czechoslovakia are not reproduced to a similar extent in Finland. Unless however the communists here and in Moscow are prepared to accept a considerable set-back and to play for a year or two a waiting game which *might* allow them to strengthen materially their hold on the people of this country, they seem to be exposed to the temptation of trying a *coup* in the hope that it might put them in a position to 'rig', or avoid, the July elections, even though its prospects of success are by no means good.[3]

[3] Dixon commented from Prague on this despatch in a letter to Bateman of 16 April 1948. Etherington-Smith concluded that there were differences between the Czech and Finnish situations and thought that the Finns were better equipped than the Czechs to resist a *coup*. 'This is largely because (*a*) the Finnish Communists, while occupying certain key positions, do not have the same hold on the organisation of the country e.g. in the civil service and trades unions, and (*b*) opposition to the Communists in Finland is stronger and better organised' (FO 371/71410, N4667/100/56).

No. 131

Sir M. Peterson (Moscow) to Mr Bevin, 7 April 1948, 5.15 p.m.[1]
Tel. No. 460 Important, Confidential, Light (FO 371/71407, N4153/83/56)

My telegram No. 439: Fenno-Soviet Treaty.[2]

Soviet press of April 7th publishes Fenno-Soviet Treaty of Friendship, Co-operation and Mutual Assistance signed on April 6th. Translation is being checked and will follow by next bag. There has been interesting contrast between treatment accorded to Finnish and other recent visiting Delegations. Whereas latter were required to accept stock Treaty, Finnish Delegation besides being invited to produce first draft, have been allowed some latitude in negotiation, including permission to refer to Helsingfors for instructions. Soviet leaders, having had previous experience of Finnish toughness, no doubt appreciated the need for more careful handling than was necessary in the case of the Balkan satellites. They had moreover, to take into account

[1] Repeated to Helsinki.
[2] Not printed.

possibility of non-ratification by Finnish Diet, or even rupture of negotiations, and with world opinion, especially after Czechoslovakia, displaying keen interest, they could ill afford such a setback. By employment of gentler tactics, which will no doubt create favourable impression in Finland, they have not only succeeded in completing network of treaties with their neighbours but have come very near to securing unconditional right to send forces into Finland when they may wish to do so.[3]

[3] Etherington-Smith commented that the final part of the last sentence 'seems to be a slight exaggeration. According to the published terms of the pact, Soviet "help" will only be given after Finland has been attacked, and even then both parties must agree. I do not think, therefore, that the pact has appreciably weakened Finland's position in any formal sense. Everything will depend on the extent to which the Finns are ready to resist Russian encroachments in practice' (FO 371/712407, N4153/83/56).

No. 132

Extract from Conclusions of a Meeting of the Cabinet held on 8 April 1948
(CAB 128/12, CM(48)27)

Finnish-Soviet Treaty

5. *The Foreign Secretary* said that the firm attitude adopted by the Finnish Government had resulted in the signature of a treaty which on the face of it preserved Finland from Soviet interference in her internal affairs and treated her rather as a neutral buffer state than as a Soviet satellite. The Soviet Government had not pressed for bases in Finland and, although in war the provisions of the treaty for prior consultation before Soviet troops entered Finland might be to little effect, Finland had at least been given a breathing space and in a few years' time, when she had completed the payment of reparations to Russia, her natural trade interests were likely to strengthen her ties with Western Europe.

No. 133

Mr Scott (Helsingfors) to Mr Bevin, 9 April 1948, 11.21 a.m.
Tel. No. 201 Important, Secret (FO 371/71407, N4241/83/56)

My telegram No. 199. Friendship Pact.[1]

President of the Republic received Mr Bottomley[2] and Mr Cohen[3] on April 7th. You will receive from Mr Bottomley a report of our conversation with His Excellency. When they took their leave I stayed behind by previous arrangement so that I might hear from His Excellency his views on recent political developments. He outlined the course of negotiations for the Soviet-Finnish pact saying that he had finally instructed the delegates that if Finnish re-draft for Articles 1 and 2 (see my telegram No. 184)[4] proved inacceptable [*sic*] to the Russians negotiations would have to be broken off. He had he said made it clear to the Finnish delegates that this redraft

[1] Not printed.
[2] Secretary for Overseas Trade, Board of Trade.
[3] E.A. Cohen, Under Secretary, Commercial Relations and Treaties Department, Board of Trade.
[4] Not printed.

represented the maximum concession which he was prepared to ask the Finnish Parliament to accept.

2. To his enquiry as to how His Majesty's Government would react to this pact I said that I had as yet no indication but I could assure him that it would be examined with the fullest measure of understanding of Finland's position.

3. I then asked how he thought events would develop in the course of the next few months and he replied that he hoped that if the pact were accepted by Parliament there would be a calm period until the July elections which would be free and secret. I said that I hoped so too but when I looked back on recent experiences of other countries where the Ministry of the Interior had been in Communist hands I could not help feeling some misgivings. His reply was that the Ministry of the Interior had not as much scope here as in other countries and that he felt that at least 80% of national police were reliable. If the elections went as he hoped and expected it should be possible to make some alteration in distribution between the political parties of the posts in the Government.

4. The Government he continued had stiffened its attitude towards Communism and I had perhaps noted that even in the matter of elections to the National Academy Communist objections to some of the candidates on the grounds of 'Fascist tendencies' had been disregarded and he had initialled the list as originally submitted to him.

5. The supporters of Communism in Finland were not he said very numerous. To this I commented that they were a compact and well organised body which gave them a substantial advantage over their opponents even though they were outnumbered. He then referred to certain positive measures which had been concerted with the Minister of Defence[5] to prevent surprises.[6]

6. His Excellency was most cordial and seemed in good health and good heart though I was told by a member of his household that he had under the strain of negotiations suffered gravely from insomnia.

[5] Yrjö Kallinen.
[6] Minuting to Hankey on General Sihvo, the Commander in Chief, Etherington-Smith wrote: '... We have had reason to feel somewhat doubtful about his reliability. We have already heard from other sources that he has been taking measures to resist a communist *coup*, but he is also reported to have been in touch with the communist Minister of the Interior, and to have told the latter that he would use the forces at his disposal against Right Wing elements, ostensibly of course to lull any communist suspicions of his preparations' (FO 371/71407, N4242/83/56).

No. 134

Mr Bevin to Mr Randall (Copenhagen), 17 April 1948
No. 142 Secret (FO 371/71367, N4688/61/15)

Sir,

The Danish Minister for Foreign Affairs called on me at his request in Paris on April 17th.

2. M. Rasmussen began by thanking me for the helpful attitude which His Majesty's Government had shown over the question of removing the remaining German refugees from Denmark during the recent conversations which M. Hvass had had in London. I told M. Rasmussen that we were doing our best and I proposed to

mention the matter to M. Bidault later in the morning and to try to persuade the French Government to take more of these refugees.

3. The conversation then turned to the question of German trade with Denmark, and I asked the Commander-in-Chief, General Robertson to join us. M. Rasmussen explained that Denmark was very anxious to resume her former trading connection with Germany, which had been most important to her, and to get over the difficulty of trading in dollars.

4. General Robertson said that he was very anxious to obtain Danish food for the combined zones, but explained that a serious difficulty existed owing to the high prices charged by Danish farmers. The Americans, who had the last word on financial matters, were most reluctant to pay these prices. I told M. Rasmussen that I thought it was not in Denmark's interest to push prices up in this way merely to suit the convenience of her farmers. It was most important to Denmark to re-establish her old trading connections and markets even at the price of some short-term inconvenience through lowering prices now.

5. Developing this theme, I told M. Rasmussen that I understood that the Danes were also charging very high prices to the United Kingdom—for instance, for potatoes. I said that I thought it was essential to world economy for prices everywhere to come down. After all, under the European Recovery Programme, America was giving Europe a fixed number of dollars which would be worth much less in terms of goods and produce if prices continued to rise. If, on the contrary, we in Europe could contribute to bring prices down, then the aid we should receive from America would be proportionately greater. I urged M. Rasmussen to reflect seriously on this and to take any suitable opportunities which might arise to pass on what I had said to his Scandinavian colleagues who were not present at this meeting in Paris.

6. I later took the opportunity of private conversations with the Netherlands Minister for Foreign Affairs and the acting Belgian Minister for Foreign Affairs to make the same point about the necessity for lowering prices.

I am, etc.,
ERNEST BEVIN

No. 135

Sir L. Collier (Oslo) to Mr Bevin, 21 April 1948
No. 110 (FO 371/71485, N4816/34/30)

Sir,

As you will have seen from the press, the Norwegian Minister for Foreign Affairs delivered on the evening of April 19th an address at the *Militære Samfund* (technically an officers' club, but in practice a forum for the discussion of all questions of the day) which was in effect a public declaration of the principles now governing Norwegian foreign policy, made in the presence of the King, the Crown Prince, the Swedish Ambassador and myself, and the Service Attachés of the United States Embassy.

2. I have the honour to transmit to you herewith a summary of the chief points of the address, translated by the Press Reader to His Majesty's Embassy from the accounts of it (none of them fully textual) which appeared the next morning in the

Oslo press.¹ From this it will be seen that M. Lange gave a frank account of the present world situation and its dangers for Norway, declared firmly that Norway would not enter into any pact with the Soviet Union, welcomed both the 'Marshall Plan' and the 'Bevin Plan', and in connexion with the latter specifically refused to close the door on the possibility of political as well as economic and cultural collaboration between Norway and the Western Powers. In that connexion, too, he made it clear that, while it was highly desirable that Norway, Sweden and Denmark should follow the same policy if possible, the problems facing the three countries were not the same, and implied that in certain circumstances Norway might have to act independently of her neighbours.

3. The statement is approved by the whole non-Communist press, though the Communist *Friheten* makes, as was to be expected, a violent personal attack on M. Lange; and the general sentiment is, I think, summed up by the King's remark to me after the meeting: 'Now we know where we are, and so does everyone else.'[2]

4. I am sending copies of this despatch to His Majesty's Ambassador at Copenhagen, and to His Majesty's Chargé d'Affaires at Stockholm.

I have, etc.,
L. COLLIER

[1] Not printed.
[2] King Haakon expanded on this comment during a private dinner shortly afterwards. See No. 136.

No. 136

Letter from Sir L. Collier (Oslo) to Mr Hankey, 22 April 1948
Top Secret (FO 371/71485, N5347/34/30G)

Dear Hankey,

I can now add something further to my letter of April 14th[1] about the Norwegian attitude towards future co-operation with the West. I met King Haakon at the *Militære Samfund,* when Lange gave his address there, as reported in my despatch No. 110 of yesterday;[2] and he asked me to dine alone with him last night and, as he put it, 'talk things over'. He told me in the course of the talk that he was very pleased with Lange's declaration: 'that is what I have been working towards for three years', he said. He also said, *à propos* of the passage suggesting that Norway might have to act independently of Sweden: 'I told him to put that in.' The Swedes he added, were willing enough to hold defence talks, but only on their own terms—which were that Norway should follow their political line, 'whereas we want them to follow ours'; and there was therefore nothing to be done with them for the time being, though there might be something to be done with the Danes.

His Majesty then went on to talk about the forthcoming staff talks and said that he hoped the Americans really could promise effective aid. If not, Norway would get the worst of both worlds, since Washington was a terribly leaky place (I nearly added: 'so was Oslo', but refrained) and the news of the talks would be sure to come out sooner or later. When I said that I was convinced that the joint planners at Washington, with the example of 1940 before their eyes, would not have authorised the promise of help

[1] Not printed.
[2] No. 135.

unless they had been sure of implementing it, he seemed comforted but remarked that in any case we had better think out what we should do when the 'link-up' of military plans became generally known. I then told him of Hauge's idea of an Anglo-Scandinavian 'Bevin Plan', mentioned in the first paragraph of my letter under reference, to see whether he had had anything to do with that: I don't think he had, but he seemed to like it. I did not do more than mention it, however, as I don't yet know, of course, how it is looked upon in London.

The King reverted to the question of the value of American promises of help when discussing the forthcoming American fleet visit, mentioned in your letter of April 19th.[1] The chief unit taking part in that visit will be a large aircraft carrier called the *Valley Forge*, and the Americans have asked permission to fly 100 aircraft from this ship from Bergen to Oslo and back, as well as to parade 500 men in Bergen. The Norwegian Government have granted permission for the flight, though they are making difficulties over the parade; and the King's comment was that the former would no doubt be an excellent piece of propaganda but would not necessarily prove that the American Air Force could come to the immediate aid of Norway in case of war, and that if it was merely 'bluff' it was not worth annoying the Russians for that. He wondered whether, in any case, the Russians would not ask permission to make a similar flight, and did not seem wholly reassured when I pointed out that they had no aircraft carriers. (I have indeed heard that the Norwegian Cabinet were divided over this question and that permission was finally given on the advice of Lange and Hauge against that of the Prime Minister and, it would now appear, of the King as well. I think Lange and Hauge were right, because the Russians are already as annoyed as they can be over Lange's statement and a show of force is the only thing that seems to impress them; but I can appreciate the King's anxiety to be sure that there is more than 'bluff' in it.)

The conversation ranged over a great many subjects, most of which were not political; but I had the impression that on these particular topics King Haakon was not merely indulging in a private after-dinner talk but would not be sorry if I passed on his views to London.[3]

I am sending copies of this letter to Randall and Henderson.

Yours ever,
L. COLLIER

PS April 29th
I now learn that as a result of fresh Norwegian representations, the Americans have withdrawn the proposal to fly their aircraft over Oslo and will fly them over Bergen only. On the other hand, the parade is to take place, apparently with 1,000 men.

---

[3] Hankey minuted on 8 May 'The Norwegians are willing enough to make defensive arrangements with the West, but it must be *effective* promise of help & not bluff. This confirms again that we cannot safely arrange anything concrete without the Americans, i.e. it would not be much use trying for a political type of pact.' Bateman commented 'I do not understand the reference in para. 2 [of Hankey's minute] to an American "promise of help": unless, of course, it was President Truman's speech. I very much doubt the wisdom of speculating, at the moment, on what the Americans may or may not do' (FO 371/71485, N5347/34/30G).

No. 137

Mr Scott (Helsinki) to Mr Bevin, 27 April 1948
No. 108 Secret (FO 1110/8, PR276/1/913G)

Sir,

I have the honour to refer to the instructions in regard to combating Soviet propaganda which were conveyed in your telegram No. 6 Circular of 23rd January[1] and subsequent Circular telegrams Nos. 10 and 13.[2] In the light of these instructions we have been doing what we can to give our anti-communist publicity more hitting power.

2. At the same time we have to bear in mind the special position of Finland, geographically and politically, and, more recently, we have to remember that she has just signed with Russia a Pact of Friendship and Mutual Aid and that it is not our policy to embarrass her Government unduly.

3. In your telegram No. 129 of 9th April[2] you sanctioned the use, for secret circulation to a selected list of Finnish politicians and officials, of extracts from Mr Dixon's despatch No. 46 of March 6th,[2] which set out in detail the procedure followed by the Communists when they seized power in Czechoslovakia. The resulting memorandum, in Finnish, is now being passed by suitable members of the Legation Staff to appropriate Finns. The document itself is only a historic record of facts now fairly widely known but conditions in Finland are such that it would not be given general distribution. I am not sure that this is a method which I would wish to use at all frequently for it seems to me to be one of those half measures which are seldom really satisfactory and which have in them certain important disadvantages.

4. In the special circumstances which obtain here I believe that our anti-communist publicity should be open e.g. by newspaper articles—*Helsingin Sanomat,* with its 170,000 circulation, *Uusi Suomi,* the organ of the Conservative party and, to a lesser extent, *Hufvudstadsbladet,* the Swedish daily paper, have been consistently resourceful and courageous in their anti-communist line; the Legation bulletin; the Labour Attaché's bulletin and the BBC Finnish Service. If, and only if exceptional factors justify such a course, should we have recourse to circulating confidential information of anti-communist character and in such cases this should be done on a very restricted scale and only through a strictly secret channel.

5. Of all these methods it seems probable that it is the BBC Finnish Service which can best be turned to account. It has already a considerable number of regular listeners and, if our experience during the war with the BBC Service to Spain may be taken as a guide, some sharp cuts and thrusts, giving point to a planned anti-communist campaign, would increase considerably the numbers of the BBC's Finnish audience.

6. I am at present having the content of the BBC's Finnish Service studied and shall hope to submit shortly some comment and suggestions as to how, if it be approved as a matter of policy, this Service might best contribute to our anti-communist publicity.[3(2)]

I have, etc.,
O.A. SCOTT

---

[1] No. 108.   [2] Not printed
[3] Ruthven-Murray, Information Policy Department, commented: 'By comparison with the other countries in 'Transcurtainia' the opportunities in Finland are great. Feature articles, which are rejected both by the sophisticated press of W. Europe and the communist press of E. Europe, are in demand by the Finnish press—they are even paid for (!)—and good use should be made of this channel.'

1948

No. 138

Sir L. Collier (Oslo) to Mr Bevin, 21 May 1948
No. 138 (FO 371/71489, N6199/173/30)

Sir,
As you will have seen from the press, the visit of Mr and Mrs Winston Churchill to Oslo, foreshadowed in your telegram No. 204 of April 27th last,[1] took place as arranged, Mr Churchill and his party arriving by air on May 11th and leaving, also by air, on May 15th; and I have the honour to report that it was eminently successful, both from the personal point of view and from that of British interests in general.[2]

2. Mr Churchill received an exceptionally warm welcome, even warmer perhaps than he would have received had he come two years ago, since the Norwegian public, without distinction of party, had felt humiliated by the circumstances in which the original invitation to him had been cancelled and realise that his speech at Fulton, which had caused the cancellation, had been justified by the course of events in Europe. His prestige, too, has been increased by his part in the proceedings of the conference at The Hague on European unity and by the publication in instalments of his latest book of memoirs in the independent and widely respected organ *Verdens Gang*. His programme, a very full one, involved speeches at the King's dinner to him in the palace on the night of his arrival, at the ceremony the next day at the University, when he received an honorary degree in history and philosophy, and at the public dinner which followed it, to the *Storting* on the morning of May 13th, and on the same day at the luncheon given by the municipality, to the people of Oslo from the balcony of the Town Hall in the afternoon, and to the Round Table Club of Norway in the evening; and on all these occasions he worthily upheld his oratorical reputation. His speech to the people of Oslo, though practically impromptu, having been added to his programme at the last moment through the efforts of His Majesty's Embassy, was particularly effective, as will be seen from the enclosed verbatim report thereof;[1] and the authorities here have thought it worthwhile to arrange for the official publication of all speeches made during the visit.

3. In these speeches and in conversations with prominent Norwegians, in particular the Ministers for Foreign Affairs and Defence, as reported in my telegram No. 202 of May 15th,[1] Mr Churchill was able, without involving himself in Norwegian politics, to lend valuable support to the efforts made by this Embassy to popularise the point of view of His Majesty's Government on the foreign political situation and the role which Norway should play in it. He said to me on his arrival: 'I have not come here to embarrass either the Norwegian Government, or my own, but I think I may be able to help both of them'; and he subsequently discussed with me the political situation here, to ensure that he had all the information necessary to enable him to do this. I am assured on all sides that he succeeded admirably and that his visit has definitely encouraged and intensified the Westward trend of Norwegian public opinion.

4. For his part, Mr Churchill has, I think, returned from Norway with a higher opinion of the Norwegian people and their Government than he was sometimes inclined to hold during the war: he seemed genuinely touched by the warmth of his reception and impressed by the ability of the leading Norwegians whom he met (and

---

[1] Not printed.
[2] Churchill had originally been invited to visit Norway in 1946, but the invitation was withdrawn after he had made his speech in Fulton. Collier's despatch of 21 March 1946 describes the background (FO 371/56284, N4710/219/30).

particularly by their capacity to make first-class speeches in English), and before he left he asked me to look through the proofs of the chapters dealing with Norway in the next volume of his memoirs to make sure that he had said nothing to offend Norwegian sentiment. Though he seemed somewhat tired at the beginning of his stay, he was in good health and spirits by the end of it and on his last evening astonished and entertained the other guests at the Embassy, from King Haakon downwards, by the number and liveliness of his anecdotes from the war years. In short, he is still Britain's most valuable travelling representative abroad—at least in this part of Europe, where he is regarded, not as a party leader but as the 'voice of England'; and his presence has reminded Norwegians, as hardly anything else could have done, that there is more in the world than the Soviet Union and the United States and made them more conscious of the nearness and reality of Britain than they have been since the first days of liberation.

I have, etc.,
L. COLLIER

No. 139

Letter from Mr Kenney (Oslo) to Information Policy Department, 26 May 1948
(FO 1110/27, PR 396/57/913)

Dear Department,

We have recently received a number of memoranda from the Information Research Department dealing with various aspects of Communism and life in Russia. The material is of such a type that it will take some time to make full use of it, but in the meantime you may be interested in the attached translation of an article by the Secretary of the Norwegian Labour Party, M. Haakon Lie, who has used some of this material—a paper entitled 'The Real Conditions in Soviet Russia'—to build his article upon.

I would like if I may to draw particular attention to this article by M. Lie, since it comes from the pen of the most vigorous and able anti-Russian propagandist in Norway, and is a prototype of the sort of material which we can use here. As you will see, M. Lie has a very skilful technique of laying damning facts about Communism before a working class audience in such a way as to give no impression of anti-Communist propaganda. Moreover, his method of allowing facts to speak for themselves is a singularly telling one and constitutes by far the best means of exposing the Russian regime without alienating a public which until quite recently was disposed *a priori* to be sympathetic to it. Note also that M. Lie accompanies all statistics and factual evidence by a full explanation of his source.

M. Lie has emphasised to me on several occasions that the main policy for our anti-Communist publicity here must be to convince the Norwegian labour movement that Communism means a sinking standard of life. Inasmuch as this is likely to be our main plank for some time to come, every scrap of information you can send us on this topic will be of help.

Yours ever,
K. KENNEY

No. 140

Letter from Mr Warner to Sir L. Collier (Oslo), 28 May 1948
Secret (FO 1110/3, PR97/1/913)

My dear Collier,
Your despatch No. 74 (189/3/48) of the 12th March,[1] in which you replied to our Circular telegram No. 6 of the 23rd January[2] about the new publicity policy, was one of the best answers we have received and was most helpful. It hardly required an official reply but you may like to know how far your suggestions are being met.

2. First let me say that we agree generally with the views you express. The situation in Norway, although presenting certain features of its own, fits fairly well into the general pattern on which we are working and I think you will find that your recommendations of a general character, *viz.* those in your paragraphs 4, 5, 9, 10 (though this is some way ahead of us yet), 12 (to a large extent) and 13 will be met as the work of Information Research Department develops and our arrangements for modifying COI output have effect. Staffing difficulties have prevented us from expanding the new Department as quickly as I had hoped, but I am fairly confident that these will be removed in the near future. If, when the department has really got into its stride, any of these suggestions have not been adequately covered, or you have special demands for Norway, I hope you will not hesitate to let me know. I can also assure you that, as you point out in your paragraph 11, Information Officers and Missions abroad will be allowed wide discretion in their presentation of material. We shall aim at catering for all tastes and that in itself means that we shall produce a lot of material which cannot be used at all posts. We must, therefore, rely on Missions making their own selection and any necessary adaptation to suit their local conditions.

3. I turn now to the specific recommendations in your paragraph 7.
(*a*) We will try to establish closer contact with the London correspondents of the Norwegian newspapers. We know very little about Messrs. Nerdrum and Martinsen and should be glad to have any information about them which your Information Department can supply. The supply of material to them on the lines you suggest is rather tricky, because it is important at any rate at present, that the Foreign Office should not emerge into the limelight as the author of anti-Communist material. When we know them better, however, we will see what can be done; perhaps Kenney can help us when he comes over.
(*b*) The question of increasing Labour Party and Trade Union visits is already under study, though not of course with exclusive reference to Norway. The difficulty is that of finance. The Labour Party is unfortunately not in a financial position to increase visits and to use Government money for this purpose might well be considered open to the imputation of using the taxpayers' money for party purposes.
(*c*) We are also overhauling the distribution of newspapers, both by His Majesty's Missions and commercially. But I am afraid there is not much hope of an increase in newsprint imports to this country according to the latest statement of the President of the Board of Trade which you will have seen by the time you get this letter.
(*d*) and (*e*) We are going to increase substantially our output of labour news, and

[1] No. 124.
[2] No. 108.

improve it considerably. And we hope to produce soon a special periodical for Trade Unionist and Labour readers (your paragraph (e)). As I have mentioned above, however, the Labour Party cannot do much more to help: though possibly the recently-established Socialist Parties information bureau may help a little.[3]

(f) and (g) fall into the category referred to in my preceding paragraph.

4. In your paragraph 12 you raise the question of co-operation in our publicity with the Americans and Western European countries on the one hand and with the Dominions on the other. By the time this letter reaches you, you will have received guidance on the former in Information Research Department Circular letter of 12th May 1948.[4] We have not reached the stage of any formal discussion with the Dominions yet.

5. There remains the final question of additional staff which you mentioned in your paragraph 14. Since you wrote a Second Secretary (Information) has been appointed and left for Oslo on the 20th May. The question of finding a translator-editor for the periodical referred to in your paragraph 7(e) will naturally have to wait until a decision about the periodical itself is reached. As regards the engagement of another shorthand-typist, however, Establishment and Organisation Department are prepared to consider this as and when the necessity arises.

6. Before I close this letter I should like to ask you how you are finding the material which Information Research Department have been sending you. I am thinking in particular of the first seven papers which you will have received, and I should be interested to hear how and in what form they went down with the Embassy's clients.[5]

Yours ever,
C.F.A. WARNER

[3] This was the Socialist Information and Labour Office, which was established in London after the Clacton conference of socialist parties in May 1946.
[4] Not printed. C.f. *IRD History Note*, pp. 18-20.
[5] The Embassy had provided an initial answer to Warner's question. See No. 139.

No. 141

Minute from Mr Etherington-Smith to Sir O. Sargent, 28 May 1948
(FO 371/71716, N6430/9/42G)

I understand that the Secretary of State will be meeting the Minister of Defence shortly to discuss the question of the supply of radar and other important military equipment to Sweden.

In view of the Swedish Government's determined policy of neutrality, the Chiefs of Staff have, at our suggestion today reviewed HMG's policy in this matter. The main considerations which make a change of policy seem desirable are:

(a) The fact that, since we have no assurance that the Swedes will co-operate with us to any extent, either in the immediate future or in the event of war, our interests might be better served if we diverted supplies of important military material, of which we are very short, to other countries (e.g. Norway) of whose co-operation we are more certain.

(*b*) The fact that much of this equipment (e.g. Radar and night fighters) might in the event of war be used by the Swedes against our own forces seeking to attack Russian objectives across Swedish territory.

The position is explained more fully in Mr Bateman's letter to General Hollis at Flag A.[1] The unofficial conclusions of the Chiefs of Staff (subject to approval by the Minister of Defence) are annexed at Flag B.[1] It will be seen that the Chiefs of Staff

(*i*) agree that we should reconsider out attitude as regards the supply of various military equipment to Sweden and propose that the Joint War Planning Staff should work out a long-term policy.

(*ii*) recommend that in the meantime the position should be explained frankly to the Swedes.

It may be pertinent to mention that the Treasury, who have been consulted unofficially, consider that from the purely financial point of view, the cancellation of these deliveries to Sweden would be of no serious moment to us.

In the meantime a very early decision is required on the following two matters:

(*a*) Two Radar AA No. 3 Mark 7 sets are ready for delivery to Sweden, but at our request the Ministry of Supply have suspended shipment. The Swedes have already made representations to us on the subject. The two sets constitute highly important equipment, which is on the restricted list and is in very short supply. If diverted, they could easily be disposed of to other countries or taken over by the War Office, who require many more of these sets for their own programme.

(*b*) Marconi's have negotiated a million pound contract for the supply of Ground Control Interception equipment (Radar) to Sweden. The contract is to be signed in Stockholm on Monday next, but Marconi's representatives will not sign until they have received clearance through our Embassy.

This equipment is being supplied as part of a plan for providing the Swedes with the nucleus for a complete ground control interception system. In addition to the items mentioned above, the Swedes have contracts with us extending up to 1951 for the supply of considerable quantities of fighter aircraft and accessories and we were proposing to negotiate further contracts for the period after 1951. The Air Ministry were also intending to release certain additional Radar equipment to the Swedes through Marconi's in three or four weeks' time.[2]

R.G.A. ETHERINGTON-SMITH

---

[1] Not printed.

[2] Bevin was consulted. He saw no reason to modify policy on the provision of military supplies to Sweden. He said that he maintained the same view that he had expressed to Undén in Paris in March (No. 129), that he did not wish to attempt to force the Swedes into aligning themselves more closely with the West than they themselves felt wise (FO 371/71716, N6430/9/42G). However, the Chiefs of Staff decided to consider the matter further. See No. 144.

No. 142

Speech by Mr Bevin to a Danish Parliamentary Delegation, 7 June 1948[1]
(FO 371/71370, N7033/2232/15)

Your Excellencies, My Lords, Ladies and Gentlemen:

I want to extend on behalf of the British Government a very hearty welcome to our Danish friends. We are very glad they have arrived for a good repast without any airsickness. In these days of austerity you have arrived in a state in which you can enjoy the evening meal.

We are glad to see you because you have come as partners in the Inter-Parliamentary Union. I have said before at other gatherings, but I will repeat, that I know of no greater aid to the development of foreign relations. I do not like to use this term 'foreign relations'. It is a distant sort of term. Shall I say 'the comradeship among peoples' which this Parliamentary Union is? Foreign Offices have a limitation to what they can do. We have to design despatches very accurately and in a form that nobody understands, and we rely upon our Ambassadors to interpret them as best they can; but the beauty of the Inter-Parliamentary Union is that you meet together; you talk the same language really, in spite of different expressions; you exchange views; you find a common inheritance and purpose. I can assure you that I, as Foreign Secretary, regard this joining together of the representatives of the people in this way as the greatest aid to my work.

Many years ago I remember being in Amsterdam and trying to reorganise the International Transport Workers after the 1914-18 war, and for three days we had a terrible time. We were trying to reorganise it on a purely national basis, and we completely failed. And then one night I had a brainwave—as I do sometimes—and in the morning got up early and drafted a new constitution on a new basis. And instead of a narrow nationalist conception I put forward what I called the 'group' idea. It was the idea that the seamen got together, the railwaymen, the dockers and so on in all these sections. I had it translated into several languages including your own, and took it down to the conference, and then I asked them to go into separate rooms no longer as nationalists but as trades, as callings, as doing the same thing, and within two hours we built up that constitution which has never been broken, and which has survived this war. I feel myself that, very often, you are a trade or a calling—in a parliamentary sense you are doing the same thing. You are legislating, you are governing, you are carrying on and expressing in law the ideals of your country and the changing aspects and desires of your people, and so if you meet your fellow parliamentarians who are all doing the same thing, I am quite sure you will arrive at conclusions and conceptions which will go to strengthen the bonds between peoples, because you are all trying to achieve the same objective.

Now, of course, in these parliamentary countries we seek to govern by consent. Of course, I must confess that sometimes to get the consent we have to put 'the Whips' on, but at any rate we govern by consent; and another thing is that we are always willing to accept the rule of the majority. How many contested things have I seen in my rather long career in conferences, in Parliaments and elsewhere—when you would think that the whole thing was going to pieces with this great tussle! Then there is a statement; a decision is recorded and everybody goes to have a drink, and the whole

---

[1] The speech was given at a dinner held in honour of the Danish delegation at No. 1, Carlton House Gardens.

country goes on in a smooth, happy and prosperous way. It is a great and wonderful idea. There is another thing about the parliamentary system which is so encouraging and which we find everywhere. It is a combination of research and study at the top, but, what is more important, it is giving expression to the upward surge from beneath; it is a happy combination. As one great transport man said to me once when I had been fighting him for a fairly substantial increase of wages, 'You know that this is not bad at all; I do not object to it, because, after all, the more you press us from beneath, the more we have to use our heads at the top'. There is a great deal in that sentence.

You are come among us—there was an invasion when I saw you arrive tonight and saw all the cars with the Danish flag. You have invaded us before—yes—but now, you see, instead of indulging in all the costly trouble of military invasion, we are indulging in a sort of amalgamation which is better and cheaper, much cheaper, especially as, apparently, we have both got overdrafts. I amalgamated fifty unions into one and formed the great transport union, but you know I always found it easier to amalgamate two unions with overdrafts than I did anybody with surpluses! So the present moment is a very convenient time to develop a Western Union. All of us have difficulties. I am sure—as an old Labour colleague of mine, whose expressions of the English language were not always accurate, used to say—'the "atomosphere" is just right'. Therefore I extend to you all a very, very hearty welcome. You will be in the House this week I have no doubt, listening to questions, wondering how Ministers can think of the answers and, if only you knew, you would wonder still more how the Civil Servants anticipate the supplementaries. They don't always come off. I will tell you a secret—a secret from the Foreign Office. Every time an Ambassador comes to see me my staff try to anticipate what he is going to ask, and so they provide me with wonderful memoranda of the answers, but up till now I have not had one Ambassador arrive with a question for which they had prepared the answer. Of course, I have always thought that there is a kind of competition between the Ambassadors and the Foreign Office. I have always thought the Ambassadors have been thinking 'After all, I bet they think "he's coming down to ask so-and-so"; so I just won't ask it'. In Parliament—this great bureaucracy they are far cleverer than that, although it doesn't always come off. For instance I remember on one occasion when the Coalition was in, that wonderful Parliamentary Secretary to the Ministry of Food, Dr. Edith Summerskill whom I have no doubt you will meet—she is a great Minister—wonderfully able—asked me something about some figures. I was stumped for an answer, so I replied that the honourable Lady's figure was all right; it was her facts that were wrong! In any case you will listen to the Parliamentary questions; you will see the Opposition over there, and I am sure our friend, the leader of the Conservatives of Denmark who is with us tonight, will judge his fellow Conservatives as to their competence and ability in handling the Ministers in this country. At any rate we are a fairly even match. I will not put it higher than that, and you will hear statements and debates. I was with some friends from America last night, and they were in the House when the Finance Bill was being debated. They had a wonderful parliamentary experience; they sat till three in the morning, and they said what surprised them was that Sir Stafford Cripps seemed to have the answers before the questions were asked. In their case they would have had to have a whole lot of experts to advise them.

Well this question time, these debates, these expressions of views, this wonderful institution has gone on for so many years, but before I sit down I would like to say this. The most marvellous thing about it is its adaptation from age to age. Originally the prerogative of the rich, originally the design of the barons, originally the protection of the propertied classes, it has gradually evolved and as the franchise has been extended, as the adult suffrage has come in, the same institution, the same procedure with adaptations has served the nation just as effectively as it served the limited numbers in its original conception. I think this evolution of things which seems just to have grown with the nation, grown with education, grown with the transfer of power from a limited number of people to the mass of the people as a whole, has maintained in this country the same solidity, the same power to govern, the same careful, studious and resolute action that has been exemplified in the whole of our history and, looking back and looking out on the great mass of our people, I think to myself 'Well, there's the girl in the store, the girl in the office, the girl in the factory, the man in the mine or the factory or the field, all arriving through their representatives at well-declared laws, well-designed developments, well-studied judgements—judgements which arise from what I call the common concept and the commonsense of the people, which is better, which is greater, which is surer than the cleverness of all the clever people in the world'. In that sense I again repeat my hearty invitation to you, and I ask our British friends to rise and drink to our Danish friends, and I desire to couple it with the name of Mr Frisch[2] who will respond to the toast 'Our Danish friends and Visitors, and the Danish People'.

[2] Hartvig Frisch, Social Democrat Minister of Education.

No. 143

Mr Scott (Helsinki) to Mr Bevin, 9 June 1948
No. 143 (FO 371/71417, N6893/140/56)

Sir,

I have the honour to refer to my telegram No. 319 of 4th June,[1] reporting that the Government of the USSR had notified the Finnish Government of its intention to help Finland by reducing by 50% the reparations deliveries outstanding at 1st July 1948.

2. Two points about the form of the notification are worthy of comment. Firstly, the emphasis laid on the proposal of the three Communist Ministers, to the exclusion of any mention of the earlier official approaches reported in my despatch No. 136 (34/10/48) of 2nd June.[1] It would seem certain that this was done with an eye to the forthcoming general elections in order that the Communists in Finland might benefit from the Soviet 'generosity'. Secondly, the statement that according to the information available to the Soviet Minister in Finland the Finnish Government had approved the proposal made by MM. Leino, Murto and Janhunen. Whilst the Soviet Government could be in no doubt that the Finnish Government would welcome any alleviation, it was definitely untrue to state that the Government had approved this particular proposal. In fact, owing to its pre-occupation with the dismissal and replacement of M. Leino, the Government had taken no action on the proposal before the notification of the alleviations arrived. The Prime Minister was, as it happened, about to attend the first Cabinet meeting on the subject when M. Savonenkov called on him with his message.

3. The explanation of the precipitate Soviet decision might be that the Soviet government, having waited a fortnight for signs of action, feared that the matter might

[1] Not printed.

be further prolonged until after the elections, and thus deprive the Finnish Communists of a useful weapon in the elections. Alternatively, they may have been aware of the fact that the Finnish Government, as reported in my despatch No. 136, would judge when it was the right time to make known all the facts regarding approaches for alleviations, and so have feared the loss by the Finnish Communists of all prestige in the matter, and have decided to forestall such an eventuality.

4. Relief is felt by all Finns, though many suspect an ulterior motive, fearing the Russians *et dona ferentes*[2]. The actual granting of alleviations has, of course, put an end to criticism of the Communist proposal as an election manoeuvre. Amongst the many expressions of gratitude by prominent persons published in the press the most sensible were those of the Governor of the Bank of Finland and the Minister of Finance. M. Tuomioja pointed out that half of the remaining reparations deliveries amounted to a value of 75,000,000 gold dollars, equal to 130 million dollars at present-day values, so that the alleviation granted could be considered to amount to 37½ million dollars per annum for the remaining four years in which reparations have to be paid. M. Törngren remarked that he was pleased but that he feared that the Finnish people would think that their difficulties were now overcome. He added that it was said that the Finnish people stood adversity better than prosperity, and that if the good news resulted in increased demands for higher wages Finland would soon find itself out of the frying pan and into the fire.

5. In their comments the non-Communists have been at pains to point out that the promise of alleviations did not materialise solely as a result of the Communist initiative, but it is obviously difficult to gain credence for such statements in the light of the wording of the Soviet notification.

6. The Communists have exploited their advantage to the full, claiming that the alleviations are the work of the Folk-Democrats and particularly of the Communists and that as a result it should be the workers who should benefit. They are linking this up with their current demands for increased wages on the grounds that the tying of wages to the cost-of-living has not proved productive from the workers point of view. They have drawn improper comparisons with Marshall Aid of which they say that 'after one year it has brought about only deterioration in the economic situation in Britain, France and Sweden', regardless of the fact that the flow of Marshall Aid 'with its political strings' to the Soviet 'gift' with no political strings, proceeding somewhat illogically to state that now the Finnish people should have no difficulty in choosing where to place their votes in July—for the party which supports friendly relations with the USSR on a basis of equality!

7. Expressions of gratitude have been sent to Marshal Stalin by the President, the Government, the Diet and numerous official and unofficial organisations.

8. I am sending a copy of this despatch to HM Ambassador in Moscow.

I have, etc.,
O.A. SCOTT

---

[2] Part of a quotation from Virgil's *Aeneid*, '*Timeo Danaos et dona ferentes*' meaning 'I fear the Greeks, even if they bring gifts'.

No. 144

Minute from Mr Bateman to Mr Bevin, 12 June 1948
Top Secret (FO 371/71716, N7144/9/42)

Supply of Arms to Sweden

On May 28th the Chiefs of Staff decided that there was a case for adapting our policy on the supply of military equipment to Sweden in accordance with her attitude towards the Western Powers; they recommended that the Swedish Government be informed that unless Sweden supported the Western Powers she could not expect to be placed in a high category for the supply of military equipment, as we should first have to provide for the needs of our Allies.

At that time the Secretary of State saw no reason to modify our policy of helping Sweden to obtain armaments and military supplies. He held to the views he had expressed to M. Undén in Paris in March and he did not wish to force the Swedes into allying themselves more closely with the West than they themselves felt wise. He had confidence that the Swedes would stand up to the Russians in case of need and he wished them to be strong enough to do so.

Since then, the Joint War Production Staff have examined this question. Their conclusions are summarised below—Flag A.[1] Moreover, certain Swedish newspapers are taking a truculent anti-British line in an effort to support M. Undén's policy for the formation of a neutral Scandinavian *bloc*—see Flag B.[2]

Recommendation

The Secretary of State may wish to reconsider the matter of the supply of arms to Sweden in the light of the views of the Joint War Production Staff. He may also wish to invite the attention of the Swedish Ambassador to the tone of the Swedish press and suggest that the Swedish Government may, in the general interest, see fit to discourage public discussion of such a delicate subject at the present time.

Considerations

The arms and military equipment which we are at present supplying, or contemplate supplying in the future to Sweden, are mainly for defence against air or sea attack. The most important items are (1) fighter aircraft, the orders for which, if fulfilled, would total about £6½ million, and (2) radar equipment, totalling about £1½ million.

The effects of giving Sweden less favourable treatment than at present would not be seriously felt during the next six months, but would begin to delay the Swedish armament programme in the course of 1949. As regards our own financial and trading position, Sweden has for the present lost some of her attractions as a customer, since we now hold a balance of £7,000,000 in *kroner*; nor would a reduction in trade this year embarrass the Board of Trade. This favourable position may be reversed next year and the position beyond 1949 cannot be forecast. If Sweden were to be denied important supplies of arms in 1949 and following years, she might refuse to supply us with timber, or with one of the essential components in the manufacture of high grade steel, of which she is the sole supplier. In general, the effect on our own armaments programme of reducing supplies to Sweden is not likely to be serious for some time to come. Alternative markets for radar equipment and aircraft exist at present; but the

---

[1] Not printed.
[2] Not printed. Following a Swedish initiative, negotiations between Sweden, Norway and Denmark for a neutral Scandinavian defence pact had begun in May 1948.

permanent loss of Swedish orders for aircraft might affect our own war potential from the early 1950s.

Two important contracts between the Swedish Government and British firms have already been signed. These are: a contract with Marconi's for the supply of radar equipment worth £¾ million, which was recently signed, with the approval of the Secretary of State, subject to the caution that Government policy might affect delivery dates (it also contains an escape clause), and a contract for the supply of 120 Vampire aircraft, delivery to begin in March 1949 (this contract also contains an escape clause). To enforce a cancellation of these contracts by prohibiting exports would be an extreme measure, but it would be possible to deny these supplies to Sweden for an indefinite period by deferring delivery dates.

Meanwhile the Swedish Government are persisting in their policy of neutrality as between East and West and have done their best to persuade the other Scandinavian countries to form with them a *Bloc* pledged to defend its neutrality against all comers. The attitude of HM Government towards Scandinavia in general and the Swedish conception of neutrality in particular has been the subject of several articles in the Swedish press. In particular, the *Stockholms Tidningen* has misrepresented the whole position. Their article, published on June 9th, seems deliberately designed to strengthen the isolationist trend in Sweden by arguing that we can give no effective guarantee to Scandinavia and alleging that we are 'indifferent' to the fate of these three countries. HM Ambassador in Stockholm considers that public opinion in Sweden and the other Scandinavian countries may be misled by this version of our policy unless steps are taken to correct it.[3]

C.H. BATEMAN

[3] In a minute of 16 June, Sargent advised Bevin that there was no reason to reconsider his policy of supplying military material to Sweden, but suggested that he should see the Swedish Ambassador to express his regret at the press campaign in Sweden. This Bevin agreed to do (FO 371/71716, N7144/9/42G).

No. 145

Letter from Mr Trevelyan to Mr Rowan (Treasury), 16 July 1948
(PREM 8/855)

[No salutation on this copy]

I enclose a copy of a letter dated July 9th 1948 from the Vice President of the Norwegian *Storting* to the Prime Minister, suggesting that a Norwegian Delegation should visit the UK to discuss closer economic collaboration between Norway and the UK. We understand that you heard of this proposal and were inclined to feel at first sight that it was a matter for the OEEC rather than for bilateral negotiation. The Foreign Secretary, to whom this view was communicated, said that in his opinion we could not accept the position that OEEC prevented individual countries within the Organisation from improving their own economic relations. He attaches great importance to developing Anglo-Norwegian economic links. He would like the matter to be studied most sympathetically and the Prime Minister's reply to be as forthcoming as possible. This question probably needs a certain amount of discussion before we send a reply and we therefore suggest that you might like to consider arranging a small party to discuss what reply should be sent. I have not copied this letter to anyone, except Pumphrey[1], but you will no doubt wish to have the papers sent to those whom you think should take part in the discussion.

H. TREVELYAN

[1] Assistant Private Secretary to the Prime Minister.

No. 146

Sir L. Collier (Oslo) to Mr Bevin, 16 September 1948, 11.08 a.m.
Tel. No. 391 Immediate, Confidential (FO 371/71488, N10065/128/30)

Norwegian Minister for Foreign Affairs sent for me yesterday to tell me the *Storting* at the end of its last session had considered in secret the question of fishing limits in the course of investigation of the proceedings of the Norwegian Government in London during the war (see my despatch No. 49, February 19th),[1] and had unanimously resolved that the 1935 decree should now be enforced. Government had felt it useless to contest the decision in view of the desire of all parties to gain the fishermen's vote; and as the trawling season was about to begin they had issued orders accordingly to the fisheries protection vessels.

2. I expressed surprise at this sudden and unprovoked action, pointing out that the Norwegian Government must expect British trawlers to be given protection against it and added that the responsibility would be with them for any incidents which might occur.

3. The Minister for Foreign Affairs whose attitude was apologetic throughout, did not deny this but maintained that the Government had no option in view of the attitude of the *Storting*. He admitted there was no change of situation on the fishing grounds which could justify their action, but read out a long statement on the history of the question, evidently prepared elsewhere, which was apparently designed to show that they were constitutionally bound sooner or later to enforce the [gr. undec] decree live. When I said that in that case we were equally bound to enforce our rights he said that he realised that a clash between the two conceptions of right was now inevitable but that between friendly Governments the result need not be tragic. I think he expects ultimate reference to The Hague.[2]

[1] Not printed.
[2] See No. 154.

No. 147

Sir O. Franks (Washington) to Mr Bevin, 24 September 1948, 8.36 p.m.[1]
Tel. No 4561 Important, Top Secret (FO 371/71716, N10363/9/42G)

My telegram No. 4525 of September 21st: Sweden.[2]
As foreshadowed in telegram under reference, Lovett today asked me to see him about Sweden and the alleged British contract for the supply to Sweden of Vampire

[1] Repeated to Stockholm
[2] Not printed.

aircraft. He handed me an *aide-mémoire*, copy of which follows by airbag, the main points of which are as follows:

(*a*) Increased efforts should be made to induce Sweden to alter its policy of neutrality which is more in the interests of the USSR than of the Western Powers.

(*b*) Although until recently Sweden has tried to persuade Norway and Denmark to adopt a policy of neutrality as the price of Swedish cooperation in a projected Scandinavian defence arrangement, the United States Government favours the continued participation of Sweden in Scandinavian defence discussions in view of the .possible beneficial effects on Swedish policy

(*c*) The United States Government will make clear to Sweden its dissatisfaction with the latter's policy and will, while refraining from forcing Sweden into an attitude unnecessarily provocative towards Russia, try to influence Sweden towards eventual alignment with the other Western Powers. For this purpose the United States is giving priority, on the limited amount of military aid available, to those countries which are willing to cooperate with the United States or Brussels Treaty signatories in security arrangements. This policy which has had some effect cannot be fully effective without British support.

(*d*) The United States Government, therefore, who were seriously disturbed at the recent sale of Spitfires to Sweden, consider that the reported sale of a further large order of Vampire jet fighters to Sweden is a far more serious development. They think it would largely nullify United States efforts to influence the Swedish Government. They believe that these aircraft orders should be viewed in the light of the military requirements of the Brussels pact signatories. Finally, they hope that the sale will be held up pending further consultation.

2. The impression left in my mind by Lovett after he had run over these points with me was that the United States Government hoped that, in the light of present circumstances, His Majesty's Government would reconsider their policy towards Sweden with a view to reaching a policy similar to that of the United States Government. A decision by His Majesty's Government to supply these up to date jet fighters to Sweden had to be considered he thought, not only in relation to its possible effect upon Swedish policy, but in relation to the urgent needs for military supplies of this kind of other Western European countries who showed themselves willing to collaborate in collective defence.

3. Lovett also said, and this is a point which is not covered in the *aide-mémoire*, that he hoped the day might come fairly soon when there was some flow of military supplies from the United States across the Atlantic. It would be impossible he emphasised to justify before Congress the supply of such supplies to Western Europe in the interests of collective defence if, at the same time, the United Kingdom were sending highly efficient and badly needed jet fighters to Sweden, which persisted in remaining neutral.

4. I might add that Lovett's tone, far from censorious, reflected real concern at this alleged sale and at the serious and far-reaching consequences which he thought it might have.[3]

[3] Commenting on the brief which he sent to Robert Lovett (Acting US Secretary of State), John Hickerson (Director of the Office of European Affairs) noted in his own handwriting: 'The language of this *aide-mémoire* is restrained, in accordance with diplomatic practice. If you concur, I hope you will "soup" this up in the oral presentation to Franks. If you will, I will be present and help in this. I feel strongly that their policy doesn't make any real sense. Why the hell should we spend money to rearm the Brussels Pact countries when they are selling jets to neutrals?' (FRUS 1948, Vol. III, pp. 253-54). Foreign Office officials were surprised by this approach, because they thought they had reached an understanding with the United States over policy towards Sweden. In a minute of 27 September, Hankey noted that the source of the problem was likely to be the US Ambassador in Stockholm, aided by jealousy on the part of American aircraft manufacturers, since the Foreign Office had frequently explained UK policy to the US Embassy in London. He added: 'At the present stage of our discussions about Western Union, I do not think it will pay the Americans or ourselves to press the Swedes too strongly as they seem to intend to do. We should be most unwise to do this until we know what, if anything, we could do for the Swedes if their association with the West in defence matters were to get them into difficulties with Russia. I think we should put this issue to the State Department at some length.' Commenting to Sargent on Hankey's draft telegram, Bateman pointed out that the State Department had been wrongly informed and that in any case Bevin had decided in May against interfering with armament exports to Sweden. The reply to Washington (FO tel. No. 10856 of 29 September) explained the Foreign Office position in detail, and concluded: 'We consider that our present policy has yielded good results as Swedish Government have dropped their previous refusal to discuss Scandinavian defence cooperation except on condition that Norway and Denmark undertook no commitments to other Powers. We are convinced that a policy of applying pressure to Swedish Government will *not* yield good results particularly as in present state of security discussions we are unable to give them any firm guarantee of support. We therefore do not propose to alter our present policy, and trust that the United States Government will on further consideration share this view' (FO 371/71716, N10363/9/42G).

No. 148

Memorandum by Mr Hankey, 30 September 1948
Top Secret (FO 371/71454, N11084/637/63G)

The relation of Sweden to Scandinavian Co-operation and Atlantic and Western Union[1]

In view of Swedish history in the last 100 years, it seems unrealistic to hope that Sweden will ever be prepared to join an Atlantic Union or the Brussels pact at any rate on equal terms with other Powers.[2] Most Swedes agree substantially with M. Undén's policy, and it is almost incredible that Sweden would go to war because e.g. Belgium or Western Germany or still more Italy had been attacked by the Soviet *Bloc*. Only in the event of a Soviet attack on Norway or Denmark is it easy to conceive of Sweden really going to war; and most Swedes conceive of Scandinavian co-operation much more in terms of co-operative neutrality than co-operative warfare.

[1] Hankey wrote a first version of this paper on 6 August (FO 371/71452, N8874/637/63G, also on FO 371/71458, N8874/3001/63G). Mason minuted on 1 September that he had discussed it with Sargent, who liked it but requested that it should be considered from the strategic aspect by the Chiefs of Staff before it was disseminated further. Hankey wrote accordingly to Hollis on 2 September (FO 371/71452, N8874/637/63G). This paper, (which came to be known as 'Hankey 1'), embodied the changes which were made in the light of their reply (FO 371/71458, N10092/3001/63G).
[2] The Brussels Treaty, between Britain, France and the Benelux countries, was signed on 17 March 1948.

1948

2. His Majesty's Embassies in Sweden and in Norway and Denmark have all therefore recommended that we should aim first at drawing Norway and Denmark into an Atlantic Pact and that we should thereafter try to attach Sweden to Norway and Denmark. The following suggestions are offered as a means of doing this.

3. (*a*) Norway and Denmark should enter the Atlantic Security Pact as full members or if necessary as members with a more limited commitment of mutual assistance as foreshadowed in the Washington exploratory conversations.

(*b*) Sweden should undertake in a separate agreement the following obligations to Norway and Denmark:

(*i*) Sweden would remain *non-belligerent* (not neutral) in any war in which Denmark and Norway are engaged but are not actively attacked (i.e. supposing they are drawn in by their obligations to Atlantic Security Pact but are not attacked by Russia or any other satellite).

(*ii*) During any such period Sweden will prepare by mobilisation if necessary to defend her territory including her air space against any *Soviet* attempt to cross or use either for any purpose civil or military. She would allow Soviet merchant vessels but not warships to use her territorial waters and would actively prevent the laying of Soviet mines. She would so dispose and use her radar services to give warning to the Danish and Norwegian service authorities of any impending attack upon them. She would co-operate so far as she could in measures of economic warfare against Russia, and would resist any Soviet attempt to prevent or dissuade her from trading with the Western Powers (iron ore, ball-bearings, timber, munitions). In this period she would not be expected to declare war or take any measure of active hostility, beyond making clear her determination to defend her territory and her solidarity in principle with Norway and Denmark.

(*iii*) Should Norway or Denmark be attacked physically by the Soviet Union or her satellites, Sweden would enter the war with all her forces and co-operate in the defence of Scandinavia as a whole in accordance with plans to be arranged in advance in inter-Scandinavian defence talks. Only in this case would Sweden be entitled to armed assistance from Great Britain, United States of America and other Western Powers.

(*iv*) Sweden would in return be entitled to the armed assistance of Norway and Denmark if attacked. This would involve the other members of the North Atlantic Security Pact, but it is unlikely that Russia would attack Sweden except as part of or as a prelude to a general attack on the west.

4. Such a system would recognise the urge of the Swedish people towards neutrality, or non-belligerency, as well as the desire of all Scandinavians for Scandinavian co-operation. It would allow the nature of the attachment of the Scandinavian Powers to Atlantic Union to shade gradually off eastwards as it were and would be less likely to provoke Russia to annex or communize Finland than a direct alliance between Sweden and the Western Powers. It would give the Danes and Norwegians all they really need from Sweden, *viz.* assurance of effective support according to prearranged plans if they are actually attacked. It would warn the Russians that they could not safely attack Sweden in isolation (though they would be most unlikely to believe that they could). By making the Swedes feel that they were backing onto something fairly solid, *viz.* Norway and Denmark with the full support of the members of the North Atlantic Security Pact, it would give the Swedes confidence, while they would only be expected to intervene if their own chance of

national safety or survival were most gravely compromised by the threat of Soviet encirclement.³

R.M.A. HANKEY

³ Kirkpatrick sent a copy of this paper to Hoyer Millar in Washington on 5 October, asking him to pass it to the State Department (FO 371/71458, N10092/3001/63G). Hankey also discussed it with Prebensen, who on 20 October replied that Lange was not in favour, because he thought that it would cause difficulties for him within the Norwegian Cabinet, and he therefore hoped that it would not be raised with the Swedes. Kirkpatrick wrote accordingly to Hoyer Millar again on 23 October 1948 (FO 371/71454, N11090/637/G). Collier reported on 1 December that the Americans had considered 'Mr Hankey's plan' but preferred an alternative whereby Norway and Denmark would be parties to the Atlantic Pact and also to a separate pact with Sweden which would oblige Scandinavian countries to come to each others defence but would not induce any action from Sweden unless Norway or Denmark were attacked nor any obligation towards Sweden on the part of the non-Scandinavian powers (FO 371/71455, N12823/637/63G). In a telegram to the US Ambassador in Sweden of 17 November commenting on Hankey's paper, Lovett wrote: 'We agree with much of its substance, but feel it would provide something too closely resembling one-way commitment to Sweden by members North Atlantic Security Pact (FRUS 1948, Vol. III, p. 272).

No. 149

Mr Bevin to Sir O. Franks (Washington), 7 October 1948[1]
Saving Tel. No. 1466 Top Secret (FO 371/71453, N10452/637/63G)

Oslo telegram No. 417 [of September 30th: Scandinavian defence and Atlantic Security].[2]

As you will see, misunderstanding arising out of our communication here has been cleared up, but there is still some doubt as to when Norwegian Government will be invited to participate in a preliminary conference to discuss the projected Atlantic Security Pact. State Department have spoken of a date 'at any time after October 15th'.

2. Norwegian Minister for Foreign Affairs spoke to me in Paris on this subject on September 28th. Full record by bag.[3] He explained the steps now being taken by three Scandinavian powers to arrange for coordinated scheme of defence and said that an undertaking had been given to Sweden that, while these discussions were proceeding, the Norwegian Government would not enter into negotiations without advising Swedish Government. If United States invitation were given now it would place them in very difficult position. He strongly urged that *no* approach should be made for three or four months, though if international situation made it unavoidable, Norwegian Government would consider it.

3. M. Lange was optimistic that it would be possible to bring Sweden into a Scandinavian Pact and so end Swedish neutrality. From that point of view it would be disastrous if American invitation were given now. He also asked whether I thought

[1] Repeated to Oslo, Copenhagen and Stockholm.
[2] Not printed. Oslo tel. No. 410 of 25 September reported that the Norwegian Chargé d'Affaires in London had reported a conversation with Sargent showing that an invitation to Norway and Denmark to join a conference to discuss Atlantic defence might be expected imminently (FO 371/71453, N10369/637/63G). This was considerably in advance of Norwegian Government expectations and would have been unwelcome. Oslo tel. No. 417 of 30 September provided clarification (FO 371/71453, N10452/637/63G).
[3] Not printed.

Norwegians should not tell Swedes of preliminary warning which they had received in Washington and London, though State Department has asked them not to tell Swedes.

4. I said I would consider matter carefully and consult United States Government to see whether invitation could not be postponed so that whole matter of Scandinavian defence and of industrial development and supply of equipment necessary for that purpose, could be worked out.

5. Danish Minister for Foreign Affairs also expressed to me on September 25th Danish Government's concern lest invitation should come before Scandinavian defence talks were concluded and Danish Ambassador had also spoken to Sir O. Sargent.

6. Please inform State Department of these developments. Invitation to Scandinavian Powers cannot presumably in any case be made until whole question of Atlantic Security has been carried a stage further in London, but I am sure it will be advantageous to let the Scandinavian Powers work out their defence arrangements among themselves before we approach them further.

7. We would see no objection to the Swedes being told confidentially of our preliminary warning, if the Danish and Norwegian Governments think that by so doing they might help on the process of weaning the Swedish Government from their policy of neutrality. We should be glad to know the views of the United States Government on this point.

8. We are sending you by bag shortly a scheme we have evolved linking a Scandinavian defence pact with the projected North Atlantic Security Pact in such a way as to meet Swedish preconceptions.[4] We should like State Department to take this into account when considering the matter.

[4] No. 148.

No. 150

Mr Bevin to Sir O. Franks (Washington), 9 October 1948, 11.30 p.m.[1]
Tel. No. 11146 Important, Top Secret (FO 371/71453, N10934/637/63G)

On October 4th I discussed with Mr Marshall in Paris the subject of Scandinavia and Atlantic Security; Mr Caffery, Mr Bohlen and Mr Roberts were also present. I explained that we had been trying to bring Sweden further in our direction. I said it was important that the three Scandinavian countries should get together. The Norwegian and Danish Governments had therefore asked that the expected approach from the United States Government should be delayed until they had had a further opportunity for discussions with the Swedish Government, which they hoped might result in maintaining the Scandinavian 'bloc'.

2. Mr Marshall said that he had been approached in the same way but he understood that the suggested delay was until January or February next. This seemed to him too long, although he agreed that the Scandinavian countries should not be embarrassed now by too much pressure on them.

[1] Repeated to Stockholm, Oslo and Copenhagen.

3. I said that the Norwegian Foreign Minister had asked me whether the Swedish Government should be informed of the possible American approach. Mr Marshall thought that this should be left to Mr Lange's judgement; I agreed with this.[2]

4. Mr Marshall said that he had not got the most recent information on all this from Washington, but he assumed that the maintenance of a Scandinavian '*bloc*' would imply maintenance of Swedish neutrality. In that case Scandinavia would be a neutral, and we should have to ask ourselves whether that would be to our advantage or not. In his view the critical point was the strait between Denmark and Sweden. If that could be made impassable in time of war, then a Scandinavian neutral '*bloc*' might not be too bad, although we had a strong interest in the Norwegian coastline and, of course, in Greenland.

5. I recalled that Stalin had spoken to me in 1945 about the Kattegat.[3] In subsequent discussions the Soviet Government had been assured that our intention was that this should remain an open waterway. We had done this at the time in order to get the Russians out of Bornholm.

---

[2] On 12 October, Collier reported by telegram that the Secretary General of the Norwegian Foreign Ministry had told him that Lange had spoken to Undén in general terms about the prospect of Norway being able to enter the defence arrangements with the Western powers, but that the Swedish reaction was not yet known. He also reported that the Norwegian Ambassador in Washington had been told by Lovett that no formal invitation need now be expected before January (FO 371/71453, N10935/637/63G).

[3] It was actually Molotov who had spoken to Bevin at the Moscow Conference of Foreign Ministers in December 1945, and he had referred to the Great Belt rather than the Kattegat: DBPO, Series I, Vol. II, Nos. 320 and 332.

No. 151

Mr Farquhar (Stockholm) to Mr Bevin, 13 October 1948, 7.58 p.m.[1]

Tel. No. 570 Top Secret, Light (FO 371/71453, N11003/637/63G).

In view of Foreign Office telegram No. 11146 to Washington,[2] I think it may be of value if I set out, as we see it, the present Swedish attitude to Scandinavian defence and Western Union.

After the meeting of Scandinavian Prime Minister in March, the Swedish Government made it quite clear that

(*a*) they intended to remain firm in their insistence on non-adherence to any Great Power *bloc*.

(*b*) that, although in principle in favour of Scandinavian unity in defence, they would only consent to enter into discussions with Norway and Denmark if they were first assured that a Scandinavian *bloc*, if formed, would be a neutral one.

2. His Majesty's Government expressed their displeasure at (*b*) above as tending to bring pressure on countries which if left to themselves would probably be willing to join the Western Union when invited to do so.

As regards the Swedish attitude in (*a*) above, we have, however, acting on instructions contained in Hankey's letter N8687/577/G of August 9th[3] refrained from trying to argue the Swedes round, preferring to leave events to speak for themselves.

---

[1] Repeated to Oslo, Copenhagen, Washington and UK Delegation to UNGA, Paris.
[2] No. 150.
[3] Not printed.

3. The Swedish Government has now modified its attitude sufficiently to authorize discussions on Scandinavian defence without any prior conditions attached. These are to start in Oslo in the immediate future and it is understood that a report to the Governments has been called for by the New Year.

4. Although the Swedish armed forces in general and perhaps some sections of the public would be prepared to see Sweden abandon neutrality and join the West, the Government is officially still as insistent as ever upon a policy of 'no entanglement' and generally the public, in so far as it thinks about these questions at all, would require a strong leader to persuade it to accept any change.

5. We have continued to act on instructions referred to in para 2. above. This policy seems to have been reasonably effective in that there has been some slight advance in the Swedish attitude (see para. 3 above). Our American colleagues have adopted a more forceful line which seems from here to have done little good with the Swedes and some harm to the Americans.

6. Whether we should continue our present policy seems to us to depend on

(*a*) whether from the strategical point of view we do or do not require Sweden to join the West. We have never had firm guidance on this point.

(*b*) if we do wish Sweden to join the West how soon we should like it to happen. We think our present policy will (subject to (*c*) below) produce results in the end but it will not do so quickly.

(*c*) whether if we are to try to persuade Sweden to join the West soon, we can give a reasonably satisfactory answer to the inevitable question of what we can do to assist her in the event of war.

7. I have shown the above to my United States colleague who appreciates the situation from our point of view and agrees generally except with the last sentence of para. 5. He points out that the Americans in talking to the Swedes are laying more emphasis on the necessity of Swedish collaboration with the West, with the object of preventing a war by a show of Western unity and strength, than on the usefulness of Sweden to the West in a war, because they are in any case not quite sure whether Sweden would be an asset or a liability.[4]

---

[4] This was discussed at a meeting of the Ambassadors from Oslo, Copenhagen and Stockholm chaired by Bateman, on 22 October. See No. 152.

No. 152

Record of a meeting chaired by Mr Bateman, 22 October 1948
Top Secret (FO 371/71454, N11864/637/63G)

Scandinavian Defence Co-operation and the Atlantic Security Pact

A meeting was held in Mr Bateman's room on October 22nd to discuss the question of Scandinavian adherence to an Atlantic Security Pact and the tactics which the Western Powers should pursue in order to achieve that object. The following were present: Mr Bateman, HM Ambassadors from Oslo, Copenhagen and Stockholm and Mr Hankey.

Sir Laurence Collier said that there was still enough Pan-Scandinavian feeling in Norway to make it necessary to proceed with caution in their 'pro-Western' policy. Their object in the present staff discussions in Oslo was to bring things to the point where, if Sweden could not be brought in, they could show Norwegian public opinion that everything possible had been done to conclude an effective system of Scandinavian defence including Sweden before Norway was faced with the question of joining a Western Security system.

It was pointed out in the discussions that it would in fact be difficult to make any effective scheme if Sweden were left out altogether. Such studies of Scandinavian defence as had been made in London showed that, while the three Scandinavian countries together might hope by 1957 to be able to defend Scandinavia for a certain time against a Soviet attack with some degree of outside assistance (if that were forthcoming), Norway and Denmark would *by themselves* be able to offer no worthwhile degree of resistance. Mr Hankey said that the Ministry of Defence had expressed the gravest doubts whether any armed help at all would be available for Scandinavia from the West and that nothing should be said to imply that it would; but it seemed clear that without the participation of Sweden the scale of help needed from the West to enable any effective degree of resistance to be offered to Soviet aggression would go very much further beyond the limits of any practical assistance that was likely to be available. It was agreed that the conclusion of an effective scheme for the coordinated defence of Scandinavia as a whole, including Sweden was an essential object at which we should aim.

All three Ambassadors made it clear that the Western Powers would inevitably be asked by the Scandinavian Powers how much armed assistance could be given to them in the event of war. Everything would in the end depend on the degree of security that could be hoped for. If no security either by their own means or with the aid of outside help could be hoped for, the Scandinavian Powers might well refuse in the end to be associated at all with an Atlantic Security Pact, though they might do their best to form an inter-Scandinavian Defence *Bloc* which would endeavour to preserve neutrality in the event of a conflict. It was agreed that this could not by itself offer any real security to the Scandinavian Powers and in the circumstances they would, sooner or later, be bound to appease the Russians and would tend to become unreliable friends of the Western Powers at UNO and at international gatherings. However awkward it might be, the discussion showed that the request for outside assistance (whatever form the assistance might take) would certainly have to be discussed at least with Norway and Denmark as soon as the question of adherence to the Atlantic Security Pact was brought to a head. (The view was also expressed that some coordination of ideas between the British and American Chiefs of Staff on this subject would be desirable before the crucial moment arrived.)

Mr Hankey said that to judge by remarks made by the new Swedish Ambassador since his arrival, the Swedes were likely to claim in the staff talks now proceeding in Oslo that they could offer to the other Scandinavian Powers arms and equipment from their spare production in Sweden (but not from stocks) and were thus in a better position to assist them than the British or Americans. Mr Farquhar said the Swedish General Staff were, however, convinced that Scandinavia must have help from the outside and, indeed, it was clear that Sweden had to import aeroplanes, radar and other arms and equipment herself. The trouble was that the Swedish General Staff could not persuade M. Undén of the true position. He thought M. Undén was slowly coming to see the light, but at the present rate of progress his attitude was unlikely to change effectively by the time the question of an Atlantic Security Pact was brought to a head at the end of the year or early in January as was now contemplated. If the present staff talks in Oslo resulted in a unanimous decision by the Scandinavian defence experts that outside assistance was essential, and that the Scandinavian Powers together could not defend their neutrality alone, this should certainly assist in educating M. Undén. Mr Farquhar said that the present Swedish Government seemed to be firmly back in the saddle and that it would be unwise to gamble on any change of personalities either at the Ministry of Foreign Affaires or at the Ministry of Defence.

The meeting then discussed the prospects of securing Swedish participation in Atlantic Security. It was agreed that it seemed out of the question to hope to secure any arrangement by which Sweden would go to war if one of the Brussels Powers, e.g. France or Belgium were attacked. The tradition of Swedish neutrality is too strong, and even if the Swedish Government were to accept such an obligation, they might not be able to implement it against the current of Swedish opinion when it came to the point. It was agreed that the most that could be hoped for was an arrangement on the lines suggested in the Northern Department memorandum enclosed in Sir I. Kirkpatrick's letter No. N10092/3001G to Mr Hoyer Millar in Washington.[1] (This was, briefly, a mutual assistance arrangement between the Scandinavian Powers, backed by the participation of Norway and Denmark in the Atlantic Security Pact in such a way that they would enter the war whenever Great Britain did so, Sweden undertaking to remain non-belligerent (not neutral) in such an event until the moment when Norway or Denmark were physically attacked when she would of course enter the war.) Even if such a scheme were achieved, Mr Farquhar expressed doubts as to how far the Swedish Government would be likely to go in their non-belligerency in favour of the Western Powers. Here again all would depend on the amount of assistance which the Western Powers could offer if Scandinavia were attacked.

Sir Laurence Collier said that from Norway's point of view the Northern Department scheme would have the great advantage that it allowed for an inter-Scandinavian defence plan and would not involve Norway too directly with France or the Benelux Powers. Norwegian opinion would, in his view, accept a departure from neutrality with less reluctance if Norway's entry into a war were directly connected only with the entry of Great Britain into war; but in any case it would require to be convinced that Norway would then get reasonably effective help.

Mr Hankey said that the Norwegian Ambassador, at his own pressing request, had been allowed to explain the Northern Department scheme to M. Lange for his private consideration and had, on October 20th, received a message back saying that M. Lange would be grateful if *nothing* could be said on such lines as it would create internal political difficulties in the Norwegian Cabinet if Sweden and Norway were treated differently and moreover any offer involving possible non-belligerency or nominal neutrality made now would discourage the Swedes from making their proper contribution. Mr Hankey had said that we would certainly follow M. Lange's wishes as we were expecting him to play the hand with the Swedes at present. It was not clear how far M. Lange hoped to get the Swedes to go. Sir Laurence Collier suggested that M. Lange might still conceivably be hoping to bring the Swedes into some sort of general association with an Atlantic Security Pact.

The meeting discussed the argument used by the Swedish Government that Sweden's direct association with the Atlantic Security Pact would lead the Russians to destroy Finnish independence. Mr Hankey said that he had been able to discuss this with HM Minister in Helsingfors. Mr Scott had expressed the view that the Russians probably would make some further demands on Finland if Sweden were directly connected with the Western Powers. They would probably ask for bases on the Finnish shore in the Gulf of Bothnia and might even also demand a more pro-Soviet

---

[1] No. 148, footnote 3.

Finnish Government, if the procedure they had followed in the Baltic States was any guide. Mr Scott did not consider that the Russians would necessarily be moved to do this if Sweden were associated with the Atlantic Security Pact only indirectly in the manner suggested in the Northern Department Memorandum. The meeting agreed that the problem of Finland was probably a secondary consideration with the Swedes though they might use the argument to support their attitude.

The meeting discussed the question of the best tactics to pursue in order to induce the Swedish Government to make their maximum contribution to Scandinavian and Atlantic Security. It was pointed out that at present the Americans seemed to favour a tough policy, including the refusal of arms and equipment, until such time as the Swedish Government altered their attitude (it was uncertain how far the Americans expected the Swedes to go). On the other hand, HM Government favoured a policy of slow persuasion and had particularly insisted on the importance of not precipitating the neutrality issue at the election. This policy had yielded favourable results but the discussion had shown that it was not working quickly enough on M. Undén. The upshot of the discussion was, however, that it would be undesirable to face the Swedes with a direct demand to declare their attitude to an Atlantic Security Pact before the proposal for the latter had made more headway and before the Western Powers were able to answer the inevitable Swedish (and, indeed, Norwegian and Danish) question what, if anything, they could do to help if Scandinavia were attacked. There was general agreement with the view expressed by Mr Farquhar that it would be better *not* to bring matters to a head with the Swedes in any way until the staff talks in Oslo resulted in a report or plan which would have to be discussed by the Scandinavian Cabinets. The limitations of any plan of Scandinavian defence in isolation should then be obvious, and we might expect to be in a better position to influence Swedish views when the whole question of defence was in the melting pot. Such a timetable would also be more likely to suit Norwegian requirements. On the other hand, we could not wait indefinitely, since failure to act when the Scandinavian defence talks were complete would risk creating a revulsion in Norwegian and Danish opinion which might result in a Scandinavian defence pact based on the Swedish Government's 'isolationist' doctrine. The three Ambassadors thought they would certainly be able to inform the Foreign Office when this moment arrived and that their Military Attachés might even be given the text of any report resulting from the talks. We could then consider the position with greater knowledge of practical possibilities and needs.

It was accordingly agreed that:

(*a*) We should not press the Swedes or other Scandinavian Powers until their staff talks resulted in a report of scheme regarding Scandinavian defence;

(*b*) We should try to get the text or at least full details of any such Scandinavian defence scheme through our respective Service Attachés;

(*c*) If that fails, then we should, with the US Government, make a joint approach for information to all three Scandinavian Governments basing our request on the evident fact that any such Scandinavian defence scheme must obviously be aimed against a common enemy and that it was sensible and prudent for us to see how far it fitted into *our* overall defence plans.

(*d*) We should make use of any discussions regarding the Scandinavian defence scheme to point out that it would be of no value unless Scandinavia was a part of, or associated with the Atlantic Pact.

Meanwhile it was agreed that it was undesirable that M. Undén should feel assured of British approval for a continued policy of neutrality in all circumstances, and that the Northern Department should consider ways and means of countering the suggestions which had appeared in the Swedish press to that effect.[2]

R.M.A. HANKEY

[2] Kirkpatrick sent a copy of this record to Hoyer Millar in Washington on 8 November. See No. 155.

No. 153

Minute of conversations with a Danish delegation, 27 October 1948
Confidential (FO 371/70550, C9099/42/18)

Agreed minute[1]

A series of seven meetings were held at the Foreign Office, London from 18th October to 23rd October between a Danish Delegation led by Mr Gustav Rasmussen, Minister for Foreign Affairs and accompanied by Mr Alsing Andersen,[2] Mr Thorkil Kristensen,[3] Mr Ole Bjørn Kraft,[4] Mr Jørgen Jørgensen[5] and Lord Henderson, Parliamentary Under-Secretary of State for Foreign Affairs, assisted by members of the Foreign Office, to discuss the various problems affecting the Danish-minded minority in South Schleswig. The whole question was reviewed in much detail and a careful examination was made of the following proposals, put forward by the Danish Delegation:

(*a*) Administrative Separation of South Schleswig from Holstein.

(*b*) Removal or reduction of numbers of refugees in South Schleswig.

(*c*) Safeguards for the cultural and civic rights of the Danish-minded population in South Schleswig.

The main reason put forward by the Danish Delegation for favouring administrative separation of South Schleswig from Holstein was that they considered this one of the principal means of ensuring democratic liberties for the Danish-minded population. The British Delegation drew attention to the political and economic difficulties involved in administrative separation. They pointed out that it would be necessary to secure French and United States approval before any alteration of Land boundaries could be made. In practice a favourable vote by the German population would be required—e.g. in a plebiscite—and even if the refugees could be excluded from voting, which seemed very uncertain, it appeared most unlikely on the facts available that a vote in favour of separation could be secured. Even if such a proposal were, contrary to expectation, to be passed by a narrow majority, it would be difficult to ensure that once a West German state were set up, the separation would be maintained, more particularly in view of the impression on the part of the German population that administrative separation of South Schleswig might be a prelude to a movement for its ultimate cession to Denmark. Attention was also drawn to the increased burden of overhead charges for the Land Government in so small an area,

[1] The agreed minute was approved by Mr Rasmussen and Lord Henderson.
[2] Former Minister of Defence and later Minister of the Interior.
[3] Former, and later, Minister of Finance.
[4] Minister of Defence, 1945, Chairman of the Conservative Party and later Foreign Minister.
[5] Former, and later, Minister of Education.

though it was pointed out that the system of Land Government might be correspondingly simplified.

The Danish Delegation emphasised the anxiety felt by the Danish Government lest the accumulation of refugees near the Danish frontier should affect the security of the frontier districts. The Delegation urged that in view of the cultural struggle in South Schleswig the situation there could not be regarded in the same way as in the rest of Germany.

Lord Henderson expressed the view that, while it was true that South Schleswig was bearing an undue share of the refugee burden, it would not be practicable to reduce the number of refugees in South Schleswig to a proportion much lower than that in other parts of Germany. It was, however, recognised that the present position called for alleviation and it was agreed that the Foreign Office would take the initiative in proposing to the other Occupying Powers in Western Germany that a joint Working Party (to include a German representative) should be set up to examine the refugee question and to see what practical measures could be taken to secure a more even distribution of refugees throughout Western Germany. It was further agreed that a representative of the Danish-minded population should be associated with the British element of the joint Working Party.

It was further agreed that the encouragement of emigration and resettlement of refugees in other areas was highly desirable, but the discussion on this subject showed that there was little hope of immediate improvement from resettlement schemes owing to the serious shortage of housing and equipment. It was agreed however that the Foreign Office would examine the possibility of providing, in any future proposals for the recruitment of German labour for employment in other countries, that as high a proportion as possible is recruited from the refugee population of South Schleswig. It was also agreed that the Foreign Office would instruct the British Military Governor to examine the Schleswig-Holstein Refugee Assistance Act when it came up for renewal in December, 1948 to see whether Article V needed modification to ensure that an unfair advantage is not given to refugee candidates for appointments to the public services in South Schleswig.

The Danish Delegation drew attention to reports that the German authorities had in several respects already used methods which did not seem consistent with the state of cultural and political freedom which it was agreed on both the Danish and British sides ought to be assured with the Danish-minded population.

As regards the safeguarding of the rights of the Danish-minded part of the population it was proposed that the South Schleswig Association as representing the cultural interests of the Danish-minded population should be invited to approach the Government of Land Schleswig-Holstein with a view to reaching an agreement on the rights to be enjoyed by the Danish-minded population and on the safeguards necessary for their preservation. In this connexion reference was made to the procedure which subsequently led to the conclusion of the arrangement in 1948 in the South Tyrol. The aim should be to reach a permanent and satisfactory solution of this problem.

An agreement to this effect might be embodied in the constitution of Land Schleswig-Holstein or possibly take the form of a Land Statute. Lord Henderson expressed the earnest hope that the Danish Government would exercise a moderating influence on the Danish-minded population's representatives in any negotiations that might take place and said that the Foreign Office for their part would through the Military Governor advise the Land Government to enter into negotiations and would use their influence to promote a satisfactory result.

No. 154

Memorandum by Mr Bevin on the Anglo-Norwegian Fishery Dispute, 8 November 1948
CP(48)257 Secret

After consultation with the Secretary of State for Scotland and the Minister for Agriculture and Fisheries, I think my colleagues should be informed of the revival of the dispute over fishing limits claimed by the Norwegian Government for the exclusive use of Norwegian fishermen. It seems essential, in order to avoid a really embittered controversy, that this question should go to the Court of International Justice and this is likely to be arranged. Moreover, this dispute, apart from its possible effect on our fishing activities on the Norwegian Coast, has assumed much greater importance because of the exaggerated claims to control the fisheries in waters off their coasts, recently put forward by the Governments of the United States of America, Mexico, Argentine, Chile, Peru and Iceland. Any concession to Norway may prejudice our position in dealing with the claims of these countries. The circumstances are as follows:

2. On 16th September, His Majesty's Ambassador in Oslo reported that the Norwegian Government had decided to enforce the Royal Decree of 1935 prescribing an extensive 'Norwegian Fisheries Zone'. This means that large areas of the waters off the Norwegian coast, which, according to the view of His Majesty's Government, are high seas and where in consequence all nations have an equal right to fish, will be closed to British trawlers.

3. The dispute about fishing limits dates from a long time back. All attempts to solve it in the 1920s were fruitless, but in 1933 a *modus vivendi* was agreed with the Norwegian Government on the basis of what has since been known as the Red Line. This line is somewhat outside the strict limits of what we recognise as Norwegian territorial waters and makes a substantial concession to Norway. It is still observed by our trawler owners who have always regarded it as a temporary expedient pending a decision by the Court of International Justice. This *modus vivendi* was upset by the Norwegian decree of 1935, which went far beyond anything that His Majesty's Government could possibly accept.

4. Attempts were made in 1938 to conclude a Fishery Convention with the Norwegians and to settle the dispute. A draft convention was agreed in Oslo between British and Norwegian delegations and was referred to the two Governments. This draft convention made further concessions to Norway, but shortly before Norway was invaded it was rejected by the Norwegian Parliament, and the British trawler owners regarded these concessions as being a breach of their conditional acceptance of the Red Line.

5. The Norwegian Parliament has now decided that the 1935 decree should be enforced. If British shipping is interfered with on banks outside the Red Line limits which His Majesty's Government recognised by the *modus vivendi* of 1933 there are sure to be unpleasant incidents and much bad blood will be created. This would be particularly unfortunate at the present time when we are anxious to draw the Norwegian and other Scandinavian Governments closer to the Western Powers.

6. His Majesty's Ambassador was accordingly instructed to express to the Norwegian Minister for Foreign Affairs the surprise and distress of His Majesty's Government at the Norwegian decision to apply without warning a measure which is known to be utterly unacceptable to us and to say that unless enforcement of the 1935

The Nordic Countries, 1944-1951

decree was deferred to allow time for consultation, relations between the two Governments could not fail to be seriously affected. His Majesty's Government were still prepared to try to reach agreement with the Norwegian Government over fishing limits, should the Norwegian Government wish to do so; alternatively, the case might be brought before the International Court of Justice at The Hague, preferably by agreement between the parties, but either country could bring it unilaterally since both countries are bound by the optional clause of the statute of the court. In any case it was most desirable that there should be an interim arrangement to regulate fishing while the matter was under discussion or pending before the court and this could, in the view of His Majesty's Government, only be based on the Red Line observed hitherto. His Majesty's Government would be glad to discuss these issues with a Norwegian delegation in London.

7. The preliminary reaction of the Norwegian Government to Sir L. Collier's communication was that a compromise was no longer possible in view of the decision of the Norwegian Parliament, and that they saw no difficulty in sending a delegation to London to discuss terms of reference to The Hague Court if that should be necessary. A final reply is expected shortly. Meanwhile, the Norwegian Government have said that the *status quo* will be preserved in the fishing areas.

8. To sum up, the best solution seems to be that an authoritative opinion on the relevant issues of international law in this case should be obtained from the Court of International Justice. Owing to the action of the Norwegian parliament, the Norwegian Government is not now in a position to give way on the claims embodied in the 1935 decree. The only settlement, therefore, which could now be negotiated would be a settlement under which the United Kingdom accepted the Norwegian decree and that would be a step which would be politically almost impossible for the United Kingdom to take in view of the strong reaction of British fishery interests. If there is no settlement by judicial decision or otherwise, incidents by fishery-protection vessels on both sides in the disputed area are inevitable. On the other hand, the Court of International Justice would lay down principles on the application of which the two Governments might be able to agree and if they did not, they could go back to the court.

9. The Legal Adviser of the Foreign Office has discussed the matter with the Attorney-General, who agrees that in the circumstances a reference of the dispute to The Hague appears to be the only practicable course to take.

E. B.

No. 155

**Letter from Sir I. Kirkpatrick to Mr Hoyer Millar (Washington),
8 November 1948**
Top Secret (FO 371/71454, N11864/637/G)

My dear Derek,
Your letter No. G3/360/48 of the 13th October.[1]
We have now been able to discuss the whole question of Scandinavian defence cooperation and its relation to a possible Atlantic Security Pact, with our

---
[1] Not printed.

Ambassadors from Oslo, Stockholm and Copenhagen and I enclose a record of the discussion.[2]

As you will see it was generally agreed that it would be better not to press the Scandinavian Powers further on this subject until their staff talks now going on in Oslo result in a report or scheme regarding Scandinavian defence, but that we should endeavour to use any such report that may be made in order to bring them to practical discussions on the relation of a Scandinavian Pact to Atlantic Security.

It seems essential that we should clear our ideas with the State Department on this subject, partly because they have been inclined at times to favour a different policy (i.e. immediate pressure on Sweden) and partly because when the time comes to take up the question with the Scandinavian Powers, and more particularly with Sweden, the representations which either of us will make will carry very much more weight if they can be co-ordinated in any manner felt locally desirable by the British and United States Ambassadors on the spot.

Provided you see no objection, we should therefore be glad if you would communicate a copy of the enclosed record to the State Department for their own Top Secret information and invite them to give us their views on the whole subject. We should like to reach some sort of understanding with them both as to the timing of an approach to the three Scandinavian Powers and as to how the matter should be handled in the three capitals concerned. For the moment we are convinced that we should do best to allow the Norwegians to handle the Swedes and to carry the Oslo staff conversations as far as they can in the right direction.

Yours ever,
I.A. KIRKPATRICK

[2] No. 152.

No. 156

Record by Mr Jebb of a meeting with M. Lange, 20 November 1948
Secret (FO 371/71455, N12650/637/63G)

Scandinavia and the Atlantic Pact
Note of Conversation with the Norwegian Foreign Minister

As predicted in Mr Hankey's letter to me, N11919/637/G of the 8th November last,[1] Mr Lange asked me to lunch with him today in order to talk about the Atlantic Pact and the present defence negotiations among the Scandinavians. The following was the upshot of our talk.

(*a*) Mr Lange is practically convinced that there is no possibility of persuading the Swedes to do anything beyond joining a Three Power Scandinavian defensive alliance based on Articles 51 to 54 of the Charter.

(*b*) It is just possible, however, that if sufficient pressure were put on the Swedes, and notably if the Americans made it clear that a policy of complete neutrality would result in no American arms, the Swedes would agree to the Three Power defensive alliance embodying some provisions designed to deny the entrance to the Baltic to both sides in the event of war in which the Scandinavian *bloc* would not be involved.

[1] Not printed.

(c) There was in any case no possibility in his view of the Swedes agreeing to join the Three Power Scandinavian Pact if Norway and Denmark, or either of them, joined a North Atlantic Defensive Alliance.

(d) In these circumstances the Norwegians would have to consider very seriously whether they could come in to any Atlantic Pact based on Article 51.

(e) If they did consider coming in, however, he thought it highly likely that they would request some limitation of Norwegian obligations so as not to be committed to e.g. going to war in the event of some Russian attack on Alaska. Mr Lange said that this was important from the point of view of Norwegian public opinion.

(f) It was still highly desirable, if possible, for any definite request for Norway to make known her attitude towards some Atlantic Pact to be deferred until at any rate the new year.

2. Mr Lange had just seen Mr Marshall, the object of his visit being to discover what, if anything, the Americans would do supply the Swedes with arms if they should maintain the attitude described above. Mr Marshall, I understand, made a guarded reply and said that he would have to consult his colleagues.[2]

3. A good deal of time was spent in my outlining for the benefit of Mr Lange the present state of our negotiations on the subject of the Atlantic Pact, largely from the technical angle. I did *not* think it wise to tell the Norwegian Foreign Minister that there was any difference of opinion between us and the French as regards a possible invitation to Italy, and indeed Italy was not mentioned in our conversation. At one stage, however, Mr Lange said that he himself trusted that Greece and Turkey, at any rate, would not come into the Atlantic Pact, and that they would be covered by some sort of collaborative assurance.

G. JEBB

[2] For a record of Lange's meeting with Marshall, see FRUS 1948, Vol. III, pp. 279-281.

No. 157

Briefing points by Mr Figg for a speech by Mr Mayhew, 23 November 1948[1]
(FO 371/71720, N12587/126/42)

Mr Mayhew may care to bring out in his speech at the Secretary of State's dinner for the Swedish Parliamentary Delegation a few points marking the similarity between the United Kingdom and Sweden in the field of social affairs.

Both countries started after the war, under Social Democratic Governments, on ambitious programmes of social reform and social services. The extent of the Swedish Government's efforts in this direction are well illustrated by the fact that her 1945 favourable balance of trade has dwindled to a deficit during the last three years; this is attributable in a large measure to the cost of her social improvement. For instance in order to satisfy the people's demand for houses energy was diverted to the building industry at the expense of her export industries. Lately, however, the National Bank of Sweden has recommended further curtailment of building permits with a view to the release of many materials for the export trade. Secondly, there has been a uniform increase in workers' wages. Compared with 1946, hourly rates have increased by almost 15%, and annual incomes by more than 13%; significantly real wages have

[1] The dinner for the Swedish Parliamentary Delegation took place on 24 November 1948.

increased by 8% and 7% respectively. The point seems important and justifies any praise we may care to bestow on Sweden for improving the standard of living.

Our difficulties may also be contrasted with those of Sweden. As we are short of coal miners, Sweden is short of iron ore miners. To overcome this difficulty, the Swedish Minister of Labour is negotiating to bring in foreign mine workers (this information was given confidentially by Swedish officials and should not be used. It is only included for Mr Mayhew's information). There is also a shortage of skilled workers in the engineering industry, a situation aggravated by the fact that the skilled men working now are approaching the retirement age. In general, industrial relations between the Government and Trade Unions in Sweden have been harmonious. Constant study by the Swedish Ministry of Labour of industrial conditions and, until the elections this year a working majority in the *Rikstag* [*sic*], has enabled the Social Democrat Government to make sure of industry's co-operation. A distinct drop in the Social Democrat majority in the *Rikstag* [*sic*] in the elections in September, combined with the now adverse balance of trade making curtailment of social programmes necessary, will doubtless exacerbate to some extent relations with industry in the near future; especially when the Government, if ever, pursues a vigorous anti-Communist campaign.

Less important points are the following:

1. Great Britain was honoured with two Nobel prizes in 1947, that for chemistry going to Sir Robert Robinson and that for physics to Sir Edward Appleton.

2. Up to September 1st this year there were 24,462 British visitors to Sweden and this was a drop of 20% over the figures last year, no doubt due to the severer currency restrictions.

3. Bread rationing has been abolished (Sept. 1948).

4. It is rumoured that, in connexion with the expert report on traffic legislation, 1944, a resolution will be tabled by the National Union of Temperance Committees recommending that no alcohol may be consumed within eight hours before driving a car. This seems to be an ingenious way of petrol rationing.

L.C.W. FIGG

No. 158

Minute from Mr Hankey to Mr Bateman, 30 November 1948
(FO 371/71455, N12650/3001/63/G)

Scandinavian Defence Co-operation and the Atlantic Pact

We have a number of indications now as to the present state of this question.

2. *The Inter-Scandinavian Defence Talks* are still proceeding in Stockholm and are to be continued in the middle of December in Copenhagen. According to the Danish Minister for Foreign Affairs (N12506 Flag A)[1] the three countries have agreed:

(*a*) that the only possible aggressor for them to consider is Soviet Russia;

(*b*) that the Northern Defence Union could not be effective without a link with the West.

3. *The Danish attitude* is explained further by Mr Randall in his letter at N12238 (Flag B).[1] See especially marked passages. The Danish Government will apparently support the Norwegian Government in resisting any conditions which ban connexion

---
[1] Not printed.

with the West and will also endeavour to speed up a decision. But Mr Randall and the US Ambassador are agreed that the Danes probably feel that we should in our own interests do our best to defend them in any event and whatever official attitude they adopted to the Western Powers, and that it is necessary to dispel this illusion in such private conversations as we may have with the authorities concerned. A useful opportunity to do this will occur when the Danish Defence Minister visits this country this week in connexion with the renewal of the Agreement about the Danish brigade in Germany.

4. *The Norwegian attitude* is explained authoritatively in the record of Mr Jebb's conversation with the Minister for Foreign Affairs, M. Lange, in N12650 (Flag C).[2] As will be seen M. Lange is particularly convinced that there is no possibility of persuading the Swedes to conclude a Scandinavian Defence Pact any members of which have any link with the Western Powers. In the circumstances the Norwegian Government would have to consider very seriously whether they should come in to an Atlantic Pact based on Article 51 of the Charter. If they did it seems highly likely that they would request some limitations of Norwegian obligations as to the circumstances in which they would go to war. M. Lange said it was still highly desirable that any further request for Norway to declare her attitude towards some Atlantic Pact should, if possible, be deferred until at any rate the New Year.

5. *The Swedish attitude* is only known to us authoritatively by what M. Lange has said. He has expressed the view (see N12650 Flag C) that the Swedes might by dint of pressure be got to agree that a Scandinavian Defence Alliance might include a provision deigned to deny the entrances of the Baltic to both sides in the event of a war in which the Scandinavian *Bloc* were *not* involved. We have written to the Chiefs of Staff to find out exactly what strategic facilities we want from the Scandinavian Powers and until we have their reply it is really impossible to say to what extent (if at all) such an arrangement could meet our needs. It seems however clear that the Swedes would in fact only take such action when the time came if they received some assurances of help against the almost inevitable Soviet reaction.

6. There seems to be no doubt that Swedish opinion is actually cooling off towards Scandinavian Defence plans and towards association with the West, e.g. an Atlantic Pact, partly because the memory of the Czechoslovak *coup* is fading and partly because the Swedish predisposition towards neutrality is again coming to the fore. The Swedish motives, and the very mixed and contradictory arguments which the Swedes are at present using are very well summarised in Mr Henderson's letter in N12507 (Flag D).[3]

7. For the purpose of bringing the Swedes to even the step mentioned above, M. Lange seems to think that American pressure as regards the supply of arms might be important. M. Lange has sounded the Americans out about this and Mr Marshall said he would have to consult his colleagues. I think pressure on the Swedes would have to be applied just the right way. Plain pressure would merely bring out their Nordic quality of obstinacy, as the Germans found. It would have to combine separation from the other Scandinavian Powers and refusal of a fairly attractive 'carrot' from our side to be effective. The Swedes, in my opinion will be pretty hard-boiled and calculating about the whole affair.

---

[2] No. 156.
[3] Not printed. Bateman commented on this point 'Arguments similar to those summarised in Mr Henderson's letter were recently used to me by the Swedish Ambassador. The Swedes *have* got cold feet' (FO 371/71455, N12650/637/63G).

8. I may mention here that the Air Ministry have just told us that the Swedes have asked for facilities to train night-fighter pilots here—we have apparently agreed to sell them a number of night fighters. I can hardly believe that it is in our interests to help the Swedes in this way at a time when we may well want to fly bombers over their territory at night and are unable to obtain any understanding as to the use which the Swedes will make of their neutrality. It would be tragic if British night fighters were used to shoot down American or British bombers. This matter will be the subject of a separate minute but meanwhile I have asked the Air Ministry to suspend action.

9. As regards *the action we are now to take*, we agreed with HM Ambassadors in Oslo, Copenhagen and Stockholm on October 22nd that we would wait until the Scandinavian talks resulted in some sort of report before we pressed the matter. We have told the Scandinavian Powers that their date line of February 1st is leaving it too late, but it looks rather as if matters were going to drag on. Nothing at least will eventuate before the talks in Copenhagen in the middle of December. Whether we can allow matters to drag on into the New Year will depend partly on the speed of progress in the Atlantic Pact talks.

R.M.A .HANKEY

No. 159

Minute from Mr Etherington-Smith to Mr Bevin, 8 December 1948
Top Secret (FO 371/71717, N13585/9/42G)

Supply of arms to Sweden

In May this year the Chiefs of Staff considered this question (see minutes at Flag A)[1] and concluded that there was a case of adapting our policy as regards the supply of military equipment to Sweden in accordance with Sweden's attitude towards the Western Powers. Subsequently, the matter was further examined by the Joint War Production Staff from a more technical aspect (see minutes at Flag B).[1] Generally speaking, their decision was that the adoption by HM Government of a policy of restricting military supplies to Sweden was a practicable one and might in the course of time have a considerable effect on the Swedes.

2. When the question was submitted to the Secretary of State on the 29th May however, (see Mr Roberts's minute at Flag C),[2] he saw no reason at that time to modify our policy of helping Sweden to obtain armaments and military supplies. He held to the view which he had expressed to M. Undén in Paris in March and he did not wish to force the Swedes into allying themselves more closely with the West than they themselves felt wise. He had confidence that the Swedes would stand up to the Russians in case of need and he wished them to be strong enough to do so.

3. When the Chiefs of Staff were informed of the Secretary of State's view, it was arranged at the same time that the matter would be kept under review and reconsidered if there was a change in the political situation e.g. if America decided to give military support to a Western Alliance (see last para. of letter at Flag D).[1]

4. Since the above decision was taken, the situation has in fact undergone a considerable change. The Swedish elections have taken place and the Swedish Government is no longer hampered by electioneering considerations in deciding on

---

[1] Not printed.
[2] See No. 141.

the policy it should pursue. Notwithstanding this fact, however, it appears from recent reports that the Swedish attitude has hardened still further and that the Swedes are even less willing than before to contemplate any association with the West. They are even showing reluctance to cooperate in the preparation of inter-Scandinavian defence plans unless the other participants pledge themselves to a policy of strict neutrality.

5. In a recent conversation with Mr Jebb in Paris (see record at Flag E),[3] the Norwegian Minister for Foreign Affairs was evidently of the opinion that some pressure should be put on the Swedes and he indicated that the form of pressure most likely to be effective would be a total denial of arms (paragraph 1(*b*)). He also revealed that he had seen Mr Marshall about this and the purpose of his approach was clearly to suggest that pressure should be applied to Sweden in this way. We do not yet know the American response to this suggestion, but we do know that the Americans have had considerable misgivings about our deliveries to Sweden of important military material such as Vampire fighters, and would like to see these deliveries curtailed,

6. Meanwhile, the Air Ministry have drawn our attention to the fact that, in addition to deliveries of ordinary fighter aircraft, we are also supplying the Swedes with a considerable number of Mosquito night fighters, some of which have already left this country. A quantity of radar is also on order. A note by the Air Ministry showing the present position in regard to military supplies for Sweden is annexed at Flag F.¹ We must expect the Americans to react very strongly when they discover that we are arming a persistently neutral Sweden with night fighters.

7. In view of the above considerations, I submit that the Chiefs of Staff should be asked to re-examine this matter and to consider whether the adoption of a more restrictive policy towards Sweden is not now desirable. If it is eventually decided that military supplies to Sweden should be reduced, we shall have to consider carefully how such a policy should be put into effect. There would be no question of presenting the Swedes with a blunt threat that unless they joined an alliance with the West we would cut off the supply of arms. The line we should take, which is a perfectly logical and legitimate one, is that as there is only a limited supply of such things as high performance fighter aircraft we have to place the available supplies where they will be most useful to us. We must therefore give prior consideration to the needs of our allies and so long as we cannot count on the Swedes being on our side in the event of a war, they cannot expect to receive the same priority as other Western countries, who have pledged themselves to fight with us. This does not mean, however, that they would get *no* supplies at all from us. We should continue to assist them with deliveries of military equipment and material as far as we could, subject to the over-riding needs of Western security, but they must expect a low priority and Powers with whom we have some sort of defence understanding will all come well before them.[4]

R.G.A. ETHERINGTON-SMITH

---

[3] No. 156.

[4] Bevin's handwritten minute was transcribed by Northern Department as follows: 'I have never urged that we should go out of (our) way to supply. On the other hand I have not wanted to stop (supplies). It is a question of availability, of priority. Our friends who enter into commitments have priority. I still believe that if handled wisely Sweden is not hopeless.' In a letter to Hollis of 23 December, Sargent cited Lange's opinion (expressed to Jebb in Paris (No. 153) that the supply of arms to Sweden should be reduced, and referred to American misgivings about continued British deliveries to Sweden of military material. He quoted Bevin's view that the treatment Britain accorded to Sweden should be governed by availability and priority, and requested that the question should be reviewed again by the Chiefs of Staff (FO 371/71717, N13585/9/42G).

No. 160

Mr Scott (Helsinki) to Mr Bevin, 15 December 1948
No. 274 Confidential (FO 371/71412, N13450/100/56)

Sir,
In paragraph 4 of my despatch No. 267 of the 8th December[1] I had the honour to inform you that, in the course of a speech which he made on the Finnish Independence Day, the President had drawn attention to the necessity for the Finns to exercise great care and caution in their dealings with the Russians. 'It should be remembered', he said, 'that even the smallest and in itself innocent and unsophisticated deed, even a childish one, may give cause for suspicion and unfounded conclusions and bring trouble both to individuals and to the whole country'.

2. One of the favourite themes of the Finnish Communists is that relations with the Soviet Government have deteriorated in recent months and that this is the fault of the Social Democrats' minority government. The Communist press has accordingly sought to interpret the passage in Monsieur Paasikivi's speech in which he referred to Finnish relations with the Soviet Union as a criticism of Monsieur Fagerholm's administration.

3. Be that as it may, recent incidents have given point to the President's warning. The Soviet Chargé d'Affaires has recently addressed two notes to the Finnish Government. In the first of these he complained that two Soviet officials, who were involved in a brawl at a circus, had been ill-treated by the police; in the second he protested against the performance in a small Helsinki Revue Theatre of *The Jaeger's Bride* about the Finnish civil war in 1918 and against the performance at the Finnish National Theatre of Sartre's *Les Mains Sales*, both of which plays were considered to express anti-Soviet sentiments. No official replies have as yet been given to these Notes. The first incident is now being officially investigated and it is reported that it arose from the two Soviet officials being drunk. The two plays had finished their runs by the time the second Note was delivered.

4. No especial significance should be assigned to the presentation of these two Notes since the incidents out of which they arose are trivial and there are no indications of their being linked with a more serious attempt to embarrass the Finnish Government. Nevertheless, the Finnish Government are taking the two matters very seriously and the extent of their appreciation of the danger of the situation in which they are placed is shown by the fact that the President has given orders for the prosecution of a Finnish citizen who is alleged to have made disparaging remarks about the Soviet Union in a public conveyance. Action will be taken on the basis of an amendment to the Criminal Code which was specially passed for this purpose on the 8th May, 1948, and which provides that persons who make or publish statements capable of jeopardising Finland's relations with a foreign power may, on conviction, be sentenced to a term of imprisonment of up to two years.

5. The Prime Minister was also sufficiently impressed by the danger of providing the Soviet Union with any pretext for picking a quarrel to devote the first part of a speech which he made in Bromarv on the 11th December, and of which I

[1] Not printed.

have the honour to enclose a summarised translation herein,[1] to the subject matter of the two Soviet Notes.

6. The second half of Monsieur Fagerholm's speech contained the following important statement of the Finnish Government's attitude towards the adhesion of Sweden to the Atlantic Pact.

> If the other Scandinavian countries commit themselves to a *bloc* which can in any manner be considered as directed against the Soviet Union, it is obvious that Finnish interests, as a result of the country's geographical position and Treaty obligations, will be intimately affected thereby, and that our possibilities of participating even in cultural and economic Scandinavian co-operation can be affected. When the political leaders in Sweden in vindication of the policy of neutrality followed by the Swedish Government often refer to consideration for Finland, this is something which we in Finland completely appreciate and note with thanks.

7. The position of Finland has no doubt been taken into account in any negotiations which there may have been with the Swedish Government. Nevertheless, it may be useful to restate it as seen from this post. From their advanced posts on the Viipuri Isthmus and their base at Porkkala, the Russians control the approaches to the capital. The Finnish Army is restricted by the Peace Treaty to 34,000 men and is ill-equipped. There is consequently no possibility of organised resistance (as opposed to guerrilla warfare) and, within a few days of the outbreak of war, the Russians could reach the Swedish frontier. If Sweden decides to associate herself more closely with the Western Powers, there is a risk that the Russians may occupy Finland as a counter-measure. From a strategical point of view this would not be of great importance since, as stated above, it is a measure which the Russians can take at any time that suits their convenience.

8. There is, however, considerable political objection to pursuing a policy which would result in the extinction of the last democratic State to survive in Eastern Europe. The occupation of Finland would mean that thenceforward the Soviet frontier from the Arctic Ocean to the Black Sea was guarded by a chain of States all alike in their subservience to the Soviet Union and in their proscription of religion, of personal liberty and of freedom of expression. Of even greater importance is the moral consideration. It is not a light thing to expose a country to the horrors of a Russian occupation. Prolonged over a period of years it might result in the disappearance of the Finnish nation as an organised entity. The Finns are a courageous people, as their recent history has shown, and if they were satisfied that the adhesion of Sweden to the Atlantic Pact would give such an accretion of strength to the Western Powers as would be likely to be a deciding factor in an eventual war, they themselves might agree that their nation should be sacrificed in the common interest.

9. This, however, is a decision which, quite intelligibly, they would not wish any other nation to take on their behalf, and it would indeed be hard to justify unless it were established that it was the only course by which the survival of European civilisation could be secured.[2]

---

[2] Hankey minuted to Bateman: 'I think this Russian pressure on Finland is really aimed at *Sweden*. It obviously is not serious, as they've just made quite a good trade agreement with Finland.' Bateman agreed with Hankey, adding 'The Swedish Ambassador told me, some weeks ago, that Sweden must have regard, in relation to the Atlantic Pact, to the possible Russian reaction in Finland. This desp. explains what was in his mind' (FO 371/71412, N13450/100/56).

10. I am sending copies of this despatch to His Majesty's representatives at Warsaw, Prague, Budapest, Belgrade, Sofia, Bucharest, Berlin, Vienna and His Majesty's Ambassadors at Moscow and Stockholm.

I have, etc.,
O.A. SCOTT

No. 161

Mr Farquhar (Stockholm) to Mr Bevin, 18 December 1948, 1.42 p.m.[1]
Tel. No. 658 Important, Top Secret (FO 371/71455, N13444/3001/63G)

My telegram 655.[2]

I saw the Swedish Minister for Foreign Affairs this morning. After a few preliminary remarks conversation turned to representations recently made by [?United States Ambassador]. I told him that I was aware of the conversation which the Swedish Ambassador in London had just had on this subject and then read out to him gist of paragraphs 2 and 3 of your telegram No. 776.[2] I derived the impression that the Swedish Ambassador's report of the conversation was not as full as what I read out.

2. M. Undén raised with me the question of supply of military equipment etc. and I told him it was a question of availability. If I could put it in such a way, it is only natural that members of a club should enjoy certain advantages not enjoyed by non members. M. Undén then went on to explain that it would be difficult for the Swedish Government to formulate their policy, and they had studied the scheme which had been prepared by the military experts of the 3 Scandinavian Powers. He indicated to me that progress was being made and that with luck this military plan would be ready for consideration by the Swedish Government before February 1st. He then went on to make a remark the full significance of which I find some difficulty in assessing. He said that it was not impossible that Sweden might have certain things to offer in exchange for military equipment. He did, however, make an allusion to Bofors and it is possible that he had in mind certain new developments in gunnery of which the Admiralty Mission which came here this month have full details.

3. The conversation was friendly throughout. I have the impression that it would be prudent to hold our hands until the Swedish Government have considered the plan drawn up by the Scandinavian military experts. It is perhaps of interest in this connexion that in subsequent conversation with the Secretary General,[3] he seemed to evince more interest than has previously been shown in commitments which may be entered into by the Atlantic Pact Powers.

---

[1] Repeated to Washington, Oslo and Copenhagen.
[2] Not printed.
[3] Hans Beck-Friis.

No. 162

Minute from Mr Hankey to Mr Bateman, 22 December 1948
Top Secret (FO 371/71453, N13444/3001/63G)

Sweden and the North Atlantic Pact
This question is evolving rather rapidly. The present position is as follows.
Swedish Attitude
2. The Swedish attitude remains unchanged in spite of the warning which the Americans have given to the Swedish Government that they could only expect to receive a very low priority for the supply of arms if they do not join the Atlantic Pact. (The precise text of what the US Ambassador in Stockholm said has now been given to us and is in N13413 (Flag A).[1] The Swedish General Staff are agreed that Sweden could not do otherwise than associate herself with the West but they have not so far been able to convert the Swedish politicians to this view (see N 13443—Flag B).[1] Mr Farquhar has discussed the question now with Monsieur Undén himself (N 13444—Flag C).[2] Monsieur Undén appears to be disinclined to be hurried in his consideration of the scheme which the military experts of the three Scandinavian powers are preparing. He seemed to regard the American communication about the supply of arms as not unnatural in the circumstances and implied that when it comes to the supply of arms Sweden might well have something to offer in return for military equipment, (even if as seems to be implied, she remains neutral).
3. On the other hand the Secretary-General of the Swedish Ministry for Foreign Affairs evinced more interest than previously in the Atlantic Pact and while the Swedish Ambassador in Oslo says that there is no hope of a Scandinavian Defence Agreement (N 13442—Flag D)[1] since the Swedish Government will not drop their insistence on neutrality, he hoped that some means could be found to keep the door open so that Sweden could come into an Atlantic Pact later *perhaps as a non-belligerent partner.*
4. Mr Farquhar maintains his previous strong recommendation that we should not apply anything which might be construed as 'pressure' to the Swedish Government. The latter have not yet definitely committed themselves to non-association with the West and until the Swedish Government refuse on political grounds to accept the military recommendations of all three Scandinavian General Staffs it seems to him wiser to lay off them, and not to bring the matter to a head (N 13443).
The Norwegian Attitude
5. Monsieur Hauge, the Norwegian Minister of Defence, has told Sir L. Collier that if it became clear that the Swedes were merely procrastinating in the Scandinavian talks which would very shortly become apparent when they are resumed on Jan.10, he thought that the Norwegian Government and probably the Danish Government too would be willing to bring the talks to an end if as now seemed probable they were given to understand from the West that they would be invited to discuss the Atlantic Pact some time in January. But he said it would be desirable to put off the invitation as long as possible, since the longer we should wait the more ready the public would be to accept the invitation when it came and

[1] Not printed.
[2] No. 161.

also because the Danes were not yet as far advanced as the Norwegians along the western road (see N 13422—Flag E).[3] The Norwegians will ask us some searching questions and a preview of this has been given to the Military Attaché. They concern the equipment which Norway would want and the facilities which Great Britain and America would expect to get from Norway in exchange for mutual aid. (N13372—Flag F).[1]

Danish Attitude

6. The Danes are still hiding their head in the sands of optimism about the outcome of the Scandinavian talks which, however, they think may last until June! (N13340—Flag G).

Discussions in Washington

7. The result of the discussions in Washington will be found in N 13400 (Flag H—see letter from Mr Hoyer Millar[1] and copy of Washington telegram No. 552 Saving behind it—Flag I).[1] It seems to be generally agreed in Washington that there is no prospect at the moment of getting the Swedes to join either a North Atlantic Pact or a Scandinavian Pact. The Americans will now take the lead in sounding the Norwegian and Danish Governments (and also the Icelandic Government) in due course as to whether they wish to participate in an Atlantic Pact and to instruct their representatives to participate in the final discussions on the text when it is elaborated. Therefore for the moment we should ignore Sweden and concentrate on Norway and Denmark, though if the Norwegians or Danes wish to do so they could explain the position in Stockholm. I think it is clear that we should approve these recommendations so far as the Scandinavian countries are concerned and inform our representatives in Stockholm, Oslo and Copenhagen accordingly; but we should add that it would be better if the American approach could be delayed until mid-January when the Scandinavian defence talks should be quite or almost concluded.

Strategic Requirements

8. Meanwhile the Chiefs of Staff have produced a most interesting paper (annexed at Flag J)[1] showing (*a*) what would be the Allied requirements for strategic facilities and (*b*) how much assistance the Allies will be able to give the Scandinavian countries if they were associated with the Atlantic Pact.

9. It appears that we will *require* the right to occupy the Faroes at the outbreak of war and 'we understand that the Americans will occupy Greenland'; and certain Naval and Air facilities in Scandinavian territories would be of great use to us as would also their resources. Apart from this, if the Scandinavian countries were to unite and follow a firm co-ordinating defence policy they could as a result of their ability to defend themselves be a valuable strategic asset even if they remain neutral. (With some outside assistance in material during peace and the prospect of maintenance during war there is a 'reasonable chance' that Norway and Sweden could jointly provide sufficient forces at least to make the Russians hesitate before embarking on a campaign in Scandinavia). On the other hand it seems clear that Norway and Denmark without Sweden are almost a pure liability, and if it were not for their shipping and their resources which we need and more particularly if it were not for the question of our occupying the Faroes, which I presume must be done by agreement, there would be something to be said on purely military grounds for leaving the Scandinavian powers out of an Atlantic Pact if we cannot have all three of them in it in some form (possibly by an interlocking arrangement

---

[3] Not printed. Hankey noted in the margin of his minute that Randall shared this view strongly.

between a Scandinavian Pact and the Atlantic Pact such as the scheme for Swedish non-belligerency proposed by the Northern Department which the State Department at an earlier stage approved with certain modifications at a working level) but we also have to look at this question from the political angle. If we do not bring the Norwegians and Danes into the Scandinavian Pact it seems clear that being left in isolation they will pursue a weaker attitude towards the Russians and may even start to appease, e.g. by voting for Russian resolutions at UNO and in other ways. This would be very bad for our interests and therefore it seems better to draw the Norwegians and Danes in under the Atlantic pact umbrella and to hope that a spell of unpleasant isolation and time for reflection will move the Swedes to attach themselves in some way at a later date to the other Scandinavian powers who will be very much better partners for them when they are strengthened and backed up by their membership of the Atlantic Pact. Therefore, on balance, I do not think that the Chiefs of Staff report should modify our decision on other grounds to approve what has been agreed in Washington (see paragraph 7 above).[4]

R.M.A. HANKEY

PS I now understand the Secretary of State wishes to discuss this question.[5]

---

[4] Kirkpatrick minuted on 22 December: 'I don't dissent, but 1. We shall lose the whole Atlantic Pact if we go in for perfection. 2. The Cabinet decision was to the effect that Norway & Denmark shd. be included if possible; but that any country which hesitated or caused delay should be immediately discarded'. Commenting on this and on the views of the Chiefs of Staff, Jebb noted on 24 December that he did not have many comments to make, other than to observe 'that we shall certainly have to explain (or rather the Americans will) to the Norwegians what, if any, military assistance could be given to them in the event of war, and I should think that this, for some time to come at any rate, would be inconsiderable except in the naval sphere. In any case, if Denmark did *not* come into the Atlantic Pact I do not see how we could obtain the use of bases in Greenland (except with Denmark's express consent) in peacetime, though in wartime no doubt they would at once be occupied, as indeed would be any bases in Iceland too.'

[5] Following further consideration by Bevin, Hankey wrote to Farquhar, Collier and Randall on 3 January to say that the Foreign Office shared the view that it would be a mistake at present to do anything which might be construed as 'pressure' on the Swedish Government. 'It would be wiser to lay off and not bring the matter to a head at present. We were glad to see . . . that your American colleague appears to have been won over to this view.' The Foreign Office agreed with the American view that they should concentrate on Norway and Denmark (FO 371/71454, N13444/637/63G).

CHAPTER IV

1949-1951

No. 163

Letter from Mr Hankey to Mr Farquhar, 3 January 1949
Top Secret and Personal (FO 371/71453, N13444/3001/63G)

[No salutation on this copy]

As you surmise, we have been considering the question of the Swedish attitude to the Atlantic Pact and of our own policy towards Sweden, particularly in the light of your recent reports ending with telegram No. 658 of the 18th December[1] (which have been most helpful to us). The Secretary of State has again considered this matter and, as the bag is just leaving, I think you may like to have the following outline of the policy which he has approved and which we propose to follow in the immediate future.

The most recent reports all suggest that the Swedish attitude on the neutrality issue and their refusal to form any closer association with the West, have remained unchanged in spite of the American warning reported in your telegram No. 656.[2] M. Undén himself does not appear to have been unduly perturbed by these representations (see your telegram No. 658) and seems disinclined to be hurried in his consideration of the defence scheme which is expected to emerge from the present inter-Scandinavian military talks. Although there is some ground for thinking that the Swedish Service Chiefs are now agreed that Sweden will have to throw in her lot with the West if it comes to war, the Swedish Ambassador in Oslo (see Collier's telegram No. 525)[2] has confirmed our previous fears that an effective Scandinavian defence arrangement would be rendered impossible by Sweden's insistence on neutrality. At the same time he evidently thinks that there is some chance that the Swedish Government might associate themselves with the Atlantic System later in some way—perhaps as a non-belligerent partner—if the door is left open for them to do so.

In the light of this situation, we share your view that it would be a mistake at the present to do anything which might be construed as 'pressure' by the Swedish Government. We agree that, as the latter have not yet definitely committed

---

[1] No. 161.
[2] Not printed. The US Ambassador to Sweden recommended to the Acting Secretary of State, Lovett, on 4 January that 'no approach to Swedes with invitation to join North Atlantic pact be made at this time either by US or Britain. I see many signs of effectiveness of our tactics in showing indifference to Swedish policy all of which would be undone if we made any approach to Swedes at this time. Let the Norwegians and/or Danes tell the Swedes about North Atlantic Pact if and when the time seems proper to them' (FRUS 1949, Vol. IV, p. 5).

themselves to non-association with the West, and unless and until they refuse on political grounds to accept the military recommendations of all three Scandinavian General Staffs, it is wiser to lay off them and not to bring the matter to a head at present. We were glad to see from your telegram No. 657[2] that your American colleague appears to have been won over to this view.

Meanwhile Washington telegram No. 552 Saving[2] (copied to you by the last bag) will have given you an idea of the way things have been developing in the Atlantic Pact talks in Washington. It now seems to be generally agreed that there is no prospect at the moment of getting the Swedes to join either a North Atlantic Pact or a Scandinavian Pact. The Americans will take the lead in sounding out the Norwegian and Danish Governments (and also the Icelandic Government) in due course—though this will probably not be before the middle of January—as to whether they wish to participate in an Atlantic Pact and to instruct their Washington representatives to take part in the preparation of a final text. Presumably they would have to be given some time (say until towards the end of January) to consider the matter. The Americans have also undertaken the responsibility of keeping the Norwegians and Danes generally informed of developments before the above approach is made.

Meanwhile, we are in agreement with the American view that during this phase we should leave Sweden alone and concentrate on Norway and Denmark; although if the Norwegians or Danes wish to do so, they could perhaps usefully explain the position in Stockholm. If we were to inform the Swedes directly of the draft provisions of the Atlantic Pact, M. Undén might well use the information to make trouble with Norwegian and Danish opinion. He would almost certainly reject an invitation to join the discussions and, having once rejected it, would be too obstinate ever to change his mind. It therefore seems better to leave the Swedes out of the picture for the moment in the hope that they will dislike the feeling of being deserted even by the other Scandinavian Powers and will ultimately try to find some way in which they can adhere directly or indirectly to the North Atlantic Pact (e.g. by some arrangement such as that suggested by the Swedish Ambassador in Oslo—see paragraph 2 above). This line of approach, which corresponds to your own recommendations, is also in line with the policy which has already been decided on here with regard to the Atlantic Pact, namely that Norway and Denmark should be included if possible, but that any country which hesitates or causes delays should be immediately discarded. It is clearly preferable that the Swedes should regret being left out in the cold and should then try to find some way of coming in, rather than that we should have to discard them owing to M. Undén's obstinate procrastination and push them still further into isolation.

I am sending copies of this letter to Laurence Collier, Alec Randall and to Derek Hoyer Millar.

R.M.A. HANKEY

No. 164

Letter from Mr Hankey to Sir L. Collier (Oslo), 11 January 1949
Confidential (FO 371/77459, N 320/1351/30)

[No salutation on this copy]

We have now received the opinion of the Law Officers regarding the question of taking the Norwegian Fisheries dispute to the Cabinet and I am sending you a copy separately for your own confidential information. Beckett[1] asked me to remind you in doing this that the Law Officers' opinion should not be referred to in speaking to the Norwegians and is utterly confidential.

As you see, the Law Officers are of the opinion that while it is impossible to forecast with any confidence what might be the ultimate verdict of the International Court, it is unlikely that the Norwegian claim to the so-called Blue Line would be accepted. They are inclined to believe, though here again they cannot advise with certainty, that the boundary which the Court might lay down would probably be somewhere between the Green Line and the Red Line. They seem confident that a submission to the International Court is in principle the right course and they do not think that any substantial concessions going beyond the Red Line should be offered to the Norwegians as a means of avoiding the risk of an adverse decision by the Court.

The next stage will be to bring the Law Officers' opinion to the Cabinet, who had doubts last time the matter was mentioned whether the matter should be taken to The Hague or not, in the event of final disagreement after the London discussions.

Meanwhile the talks with Dr. Bull have continued yesterday and today and after very nearly breaking down in the early stages, the Delegations have now got down to discussing possible lines for fishing limits in detail. The proposal we have been considering is that in the southern part of the fishing areas the line should be more or less the same as the Blue Line (i.e. the 1935 line) whereas in the north the line should correspond more or less to the Green Line (i.e. 4 mile limit with 10 mile base lines).

The Norwegians began by saying that the Green Line in the northern part was absolutely out of the question for them, but at our invitation made a counter proposition which is now being developed in discussion. I think it is not impossible that we may agree to recommend to the Governments a compromise proposal which will in fact be the Green Line in parts and also approximate to the Red Line in parts. But both sides seem very doubtful whether there is any chance of getting the respective industries to agree to such a line. If something of this sort can be agreed, we have some grounds for hoping that we might be able to get a sensible *status quo* agreement. We are particularly anxious to get this if possible even if it involves some derogations from the Red Line and even if it involves only a 'lenient enforcement' arrangement on the Norwegian side, because otherwise claims and incidents will pile up and, I am afraid, create so much ill-will that it will be very much harder to reach any settlement of the main question—to say nothing of the effect on our relations with Norway and even on the problem of Norway's attachment to the Atlantic Pact. We recognise that we must now allow the Norwegians to trade on our forbearance in this matter. But Beckett is very anxious

[1] Sir W.E. Beckett was Legal Adviser to the Foreign Office.

that we should remember the atmosphere in the International Court in case the matter should ultimately come there. The Corfu case has been a gift to the critics of this country who grumble about the British Navy sailing up and down 'trailing its coat', and Beckett fears that the atmosphere at the Court would not be at all improved if the British Fishery Protection vessels had been involved in serious incidents within an area claimed by the Norwegians even though we maintained that it formed part of the high seas. This, together with the delay in securing the Law Officers' opinion and Cabinet authority to take the matter to The Hague in the event of final disagreement, explains the reluctance we have shown in London to precipitate matters. We have, however, now persuaded the Admiralty to provide two or three Fishery Protection vessels for the coming season off the Norwegian coast with instructions to collect independent evidence of any incidents that may occur and to warn the Norwegians in every case that interference by them with British vessels outside areas where we recognise their competence will inevitably be followed by financial claims (I am quoting this from memory; the instructions I believe are not yet finally drafted).

From the long term point of view, we very much hope that the present discussions in London may result in a Line which will be agreed on both sides, even if this has to be imposed by governments on the industries concerned—though this will clearly be very difficult for the Norwegian Government and will not be easy for us. There seem to be real advantages in settling this question by agreement if we possibly can and I think Dr. Bull feels very much the same about it. At the worst I should hope that we may possibly be able to agree on a Line which will form the basis of a *status quo* understanding while the matter is taken to The Hague court, since it may be 9 months or a year before we have a decision.

R.M.A. HANKEY

No. 165

Sir L. Collier (Oslo) to Mr Bevin, 12 January 1949, 11.06 a.m.[1]
Tel. No. 11 Important, Secret (FO 371/77391, N390/1071/63G)

Stockholm telegram No. 12: Scandinavian Defence.[2]

I learn from a reliable Norwegian source that at the Karlstad meeting[3] the Swedes offered to supply from Bofors all Norwegian requirements of war material. This taken in conjunction with the remarks by the Swedish Minister for Foreign Affairs reported in Stockholm telegram No. 3[2] seems to show that the Swedish Government expects the Western Powers, by providing means for increasing Bofors production, to enable Sweden to remain outside the Atlantic Pact and perhaps keep Norway out as well. If so I venture to agree with Farquhar that it is for consideration whether M. Undén should not be disillusioned as soon as possible.

2. The same source reports that the Norwegian Government are ready to accede to the Atlantic Pact on two conditions:

---

[1] Repeated to Stockholm, Copenhagen and Washington.
[2] Not printed.
[3] The Prime Ministers, Foreign Ministers and Defence Ministers of Sweden, Norway and Denmark met in Karlstad, Sweden, on 5-6 January 1949 to discuss a Scandinavian defence pact.

(1) that Norway will receive instant help if attacked and
(2) that the additional war material which she requires can be obtained immediately (i.e. within the next few months).

The source is in touch with the Minister of Defence but this goes beyond what the latter said last month as reported in my letter to Hankey of December 15th.[2]

No. 166

Minute from Mr Hankey to Mr Bateman, 13 January 1949
(FO 371/77391, N390/1071/63G)

The latest telegrams from Oslo and Copenhagen seem to show that the Scandinavian powers are very much impressed by the Swedish offer of a Scandinavian Pact even though it is apparently made on a condition of neutrality. This is (from their point of view) admittedly a very great advance by the Swedes and if only some way could be found round the condition of neutrality which the Swedes make it would be of great advantage for ourselves, since we do not need very much from the Danes and Norwegians, and from a defence point of view they are, without the Swedes, a not inconsiderable liability.

2. The talks held in Washington just before Christmas led to the conclusion that for the time being we should let the Swedes alone and try to draw the Norwegians and the Danes into an Atlantic Pact in the hope that the Swedes would later make defence arrangements with them in their own interests.[1] It is possible that this may still be our best course, but from Copenhagen telegram No. 10 (Flag A)[2] it appears that the Danes have already run out and the Norwegians now seem likely to make impossible conditions about coming into the Atlantic Pact (see Oslo telegram No. 11—Flag B).[3]

3. We are expecting further information from Oslo for which we have telegraphed, but meanwhile I have been considering whether in the last resort we should not make quite a different arrangement to provide both for a Scandinavian Pact which would buttress Scandinavia and give us substantially the defence facilities which we need. The suggestion is contained in the annexed memorandum which has been prepared after discussion with Brigadier Price in the Ministry of Defence.

4. If this proposal is thought worthy of further examination the first step would be to send the memorandum to Washington for discussion with the State Department. The joint planners or Chiefs of Staff organisation might, in Brigadier Price's view, consider it simultaneously.

5. The matter is very urgent because the Scandinavian discussions are clearly coming to a head at the end of this month and if we are to exert an effective pull on the Danes and the Norwegians we must obviously be prepared to do it now.

---

[1] See the Report of the International Working Group to the Ambassadors' Committee, 24 December 1948 (FRUS 1948, Vol. III, pp. 333-43).
[2] Not printed.
[3] No. 165.

Scandinavian Defence and the Atlantic Pact

As Norway and Denmark are by themselves rather a defence liability to the Atlantic Powers, it is most desirable that they should be buttressed by a Scandinavian Defence Pact if possible.

2. We have already devised a possible system to meet this difficulty in agreement with the State Department and our own Chiefs of Staff. Briefly our proposal was that the Norwegians, Danes and Swedes should conclude a Scandinavian Defence Pact but only Norway and Denmark should join the Atlantic Pact. In the event of Norway and Denmark being involved in war through their membership of the Atlantic Pact but not being physically attacked, Sweden would remain *non-belligerent* and would only enter the war if Denmark or Norway was physically attacked. In the event of Sweden being attacked Norway and Denmark would go to her assistance in accordance with the Scandinavian Pact but Sweden would only be entitled to immediate *consultation* with the Western Powers. It is believed that M. Lange, who is aware of this proposal, suggested something of the sort to M. Undén who rejected it in the recent Scandinavian discussions.

3. Sweden's insistence in the Scandinavian Defence negotiations that a Scandinavian *bloc* should be *entirely neutral* and that no members of it should be connected with the Atlantic Pact would, if persisted in, make a system such as this impossible. It might, however, be conceivable to find a solution which could be made acceptable to the Swedes in another way. Such a plan might be as follows:

(*a*) Sweden, Norway and Denmark conclude a Scandinavian Pact of Mutual Assistance.

(*b*) Denmark and Norway do not join the Atlantic Pact but they make the following arrangements with Great Britain and America:

(*c*) Great Britain receives naval facilities in the Faroe Islands which are not covered by the Swedish offer of the Scandinavian Pact (the Chiefs of Staff say that we require such facilities in the event of war.)

(*d*) The US get bases in Greenland which are also not covered by the Swedish offer.

(*e*) The Norwegians undertake to prevent shipping hostile to the Atlantic Powers from infiltrating along their coast line as happened at the beginning of the last war.

(*f*) Denmark and Norway undertake to defend their territory (including territorial waters) and independence against direct or indirect aggression to the best of their ability in accordance with article 51 of the Charter (which is the same general undertaking as is given by the members of the Atlantic Pact).

(*g*) Norway and Denmark also agree to make provisional plans with British and American staffs so that in the event of being attacked and asking for assistance this can be given so far as it may be possible.

(*h*) In return for these undertakings by Norway and Denmark and for the Swedish guarantee of these two countries in the security of which Great Britain and America are interested, His Majesty's Government and the US Government agree to continue to give the Danish, Norwegian and also Swedish governments such help as may be in their power in the supply of arms and equipment and technical advice.

4. Such a system would not compromise the neutrality of any of the Scandinavian powers though it would more or less turn them into friendly or non-belligerent neutrals and it might, therefore, be possible to secure Swedish agreement to it. It is clear that the Swedes are very worried about the supply of

arms. Stockholm telegram No. 19[1] says the three Commanders-in-Chief of the Swedish armed forces are all equally alarmed lest a policy of isolation might jeopardise the armament and modernisation of the Swedish armed forces, and the fact that the Swedish Ambassador has canvassed almost every senior member of the Foreign Office who has anything to do with the Atlantic Pact and has particularly emphasised the desirability of our continuing to supply arms to Scandinavia even if it is not neutral, seems to show quite clearly that the Swedes are not feeling at all sure of their position. If we are fairly tough about the supply of arms it may therefore be possible to induce the Swedes to come some distance to meet us.

5. The system outlined in para. 3 above would also have the advantage that by leaving Scandinavia neutral it would give the Russians less excuse to occupy Finland, a consideration which weighs very much with the Swedes though it seems clear that the Russians could occupy Finland at any time if they really wished to do so.

6. While the British defence link with Norway and Denmark would probably be preserved, the system outlined above has the disadvantage that the Scandinavian countries would definitely be wedded to a policy of neutrality and semi-isolation under Swedish leadership, and we should probably have to accept that they would drift away into a passive and weak-kneed policy in political matters towards the Soviet Union and might even on occasion appease the latter in fairly important questions. From our point of view it is therefore very much less satisfactory than the plan outlined in paragraph 2 above.[4]

R.M.A. HANKEY

[4] Bateman minuted on Hankey's proposal: 'This is an ingenious plea either (*a*) to put the Hankey-Hickerson plan to the Swedes now or (*b*) to tell the Swedes that arms would be supplied from the West only if they allowed some freedom to Denmark and Norway to make strategic plans with the West. The first alternative is preferable and could be put to the Swedish MFA if the US Govt. agree.' Hankey added: 'Discussed with Sir G. Jebb in the light of Oslo tel. No 23 since received.' See No. 168. (FO 371/77391, N390/1071/63G).

No. 167

Letter from Mr Farquhar to Mr Hankey, 13 January 1949
Top Secret (FO 371/77400, N552/1074/63G)

My dear Robin,

The situation, as far as Sweden is concerned, seems to be changing rather rapidly as a result of the American approach (which may or may not have been well timed) to the Danes and Norwegians and what we know of the decisions taken at the Karlstad meeting. I hope you will not mind if I go in for a bit of 'thinking aloud' and inflict these thoughts on you in a somewhat disjointed form so as to catch today's bag.

A. Up to a certain point it may be true, as M. Rasmussen claims, that Sweden's offer to enter a Scandinavian defence alliance under which an attack on any of the signatories would be held to be an attack on all was a 'remarkable and historic commitment' (Copenhagen telegram No. 10).[1] There is a school of thought in Sweden which envisages the next war somewhat as follows: When the Russians start sweeping forward into Europe they would obviously gobble up Denmark and would in all probability try to take possession of at least the Northern part of the West coast of Norway. If they did that—and who could stop it—there would be no point in Russia invading Sweden. It would be a waste of manpower. Sweden therefore need only bow her head to the storm and indulge in a policy of appeasement; she would thereby avoid physical invasion. She could lie low in a position of inglorious encirclement and neutrality until such time as the Western Powers stage a comeback. This opinion is held more in political than in military circles.

But is this such a 'remarkable and historic' commitment when you add on to it M. Undén's proviso that there was little hope of a Scandinavian defence pact if any one of the three Scandinavian powers were to enter into any other and outside commitment (para. 5 of my telegram No. 11)?[1] It would seem that so far neither M. Rasmussen nor M. Lange have admitted this in conversation with Randall and Collier. But I am inclined to think that he did say so since otherwise why should M. Rasmussen have begged Randall to represent to you 'Denmark's dilemma'?

B. In assuming that M. Undén did say this, is he or is he not exercising on Denmark and Norway that very pressure which he promised not to exert (your despatch No. 152 of June 18th[1] and my telegram No. 392 of the 29th June)?[1]

C. It is difficult to resist the conclusion that Messrs Erlander, Undén and Vougt were rather overselling Sweden as a powerful military state full of confidence in their armed forces and fully capable of supplying the military needs of all three Scandinavian powers. Both I and Collier have already raised the question of Bofors' capacity (my telegram No. 12 of the 8th January[1] and Oslo telegram No. 11 of the 12th January)[2] and I needn't develop this any further. I am, however, wondering whether the Swedish Prime Minister and Foreign Minister were talking out of ignorance or whether the first two had been misinformed by Vougt. It is difficult to believe that their own Service chiefs have not given them the facts of the case.

But apart from overselling Bofors, these three Swedish politicians seem to have been overselling their country as a military factor, and ignoring the warnings which have been repeatedly given to them by their Service Commanders-in-Chief. It would be presumptuous of me to pose as a military expert and you can always get a good appreciation of what the Swedish armed forces could do in the face of an unprovoked aggression from Russia from the Chiefs of Staff Committee and the Service Departments. As I understand it, however, the Swedish army can put about 8 divisions and 3 independent brigades in the field. There are one or two snags to this. In the first place their regular army of 13,000, plus 23,000 conscripts now under training, is only in theory available to meet a sudden attack. It is not organised as a field force. In the second place it would take her about 3 months to mobilise her 8 divisions, etc. The Swedes have a nice little air force and they hope to make it still nicer and larger as long as we go on delivering to them all those jet propelled fighters, heavy ground radar, etc., we have promised them. It is perhaps of interest that Nordenskiöld (C-in-C, Swedish Air Force), who talks very openly and sometimes indiscreetly, has at various times during the past summer estimated

---

[1] Not printed.
[2] No. 165.

that his air force could, without outside aid, remain in the air against the Russians for about three weeks. The Swedish navy could, I understand, give quite a good account of itself and cope with a seaborne invasion *for as long as* it has adequate air cover. Nordenskiöld once remarked to me rather bitterly that he wished his opposite number in the Swedish Navy, and also his civilian Minister of Defence, would realise that ships were no use without planes, and didn't Admiral Phillips make that discovery in the last war?[3] Now if Sweden is proposing to rush to the aid of gallant little Norway and brave little Denmark, how many divisions does she want to guard her own metropolitan territory (it is a long way from Malmö to her northernmost frontier, northeast of Narvik) and at the same time send enough divisions to Denmark to seal off even a part of that territory? A little thin on the ground?

D. Our best friends in Sweden, i.e. those who are strongest for co-operation with the West, are the Service Chiefs. They are about to warn the politicians that if Sweden opts for neutrality or rather isolation, the tap is likely to be turned off by the Western Powers and that Sweden will not get the arms, etc., she must have. If the politicians ignore these warnings and we go on supplying them with essential military equipment, our friends are made to look like fools and M. Undén & Company can almost adopt the attitude of Hitler to his Generals.

E. If Norway and Denmark adhere to the Atlantic Pact they clearly expect to get arms from the West. In fact in their opinion they feel that politically it is a risky step for them to take but they are prepared to do it if they can be quickly rearmed. What would these two countries think if after they had taken the plunge they found Sweden was getting exactly the same by having remained on the beach? From what I can gather from what I know of the draft of the Pact, those of the participating powers that *can* supply military equipment are going to do so to the others on a sort of Lend-Lease basis and that 'no questions of finance' should be involved. (Para. 2(*iii*) and (*v*) of Washington telegram No. 24 of the 3rd January).[1] It would be rather awkward if we had to tell the Norwegians that we couldn't give them any jet fighters on account of a previous contract with the Swedes.

F. To sum up:
(1) The Swedes *are* exercising indirect pressure on Norway and Denmark. In doing so, M. Undén is doing what he said he would not do.
(2) The Swedes *are* overselling their country as a military factor. Their politicians may be doing it out of ignorance but I have a suspicion that these very upright gentlemen are also being a little bit 'slick'.
(3) As soon as we become signatories of the Atlantic pact we automatically undertake enlarged commitments in the way of the provisions of military material, etc. Would it be unreasonable if we then served notice to the Swedes as indicated in para. 3 of your telegram No. 10856 to Washington of the 29th September?[1]
(4) In view of the last paragraph of your letter N 13444/637/G of the 3rd January,[1] I would not suggest any further direct approach to Undén from this post, but there might be advantage in reminding the Norwegians, and the Danes, of Undén's undertaking, which he agreed could be communicated to the Governments of those two countries, and also in giving the Norwegians enough dope to enable them to debunk Sweden's claim to be an arsenal for Scandinavia. Such a move would seem to fit in with the suggestions contained in Collier's telegram No. 11 of the 12th

---

[3] Admiral Sir Tom Phillips commanded Task Force Z, which included the *Prince of Wales* and the *Renown*, both of which were sunk by Japanese aircraft off Malaya on 10 December 1941.

January.
I am sending copies of this letter to Laurence Collier, Alec Randall and Derek Hoyer Millar.

Yours ever,
H. FARQUHAR

No. 168

Sir L. Collier (Oslo), to Mr Bevin, 14 January 1949, 8.09 p.m.[1]
Tel. No. 23 Top Secret, Light (FO 371/77391, N459/1071/63)

Your telegram No. 38: Scandinavian Defence.[2]

Norwegian Minister for Foreign Affairs tells me that the timetable is as stated in my telegram No. 19[2] and that there is no question of requesting the postponement of the invitation to discuss the Atlantic Pact until the second half of February. On the contrary Norwegian and Danish Ambassadors at Washington have just been instructed to inform the United States Government that their Governments require time until February 1st to consider the report of the Technical Defence Committee which has now held its last meeting at Oslo after which they will be ready to receive the invitation. When that comes however they will put before the United States Government (and His Majesty's Government as well) considerations arising out of the special conditions in Scandinavia.

2. The Minister for Foreign Affairs said the meaning of this last statement was that at Karlstad the Swedes while repeating that they could not defend Denmark with their own resources (please see my telegram No. 10)[2] had undertaken to defend Denmark as well as Norway, if these resources were supplemented from the West. They accordingly proposed that the United States Government should be asked to supply armaments to a Scandinavian Defence Union which would not join the Atlantic Pact for fear of precipitating a militarist [*sic*] attack on Sweden but would ensure that all three States would fight if one were attacked though not otherwise.

3. The Danes had supported this proposal because they were desperately afraid that Denmark would be the first Scandinavian country to be attacked and would not receive from the West the immediate help which could be expected from Sweden under this plan. The Norwegian Minister for Foreign Affairs had pointed out that as he had twice been told by Mr Marshall, the United States Government were unalterably opposed to providing assistance of this sort to Governments which [?entered into] no reciprocal obligations towards them; but the Swedes and Danes urged that they might change their view if the proposal was made to them by all three Scandinavian Governments and the Norwegians finally agreed to join in putting the question because, as the Minister for Foreign Affairs said to me, 'there are more isolationists, even in Norway, than would appear from the press and it is important to give them no handle for saying that we have not done our utmost to preserve Scandinavian solidarity'.

4. The Minister for Foreign Affairs indicated that the attitude of the Danish Minister for Foreign Affairs had not been very loyal. At Karlstad he had originally supported a Swedish proposal that Scandinavian Defence Union should be formed on the Swedish terms and should ask then for arms from the United States

---

[1] Repeated to Copenhagen, Stockholm and Washington.
[2] Not printed.

Government, thus presenting them with a *fait accompli* which the Norwegians had rejected as patently dishonest. He had not kept his promise to regard the Karlstad conversations as confidential and he now seemed to be inspiring tendentious articles in the Danish press. His idea that secret understandings about Western military help could be combined with adherence to a disarmed neutrality was impracticable and disingenuous: these could never be kept from the Swedish Government who were determined not to be a party to anything which the Russians could regard as provocation and would repudiate any Defence Union which did not remain on a basis of neutrality. He thought neither Danish nor Swedish Ministers for Foreign Affairs capable of viewing the situation objectively owing to their panic fear of Russia. For his own part, he thought that the Russians were no more, probably less, likely to attack Sweden at once if she joined in the Atlantic Pact than if she did not, nor did he see how far the United States Government and His Majesty's Government could be expected themselves to provide means of enabling the Scandinavian countries to refuse to play their part in the common defence of the West.

5. I venture to agree with this estimate and in view of Copenhagen telegram No. 14,[2] to express the hope that we shall not support the plans of the Danish Minister for Foreign Affairs for fear of being accused of splitting Scandinavian unity. The Norwegian Minister for Foreign Affairs intimated to me that he could help us to deal with that argument and I think that he can be trusted to do so effectively when the time comes.[3]

---

[3] Hankey noted that the timetable was now clear. He highlighted Collier's recommendation in paragraph 5 that 'we should *not* answer this question in the affirmative for fear of splitting Scandinavian unity. Sir L Collier has always emphasised to us the danger that the Swedes would pull the Norwegians and the Danes altogether away from us if they possibly could. The underlined passages in Oslo telegram No. 19 seem to show that the Norwegian Government intend to come into the Atlantic Pact if the answer is in the negative. But it will be hard to meet their defence needs in such conditions' (FO 371/77391. N459/1071/63G).

No. 169

Mr Bevin to Mr Farquhar (Stockholm), 16 January 1949, 11.55 p.m.[1]
Tel. No. 30 Important, Top Secret (FO 371/77392, N547/1071/63)

During the last few days Swedish Ambassador[2] has approached several officials in this Department on the subject of Scandinavian defence. His purpose was clearly to sound our reactions on latest developments before his return to Stockholm for consultation.

2. Ambassador was at pains to prove that it was in fact to the interest of the Western Powers to accept and support an effective Scandinavian defence arrangement such as Sweden was now prepared to conclude with Norway and Denmark. The Swedish Government he said, were definitely not prepared to join the North Atlantic Pact and the other two Governments would have to choose between adherence to the Pact and the proposed Scandinavian system, for they could not have both. While the Norwegians seemed to have decided on the former alternative, the Danish attitude was less certain. But would it not really be to the

---

[1] Repeated to Washington, Oslo and Copenhagen.
[2] Gunnar Hägglöf.

advantage of Britain and America if these two countries formed a neutral Scandinavian *bloc* with Sweden? Such an arrangement would provide a more effective deterrent to aggression than a divided Scandinavia, the more so as it seemed that at present Britain and America could give Norway and Denmark very little help if they were attacked. Sweden had taken an unprecedented step in offering to enter into such an arrangement and moreover she would herself provide the bulk of the armaments required, thus relieving the United States and United Kingdom of the burden they would have to shoulder if Norway and Denmark were directly dependent on them for arms. Some assistance in the way of military supplies from the West would however still be required and the Swedish Government had therefore been alarmed by recent statements of the United States Ambassador in Stockholm threatening the cessation of American deliveries unless Sweden joined the Atlantic Pact. The Ambassador wished to know whether this was the considered view of the United States Government. He urged that such a policy would in fact be contrary to the interests of the Western Powers, who should welcome the establishment of a firm Scandinavian defence system and do everything in their power to strengthen it.

3. It was made clear to the Ambassador at the outset that whatever reasons the Swedish Government might have for their attitude over the Atlantic Pact we looked to them not to exert pressure on the other two Scandinavian Governments. Ambassador emphatically denied that there was any question of this.

4. It was explained to him that we considered it extremely improbable that adherence of Norway and Denmark to the Atlantic Pact would precipitate any aggressive Soviet move. The Russians would be more likely to be encouraged to pursue an expansionist course if the West appeared confused, weak or disunited and therefore the more countries associated themselves with the Atlantic Pact (even though, in the unlikely event of war in the near future, it might not be possible to provide immediately for the defence of every part of every country) the less likely would the Russians be to take any military action. On the other hand the formation of neutral *blocs* such as that now proposed for Scandinavia was more likely to increase the danger to the rest of the world which was prepared to assume obligations of self-defence.

5. Ambassador was informed that after careful consideration we had definitely decided that a neutral Scandinavian *bloc* was not in our interests. Scandinavian countries were too weak in our view either to deter, or offer effective resistance to, the Russians without outside help and we were equally convinced that in view of its strategic position Scandinavia could not hope to keep out of any war between Russia and the West. Under the Vandenberg Resolution[3] it would be extremely difficult for the United States to supply arms to a Scandinavian *bloc* which remained entirely neutral. Furthermore, what assurance would we have that Scandinavian neutrality, which we were asked to support along with deliveries of military material, would not for so long as it lasted be applied in a one-sided manner to our military disadvantage? We were naturally interested in the defence of Scandinavia, but experience of the last war had unfortunately taught us that it was unprofitable, in the absence of definite guarantees, to dissipate resources which we needed for ourselves and our Allies in order to supply Nations who refused to make defence plans with us. While the Ambassador, who was clearly

---

[3] The Vandenberg Resolution, passed in the Senate in June 1948, supported the association of the United States, by constitutional procedures, with regional or collective security arrangements.

worried over this question, was not told positively that no arms would be forthcoming for countries who remained neutral, it was made clear that in allocation of limited supplies our Allies would naturally have preferential treatment.

6. It was further pointed out to the Ambassador that the Western Powers had not sought to dissuade the Norwegians and Danes from making defence arrangements with the Swedes—on the contrary, they had encouraged them to do so—and it was only the Swedes who had taken the line that Norway and Denmark *must choose* between the Western powers and a Scandinavian *bloc*. This seemed to us both regrettable and illogical, since we all had the same political aggressor in view, and, to turn his question round, would it not really be in Sweden's interest if Norway and Denmark were associated with the Atlantic Pact and were greatly strengthened thereby? Would it not then also be to Sweden's advantage to make defence arrangements with Norway and Denmark so as to prevent the encirclement of Sweden which might result from a Russian attack on these countries? Ambassador seemed rather to agree, but said that Sweden did not want to be involved if, for instance, Norway went to war as a result of a Soviet attack on Western Europe. It was suggested to him that with a little ingenuity a system could no doubt be devised whereby Sweden would only become directly involved if Norway or Denmark were physically attacked (this would be the position under the Northern Department plan; which it appears was mentioned by Norwegian Minister for Foreign Affairs in recent Scandinavian discussions but rejected by the Swedes).

7. In reply to his questions Ambassador was generally informed of the present state of negotiations in Washington and future prospects, particularly as regards position of Italy (if she did not join the Pact), Greece and Turkey. It was indicated that it was hoped that there would be agreement on some form of collective assurance to these countries.

No. 170

Sir L. Collier (Oslo) to Mr Bevin, 17 January 1949, 2.29 p.m.,[1]
with minute by Mr Hankey
Tel. No. 25 Important, Top Secret (FO 371/77392, N551/1071/63G)

My telegram No. 23: Scandinavian Defence.[2]

On January 15th I discussed the position with the United States Ambassador as instructed in your telegram No. 38.[3] He told me spontaneously of recommendations of United States Ambassador at Copenhagen and added that he was advising State Department to reject them,[4] which indeed they seemed to have done already to judge from their statement published in the press that morning confirming declarations that United States Government would not supply arms to

---

[1] Repeated to Copenhagen, Stockholm and Washington.
[2] No. 168.
[3] Not printed.
[4] For the US Ambassador's report of this meeting, see FRUS 1949, Vol. IV, pp. 34-36. He wrote: 'I believe that any support of such fallacious and weak-kneed Danish policy at this critical point would be disastrous in its consequences to Norway and to Norwegian morale. By espousing or offering slightest encouragement to such course we might not only lose Denmark as prospective member Atlantic Pact, but would undermine whole Norwegian position.'

countries refusing to enter obligations towards them. (This is reported in the Washington press as the death blow to Karlstad proposals.)

2. Ambassador said that he thought his colleague must have gone 'haywire'. He could not see there was any real change in Swedish policy. Sweden had always been willing and indeed anxious to obtain arms from the West and though the Karlstad plan implied that she would receive these on a more systematic basis it did not commit her to doing anything new in return for them except to defend Denmark as well as Norway ([?to whom] she had promised defences in any case) while on the other hand it would definitely keep Norway as well as Denmark out of the Atlantic Pact. He could see no evidence that the Swedish Government were weakening in their determination to have nothing to do with the Pact and to keep Norway and Denmark out of it if possible and he thought that the Danish Prime Minister must have had his tongue in his cheek when he suggested that acceptance of the Karlstad plan would bring Scandinavia into the Pact within six months. In his view result would be exactly contrary since Western Powers by accepting the principle of Scandinavian neutrality would have convinced public opinion in all three countries that they themselves did not believe anything more was required and Swedish Government would not fail to point this out if asked to go further in future. Norwegian willingness to accept Atlantic Pact was the only firm foundation on which we could build. If we let that go we should lose substance for the shadow, but if we held on to it we might bring the Danes round now and perhaps the Swedes themselves later on when they realised full disadvantages of isolation.

3. Above views are also held by Counsellor of United States Embassy (who is more experienced than the Ambassador) and I entirely agree with them. The Ambassador proposes to ask Danish Ambassador if he can influence his Government in the right direction and I propose to do likewise if you see no objection.

Minute from Hankey to Bateman 20 January 1949

Please see also Stockholm telegram No. 30 (Flag A),[3] Copenhagen telegram No. 19 (Flag B)[3] and Washington telegram No. 20 Saving (Flag C)[3] submitted herewith.

The following main points emerge from these telegrams:

(*a*) The State Department have informed the Scandinavian Governments that the Vandenberg Resolution definitely precludes the supply of arms to a neutral Scandinavian *bloc*.

(*b*) The Swedes have received the intimation, which merely repeats what was said to them last November, with equanimity (see Stockholm telegram No. 30 (Flag A)).

(*c*) The Danes were at first upset at a move which they think will split Scandinavian solidarity; but the Danish Minister for Foreign Affairs said he *supposed* that Norway would now accept an invitation to discuss the Atlantic Pact and that Denmark *would in all probability* join her. The Danish attitude is still rather wobbly (see Copenhagen telegram No. 19 at Flag B).

(*d*) In the telegram in this jacket Sir L. Collier says that he and his American colleague are both convinced that if the Western Powers once accept the principle of Scandinavian neutrality the Swedes are sure to lead Denmark and Norway away from the Western Powers. Norwegian willingness to accept the Atlantic Pact is the only firm foundation on which we can build and if we hold on to it we might bring the Danes round now and even perhaps the Swedes themselves later on when they realise the full disadvantages of isolation. There is much force in Sir L. Collier's views (and he has been consistently right so far in this question). All the same I think in our own interests we should try to get the Scandinavians to accept a system of interlocking pacts if we possibly can. A draft to Washington has been submitted on this separately.

(*e*) Finally Washington telegram No. 20 saving (Flag C) confirms what we have surmised, that the Icelandic Government (who will be represented at the Oslo meeting on January 28th and 29th) will be guided by the attitude of Denmark and Norway. I think it is very important that the Icelanders should be in the Atlantic Pact and this is an additional consideration in favour of Sir. L. Collier's views.

R.M.A. HANKEY

No. 171

Minute from Mr Hankey to Mr Bateman, 25 January 1949
Top Secret (FO 371/77729, N726/1194/42G)

Armaments Production of Bofors A.B.

Please see also Mr Farquhar's letter in N552/1074/63G (Flag A)[1] and CoS letter at N4929/G (Flag C).[2]

In his telegram No. 12 (Flag G)[2] Mr Farquhar suggested that Monsieur Undén's claims that Bofors arms production was capable of covering the bulk of defence requirements of all three Scandinavian countries—and indeed of supplying some of the arms needed by Western Union—was greatly exaggerated. This matter has now been examined by JIB and the paper in this jacket generally confirms Mr Farquhar's view. It shows that, while Bofors are outstanding in the field of research and design, they are not organised for mass production and the contribution which they could make would be very small quantitatively. A further JIB paper, attached at Flag I,[2] shows that Sweden's other arms production, while not negligible is not sufficient to affect this conclusion.

Both Mr Farquhar and Sir L. Collier have recommended that we should take steps to expose the exaggerated nature of the Swedish claims regarding Sweden's military potential, which have been freely used by the Swedes in their recent attempt to dissuade the Norwegians and the Danes from entering into the Atlantic Pact. It seemed worthwhile to send the JIB paper to Sir L. Collier and Mr Randall and authorise them to make judicious use of this information in conversation with the Norwegian and Danish Ministers for Foreign Affairs if they still see fit and if a suitable opportunity occurs so that they should at least know the correct position in reaching this decision. A letter has been sent by the bag that left this afternoon.

Mr Farquhar's letter at Flag A makes four further points, namely:

(*a*) That Monsieur Undén has broken his undertaking, given personally to the Secretary of State last March, not to exert pressure on Norway and Denmark to

[1] No. 167
[2] Not printed

prevent them from collaborating more closely with the West. (This point has already been dealt with in recent minutes).

(*b*) That, in addition to exaggerating the importance of Bofors, the Swedes have also exaggerated the capacity of their armed forces to defend Scandinavia effectively.

(*c*) That if Sweden remains neutral and we continue to supply her with essential military equipment, this will embarrass and discourage our friends in Sweden, notably the Swedish Service Chiefs.

(*d*) If Norway and Denmark join the Atlantic Pact while Sweden remains strictly neutral it will be awkward if Sweden gets just the same treatment as the others regarding the supply of arms, and there might also be very awkward questions of priority between them. Mr Farquhar has suggested that it might therefore be desirable for us in certain circumstances to invoke the *force majeure* clauses which are contained in most of our contracts with the Swedes.

Points (*c*) and (*d*) raise again the vexed question of our policy with regard to the supply of arms to Sweden. This question was recently re-examined by the Chiefs of Staff, who decided (see letter to Sir Orme Sargent at Flag C),[2] that no alteration in our existing policy was called for at present. I think, however, that if, as now seems quite possible, Norway and Denmark join the Atlantic Pact and Sweden persists in her policy of neutrality, it will be very difficult for us to continue our present practice as regards military deliveries to Sweden, at least where it involves supplying her with important and scarce material which is urgently needed by our allies. In points (*c*) and (*d*) above, Mr Farquhar has drawn attention to the two objections to this course. There is also the further objection that, since the United States Government will apparently have been precluded under the Vandenberg Resolution from supplying arms to neutrals, there would be an awkward divergence of policy, which might cause us increasing difficulties with the Americans if we did not revise our treatment of Sweden in the matter of arms deliveries to conform more closely to that of the United States Government. This can, however, be left over for further consideration after the attitude of the three Scandinavian countries towards the Atlantic Pact has finally crystallised itself.[3]

R.M.A. HANKEY

---

[3] Bateman commented 'We shall, I think, be better able to consider this question in (say) three months' time. There are strong arguments for and against continuing our present policy' (FO 371/77729, N726/1194/42G).

No. 172

Letter from Mr Hankey to Sir L. Collier (Oslo), 25 January 1949
Top Secret and Personal (FO 371/71485, N3492/34/30)

[No salutation on this copy]

Ryder[1] came to see me this morning and elaborated your views more or less as stated in your telegram No. 35.[2]

---

[1] Naval Attaché, British Embassy, Oslo.

1949-1951

You will by now have seen my personal telegram (I have not got the number of it yet) telling you that we have dropped the ideas of interlocking pacts because we do not want to upset the Norwegian decision. Moreover in view of Farquhar's last letter it seems obvious that we shall not in any case succeed in bringing about any change in the Swedish attitude.

I am sorry myself that we have not been able to make anything of the plan of interlocking pacts because I foresee that when it comes to the point it will be impossible for us to persuade the Norwegians that they are in fact going to get real security out of the Atlantic Pact if Sweden is not connected with them also. We have always understood from you that the Norwegians will have some very awkward questions to ask us about the amount of assistance they will get, but the studies which our Chiefs of Staff have carried out show quite clearly that the amount of outside aid needed to defend Norway without the help of Sweden is far beyond anything which is remotely likely for us to be able to provide at any foreseeable time in the early stages of a war. I don't think such a solution will give them much satisfaction and our own service authorities are worried at the commitment involved. Of course to some extent the Norwegians will already have thrown their lot in with us when they reject the Swedish offer (if they do so in the end) and thus the die will already be cast. But I foresee that we shall have a most difficult passage with Hauge or whoever goes to Washington. I am only slightly comforted by his very interesting remark recorded in your telegram No. 35 that 'what Norway needed was not so much a detailed plan for specific military help or supplies, as inclusion in a defence system . . .'[3]

So far as the plan for interlocking pacts is concerned, I listened carefully to what Ryder had to say but I still cannot see that the Norwegians would be in any way placed in a worse position than the Swedes. The Atlantic Pact will probably not provide for automatic entry of all members into war on aggression occurring though it will provide for the giving of maximum possible assistance and presumably a greatly improved supply of arms before the outbreak of war. Under this system of interlocking pacts Norway would thus get maximum assistance from all the Atlantic powers and from Sweden if attacked. In return she would give reciprocal undertakings. But the Swedes would give a reciprocal obligation only to the Norwegians and Danes and would get nothing from the other Atlantic powers except an undertaking to consult if Sweden were attacked. The position of Sweden and Norway thus simply is not comparable either as regards obligations or benefits.

I still have not been able to discover how or why this misunderstanding suddenly excited and worried Hauge so much but Prebensen is very keen on the interlocking pact idea (though we may not have told him the latest form of it) and as he has seen a good many senior members of the Office recently someone may have said something to him about it, I suppose. No doubt internal political considerations in a matter such as this also tend to make Hauge rather ticklish.

In this connection you may be amused to hear of an extraordinary episode last week when I got a message [. . .][4] saying that Hauge had had a message through his Military Attaché here who had heard something from Prince George of

---

[2] Not printed. This telegram reported that Hauge had heard of the proposal to suggest interlocking pacts combining a Scandinavian Pact with Norwegian and Danish adherence to the Atlantic Pact, and had expressed his reservations to Collier. See No. 173.

[3] Ellipsis in original.

[4] A phrase is here omitted.

Denmark, the Danish Military Attaché,[5] who had heard something from Reventlow of a conversation with me in which it was implied that we were not particularly anxious to have Norway in the Atlantic Pact after all, and could it possibly be true?!? Obviously we had no difficulty in disposing of that one, but it was to me an astonishing revelation of the misunderstandings which can occur.

Meanwhile so far as I can divine the Secretary of State's feeling, it seems to be in favour of getting Norway and Denmark into the Atlantic Pact in present circumstances but considerable reluctance to apply any pressure particularly to Denmark, as she is so very exposed and we can really do so little to help her when it comes to the point.[6]

By the way, please don't refer to the proposal for interlocking pacts as the 'Hankey Plan' any more. The joke wasn't appreciated overmuch in high quarters!!

R.M.A. HANKEY

[5] Assistant MA, March 1948; Acting MA, September 1948; MA, March 1952 - 1986.
[6] No. 173.

No. 173

Minute from Mr Hankey to Mr Bateman, 26 January 1949
Top Secret (FO 371/77392, N684/1071/63)

Sir O. Sargent has said that he does not understand Oslo telegram No. 35.[1]

I think that the matter will be clear to him from the annexed paper and also from the minute at Flag H with a draft Cabinet Paper now requested by the Secretary of State and submitted in the same box as this file.[2]

Briefly the situation is that the Norwegian Minister of Defence has expressed grave doubts about any scheme of interlocking pacts by which Norway and Denmark would join both the Atlantic Pact and the Scandinavian Pact (jocularly referred to by Sir L. Collier as the 'Hankey Plan' in his telegram No. 35, presumably because I started the original form of the idea though it has since been much altered).

Sir L. Collier thinks that if we were to make this proposal now (as we had been contemplating) we should risk upsetting the Norwegian decision to join the Atlantic Pact which he thinks is otherwise fairly certain.

In the circumstances the Secretary of State has come to the conclusion that it would be better for us to let matters take their course and for the Norwegians and, if possible, the Danes to come into the Atlantic Pact in the hope that Sweden will afterwards regret her complete isolation and make some private defence arrangements with them.[3]

[1] See No. 172, note 2.
[2] Not printed.
[3] Jebb minuted on 26 January: 'I think the Secretary of State's decision was right in view of the latest hopeful reports as to the willingness of Norway and perhaps Denmark also to come into the Atlantic Pact. If by any chance they don't we might revive the 'Hankey Plan' or some variant of it' (FO 371/77392, N684/1071/63G).

The Cabinet paper explains the situation briefly to the Cabinet and the grounds for this decision.

R.M.A. HANKEY

No. 174

Sir L. Collier (Oslo) to Mr Bevin, 31 January 1949, 4.28 p.m.[1]
Tel. No. 51 Immediate, Secret (FO 371/77397, N1015/1073/63G)

Moscow telegram No. 75: Norway and the Atlantic Pact.[2]

The Secretary General of the Norwegian Ministry of Foreign Affairs[3] told me this morning that the Soviet note[4] was presented on Saturday night and in [*sic*] simultaneously with statements in the Moscow press and wireless and that the Norwegian Government intended to reply immediately and with equal publicity taking the line that they welcomed the opportunity to make their attitude clear. After the reply had been sent and published the Minister for Foreign Affairs would speak in the *Storting* on February 2nd probably in public session on the whole question of Scandinavian defence and the Atlantic Pact and would ask for authority to accept an invitation if received to discuss entry into the Pact. This he would probably obtain without great difficulty in view of the general indignation aroused by the Soviet action and he would then be able to say in reply to approach already made that a formal invitation would be acceptable.

2. I asked whether that meant that the Minister for Foreign Affairs wished formal invitation to be further postponed and the Secretary General replied that this was so though there should be no need for postponement after the end of this week. He hoped indeed there would be no postponement after that as the time was now ripe for action on our part. We could if we liked send a formal invitation now if we did not make it public until after the *Storting* debate. In that case the Minister for Foreign Affairs would merely put it aside for consideration at the end of the week. When I asked how this time table squared with the statement by the Minister for Foreign Affairs in this morning's press to the effect that no step was to be expected from the Western Powers in the near future and that the next move lay with Norway the Secretary General said that the 'near future' meant the next few days and move by Norway referred to the reply to informal approach.

3. I then asked whether the time table applied to Denmark as well. The Secretary General said that while the Danes at the Oslo meeting had shown no signs of making up their minds we should in his private opinion be well advised to send them formal invitation at the same time as it was sent to the Norwegians, whether or not they had made any reply to informal approach at that time. If we waited for a reply to that or asked for one they might procrastinate indefinitely whereas they would find it difficult not to follow Norway's lead if faced with a definite and immediate choice.

[1] Repeated to Copenhagen, Stockholm, Washington and Moscow.
[2] Not printed.
[3] Rasmus Skylstad.
[4] The Soviet note of 29 January asked for clarification of the Norwegian Government's position with regard to the Atlantic Pact.

4. The Secretary General said the meeting at Oslo proceeded exactly as expected.[5] The Swedes were quite intransigent and even the Danes realised that nothing could be done with them. He added that the Russian note seemed to have provoked something like panic in the Swedish Ministry of Foreign Affairs who kept my Swedish colleague on the telephone all yesterday. One of their enquiries concerned a report of troop concentrations in North Norway apparently originating from London *Sunday Pictorial*. The Norwegian Government had authorised a *démenti* but were not publishing it here as the rumour had not reached the Oslo press.

5. The United States Ambassador in reply to request reported in my telegram No. 47[6] was authorised to tell Minister for Foreign Affairs that the passage in President Truman's inauguration speech promising help to the countries willing to collaborate with the United States in the maintenance of peace applied specifically to the points in question. He left messages to this effect with the Minister for Foreign Affairs on the night of January 29th and the Swedish rumour now seems to have been effectively scotched.[7]

---

[5] Following the conference at Karlstad, there were further meetings in Copenhagen and Oslo in late January which discussed Atlantic security.

[6] Not printed.

[7] Hankey noted Skylstad's recommendation that the Danes should be approached in parallel with the Norwegians, and recommended that Randall be consulted to see if he agreed with this advice. He assumed that the Norwegians would also be consulting the Americans and that there would be no undue difficulty about giving them the invitation and the draft text at the same time. He discussed this with Jebb, and later with Bevin, who requested that a telegram be sent to Washington drawing attention to the possibility of heavy Soviet pressure on Scandinavia if they thought that the Americans were going to obtain peacetime bases there (FO 371/77397, N1046/1073/63G). This point was included in FO tel. No 1291 to Washington of 2 February, which also made clear that invitations could not be issued to other Governments until the text had been agreed by Cabinet, and that this would be done shortly (FO 371/77397, N1015/1073/63G). The text of the paper to Cabinet is contained in a memorandum of 2 February (FO 371/77394, N1151/1071/63G).

No. 175

Sir L. Collier (Oslo) to Mr Bevin, 1 February 1949, 7.40 p.m.[1]
Tel. No. 59 Top Secret, Light (FO 371/77397, N1046/1071/63)

My telegram No. 51: Norway and the Atlantic Pact.[2]

Norwegian Minister for Foreign Affairs sent for the United States Ambassador and me this afternoon, told us that the reply to the Soviet notes [*sic*][3] had just been handed over to the Soviet Ambassador, gave us copies of the text which will appear in the press tomorrow morning and drew attention to the passage stating that the Norwegian Government would now 'investigate in what form and in what conditions the Norwegians could take part in a system of regional security for the Atlantic countries' and also to the passage declaring that Norway would not enter into any treaty granting bases for foreign forces on Norwegian territory 'so long as she was not attacked or exposed to threats of aggression'.

---

[1] Repeated to Copenhagen, Stockholm, Washington and Moscow.

[2] No. 174.

[3] The Soviet Government delivered a further note on 5 February in answer to the Norwegian response. See No. 178.

2. The Minister for Foreign Affairs explained that the second passage did not mean that Norway would not prepare bases of her own for allied forces to use completely or hold preliminary staff talks with the Allies for eventual use of such bases and for planning defensive measures in general—on the contrary it was precisely on this point inter-Scandinavian conversations had broken down, the Norwegians declaring that such consultations were essential for the Scandinavian defence and the Swedes refusing them at any price.

3. The meaning of the first passage was that the Norwegian Government would now reply to approach made by the British and United States Governments by putting through the Ambassadors in London and Washington certain questions designed partly to elucidate the points of principle in the draft of the Atlantic Pact and partly to ascertain how much material assistance Norway could expect in building up her armed forces if she joined the pact and how soon that would be forthcoming (as foreshadowed in my telegram No. 11).[4] The Ambassador in London would be returning February 4th and would ask for personal appointment with you on February 5th while the Ambassador at Washington who would arrive February 6th would ask to see the Secretary of State on February 7th. He realised that some of the questions might be difficult to answer fully or quite satisfactorily but the Norwegian Government required all the help we could give them in recommending the Atlantic Pact policy to the *Storting* and to public opinion. Moreover Norway without Sweden (and perhaps without Denmark too for the time being since he doubted whether she would join the pact at the same time as Norway) would obviously need more material help than if she brought the rest of Scandinavia with her.

4. When answers to the questions had been considered the Norwegian Government would ask the *Storting* for authority to join in the discussions on the Atlantic Pact, a step they could not take without Parliamentary approval though they realise the need for haste. The debate in the *Storting* now fixed for February 3rd would deal with *inter alia* Scandinavian discussions and with the Soviet note and reply thereto but would not if he could help it discuss the terms on which Norway could enter into the Atlantic Pact.

5. In reply to questions by the United States Ambassador and me the Minister for Foreign Affairs said that text of Soviet note (described by the Soviet Ambassador as a 'declaration') was as given in the press but it did not cover a longer document as stated by Tass and it was presented without comment.

6. In conclusion Minister for Foreign Affairs emphasised the need for helping the Norwegian Government with their public. Communist and Swedish propaganda here had been intense (please see in this connexion my telegram No. 11 to Stockholm)[5] and there would probably in any case be enough discontent in the Labour Party to assist the Communists in the general election this autumn. As I have reported the Minister for Foreign Affairs has had to fight hard to put through his policy on which he has staked his political future and he certainly deserves all the help we can give him.[6]

[4] No. 165.
[5] Not printed.
[6] For the US Ambassador's report on this meeting, see FRUS 1949, Vol IV, pp. 60-62.

No. 176

Mr Farquhar (Stockholm) to Mr Bevin, 1 February 1949, 7.52 p.m.[1]
Tel. No. 42 Top Secret (FO 371/77403, N1098/1076/63G)

My Air Attaché has just been informed by Colonel Bjuggren, Commander of Swedish Air Force Staff College, who has recently been in Finland, that according to certain senior Finnish Army officers, Finland intends, in the event of Norway joining the Atlantic Pact, to place a number of airfields at the disposal of the Russians. Finnish explanation of this action is that they consider that the Russians will almost certainly occupy Finland as soon as Norway joins the Atlantic Pact or at least demand the use of Finnish airfields and the Finns hope that by forestalling Soviet Russia's request they may better their own position.

2. Source is one of the few Swedish Air Force officers who served with Finnish forces against Russia and he therefore has the confidence of the Finns. Air Attaché in reporting the above to Air Ministry will grade it A2.[2]

[1] Repeated to Oslo, Helsinki, Copenhagen and Washington.
[2] This telegram caused considerable concern within the Foreign Office. Bevin asked for briefing before a meeting with the Minister of Defence on 5 February. After obtaining comment from Scott, Hankey informed Bevin's Private Secretary on 5 February that reporting from Helsinki confirmed his view 'that no great importance should be attached to the Swedish story that if Norway comes into the Atlantic Pact the Finns will offer bases to the Russians. It's just a Swedish story designed to choke Norway off the Atlantic Pact in my view.' Bevin commented on this briefing: '*Keep me informed.* It is clear now I think that we shall get a reaction by Russia if there is any Pact with a country which touches their frontier' (FO 371/77403, N1387/1076/63G). On Bateman's instructions, Hankey subsequently wrote to Farquhar to inform him of the consequences of his telegram ('which threw some quarters here into a temporary flap') and to suggest that if in future he was not completely certain of his information, he should send a report personally to one of them, to allow them to decide its distribution (FO 371/77493, N1098/1076/63G).

No. 177

Mr Bevin to Mr Farquhar (Stockholm), 3 February 1949
No. 22 Top Secret (FO 371/77400, N1245/1074/63G)

Scandinavian Countries and the Atlantic Pact: Policy of the Swedish Government

Sir,

The Swedish Ambassador called on me at his request today to inform me of the recent discussions between the three Scandinavian countries in connexion with which he had recently been summoned home by his Government for consultation.

2. M. Hägglöf explained to me that the Swedish Government was anxious to arrange for the joint defence of the Scandinavian area as a whole, although in reply to a question from me he confirmed that they intended any Scandinavian *bloc* to remain neutral, and preferred to keep Scandinavia outside the Atlantic Pact. Their main anxiety was to avoid provoking the Soviet Union to occupy Finland, which would be a matter of serious concern to Sweden.

3. M. Hägglöf explained that Denmark was for practical purposes defenceless, having neither trained men nor weapons. Norway was in a rather better position, and could no doubt obtain more weapons from outside. But Sweden was the only

military power in Scandinavia. She had 1,000 aircraft, a navy which was very useful in the Baltic, and she could put 600,000 men in the field in case of mobilisation. The Swedish Government therefore felt that it was in the general interest for all three Scandinavian countries to stand together, and for Norwegian and Danish military strength to be built up in a joint system which we could rest assured would never be used against the West, and which would have a deterrent effect upon the Soviet Union while avoiding the occupation of Finland. Even if Norway were to join the Atlantic Pact, there was nothing to show that she could then be quickly and adequately armed. The general Swedish conception for the defence of the West was, therefore, twofold: (1) An Atlantic Pact to which the Scandinavian Powers would not be parties and which would cover the Western frontiers of Europe and (2) as a support to this pact, there would be a Scandinavian *bloc*, which, although neutral, would in fact contribute to the safeguarding of the West, and prevent the territory or the raw materials of Scandinavia ever being used against the West.

4. The talks between the Scandinavian Ministers had revealed a fundamental difference of opinion, which represented an honest divergence of view, but which it was quite impossible to reconcile. Norway, while willing to consider participating in a Scandinavian *bloc*, wanted to remain free to join the Atlantic Pact. The talks had been friendly and frank, and the Ambassador reminded me that this was the first time in the many years since Sweden had adopted a policy of neutrality that the Swedish Government had been willing to consider participating even in a Scandinavian Pact.[1]

5. I told the Ambassador that His Majesty's Government had exerted no pressure on any of the Scandinavian countries and that we had thought they should each be left free to decide on their policy for themselves. I reminded him, however, that the state of Europe a year ago had been very different and much less secure. If other European countries had then preferred to remain neutral it might have been impossible to build up an organisation for Western Europe capable of checking Communist aggression.

6. Finally, the Ambassador tried to obtain from me some information about the contents of the proposed Atlantic Pact, but I said that I could not give him any information on this at present.

I am, etc.,
ERNEST BEVIN

[1] For an American description of Swedish reactions to the Oslo conference, see FRUS 1949, Vol. IV, p. 63, containing an account of a discussion between Matthews, the American Ambassador to Stockholm, and Boheman, the Swedish Ambassador to Washington.

No. 178

Brief for Mr Bevin before a meeting with M. Prebensen, 7 February 1949
(FO 371/77397, N1341/1071/63)

When the Norwegian Ambassador calls on the Secretary of State at three o'clock this afternoon, he may raise the following points:

(1) The timing of the invitation to Norway to join discussions on the Atlantic Pact.

The Nordic Countries, 1944-1951

(2) The questions he has been instructed to put to the Secretary of State. (These questions are reported in Oslo telegram No. 73 attached—Flag A).[1]

(3) The Soviet Note to Norway of February 5th (Flag B).[2]

Invitation to join Atlantic Pact Discussions

2. The text of the Atlantic Pact must be finally agreed in Washington and approved by the Cabinet before a formal invitation can be issued to the Norwegian Government. The Minister of State told the Norwegian Chargé d'Affaires on February 4th that it was the intention to issue an invitation about the middle of this week or shortly afterwards. It now seems unlikely that the text will have been agreed and approved by the Cabinet in time for this to be done; Mr Acheson[3] has not yet, so far as we know, met the Ambassadors of the Western Union powers and Canada to settle outstanding points in the text. Mr Bevin may, therefore, wish to make it clear to the Norwegian Ambassador that the invitation may not be issued as soon as we had hoped, though it will be forthcoming very shortly.

M. Lange's Questions

3. The answers to the questions reported in Oslo telegram No. 73 (Flag A) are as follows so far as they can be given at once.

(*a*) *The area to be covered by the Pact* is still under discussion. Points such as the inclusion of Spitzbergen should really be discussed at Washington in the conference on the Pact.

It may be noted here that Spitzbergen is already covered by a Treaty of 1920 to which the United Kingdom and USA are signatories and to which the USSR acceded in 1935. This Treaty provides for Spitzbergen to be a demilitarised territory under Norwegian sovereignty. If it were to be included in the Atlantic Pact some provision would have to be made so as to ensure that Pact did not conflict with the 1920 Treaty.

It would seem a tactical mistake to admit that we may be faced with a clear choice between the inclusion of Italy and the inclusion of Norway in the Atlantic Pact. Mr Bevin may wish to say that we ourselves are not convinced that Italy should be in the Pact; but no doubt M. Lange will be discussing this point with the State Dept. in Washington. If it is finally decided to include Italy, we hope that Norway will reconsider any objection she may now have to Italian adherence.

(*b*) *The question of Norway's defence contribution* under the Atlantic Pact can only be settled by discussion between the participating powers. This could take place first at the Conference in Washington and even better, afterwards within the framework of the defence organisation to be set up. The Atlantic Pact provides for all parties to do their best but we do not think Norway would be embarrassed by such a provision.

(*c*) We are finding out whether we can expedite *deliveries of war material already on order*. It seems doubtful, as we are already doing our best to meet the requirements of our friends. See separate note by the Ministry of Defence (Flag C).[1]

(*d*) The question of *Norway's strategic importance,* like question (*b*) above, is one which can only be decided by discussions in which all the countries in the

---

[1] Not printed.

[2] This was the Soviet note responding to the Norwegian Government's note of 1 February, which answered the original Soviet note of 29 January, requesting information about the attitude of the Norwegian Government to the Atlantic Pact. See No. 175.

[3] US Secretary of State.

Pact will work out the essentials for their common defence—i.e. the question can only be discussed within the framework of the defence organisation to be set up.

Soviet Note to Norway

4. The Secretary of State will be aware that the Soviet Government have addressed another Note to the Norwegian Government (see cutting annexed at Flag B)[1] saying that the Norwegian Government have failed to give a clear answer to the Soviet Government's previous questions about bases which was of special importance as the two countries had a common border. The Soviet Government said there was no ground whatever for thinking that Russia might attack Norway and offered a non-aggression pact.

5. It may be presumed that any such treaty would contain the usual Soviet clause about neither party engaging in any alliance or coalition aimed directly or indirectly or in any other way against the other party and that the Soviet Government would thereafter say that the Norwegians had infringed such a provision by joining the Atlantic Pact. Present indications are that the Norwegians will reject the Soviet offer, though it may be presumed that M. Lange will discuss the question in Washington.

6. The Secretary of State will have seen in this connexion Moscow telegram No. 95 (Flag D)[1] in which Sir M Peterson suggests that possibly the Soviet Union might be preparing to ask for bases in Finland or even to occupy the country with a view to putting direct pressure on the Scandinavian countries and to frighten them out of joining the Atlantic Pact.

7. The Ambassador seems to share our view and that of HM Minister in Helsingfors that the story about the Finns giving bases to the Russians out of sheer panic contained in a recent telegram from Stockholm[4] is not entitled to credence and like ourselves suggests that it is being disseminated by the Swedes for their own purposes.

8. We must clearly expect the Soviet Government to do their utmost to put the Scandinavians off joining the Atlantic Pact but on the whole the Scandinavians will be very much more open to Soviet pressure and liable to be swayed into isolation and appeasement if they do not join the Atlantic Pact and are left divided and alone. It therefore seems better that we should encourage the Norwegians not to be deflected by this 'huffing and puffing' from Moscow. The Russians can after all occupy Finland or demand bases there at any time (as they did in the case of the Baltic States), and we have always thought that they would be quite likely to do this when it suited them.

9. I may add that we have absolutely no information to confirm the suggestion in paragraph 2 of Moscow telegram No. 95[1] that the Kremlin may possibly be contemplating any other form of offensive action in Scandinavia or elsewhere though we are constantly on the lookout for it.

10. To sum up, the whole episode seems to confirm that Norway will be better in the Atlantic Pact than out of it especially as the attitude of Denmark and Iceland will be guided by that of Norway.

R.M.A.HANKEY

[4] No. 176.

No. 179

Mr Bevin to Sir L. Collier (Oslo), 7 February 1949
No. 29 Top Secret (FO 371/77394, N1305/1071/63G)

Scandinavian Defence and the Atlantic Pact

Sir,

The Norwegian Ambassador called on me today to inform me of the result of the discussions in Oslo on the Scandinavian Pact, and also to give me some idea of the questions which his Foreign Minister would put to Mr Dean Acheson[1] while in the United States. M. Prebensen said that the discussions in Oslo between the Scandinavian Powers had been very cordial, and great understanding had been achieved, but they had not been able to get agreement.

2. For my guidance, the Ambassador handed me four documents, which are attached:[2]

(*a*) A statement showing the Swedish point of view, beyond which the Swedish Government would not go.

(*b*) A proposal by the Norwegian Government for a Scandinavian Defence Union.

(*c*) Questions which M. Lange will put to Mr Acheson. (This document was handed to me in the strictest confidence.)

(*d*) Further notes for M. Lange's use during his visit to the United States.

3. The Ambassador asked me whether I could give him the view of His Majesty's Government in the United Kingdom on all this. I told him that we had not yet got the final draft of the Atlantic Pact, which would have to be submitted to the Cabinet here, and presumably to Governments in the other participating countries, before any further invitations were issued. Until I had this I could not give the Ambassador any clear statement. But I had no doubt that his Foreign Minister in the United States would know pretty well by now what was in it. I had expected the draft to be here this week, but the Ambassadors had not yet met the United States Secretary of State, though they might do so this week.

4. The Ambassador then asked me how I thought the Russian attitude might develop. I told him it was difficult to say, but my view was that Russia, who had carried on a Communist offensive, now found it very difficult to achieve her aims simply by these methods. Russia's policy had really necessitated the setting up of the Western European Organisation and the proposed Atlantic Pact, which she was at the moment desperately trying to prevent from becoming an accomplished fact. On the other hand, it was true that the organisation of Western Europe had called a halt on the Communist offensive, and everybody had gained from that. I thought that if the pact went through and was satisfactory it might in the end lead to discussions and possibly to a settlement between the West and the East.

5. The Ambassador then asked me whether I thought that Russia, in order to show her resistance to the Atlantic Pact and Norwegian entry into it, might invade some part of Norway. I said I did not think she would take that step, but, of course, every move would have to be watched.

6. The Ambassador then asked me whether it was still out of the question to create a situation in which the Scandinavian countries could act together, and

---

[1] An account of Acheson's meeting with Lange on 7 February is contained in FRUS 1949, Vol. IV, pp.66-68. See also No. 183.
[2] Not printed.

whether it might not still be possible, by further study, to create an opportunity for Scandinavia to be associated in some way with the Atlantic Pact. I replied that we had placed no pressure on the Scandinavian countries, either separately or collectively, to do anything, but before I could examine the question afresh I must look into the actual draft of the pact when it was completed.

7. The Ambassador then spoke to me about the internal situation in Norway. He pointed out that, while many people, both in other parties and the Labour Party, were solidly in favour, there was a big section of the Labour Party who were not so favourable to the Atlantic Pact, while at the same time anxious to be aligned with the West. The feeling of this group was that Norway ought to exercise very great care before breaking with Sweden, and there was a strong body of opinion in this sense in Norway, which the Norwegian Government was bound to take into account.

8. I told the Ambassador that we would keep him and his Government informed of every development.

9. The Ambassador told me that M. Lange would like to call on me on his return from the United States and I said I would be glad to see him.

10. Copies of this despatch are being sent to His Majesty's Ambassadors, Copenhagen, Stockholm, Washington and Moscow.

I am, etc.,
ERNEST BEVIN

No. 180

Mr Bevin to Sir A. Randall (Copenhagen), 8 February 1949
No. 31 Secret (FO 371/77395, N1396/1072/63G)

Conversation between the Secretary of State and the Danish Ambassador: Denmark and the Atlantic Pact

Sir,

The Danish Ambassador called on me today to discuss the question of the Atlantic Pact. He explained to me Denmark's position and the difficult decision before her. Denmark had pacifist traditions and the Danish population since 1864 had felt that it was no use attempting to fight, and that Denmark must just take what came if war broke out. However, in the light of the present situation Denmark had made arrangements for the organisation of armed forces numbering 100,000 and she was anxious to play her part should anything unfortunate happen. But Denmark was very desirous of not splitting Scandinavian solidarity, and felt that she could render greater service to this end if she joined a Scandinavian *bloc*. Strategically, she felt that unless she went in with Sweden she could do nothing as far as the entrances to the Baltic were concerned, and accordingly she was extremely nervous over the present position. The Danes in their hearts wanted to be with the West, but they asked His Majesty's Government to take into account the situation in which they found themselves.

2. I pointed out to Count Reventlow that it had not yet been decided to send an invitation to Denmark. The Atlantic Pact was not through, and a final decision still had to be taken by His Majesty's Government. Then invitations would be sent out to other States in the light of further discussions. In reply, the Ambassador said that

what worried him was that his Government had been told in very definite terms by the Americans that, if Denmark could not see her way clear to joining the Pact, then she could not have arms, and what arms there were would be used solely for those who joined the Pact. He said this was giving him and his Government the greatest anxiety. I explained to the Ambassador that it was not a matter of antagonism to the Scandinavian *bloc*, or of putting pressure on them. The facts were that both America and ourselves had only a certain amount of industrial capacity which we could reserve for defence needs, and the question was: How could that production be used best? There was the Brussels Treaty already in existence and the Americans had pledged themselves to develop the armies of France, Belgium and Holland in co-operation with ourselves. Who should have the priority, the partners to the Atlantic Pact, or those outside it, however sympathetic they might be? That was the issue that had to be decided. I pointed out to the Ambassador that the situation had been much worse a year ago when the Russians seemed to be sweeping over the whole of Europe with their Communist propaganda. There had, however, been a check and while the Russians had recently indulged in a clever peace move, the salutary thing was that they had deceived no one. After all, the question before us was whether the Western races would survive or not. That was the anxiety that was exercising all our minds.

3. For the rest, the Ambassador spoke on the same lines as he had spoken to Mr Hankey when he called on him on 4th February. A record of this conversation is attached.[1]

4. I did, however, finally make it clear that His Majesty's Government were not putting any pressure upon the Danish Government. The Ambassador then asked whether, if the Danes were not able to join the Atlantic Pact, His Majesty's Government would consider the continuation of the collaboration which now existed between Denmark and the United Kingdom. On that I said I would consult the Minister of Defence.[2]

5. I am sending copies of this despatch to His Majesty's Ambassadors at Oslo, Stockholm, Washington and Moscow.

I am, etc.,
ERNEST BEVIN

[1] Not printed.
[2] The Danish Ambassador to Washington also briefed Acheson on the Oslo meeting on 9 February: see FRUS 1949, Vol. IV, p. 88.

No. 181

Sir O. Franks (Washington) to Mr Bevin, 8 February 1949, 9.55 p.m.
Tel. No. 785 Top Secret (FO 371/77394, N1150/1071/63)

My telegram No. 749—North Atlantic Pact.[1]
Meeting with Acheson this afternoon was principally concerned with Norway. I will telegraph separately on the other issues raised.

[1] Not printed.

2. As regards Norway, Acheson said that the conversations with Lange had shown that although the latter agreed that there were strong links between Norway and the North Atlantic Powers, he was concerned at the prospect of splitting Scandinavian solidarity. Lange was therefore anxious to be certain that the participation of Norway in the North Atlantic Pact was definitely desired by the other Governments, or alternatively, to know whether the inclusion of Norway in a Scandinavian Defence Pact on the lines suggested by the Swedish Government (see my telegram under reference) would serve the interests of the North Atlantic Powers equally well. He had explained that under such a Scandinavian defence agreement the three Governments would, as a result of Swedish insistence, be precluded from any sort of association with the North Atlantic Powers, and that nothing in the nature of staff talks with these Powers could be allowed. Lange had indicated however that he thought that the Swedes might not object if Norway and Denmark were to make some special agreements with the North Atlantic Powers in respect of their overseas territories—i.e. Greenland and Spitzbergen. Lange had made it pretty clear that he was personally not greatly enamoured of this idea of a Scandinavian Defence Pact, and that he himself doubted whether it would be sufficiently effective to justify the three Scandinavian Governments in asking for outside military assistance (as the Swedes evidently contemplated). He implied that the Norwegian Government would not wish to join the Scandinavian Pact unless they were assured of the prior approval of the North Atlantic Powers. He also implied that Norway would be very reluctant to join without an assurance of military supplies from the West.

3. Acheson then said that in view of this approach by Lange, it was urgently necessary for the North Atlantic Powers to decide whether their own interests would best be served by the participation of Norway, and perhaps Denmark, in the North Atlantic Pact, or by the formation of a Scandinavian Defence Pact on the lines suggested by Sweden. If the second alternative were adopted, it would however be essential from the American point of view that Iceland should be a member of the North Atlantic Pact, and that some special arrangement on the lines suggested above to cover Greenland be in force.

4. The meeting then considered the political implications of the question. It was agreed that if Norway were now to decline to join the North Atlantic Pact, or indeed if the other Governments decided not to invite her participation, this would provide the Swedish Government with a very strong propaganda case. Furthermore the creation of a neutral Scandinavian *bloc* would weaken the general position of the North Atlantic Powers and enhance Russian prestige. There might also be unfortunate political repercussions in Norway. There was also the most important point that if Norway and Denmark were not to join the North Atlantic Pact, Iceland would be very unlikely to come in.

5. It was generally agreed however that, before any conclusions could be reached, the views of Governments on the military implications of the question must be obtained. Since Acheson was anxious if possible to give Lange some indications of the views of the North Atlantic Governments before Lange's departure on the afternoon of February 11th, it was agreed that the various representatives would at once ask for guidance on the relative advantages and disadvantages from the military point of view of the two alternatives mentioned in paragraph 3 above. The American and Canadian representatives undertook to consult their respective Chiefs of Staff, and it was agreed between the Brussels representatives that the quickest way of getting an agreed European military point

of view would be to ask that the matter be submitted to the Permanent Military Committee of the Brussels Powers without delay.

6. Subsequently at a hurried meeting of the Working Party certain questions which it was thought that the military authorities might usefully answer were drawn up. These are contained in my immediately following telegram.[1] I should be grateful if the whole question could be brought to the attention of the Military Committee at once and if at the same time the other Brussels Governments could be informed of what is being done.

7. Since Acheson is anxious to have another meeting before Lange leaves on February 11th, I should be grateful for your very early instructions on these questions concerning Norway both from the political and the military points of view.

8. Since drafting the above, I have heard from the State Department that it may be possible for the views of the United States Chiefs of Staff to be communicated to the American representative on the Military Committee in the course of tomorrow.[2]

[2] See No. 182.

No. 182

Minutes by Mr Bateman, Sir G. Jebb and Sir O. Sargent, 9 February 1949
Very Urgent (FO 371/77398, N1473/1073/63G)

Sir G. Jebb

You will see from telegrams Nos. 785[1] and 786[2] from Washington that the negotiators of the Atlantic Pact in Washington are now anxious to have the opinion of the Permanent Military Committee of the Brussels Powers on the question of whether the strategic interests of the West will best be served by persuading Norway to join the Atlantic Pact or by allowing the Swedes to have their way in concluding a self-contained Scandinavian Mutual Defence Pact based on neutrality (See marked portions of Flag A and the actual questionnaire to be put to the Permanent Military at Flag O).[2]

The latest opinion of our own Chiefs of Staff will be found at Flag E,[2] from which it is reasonably clear that the Chiefs of Staff are now inclined to favour a Scandinavian Defence Pact based on neutrality.

The Chiefs of Staff are discussing this matter this morning and Mr Hayter is with them.

The point is however that Washington want a reply to these telegrams before the Norwegian Minister for Foreign Affairs leaves on February 11th. This means that we have about 24 hours in which to send Washington the views of the Permanent Military Committee.[3]

[1] No. 181.
[2] Not printed.
[3] For the views of the US Joint Chiefs of Staff on the relation of Scandinavia to the Atlantic Pact, dated 10 February, see FRUS 1949, Vol. IV, pp. 95-101.

I do not know whether we communicate direct with the Permanent Military Committee or whether this will be done by our Chiefs of Staff. Perhaps you can let me know the answer to this question.

C.H. BATEMAN

I induced the Permanent Commission this morning to instruct the Military Committee to consider the American questionnaire *this afternoon* and, if possible, produce a report within 24 hours.

G. JEBB

Sir Orme Sargent
The following represent my provisional views on the latest stage of negotiations regarding Norway's participation in the North Atlantic Pact (Washington telegrams Nos. 785, 786 and 787).[2]

If we suppose that the Soviets would, in fact, take no positive action (except possibly the occupation of Finland) against the West, if Norway and Denmark joined the Atlantic Pact, it would probably be to our advantage that they should do so, for the following main reasons:

(*a*) Iceland would then come in too and the United States would be in a fair way to obtaining her bases in Greenland and in Iceland;

(*b*) Staff talks would be possible between Norway and Denmark and the other Atlantic Powers;

(*c*) The defence of, at any rate, the western part of Scandinavia, could be coordinated over a period of years, with the defence of the rest of Western Europe;

(*d*) Sweden might quite likely, after a period of time, be compelled to abandon her neutrality and make certain arrangements with the Atlantic Powers as well.

On the other hand, if we believe that the Russians really would risk a general war, in the event of Norway and Denmark joining the Atlantic Pact, then we must conclude presumably, that the balance of advantage would lie in the constitution of some neutral *bloc*, under the leadership of Sweden, which would at least:

(*a*) not provoke the Russians, and

(*b*) provide some—though no doubt not much—security for Scandinavia against a Russian attack in the event of a war nevertheless occurring in the future.

G. JEBB

A neutral Norway and Denmark means a neutral Greenland and Iceland. Of course in a crisis the United States Government would seize both these territories in defiance of International Law, but they would not have been able to make arrangements in peacetime for the use of these territories in war and it is this to which, I gather, they attach particular importance.

It has been argued that Norway pledged to come into a war with us without Sweden might constitute a military liability, but against this a neutral Norway unable to defend its neutrality, would be liable to have its northern territory—including the all-important port of Narvik—overrun by the Russians before the Swedes could intervene (if they ever did). Such a *fait accompli* would, as we knew to our cost in the last war, have very serious effects on our position in the North Sea and convert our strategy there from the offensive to the defensive.

If Norway joins the Atlantic Pact there is of course the risk that the Soviet Government will take some action which will precipitate a crisis. The Russians are counting on us not to dare to face this danger.

For instance it has been suggested that they might occupy Finland, but this is by no means certain seeing that as General Hollis has pointed out this would not improve their strategic position in any way.

What is more likely is that they would intensify their pressure on Sweden so as to prevent her from entering into any defence arrangements with Norway or Denmark even on the basis of neutrality, and on Denmark in order to obtain the closing of the Belts[4] to all foreign warships. But even if they succeeded in these objectives would it really be very serious? The assistance of Sweden bent on neutrality would in any event be very problematical and probably come too late to be of any use to Norway and the closing of the Belts to our warships would not worry us much since we are not likely to want to operate in the Baltic.

All this is problematical but what is absolutely certain is that if Norway does not join the Atlantic pact it will be recognised throughout the world as a Soviet victory—to be followed I should think by a further diplomatic offensive in order to forbid the formation of even a neutral Scandinavian pact.

O.G. SARGENT

[4] The two straits in the Danish archipelago leading into the Baltic.

No. 183

Record of Conversation between the Secretary of State for Foreign Affairs and the Norwegian Minister for Foreign Affairs on 14th February 1949[1]
(FO 371/77398, N1656/1073/63G)

Present:
United Kingdom
Secretary of State for Foreign Affairs
Sir Gladwyn Jebb
Mr Bateman
Mr Etherington-Smith

Norway
Norwegian Minister for Foreign Affairs
Norwegian Ambassador
M. Oscar Torp

A. *Atlantic Pact*
The Norwegian Foreign Minister said he would begin by giving an account of what had passed during his recent conversation in Washington.

[1] Enclosed in despatch No. 34 Top Secret to Collier, 14 February 1949.

2. He had explained to Mr Acheson what had happened in the inter-Scandinavian defence discussions and had emphasised the advantage of a Scandinavian solution of the problem, if it could have the understanding and support of the United States and United Kingdom. The arrangement would then have been on a neutrality basis technically speaking without any formal link with a general Western security system, but it would nevertheless have had its basis in a common interest with the West. He had also pointed out the risks which Norway would have to run if she took an independent course by adhering to the North Atlantic Pact. Denmark might not be able to follow her in this course, at least in the immediate future, owing to her more difficult internal situation. There was also another risk which was of common concern to the West—namely, that of the Communists strengthening their position in Norway, particularly by renewed infiltration into the trades unions. In 1945 and for a short while after the end of hostilities the Communists had had some influence in some of the unions, i.e. Seamen's and Building trades unions, and some of the export industries. Since that time they had been steadily driven back and had lost most of their key positions. It was estimated that if an election were to be held now the Communist vote, which in 1945 amounted to 11 per cent, would be about halved. If Norway embarked on an independent course away from the rest of Scandinavia, and if, as seemed highly probable, the Russians brought strong pressure to bear on Norway (though he did not think this would extend to military action), the effect might well be to cause a split in the Norwegian Labour Party. There was a section in the party which had never hitherto felt strong enough to challenge by a formal vote of non-confidence the policy approved by the majority, but which might now do so. They would probably not join forces with the Communists but their action might undermine the morale and weaken the determination of those who were fighting the Communists in the unions. The Communists were now playing the peace card for all they were worth, saying that Norway could have peace if she went with Sweden. This propaganda had a certain effect and was liable to weaken the fighting spirit of the Government's supporters in the unions. There was also going to be a general election in Norway in October and a party conference was being held on 17th February to discuss the election programme, after which the Government would prepare their campaign. If there was a split in the party, it would obviously weaken their leadership. Yet another consideration was that Norwegian military experts estimated that close military co-operation with Sweden would have certain advantages from a general point of view, i.e. it would give greater depth to the Norwegian defences, but the serious disadvantage of such co-operation with Sweden would be that it would preclude effective preparatory planning of co-operation with the Western Powers. The Norwegian Government had allowed the Scandinavian negotiations to break down over this point, as they felt that under such conditions Western help would come too late and be ineffective.

3. M. Lange said that he had asked the Americans whether they could say at this stage what would be the practical effect of Article V of the Atlantic Pact and whether it would constitute a quasi-automatic commitment. He had been told that there could be no automatic commitment. Any attack on one of the signatories would, under the terms of the Pact, be equivalent to an attack on the United States, but in view of the constitutional position and the limited powers of the President as Commander-in-Chief, there could be no definite assurance of immediate United States military assistance, though the delay might be very brief. M. Lange had been

somewhat disappointed with this answer, but it was evidently as far as the Americans were prepared to go.

4. M. Lange had asked the United States authorities whether it would be possible for any forces, particularly air and aircraft carrier units, to be kept in readiness to go to the assistance of Norway if she was attacked. He had been told that the stage had not been reached where such a measure could be taken and that the decision would rest with the consultative body to be set up under the Pact. It was clear, M. Lange said, that nobody could be sure beforehand what would be the first move in an emergency and whether Norway could expect immediate help. On the other hand it was certain that, unless Norway participated in the common planning beforehand, no immediate assistance would be forthcoming.

5. The Americans had been unable to give him any positive answer as to what would happen if Norway were attacked during the interim period before the Pact came into force. President Truman had, however, said that, although under the United States Constitution there would be no actual commitment, an attack on any part of Norwegian territory would be viewed with the very gravest concern. M. Lange remarked that he thought it in fact improbable that the Russians would take any military action during this interim period. The Norwegian Government had no evidence that the Russians were contemplating any such move either against Norway proper or against Spitsbergen. There was, however, a good deal of nervousness in Northern Norway and he thought the Russians would try to play on Norwegian nerves by intensified propaganda and diplomatic pressure. Although the Americans had given no positive guarantees, they had shown great sympathy for Norway's difficulties in this connexion and a very real understanding for the problems in general.

6. M. Lange had asked President Truman whether he would consider the question of issuing a declaration of support for Norway, but the President said that he did not at the moment feel free to take such a step. Congressional opinion would have to be consulted before he could say anything further on the matter.

7. As regards military supplies, the Americans had said that there were at present certain surplus items available but that, while there was no intention of using this as a means of pressure, countries adhering to the Pact would naturally have a better claim. As regards future supplies, it was not yet possible to say how these would be allocated.

8. In the light of all that he had been told in Washington, M. Lange thought that his recommendation to the Norwegian Government and *Storting* would be to wait and not to force matters until more was known about the form which the Pact would take and the attitude of the American Congress. Mr Acheson had indicated that the preparatory talks and the necessary consultations with congressional circles would in any case take some time. At his party conference on 17th February he (M. Lange) therefore proposed to ask for approval of the Government's past action and to be allowed a free hand for the future. He himself was convinced that the Russians would only be stopped if there was solidarity in the West. He did not propose to send an immediate answer to the latest Soviet note, but he thought that the Norwegian Government's eventual reply might be to the effect that there was no need for a non-aggression pact with the Soviet Union, and that while they knew that Russia had no aggressive intent, they considered that the position was already fully covered under the United Nations Charter. He had considered the suggestion that Norway might say that she had no objection to concluding a non-aggression

pact with Russia in addition to joining the Atlantic Pact, but on the whole he did not think this advisable.

9. The Secretary of State said that he was in general agreement with M. Lange's point of view. As he knew, he had purposely refrained from trying to hasten Norway's decision with regard to the Atlantic Pact because he had feared that the matter might come to a head before everyone was ready. He asked if Sweden was pressing Norway to make an immediate choice between the two pacts.

10. M. Lange said that this was not the case. Sweden had, however, approached Norway immediately after his speech of 19th April 1948, and the Swedes had offered their co-operation provided Norway and Denmark accepted Sweden's neutrality policy. This meant that Sweden would in fact control Norwegian foreign policy. It was also important to note that the Swedish offer was not unconditional. It was subject to two conditions, namely:-

(*i*) That the Norwegians accepted Swedish foreign policy.

(*ii*) That they should be assured of getting Western military assistance on terms which were acceptable both politically and economically.

11. The Secretary of State said that he quite agreed that matters should not be hurried. The first thing to agree on was the Pact and see what form it took. It now appeared that the effect of article V might be whittled down and the French were worried about this, but no doubt these difficulties would be overcome.

12. As regards arms, the Secretary of State pointed out that under the Brussels Pact there was a joint supply board to determine allocations. Owing to the strained economic position, however, His Majesty's Government had to strike a balance as to how much productivity should be set aside for military purposes, and how much should be left for other requirements. This was a difficult matter and it was also necessary for the United Kingdom to co-ordinate their measures with the other countries concerned, such as the United States and Canada. There was also the further and very important point, which the Swedes did not seem to have appreciated, that we were getting to a point where armaments were so expensive that no one country could stand the strain and the system would need to provide a common budget to provide for the common defence. It was not merely a question of whether we could provide Norway, say, with a certain amount of rifles. It would be necessary to deal comprehensively with the defence requirements of all the countries concerned, and he had already initiated discussion of this aspect of the question in the Brussels organisation. Consequently it was completely unrealistic for Sweden to talk about getting arms from the West while making no contribution herself. By co-ordination among the different countries, it would be possible considerably to reduce the general burden and increase the effectiveness of the defences. But this, of course, involved that the participating countries should not merely be signatories of a pact, but loyal members of a system whose co-operation would extend to many other fields. Mutual help in the economic sphere, which was already being developed through the OEEC, was merely another aspect of this universal co-operation. But you could not belong to the system and measure the amount of co-operation you were prepared to give. He thought that Sweden had not considered these implications fully enough and more time was required before they were fully understood.

13. As regards the Soviet offer of a non-aggression pact with Norway, the Secretary of State said that the Norwegian Government would no doubt act as they thought best, but he would not be in favour of accepting, though there was no need

for the reply to be provocative. He did not believe that Russia would attack Norway, though there might be more Soviet notes.

14. M. Lange remarked that the whole opposition to the Government's policy in Norway came from within the Labour Party. They feared that the Government were provoking a crisis with Russia and splitting Scandinavia instead of uniting it.

15. The Secretary of State said that in 1946 the Left wing of his own party had harboured similar fears about entering into pacts, but they had since come round and were now as eager as anyone to promote an effective Western security system.

16. M. Lange said it was important that he should be able to assure the Norwegian cabinet that there was no real reason for thinking that they had aggravated the international situation.

17. The Secretary of State said that he did not think this was so. He would, however, have preferred matters to develop more slowly. But it would be disastrous, and a victory for the Russians, if Norway renounced the Atlantic Pact and joined a Scandinavian Pact on the conditions M. Lange had mentioned. If M. Lange asked him whether Norway should join the Atlantic Pact, he would feel unable to give him definite advice at this stage, as the Pact had not yet taken final shape. All he could say was that His Majesty's Government and the British Parliament accepted the wisdom and rightness of such a pact, though they would require more details before making a final decision.

18. M. Lange said that this was exactly the Norwegian standpoint. The final decision would rest with the Norwegian Parliament. As the Pact was still in a preparatory stage, his advice would be to wait. But there were some who thought that, if Norway did not join now, she would be in a worse position over arms. He had gathered from Mr Acheson, however, that some delay would not make much difference and that Norway would always be welcome. He realised, nevertheless, that the sooner Norway entered into close military co-operation with the Western Powers, the sooner she could expect to get supplies.

19. Sir G. Jebb explained that the advantage of attending the conference which was to be held in Washington would be that the country concerned would take part in the final drafting and would thus have an opportunity of securing modification in the text. A country which did not join the Pact at the outset would not be included in the initial allocation of arms. But two or three months' delay in acceding would probably not matter from this point of view.

20. M. Lange observed that if Norway delayed too much, however, the Russians might say that they had scored a point.

21. The Secretary of State said that this was also his view. But if Norway joined the Pact and then during the interim period Russia took some aggressive action against her (which, however, he thought unlikely), there was no complete assurance that the United States and the United Kingdom would be able to assist her effectively. For this reason he did not like to press Norway, as the Pact had not yet finally been worked out and he did not wish to lead her into a false position. Therefore, he thought that it would be advantageous to wait, but that once the Pact was ready there should be quick action. It was all a matter of timing and tactics.

22. M. Lange agreed, adding that his main concern was (1) to keep his party in line, (2) not to push matters so far as to provoke the Russians.

23. The Secretary of State then asked about the position of Greenland, the Faroes and Iceland.

24. M. Lange said that Iceland, being an independent country, was not directly affected. As regards Greenland, Senator Vandenberg had told him in Washington

(though this might be an extreme view) that, unless the United States could be sure of bases there, he would have no interest in the Atlantic Pact. When asked by the State Department about the position as regards Greenland and Spitsbergen if a neutral Scandinavian *bloc* was formed, M. Lange had told them on his own authority that he did not think that the Swedes would object to the grant of facilities in these territories; and the Swedish Ambassador later told him that he had given the same opinion. On the other hand, from Denmark's point of view the advantage of a neutral Scandinavian solution was that it would prove less objectionable to the Russians, but this advantage would be lost if Greenland was handed over, as they thought that this would be most likely to provoke the Russians. The Danes were very nervous about Bornholm and thought that the Russians might occupy it if Denmark joined the Atlantic Pact. There were also people in Norway, particularly in the North, who thought that any talks and preparations with the Western Powers would be sufficient to provoke the Russians to lay hands on Eastern Finmark. He did not himself think this likely, but one could not be absolutely certain.

25. The Secretary of State said that he had seen no sign of such Soviet intentions. Once the Pact was concluded and they knew that any move would mean the risk of war, he did not think the Russians would move. This applied also to Bornholm. But while matters were undecided one could not be certain.

26. Sir G. Jebb pointed out that, if a neutral Scandinavian pact was concluded, Denmark would not be protected.

27. The Secretary of State said that you could not buy peace nowadays, as the experience of Belgium and Holland had provide in the last war; a country could not expect guarantees unless it was prepared to assume obligations.

28. M. Lange mentioned that the Americans had told him (when asked if the southwest coast of Norway was of such concern to them that they would take action to prevent the Russians from securing control of it) that it was not of vital interest to the United States itself, but that as it was important to Britain it was also important to them. Moreover, Mr Marshall had said that the whole coast of Norway was so important that in any future war the contending Powers would inevitably race to control it.

29. The Secretary of State, in summing up, said that he understood M. Lange to think that Norway was not called on to take a definite decision as yet, but that her sympathies were with the West.

30. M. Lange assented. Norway might have to go slow, but this did not mean that she would not come in before the Pact was concluded.

31. The Secretary of State said that he held the same view. America was a powerful country and it seemed desirable that there should be some balance between her and Europe. The more co-ordinated strength was grouped in Europe, the more equal would be the balance with the United States. It would be a good thing from America's point of view if she did not have a complete ascendancy and this was one reason why he hoped that Sweden might come in. Moreover, when American economic aid ceased after 1952, effective organisation in Europe would be absolutely essential.

32. M. Lange thought that there should be no illusion about Sweden coming in for at least some years. But he had nevertheless been encouraged that M. Undén, who when he saw him after the United Nations Assembly meeting had been against participation in the Council of Europe, had now agreed to join.

The Nordic Countries, 1944-1951

33. M. Lange asked finally about the position over Italy, pointing out that it would be more difficult to handle the question of the Atlantic Pact in Norway if Italy was included.

34. The Secretary of State explained that France and also the United States were in favour of Italy being brought in and that, as Italy had herself asked for an invitation, it might be difficult not to invite her.[2]

B. *Anglo-Norwegian Economic Relations*

35. The Secretary of State went on to tell M. Lange that the Cabinet had now approved proposals for achieving closer economic co-operation between the United Kingdom and Norway. M. Lange said that he was very glad to hear this. The Norwegian Minister of Commerce, M. Brofoss, was taking a preliminary draft agreement with him to Paris and hoped to discuss it with Sir Stafford Cripps.

C. *Fisheries Dispute*

36. The Secretary of State referred, in conclusion, to the dispute regarding fishing rights off the coast of Norway and enquired how this matter stood.

37. M. Lange said that before he left Oslo for Washington he had attended a meeting of the Foreign Affairs and Fisheries Committees of the *Storting*, when it was agreed to recommend the 'Yellow Line' to the *Storting* as a *modus vivendi*. He thought that this proposal would go through. Once it was agreed by the *Storting*, the Government could alter the instructions to the coastal authorities and the outstanding cases involving British vessels could be settled in an equitable manner. It would then remain to decide whether to go to The Hague Court on the main issue or whether to settle it by a direct agreement on the lines proposed after the recent discussions. He personally thought that the latter was preferable and believed that there was a good prospect of the *Storting* agreeing to such a solution for a limited period of years.

---

[2] In a telegram to Oslo (No. 198 of 16 February), which summarised this conversation, Bevin concluded: 'From this discussion, which was most friendly, I was left with the impression that M. Lange takes a sober view of the situation and maintains his belief that Norway's interest lies in a firm link with the West. He was evidently worried over the possibility of a split among Labour opinion in Norway and anxious not to play into the hands of the Communists. He will clearly do what he can to avoid provoking the Russians, but in this delicate situation there is obviously a danger that the Norwegian Government may lose their initiative and fight shy of any decisive action for fear of the risks attached to it' (FO 371/77398, N1656/1073/63G).

No. 184

Minute from Mr Bevin to Sir S. Cripps, 14 February 1949
Secret and Personal (FO 800/500, SC/491)

Chancellor of the Exchequer

As the Swedish Foreign Minister, M. Undén, is going to Paris to attend the forthcoming session of the OEEC Ministerial Committee of Nine, it is probable that you will meet him when you are yourself in Paris this week.

2. M. Undén has been doing his best to persuade the other Scandinavian countries to join a neutral *bloc* in Scandinavia and, while we are of course sympathetic to the idea of a closer link between the Scandinavian countries, providing for mutual defence arrangements, we do not wish this *bloc* to be neutral to the extent of preventing defence arrangements between Norway and Denmark

and the Atlantic Powers, if Norway and Denmark should so desire now or later. A neutral *bloc* would also raise very awkward issues in regard to Iceland and Greenland.

3. Our policy throughout has been to leave all three Scandinavian countries free to make their own choice. M. Undén, however, although he gave me an undertaking last year that Sweden would not bring pressure to bear on Norway and Denmark to stay out of the North Atlantic Pact, has in fact used considerable pressure. The whole question of Norwegian and Danish adherence to a North Atlantic Pact has now reached a most difficult and delicate stage. I thought I had better warn you of this, in view of your absence from London last week, in case M. Undén raises this question with you in Paris.

ERNEST BEVIN

No. 185

Letter from Sir L. Collier (Oslo) to Mr Hankey, 23 February 1949
Top Secret (FO 371/77398, N1985/1071/63G)

Dear Hankey,

There will not be time before this bag leaves to send home my official account of the proceedings in the Norwegian Labour Party meeting and other events here since Lange's return from Washington and London;[1] but I am writing this letter now to give you a picture of the salient points in the situation as I see it now.

Lange won an even more decisive victory at the party meeting than had been generally expected; and in the opinion of Inman, my acting Labour Attaché, who was present throughout (even during the closed session), this was mainly due to the realisation by all the Norwegians concerned that the Karlstad plan was now out of the question and that the alternatives for Norway were no longer the Atlantic Pact or a Scandinavian defence pact, but the Atlantic Pact or complete isolation. The only persons present who did not seem to realise this were the Swedish and Danish journalists, who had become the victims of their own propaganda and were quite ludicrously cast down when the result of the voting was announced. So, it appears, was the Danish Prime Minister, who even talked about resignation and whose whole attitude was, as described in my telegram No. 108,[2] one of bewildered defeatism. The Swedish Prime Minister, on the other hand, seems to have expected the result and taken it calmly; and the Norwegians in general now seem to feel more respect for the Swedes, who at least know their own minds, wrong-headed though they may be, than for the Danes, who go about wringing their hands and saying they don't know what to do. Skylstad,[3] as also reported in my telegram No. 108, spoke to me bitterly of language used by Rasmussen to the American 'Marshall Plan' correspondents now touring Scandinavia, which, he said, was 'pure defeatism'. (I don't know exactly what Rasmussen said, but no doubt we shall hear from Copenhagen). The Norwegians have also noted with interest, though without much expectation of practical consequences, the statements of Generals Nordenskiöld and Petri, the tergiversations of M. Vougt and other signs

---
[1] See Nos. 179 and 183.
[2] Not printed.
[3] Secretary-General, Norwegian Foreign Ministry.

that Swedish opinion is no longer solid behind the Swedish Government. A recent leading article in *Aftenposten* is entitled 'Norwegian unity: Swedish disunity'.

This does not mean, however, that all is now plain sailing for Lange, who certainly did not get at Washington all the information he will need to put before the *Storting* when the time comes for their final decision. I believe it surprised him, as it undoubtedly surprised my United States colleague as well as me, to find Washington so unprepared for his questions that Acheson, for example, could not even say whether or not the Atlantic Pact would cover Spitsbergen (in our view it obviously must, since to exclude that territory would be equivalent to notifying the Russians that they were free to seize it);[4] and he would have been still more surprised had he known—which I hope and believe he did not—that the military implications of the question whether Norway should join the Atlantic Pact or a 'neutral' Scandinavian defence union had not been considered until after his arrival (see Washington telegram No. 785),[5] although the question had been on the *tapis* for at least a month previously. (I suppose I shall see in due course a copy of the military appreciation mentioned in that telegram, though it is now mainly of academic interest).[6] As regards arms supplies, too, the position still seems vague, though I gather that the Norwegians are comforted by the Secretary of State's assurance that the arms requirements of all the Atlantic Pact countries will be dealt with in common. (Incidentally, can I assume that Mr Bevin's remarks on this subject, as reported in paragraph 12 of the record,[7] have been passed on to the Swedes? I should think they might do a lot of good in Stockholm).[8]

Lange's visit, then (though I note that the Secretary of State is inclined to deprecate its timing) has achieved not only its declared object of providing the Norwegian Government with enough material to convince public opinion that it is desirable *in principle* to enter the Atlantic Pact, but also the further object of stirring up the Americans and making them, in their own phraseology, 'get down to brass tacks'; and I doubt whether anything short of that could have produced this double result.

I am sending copies of this letter to Randall, Farquhar and Hoyer Millar.

Yours ever,
L. COLLIER

PS A fairly authoritative account of the Norwegian Government's present attitude will be found in the *Daily Telegraph* for February 21st. Goulding, the *Telegraph* correspondent, got it from Lange's brother in law.

---

[4] Commenting on this, Etherington-Smith observed that the revised wording of the Pact should cover Spitsbergen automatically.

[5] See No. 181.

[6] Northern Department were not willing to send a copy of this appreciation to Oslo, because the American Chiefs of Staff had asked that their views should be treated with the utmost secrecy.

[7] No. 183.

[8] Replying to Collier on 8 March, Hankey wrote 'We have taken no special action to convey these remarks of the Secretary of State to the Swedes. I think in fact that the Secretary of State's feeling at the time was that the Swedes should rather be left to discover these truths for themselves as the reality of the situation becomes more apparent to them. As you know, he is strongly of the opinion that no pressure should be applied to them and our present policy is to leave them very much to themselves in the hope that they will gradually come to realise the practical disadvantages of the isolationist course which M. Undén has chosen for them, and may be willing to co-operate to some extent with the West, or at least with their Scandinavian neighbours (which would probably meet our requirements almost as well)' (FO 371/77399, N1985/1073/63G).

No. 186

Minute from Mr Etherington-Smith to Mr Hankey, 3 March 1949
(FO 371/77357, N2174/1015/56)

In the course of a conversation which I had with him yesterday morning the Finnish Minister asked me what I though of the present situation in Scandinavia, particularly in view of the probability that Norway and Denmark would shortly accede to the Atlantic Pact. I said that I personally thought that this development would prove a stabilising factor in Scandinavia as well as elsewhere. Experience had taught us that the Russians only respected strength and if the countries of the West got together and made it clear that they would jointly resist attack on any one of them, I thought that the Russians would be far less likely to press their aggressive policy so far as to precipitate a war.

M. Wuori referred to the possibility that the Russians might make some move to redress the balance of power in their favour in view of the probable adherence of Norway and Denmark to the Atlantic Pact. There had been no evidence so far of any intensification of Soviet diplomatic and political pressures on Finland, but he did not think that the possibility of some move could be altogether excluded. The Soviet Minister to Finland, Savonenkov, had recently returned to Helsinki, and although it appeared that his absence had been genuinely due to health reasons, his return at this stage might nevertheless possibly have some political significance.

M. Wuori went on to say that, as regards the possibility that the Russians might exert pressure inside the country through the Finnish Communists, the Finnish Government were well prepared to meet such a threat. They were confident of being able to prevent the Communists from starting up any serious trouble e.g. in the form of big strikes. As regards the alternative possibility that the Russians might bring overt pressure to bear and might even move troops into Finland, M. Wuori indicated that he had no reason to believe that any such action was imminent. Nor did he see what the Russians would gain by it. It would, he said, inevitably tend to push Sweden into the Atlantic Pact. It would also arouse world opinion, particularly American opinion, and, although he had no illusions that the West would be able to give Finland any effective help in such circumstances, it would assist them to consolidate the system which was being built in the West in opposition to Russia.

M. Wuori added that, as indicated in the recent statement by the Finnish Prime Minister, an attempt would probably now be made to form a coalition Government in Finland. Some Finnish politicians, however, had felt that there might be some advantage in bringing the Communists into such a Government and that they could be relegated to one or two minor posts. He did not however himself think that this would be possible. The Finnish Communists, like the Communist parties in the West and elsewhere, had recently been taking a much more dogmatic and intransigent line and, whereas they had previously been prepared to co-operate to some extent with other parties, particularly the Socialists, they were less ready to do so now and were much more exacting in their terms. He did not think, therefore, that if they were asked to join a Government, they would be willing to do so unless they were offered some key posts such as the ministries of the Interior or Foreign Affairs, which he seemed to recognise as being clearly undesirable. On this question I repeated to M. Wuori the familiar arguments against allowing the Communists to participate in a Government at all.[1]

R.G.A. ETHERINGTON-SMITH

[1] Hankey copied this minute to Helsinki and Moscow. The Finnish Legation in London maintained frequent contact with the Foreign Office in the first three months of 1949, raising a range of concerns about the possible implications for Finland if Norway and Denmark were to join the Atlantic Pact. For example, Vuori accompanied Söderhjelm, leader of the Swedish Party in Finland, to a meeting with McNeil on 18 February. Söderhjelm asked what might happen if, after Norway and Denmark (and possibly even Sweden) had joined the Atlantic Pact, the Russians were then to put pressure on the Finns. Would Britain press Finland to enter some sort of defensive alliance, or what advice might Britain offer them? McNeil replied that this was a hypothetical question, but he expected that in such circumstances Bevin would be prepared to do whatever the Finns themselves wanted (FO 371/77403, N1756/1076/63G).

No. 187

Letter from Count Reventlow (Danish Ambassador) to Sir I. Kirkpatrick, 7 March 1949
(FO 371/77351, N3119/1821/15)

My dear Sir Ivone,
On the 15th February the last German refugee left Denmark. As you know the presence of the great number of refugees constituted an extremely heavy burden upon Denmark. It is, therefore, felt as a great relief that the refugees have now at last all been removed and my Government are grateful to His Britannic Majesty's Government for the ready help which they have throughout rendered in this matter. You yourself have been quite particularly helpful and I have received instructions to express to you my Government's gratitude.[1]

Believe me,
Yours sincerely,
REVENTLOW

[1] Kirkpatrick marked this letter to Bevin, commenting: 'You took an interest in this. It is a small matter. But a settlement of any problem is always something.' Bevin requested that Sir John Anderson should be informed (FO 371/77351, N3119/1821/15).

No. 188

Letter from Sir A. Randall (Copenhagen) to Mr Hankey, 8 March 1949
Top Secret (FO 371/77396, N2497/1072/63G)

Dear Robin,
Collier's Top Secret letter G12/148/49 of February 23rd[1] and in particular remark about the Danish Prime Minister's 'bewildered defeatism' and the Danish Foreign Minister's 'pure defeatism', seem to call for a brief comment.
As regards the first I would refer you to the last paragraph of my letter G11/134/49 of 23rd February,[2] and add that the steadfast adherents of the Atlantic

[1] No. 185. [2] Not printed.

Pact here now express admiration for the Danish Prime Minister's tactics which succeeded so well in bringing his party rapidly to a complete change of view. The 'bewildered defeatism' did not last long!

On the subject of Rasmussen's declarations reported in the Danish press of the 13th February, I did not worry you with these as they contained nothing new. If, however, Skylstad had read the whole of Rasmussen's remarks to the American correspondents I do not think he would have spoken of 'pure defeatism'. In private talks with me Rasmussen is given to a rather defeatist attitude, but in his public statements he expounds his Government's policy from which, at the time of the interview in question, Norway did not dissent, namely, that the best solution for the Scandinavian defence problem would have been a defence agreement between all three countries. As I have all along insisted, the Norwegian Government have always been in a far happier position both because they have the backing of a united public opinion, and because Norwegian defence possibilities are vastly greater than Denmark's. So I hope that there will not be too much display of Norwegian 'superiority'. This has in the past not improved Norwegian relations with Sweden and it would be a pity if, at a time when Denmark is preparing to go into the Atlantic Pact, Dano-Norwegian relations are disturbed for any cause. To put it frankly, the Danes feel that the Norwegians, from their relatively sheltered strategic position, have been showing a tinge of self-righteousness. This does not excuse the annoying Danish habit of 'wanting to have it both ways' and showing extreme dilatoriness, but I hope I have made it clear that the very difficult domestic political situation here was at least a partial defence, (see my despatch No. 41 (G11/100/49) of 11th February 1949),[2] and if in the future the Danes and Norwegians are to work as equal partners in the Atlantic Pact (no easy job as far as Denmark is concerned) the path will be made smoother if Norway does not too much insist on her having possessed a monopoly of courage and decision.[2]

Yours ever,
A.W.G. RANDALL

PS I am sending copies of this letter to Oslo and Stockholm.

[2] Hankey commented: 'It's so hard to divine how much of the "superiority" comes from Sir L. Collier himself!'

No. 189

Mr Bevin to Mr Baxter (Reykjavik), 9 March 1949
No. 18 Secret (FO 371/77402, N2412/1075/63G)

Sir,
At the request of the Icelandic Prime Minister[1] I saw M. Harald Gudmundsson, who is here negotiating the question of fish on behalf of the Icelandic Government.

2. M. Gudmundsson asked me questions about the Atlantic Pact; for example, whether the Icelandic Government would be involved except as regards the

[1] The request from Stefán Stefánsson was not made directly to Bevin: it was passed to his Private Office by Morgan Phillips, General Secretary of the Labour Party, whom Gudmundsson had originally approached with his letter of introduction. Gudmundsson was a former Minister of Labour and a former President of the Icelandic *Althing.*

The Nordic Countries, 1944-1951

establishment of foreign troops in Iceland, what they would have to do with regard to bases and whether, if Iceland could be used in case of war as it was in the last war, there was any need for them to join the Pact.

3. In regard to these questions, I told him that I was severely handicapped because the Pact was private and confidential and it was extremely difficult for me to discuss it. I thought that in a few days' time his Government would be approached on the subject and the correct thing to do was for them to put these questions between then and the day of signature; they would have ample time. I should be willing to see their representative immediately I was free to discuss the Pact.

4. He informed me that their difficulty was that for 700 years they had been defenceless and had had no army or anything of that kind, and the people would be very reluctant to join any Pact.

5. I told him with regard to the latter point that, if he was not a member of the club, it would be difficult to guarantee to him the benefits of the club. He said he quite understood.[2]

6. He then told me of the difficulties associated with the price of fish which he was now negotiating with his delegation in London.

7. Copies have been sent to Washington and Paris.

I am, etc.,
ERNEST BEVIN

[2] Icelandic reservations about the Atlantic Pact had been raised with the Americans in January: see FRUS 1949, Vol. IV, p. 22.

No. 190

Letter from Sir L. Collier (Oslo) to Mr Hankey, 18 March 1949
Top Secret (FO 371/77396, N2886/1072/63)

Dear Hankey,

I see from my copy of Randall's letter to you of March 8th[1] that the remarks in my letter of February 23rd[2] about the attitude of Hedtoft and Rasmussen during the final discussions on Norway's adherence to the Atlantic Pact, have roused Randall to defend them against Norwegian criticism.

2. It was not, however, on Norwegians alone that Hedtoft, when here, made the impression of a man much annoyed at being forced to make up his mind. He made the same impression on the Danish journalists who accompanied him (they were in touch with my Press Attaché, who has a Danish wife): indeed, his language to them about Lange was, to put it mildly, more than peevish. I did not go into this at the time, since it was not likely to affect his permanent policy; but if it got known to the Norwegians, as it probably did, they might well be excused for taking a dim view of it and of him.

3. It is also common knowledge here that Hedtoft's hesitations lasted up to the very moment of his departure. Oxholm, the Danish Ambassador, told me the other day that Hedtoft's last words to him, as he said goodbye at the railway station,

[1] No. 188.
[2] No. 185.

were: 'What on earth shall I do now?', in reply to which he had shouted as the train was leaving: 'There is only one thing to do'—'so I hope', he added with a grin, 'that I had some share in bringing about his sudden conversation when he got to Copenhagen'.

4. As regards Rasmussen, again, it is not only the Norwegians who have commented on his tendency to express 'alarm and despondency'. I knew him fairly well when he was Counsellor of the Danish legation in London, and although I found him a great improvement on his chief, Reventlow, 'the last of a long line of maiden aunts', he showed nothing like the determination of, say, Christmas Møller.

5. I have heard it said (and not by a Norwegian) that Norway has been fortunate in the past year or so to have been led by intelligent and determined men like Gerhardsen, Lange and Hauge, whereas Sweden has been led by men who were determined but not intelligent, like Undén and Wigforss, and Denmark by men who were intelligent but not determined, like Hedtoft and Rasmussen; and though this, of course, is too much of an epigram to be wholly fair there is, I think, a good deal of truth in it.

6. In short, if people here have a wrong impression of the Danish Government's attitude, as Randall suggests, that has not been due to Norwegian 'superiority', but to the actions and language of the Danish leaders themselves; and if, as now seems, fortunately, to be the case, these have come into line with Norwegian actions and language, then he will have no reason to fear a disturbance of Danish-Norwegian relations on this score.[3]

7. I am sending copies of this letter to Randall and Farquhar.

Yours ever,
L. COLLIER

[3] Davidson commented to Hankey: 'Sir L. Collier wins Round 2 easily. Indeed his fifth paragraph is almost a knockout' (FO 371/77396, N2886/1072/63).

No. 191

Sir A. Randall (Copenhagen) to Mr Bevin, 30 March 1949
No. 97 Top Secret (FO 371/77396, N3157/1072/63)

Sir,
Now that the Danish *Rigsdag*, by a large majority in both Houses had, as reported in my telegrams Nos. 18 and 19 Saving, of 25th and 26th March,[1] authorised the Danish Government to sign and ratify the Atlantic Pact it is, I think, of some interest to analyse the national sentiment and estimates for the future which accompany this historic decision. Since it was taken I have had conversations with two or three Danish Ministers, in particular a long talk on 25th March with the Minister of Defence, and the following account is based largely on these informal discussions.

There is, I think, no doubt that the mood of the country is one of resignation to the inevitable rather than enthusiastic adherence to and confidence in the new alliance. I have not met a Danish Minister who did not inform me that Denmark

[1] Not printed.

would have greatly preferred the Scandinavian defence-union on a basis of neutrality; and it is clear that the Prime Minister correctly sensed the feeling of the country in delaying the decision to enter the Atlantic Pact until it was shown, beyond any kind of question, that the Scandinavian union was and, for an indefinite period would remain, an empty dream. He has been much praised for his tactics which effected so rapid a change in the mood of the Socialist Party (in the *Rigsdag* and the Party Executive, at any rate; there is said to be a good deal of unwillingness in the rank and file in the country). But I think he, and certainly other Ministers, have an undercurrent of regret and even resentment that the pace was forced by the Norwegians and Americans, so that unity with Sweden which the Karlstad plan promised could not be achieved. This is combined with a relief, which other Ministers have expressed to me, that the great decision has at last been taken, moreover, as the Minister of Defence told me, with the full approval of the Swedish Government, or at least of the Swedish Prime Minister. Indeed, so Mr Rasmus Hansen informed me in confidence, Mr Erlander had at the last actually advised Mr Hedtoft to decide in favour of the Pact.

There is a practical side to the extreme importance which the Danish Government attaches to Swedish policy. Without Sweden, as Mr Rasmus Hansen said to me, the naval defence of the Sound is impossible. He also remarked that Denmark would like the use of the South Swedish airfields, while, in an emergency, the partial evacuation of civilians from Copenhagen to Sweden would, he said, be desirable. Sweden was now, he went on, in an irritated, distrustful and alarmed state of mind. It was of vital interest to Denmark that some way should be found of soothing Swedish feelings and removing the impression that Sweden had missed her chance and was now a subject of indifference to the West. I told Mr Rasmus Hansen that it seemed obvious to me that a weak Sweden would not be in the interests of peace, and he said that he was glad to hear me say this. Had the Scandinavian Defence Agreement been practicable, he thought Sweden could have been brought round to some kind of link with the West within six months.[2] Now I have heard that members of the Danish Government are saying that it will require two years, unless meanwhile the Soviet government makes an aggressive move in Finland. I remarked to Mr Rasmus Hansen that I hoped Moscow was aware of this estimate of Sweden's possible reactions, and the Minister said that he thought this was so.

It is clear to me that, although the Danes will now begin asking with some insistence for more military supplies, their more immediate preoccupation is with Sweden. The fairly far-reaching discussions which have been going on between the Swedish and Danish Naval Commanders-in-Chief seem to have come to an end; it is obviously desirable that they should be taken up once more and that in general some way should be found of keeping close contact between the planners of defence on both sides of the Sound. The Danes evidently think this will not be so difficult as it will be to restore Swedish-Norwegian relations to what they were before the Atlantic Pact discussions. As I have often mentioned, the Danish attitude towards the Swedes is fundamentally different from the Norwegian, and it may be that in the renewed approach to Sweden which the Danes think so desirable they may have that same mediatory role to play as they attempted over the main Pact negotiations.

---

[2] Hankey annotated this statement: 'We always doubted this and still do!'

As regards Denmark's own share in the Pact I think one can say that there is a certain feeling of confidence in its moral and deterrent value. Certainly I have noted an absence of the state bordering on panic which existed here about twelve months ago. The text of the Pact has been much praised to me by Danes for its firm yet unprovocative character. There is a certain puzzlement over the mildness of the Russian reactions so far; but if the 'nerve-war' is intensified I think it will cause less worry now than it would have done last year. At the same time the Government's quick conversion, and above all that of the Minister for Foreign Affairs, should not obscure the fact that every effort will be made to avoid frightening the Danish people with the belief that they have been committed to an automatic military alliance. In the final debate Mr Gustav Rasmussen was at some pains to emphasise that Denmark would remain her own judge whether to go to war, and that she had not agreed to any foreign bases in Denmark, or committed herself in regard to Greenland, the role of which in plans for Atlantic defence remained to be determined. The Danish opposition to the Atlantic Pact is by no means exclusively Communist or anti-Western. There is a solid element of pacifism, and although some of the Radical intellectuals who signed petitions against the signature might almost be classed as 'fellow-travellers', many are rather of that old-fashioned type of optimistic liberal which, despite all experience, thinks a modest neutral role would have been safer for the country. I know the Prime Minister was deeply disappointed that he was unable to carry the Radical Party with him; the links between them and the Socialists are of long standing, and Mr Hedtoft's embarrassment over breaking them with this decision is said to have been exceeded only by the Radicals' embarrassment at finding themselves in the same lobby as the Communists. Internal politics will therefore continue to play some part in Denmark's policy when once the ratification faces her, it may be, with practical decisions. The Defence Minister told me that he felt sure the majority which had approved the signature of the Pact would support the Government in providing for any financial sacrifices which might be necessary. But these will be closely scrutinised by the opponents of the Pact, and will obviously give an opportunity to Communist propaganda. So, too, will any suggestion of reducing Denmark's trade with the East; suggestions on these lines, if it is necessary that they should be made, should be framed with the greatest tact.

Communist agitation here has not, so far, gone beyond the crude propaganda about 'leading the country into war', concentrated on the allegation that the Pact stabilises the capitalist order and, as a follow-up from the Marshall Plan, puts Denmark even more completely under American control. This can be met by emphasis on the constructive side of the Pact, illustrated in Article 2. This social and economic side of the Brussels Pact made the most favourable impression here, and contributed I think, to the willingness with which the Danish Government agreed to take part in the Council of Europe discussions. In private talk Danes, to justify their pessimism, dwell excessively on the military aspects of the Atlantic Pact; for public consumption I think it is important that this should be paralleled with the constructive moral and economic aspect of the new alliance. The revolutionary nature of the decision which Denmark has taken will perhaps begin to cause apprehension in the months to come unless it is appreciated that the United States has also made a revolutionary decision, and the United Kingdom and

Canada, with the resources of the colonies, have determined to play their part with all the power they can muster in the re-establishment of Europe.[3]

I am sending copies of this despatch to His Majesty's representatives at Oslo, Stockholm and Washington.

I have, etc.,
A.W.G. RANDALL

[3] Etherington-Smith minuted to Hankey: 'We can certainly agree with Sir A. Randall's view in para. 4 that Danish-Swedish service contacts & joint planning for defence should be encouraged. This is precisely what we are hoping for, i.e. that Sweden will gradually be drawn into practical co-operation with her two Western neighbours' (FO 371/77396, N3157/1072/63).

No. 192

Dr Thornton (Reykjavik) to Mr Bevin, 4 April 1949
No. 28 Confidential (FO 371/77402, N3868/1075/63)

Sir,

In my telegram No. 54 of 30th March,[1] I had the honour to report that the Icelandic Government had on that day secured the approval of Parliament to Iceland's participation in the North Atlantic Pact. The vote was taken after three of the stormiest days in the history of the modern *Althing* and was followed immediately by demonstrations which were both unprecedented and largely unexpected.

2. As has been previously reported, opposition to participation has recently diminished. The decision of Norway and Denmark to participate, the publication of the text of the Treaty and the assurance that Iceland would not be called upon to provide military bases in peacetime did much to allay the fears of all but the extreme nationalists, who regarded any alliance as a potential threat to Iceland's language and culture. The Communists, who had been playing upon these fears and posing as the defence of Icelandic independence, were thus deprived of their strongest line of propaganda.

3. The Minister for Foreign Affairs[2] and his two colleagues, the Minister for Education (Progressive) and the Minister of Commerce and Communications (Labour)[3] returned from Washington on 29th March and it was expected that the North Atlantic Pact would be debated in the *Althing* on 25th or 26th March. Its postponement over that weekend was decided upon, for reasons that, in the light of after events, appear sound.

4. In proportion as the non-communist opposition decreased, so had the violence of the communist opposition increased. Protest meetings were convened. Resolutions passed, headlines daily screamed abuse at the 'puppet' government and 'land-sale clique' and announced that the Icelandic people should and would prevent the proposed treachery and forbid the parliament to betray the country. On a slightly more dignified level, the Communists in parliament tabled a motion of non-confidence in the Government which clearly had to be disposed of before the

[1] Not printed.
[2] Bjarni Benediktsson.
[3] Eysteinn Jónsson and Emil Jónsson.

Pact itself was debated. The Communists proposed to base their case not only on the question of the Pact, but also on the record of the economic misdeeds of the Government, of which the trawler strike was to be cited as the last damning example. There was reason to believe that the communists had been largely responsible for the rejection of the first mediation proposals by the seamen, and for the prolongation of this strike. The Government therefore decided with eleventh hour discretion that the strike must be settled and some at least of the trawlers out of the harbour before they dealt with this motion, in order not only to weaken the Communists' argument but also, and this was apparently considered more important, to lessen the risk of anti-government demonstrations by the seamen. The Government appealed to the trawler-owners and men and, as reported in my telegram No. 50 of 28th March,[1] agreement was reached on 27th March and the first trawlers put to sea on that day.

5. The Government still however took the Communist threats more seriously than did many of the public. During the weekend of 26th-27th March police reserves were called up and, I was informed, the force was issued with steel helmets and truncheons. The Communist paper meanwhile published warnings to the public and instructions for dealing with tear gas. The Conservatives mobilised all party members and proceeded to man the Conservative headquarters, a large building in the parliament square, ready and undoubtedly willing to move across should the Communists attempt to rush the house at any time during the forthcoming debates. As a further sensible precaution all guest tickets for the *Althing* were withdrawn and members were issued with three new tickets each.

6. The three Government parties had officially declared themselves in favour of participation. There were certain dissenters in the Labour and Progressive ranks but it was clear that the Government was certain of 36-37 votes out of the total 52: it was equally certain of 10 Communist votes against. The Minister for Foreign Affairs continued however to hope that some at least of the dissenters might be won over, the Progressive and Labour amendments to the Bill (see Paragraph 9 below) possibly withdrawn, and opinion in the country favourably solidified, if emphasis were publicly to be laid on the fact that Iceland as an unarmed nation could not and would not be expected to declare war in implementation of Article V of the Treaty. This question had been discussed with the State Department and on 26th March, an official statement on the discussions (of which a translation is attached)[1] was issued to the Icelandic press. The amendments were not withdrawn, and, so far as can be judged, this statement had no effect on the final voting or on public opinion. The Minister for Foreign Affairs was made aware of your objections Sir, and of those of the State Department, to any insistence on Iceland's 'special' position (my telegrams Nos. 51 and 56)[1] and it appeared that before the beginning of the debate on 28th March, he had decided to face the House with the issue of participation, without attempt at further conciliation.

7. The debate on the motion of non-confidence took place on the evening of 28th March and ended with a vote of 9 to 37 against: there were 5 abstentions (Labour and Progressive) and one absentee (Communist). The Communist speeches followed the expected line of abuse and threats, which have become so familiar during the last three months, and even the United States Minister who, possibly tactlessly, was in the visitors' gallery with some of his staff, was not spared.

8. The debate on the Government bill for participation in the Pact began on Tuesday morning, 29th March and continued until the following afternoon, 30th

March. The Communists summoned a final towns-meeting for 1 p.m. on 30th March and, supported by the communist-controlled Reykjavik labourers' union, ordered all workers to down tools for the rest of the day. The Government, fearing that the meeting would adjourn en masse to the parliament square and, there possibly attempt to enter the *Althing*, promptly issued handbills summoning all peaceful citizens to go at that time to the square in token of their desire that the lawfully elected parliament should continue its deliberations without disturbance. Despite all the disturbances that followed, this manoeuvre was successful insofar as there seems to be no doubt that the majority of the crowd in the packed square were indeed peaceful citizens and that only the advance guard of the communist meeting had found strategic positions in front of the main doors of the *Althing*.

9. Within the *Althing*, the debate proceeded as foreseen. The Communist leaders repeated their previous arguments of treachery and, even by the accepted standards of Icelandic debate, passed all bounds of personal invective, completely outstripping the resources of all available Icelandic dictionaries. The two amendments were taken first and both were defeated by 36 votes to 16. The first, a Progressive amendment, proposed that participation should be decided by a plebiscite, the second, a Labour amendment, proposed that participation should be conditional upon an immediate revision of the Keflavik agreement. Both amendments also demanded formal recognition by all participants of Iceland's special status as an unarmed nation that never intended or would be required to arm. The voting on the Government bill then took place with 37 votes (19 Conservative, 11 Progressive and 7 Labour) against 13 (10 Communist, 1 Progressive and 2 Labour) and 2 abstentions (Progressive). Iceland was thus formally admitted to participation in the North Atlantic Treaty. The House adjourned and the waiting crowds heard the result as the flag was lowered on the building.

10. In the chaos that followed it is doubtful whether any one of the 'peaceful citizens' there assembled had any idea of the sequence of events, but now that the smoke and gas have somewhat cleared, it is possible to reconstruct the scene from the accounts of the people both inside and outside the *Althing*. As the house rose, the police within the building asked that members should remain inside until the crowd had dispersed somewhat, and a way could be made for the ministers' cars. At this point, the leader of the Communist party thrust his head out of one of the windows—the debating hall faces onto the square—and shouted to the crowd that they were prisoners in the *Althing*. It had been noticed that one of the other Communists had previously slipped out before the result was formally declared and it seems more than probable that he had given some sign to his supporters in the crowd. Certainly at precisely that moment a well-aimed stone smashed one of the windows, immediately followed by others, which wrecked the doors and, aimed up at the chamber, went through, reaching as far as the Speaker's chair, with a shower of glass. There was shouting, more stones and eggs. The police went into action to reach the culprits nearest to the building and with the raw materials of the square rock gardens flying through the air, they dispersed the crowd with tear gas. As a sidelight on the result it might be said that the citizens of Reykjavik have seldom been seen to move so quickly or to be so unanimous in their desire for plain water, as they rushed towards the lake, by this Legation, seeking to stem their tears with dampened handkerchiefs. Several policemen were severely injured in the melée: arrests were made of the more obvious inciters of the mob, including a young woman who smacked the Prime Minister's face as he came out of

parliament. The disturbances continued intermittently throughout the night during which all the windows of the Conservative headquarters were smashed and many shops suffered. The Minister for Foreign Affairs left that same evening for Washington.

11. The predominant feeling in Reykjavik, I cannot of course judge that of the countryside, appears to be one of shock. A majority of by no means unthinking people here have previously been convinced that, whatever happened in other countries, in Iceland at least, Communists were good citizens at heart, and that, in any crisis, they would be Icelanders first and Communists second. The Communists themselves have played up to this conception and, recently, have been at pains not to commit themselves to any declarations on the lines of those made by Monsieur Thorez and Signor Togliatti.[4] At the same time, the ordinary honest citizen naturally did not believe that the Communist threats of local violence would be translated into action, and it was in this belief, that people obeyed the Government's injunction and went to the parliament square on 30th March, many with their families including young children. The events of that afternoon have undoubtedly shaken this belief. The police did not provoke the crowd and clearly the supporters of the Government would not attack each other. There can be no other interpretation than that the Communists intended to cause and did indeed deliberately start the disturbance.

12. It is too early to assess the lasting effects of these events. At present, the prestige of the Government is higher than it has been for some time, people appear to be relieved that during the past ten days the Government has at last shown strength of mind and has taken action: the only criticism is that they did not act sooner over the trawler strike, and more drastically with the Communist hooligans.

13. The Communists on the other hand appear to have lost what remained of the uncertain ground gained during the past few months. That the *Althing*, symbol of so much of Iceland's history, should have been attacked, is regarded as a personal hurt by many who are themselves not enthusiastic supporters of the Government. The material damage is fortunately inconsiderable; already most of the windows have been replaced. It would possibly be well if the crack in the wall of Iceland complacency were not so swiftly and easily repaired.

I am sending a copy of this despatch to HM Ambassador at Washington.

I have, etc.,
C.G. THORNTON

[4] Leaders of the French and Italian Communist Parties.

No. 193

Mr Bevin to Mr Crowe (Oslo), 6 May 1949
No. 110 Secret (FO 371/77398, N4187/1073/63G)

Sir,

When he called on me today the Norwegian Foreign Minister, M. Lange, referred to the defence arrangements which would need to be made for the implementation of the North Atlantic Treaty.

2. M. Lange said that, even though the Swedish Government took a very neutral attitude, he felt that it was in the interests of the Atlantic Powers that Swedish

defence requirements should be met so far as possible. He mentioned in particular aircraft and radar and said that, from the point of view of Norwegian defence, it was desirable that the effective radar screen should be as far to the east as possible.

3. I said that I was inclined to agree with M. Lange about this. It was certainly desirable for the defence of Scandinavia to be organised in as much depth as possible, and I felt confident that the Swedes would never side with the Russians. The Americans had been a little dogmatic in the past about the supply of arms to Sweden, but I thought that recently there had been less difficulty on this head. Meanwhile, no orders for Sweden had been cancelled though there would inevitably be difficult questions about priorities when the Atlantic Pact supply programme came to be worked out. M. Lange agreed, and said that Norway would also wish to press certain priority claims at that point.

4. M. Lange then asked whether anything had been decided about the location of the various organisations to be set up under the Atlantic Treaty. I said that this had not yet been settled, and I was reluctant to raise a question which might possibly be a source of further difficulties until the treaty had been ratified, and until I had had further time to reflect on it. M. Lange said in this connexion that he realised that it would be necessary for Norwegian planning to be co-ordinated with the defence plans of the other North Atlantic Powers. He felt, however, that Norway and Denmark shared with Great Britain, Canada and the United States a rather special interest in the North Atlantic area, and that something might well be lost if they were merely asked to join in the Brussels Pact machinery in which France would no doubt emphasise the special interests of the more southern part of Western Europe. I said that I thought the Brussels Pact organisation would certainly have to continue for some time. I felt that there were two aspects of the North Atlantic defence problem. First of all there was the problem of where the first impact of any attack should be met. We had nearly come to grief both in 1914 and 1939 because no adequate preparations had been made, and also because there was no united and agreed concept on how the impact should be met. On the other hand, there were most complicated problems of how the conduct of air defence and naval warfare in the area was to be fitted in, and it was necessary to have the correct conception of what was required or the necessary equipment and supplies would not be sent where they were most needed. I felt, therefore, that there was much force in what M. Lange said.

5. Copies of this despatch have been sent to Brussels, Paris, Washington, Copenhagen, and Stockholm.

I am, etc.,
ERNEST BEVIN

No. 194

Letter from Mr Hankey to Mr Scott (Helsinki), 9 May 1949
Top Secret and Personal (FO 371/77363, N4240/10338/56G)

Dear Oswald,

You may be interested to hear that Wuori told me on May 4th that he had recently been asked to dinner by the Soviet Ambassador. He said that Zaroubin was accompanied only by the new Counsellor, Korovin. They spoke mostly in English as Wuori is forgetting his Russian.

After filling him and themselves up with vodka (from which, he said with a glint in his eye, he thought they suffered more than he did), Zaroubin asked Wuori to tell him plainly what were the relations between the Finnish Government and the new military organisation of Western Europe. Surely, he said, there were Finnish officers in Lord Montgomery's new staff and in this connexion he referred to the presence of Marshal Mannerheim in Switzerland. Wuori said that he had little difficulty in dealing with this accusation. He told Zaroubin that Mannerheim was much too old and too ill to take any interest in such matters. There were of course many Finnish officers abroad as a result of the events of the last ten years. They were mostly of Fascist sympathies and one was even training the United States Army in winter manoeuvres in Alaska. On the other hand, as he told Zaroubin, it was surely a considerable advantage both to the Finnish Government and to the Soviet Government that they should not be inside Finland at the present time. The Finnish Government had nothing to do with the Western European Organisation.

Zaroubin and Korovin pressed him a good deal about his relations with us and he told them that the Foreign Office, while suspicious of the Finnish communists, was entirely in favour of the foreign policy of the present Finnish Government, namely, pursuing friendly relations with the Soviet Union. Zaroubin was rather disbelieving about this and suggested that the Finns were preparing military aerodromes for use by the Americans.

I asked Wuori what interpretation he placed on this interview. He said he was a little afraid that it might be a prelude to very much stronger pressure on Finland. He recalled that in 1939 the Soviet diplomats in a number of capitals had interviews rather on these lines with their Finnish colleagues. On the other hand, he agreed when I suggested that the circumstances looked more as if they were trying to get information out of him, particularly their letting the vodka flow so freely first. I said we had a number of indications that the Russians might be genuinely worried about military preparations in the West, and they were certainly doing their best to get information on the subject. The Soviet Embassy lived in a state of very great seclusion and it would be surprising if they did not try to use people like Wuori with a large number of western contacts in order to increase the information available.

I should be glad to know whether you have any indications of the Russians in Helsinki adopting a different attitude towards the Finns locally.

Wuori asked that we should treat what he had said with the utmost secrecy and I should be grateful if you would regard this as absolutely Top Secret.

R.M.A. HANKEY

No. 195

Leading Personalities in Norway, 23 June 1949 (extract)[1]
Confidential (FO 371/77434, N 5959/1012/30)

Halvard Manthey Lange

Born 1902 at Oslo, the son of the late Christian Lange, Norwegian delegate to the League of Nations and a leader in the pacifist movement. He read philology and afterwards travelled widely, studying social affairs and labour conditions in many European countries, including Great Britain, where he worked in the London School of Economics; and at the age of 21, he was appointed secretary of the International Pacifist Union in London. Thereafter he was employed as a school teacher, served on the Oslo Municipality from 1932 to 1934, and in 1933 became a member of the central executive of the Norwegian Labour Party. Shortly before the outbreak of war he became headmaster of the Workers' Educational Association residential college; but he was dismissed by the Germans and interned at Sachsenhausen, whence he returned after the liberation with M. Gerhardsen (*q.v.*), succeeding M. Lie (*q.v.*) as Minister for Foreign Affairs on the latter's appointment as Secretary-General of the United Nations Organisation. A highly cultivated man of the academic type and the author of a number of books on historical and social subjects, he has more background than his predecessor, but it was not clear when he was appointed whether he would have equal will-power. In the event, however, he has proved to be a man of even greater determination, as well as higher moral character; and he has succeeded, with the help of the Prime Minister, in giving a definitely 'Western' orientation to Norwegian foreign policy, in outwitting the Russians in the 'Spitzbergen crisis' at the beginning of 1947 and in preventing the Swedish Government from imposing their isolationism on the whole of Scandinavia. A first-class linguist, speaking excellent English and French (the latter a rare accomplishment in Norway), he is a clear speaker and an attractive talker, having a wide range of interests, a modest manner and a considerable sense of humour. In 1947 he suffered a serious and prolonged illness, a delayed result of his imprisonment in Germany, from which, however, he now seems almost completely recovered. He has married twice, his present wife, a young and attractive woman, being the daughter of *Stortingspresident* Monsen (*q.v.*). M. Lange's prestige has been greatly increased by the developments of 1948 in foreign affairs: he is known to have been the protagonist of the Atlantic Pact policy in Norway, and to have shown great skill and determination in bringing, first the Prime Minister and the Cabinet and then the Labour Party and the *Storting* round to his point of view, while countering Swedish attempts to upset him; and he is now a European figure, head and shoulders above the foreign ministers of the other Scandinavian States, while his reputation with the Norwegian public rivals that of M. Gerhardsen.

---

[1] At this time, Leading Personalities Reports were prepared by embassies on an irregular basis every few years and submitted to the Foreign Office. They contained biographical sketches and historical details of key personalities, mostly from the political and military leadership.

No. 196

Sir A. Cadogan (New York) to Mr Bevin, 13 October 1949, 10.28 p.m.
Tel. No. 2164 Confidential (FO 1110/254, PR3086/64/913)

Following for Information Research Department and Northern Department.

Icelandic Delegation have approached us for anti-Communist material which might effectively be used by Icelandic Minister for Foreign Affairs in forthcoming election campaign where Communists form principal opposition party. Icelandic Minister for Foreign Affairs is particularly interested in authentic material such as texts of [?laws] and statements by Government speakers in Communist controlled countries. We are communicating to Icelandic Delegation here material on Hungary, Bulgaria and Roumania taken from our brief and extracts from 'points of issue' but you may wish to supplement this by material covering Czechoslovakia, Poland and the Soviet Union.

2. To be of use material must reach Reykjavik not later than October 20th as elections take place on October 23rd. Material should be communicated to Icelandic Minister or Chargé d'Affaires in London for urgent confidential transmission to Iceland Minister for Foreign Affairs personally.[1]

---

[1] In a telegram from Reykjavik of 17 October, Baxter advised that it would be better for the material to reach the Minister for Foreign Affairs under cover of a personal letter from the Icelandic Minister in London. He pointed out that 'It might embarrass the Minister for Foreign Affairs to receive personal communications of this kind from British or American Legations here. His opponents are always accusing him of being merely the mouth-piece of Anglo-Saxon powers who tell him what to say' (FO 1110/254, PR3118/64/913). The Icelandic Minister complied with the request to write a covering letter, although in order to meet the deadline the material was sent in a Foreign Office bag via the Embassy in Reykjavik (FO 1110/254, PR3086/64/913).

No. 197

Sir A. Randall (Copenhagen) to Mr Bevin, 29 October 1949, 3.25 p.m.
Tel. No. 318 Priority, Confidential (FO 371/77341, N9366/1153/15)

Announcement of sharp increase in British coal export prices has called forth sharp protests in the Danish press. Price increase is regarded here as particularly unfortunate, following so soon after the admittedly guarded statement of leader of British Trade Delegation that no such increase was foreseen, and in Danish eyes an aggravating factor is that the Coal Board represents the state-owned coal mines. Press generally take the line that the coal price amply justifies the caution of the Danish side in declining to negotiate Trade Agreement for 1950 in the fluctuating price situation. Danish Government is consulting with the interested bodies and it is expected that representations will be made in London early next week. Less responsible press comment even talks of a trade war between the two countries, and the possibility of holding up shipments of Danish food produce to the United Kingdom unless the principle of price review is conceded from the British side.

From the point of view of Anglo-Danish relations the announcement was most unfortunately timed, and I should welcome early and all possible guidance as to the explanations which I could give here. Danes have previously objected to our differentiation in prices for home consumption and for export, and the Minister of

Commerce points out that this marginal discrimination has now been further increased. He added, and this point has also been made in the press, that the coal price increase is a retrograde step at a [?time] when efforts are being made to liberalise trade and promote economic viability in Europe.[1]

[1] Bevin took this problem up with the Prime Minister. See No. 200.

No. 198

Minute from Mr Falla to Mr Bevin, 31 October 1949
(FO 371/77725, N9782/1192/42)

When the Swedish Ambassador sees the Secretary of State tomorrow, he may mention the question of the supply of Radar AA No. 3 Mark 7 sets to Sweden.

2. Monsieur Hägglöf raised this matter in a memorandum which he left with the Head of Northern Department on the 28th September (flag A).[1] Briefly the position is that in December 1947 the Swedish Government placed an order for 35 of these sets with the British Thomson Houston Co. (BTH). Two sets were delivered to them in May last year and were fully paid for. It was further promised that the balance would be delivered to Sweden from August 1949 at a rate of more than one a month. The Swedes have made an advance payment of £100,000 (out of a total of £350,000) for these remaining 33 sets. However, the Swedes were informed by BTH last month that it would be impossible to supply any further sets for the present, as all available production was required by the UK authorities for their own use.[2]

3. Enquiries have since shown that this statement by BTH is basically correct. At a meeting of the JWPS (Joint War Planning Staff) Arms Working Party last week it was revealed that production of these sets has fallen far short of expectations, with the result that the War Office have been unable to cover their own requirements for UK defence (a copy of a note by the Ministry of Supply on the production position is attached at flag B).[1] Steps are now being taken to increase production and it is hoped that a greatly enhanced output can be achieved in about 18 months. But for the present not more than ten sets can be made available for export between now and the end of March—and even this is subject to confirmation by the War Office (which is still awaited) that they do not require these sets themselves. If the War Office relinquish their claim it is proposed to allocate the sets to Sweden, Norway and Denmark in the proportion of 6, 3 and 1. It will be impossible to tell how many sets will become available for export after next March until we know what War Office requirements will be for the following year.

4. Until War Office clearance has been obtained for the ten sets referred to above it is impossible to give the Swedes any assurances regarding future deliveries. Should the Swedish Ambassador raise this matter therefore, I think that the Secretary of State can only tell him that deliveries to Sweden have unfortunately been delayed owing to an unexpected shortfall in production, that the

[1] Not printed.
[2] Wilford minuted to Bevin that Northern Department had requested him to add that there was in the contract a *force majeure* clause so that there would be no question of the Swedes having a case against BTH for failing to fulfil a commercial contract.

question is being looked into and that we hope to be able to give him some further information about deliveries in the near future.

5. There is however another aspect of this question which should be considered before we decide how soon and at what rate we can supply these radar sets to Sweden—namely how far these deliveries are compatible with our obligations to members of the Atlantic Pact, particularly Norway and Denmark. Our policy in regard to the supply of arms to Sweden, as approved by the Secretary of State, has hitherto been to provide Sweden as far as possible with the material she requires, subject to the proviso that our Allies should have first claim on any available supplies. (See the Secretary of State's minute at flag C.)[1] Up to now we have always been able to show that the arms which we were sending to Sweden were not required by our Allies and this has enabled us to meet criticism, which has been voiced on several occasions in American quarters. In the case of these radar sets, however, the total Swedish requirements (50 sets) compete with Norwegian requirements (22 sets) and Danish requirements (1 set). It is therefore important to avoid creating an impression that we are favouring the Swedes to the detriment of our own Allies and that we should be able to justify whatever course we take in the case of American criticism. I would submit, however, that the proposed allocation of the ten sets now available in the ratio of Sweden 6, Norway 3 and Denmark 1 provides a reasonable solution and one which can be defended. It should be borne in mind that the Swedes placed their order considerably before the Norwegians placed theirs and it is more than twice the size of the Norwegian order. While we do not wish to supply the Swedes in preference to the Norwegians, it seems equally wrong that the Swedes should have to wait until the whole Norwegian order has been completed before they receive any sets themselves. The logical course, in fact, seems to be to fulfil the two orders *pari passu* and this is what the allocation now proposed is intended to do.[3]

The above is agreed with Economic Relations and Western Departments.

P.S. FALLA

[3] Bevin commented: 'If what is now said is correct why did we take the order, what has been done about production, we need the money. The whole business is unsatisfactory.'

No. 199

Minute from Mr Henniker-Major to Sir R. Makins, 1 November 1949
(FO 371/78136, UR11040/332/98)

Scandinavian Regional Grouping

The attached telegram from Paris[1] reports that Norwegian Ministers at the OEEC discussions there have approached the Chancellor with a proposal that they should come forward with a Resolution at the Council tomorrow for a Scandinavian regional grouping. They would like us to be associated with this group, though they would not of course mention this in the Resolution. The Chancellor has agreed to see the Ministers of the three Scandinavian countries tomorrow morning, and enquires whether the Secretary of State would be prepared to continue the talks with them after his arrival.

[1] No. 1246 of 1 November (not printed).

From the Foreign Office point of view there seems to be great advantage in encouraging this approach, and it is suggested that we should listen sympathetically to the proposals of the Scandinavian countries. It would help to allay the suspicions of the Americans and others that we were opposed in principle to joining any regional grouping in Europe, even if this would not harm us economically, if we were able to indicate that we were seriously considering a proposal to join a group of this kind.

It should also be borne in mind that almost alone among the Europeans the Scandinavians have been consistently friendly towards us lately. During the difficult wrangles over the Division of Aid when we were being attacked by everyone else, the Norwegians and the Danes rallied to our support and urged that we should be given fair treatment.

Politically also our association with such a group might strengthen the Scandinavians in overcoming their scruples about abandoning the policy of neutrality. It is true that the Norwegians and the Danes have already taken the plunge by their signature of the Atlantic Pact, but a move of this kind might help to bring the Swedes fully into Western Europe as well. It will be remembered that we recently agreed to the Norwegian proposals for closer economic co-operation. These proposals were made by the Norwegians largely because they wanted to show their population that they were gaining some tangible advantages in return for their abandonment of neutrality. As a result, an Anglo-Norwegian Committee was set up which met for the first time in the summer in Oslo. Though the Committee then did useful work it could not accomplish many spectacular results. The Norwegians may perhaps have been disappointed over this, and a sympathetic response to their suggestion now might serve to convince them that we are in earnest in our desire for closer economic co-operation with them. I am not sure whether the economic objections to a proposal of this kind are very serious. At first sight it does not appear that they are. We have no real balance of payments difficulties with the Scandinavians, though we may in future have some with Denmark and Sweden. The Danes, for instance, showed in their Long Term Programme that they were expecting to earn some gold and dollars from us in 1952. These balance of payments difficulties are however nothing like so serious as those which exist between Holland and Belgium and which are at the moment proving a stumbling block to the final establishment of Benelux. On the whole it also seems that our economy and those of the Scandinavian countries are largely complementary, though there would undoubtedly be some difficulties with the farmers if we were to enter into some regional grouping with Denmark.

It seems possible that our association with a Scandinavian regional grouping might eventually lead to some wider grouping of the Northern European countries, eventually embracing Germany and the Netherlands, which would be parallel with a similar Latin grouping comprising Belgium, France, Italy and possibly others.

It is suggested that the Secretary of State should agree to continue these talks with the three Scandinavian Ministers when he is in Paris. These talks would naturally have to be of a very exploratory nature with a view to finding out what the Scandinavians have in mind.[2]

---

[2] This document describes the beginning of the process which led to the formation of UNISCAN, an organisation comprising Britain and the Scandinavian countries whose purpose was to promote economic collaboration. Bevin agreed to continue the discussions after his arrival in Paris. See No. 201.

I submit a draft telegram.

J.P.E.C. HENNIKER-MAJOR

No. 200

Minute from Mr Bevin to Mr Attlee, 7 November 1949
Confidential (PREM 8/961)

Prime Minister

I have been very disturbed about the sudden announcement of the increased price of coal exported to Denmark.[1] I find that in other countries too there are serious reactions to this announcement by the Coal Board. The British Government made no previous announcement and in fact did not know that the action was going to be taken. I assure you that in these days such developments cannot fail to have very serious repercussions on our relations with other countries.

2. During the negotiations with the Danes on food and in order to obtain the maximum supplies, we co-operated with the Ministry of Food to the best of our ability to assist in getting desirable results. I feel that it is imperative that there should be co-ordination between these nationalised industries, the production Ministries, the purchasing Ministries and ourselves, so that our policy may be kept on an even keel in dealing with these countries.

3. We really cannot go on as if we have not socialised anything and as if we were living in pre-war days. This is one of the difficulties that arise when we take over these vast undertakings, but it is one that can be easily handled if the Ministers concerned and the Boards will co-operate in the correct manner.

4. I trust therefore that this will not be passed over lightly, but that you will take steps towards the issuing of a directive, which in my view ought to be strictly followed.[2]

ERNEST BEVIN

[1] No. 197.
[2] Attlee replied to Bevin that the issue had already engaged his attention, that he had seen Ministers, and that the general question would shortly be discussed.

No. 201

Mr Bevin to Sir L. Collier (Oslo), 20 November 1949, 1.20 p.m.[1]
Tel. No 727 Secret (FO 371/78136, UR11706/332/98)

Scandinavian Regional Group.

You will recall and will no doubt have seen copies of the important statements on Western European economic integration made by the Chancellor of the Exchequer and Mr Hoffman, Economic Co-operation Administrator, to the Council of Organisation for European Economic Co-operation (OEEC) in Paris on

[1] Also addressed to Stockholm and Copenhagen, and copied to Reykjavik, Helsinki, OEEC Paris and Washington.

the 1st November (see my No. 404 Intel of the 4th November).[2] The Resolution which the Council adopted on the 2nd November recognised 'that it may be desirable to provide for a closer economic and monetary association on a regional basis for some of the member countries where the requisite conditions already exist ...' (see my No. 407 Intel).[2]

2. In the light of the discussions in the OEEC the Norwegians approached the Chancellor of the Exchequer as reported in Paris telegram No. 1246 (of the 1st November)[3] from UKDel to OEEC. Subsequently, after receipt of my telegram under reference, the Chancellor discussed on the 2nd November with Messrs. Undén, Lange, Brofoss and Rasmussen in Paris the possibility of associating an economic grouping between the Scandinavian countries participating in OEEC with the United Kingdom and the sterling area. It was agreed that His Majesty's Government and each of the Scandinavian Governments would look into the matter further with a view to exchanging preliminary ideas and having a more extensive discussion at the ministerial level when next the Council of OEEC meets.

3. As you will be aware M. Lange announced during the OEEC Ministerial meetings that the 3 Scandinavian countries would be notifying a further step towards their own economic association before the end of the year.

4. For your own information there has since been inter-departmental consideration of the implications of this idea, and of possible ways in which we could assist in the formation of a Scandinavian economic group as well as of the ways in which it would be associated with the United Kingdom and the sterling area. It is not possible for us to evolve a more definite scheme until we know more of how the Scandinavians are thinking but we hope to be ready to submit certain proposals to them soon. A paper is being prepared for submission to Ministers giving the results of the preliminary consideration here and you will be informed of further developments as soon as possible.

5. We would be very interested to receive any information you may have gathered as to developments at your end.

[2] Not printed. Ellipsis in original.
[3] Not printed, though see No. 199.

No. 202

Letter from Mr Lambert (Stockholm) to Mr McNeil, 1 March 1950
No. 78 Confidential (FO 371/86909, NW1016/4)

Sir,
I have the honour to report that, as was to be expected, the British General Election has been followed with the keenest interest by all sections of the informed Swedish public. The campaign has been very well and, on the whole, very sympathetically reported by all the leading newspapers, some of which had sent special correspondents to London for the purpose; and a member of this Embassy was told at the Social Democratic Party headquarters yesterday that rarely if ever had an election in a foreign country been given so much space in the Swedish press.

2. In the eyes of the Swedish Government much depended on the outcome. I have no hesitation in saying that to most Swedes Great Britain is still the keystone of the western arch. Consequently, as the Prime Minister remarked to me yesterday, any sign of instability or the prospect of a prolonged political crisis at Westminster is most unwelcome. Moreover the fortunes of Labour in the United Kingdom tend to affect the credit of Social Democracy in this country in a general way. Nationalisation is not likely to be an issue in Sweden in the foreseeable future; on the other hand if a second election were to be held in the United Kingdom during the course of the summer it might be expected to exert some influence on the course of the Swedish municipal elections, which are due in the middle of September. This being so I was not surprised to hear two of the Social Democrat Party Secretaries, who were listening to the BBC at my house on election night, exclaiming, each time a Labour victory was announced, 'another gain for us'.

3. Indeed members of the Swedish Government were not only deeply interested in the British elections, but were even positively nervous about the outcome. The Foreign Minister, whom I met at a dinner party during the election campaign, gave me the impression that he was distinctly worried; and the Naval Attaché detected similar symptoms in the Minister of Defence at about the same time. In the small hours of February 24th the Information Secretary and I sounded the Prime Minister, who was among the guests at my house on that occasion, on the causes of this apparent anxiety. To our astonishment he replied that Mr Hjalmarsson, the Swedish Conservative Leader, had definite information from Conservative circles in London that if the Conservatives returned to power they would probably revise the policy of HM Government towards Scandinavia. Although Mr Erlander did not actually say so, he can only have had in mind an attempt to force Sweden into the Atlantic Pact. The Prime Minister is by no means an expert on foreign policy but it is surprising that he should apparently have listened to Mr Hjalmarsson rather than his own Ministry for Foreign Affairs who, as I learned the same evening from a conversation with the Secretary General, are not in the least nervous of any such change of policy.

4. Now that the result of the election is known the Swedish Government may feel that for the time being at any rate they will not be faced with a new situation as regards their freedom from alliance. The Prime Minister has welcomed the election as a Labour victory in the following declaration, which was published on February 26th: 'The British elections were a success for Labour, even though it was narrow. As the leader of the Swedish Social Democrats I should therefore like to describe the outcome as an encouragement. It is satisfactory that, after all, the result was a Labour majority. Its insignificant size would not mean anything in Sweden, but with the political system they have in Britain it will, of course, be more difficult for the Government party to master the situation. To a Socialist it is stimulating to see the tendency in both Britain and Scandinavia where the elections have yielded the same result despite the severe strain on the Socialist parties.'

5. The Swedish Government naturally welcome the continuance of Labour in office. It is only fair to add, however, that, taking the larger view, their main desire is to see a government with a working majority installed at Westminster which would be able to take firm decisions on international questions of importance to Sweden as well as to other members of Western Europe. Many Swedes are also nervous about United States foreign policy, which they conceive to be erratic and unpredictable, and they look to HM Government to exert a stabilizing influence.

The course of events will therefore be very closely and anxiously followed by the political leaders of this country.

6. I am sending copies of this despatch to HM Representatives in Copenhagen, Oslo and Helsingfors.

I have, etc.,
A. LAMBERT

No. 203

Minute from Mr Etherington-Smith to Mr Harrison, 8 March 1950
(FO 371/86437, NF10338/34)

The Finnish Minister joined me as I was walking back to the office after the luncheon at the Finnish Trade Delegation this afternoon and again spoke to me of the difficulty of his personal relations with the Soviet Embassy here. He said that there had lately been a noticeable increase in the pressure to which he was being subjected by the Russians to supply them with information. They had told him quite frankly that they were completely isolated here and found great difficulty in keeping themselves informed of what was going on. To this he pleaded that he was in much the same position himself, but he had difficulty in persuading them of this. Apparently their inclination to make use of him as an informant dates from the period immediately after the war when he was a member of the Finnish Government and had acted as a go-between with the Russian members of the Control Commission.

M. Wuori told me that the subject in which the Russians showed greatest interest was that of the political situation in Scandinavia and the latest developments there. He went on to make the interesting disclosure that the Russians have indicated to him that they suspect that the Swedes have come to a tacit understanding with the Norwegians and Danes regarding joint co-operation in the event of war. He did not know whether the Russians had any solid ground for this suspicion, but he made it pretty clear that he himself thought that it might well be justified. He said that he knew, for instance, that the Norwegian and Danish embassies here had recently received instructions to avoid all further references to their attempts to persuade the Swedes to join the Atlantic Treaty and he regarded this as an indication that some understanding had been arrived at with the Swedes. I told him that I had no reason to believe that any understanding of this nature had been reached and I said that I hoped he would be able to dispel the Soviet Embassy's suspicions. He said that he certainly intended to do his best to do so, but he was not sure whether he would succeed. He did not seem to have quite decided whether the Russians had genuinely formed this suspicion or whether they were simply creating a pretext for an impending campaign against the Swedes, which he also seemed to consider a possibility.

Whether the Soviet suspicion is genuine or not, this development is of some interest and we must clearly be prepared for the issue to be pressed further by the Russians. We do not know, of course, whether they have got wind of the military discussions which the Swedes have recently had with the Norwegians and the Danes. In any case it seems to me highly probable that this is the beginning of a new move in the war of nerves designed to scare the Swedes from making any tacit plans with Norway and Denmark, let alone with the UK.

In conclusion, M. Wuori reiterated how embarrassed he was by the Russian requests for information. In view of Finland's difficult position he could not reject these approaches. He hoped, however, that this would not be held against him by us. I assured him that we fully understood that he could not avoid maintaining these contacts with the Soviet Embassy.[1]

R.G.A. ETHERINGTON-SMITH

[1] Soviet Department commented: 'The Russians do seem to be showing some interest in Sweden at the present time; the most recent Peace Congress was held at Stockholm (where considerable emphasis was placed upon "neutrality" as a way of undermining the North Atlantic Treaty) while an important article in *New Times* has "warned" the Swedish Government that it does not consider their present degree of neutrality as good enough' (FO 371/86437, NF10338/34).

No. 204

Minute from Mr Etherington-Smith to Mr Harrison, 11 April 1950
Top Secret (FO 371/86167, N1194/1)

Scandinavian Views on Defence Policy

The question how Sweden, Norway and Denmark can best protect themselves against a future attack from the East continues to be hotly debated in all three countries, and, although the position has not changed fundamentally, it may be convenient to summarise briefly the main trends of current Scandinavian opinion.

2. After the spirit of excitement and, one might almost say, recklessness which prevailed at the time of the decision of Norway and Denmark to join the Atlantic Pact, there has undoubtedly been some cooling off of enthusiasm for the Pact in both countries. This is partly the inevitable result of the absence of any major political developments since the Pact was concluded and of the unsensational manner in which the groundwork for the implementation of the Pact has been carried out. It may also reflect a growing realisation of the meagre assistance to be expected from the West in the event of war. At present the extremely limited scale of such assistance is fully realised by only a small number of officials, since we have not yet committed ourselves officially regarding the nature and scale of the assistance which we can provide; but we shall presumably have to make some statement in the end and we must be prepared for the feeling of disappointment in Norway and Denmark to increase as soon as the position is more widely known, though this tendency may be counteracted by the arrival of military supplies from America and the generally increasing sense of confidence resulting from the strengthening of the North Atlantic defence system as a whole. Thirdly, there are indications of growing concern in Norway and Denmark regarding the cost to both countries of strengthening their defences as required by the Pact, and there is some tendency for public opinion to expect, not only that the necessary military material will be provided *gratis,* but even that Norway and Denmark should be compensated for the increased cost of maintaining a much bigger military establishment. These factors, and particularly the second, seem to have had the effect of making certain circles in both countries turn their thoughts once again

towards Sweden and to consider whether some form of defence co-operation with that country, based on the idea of Scandinavian neutrality, would not be possible.

3. As regards Sweden, it is clear that the official policy of the Swedish Government remains as firmly wedded to neutrality as before. This has been confirmed most recently by the Swedish Foreign Minister's outspoken speech before the *Riksdag* on March 22nd in which he came out flatly against even technical co-operation with Norway and Denmark. We have also learned that the indiscretions of General Jung, the Swedish Commander-in-Chief, caused a temporary suspension (presumably on Government orders) of such contacts as existed between the Swedish Defence Staff and their Danish and Norwegian colleagues.

4. Nevertheless, there are certain favourable developments to be noted. It is a fact that military discussions between the Swedish, Norwegian and Danish authorities at a service level have taken place in the past and will no doubt be resumed in due course. The Swedish Service Chiefs are, indeed, reported to be pressing the Government to approve a complete plan for practical military co-operation with the Norwegians and the Danes. Secondly, the Swedish Service Chiefs appear more than ever convinced of the importance, in Sweden's own interest, of military collaboration with the West (c.f. the proposed meeting during the summer between British and Swedish Admirals). Thirdly, it is significant that, in an address to a group of officers delivered in the presence of both the Prime Minister and the Minister of Defence, the Commander of the Swedish Navy emphasised the danger threatening Sweden from the East and made it clear that he did not seriously contemplate the possibility that Sweden could escape being involved in the event of a Soviet attack on Scandinavia. Finally, the advantages to Sweden of making some defence arrangements with Norway and Denmark are again being canvassed in public discussions. The new leader of the Conservative Party has made himself the advocate of inter-Scandinavian military co-operation, and a proposal to revive the 'Karlstad Plan' for a Scandinavian Defence Union in a somewhat altered form has recently appeared in a Swedish Liberal newspaper.

5. As indicated above, the Swedish Government still remains firmly opposed to any departure from strict neutrality. The position has not therefore altered fundamentally. But at the same time there has been a movement in the direction of inter-Scandinavian collaboration in two respects:

(*a*) by the maintenance and development of Service contacts, with or without ministerial approval, with Norway and Denmark, and,

(*b*) by the increasing number of public statements pointing out the advantages of inter-Scandinavian co-operation.

It would seem, therefore, that Swedish opinion is at least beginning to develop a more realistic approach to the whole problem and there appears to be a newly-awakened desire to find a solution which would enable Sweden to make essential plans with Norway and Denmark, while preserving her formal neutrality.

6. As a corollary of the above, it is not without interest that, according to the Finnish Minister, the Soviet Embassy in London have intimated to him their suspicion, presumably derived from Moscow or Stockholm, that the Swedes have reached a tacit understanding with the Norwegians and Danes regarding joint co-operation in the event of war.

R.G.A. ETHERINGTON-SMITH

No. 205

Mr Scott (Helsinki) to Mr Younger, 12 April 1950[1]
No. 78 Secret (FO 371/86446, NF1121/13)

Review of Finland's economic and social developments

Sir,

The reassumption of office by President Paasikivi for a further period of six years leads one to reflect upon what has been achieved during the four years which have passed since Marshal Mannerheim resigned the presidency and his Prime Minister succeeded him in that office.

2. Finland's four major problems during these four years have been the punctual discharge to Russia of her reparations liabilities, assessed under the terms of the armistice at 300 million United States dollars at their 1938 value, but subsequently reduced to $226,500,0000; the rebuilding of her foreign trade; the resettlement of her refugees and ex-servicemen; and how to check the tendency of wages and prices to mount uncontrollably, with all the social and labour problems to which such a development would give rise.

Reparations

3. During the past six years reparations payments have by a great national effort been met as they fell due and such fines as Finland has incurred on two occasions have been remitted by her Soviet creditor with a gesture of magnanimity. With two and a half years in which to complete these payments, Finland is faced with the delivery of only $39.3 million worth of reparations goods—a burden which should be well within her strength.

Foreign Trade

4. Finland has worked assiduously to rebuild her foreign trade, to re-knit old trade relations and to develop new ones. She has to this end concluded trade agreements with twenty three countries during the past year, but costs of production are inordinately high and it remains to be seen whether the two devaluations of the Finnmark totalling 17½ per cent against sterling which were carried through in July and September last will enable her export trade to keep its hold in foreign markets. The revival of German trade competition begins to form an additional cause of anxiety. In 1949 about 56 per cent of Finland's trade was done with countries members of the OEEC and 19½ per cent with the Soviet orbit; this latter figure showed an increase of 6½ per cent since 1947, and was mainly at the expense of trade with the Western Hemisphere.

Refugee resettlement

5. Even harder than the re-establishment and maintenance of foreign trade is the problem of resettlement of 35,000 refugee farmers' families from Karelia and the leased territory of Porkkala, and of some 120,000 ex-servicemen to whom it was promised that they would after the war be allotted small holdings to be derived from the break-up of the so-called large estates—only 0.2 per cent of the cultivable land is accounted for by holdings of 100 hectares or more. Political considerations made this course almost inevitable; but even when the decision was taken there were misgivings as to the effects of this policy on the quantity and quality of agricultural production and these misgivings are already proving to be all too

---

[1] Kenneth Younger, the Minister of State, was in charge of the Foreign Office while Bevin was in hospital, from 11 April to 4 May.

justified. Finnish soil is not in general of a quality to make its small-scale cultivation economic, many of the ex-servicemen had no previous farming experience, many too are reluctant to put in the hours of ungrudging labour which successful cultivation of a smallholding demands, and all too many are already taking up the attitude that the Government put them on the land and it is therefore up to the Government to assure them a reasonable livelihood. It is natural therefore that there are many who take a gloomy view of the long-term consequences of an experiment carried out in defiance of the lessons of technical knowledge and experience, and there are those who say that it will cost the country far more than the reparations payment to Russia.

Wages and prices

6. Lastly and most intractable of all the four problems mentioned is the problem of wages and prices and their combined influence on the costs of production.

7. In 1938 Finland was a country where life was cheap and wages and costs of production correspondingly low. In 1948 it was calculated that the cost of living (perhaps a slightly higher standard) had risen seven times above the 1938 figure; that wages in industry had risen eleven to thirteen times for male and female industrial labour and twelve to sixteen times for agricultural labour.

8. The price of a standard of sawn timber (class IV) in 1938 was £12.17s.6d and of a ton of chemical sulphate and mechanical pulp £7.5s.0d and £4.8s.0d respectively. A thousand kilograms of wheat or rye cost Fmks 2,900 and Fmks 2,250 at Fmks 227 = £1 and a kilogram of butter cost Fmks 29. Comparable figures today are:

Sawn timber (Class IV): £43 per standard
Chemical sulphate pulp: £27 per ton
Mechanical pulp: £15 per ton
Wheat: 20,000 Fmks per 1,000 kilog
Rye: 20,000 Fmks per 1,000 kilog
Butter: 340 Fmks per kilog

9. On 15th February this year the system by which wages were pegged to a cost of living figure rising 5½ per cent for each 5 per cent increase in that figure, and which had achieved a considerable measure of success, was summarily discarded for political rather than economic reasons, and the country appears to be entering on a fresh period of labour unrest with widespread demands for further wage increases which will be reflected in increased cost of production, both of articles for home consumption and for export, without prospect of real advantage to the workers (for climbing prices can always outstrip wages) and with increased hardship for the armed forces, police and civil servants whose wages here as elsewhere are among the last to be increased. The extent of this hardship may be judged by the fact that the salary of a Cabinet Minister before deduction of tax—and in a country where the cost of living is at least 50 percent higher than in the United Kingdom—is just over £1,000 per annum and of a captain (married) in the army £500 a year after nine years' service.

10. What are the prospects which confront President Paasikivi as he enters on his second term of office?

11. He has a new Government based on a narrow coalition recruited from Agrarian, Progressive and Fenno-Swedish Parties whose parliamentary representation is fifty six, five and fourteen members respectively, seventy five out of the 200 members of the Diet. It is led by the astute M. Kekkonen, former Speaker of the Diet, whose ability is widely conceded, though many—and even

some of his followers—question his political reliability. But with the next general election only fifteen months away and a lot of difficult problems awaiting urgent solution, no one seems anxious to displace him and take on his burdens.

12. Financially the country's position looks precarious with a budget deficit in 1949 of almost 7,000 million Fmks (£10.5 million) which, according to preliminary estimates, may rise to as much as 12,000 Fmks (£18 million) in 1950. Taxes are already high for a country which is by no means wealthy. Public indebtedness has risen to 37 times its 1938 level but, at the present exchange rate, is equivalent to not more than £52 per head of the population—perhaps a relatively low rate (even for a poor country) when compared to Sweden's rate of £130 and our own of over £500.

13. Industry and agriculture are hampered alike by high labour costs and relatively low productivity and industry must look forward to the time when in 1952 with its reparations deliveries completed it will have to find other outlets for many of its products at prices less attractive than those paid by the Government for whom punctual delivery of the yearly quotas has been the prime consideration. Nor are the prospects for agriculture encouraging for there are many operations which can only be economically carried out with cheap labour or advanced mechanisation and Finnish agriculture does not possess the former and is ill adapted for the latter. It may therefore prove well-nigh impossible to re-establish at competitive prices, unless some form of subsidisation is resorted to, her useful export market in bacon and dairy products, which amounted to almost £3 million in 1938 (about 10 per cent of total exports).

14. The country's well-organised and exploited forest reserves are still her chief source of wealth and revenue, but even here prospects looked black in 1949 owing to high labour costs and continued so until the situation was eased for her pulp, paper and timber industries by devaluation of the Finnmark in July and later by the rise of world prices for these products, following the wider devaluation of European currency in September last.

15. Unemployment is not a serious problem yet but the standard of living in the rural areas of central and north-central Finland is very low and likely to remain so unless and until it becomes possible to develop the mineral resources which are known to exist in this area; a process, which even with the greatly increased provision of cheap electric power must still prove exceedingly costly and one which the State may be unable to carry out with the rapidity which the social distress of the area demands. It is chiefly in this area and in the woodworking and timber shipping ports of Kemi, Oulu and Raahe on the west coast that communism continues to develop and to press forward with its efforts to tighten discipline and improve 'security' within its ranks. The fact that the Communist party has temporarily been denied participation in the Government, though a cause for satisfaction, should not be taken as an indication that the power of communism is yet on the wane.

16. It would seem then that the problems which confront the President as he begins his second term of office are scarcely less than those which confronted his country during his first term. As a field for investment Finland's prospects in the next six years are not such as would attract an international banker who based his judgements on a purely factual analysis and did not allow his logical deductions to be influenced by human and psychological considerations.

17. Finland's history, however, has been the story of a long succession of struggles to survive; the will to live is still there and I can see no signs that the

difficulties of the last ten years have impaired it. His country's climate—so strong an influence on national character—has made the Finn tough and stubborn, hard to discourage and not easily swayed by emotion. With these characteristics he may, unless physically overrun by his Eastern neighbour, overcome the very considerable difficulties which confront him, and the second half of this decade may prove a period of economic and social development such as he experienced between 1930 and 1940.

I am sending copies of the despatch to the Treasury and the Board of Trade.

I have, etc.,
O.A. SCOTT

No. 206

Mr Younger to Mr Beeley (Copenhagen), 21 April 1950
No. 94 Secret (FO 371/86363, ND1015/7G)

(1) *Anglo-Danish Relations;* (2) *German Rearmament*

Sir,

The Danish Prime Minister, Mr Hedtoft, called this morning accompanied by the Danish Ambassador. He said he did not wish to discuss in any detail the problems of Anglo-Danish relations. He gave me, however, a brief account of the difficulties for his country which had followed upon devaluation. He had felt obliged to follow our devaluation almost automatically owing to Denmark's dependence on the British market, but he had been strongly criticised in Parliament for doing so. He said that any further devaluation would be very unfortunate for Denmark and particularly unfortunate for him and his party. He said he presumed that we were not expecting any further devaluation and I assured him that this was the case.

2. He then asked about the agenda for the Tripartite talks, with particular reference to Germany, and I told him that all the major aspects of this problem were sure to come up. He said that he was in difficulties internally about Danish defence measures as a result of the attitude of the Western Powers to the rearmament of Germany. His opponents, both Communist and Conservative, have been pointing out that the German Social Democrats and the Western Powers are opposed to German rearmament partly upon the grounds that any such measure would be a provocation to the Soviet Union. His opponents therefore argue that the same applies to Danish rearmament. The Prime Minister said that Danish opinion finds it very hard to accept the situation that all the Western democracies, including Denmark, should share in heavy defence burdens while Western Germany remains, from that point of view, a vacuum. He admitted that in putting these views recently to the Norwegian Government he had found that they were not in agreement with him. I told him that, while we all appreciate that the present situation in Germany leads to many anomalies, our view has been that it would be most inadvisable to single out the problem of German rearmament and to deal with it before even bigger questions relating to the unity of Germany, or the Western reorientation of Western Germany, had been fully thrashed out.

I am, etc.,
K.G. YOUNGER

No. 207

Record of meeting between Sir P. Dixon and M. Hägglöf, 10 July 1950
(FO 371/89895, WU10712/19)

The Swedish Ambassador called this afternoon and raised the question of the Council of Europe.[1] He expressed considerable restiveness about the Council which he said had produced no positive results. I put it to him that the value of the Council did not perhaps lie in producing positive results; its value was rather as a forum for European opinion.

In particular the Ambassador said that his Government hoped that there would be no question of OEEC derogating from its authority in defence to the Council of Europe. The Swedish Government were much impressed by the efficiency of the OEEC and the progress which it was making. I told M. Hägglöf that I could not believe that HM Government would wish in any way to weaken the authority or efficiency of OEEC in favour of the Council of Europe.

The Ambassador thought that the Human Rights Commission was perhaps the most important work being undertaken by the Council of Europe, and he urged that we should fall in with a compromise suggestion which he alleged was supported by the French Government and which would provide for optional submission by Governments to a Court of Human Rights. I replied that as a Colonial Power we were obliged to watch the question of a Court of Human Rights with great care, and I could not commit myself to define our attitude towards this compromise proposal.

P. DIXON

[1] The Council of Europe, founded for the purpose of promoting European integration, was established by a treaty signed in London on 5 May 1949 by the United Kingdom, Norway, Sweden, Denmark, Belgium, France, Ireland, Italy, Luxembourg and the Netherlands.

No. 208

Mr Baxter (Reykjavik) to Mr Bevin, 15 August 1950, 6.20 p.m.
Tel. No. 70 Top Secret (FO 371/86501, NL1022/6)

Your telegram No. 3576 to Washington: Defence of Iceland.

Recent Naval visits followed by a few isolated newspaper articles have begun to prepare the way but the Icelandic public are as yet very far from accepting the principle that they ought to improve their defences. No member of the Government has yet given a definite lead and there are some grounds for supposing that certain Cabinet Ministers might be very difficult indeed if the problem were to come suddenly to a head. A crisis might at the worst lead to a split between the Conservative and Progressive parties and the fall of the present Coalition Government.

2. In these circumstances I wonder whether useful process of educating Icelandic opinion might be continued by the Norwegian Foreign Minister who is due to visit Reykjavik on 28th August for some days for the Conference of Scandinavian Foreign Ministers. He would probably have the opportunity of talking the matter over with each of the members of the Iceland Cabinet, and

pointing out that Iceland's complete defencelessness is a potential danger, not only to herself but also to Norway and other members of the Atlantic Defence Pact.[1]

[1] Northern Department agreed that a request should be made to the Icelandic Government to take steps to improve Icelandic defences, but were also aware of the need to respect Icelandic sensitivities and of the attraction of an indirect approach which avoided British or American involvement. A telegram was sent to Oslo (No. 268 of 24 August) instructing Collier to approach Lange (who was shortly due to visit Reykjavik) with a request for him to exert his influence on the Icelandic Government. It stressed that Collier 'should impress on M. Lange that his approach should stem entirely from his own initiative. He should on no account give any impression whatsoever that he has been briefed either by the British or the Americans to make this approach' (FO 371/86501, NL1022/6). Lange told Collier that most of the Icelandic Cabinet was in favour of some sort of 'Home Guard', but that the Socialist party was divided (Oslo tel. No. 26 Saving of 7 September 1950). In the event, the Icelandic Government agreed that Benediktsson, the Foreign Minister, should enter into general discussions of Icelandic peacetime defence when he visited New York later in September (FO 371/86501, NL1022/14).

No. 209

Minute from Mr Bevin to Mr Attlee, 30 August 1950
(PREM 8/1402)

Prime Minister

I was very much concerned recently to hear that there was some question of having to break our contract for coal exports with Denmark and Sweden, owing to a shortage of supplies. I accordingly arranged a meeting with those available at the Ministry of Fuel and Power and the Board of Trade, namely Bottomley and Robens, and enclose a copy of a record which I think you will find self-explanatory.

2.. I had hoped that as a result of our meeting the Ministry of Fuel and Power would have found ways out of the difficulty which did not even mean asking our Danish and Swedish customers to let us off our contracts by supplying over a longer period. However, as you will see from the attached copy of a letter from Robens dated August 29th, the Ministry of Fuel and Power are concentrating on postponement as a way out of the difficulty, and will not know the chance of success until September 5th. As I shall be leaving on September 7th for New York this hardly leaves me time to put this matter as a policy issue to the Cabinet, as I would wish to do before there is a question of breaking contracts. I suggest that you should ask the Minister of Fuel and Power to let you know how matters stand before the Cabinet meeting on September 6th, and would be most grateful if you would keep an eye on the question after my departure.

3. I feel sure you will agree that it would be wrong to prejudice our international relations and good name for the sake of a ludicrously small margin of 500,000 tons out of a total production of 200,000,000 tons. This is what I was being asked to agree to.[1]

ERNEST BEVIN

[1] Attlee asked for briefing from the Minister of Fuel and Power. Robens replied on 1 September that the level of stocks was lower than anticipated. The contract with Denmark required the delivery of 2.0 million tons, that with Sweden 1.47 million tons. He now expected to be able to ship 1.8 million tons to Denmark and 1.32 millions tons to Sweden. 'Although . . . these figures appear small . . . I am satisfied . . . that in the position in which we find ourselves those tonnages could only be provided for export by reducing the coal needed for our gas works and domestic consumers below the safety level.' Bevin found this unsatisfactory and obtained agreement to address the Cabinet before his departure for New York. It was agreed to send Lord Hyndley, Chairman of the National Coal Board, to Scandinavia to seek understanding and acceptance of the British position, and he reported that this had been achieved. The situation worsened in October when a further shortfall was expected, and Bevin wrote again to Attlee on 28 October to express his concern. He subsequently put up a paper to Cabinet entitled 'The Importance of Coal Exports in the Foreign Relations of the United Kingdom' (CP(50)23 of 3 November). There were further cuts, but in January 1951 the recommendation was accepted that further reductions should be deferred until a serious fuel crisis developed (PREM 8/1402).

No. 210

Minute from Mr Harrison to Mr Bevin, 4 September 1950
Secret (FO 371/86948, NW1193/5)

The Swedish ambassador called on me this afternoon at his request to enquire about the export of Vampire airframes to Sweden.

The general position is that, after the export of jet aircraft had been temporarily suspended by order of the Prime Minister, the Minister of Defence was invited to review our commitments for the supply of arms to foreign powers. This review has now been agreed between the Ministry of Defence and the Foreign Office and submitted to the Prime Minister, who has approved the Minister of Defence's recommendations.

The following will be the effect on Sweden. Under existing arrangements, the Swedes send engines, instruments and guns to de Havillands, who build airframes around them. The completed aircraft is then flown back to Sweden by Swedish pilots. The Swedish Ambassador claims that the contract is for some 300 aircraft, delivery to be completed some time next year. (The Ministry of Defence's paper speaks of only 243 aircraft.)

I told M. Hägglöf that, as I understood the position, permission would now be given for four completed aircraft to be flown back forthwith to Sweden and that work would be completed on the airframes at present under construction. But I understood that thereafter de Havillands' contract would be abrogated or at all events suspended. I undertook to verify the exact position and let the Ambassador know.

M. Hägglöf said that his Government must inevitably take an extremely serious view of the matter if it were confirmed that the contract would be interrupted. He said he would like to give me various arguments in favour of the Swedish case:

(1) De Havillands had always been understood to have welcomed the Swedish

order since it enabled them to expand their factory at (I think) Chester.

(2) The Swedish Government would be justified in feeling extremely ill-used in that they might quite well have laid down factories in Sweden where they might have made airframes themselves. (I understand the contract dates back three or four years.)

(3) The Swedish air force have so far taken delivery of some 100 out of the 300 aircraft. If delivery of the remaining 200 were interrupted just when the flow was accelerating, it would throw the whole of the Swedish air force out of balance. This could hardly be to the advantage of Western defence.

(4) A British Purchasing Mission had recently been in touch with Bofors and were, M. Hägglöf understood, on the point of concluding a contract for the purchase of the latest Bofors anti-aircraft gun. Bofors were also supplying guns to France and the Netherlands. It would be seen therefore that there was a two-way flow of armaments. M. Hägglöf was too good a diplomat directly to link the sale of Bofors guns with the delivery of airframes; but the thought was there.

(5) M. Hägglöf also referred delicately to the Prime Minister's remarks in his broadcast on Saturday night about the sanctity of prior trade commitments to the Soviet Union.

I told M. Hägglöf that both for political and trade reasons there had been the utmost reluctance to interfere with the Swedish arrangements with de Havillands. It was due solely to the overriding strategic necessity, arising out of the international developments of the past two months.

M. Hägglöf said that, if what I told him was confirmed (I shall be seeing him on September 7th), he would feel bound to take the matter up at a high level, possibly with the Prime Minister, since it was a matter of the highest importance to his Government.[1]

G.W. HARRISON

[1] Bevin commented: 'I feel all this is getting into a mess and should be re-examined to get a clear policy' (FO 371/86948, NW1193/5). Hägglöf saw Attlee on 8 September: Attlee subsequently requested that the question should be reconsidered by Ministers at the Defence Committee meeting later that day. The brief prepared for McNeil for that meeting emphasised concern that, if the de Havilland contract were overridden, this could have repercussions on wider trade relations with Sweden which could extend as far as Bofors armaments (FO 371/86948, NW1193/6). It was decided that the contract should be proceeded with and that Vampire aircraft awaiting delivery should be despatched. Harrison wrote accordingly to Hägglöf on 13 September (FO 371/86948, NW1193/5).

No. 211

Letter from Sir H. Farquhar (Stockholm) to Mr Harrison, 26 October 1950
Top Secret (FO 371/86947, NW1192/9)

My dear Geoffrey,

On the 30th September Captain Wyburd, the Naval Attaché, had an interesting conversation with the Swedish Minister of Defence and a record of this conversation was sent to the DNI under his reference sheet No. 347 of September

30th.[1] You may by now have seen a copy of it. You will notice that in paragraph 5 M. Vougt assumed that as long as Norway was in Western hands it would be possible to supply the West coast Swedish ports even if Denmark was in Soviet hands. Captain Wyburd added that 'M. Vougt seemed to take it for granted that His Majesty's Government would be prepared to make such supplies available to Sweden'. Captain Wyburd has now received a reply to this communication from the DNI (Admiralty reference NID 08366/50 of the 16th October).[1] The DNI encourages Captain Wyburd to 'have further talks on similar lines' and, in paragraph 5, goes on to state that, in the event of either Denmark and/or Norway being invaded, the chances of Sweden receiving any further supplies are very small '*if she is not a member of the Atlantic Pact*'. I admit, of course, that this is a question of wording and drafting and Captain Wyburd is not expressly told to impart this information to the Swedish Minister of Defence. We would, however, like to be quite clear as to whether or not Captain Wyburd should speak to M. Vougt in the sense of this paragraph 5 before we take further action. I should also like to be sure that I am right in assuming that the word 'supplies' covers all cargoes and not only war equipment.

2. Captain Wyburd wants me to point out that as far as he is aware the Swedes have based all their plans on the assumption that if Denmark were to be invaded supplies would nevertheless continue to come in through West coast Swedish ports. If he tells the Minister of Defence that this is a rather risky assumption the Swedes would presumably have to change all their plans, which would be a very serious matter for them, and might have all sorts of consequences. The point is, ought we to warn the Swedes and, if we do so, is there a risk of their interpreting our warning as a form of pressure to force them into the Atlantic Pact? You will remember that in paragraph 3 of my Confidential letter to you 221/15/50 of the 19th October[1] I told you that fears were being expressed in certain Swedish circles that HMG might be flirting with the idea of using the 'Vampire' contract as a lever to push the Swedes into the Pact.

3. For convenience of reference I enclose herein Captain Wyburd's record of conversation with the Minister of Defence and the DNI's reply thereto.[2]

Yours ever,
H. FARQUHAR

[1] Not printed.
[2] Not printed. Despite two reminders from Farquhar (Stockholm tel. No. 359 of 8 December 1950 and his letter of 10 January 1951), Harrison did not reply to this letter until 15 January 1951. See No. 214.

No. 212

Sir L. Collier (Oslo) to Mr Bevin, 22 November 1950
No. 281 Restricted (FO 371/86535, NN 1015/18)

Sir,
Now that, after a quarter of a century, I am about to sever an official connexion with Norway which has lasted in one form or another since I entered the Northern Department of the Foreign Office in 1925, it may be of interest if I put on record my final impressions of the political and social state of the country and its relations

with Britain, as I remember one of my predecessors, the late Sir F Lindley, to have done when he left Oslo in 1929. I accordingly have the honour to submit a summary of these impressions in the following paragraphs.

2. As you are aware, Norway is a large country with a small population and no great natural resources, apart from water-power, timber and fish. Her people, however, have built up considerable national wealth, mainly from the profits of a very large merchant marine, and their standard of living, though not as high as in the neighbouring countries of Sweden and Denmark, is far above the average for Europe as a whole. Their standard of education is also well above the average; and as they are an intensely literate people, devoting perhaps more time to reading, both for pleasure and for profit, than any other nation except the Icelanders, they approach as nearly as any to the ideal of an instructed democracy. This is not to say that they approach it at all closely: it cannot honestly be claimed here, any more than elsewhere in the world, that the 'man in the street' has anything like a satisfactory understanding of all the political and economic problems on which democratic theory requires that he should form an opinion; but it can be said, at least, that he usually approaches such problems with a better background of general knowledge and less tendency to passion and prejudice than is shown by most of his fellows abroad. He is now free, as a rule, from either religious or political fanaticism; and though he has been prone in the past, and is still prone to some extent, to exhibitions of a rather childish nationalism, as exemplified in the *Landsmål* movement and other attempts to 'purify the language', change geographical names, etc., the impetus of these movements seems to be slackening and they are now mainly confined to the more backward rural parts of Western Norway. It is only where the Norwegian thinks his material interests to be vitally concerned that he shows unreasonable obstinacy, as in the dispute on fishery limits.

3. It follows from this that Norwegian politics have become—what they do not seem to have been in the nineteenth century—reputable, sober and almost dull. The fundamental principles of the democratic State are now so fully accepted by all parties (except the negligible minority of Communists) and the principles of Norwegian foreign policy have been so clearly defined and become so firmly established in the last few years, that political argument is now almost confined to economic issues; and though there is here plenty of disagreement in principle, the argument is conducted on actual lines, with comparatively little appeal to passion and hardly any of the 'spell-binding' emotional oratory which characterises the similar argument in America or, for that matter, in the 'Celtic fringe' of Britain. Indeed, political oratory, as such, is regarded with some distrust: it is still practised by some of the older politicians such as M. Hambro, the Conservative leader, but his style is now more admired than imitated. Politics, moreover, is a comparatively clean trade in Norway. Accusations of corruption are rare, as are personal attacks and 'smear' campaigns: after last year's general elections, for example, members of the United States Embassy expressed to me their astonishment that the Prime Minister was never opposed, even by the Christian People's Party, on religious grounds, though he is well known to be an agnostic, nor the Minister of Finance on personal grounds, though he was one of the *Stortingsmenn* who voted for the King's abdication in 1940, under German pressure. These elections proved, however, that in Norway lack of political passion does not imply lack of political interest, for the proportion of electors voting was very high, the attendance at political meetings was large and the amount of political literature distributed and

apparently read was almost a record. The worst that can be said of Norwegian politicians is that some of them, such as the notorious M. Oksvik,[1] are not above electoral 'gerrymandering', that there is probably some foundation for the general belief that membership of the Labour Party is a passport to advancement in government service, and that the Labour Party and Trade Union leadership, having obtained what appears to be an indefinite lease of political power, is inclined to ignore the rights of minorities and to rule both its own followers and the country at large in a somewhat dictatorial fashion.

4. Political conditions of this sort form a good basis for a firm and sensible foreign policy; but they do not, of course, ensure of themselves that such a policy will be adopted, and it is Norway's good fortune rather than merit that the conduct of her foreign affairs has lain, during the critical years in which the present world conflict with Soviet Communism has developed, in the unusually capable hands of M. Halvard Lange, probably the ablest Foreign Minister in Norwegian history. M. Lange, as I have reported elsewhere, had no easy task in convincing, first the Prime Minister, then the other members of the Cabinet and then the parliamentary Labour Party and the electorate as a whole, that Norway's interests required whole-hearted collaboration with the West and complete rejection of the pre-war ideal of neutrality; but once he had succeeded there was no question of going back on this policy and no difficulty in persuading the Norwegian public to follow it out to its logical conclusion, even in such matters as German rearmament, which their feelings would have led them to oppose, or the onerous and expensive defence measures now being put into force. This is an astonishing change to anyone acquainted with the sentimentally pacifist and naively idealistic Norway of the 1920s as depicted, for example, in *Jérome à Soixante Degrés Latitude Nord* (a book whose satire came so close to the truth that it can still hardly be mentioned in Oslo);[2] but Norwegians, unlike the proverbial Bourbons, are capable of learning from experience and they now, with few exceptions, take a much more realistic view of the state of the world and the possibilities of reforming it. It should not be assumed from this, however, that the idealistic and humanitarian spirit of Nansen is still not very much alive in them. Indeed, one of the chief causes of the speedy acceptance of M. Lange's views was the support which they received from left-wing idealists such as the poet Øverland, who regard Moscow Communism as the chief enemy of human liberty and I have been warned from more than one quarter here that it would put a severe strain on Norwegian adherence to the Atlantic Pact if it were extended, as is sometimes advocated in America, to include so obvious an enemy of liberty as General Franco.

5. A consequence or corollary of this development has been the unexpectedly complete maintenance of the close relations with Britain which developed during the war after the fateful year 1940. It hardly seemed possible to me, when I came here in 1945 just after the liberation of Norway, that Anglo-Norwegian relations, then at the crest of the wave, should not subsequently suffer some diminution in cordiality, if only through a natural reaction from the emotional high tension of the war years: there was a strong tradition of neutrality in Norway and several grounds for friction with her former allies, and if the Soviet Government had played their cards with skill they might have taken advantage of these factors and of the considerable Russophile feeling existing in Norway at the end of the war to drive a

---

[1] Olav Oksvik was a member of the Norwegian Labour party and a representative in the *Storting* from 1928-53. He was Minister of Agriculture from 1947-48.

[2] Maurice Bedel, *Jérôme 60 degrés latitude nord* (Paris: Gallimard, 1927).

serious wedge between the two countries at the critical moment when they embarked upon open opposition to British interests. As you are aware, however, their actions, beginning with the 'Spitsbergen demands' of 1946, opened the eyes of almost all Norwegians and drove such of them as might have been wavering, back into the arms of the West; and though the Western grouping was now perforce based fundamentally on the United States, it was Anglo-Norwegian, rather than American-Norwegian relations which derived the chief benefit from this movement of opinion. In spite of the influence of the numerous Norwegian-Americans (or perhaps partly because of it, since these hybrids are not as a rule popular in Norway), the Norwegian is essentially a European with no great liking for the 'American way of life' and, indeed, with a certain prejudice about it, particularly if he is a member of the Labour Party: his political and social ideals are those of Britain (or at least of Left-Wing Britain) rather than those of America, and the members of the present Norwegian Government have discovered, during and since the war, the affinity of their political and social ideas with those of the British Labour movement, which had previously been obscured by their closer contacts with German Social Democracy. At the same time, the Norwegian, though consciously a European, is not a European federalist in the Strasbourg sense: on the contrary, he instinctively distrusts the Franco-Italian approach to European problems (an Italian once complained to me that Norwegians would 'never take Latins seriously'), and his ideal is Atlantic co-operation rather than Continental federalism. These negative influences, aided, it can fairly be claimed, by some positive British contributions such as the good impression made by General Thorne and his troops after the liberation, have produced a situation in which, as a much travelled Englishman has recently observed with surprise, 'Norway is the one country in Europe where the English are positively popular and, indeed, more popular than any other foreigners'; and this situation seems likely to continue so long, at least, as both countries retain their present governments and face the same common enemy.

6. The above picture of a reasonable but determined people with unusually pro-British sentiments would, however, be too rosy without reference to the great shadow overhanging Norwegian life, the uncertain economic situation. As is well known, the average Norwegian is not very industrious; and having attained a comparatively high standard of living without having had to work very hard for it, he finds it difficult to believe that this standard cannot be maintained in the future without greater effort than has been required of him in the past. The government have done their best to ensure that the productivity of Norwegian industry is restored to more than its pre-war level, by a policy of capital investment financed by low interest rates, heavy taxation and the severe restriction of luxury imports; but, at the same time, the Trade Unions, with their connivance, have secured wage increases which have made Norwegian labour as expensive as any labour in Europe, and the two policies combined have created a situation of 'concealed inflation' within the country which reduces incentive by leaving a workman with very little on which to spend his increased earnings, while it raises costs all round and puts the export industries under an almost insuperable handicap in competition with their foreign rivals. At the moment these developments are counteracted to some extent by the abnormally high level of shipping freights and of prices for whale oil, resulting from the Korean war and the international crisis; but it seems inevitable that, when this 'crisis situation' is over, the Norwegian workman will be faced with the choice between much harder work and a fall in his standard of

living, and few observers here believe that he will choose the former alternative. There are, indeed, already signs that the regime of austerity and hard living, prevalent here during and immediately after the war, is about to return. The working-class Norwegian is perhaps better fitted to endure such a regime than his fellows in America or Britain, for his wants are comparatively simple and his pastimes (skiing, etc.) are still those of a countryman, so that he does not, like the American, feel entitled to a car and a television set or, like the Englishman, to a round of dog races and football matches; but he will not enjoy the increasing austerity and, though his strike record has hitherto been much better than that of British labour, he may well be tempted to strikes and other unsocial acts if he thinks, as the Communists are already trying hard to make him think, that other classes in the community are not being 'squeezed' sufficiently by the government. It is difficult to see, however, how a further 'squeeze' can be applied to any class, since Norwegian taxation is already a crushing burden on the professional man and a considerable obstruction to business efficiency. (The taxation of shipping companies, for example, is even heavier than in Britain and is making the modernisation of the merchant fleet increasingly difficult, as I am assured by a British shipping expert.)

7. Another shadow in the picture, less pronounced and definite but still serious, is the lack of organisation and the casual attitude to serious problems which characterises so many branches of Norwegian national life. The Norwegian is an individualist in practice, even though he is a socialist in theory, and believes, like the Englishman, in 'muddling through'; and the effects of this attitude can be seen in almost every branch of Norwegian activity, with the striking and somewhat inexplicable exception of shipping, which is managed with care and skill on what is often a very small margin between costs and profits. They are most serious, perhaps, in the organisation of the Armed forces which, I am assured by my Service attachés, will never be able to play their proper part in the defence of Western Europe, in spite of the excellent human material of which they are composed, unless they are thoroughly reformed under foreign control or at least with foreign advice; but the trouble is found in almost every service requiring organisation, from the railways to the post office and the customs, and when I am assured that there has been an improvement in nearly all services since pre-war days, I can only wonder what they can have been like then. Norwegians will speak freely of the contrast with Sweden in this respect, which can be observed at once by anyone crossing the frontier; but this seems merely to make them dislike the Swedes for their 'Teutonic efficiency' rather than attempt to bring their services up to the same level. As a Swedish friend said to me, 'I though *mañana* was a Spanish word until I came to Norway'.

8. When all is said, however, the picture of present-day Norway which I shall carry away with me and which I believe to be substantially true—at any rate I have done my best to form it without prejudice—is one of a country possessing most of the best elements in European civilisation, inhabited by a people brave to recklessness, generous to a fault, amiable (when sober), tolerant and easygoing in most matters, including their matrimonial relationships, physically rather lazy but mentally alert, though in an intellectual rather than an artistic direction (one has only to see the town hall here and that in Stockholm to realise their deficiency in artistic sense, even as compared with their next-door neighbours), who believe

firmly in the free development of human personality and are ready for almost any sacrifice to ensure that that development shall continue.[3]

I am sending copies of this despatch to His Majesty's Ambassadors at Copenhagen and Stockholm.

I have, etc.,
L. COLLIER

[3] This despatch was circulated quite widely within the Foreign Office. Noble marked it up to Bevin with the comment: 'This is an excellent study of Norway by a shrewd observer. From what little I know of Norway and the Norwegians (I am married to one) I can endorse all he says. The Norwegian habit of thought differs little from ours; as the two countries share many common interests, a close understanding is not too difficult. Sir L. Collier's tribute to M. Lange is well justified and fortunately he is a relatively young man.' Bevin noted: 'Very interesting' (FO 371/85535, NN1015/18).

No. 213

Minute from Sir H. Rumbold to Northern Department, 1 December 1950
Confidential (FO 371/87092, UR325/179)

The Uniscan Meeting in Oslo November 23rd 25th

ER(L)(50)279 of 1st December[1] within comprises (*a*) the United Kingdom minutes of this meeting, taken by Mr Burrett who acted as secretary to the United Kingdom delegation; and (*b*) the record agreed with the other delegations.

2. The brevity and comparative emptiness of the second document lead one to ask how valuable these meetings really are. Would it, one wonders, be more sensible to have longer intervals between meetings which produce such negative results?

3. The answer is, I think, that the value of Uniscan must be estimated by reference to the political and imponderable advantages which we derive from the fact of its existence rather than to the actual results of the individual meetings. These meetings are worth holding with undiminished frequency in order to foster the impression that the organisation is full of vitality even though their results may indicate the contrary.

4. I believe that the Scandinavian Governments look at it this way too. When we were going into the first meeting one of the Swedes remarked to me that he supposed that the first business of the meeting would be to write the report.[2] But although the Swedes may be cynical about the actual business performed by Uniscan the composition of their delegation at this last meeting and the obvious sincerity with which they welcomed the prospect of the next meeting being held at an early date in Stockholm showed, I think, that they set quite a high value on the organisation. M. Skaug, the Norwegian, told me, moreover, that the leader of the Swedish delegation, M. Hammarskjöld, was 'our best bet in Sweden': he was completely Atlantic-minded, he did his best at every turn to guide Sweden away

[1] Not printed.
[2] In an earlier minute of 20 October, when there were difficulties about arranging this meeting, Makins had commented 'Uniscan was brought into being largely for the benefit of the Scandinavian countries & we must try to fit in with their ideas about meetings and agenda as far as we can' (FO 371/87092, UR325/158).

from the path of neutrality, and he was powerful. Thus to a man like M. Hammarskjöld Uniscan may appear like the opening in the wall of a cell in which he finds himself imprisoned; he can look out through it at the outside world even though it is too small actually to pass through.

5. The same scepticism about the actual value of the business of Uniscan was betrayed by the leader of the Danish delegation, M. Wærum. When we were drawing up the record at the last meeting he tried to persuade his colleagues to agree that it should contain some reference to the session having 'decided' something or wishing to 'recommend' something to Governments. The latter would think it very futile, he said, if the record submitted to them described the session as having only 'noted' this or 'discussed' that. He had eventually to admit that this was in fact all that we had done. But in spite of this evident feeling of frustration M. Wærum obviously enjoyed the opportunities presented to him of airing his grievances. He made the most of these, particularly on the subject of 'liberalisation' and tariffs.

6. The Norwegians would certainly be mortified if we took any steps to wind up or curtail the activity of Uniscan. They are conscious of being politically nearer to us and more in sympathy with our general outlook than are the other two, and this feeling gives them a special reason for liking Uniscan. M. Skaug said at the end that he had regarded the meeting as a test case that would show whether Uniscan could serve rather different purposes from those originally intended in the Uniscan declaration, i.e. as a place in which to exchange views rather than to take decisions. He said that in his opinion it had passed this test very successfully.[3]

H.A.C. RUMBOLD

[3] Etherington-Smith supported these conclusions and minuted on 22 December: 'So far as the Scandinavians are concerned, I think that the arrangement holds attractions not only as a link with the UK, but also as a demonstration of *inter-Scandinavian* co-operation. Ever since Norway and Denmark joined the Atlantic Pact, Scandinavia has been split politically, a fact of which all three countries are uneasily conscious. There has therefore been an increased desire to develop practical co-operation in other non-political fields but plans for closer economic integration have not yielded any notable results. From this point of view, Uniscan has been welcomed as evidence of regular consultation and a common endeavour to adjust economic policies'. Berthoud and Makins generally agreed, and Makins commented to Strang on 2 January 1951: 'HMG could not propose its discontinuation without doing grave damage to our relations with the Scandinavian countries, though we could acquiesce if the Scandinavians at any time wished to stop it. In fact, if it does us little positive good, it certainly does us no harm, and from the political point of view I should say that there was advantage in keeping it going well' (FO 371/87092, UR325/179). See No. 214.

No. 214

Minute from Sir R. Makins to Sir W. Strang, 13 January 1951
(FO 371/94261, UR3225/3)

Uniscan

It is worth recording that Mr Hammerskjöld in Paris made a passing reference to Uniscan. He said that some people might think that the work it was doing was not of the highest importance or very constructive. On the other hand, the meetings were always very well attended and very cordial. The French had shown particular curiosity and had been unwilling to believe that these meetings of highly placed officials of the four countries were not up to some important business. Mr Hammerskjöld said that for his part he attached great importance to the maintenance of Uniscan. In certain circumstances he thought it would have a considerable role to play. I said that we also attached importance to Uniscan being maintained.[1]

R.M. MAKINS

[1] Etherington-Smith minuted on 22 January: 'I am not surprised to find Mr Hammerskjöld expressing these views. It is understandable that Sweden, who has cut herself from Norway and Denmark and the West politically, should want to maintain and even strengthen her links with the West in non-political fields (FO 371/94261, M3225/3).

No. 215

Letter from Mr Harrison to Sir H. Farquhar (Stockholm) 15 January 1951
Secret (FO 371/86497, N1192/12)

Dear Harold,

I much regret the delay in replying to your letter 288/1/50G of the 26th October,[1] to which you referred in your telegram No. 359 of the 8th December,[2] and again in your letter of January 10th,[2] about the supply of materials to Sweden in wartime.

We have considered this question in the light of the latest developments as regards deliveries to Sweden and of future prospects so far as they can be foreseen. I do not think, however, that there is anything we can say to the Swedes at present which would add materially to their existing information on this subject. They must be well aware that, as a country which has elected to stay outside our Western defence system, they cannot expect to receive the same consideration as countries which are members of the Group. This was made quite clear at the time of the signature of the Atlantic pact and in the subsequent period, when it was pointed out that the needs of our Allies would inevitably have prior attention and that only after these had been satisfied could other countries' requirements be met—so far as this was in fact possible given available supplies. The Swedes can therefore hardly be in any doubt as to the position and equally it must be clear to them that the above statement will apply *a fortiori* in the event of the Western Powers being involved in war with Russia, when available supplies of key materials will have to be even more strictly rationed. Subject to this proviso, however, it remains our wish to provide Sweden with the materials and equipment she requires and, so far as we can foresee, this policy should still hold good in the event of war, assuming that Sweden continues to maintain an effective military establishment and that she can be expected to defend herself if attacked. I do not think that it is possible for the present to say more than this, or to give any precise indication of the nature and quality of supplies which we might be able to deliver to the Swedes in the event of war. The answer to this question must depend on the particular circumstances prevailing if war does occur.

[1] See No. 211.
[2] Not printed.

In the light of the foregoing, we would have thought that the facts of the position are already so clear to the Swedish authorities as to render unnecessary any further explanation on the lines suggested in the DNI's letter to the NA of 16th October. I agree that we do not want to give the Swedish Government grounds for thinking that we are exerting pressure on them to join the Atlantic Pact; but it would surely be difficult for them to maintain that the attitude outlined above, which merely consists of pointing out that we have certain prior commitments to our Allies which we are bound to fulfil before we can consider Swedish requirements is open to such an interpretation. Nor is it consistent with the fact that we are continuing to supply them with Vampire air-frames (although it is true that we have had to cut down on certain other items, including an important machine for making 'Ghost' engine components, the delivery of which had to be cancelled recently in the interests of our own re-armament programme).

Our own inclination would therefore be to let the question of supplies for Sweden rest, since, as I say, the Swedes can hardly be in any real doubt as to the position and this does not seem the moment to rub it in.

I have consulted the DNI, who agrees and will, I understand, send Wyburd a separate line.

Yours ever,
G.W. HARRISON

No. 216

Minute from Mr Wilford to Mr Barclay, 2 August 1951
(FO 371/94696, NN1631/12)

I attach another Minister's holiday plan. Again you will see that it is Norway. Mr N-B will dead heat with P.M. for arrival at Oslo.[1]

As you will see the P.M. has already approved, though the Minister has never sought the S. of S.'s approval. I suppose therefore that we shall have to give approval and I have told Powell this.

It does seem a bit hard on Michael Wright[2] if on nobody else to have half the Cabinet on his doorstep!

It'll be easier to transport Sir N. Brook[3] to Norway if a Cabinet meeting is required!

K.M. WILFORD

---

[1] This minute reflected the reaction of Morrison's Private Office to the fact that four Ministers were planning to go to Norway on holiday in August 1951, visits which Attlee and Morrison combined with official and party talks in Oslo. Attlee (who scarcely ever holidayed abroad) visited Oslo from 10-12 August, and Morrison from 28-29 August. The other two Ministers were Philip Noel-Baker (Minister of Fuel and Power), who visited the widow of Fridtjof Nansen, and George Tomlinson, the Minister of Education.
[2] Ambassador to Oslo.
[3] Cabinet Secretary.

No. 217

Mr Morrison[1] to Mr Lambert (Stockholm), 6 September 1951
No. 170 Top Secret (FO 800/657, SC/51/5)

Sir,

During the few days I was in Sweden on holiday, I was honoured by an invitation from the King and Queen to lunch. It was particularly gratifying that Her Majesty was present as she has been abstaining from public activities owing to illness. She seemed to be in good health, and we talked a good deal during the lunch, where I sat next to her. The Swedish Prime Minister and the Governor of Halland were also present.

2. After lunch His Majesty took me into the conservatory, where we had a private talk for about fifteen or twenty minutes about general affairs. One point I should record. I indicated that we had a great respect for Sweden. We were glad she was re-arming, for the best guarantee of the peace of the world in existing circumstances was that the free and democratic countries taken together should be strong. His Majesty agreed. I then ventured to put the point to him that, if Norway and Denmark were invaded, would Sweden think it right not to declare war? He said that he was inclined to think it would be best not to declare war, even in those circumstances. Later on, when I took the point up with the Prime Minister, he said it would depend upon the conditions, but there was force in what the King had said, for Sweden might be of more assistance to Norway and Denmark if she were not herself overrun. He was not dogmatic about the point, however. He told me that the Swedes themselves would fight if attacked.

3. During my conversations with the Prime Minister I put to him the problems about collaboration on defence on the lines previously agreed. The Prime Minister was surprised to hear that we had not got sufficient information, because he had the clear impression that such information had been supplied. I told him that the Swedish authorities had kindly given us a memorandum, and I could not easily answer him in detail as to what information we still lacked. Evidently the Chiefs of Staff in London held that more information was needed though they were appreciative of the information which had been supplied. In these circumstances, would it not be best for some talks to take place privately through Service channels to see what further information we wished to have, or for that matter what further information the Swedes would like, and then we could see to what extent and in what manner the information might be supplied. I said that the element of personal consultation was important, first of all in relation to the requests for information, which either Government must be free to refuse; and secondly if and when private exchanges of views were to follow from time to time without publicity. I said I perfectly understood why the idea of the Swedish Minister of Defence coming to Britain had been dropped, and had no complaint about it. The problem remained, however, and I asked the Prime Minister to give consideration to the suggestion I had made, impressing upon him, of course, that I was speaking informally and that I knew he would be careful to handle it in a way that would not involve any bad feeling on the part of the Swedish Foreign Minister. On this last point he was quite sure that I need not be apprehensive.

[1] Herbert Morrison had succeeded Bevin as Foreign Secretary on 9 March 1951.

4. Mr Erlander, with whom I am on Christian name terms, did not respond immediately to my suggestion that some contact could be effected between the Service people in the manner suggested. In the first place, he rather inclined merely to take note of it. I pressed him again, and he said he would certainly give it thought and consideration.

5. The talk was very friendly and informal throughout. Indeed our relations are such that it could not well be otherwise.[2]

6. The above is for your personal information only and should in no way be used.

7. I am sending copies of this despatch to His Majesty's Ambassadors at Washington and Paris.

                                        I am, etc.,
                                      H. MORRISON

---

[2] Erlander recorded his impression of their conversations in his diary: Sven Erlander (ed.), *Tage Erlander. Dagböcker 1950-1951* (Hedemora: Gidlunds Förlag, 2001), p. 342 (entries for 1 and 2 September).

Index

Acheson, Dean G. xxiv, xxix, liii-liv, 310–12, 314–16, 319–22, 326
Afanasiev, S. A. 192
Aftenposten 224, 326
Air Disarmament Wing 77
Alexander, Albert V. xxix, 229
Alexander I, Tsar of Russia 108, 115
Allen, W. Dennis xxix, xxxvii, xliv, 37–9, 103, 157–8
Allied Control Commission (ACC) (Finland) xvi, 45, 90, 158
Alta 144
Althing (Icelandic Parliament) xxi, xxiv, liv, 207, 329, 334–6
Anderson, Alsing xxix, 271
Anderson, Sir John xxix, xxxvii, 31–2, 35–7, 328
Andvord, Rolf xi, xxix, 4, 13–14, 32, 203
Anti-Comintern Pact 120–1
Appleton, Sir Edward 277
Arbeiderbladet 84, 98, 124–5, 131
Arctic bases *see* Greenland, Iceland, Spitzbergen
Arctic Sea/Ocean ix, xi, xvi, 149, 282
Atlantic Ocean 15, 23, 175, 179, 216, 222, 231, 261
Atlantic security pact xii, xxiii-xxv, liv, 287–369; Denmark 285–6, 295, 313–14, 328–9, 331–4; Finland 282, 327–8; Iceland 329–30, 334–7, 355–6; Norway liii, 284–5, 295, 305–7, 309–11, 318–24, 337–8; Scandinavian Pact of Mutual Assistance 275–80, 290–3; Sweden 284–6, 308–9, 346–8, 358–9, 366–7
Atlantic Treaty *see* Atlantic security pact
Attlee, Clement xv, xx, xxix, xlvii, lvi, 60–1, 118–19, 139–42, 151–2, 166–9, 173–4, 201–4, 345, 356–8, 367
Australia 69–70, 201

Balfour, Arthur J. xxxviii, 43
Baltic Sea ix, xiii, xvii, 3, 16, 22, 29, 33, 73–4, 119, 122, 168, 179, 216, 275, 278, 309, 313, 318
Baltic States 186, 270, 311
Barclay, Christopher F. R. xxix, 139
Barclay, Roderick E. xxix, lvii, 367
Barents Sea 4
Barker, Gen. R. 75–6
Barry, R. H. 178–82
Bateman, Charles H. xx-xxiv, xxix, xlvii, l, lii-liv, 206–9, 213–14, 239, 242, 253, 258–9, 262, 267–71, 278, 282, 284–6, 291–3, 301–5, 316–24
Baxter, Charles W. xxi, xxix, xlvii, liv, lvi, 206–9, 329–30, 341, 355–6
Bay, Charles U. xxix, 156
Beale, Capt. 7–8
Bear Island 148–53, 176–7
Beck-Friis, Gen. Hans xxix, 24, 283
Beckett, Sir W. Eric xxix, 158, 289
Bedel, Maurice 361
Beeley, Harold xxix, lvi, 454
Beichmann, Gen. Fredrik 220
Belgium 130, 143, 145, 155, 179, 181, 245, 314, 323, 344, 355 *see also* Benelux countries
Benediktsson, Bjarni xxv, xxix, 334, 356
Benelux countries xix, xxii, 211, 213, 222, 231, 234–5, 262, 269, 344
Berg, H.C. xxii, 86–7
Berg, Lt-Gen. Ole xxix, 82, 86–7
Bergen 48, 144–5, 247

Index

Berlingske Tidende 81
Berthoud, Eric A. xxix, 365
Bertil, Prince of Sweden 169
Bevin, Ernest xi-xxix, xxxviii, xxxix, xlii-xliv, xlvi-li, liii-lvi, 33, 39, 42–66, 68–85, 90–110, 115–26, 137–9, 142, 147–65, 170–3, 182–99, 204–6, 209–16, 219–50, 253–66, 279–83, 296–301, 305–38, 341–6, 351, 355–64, 368
Bevin Plan xlix, 220, 246–7
Bidault, Georges xxix, 232–6, 245
Bjuggren, Col. Bjørn 308
Black Sea 33, 282
Bofors 283, 290, 294, 358; armaments production 301–2
Boheman, Erik xxix, 22–5, 195–9, 309
Bohlen, Charles E. 265
Bornholm xiii, xx, xxi, xxxvii, xl, 16–17, 29–30, 46, 54, 57, 59, 61, 77–9, 121, 122, 136, 266, 323
Bosley, R. W. 42, 67
Bottomley, Arthur G. xxix, 243, 356
Bovenschen, Sir Frederick xxix, 2
Braun, Eva xxv, xliv, 157–8
British Broadcasting Corporation (BBC) 248
British Thomson Houston Co. 342
British zone of Germany 154–5, 198
Brofoss, Erik xii, xxix, 99, 118, 324, 346
Brook, Sir N. 367
Brussels Treaty (1948) xxii, 234, 238, 239, 262, 314–15, 333, 338; Permanent Military Committee 316–17
Buhl, Vilhelm xxix
Bulgaria 39, 43, 91, 341
Bull, Dr. 289–90
Butler, R. A. xix, xxix, 194–5
Byrnes, James F. xx, xxix, 55, 59–62, 65–9, 148

Cabinet Overseas Negotiation Committee 201–2
Cabinet Overseas Reconstruction Committee xiii, 50–4, 65–6
Cadogan, Sir Alexander M. G. xxix, lv, 15, 33, 42, 77, 80, 341
Caffery, J. 265
Canada xxii, 3–4, 150–1, 153, 156, 176–8, 181, 201, 222–3, 231, 310, 315, 321, 334, 338
Caplan, D. 39, 41, 161
Carlsson-Mounsey Agreement (1939) 21–2

Cavendish Bentinck, V. 50
Chamberlain, Neville 125
Chiefs of Staff Committee 82; Joint Intelligence Sub-Committee xviii, 82
Christiansen, A. 183
Christina, Queen of Sweden (1632–54) 190
Churchill, Sir Winston xi-xii, xxix, xxxvii, l, 5, 14, 16–17, 46, 68, 234; Norway visit (1948) 249–50
Citrine, Sir Walter xxix, 100
Cohen, E.A. 243
Colban, Erik xi, xxix, 1, 86
Collier, Sir Laurence xii-xvii, xxi-v, xxix, xxxvii-xlvix, l-lvi, 13, 32–3, 47–9, 70–1, 82–90, 97–106, 124–6, 131–3, 147–57, 164–5, 177, 192, 199–204, 210, 223–33, 245–52, 260, 264–9, 274, 284–307, 312–13, 318, 325–31, 345–6, 356, 359–64
Committee on European Economic Co-operation (CEEC) 235, 238
Communism 204–6, 240–2; Finland 281–3, 327; Iceland 206–9; Norway 223–30, 246
Communist Information Bureau (Cominform) xxiv
Council of Europe 323, 333, 355
Court of International Justice 274
Crawford R. Stewart xxix, 136
Cripps, Sir R. Stafford xxix, liv, 24, 255, 324–5
Cromwell, Oliver 190
Crossman, Richard xxix, 203
Crowe, Eric E. xxx, liv, 337–8
Cumming, Cdr. A. P. 144–5
Czechoslovakia xvii, xxi, xxiii, 2, 38, 125, 196, 215, 222, 226, 228–9, 231, 234–5, 237–43, 248, 278, 341

Dahl, Gen. Arne D. xliii, 144–5
Daily Telegraph 326
Danielsen, A. xxii
Dansk Samling 52
Davidson, Alan E. xxx, 331
Denham, Capt. Henry M. xxx, 96
Denmark xiii-xv, 182–4; economic situation 182–4; military delegation to UK 142–6, 154–5, 157–8, 271–2; parliamentary delegation to UK (1948) 254–6; relations with Soviet Union 119–24; trade with Germany

Index

235–6; trade and financial relations with UK 170–3, 201–2, 341–2, 354
Dewing, Gen. Richard H. 30
Diet, Finnish 217–18, 352
Dixon, Sir Pierson J. xxx, lvi, 239–42, 248, 355
Douglas, Gen. Archibald xxx, 25, 97
Dumbarton Oaks Conference (1944) 15

Economic Intelligence Department (FO) 141
Economist 184
Eden, R. Anthony xi, xiv-xv, xx, xxx, xxxvi, 2–11, 14–37, 80, 184
Eickhoff, J. 197
Eire *see* Ireland
Elster, Torolf xxx, 98, 203
Enckell, Carl xvi-xvii, xxx, xxxix, xlvi, 57–8, 91, 107–10, 115–17, 196–9, 215–17
Eriksen, Kristian 145
Erlander, Tage F. xxx, 167, 214, 294, 332, 347, 368–9
Establishment and Organisation Department (FO) 252
Etherington-Smith, Raymond G. A. xxx, xlviii, l-li, liv-lv, 216, 218, 242–4, 252–3, 279–80, 318–24, 326–8, 334, 348–50, 365–6
European Recovery Programme (ERP) (Marshall Plan) xi, xlix, 203, 208–14, 222, 234, 238–9, 245–6, 257, 325, 333
Ewart, W. 7, 33

Fagerholm, Karl-August xvii, xxx, 218, 281–3
Falla, Paul xxx, lv, 342–3
Faroe Islands 46, 285
Farquhar, Sir Harold L. xxiii, xxx, li-liii, lvi, 268–70, 283–8, 290, 293–9, 301–3, 308–9, 326, 331, 358–9, 366–7
Feaveryear, A. 188–9
Federspiel, Per xxx, 123
Feiandt, R. von 68
Feodorov, M. A. N. 241
Figg, L. C. li, 276–7
Finland xv-xviii, 39–42, 281–3; Armistice Agreement 2–4, 72, 100; British policy 158–64; British Week in Helsinki (1947) 173–4; delegation to Moscow 193, 348–9; economic and social review 351–4; economic relations with Soviet Union 129–30, 139–41, 184–8; Independence Day 281; peace treaty 137–8, 158, 282; prospective pact with Soviet Union 20–1, 37–9, 43, 115–17, 199; reparation deliveries 63–4, 256–7; reparations agreement 130; Treaty of Friendship, Co-operation and Mutual Assistance with Soviet Union (1948) xii, xvii, xxi, xlix, 214–20, 242–4, 248; War Guilt Tribunal xli, 90–1
Finnish-Soviet Union Society 162–3
Finnmark 34–5
Flensborg/Flensburg xiii, xxv, 31, 45, 53, 75–6, 80
Fog, Prof. Mogens xxx, 123
France xix, xxii, 23, 27–8, 39, 70, 130, 151–2, 176, 179, 181, 192, 222, 231–2, 234, 242, 257, 262, 269, 314, 324, 338, 344, 355, 358
Francke, Maj. Karl 96
Franco, Gen. Francisco 361
Franks, Sir O. l-li, liii, 260–2, 264–6, 314–16
Freeman, Maj. J. 144
Freeman Matthews, H. 192
Frenckell, E. von 68
Frihedsfonden 158
Frikorps Danmark 120
Frisch, Hartvig xxx, 256

Garner Smith, Col. Kenneth J. G. xxx, 103, 199–200
Gartz, Åke xxx, 116
Gathorne-Hardy, G. A. ix
George, Prince of Denmark 303–4
Gerhardsen, Einar xxi, xxx, 84, 331, 340
German re-armament 354
German-Soviet non-aggression pact (1939) 23, 120, 126–9
Germany: British zone xiv, 46, 53, 71, 82, 106, 142, 145, 154; citizens of Danish origin xiv; collapse (1918) 19; Control Commission xiv, 41; Danish minority 44, 51; Danish troops xiv, 126, 141–2, 154, 155, 278; Denmark, trade with 235; exports 172; Finnish imports from 34; Norwegian fish exports 70; Norwegian Military Mission to Germany 47; Norwegian troops 107, 118, 119, 210; pro-Swedish elements 23; rearmament (post-WWII) 354; refugees 46, 80, 136, 165; Russia invasion 6, 7, 23, 24,

Index

120, 126; Russian reparations 115, 116; Sweden saved by Russia (WWII) 6; Swedish appeasement xviii, 7, 93; Swedish exports (WWII) 26–8; Swedish iron ore ix, 22; World War Two x, xii, xiii, 2–3, 4, 14, 21
Gibraltar 74, 231, 234
Gollancz, Victor 132
Gördeler, Carl F. 24
Göring, Marshal Hermann 23, 122
Gothenburg safe-conduct traffic 25–6
Great Belt 119, 122, 266, 318
Greece 39, 77, 236–7, 276, 299
Greenland, US bases in xx, 55 77–8, 122, 150, 169, 175–6, 266, 285–6, 292, 315, 317, 322–3, 325, 333
Grundy, J. B. C. 68
Gudmundsson, Harald 329–30
Gulf of Bothnia 6, 269–70
Gulf of Finland 3, 6
Gundersen, Oscar C. xxx, 200
Günther, Christian xviii, xxx, 6–7, 17–20, 24, 194
Gustaf V, King of Sweden xxx, xlvi, 25, 167, 191–2
Gustav VI, King of Sweden xxx, lvii, 368

Haakon VII, King of Norway xxx, 89, 246–50
Hadow, Robert H. xxx, 217
Hägglöf, Gunnar xx, xxx, 308, 342, 355, 357–8
Haigh, A. Anthony H. xviii, xxx, xxxvi-xxxvii, 7, 11–12, 20, 37–9
Halford, Aubrey S. xxx, xliv, 157–8
Halifax, First Earl of (Edward Wood) xix, xxxvi, xxxix, 6, 14–16, 61–2, 66, 68–70
Hambro, Carl J. 32, 360
Hammarskjöld, Dag xxx, 364–6
Hangö (Hanko) 3, 6, 72
Hankey, Hon. Robert M. A. xvi-xix, xxi-xxiii, xxx, xlii-xliv, xlvi-lv, 95–7, 103–4, 110, 117–18, 124–57, 164, 178, 187, 193–204, 213–18, 239, 244–7, 262–9, 282, 284–97, 301–6, 314, 325–34, 338–9
Hansen, Hans xxx, 52, 75–6
Hansen, Rasmus xxx, 332
Hansson, Per Albin xxx, 28, 167–8
Hansteen, Gen. Wilhelm 2
Harrison, Geoffrey lvi, 348–50, 357–9, 366–7

Hauge, Jens Chr. xii, xxiii, xxx, 88–9, 118, 200–4, 210, 229, 247, 284, 303, 331
Hayter, William G. xxx, 316
Healey, Denis xxv, xliii, xlv, 138, 164, 187–8
Hedin, Sven23
Hedtoft, Hans xxx, 122, 212, 330–3
Heligoland 122
Helset, Maj.Gen. Olaf xxxi, 200
Helsingfors *see* Helsinki
Helsingin Sanomat 248
Helsinki 110–15, 219–20, 311
Helo, Johan xxx 63
Henderson, James T. xxxi, xlviii, 166, 220–1, 247, 278
Henderson, Lord (William W.) xxxi, 271–2
Henniker-Major, John P. xxxi, lv, 343–4
Heppel, Richard P. xxxi, 138
Hickerson, John 262
Hicks, Maj.Gen. 143
Higgs, L. Rudolph 10
Hillilä, Karlo xxxi, 11, 116
Hitler, Adolf 23–5, 124–5, 157–8, 223, 295
Hjalmarsson, Jarl xxxi, 347
Hoffman, Paul 345
Holland *see* Netherlands
Hollis, Maj. Gen. Leslie C. xxxi, xxxvi, xxxviii, 1–2, 46, 54–6, 253, 262, 318
Holt, Adm. John G. 30
Hood, Viscount (Samuel) xxxi, 40
Howie, Capt. R. H. xxxi, 39–42, 72, 90–1
Hoyer Millar, Sir Derek R. xxxi, li, 172, 264, 269, 274–5, 285, 288, 296, 326
Hufvudstadsbladet 248
Hull, Cordell xxxi, 175–6
Hull-Kaufmann Agreement (1941) 77
Hulley, B. 68
Human Rights Commission lvi, 355
Hungary 39, 43, 91, 184, 186, 215, 341
Hvass, Franz xxxi, 43–7, 136, 244
Hyndley, Viscount (John) xxxi, 357

Iceland xx-xxi, bases 59–62, 65–6, 68–70, 104–6, 175, 207–8; Communism 335–7; defence 355–6; delegation to UN 341
Information Policy Department (FO) 227, 250

Index

Information Research Department (IRD) (FO) xxiv-xxvi, 205, 251–2
Inman, John xxxi, 156
International Nickel Company 4
International Socialist Conference Committee (COMISCO) 187
Inverchapel, Lord (Sir Archibald Clark Kerr) xi, xxi, xxxi, xxxvi, xlviii, 4–5, 221–3, 228
Iran 121, 150, 222, 228, 236
Ireland (Eire) 14, 222, 355
Italy xvi, 42, 151–2, 165, 176, 204, 223, 231, 234, 237, 239, 262, 276, 299, 310, 324, 344, 355

Japan 14–16, 37, 48, 58, 151–2, 176, 295
Jebb, Sir H. M. Gladwyn xxxi, xxiv, li, liv, 15, 182, 278, 280, 286, 293, 304, 306, 316–24
Jellicoe, Earl (George) xxxi, xlv, 165–6
Jerram, Sir Cecil B. xviii-xix, xxv, xxxi, xxxvii, xli-xlii, xlv-xlvii, xlix, li, 29, 35–7, 50, 92–7, 117–18, 126–9, 166–9, 189–92, 193–6, 236–9
Johnson, Herschel V. xviii, xxxi, 35–6
Joint Intelligence Committee *see* Chiefs of Staff Committee
Joint War Planning Staff (JWPS) xlv, 342
Joint War Production Staff 258, 279
Jones, E. M. 104–5
Jónsson, Emil 334
Jónsson, Eysteinn 334
Jørgensen, Jørgen 271
Jowitt, Lord (William A.) 118
Jung, Gen. Helge V. xxxi, 96, 214, 350

Kallinen, Yrjö xxxi, xlvi, 196–7, 217–18, 244
Kansallis Osake Bank 102
Karelia 34, 56, 58, 108–10, 111, 112, 115, 351
Karlstad Plan 296–7, 300, 306, 325, 332, 350. *See also* Scandinavian defence
Kattegat 122, 266
Keflavik 207–8, 336
Kekkonen, Urho xxxi, 67, 116, 352
Kenney, C. (Kit) xxxi, 89, 131–3, 250–1
Kenney, Rowland xxxi, 1, 84–5, 88–90, 103
Kerr, Sir Archibald J. K. Clark *see* Inverchapel, Lord
Kiel Canal 45, 53, 75

Kilpi, B. 240
Kinna, Peter F. xxxi
Kirkpatrick, Sir Ivone A. xiv, xxxi, li, liv, 133–5, 264, 269, 271, 274–5, 286, 328
Kivimäki, Toivo M. xxxi, 90
Kivinen, Lauri xxxi, 63, 67
Koht, Halvdan 164
Kollontay, Aleksandra M. xxii, xxxi, 22–3
Korovin, Alexey A. 338–9
Kraft, Ole Bjørn xxxii, 213, 271
Kristensen, Thorkil xxxii, 271
Kukkonen, Antti xxxii, 90
Kuusinen, Otto W. xxxii, 109, 161, 186
Kuznetsov, N. 192

Labouchere, George P. xxxii, 17–20
Lambert, Anthony E. xxxii, lv, lvii, 346–8, 368–9
Lamming, G. N. xxxii, 128
Landsmål movement 360
Lange, Christian 83; Nobel Prize (1921) 83
Lange, Halvard M. xii-xiii, xix, xxii-xxiii, xxxii, xli, xliv, xlvii-xlvix, li-lii, liv, 83–8, 125, 147–50, 156–7, 165, 200–4, 210, 221, 228–33, 238–9, 246–7, 264–9, 276–80, 292, 294, 310–26, 331, 337–8, 340, 346, 356, 361–4
Langhelle, Nils xxxii, 84
Laski, Prof. Harold 83
League of Nations 66
Ledward, Richard T.D. xxxii, 187–8
Leino, Yrjö xxxii, 67, 117, 185, 217, 256
Lenin, Vladimir 226
Leningrad 64, 72, 171
Leskinen, Väinö xxv, xlv, 187–8
Lie, Haakon xxv, xxxii, 98, 250
Lie, Trygve xi-xiii, xxxii, xli, 1–5, 12–13, 32, 39, 47–9, 70–1, 82–9, 103, 119, 147–8, 156–7, 340; departure from office 85–7
Lindley, Sir F. 360
Linkomies, Edwin xxxii, 90
Little Belt 119, 122, 318
London Press Service 206
Lovett, Robert A. xxxii, 228, 260–2, 264, 287
Luukka, Eemil V. xxxii, 67
Luxembourg 355 *see also* Benelux countries

375

Index

Mackenzie King, William L. xxxii, 223
Mackenzie-Johnstone, Henry B. xxxii, 213
McNeil, Hector xxxii, xliii, xlvii, 99, 138, 141–2, 164, 202–4, 209–10, 328, 346–8, 358
Magill, Col. J. H. xvi, xxxii, xl, 39, 67, 72–4, 91
Makins, Sir Roger M. xxxii, lvi, 343, 364–6
Malkin, Sir H. William xxxii, 15
Mallet, Sir Victor xviii, xxxii, xxxvi-xxxvii, 6–7, 17–29, 138, 194–5
Mannerheim, Field-Marshal C. Gustaf E. xvi, xxxii, xli-xlii, 11, 67, 92, 115–16, 339, 351; resignation 100–2
Marconi 253, 259
Markos, Gen. Vafiades 237
Marshall, George C. xxii, xxxii, li, 152, 203, 223, 228, 237, 265–6, 276, 280, 296
Marshall Plan *see* European Recovery Programme
Martin, Kingsley 132
Masaryk, Jan xxxii, 125
Matthews, H. Freeman 309
Mayall, Alexander L. 96
Mayhew, Christopher xiv, xxiv, xxxii, xliv, li, 138, 144–6, 276–7
Mills, G. H. 178–82
Minesweeping Commission 81
Ministry of Aircraft Production 83
Ministry of Fuel and Power 356–7
Møller, G. L. J. Christmas xiii-iv, xxxii, 29–31, 45–7, 53–4, 57, 77–9, 123
Molotov, Vyacheslav xi-xii, xxxii, xxxvi, xxxix, xliv-xlv, 4–5, 13–14, 22–3, 32, 64, 122, 147–53, 157, 164–5, 166, 177, 192, 199, 237–9
Monsen, Christian F. 340
Montagu-Pollock, William H. xxxii
Montgomery, Viscount (Bernard) 339
Morgenbladet 89–90, 125
Morrison, Herbert xxxii, lvii, 367–9
Mosquito night fighters 280
Mountbatten, Lord Louis 192

Nansen, Fridtjof 367
National Coal Board xv, 341, 345, 357
Netherlands 45, 130, 176, 179, 181, 245, 314, 323, 344, 358 *see also* Benelux countries
New Zealand 69–70, 141, 201, 205

Nielsen, Edgar E. M. xxxii, 166
Noble, Sir Andrew N. xxxii, 364
Noel-Baker, Philip xxxii, 367
Nordahl, Konrad xxxiii
Nordenskiöld, Gen. Bengt xxxiii, 220–1, 294–5, 325
North Atlantic Treaty *see* Atlantic security pact
North Sea 23, 132–3, 179, 318
Northern Department (FO) xxxix, xlv, xlix, 12–14, 59–60, 64–6, 75, 197, 280, 364–5
Northern Norway Military District 144
Norway xi-xiii, 222–33; armed forces 102–4, 118–19, 210; Atlantic security system 222–3; cooperation with UK 259–60; Communism 223–30, 319; economic relations with UK 324; fisheries dispute with UK 273–4, 289–90, 324; Labour Movement 97–100, 225–33, 319, 325; military mission to Germany 47–9; *Militære Samfund* 245–6; Mutual Aid Agreement with UK 48–9, 70; political and social review 359–64; Round Table Club 249; trade unions 99, 231–3, 319; whaling factories 48
Novikoff, A. 164
Nuremberg Trials 168
Nygaardsvold, Johan xxxiii, 156

Oftedal, Sven xxxiii, 84
Oksvik, Olav 361
Organisation for European Economic Co-operation (OEEC) 324, 345–6
Orlov, Pavel xxxiii, 8–10, 42, 109, 129
Ottawa Agreements (1932) 120
Oxholm, Oscar O'N. xxxiii, 330

Paasikivi, Juho K. xvii, xxxiii, xli, xlix, 11, 196–9, 281, 351; election 100–2
Pakenham, Lord (Frank) xiv, xliv, 145–6
Paris Peace Conference (1946) 125, 137–8
Pekkala, Mauno xxxiii, 11, 67, 199, 217
Persia *see* Iran
Peter the Great, Tsar of Russia 73
Petersen, Harald xxxiii, 165
Peterson, Sir Maurice D. xxxiii, xlix, 242–3, 311
Petri, Gen. 325
Petsamo 111; nickel mines 3–4

Index

Phillips, Adm. Sir Tom 295
Phillips, Morgan xxxiii, 138, 329
Pickford, Frank xlii, 110–15
Poland 18, 21, 38, 90, 129, 133, 166, 168, 171, 231, 235, 341
Political Intelligence Department (FO) 227
Porkkala 111–12
Portugal 67, 69, 222
Potsdam Agreement (1945) 80
Potsdam Conference (1945) xvi, 192
Prebensen, Per P. xxxiii, 147–51, 303, 309–12
Price, Brigadier 291
Prytz, Björn xix, xxxiii, xlvi, 193–6
Pumphrey, John L. xxxiii, 260

Quisling, Vidkun A. L. J. xxxiii, 25

Ramsay, Henrik xxxiii, 90
Randall, Sir Alec W. G. xiii-xv, xxiv, xxxiii, xxxvii-xxxviii, xl, xlii-xlvix, liii-lv, 29–32, 44–7, 53, 57, 75–81, 119–24, 136–46, 154, 170–3, 182–9, 211–13, 233–6, 244–7, 277–8, 285–8, 294–6, 301, 306, 313–14, 326, 328–34, 341–2
Rangell, Jukka W. xxxiii, 90
Rasmussen, Gustav xxii-xxiii, xxxiii, xlvii, xlix, liii, 43–5, 77, 81, 121–2, 136, 141–2, 211–13, 233–6, 244–5, 271, 293–4, 325, 329–33, 346
Red Star (Moscow) 212
Refugees 34; Danish 27; German in Denmark 136–7, 165–6; Karelian 56–8, 108–10, 111–15, 351
Reid Brown, Harry W. xl, 82–3
Reinikka, Tyko xxxiii, 90
Reuter, Prof. O. 68, 162
Reventlow, Count Eduard xiv, xxxiii, xl, liv, 78, 122, 154, 197–8, 304, 313, 328, 331
Ribbentrop, Joachim von 22–3
Riksdag (Swedish Parliament) *xiv, xxiv* 129, 167–8, 213, 277, 331–2, 350
Robens, Alfred 356–7
Roberts, Frank K. xxxiii, xxxix, 64, 135, 265, 279
Robertson, Gen. Brian H. xxxiii, 165–6, 245
Robinson, Sir Robert 277
Romania/Roumania 4, 38–9, 43, 63, 90–1, 215, 341
Ronald, Sir Nigel B. xxxiii, 1

Rose, E. Michael xxxiii, 136–7
Rosen, Count Carl von 191
Rothnie, Alan K. xxxiii, 81
Rowan, Mr, 259–60
Rumbold, Sir Horace A. C. xxxiii, lvi, 78, 364–5
Russia *see* Union of Soviet Socialist Republics (USSR)
Russell, Bertrand 132
Ruthven-Murray, B. 248
Ryder, Cdr. Robert E. D. xxxiii, 302–3
Ryti, Risto xxxiii, 90

San Francisco Conference (1945) 18–20
Sanness, John 156
Sargent, Sir Orme G. xi, xiii, xxiv, xxxiii, xxxvi-xxxix, xli-xliii, xlvi-xlvii, l, liv, 1–2, 12–17, 33, 39, 43–50, 54–5, 70–1, 85, 102–4, 126–38, 182, 193, 201–2, 214–16, 239, 252–3, 262–4, 280, 302, 304, 316–18
Savonenkov, Lt-Gen. Grigori M. xxxiii, 8, 91, 215, 217, 241, 256
Scandinavian defence xxi-xxiv; British backing 180–1; co-operation 267–71; mutual defence pact 178–82, 293–301, 304, 312–16, 332; policy 349–50; strategic value 179. *See also* Atlantic security pact, Karlstad Plan
Scandinavian regional grouping 343–6
Scavenius, Erik xxxiii, 120
Scharffenberg, J. 88
Schleswig-Holstein *see* Slesvig-Holstein
Schleswig, South *see* Slesvig, South
Schmidt, P. 23
Scott, Sir Oswald A. xxxiv, xlvi, xlviii, xlix-li, lvi, 193, 196–7, 214–19, 239–44, 248, 256–7, 269–70, 281–3, 338–9, 351–4
Shepherd, Francis M. xvi-xvii, xxiv, xxxiv, xxxvi-xlv, 7–21, 33–42, 56–8, 63–4, 67–8, 72–4, 90–2, 100–2, 107–10, 115–17, 129–30, 133–5, 139–41, 158–64, 173–4, 184–6
Shepherd, Sir Edward H. G. xxxiv, 104–6
Sihvo, Gen. Aarne xxxiv, 244
Skagerak 26
Skaug, Arne xxxiv, 364–5
Skyddskår 10
Skylstad, Rasmus *xxxiv*, 305–6, 325, 329

Index

Slesvig-Holstein 31, 51–2, 80–1, 198, 2871–2
Slesvig, South 50–4, 75–6, 81, 141–4, 189, 197–8, 271–2
Söderberg, Gen. Nils 221
Söderhjelm, Johan O. xxxiv, 328
Soteva 63–4
Sound, the 74, 119, 122, 332
Soviet Union *see* Union of Soviet Socialist Republics (USSR)
Spaak, Paul-Henri xxxiv, 86
Spain 12, 99, 165, 169, 222, 248
Special Counter Intelligence (SCI) 157–8
Special Forces Association Provident Fund 158
Spitsbergen/Spitzbergen 32, 147–53, 155–7, 164–5, 192, 231, 234, 315, 320, 323, 326, 362; Arctic bases 176–7; Convention 13; V weapons 150–3
Ståhlberg, K. 101
Stalin, Marshal Joseph xvi-xvii, xxxiv, xlviii, 37, 63–4, 116, 122, 165, 174, 186, 214–17, 226, 236–9, 257, 266
Stapleton, Grp. Capt. Deryk C. xliv, 152–3
Stauning, Thorvald xxxiv, 120
Steel, Christopher (Kit) E. xxxiv, xl, 17, 53, 75–6, 80
Stefánsson, Stefán J. xxxiv, 329
Steffens, Gen. W. 47
Steinþórsson, Steingrímur xxxiv
Stevens, J.F. 178–82
Stockholms Tidningen 259
Storting (Norwegian Parliament) l, liii, 32–3, 82, 85, 88–9, 98, 106, 147–9, 156–7, 164–5, 249, 259–60, 305–7, 320, 326, 340; Foreign Affairs and Fisheries Committees 324
Strang, Sir William xxxiv, xl, lvi, 45, 51, 75–6, 365–6
Strömbäck, Vice-Adm. Helge xxxiv, 49–50
Summerskill, Dr. Edith 255
Sunday Pictorial 306
Supreme Headquarters Allied Expeditionary Force (SHAEF) xiii, 17, 28–30
Supreme Soviet of the Karelo-Finnish SSR 109
Sutton Pratt, Brig. Reginald xxxiv, 96
Svalbard *see* Spitzbergen

Svenska Diamantbergborrnings A/B 36
Svento, Reinhold xvi, xxxiv, 11, 20, 58
Sweden xviii-xx, 11, 189–92; air force 22, 93, 220–1; annual review (1944) 11–12; armed forces 92–7; Communist Party 127; defence staff 178–82; iron ore 21, 277; naval visits 49–50; political events (1946) 166–9; Scandinavian co-operation and Atlantic and Western Union 262–4; Social Democratic Party 128; staff college 308; supply of military equipment 252–3, 258–9, 279–80; trade unions 127, 277; trade and payments agreement with Soviet Union 168; trade with Germany 21–9; uranium 36–7
Swedish ball-bearing company (SKF) 26–7
Swedish Match Company 24
Switzerland 18, 339

Talbot, Milo J. R. xxxiv, 197
Tanner, Väinö xxxiv, 90, 160
Terboven, Josef A. H. xxxiv, 25
Thomas, C. L. xxxiv, xlii, 11–115, 163
Thorez, Maurice 337
Thorne, Gen. Sir Andrew xxxiv, 2, 48–9, 70
Thornton, Dr. C. Grace xxiv, xxxiv, liv, 334–7
Thors, Ólafur xxxiv, 16
Tito, Marshal Josip B. 31
Togliatti, Palmiro 337
Tomlinson, George xxxiv, 367
Törngren, Ralf J. G. xxxiv, 257
Torp, Oscar F. xxxiv, 88–9, 318–24
Tousieng, Lt. Gen. P. 75
Tranmæl, Martin xxxiv, 84, 98
Trevelyan, H. l, 259–60
Tromsø 144–5, 196
Trøndelag 2
Trondheim 2, 22
Truman, President Harry S. xxxiv, x, 204, 247, 306, 320
Tuomioja, Sakari xxxiv, 257
Turkey 157, 222, 228, 230–1, 236–7, 276, 299
Turku 162

Undén, Bo Östen xviii-xxii, xxxiv, xli, xlix, liv, 94, 97, 203, 213–14, 236–9,

Index

253, 258, 262, 266–70, 279, 283–4, 287–95, 301, 323–6, 331, 346
Union of Soviet Socialist Republics (USSR): Control Commission 10, 348; Denmark, relations with 54, 55; Fenno-Karelian Republic 109; Finland, diplomatic relations 3, 43, 158, 199, 257; Finland, mutual pact against German aggression ix, xvi, 20, 214–5; Finland, trade relations 34; Finnish anti-Russian attitude 8; Finnish fears of xvii, 10; Finnish reparations 256; German attack 6, 7, 23, 24, 120, 126; Norwegian fears of xxi, 2, 322; Norwegian Government negotiation (post WWII) 13, 151, 152; Sweden, relations with 12, 95, 117, 261; Sweden saved by (WWII) 6, 23; Trade and Payments Agreement 168; trade with Western Europe 243
UNISCAN xi, lvi, 364–6
United Nations Organisation (UNO) ix, xii, xvi, xxiv-v, 2, 15–16, 38, 59–2, 65, 66, 68–9, 84, 88–9, 91, 94–6, 107–8, 122, 124, 128–9, 147, 151, 153, 164, 167, 169, 177, 203, 219, 230, 237, 268, 286, 323, 340; Charter 38, 55, 60, 65–6, 91–6, 177, 231–2, 320; Security Council 147–9, 153
United States of America (USA): Atlantic Pact (Article V) 319; Denmark's Atlantic Pact membership 314; German exports, dollar payments for 235; Greenland bases, role of 176; Iceland air-bases 16, 55, 59, 60, 65, 104, 168; Iceland and Portugal, post-war base requirements in 69; Iceland, US forces in 175; Iceland's Atlantic Pact membership 315; industrial capacity 314; military supplies 320, 349; Norway, relationship with 247, 363; Norway's Atlantic Pact membership 320, 326, 361; role in world affairs 169; SKF (Swedish ball-bearing company) assets 27; Spitsbergen, demilitarisation of 177; Spitsbergen treaty (1920) 148; Sweden, arms supply to xx, 260–2, 276, 284, 338, 343; Sweden, influence in 169; Sweden, trade with 29; Sweden's Atlantic Pact membership 327, 332
Uusi Suomi 248

Vachitov, Col. V. 8
Vampire fighter aircraft xx, 259–62, 280, 357–9, 367
Vandenberg, Sen. Arthur H. 322–3; Vandenberg Resolution 298, 300–2
Varjonen, U. 187
Verdens Gang 249
Versailles Treaty (1919) 51
Vogt, Benjamin xxxiv, 90
Vorley, N. 145
Vougt, Allen G. F. xxxiv, 93–4, 294, 325, 359
Vuolijoki, H. 64
Vuori, Eero A. xxxv, 56–8, 86, 89, 193, 199, 327–8, 338–9, 348–9
Vyshinsky, Andrey xxxv, 121

Waddams, Rev. Herbert 9
Waerum, Ejnar xxxv, 189, 365
Wallenberg, J. 23–5
Walsh, James M. xxxv, xxxvii, xli, 42, 57, 100–2
Walstad, B. 36
Warbey, William N. xxxv, 99
Ward, John G. xxxv, 104
Wardrop, James C. xxxv, xlii, 106–7, 131
Warner, Christopher F. A. xi, xiv-vi, xxiv, xxxv, xxxvii-xli, 1, 1–2, 39–42, 49–56, 67–8, 76–92, 97, 102–4, 125–6, 130–8, 164, 194–9, 251–2
Warr, George M. xxxv-xxxvii, xl-xlv, 7, 11–13, 21, 39–42, 58, 71–8, 85, 92–7, 104–6, 110, 136–7, 142–4, 154–5, 165–6
Warren, Avra xxxv, 217
Westring, C. A. H. xxii
Whitelocke, Bulstrode 190–2
White Sea 4
Width, Trygve xxxv, 89–90
Wied, Prince Victor zu xxxv, 7
Wigforss, Ernst J. xxxv, 331
Wilford, Kenneth M. xxxv, lvii, 342, 367
Williams, T. 118
Winant, John G. xxxv, 35–6
Wold, Terje xxxv, 156
Wood, Edward *see* Halifax, First Earl of
World Organisation *see* United Nations
Worm-Müller, Prof. Jacob S. xxxv, 156
Wright, Michael R. xxxv, 104, 367
Wuori, Eero A. *see* Vuori
Wyburd, Capt. Derek 358–9

Index

Younger, Kenneth G. xxxv, 351–4
Yugoslavia 20, 38, 39 133, 136

Zaroubin, Georgi N. xxxv, 338–9

Zhdanov, Gen. Andrey xvi, xxxv–xxxvi, 7–11, 37–8, 41–2, 161
Zilliacus, K. 138
Zorin, Valerian A. xxxv, 241